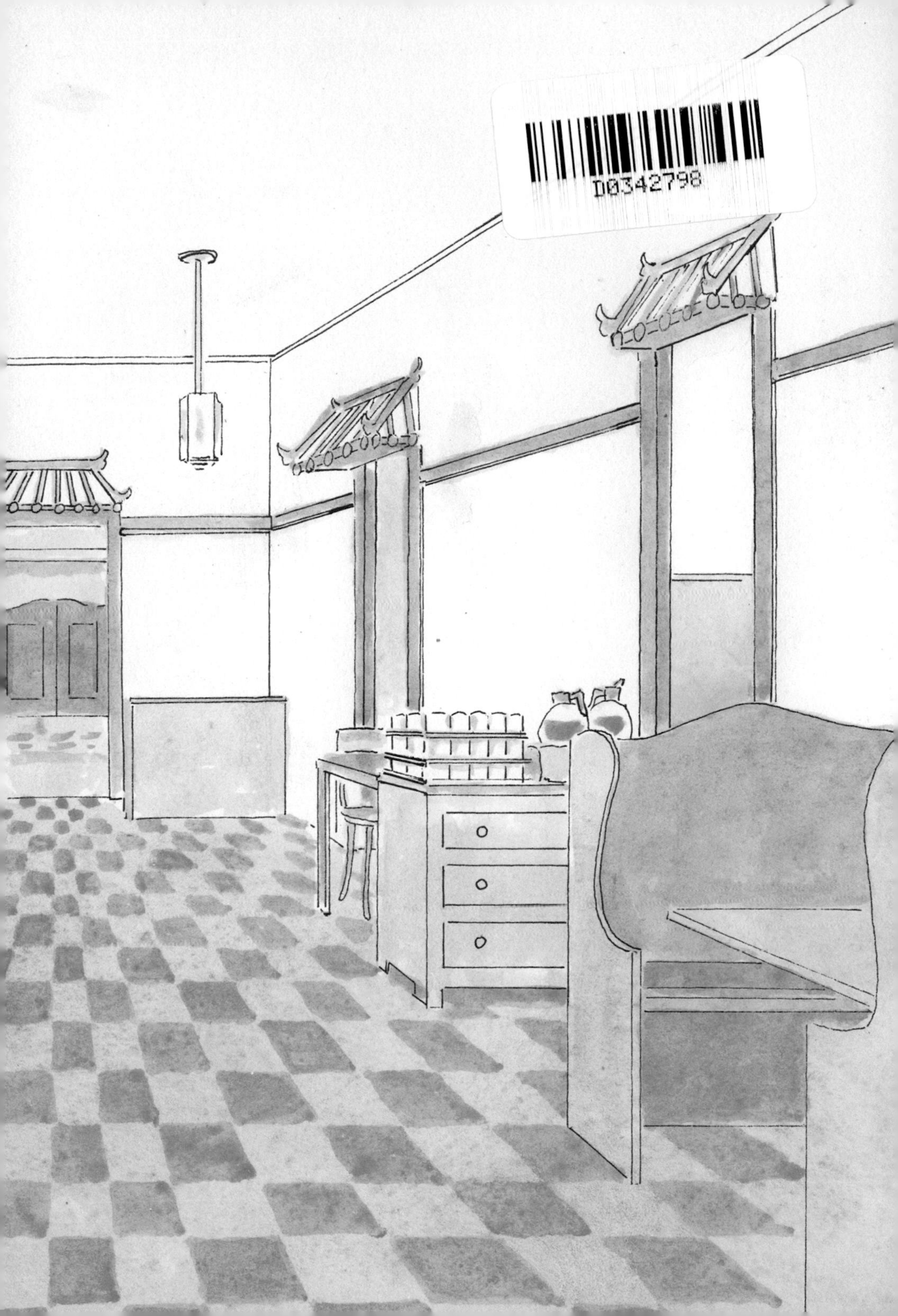

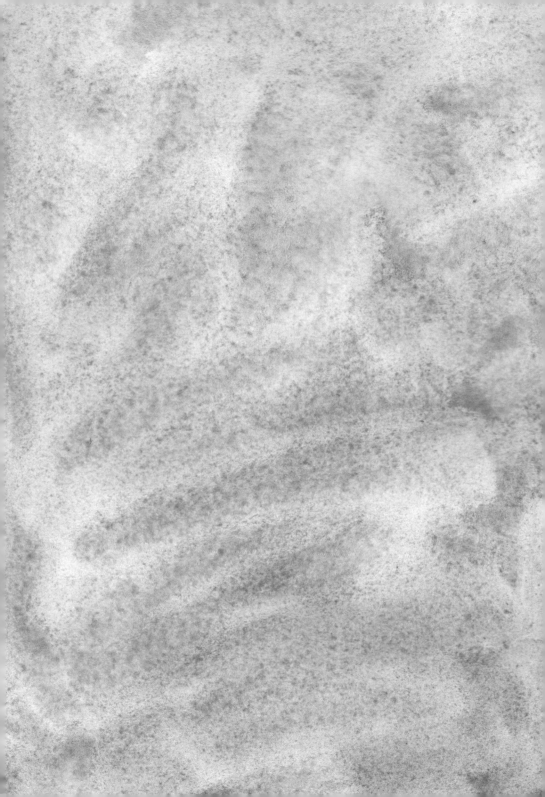

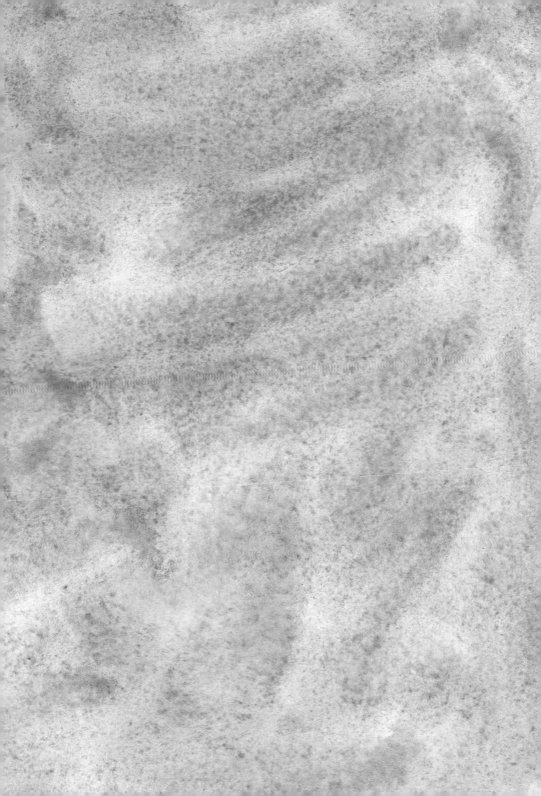

Over

Over easy
33305233447352
6an   06/18/15

Easy

Mimi Pond

drawn & quarterly

ENTIRE CONTENTS © COPYRIGHT 2014 BY MIMI POND.
ALL RIGHTS RESERVED. NO PART OF THIS BOOK (EXCEPT SMALL PORTIONS
FOR REVIEW PURPOSES) MAY BE REPRODUCED IN ANY FORM WITHOUT WRITTEN
CONSENT FROM MIMI POND OR DRAWN & QUARTERLY.
THE POEMS ON PAGES 168, 252-253, 254, 256, AND 257
WERE WRITTEN BY JOHN VEGLIA. THE CONTENTS ARE
COPYRIGHT © 2014 JOHN VEGLIA AND HIS HEIRS.

DRAWNANDQUARTERLY.COM

FIRST HARDCOVER EDITION: APRIL 2014
SECOND PRINTING: NOVEMBER 2014
10 9 8 7 6 5 4 3 2
PRINTED IN CHINA

LIBRARY AND ARCHIVES CANADA CATALOGUING IN PUBLICATION
POND, MIMI, AUTHOR
  OVER EASY / MIMI POND.
ISBN 978-1-77046-153-6 (BOUND)
  1. GRAPHIC NOVELS.   1. TITLE.
PN6 727. P66094 2014   741. 5'973   C2013-906 213-0

PUBLISHED IN THE USA BY DRAWN & QUARTERLY,
A CLIENT PUBLISHER OF FARRAR, STRAUS AND GIROUX
ORDERS: 888. 330. 8977

PUBLISHED IN CANADA BY DRAWN & QUARTERLY,
A CLIENT PUBLISHER OF RAINCOAST BOOKS
ORDERS: 800. 663. 5714

PUBLISHED IN THE UNITED KINGDOM BY DRAWN & QUARTERLY,
A CLIENT PUBLISHER OF PUBLISHERS GROUP UK
ORDERS: INFO @ PGUK.CO.UK

THANKS

I COULD NOT HAVE FINISHED THIS BOOK WITHOUT THE ENDURING LOVE, FAITH, AND SUPPORT OF MY WONDERFUL FAMILY - MY HUSBAND WAYNE WHITE, AND OUR CHILDREN, WOODROW AND LULU WHITE.

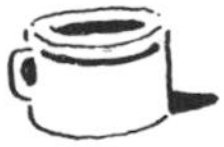

I WORKED IN A RESTAURANT IN OAKLAND, CALIFORNIA, OVER THIRTY YEARS AGO, WHERE I KNEW FROM THE VERY FIRST DAY THAT I WAS PART OF A STORY. FOR THE YEARS THAT WE LIVED THAT STORY AND THE YEARS OF HELPING ME TO PROCESS IT, I OWE A HUGE DEBT TO:

PETER BRADY, JIMMY BROWN, SHERRY JEAN COOPER, HAYDEN DUNN, ELLEN FOSTER, MARY FOSTER, CHRIS KAMMLER, DENIS KELLY, GEORGE MARINO, HEATHER MUNRO PIERCE, GARY LAMBERT, GLENN LAMBERT, AND CHRIS ORR.

LYNN PERIL, MARY RICCI, MARYEDITH BURRELL, AUDREY BROWN: THANKS FOR BEING EARLY READERS.
THANKS TO ALL THE LIT LIST GALS FOR THEIR SUPPORT.

PRAISE BE TO POE BALLANTINE FOR BEING A LIFELINE IN THE E-MAIL WILDERNESS AT THE TURN OF THE 21ST CENTURY.

THANK YOU TO KARL SCHAEFER FOR GIVING ME A PLACE TO GO WHEN THIS BOOK WAS A MERE EMBRYO.

THANKS TO RUTH SHAVIT AND THE SILVERLAKE INDEPENDENT J.C.C. FOR SAYING, "WHY DON'T YOU WORK HERE?"

THANKS TO BETH RUDIN DEWOODY, CLAUDIA GLENN BARASCH, AND SHELLY HIRSHON FOR BEING ON THE BOARD OF DIRECTORS OF THE MIMI POND SELF-RESIDENCY PROGRAM OF 2012.

THANKS TO THE ROBERT RAUSCHENBERG FOUNDATION FOR A LIFE-CHANGING RESIDENCY IN THE SPRING OF 2013.

THANKS TO JULIE FOWLER, PAUL CRAWFORD, AND ISLAND MOUNTAIN ARTS IN WELLS, B.C., CANADA.

THANKS TO TODD OLDHAM AND TONY LONGORIA FOR THE LOVE AND SUPPORT.

THANKS TO THE AWESOME INDOMITABILITY OF MY AGENT, PAUL BRESNICK.

THANKS TO ART SPIEGELMAN, FOR TELLING ME I SHOULD JUST DO IT.
THANKS TO THE COOLEST PUBLISHER IN THE WORLD, DRAWN AND QUARTERLY - CHRIS OLIVEROS, TOM DEVLIN, PEGGY BURNS, AND THE WHOLE CREW.

FINALLY, THIS BOOK IS FOR JOHN VEGLIA, AND FOR ANYONE WHO HAS EVER WORKED AT MAMA'S ROYAL CAFE IN OAKLAND, CALIFORNIA.

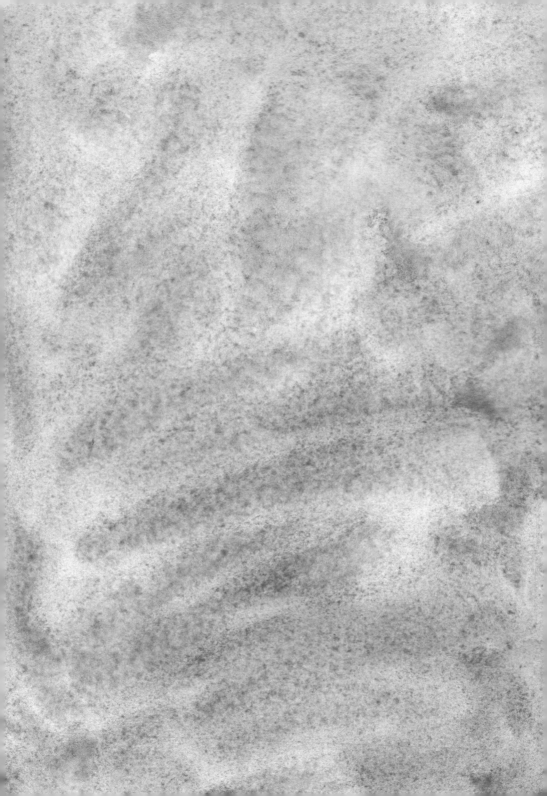

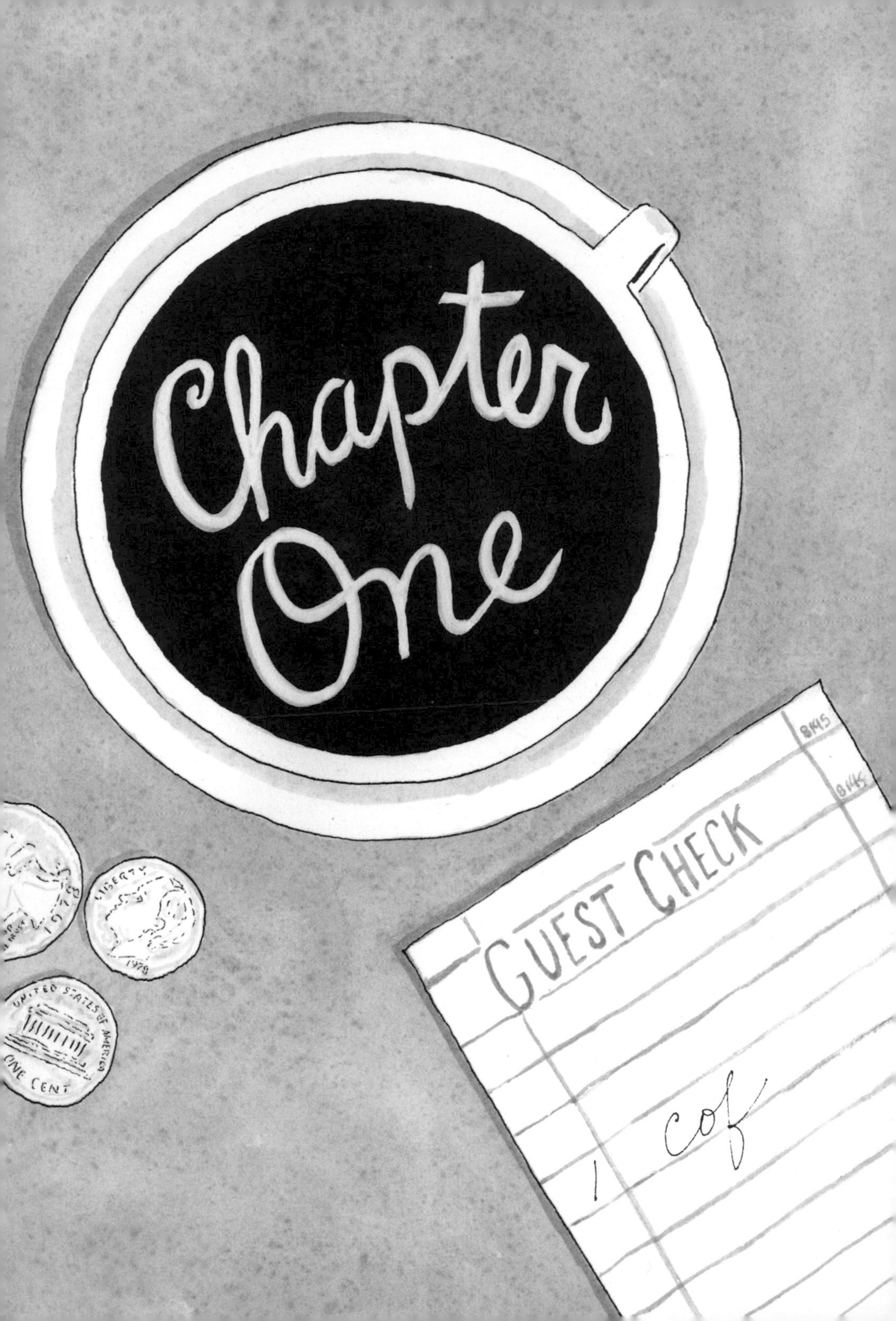
Chapter One
GUEST CHECK
1 cof
LIBERTY
1979
UNITED STATES OF AMERICA
ONE CENT

MAY 23, 1978. MIDAFTERNOON. I AM THE ONLY CUSTOMER.

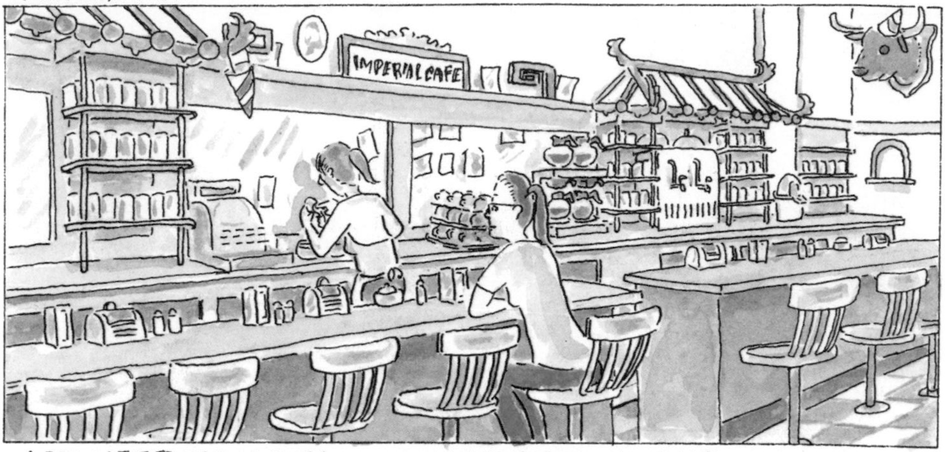
IMPERIAL CAFE

A BELL ON THE FRONT DOOR RINGS AS SOMEONE ENTERS.

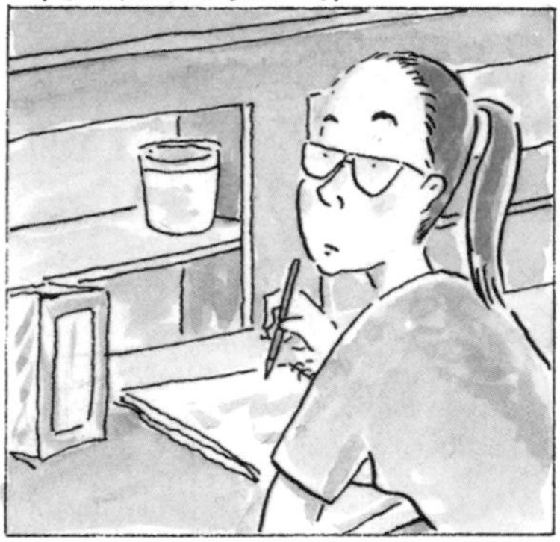

A MAN NIMBLY TWIRLS HIMSELF BEHIND THE COUNTER AND OVER TO THE REGISTER.

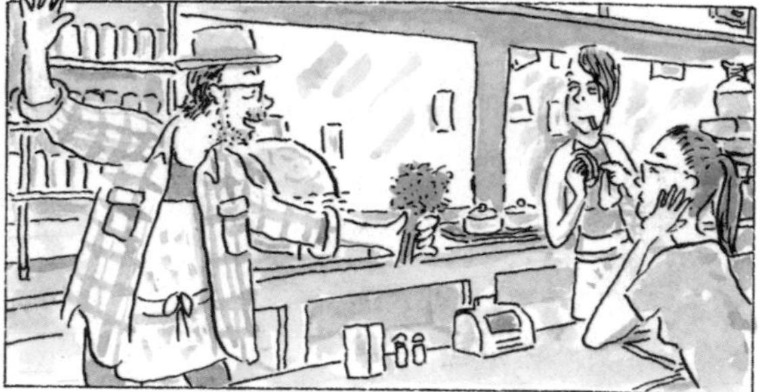

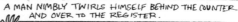

THAT TURNED OUT TO BE A DISTINCTIVELY LAZLO-LIKE DIP AND TWIRL HE'D DO.

NOW THAT I THINK ABOUT IT, HE WAS PROBABLY HIGH. DOES IT MATTER?

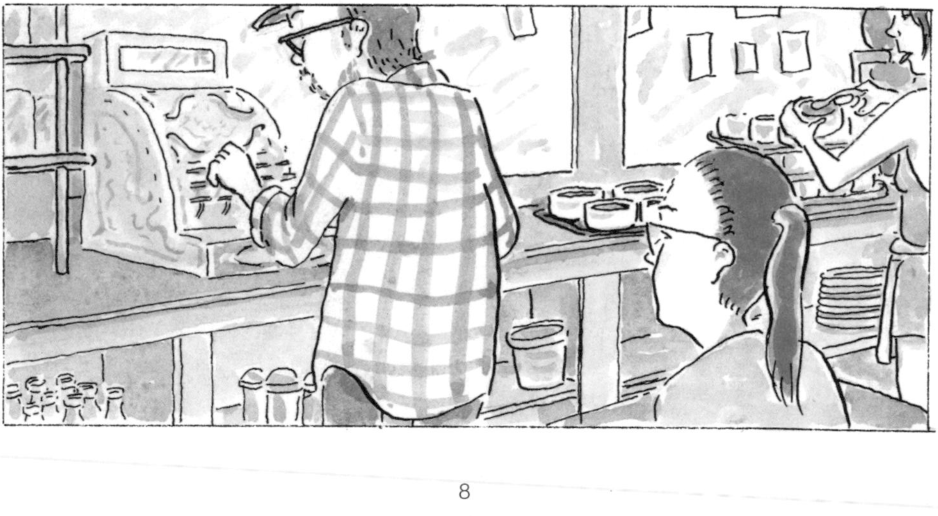

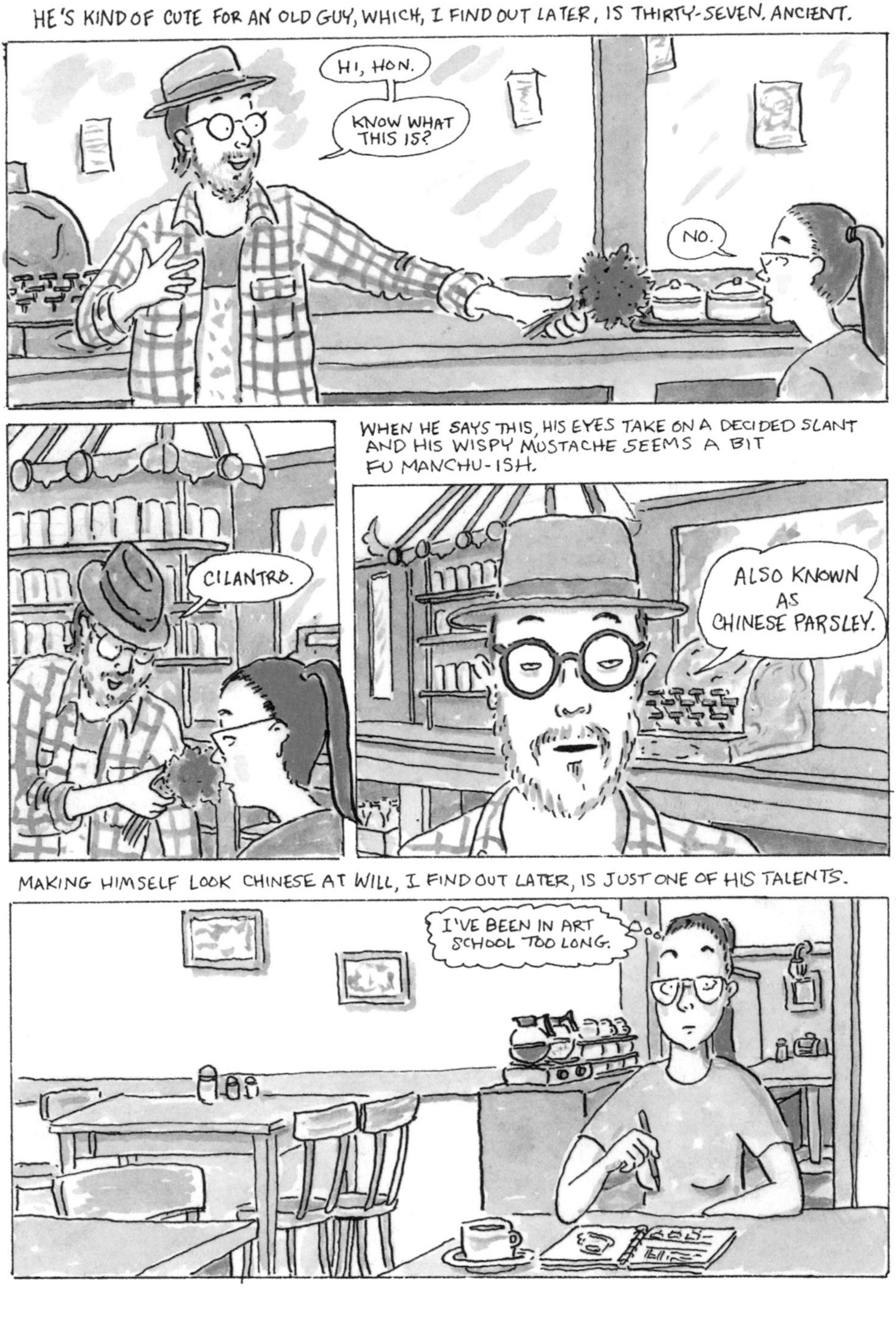
HE'S KIND OF CUTE FOR AN OLD GUY, WHICH, I FIND OUT LATER, IS THIRTY-SEVEN. ANCIENT.
HI, HON.
KNOW WHAT THIS IS?
NO.
CILANTRO.
WHEN HE SAYS THIS, HIS EYES TAKE ON A DECIDED SLANT AND HIS WISPY MUSTACHE SEEMS A BIT FU MANCHU-ISH.
ALSO KNOWN AS CHINESE PARSLEY.
MAKING HIMSELF LOOK CHINESE AT WILL, I FIND OUT LATER, IS JUST ONE OF HIS TALENTS.
I'VE BEEN IN ART SCHOOL TOO LONG.

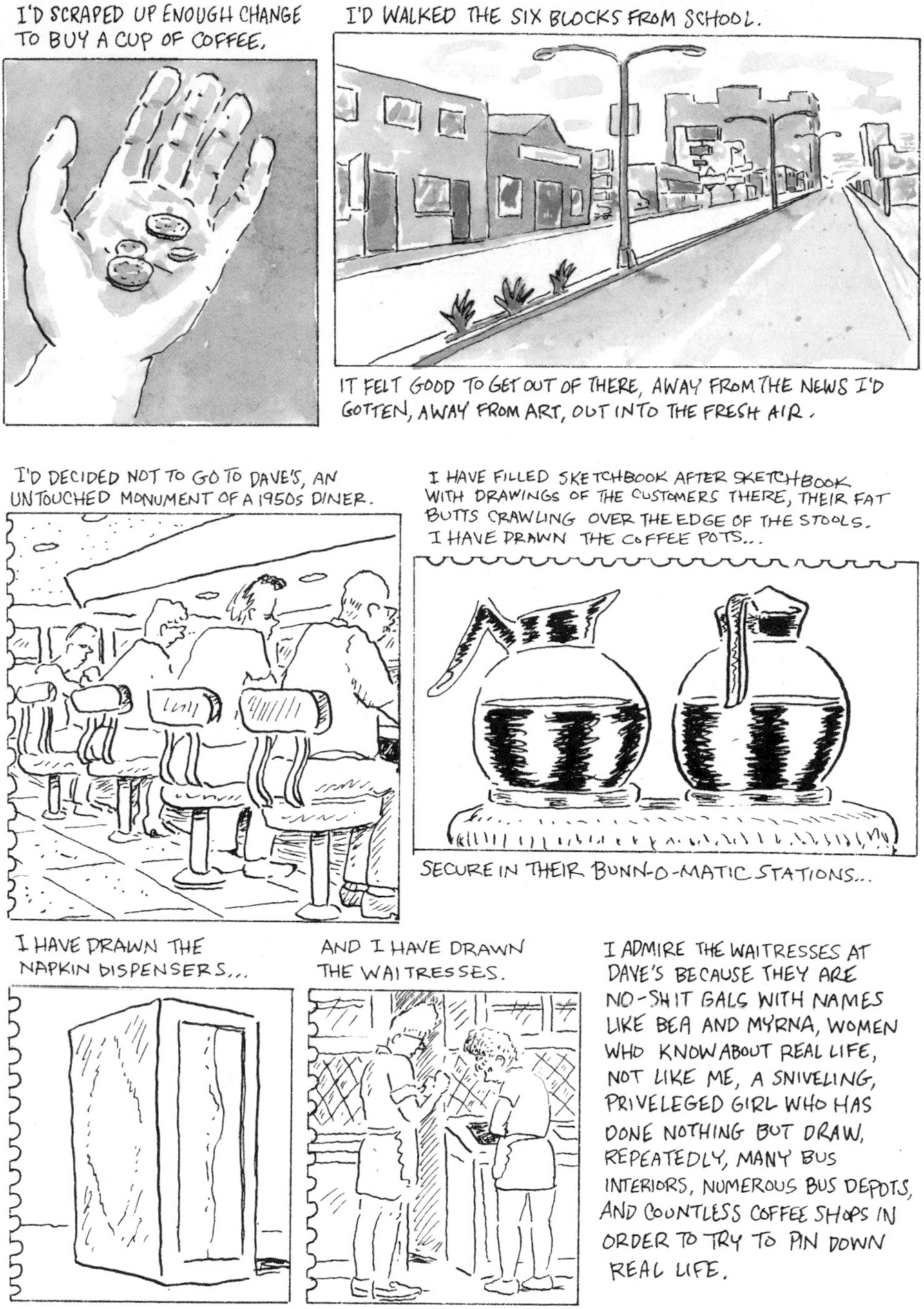
I'D SCRAPED UP ENOUGH CHANGE TO BUY A CUP OF COFFEE.
I'D WALKED THE SIX BLOCKS FROM SCHOOL.
IT FELT GOOD TO GET OUT OF THERE, AWAY FROM THE NEWS I'D GOTTEN, AWAY FROM ART, OUT INTO THE FRESH AIR.
I'D DECIDED NOT TO GO TO DAVE'S, AN UNTOUCHED MONUMENT OF A 1950s DINER.
I HAVE FILLED SKETCHBOOK AFTER SKETCHBOOK WITH DRAWINGS OF THE CUSTOMERS THERE, THEIR FAT BUTTS CRAWLING OVER THE EDGE OF THE STOOLS. I HAVE DRAWN THE COFFEE POTS...
SECURE IN THEIR BUNN-O-MATIC STATIONS...
I HAVE DRAWN THE NAPKIN DISPENSERS...
AND I HAVE DRAWN THE WAITRESSES.
I ADMIRE THE WAITRESSES AT DAVE'S BECAUSE THEY ARE NO-SHIT GALS WITH NAMES LIKE BEA AND MYRNA, WOMEN WHO KNOW ABOUT REAL LIFE, NOT LIKE ME, A SNIVELING, PRIVELEGED GIRL WHO HAS DONE NOTHING BUT DRAW, REPEATEDLY, MANY BUS INTERIORS, NUMEROUS BUS DEPOTS, AND COUNTLESS COFFEE SHOPS IN ORDER TO TRY TO PIN DOWN REAL LIFE.

I SHOULD ALSO ADD THAT I HAVE SPENT TOO MUCH TIME ALONE IN MY ROOM WITH TOM WAITS ALBUMS.

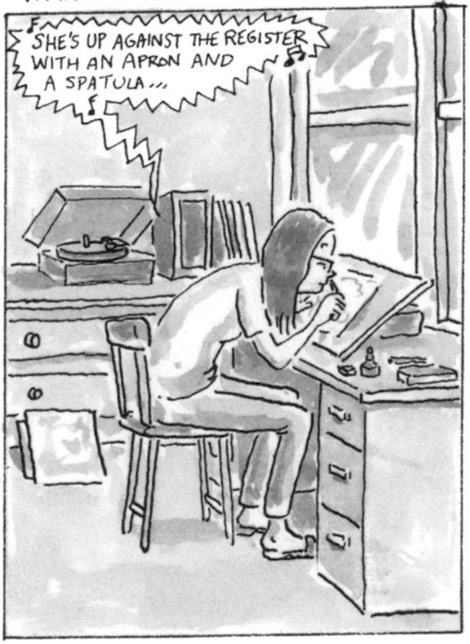
SHE'S UP AGAINST THE REGISTER WITH AN APRON AND A SPATULA...

THESE WAITRESSES ARE NOT DISPOSED TO THINK KINDLY OF ME. ART STUDENTS ARE NOT GOOD TIPPERS.

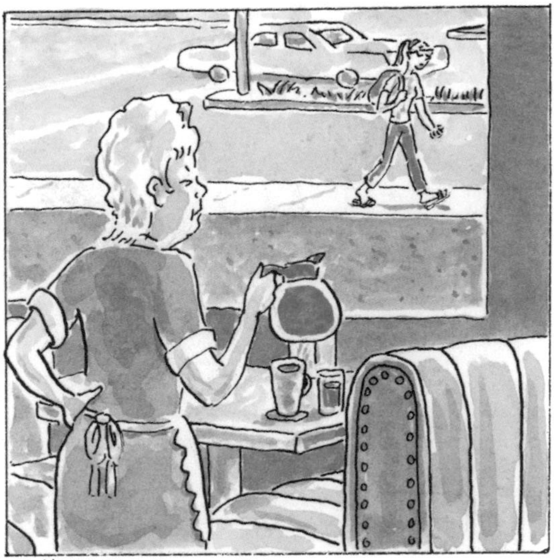

I NEED SOMETHING NEW.

I GET TO THIS PLACE. I'D ASSUMED IT WAS AN ABANDONED CHINESE RESTAURANT.

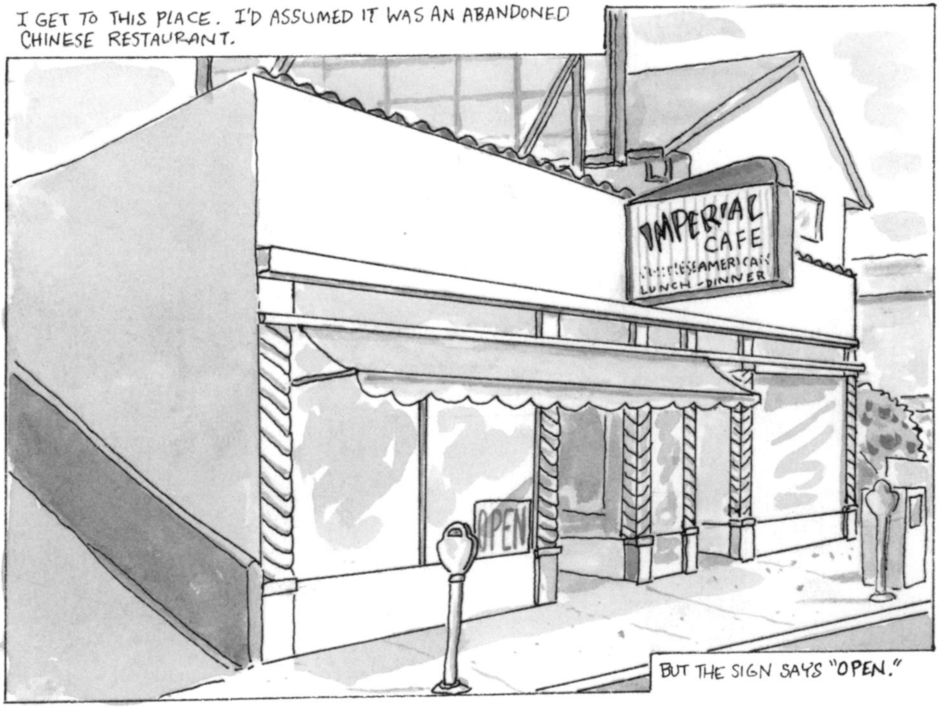
IMPERIAL
CAFE
LUNCH - DINNER
OPEN
BUT THE SIGN SAYS "OPEN."

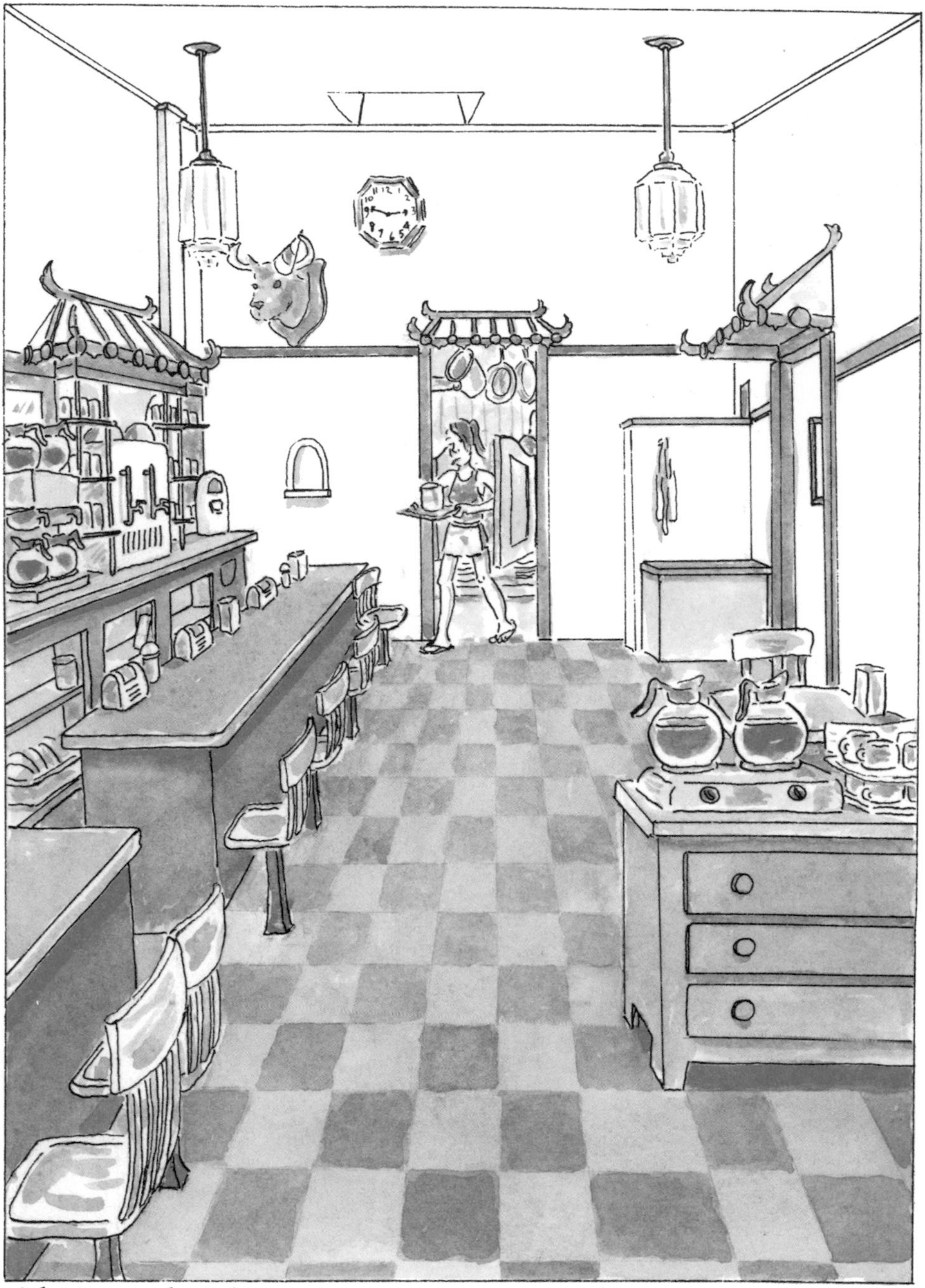

THE MINUTE I OPEN THE FRONT DOOR, THE SMELL OF COFFEE IS OVERWHELMING AND NARCOTIC.

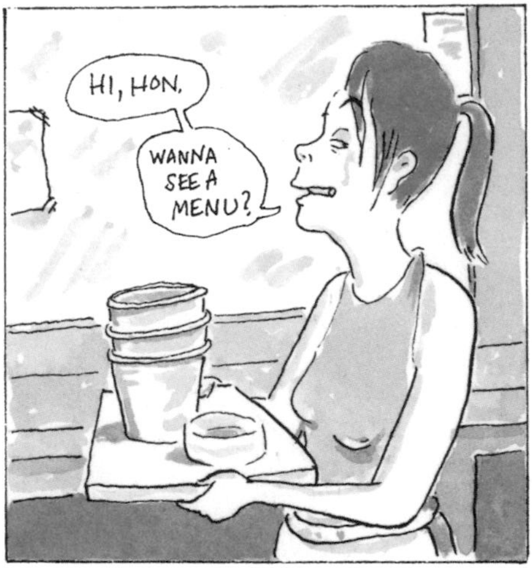
HI, HON.
WANNA SEE A MENU?

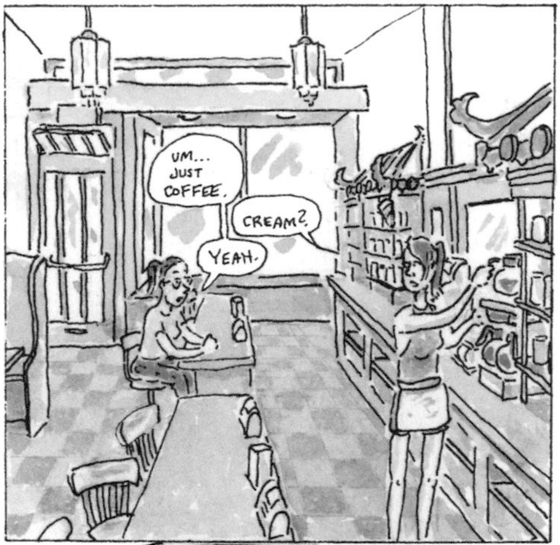
UM... JUST COFFEE.
CREAM?
YEAH.

TO MY SURPRISE, INSTEAD OF A TEENY, FACTORY-SEALED PLASTIC CONTAINER OF NON-DAIRY PRODUCT LIKE THEY GIVE YOU AT DAVE'S...

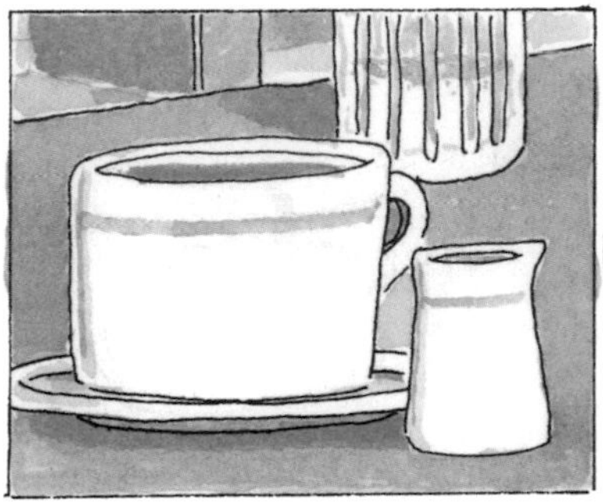

SHE GIVES ME A TINY BEAKER OF REAL CREAM ALONG WITH MY COFFEE.

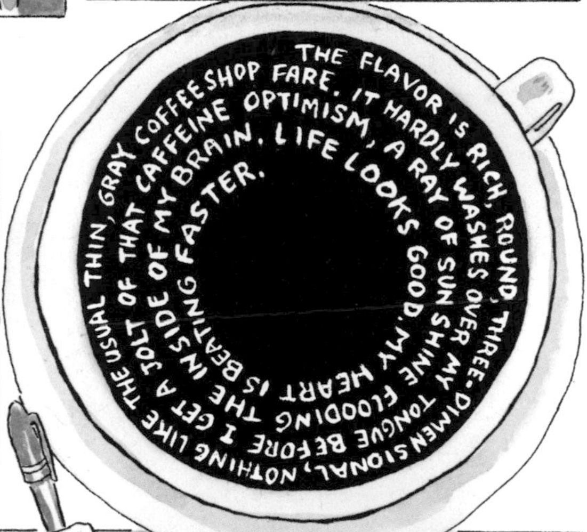
THE FLAVOR IS RICH, ROUND, THREE-DIMENSIONAL, NOTHING LIKE THE USUAL THIN, GRAY COFFEESHOP FARE. IT HARDLY WASHES OVER MY TONGUE BEFORE I GET A JOLT OF THAT CAFFEINE OPTIMISM, A RAY OF SUNSHINE FLOODING THE INSIDE OF MY BRAIN. LIFE LOOKS GOOD. MY HEART IS BEATING FASTER.

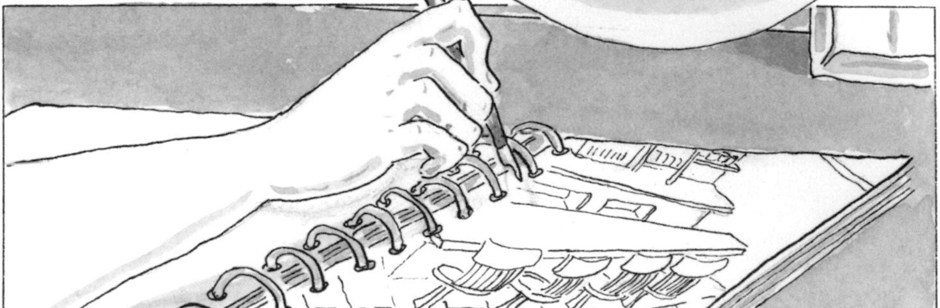

EVEN THOUGH I TOLD MYSELF I WOULDN'T, I PULL MY SKETCHBOOK OUT OF MY BACKPACK AND GET OUT MY FOUNTAIN PEN. I BEGIN TO DRAW THE WHOLE TABLEAU HERE.

AND NOW THIS GUY WHO IS NOT CHINESE, WHO HAS TWIRLED IN WITH THE CHINESE PARSLEY, PLOPS DOWN ON THE SEAT NEXT TO ME.

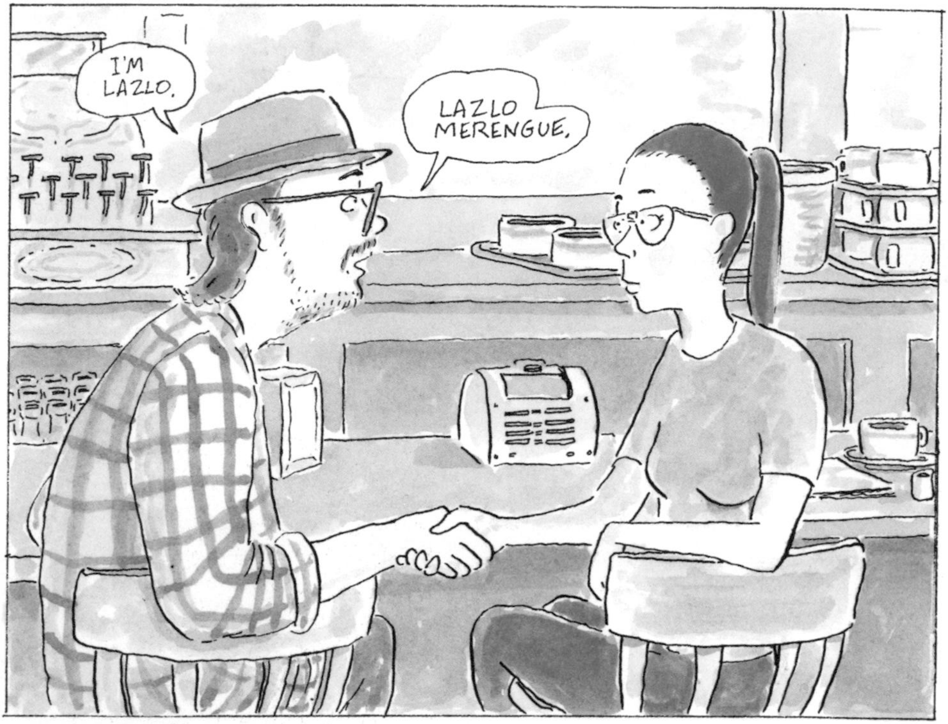
I'M LAZLO.
LAZLO MERENGUE.

I INSTANTLY RECOGNIZE THE COMIC, DRUGGY ALTER EGO. IT'S ONE OF THOSE THINGS PEOPLE ANYWHERE FROM TWO TO TWENTY YEARS OLDER THAN ME LIKE TO DO- GIVE THEMSELVES SILLY ALIASES:

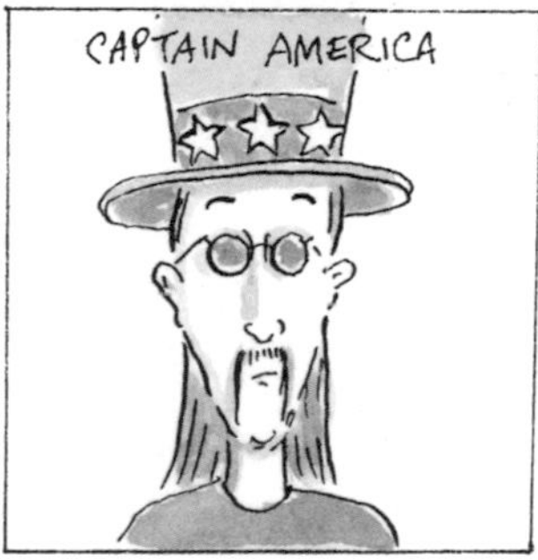
CAPTAIN AMERICA

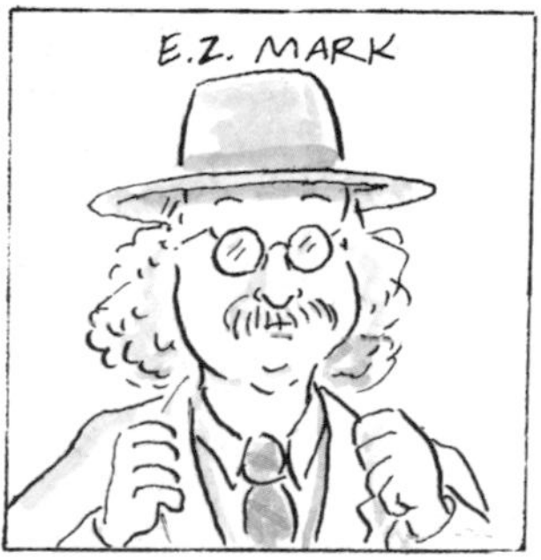
E.Z. MARK

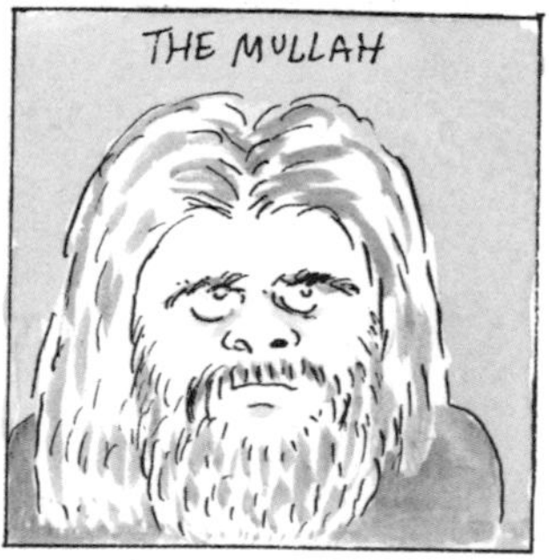
THE MULLAH

THE SUBTEXT IS THE CONCEIT THAT THEY ARE ACTUALLY SO SUBVERSIVE AND DANGEROUS (SOMETHING TO DO WITH DRUGS OR REVOLUTION) THAT THEY MUST TRAVEL UNDER ASSUMED NAMES. I MISSED THE COUNTERCULTURAL BOAT BY BEING JUST A LITTLE TOO YOUNG. I USED TO REGRET THAT. THE LAST COUPLE OF YEARS, THOUGH, THE WHOLE HIPPIE THING HAS STARTED TO GET ON MY NERVES.

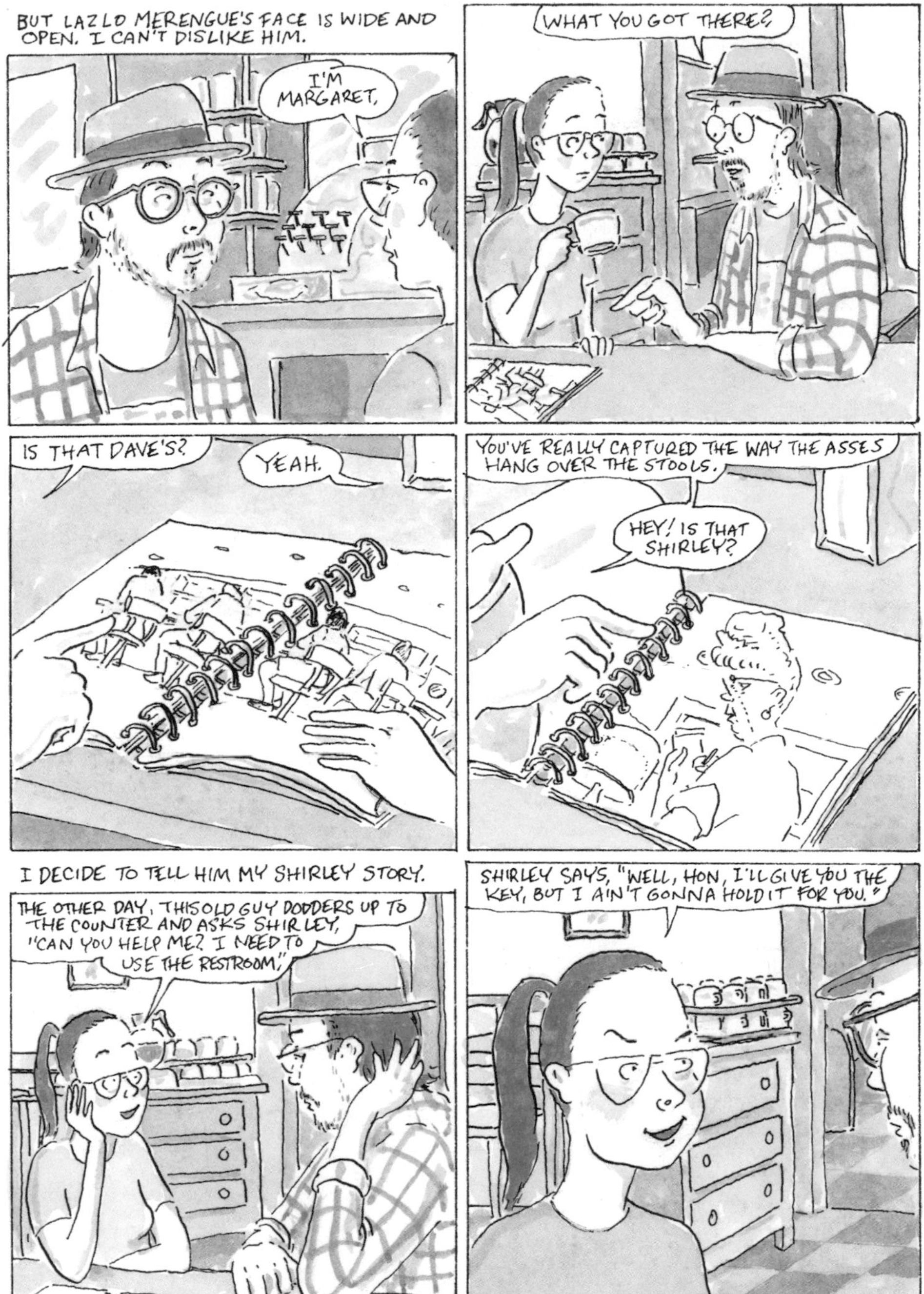
BUT LAZLO MERENGUE'S FACE IS WIDE AND OPEN. I CAN'T DISLIKE HIM.
I'M MARGARET.
WHAT YOU GOT THERE?
IS THAT DAVE'S?
YEAH.
YOU'VE REALLY CAPTURED THE WAY THE ASSES HANG OVER THE STOOLS.
HEY! IS THAT SHIRLEY?
I DECIDE TO TELL HIM MY SHIRLEY STORY.
THE OTHER DAY, THIS OLD GUY DODDERS UP TO THE COUNTER AND ASKS SHIRLEY, "CAN YOU HELP ME? I NEED TO USE THE RESTROOM."
SHIRLEY SAYS, "WELL, HON, I'LL GIVE YOU THE KEY, BUT I AIN'T GONNA HOLD IT FOR YOU."

LAZLO THROWS BACK HIS HEAD AND CACKLES. HE HAS SUCH A WELCOMING LAUGH.

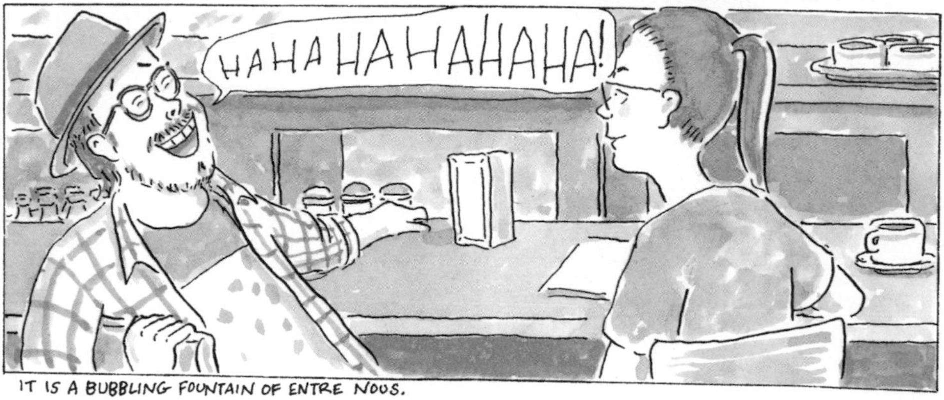
HAHAHAHAHAHAHA!

IT IS A BUBBLING FOUNTAIN OF ENTRE NOUS.

HE CERTAINLY IS FORTHCOMING, A SWITCH FROM THE BROODING, WILLFULLY OBLIQUE BOYS WHO'VE BEEN DRIVING ME CRAZY FOR THE LAST THREE YEARS OF ART SCHOOL. ABRUPTLY, I BLURT OUT:

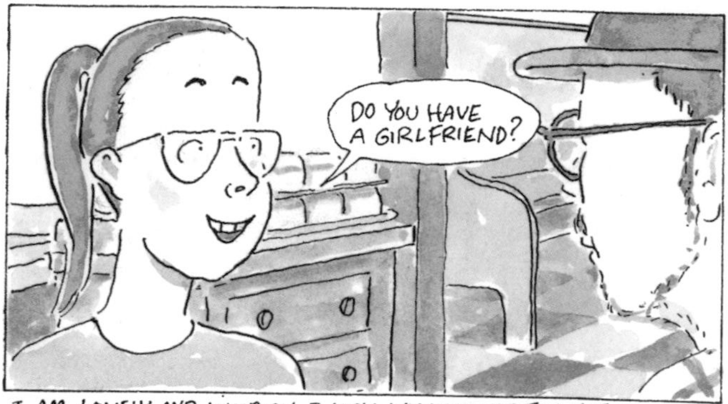
DO YOU HAVE A GIRLFRIEND?

I AM LONELY AND LUMPISH. I LACK ANY INSTINCT FOR THE FEMALE MYSTERY.

THERE IS ONLY THE SMALLEST AWKWARD HALF-BEAT.

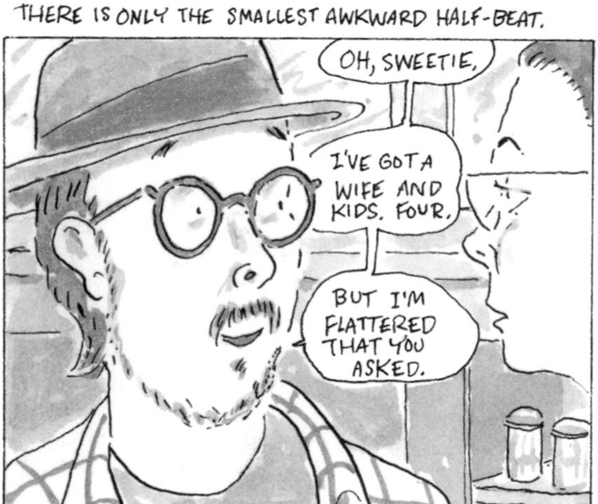
OH, SWEETIE,
I'VE GOT A WIFE AND KIDS. FOUR.
BUT I'M FLATTERED THAT YOU ASKED.

HE PICKS UP MY SKETCHBOOK AGAIN.

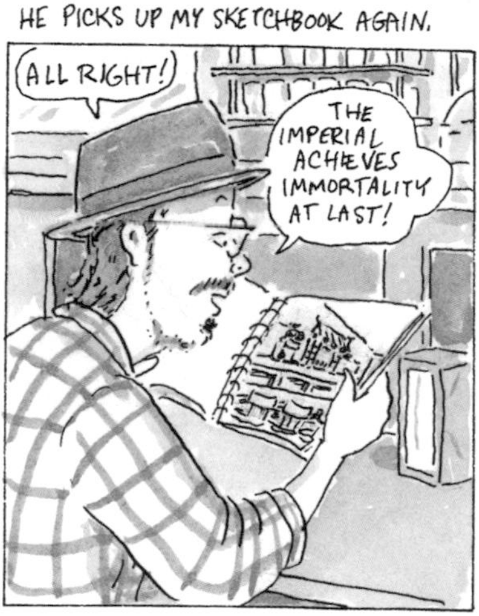
ALL RIGHT!
THE IMPERIAL ACHIEVES IMMORTALITY AT LAST!

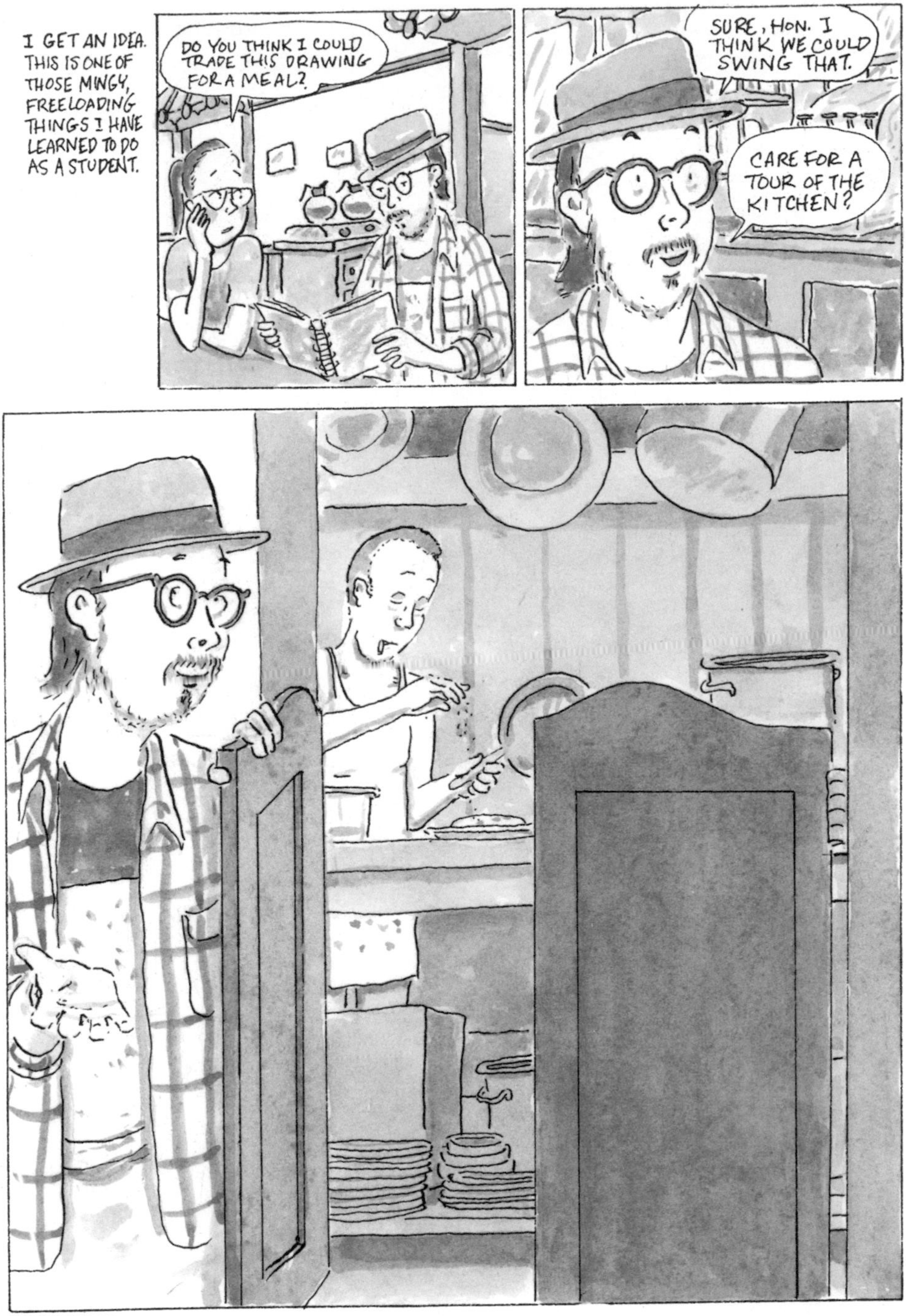
I GET AN IDEA. THIS IS ONE OF THOSE MINGY, FREELOADING THINGS I HAVE LEARNED TO DO AS A STUDENT.
DO YOU THINK I COULD TRADE THIS DRAWING FOR A MEAL?
SURE, HON. I THINK WE COULD SWING THAT.
CARE FOR A TOUR OF THE KITCHEN?

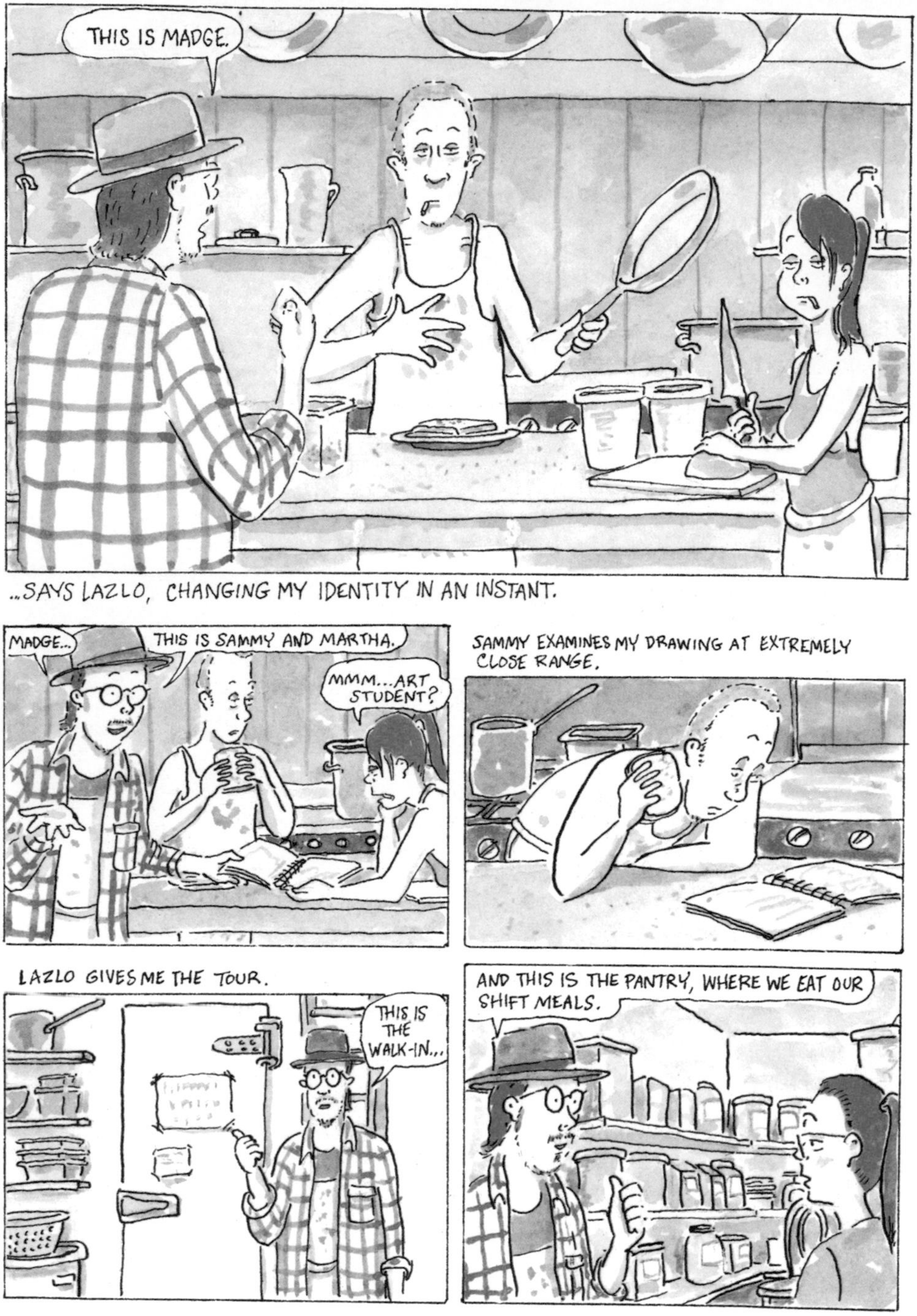
THIS IS MADGE.
..SAYS LAZLO, CHANGING MY IDENTITY IN AN INSTANT.
MADGE...
THIS IS SAMMY AND MARTHA.
MMM...ART STUDENT?
SAMMY EXAMINES MY DRAWING AT EXTREMELY CLOSE RANGE.
LAZLO GIVES ME THE TOUR.
THIS IS THE WALK-IN...
AND THIS IS THE PANTRY, WHERE WE EAT OUR SHIFT MEALS.

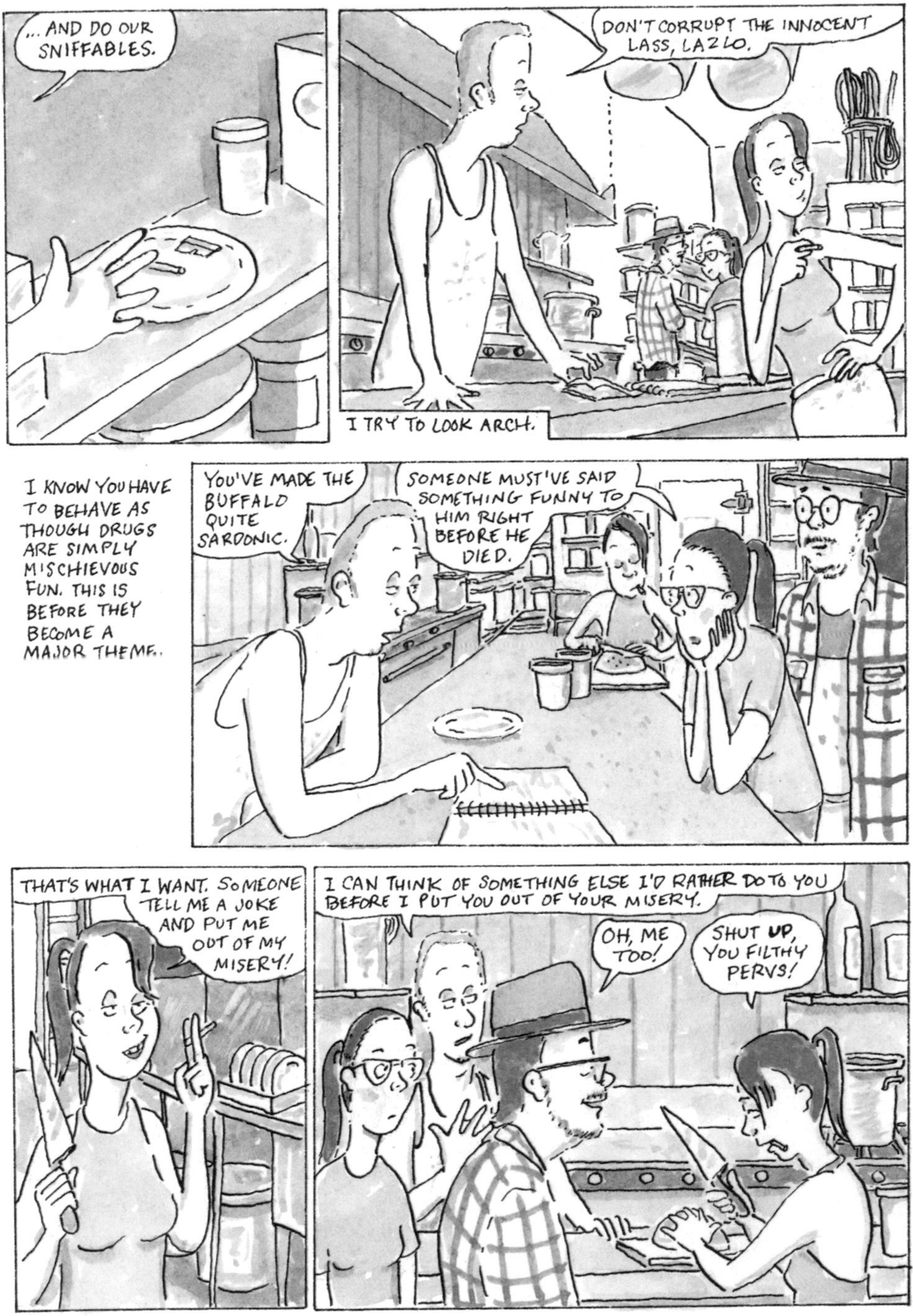

... AND DO OUR SNIFFABLES.
DON'T CORRUPT THE INNOCENT LASS, LAZLO.
I TRY TO LOOK ARCH.
I KNOW YOU HAVE TO BEHAVE AS THOUGH DRUGS ARE SIMPLY MISCHIEVOUS FUN. THIS IS BEFORE THEY BECOME A MAJOR THEME.
YOU'VE MADE THE BUFFALO QUITE SARDONIC.
SOMEONE MUST'VE SAID SOMETHING FUNNY TO HIM RIGHT BEFORE HE DIED.
THAT'S WHAT I WANT. SOMEONE TELL ME A JOKE AND PUT ME OUT OF MY MISERY!
I CAN THINK OF SOMETHING ELSE I'D RATHER DO TO YOU BEFORE I PUT YOU OUT OF YOUR MISERY.
OH, ME TOO!
SHUT UP, YOU FILTHY PERVS!

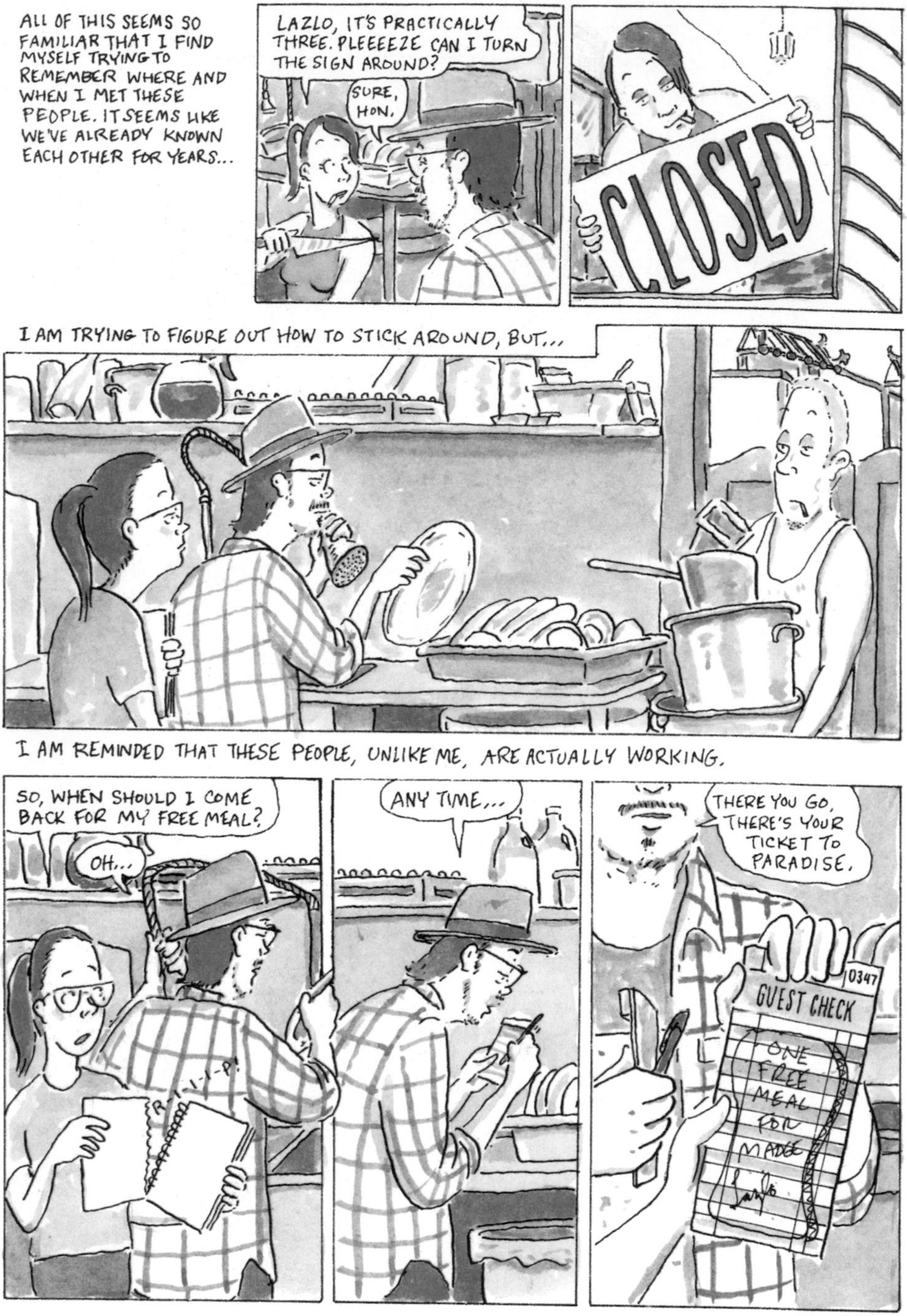
ALL OF THIS SEEMS SO FAMILIAR THAT I FIND MYSELF TRYING TO REMEMBER WHERE AND WHEN I MET THESE PEOPLE. IT SEEMS LIKE WE'VE ALREADY KNOWN EACH OTHER FOR YEARS...
LAZLO, IT'S PRACTICALLY THREE. PLEEEEZE CAN I TURN THE SIGN AROUND?
SURE, HON.
CLOSED
I AM TRYING TO FIGURE OUT HOW TO STICK AROUND, BUT...
I AM REMINDED THAT THESE PEOPLE, UNLIKE ME, ARE ACTUALLY WORKING.
SO, WHEN SHOULD I COME BACK FOR MY FREE MEAL?
OH...
R-I-I-P!
ANY TIME,...
THERE YOU GO, THERE'S YOUR TICKET TO PARADISE.
0347
GUEST CHECK
ONE FREE MEAL FOR MADGE

I GREW UP IN AN UGLY CRAFTSMAN HOUSE IN SAN DIEGO.

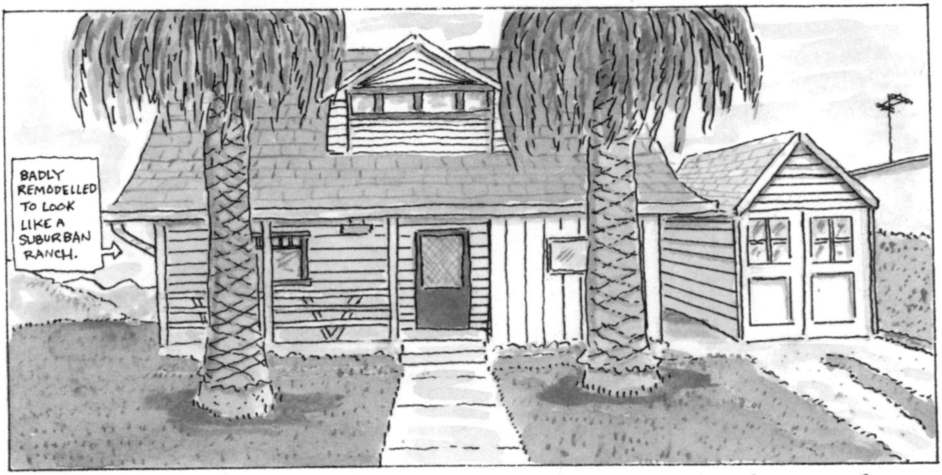
BADLY REMODELLED TO LOOK LIKE A SUBURBAN RANCH.

WHERE WE LIVED IN SAN DIEGO WAS A HIGH MESA, ON A CANYON ABOVE A VALLEY THAT WENT DOWN TO THE OCEAN.

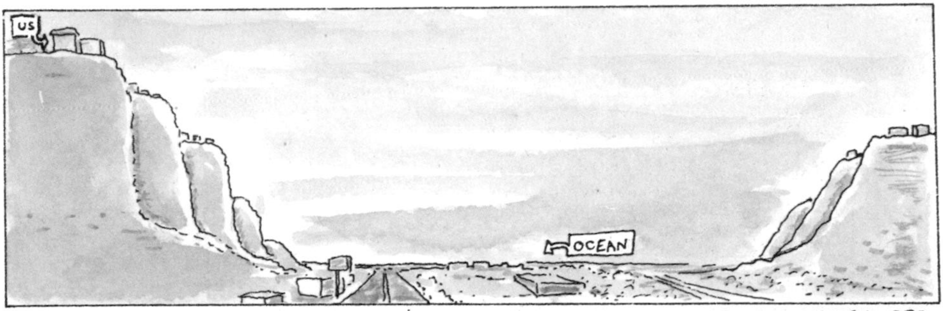
US
OCEAN

IT WAS LIKE LIVING ON A TABLE TOP IN THE MIDDLE OF AN UNSHADED PICNIC AREA. I DON'T REMEMBER EVER NOT BEING BLINDED BY THE ALMOST-WHITE SUNLIGHT WHEN I WENT OUTSIDE, THAT COULD HAVE BEEN BECAUSE INSIDE, THE LIVING ROOM AND DINING ROOM STILL HAD THE ORIGINAL CRAFTSMAN WAINSCOTING. IT WAS A COOL, DARK SANCTUARY OF BEAT-UP FURNITURE AND PILES OF LIBRARY BOOKS.

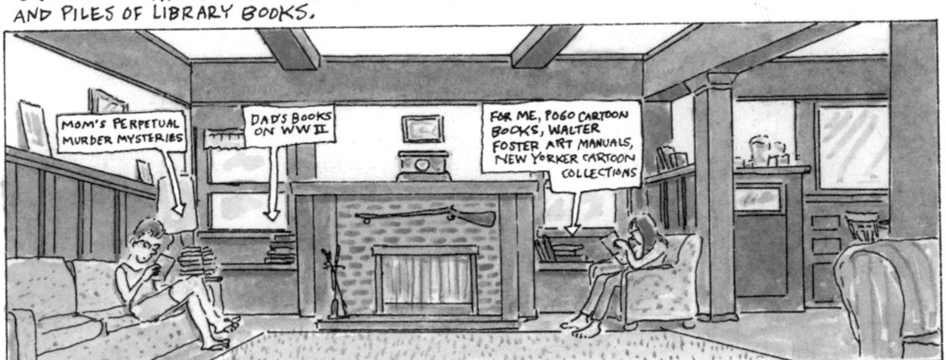
MOM'S PERPETUAL MURDER MYSTERIES
DAD'S BOOKS ON WW II
FOR ME, POGO CARTOON BOOKS, WALTER FOSTER ART MANUALS, NEW YORKER CARTOON COLLECTIONS

DAD HAD WANTED TO GO TO ART SCHOOL, BUT HIS FATHER WOULDN'T LET HIM. HE JOINED THE NAVY TO GET OUT OF DETROIT. HE WAS A SAILOR WHEN HE MET MY MOM IN SAN DIEGO IN 1953. SHE WAS A TELEPHONE OPERATOR. IT SOUNDED LIKE A BROADWAY MUSICAL TO ME, BUT OF COURSE IT WASN'T. THEY **HAD** TO GET MARRIED. "WE WERE GOING TO ANYWAY," MY MOTHER SAID DEFENSIVELY, YEARS LATER, WHEN WE FIGURED IT OUT.

THEY PROBABLY WOULD HAVE BEEN BEATNIKS, IF THEY'D HAD MORE CONFIDENCE, IF THE FIFTIES AND PARENTHOOD HADN'T ERODED THAT DREAM. BUT WE STILL LISTENED TO WOODY GUTHRIE 78s, WORSHIPPED PETE SEEGER AS A SAINT, WATCHED HOOTENANNY ON A TEN-INCH SCREEN,

DAD TAUGHT ME HOW TO THROW DARTS—BY USING A PICTURE OF RICHARD NIXON AS A TARGET. MAD MAGAZINE WAS OUR COMMUNIST MANIFESTO.

DESPITE THIS INDOCTRINATION, I STILL HAD TO WEAR UNDERSHIRTS AND EAT TUNA SANDWICHES, WASH BEHIND MY EARS, AND GO TO CHURCH. METHODIST,

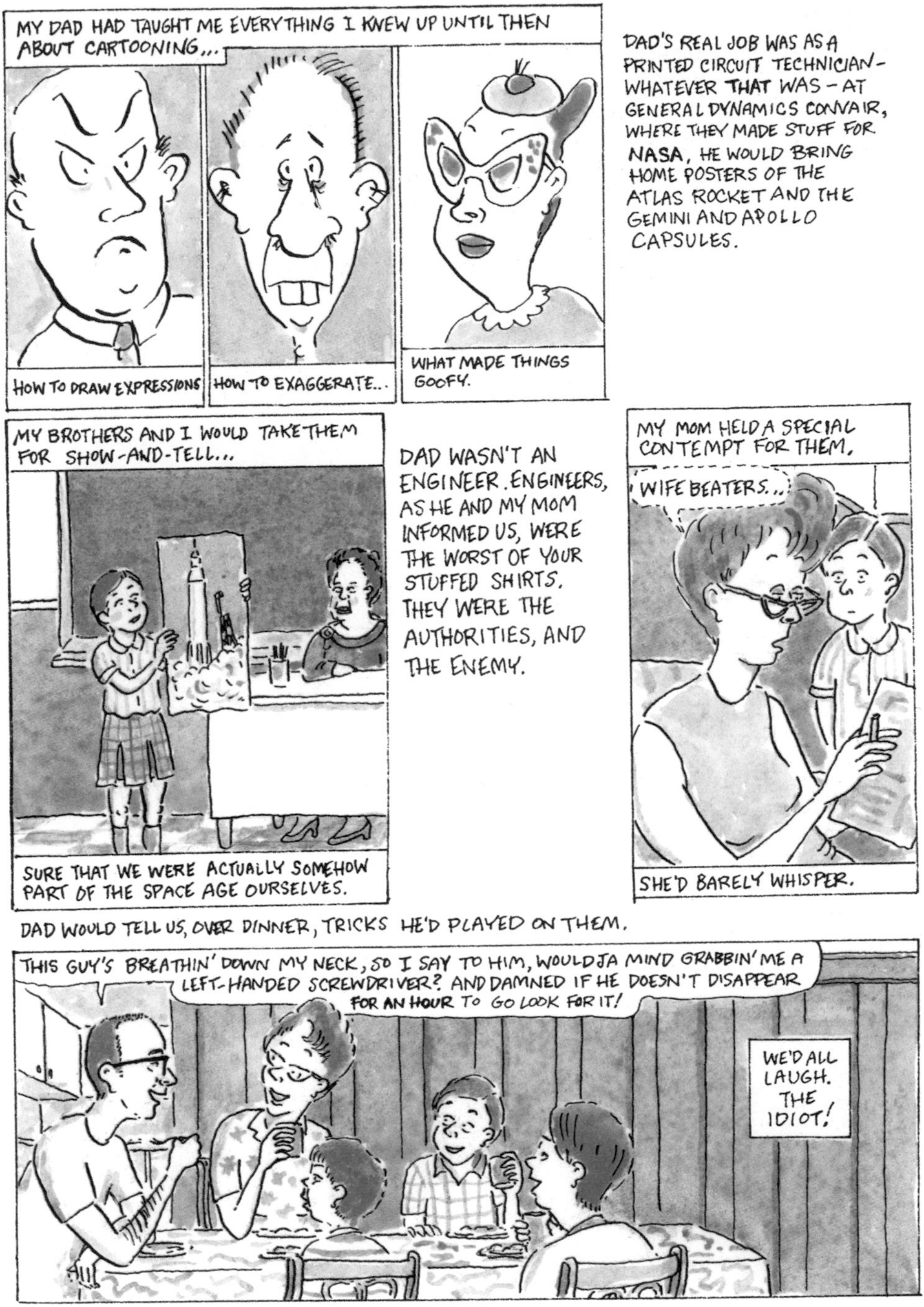

MY DAD HAD TAUGHT ME EVERYTHING I KNEW UP UNTIL THEN ABOUT CARTOONING...
HOW TO DRAW EXPRESSIONS
HOW TO EXAGGERATE...
WHAT MADE THINGS GOOFY.
DAD'S REAL JOB WAS AS A PRINTED CIRCUIT TECHNICIAN - WHATEVER THAT WAS - AT GENERAL DYNAMICS CONVAIR, WHERE THEY MADE STUFF FOR NASA. HE WOULD BRING HOME POSTERS OF THE ATLAS ROCKET AND THE GEMINI AND APOLLO CAPSULES.
MY BROTHERS AND I WOULD TAKE THEM FOR SHOW-AND-TELL...
SURE THAT WE WERE ACTUALLY SOMEHOW PART OF THE SPACE AGE OURSELVES.
DAD WASN'T AN ENGINEER. ENGINEERS, AS HE AND MY MOM INFORMED US, WERE THE WORST OF YOUR STUFFED SHIRTS. THEY WERE THE AUTHORITIES, AND THE ENEMY.
MY MOM HELD A SPECIAL CONTEMPT FOR THEM.
WIFE BEATERS...
SHE'D BARELY WHISPER.
DAD WOULD TELL US, OVER DINNER, TRICKS HE'D PLAYED ON THEM.
THIS GUY'S BREATHIN' DOWN MY NECK, SO I SAY TO HIM, WOULDJA MIND GRABBIN' ME A LEFT-HANDED SCREWDRIVER? AND DAMNED IF HE DOESN'T DISAPPEAR FOR AN HOUR TO GO LOOK FOR IT!
WE'D ALL LAUGH. THE IDIOT!

THE '70s

I KNEW, EVEN IN HIGH SCHOOL, THAT I HAD GOTTEN A RAW DEAL. THE '70s, YOU COULD JUST TELL, EVEN BY '73, WERE GOING TO BE LAME. THE '60s HAD BEEN SO EXCITING, BUT NOW THE WAR WAS OVER. WATERGATE HAD TURNED POLITICAL IDEALS INTO A JOKE, AND EVERYONE WAS JUST TREADING BONG WATER. I HAD DESPERATELY WANTED TO BE A HIPPIE, BUT NOW I COULD SEE THAT SHIP HAD SAILED. ALL THAT WAS LEFT WAS A KIND OF BROWN HIPPIE RESIDUE: THE CARPENTERS, NEIL DIAMOND, SANTANA– OUR CHEERLEADERS EVEN DID A PRECISION ROUTINE TO "OYE COMO VA" AS PERFORMED IN A STACCATO, MILITARISTIC MARCH-TIME BY THE PEP BAND. TALK ABOUT NOT GETTING IT. IT WAS ENOUGH TO TURN ANYONE INTO A NIHILIST. THE WHOLE CARTOONIST DREAM? EVERYONE KNEW THERE WERE NO WOMEN CARTOONISTS. IT SEEMED LIKE A CHILDISH DREAM AT THIS POINT. I STILL LIKED ART, BUT I'D SUNK INTO A MORASS OF DOUBT AND UNCERTAINTY. I GRADUATED FROM HIGH SCHOOL A YEAR EARLY. (I'D BEEN GOING TO SUMMER SCHOOL MY ENTIRE LIFE, ANOTHER ONE OF MOM'S BRIGHT IDEAS.) MY PLANS FOR THE FUTURE WERE VAGUE. MY PARENTS MADE IT CLEAR: THERE WAS NO MONEY FOR COLLEGE. IF I WANTED TO GO, I'D HAVE TO APPLY FOR SCHOLARSHIPS AND LOANS ON MY OWN. I JUST WANTED TO ENJOY NOT BEING IN SCHOOL FOR A WHILE.

I'D TAKEN A PERMANENT HORIZONTAL POSITION ON OUR HERCULON COUCH THAT SUMMER. THEN MY MOTHER LAID DOWN THE LAW:

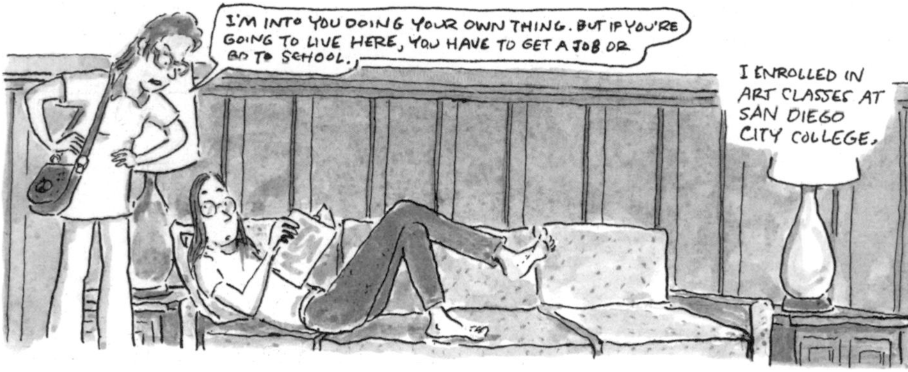
I'M INTO YOU DOING YOUR OWN THING. BUT IF YOU'RE GOING TO LIVE HERE, YOU HAVE TO GET A JOB OR GO TO SCHOOL.
I ENROLLED IN ART CLASSES AT SAN DIEGO CITY COLLEGE.

MOM WAS PLEASED. SHE HAD GONE THERE HERSELF, STARTING WHEN WE WERE IN OUR EARLY TEENS, TO FINALLY EARN HER ASSOCIATE'S DEGREE. THIRSTY FOR KNOWLEDGE AS SHE WAS, STUCK AT HOME AND IN BAD PART-TIME JOBS ALL THOSE YEARS, SHE WAS GUNG-HO ON THE PLACE.

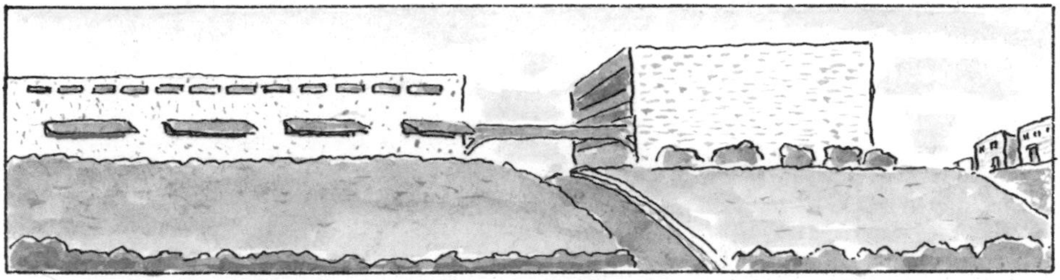

SDCC, RIGHT DOWNTOWN, MORE RESEMBLED A LOW-SECURITY CORRECTIONAL FACILITY THAN THE COMMUNITY COLLEGE CAMPUS IT CLAIMED TO BE.

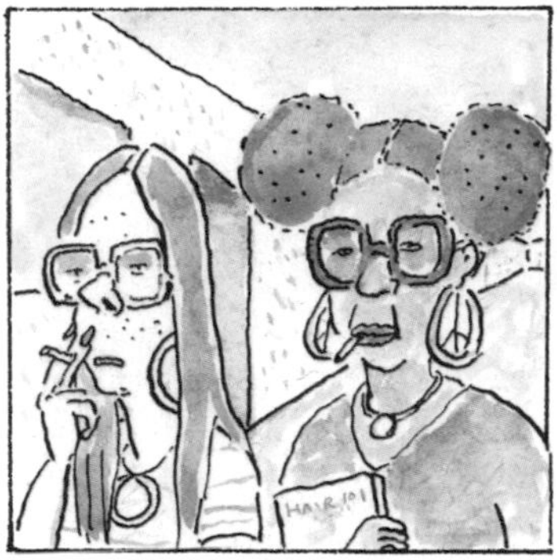
HAIR 101

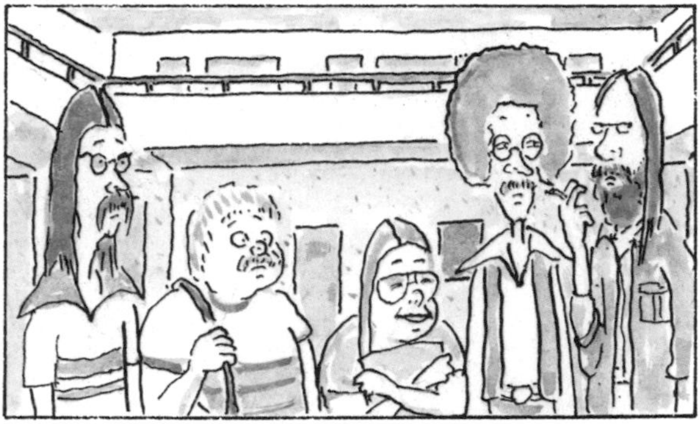

THERE WERE TWO SEPARATE TYPES OF STUDENTS THERE–YOUR WORKING-CLASS VO-TECH TYPES, AND YOUR MORE HIGHBROW INTELLECTUALS–MOSTLY EITHER RECENTLY-RETURNED VIETNAM VETS, HIPPIES, OR VIETNAM VETS-TURNED-HIPPIES, (READ: METHADONE OUTPATIENTS)–ALL OLDER.

IT STARTED TO BUG ME THAT NO MATTER WHAT YOU SAID TO THEM, ANY OF THEM, THEY WOULD SMILE BEATIFICALLY AND BOB THEIR HEADS UP AND DOWN IN AGREEMENT.

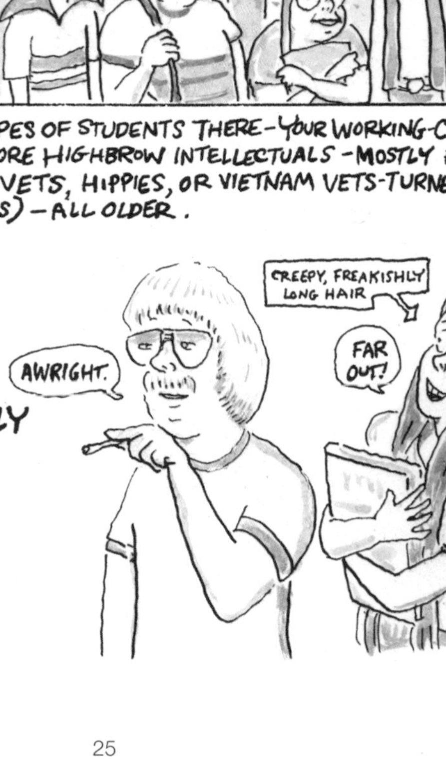
AWRIGHT.
CREEPY, FREAKISHLY LONG HAIR
FAR OUT!

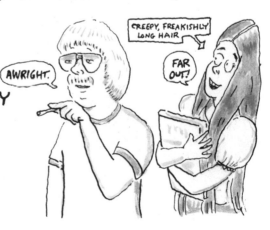

EVEN THOUGH THERE WERE DRAWING CLASSES, I FELT COMPELLED TO TAKE CRAFTS. EVERYONE, THEN, WAS INTO MAKING SOMETHING, MOSTLY...

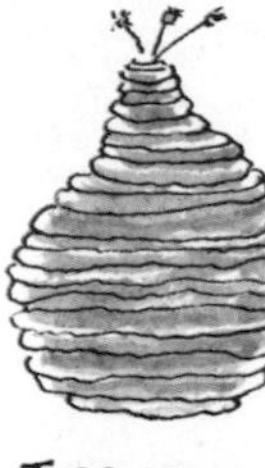

TURD-LIKE CERAMICS...

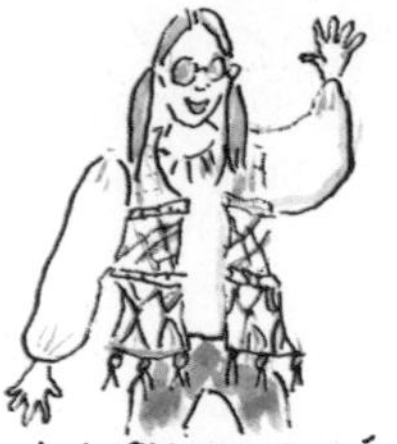

LUMPY MACRAMÉ VESTS...

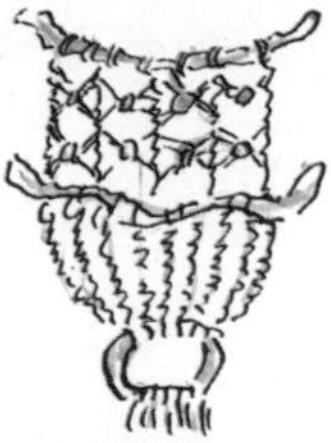

OR HIDEOUS WALL HANGINGS.

EVERYONE, THEN, LIVED ON FOOD STAMPS, OUT NEAR THE BEACH. EVERYONE, THEN, HAD A LOT OF PARTIES. THESE PARTIES ALWAYS FEATURED ROSÉ WINE, A LOT OF POT, AND SEALS AND CROFTS OR LOGGINS AND MESSINA ON THE STEREO. WHAT DID THEY TALK ABOUT? ASTROLOGY, WHERE TO SCORE THE BEST WEED, HOW TO MAKE A TERRARIUM FROM A WINE BOTTLE (TURNS OUT YOU HAD TO HAVE THAT SNAKY TOOL WITH THE LITTLE GRABBY THING ON THE END.)

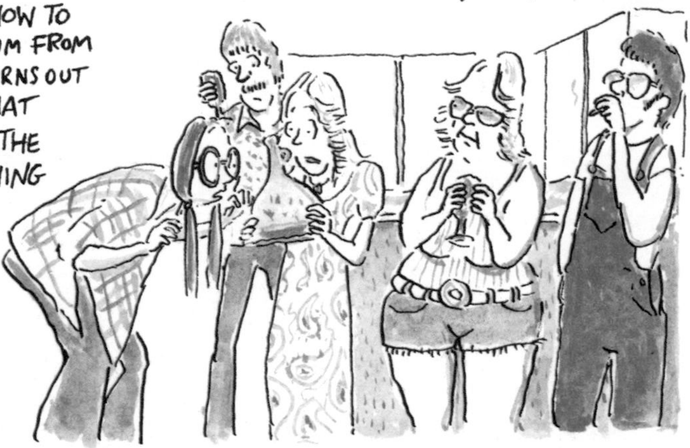

MORE THAN ONCE, I'D BEEN CORNERED ON AN INDIAN BEDSPREAD-COVERED COUCH BY SOME GUY WHO'D EARNESTLY SING RIGHT **AT** ME. NOW, **THAT** WAS HELL. HONESTLY, THIS WHOLE MELLOW DEAL WAS BECOMING PRETTY ANNOYING. I LOOKED AROUND THE ROOM AT THEIR VACANT FACES AND WONDERED, "WHAT HAVE THEY GOT TO BE SO HAPPY ABOUT?" I KNEW THEY WEREN'T. THEY WERE JUST PUTTING ON AN ACT SO EVERYONE WOULD THINK THEY WERE SPIRITUALLY EVOLVED, OR AT LEAST HIGH. OF COURSE, THEN, BEING HIGH **WAS** BEING SPIRITUALLY EVOLVED.

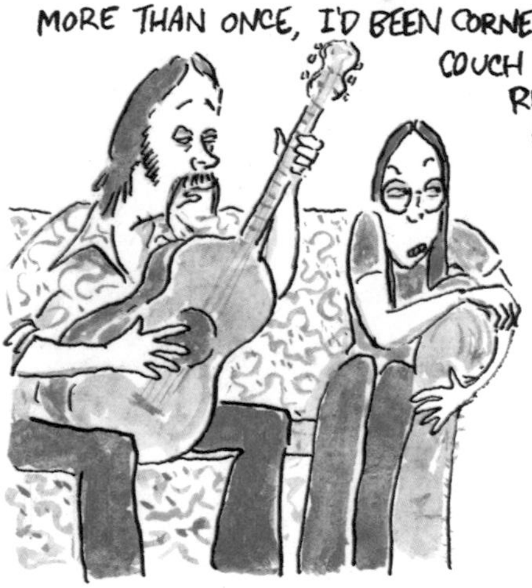

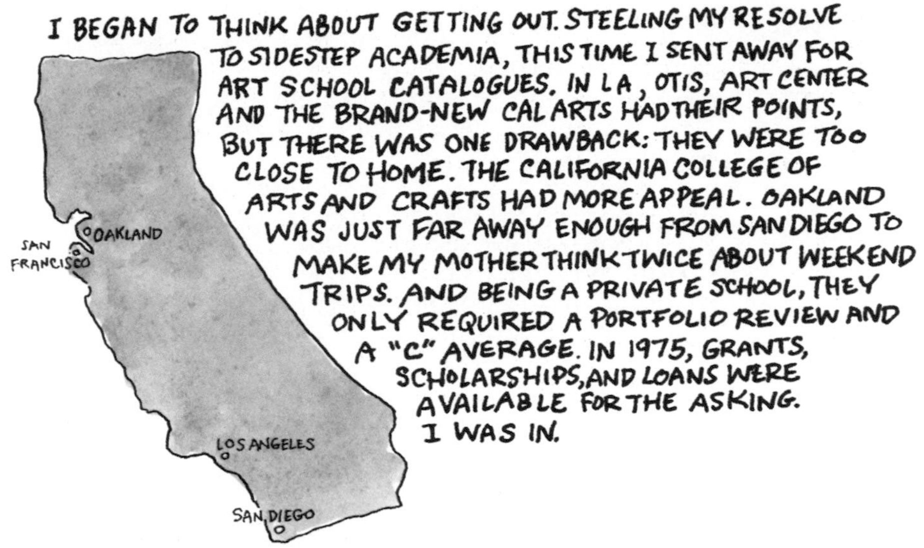
I BEGAN TO THINK ABOUT GETTING OUT. STEELING MY RESOLVE TO SIDESTEP ACADEMIA, THIS TIME I SENT AWAY FOR ART SCHOOL CATALOGUES. IN LA, OTIS, ART CENTER AND THE BRAND-NEW CAL ARTS HAD THEIR POINTS, BUT THERE WAS ONE DRAWBACK: THEY WERE TOO CLOSE TO HOME. THE CALIFORNIA COLLEGE OF ARTS AND CRAFTS HAD MORE APPEAL. OAKLAND WAS JUST FAR AWAY ENOUGH FROM SAN DIEGO TO MAKE MY MOTHER THINK TWICE ABOUT WEEKEND TRIPS. AND BEING A PRIVATE SCHOOL, THEY ONLY REQUIRED A PORTFOLIO REVIEW AND A "C" AVERAGE. IN 1975, GRANTS, SCHOLARSHIPS, AND LOANS WERE AVAILABLE FOR THE ASKING.
I WAS IN.
OAKLAND
SAN FRANCISCO
LOS ANGELES
SAN DIEGO

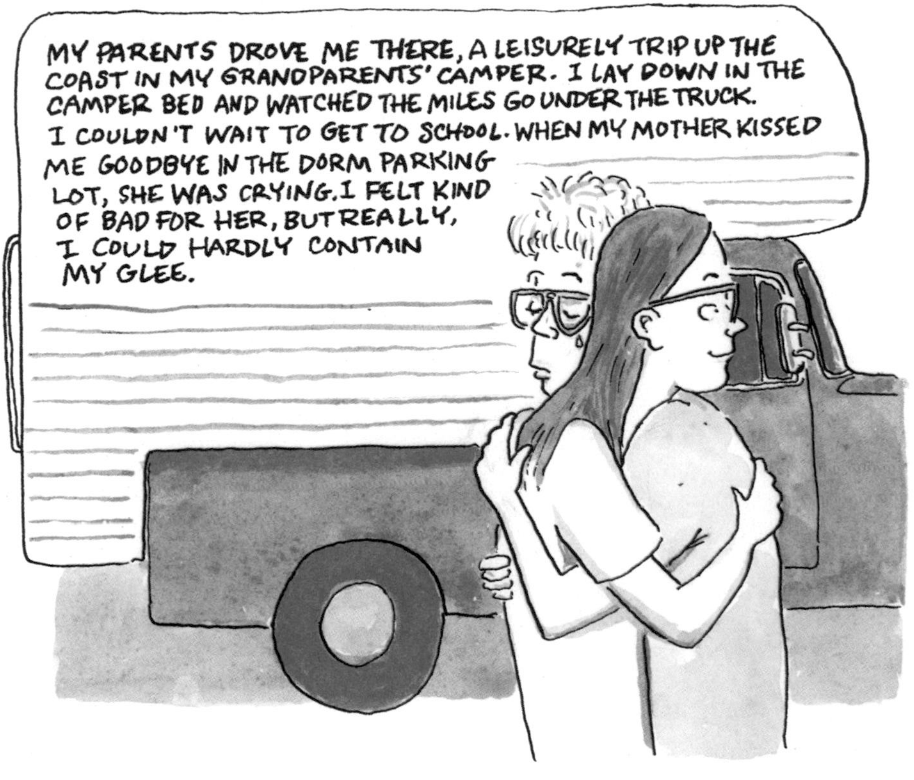
MY PARENTS DROVE ME THERE, A LEISURELY TRIP UP THE COAST IN MY GRANDPARENTS' CAMPER. I LAY DOWN IN THE CAMPER BED AND WATCHED THE MILES GO UNDER THE TRUCK. I COULDN'T WAIT TO GET TO SCHOOL. WHEN MY MOTHER KISSED ME GOODBYE IN THE DORM PARKING LOT, SHE WAS CRYING. I FELT KIND OF BAD FOR HER, BUT REALLY, I COULD HARDLY CONTAIN MY GLEE.

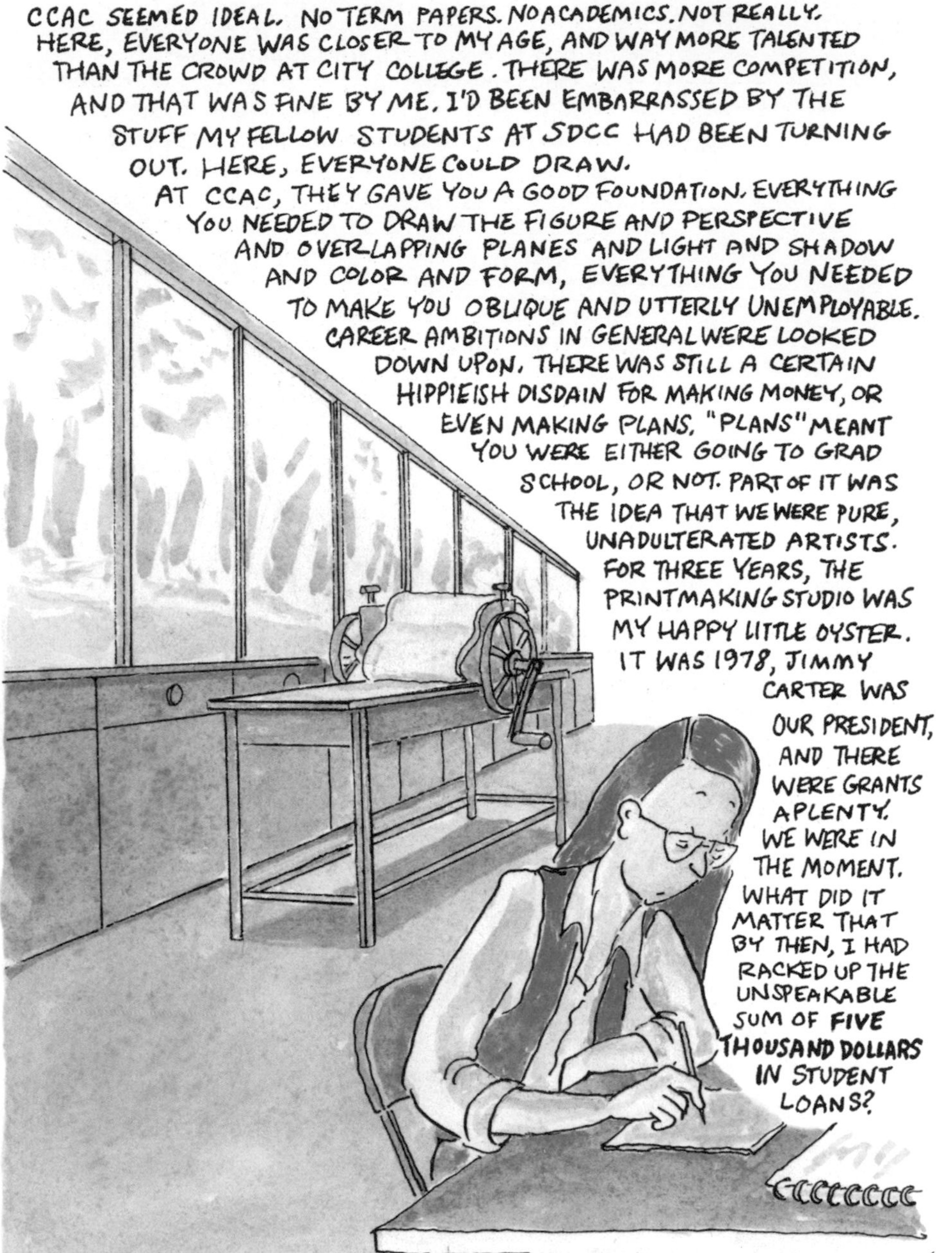
CCAC SEEMED IDEAL. NO TERM PAPERS. NO ACADEMICS. NOT REALLY. HERE, EVERYONE WAS CLOSER TO MY AGE, AND WAY MORE TALENTED THAN THE CROWD AT CITY COLLEGE. THERE WAS MORE COMPETITION, AND THAT WAS FINE BY ME. I'D BEEN EMBARRASSED BY THE STUFF MY FELLOW STUDENTS AT SDCC HAD BEEN TURNING OUT. HERE, EVERYONE COULD DRAW.
AT CCAC, THEY GAVE YOU A GOOD FOUNDATION. EVERYTHING YOU NEEDED TO DRAW THE FIGURE AND PERSPECTIVE AND OVERLAPPING PLANES AND LIGHT AND SHADOW AND COLOR AND FORM, EVERYTHING YOU NEEDED TO MAKE YOU OBLIQUE AND UTTERLY UNEMPLOYABLE. CAREER AMBITIONS IN GENERAL WERE LOOKED DOWN UPON. THERE WAS STILL A CERTAIN HIPPIEISH DISDAIN FOR MAKING MONEY, OR EVEN MAKING PLANS. "PLANS" MEANT YOU WERE EITHER GOING TO GRAD SCHOOL, OR NOT. PART OF IT WAS THE IDEA THAT WE WERE PURE, UNADULTERATED ARTISTS.
FOR THREE YEARS, THE PRINTMAKING STUDIO WAS MY HAPPY LITTLE OYSTER.
IT WAS 1978, JIMMY CARTER WAS OUR PRESIDENT, AND THERE WERE GRANTS APLENTY. WE WERE IN THE MOMENT. WHAT DID IT MATTER THAT BY THEN, I HAD RACKED UP THE UNSPEAKABLE SUM OF **FIVE THOUSAND DOLLARS** IN STUDENT LOANS?

AND THEN, THE WORLD SIMPLY SHIFTED ONE DAY, FROM INDIAN GAUZE TO BLACK LEATHER.

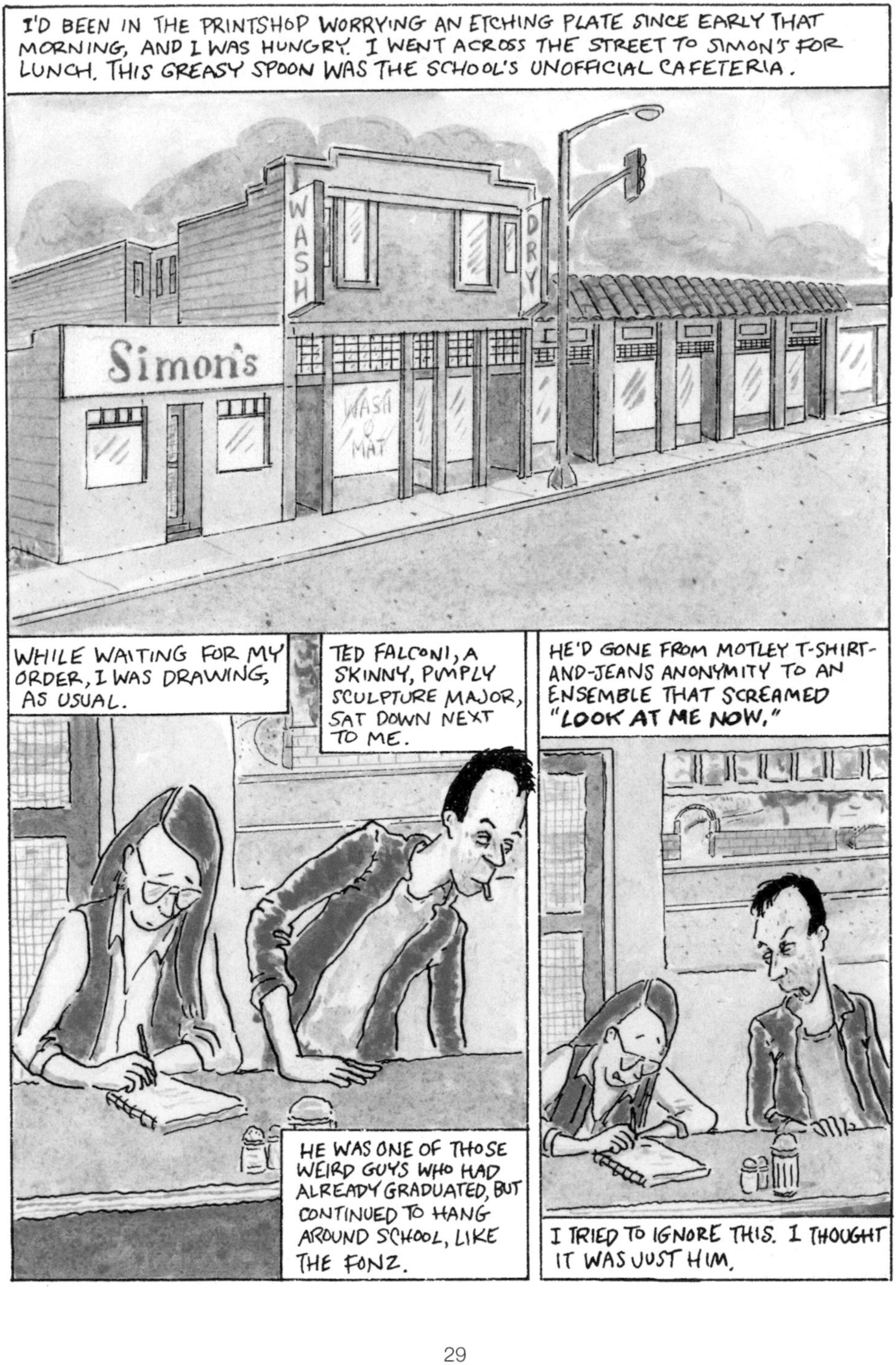
I'D BEEN IN THE PRINTSHOP WORRYING AN ETCHING PLATE SINCE EARLY THAT MORNING, AND I WAS HUNGRY. I WENT ACROSS THE STREET TO SIMON'S FOR LUNCH. THIS GREASY SPOON WAS THE SCHOOL'S UNOFFICIAL CAFETERIA.
WASH
DRY
Simon's
WASH O MAT
WHILE WAITING FOR MY ORDER, I WAS DRAWING, AS USUAL.
TED FALCONI, A SKINNY, PIMPLY SCULPTURE MAJOR, SAT DOWN NEXT TO ME.
HE WAS ONE OF THOSE WEIRD GUYS WHO HAD ALREADY GRADUATED, BUT CONTINUED TO HANG AROUND SCHOOL, LIKE THE FONZ.
HE'D GONE FROM MOTLEY T-SHIRT-AND-JEANS ANONYMITY TO AN ENSEMBLE THAT SCREAMED "LOOK AT ME NOW."
I TRIED TO IGNORE THIS. I THOUGHT IT WAS JUST HIM.

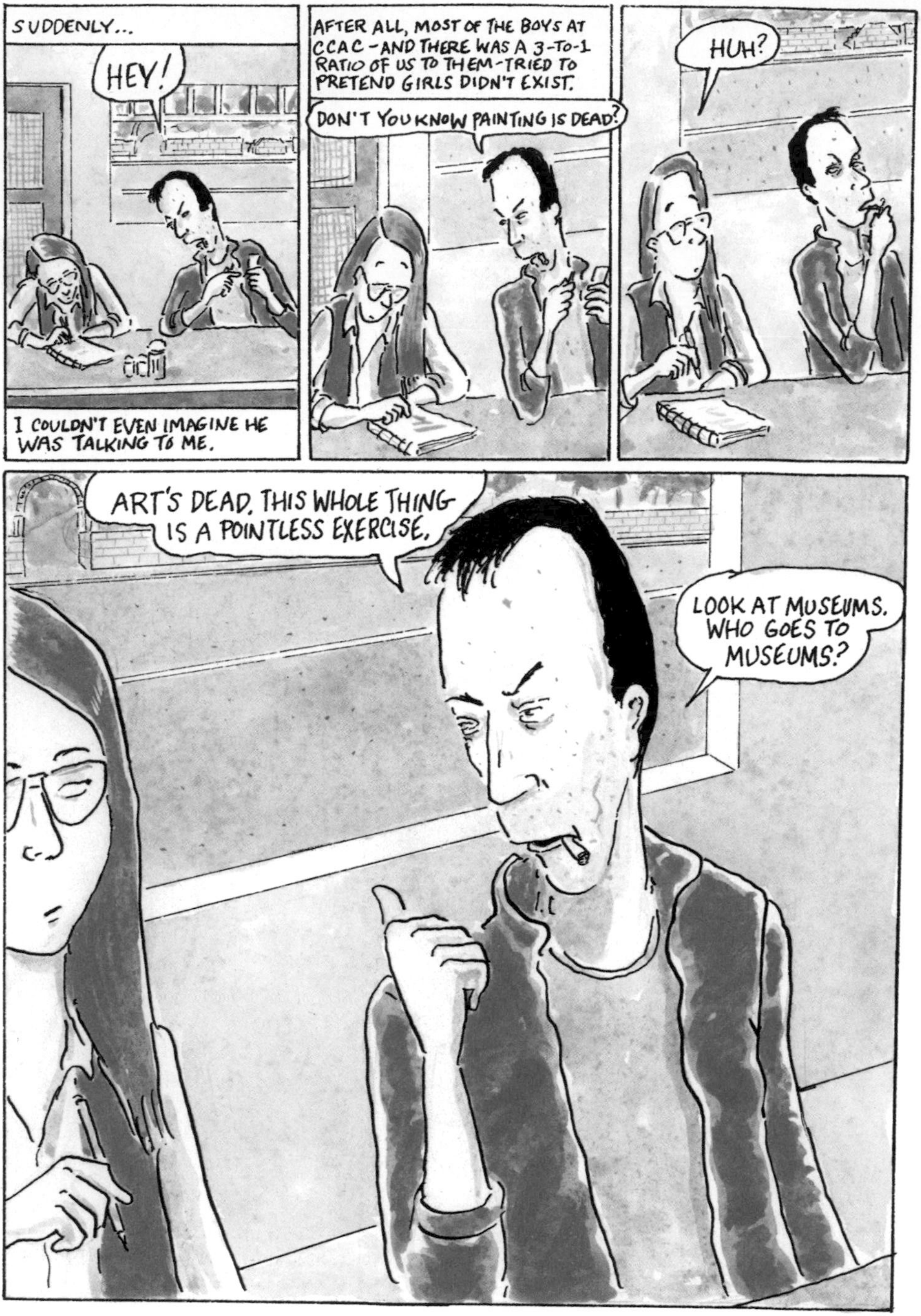

SUDDENLY...
HEY!
I COULDN'T EVEN IMAGINE HE WAS TALKING TO ME.
AFTER ALL, MOST OF THE BOYS AT CCAC - AND THERE WAS A 3-TO-1 RATIO OF US TO THEM - TRIED TO PRETEND GIRLS DIDN'T EXIST.
DON'T YOU KNOW PAINTING IS DEAD?
HUH?
ART'S DEAD. THIS WHOLE THING IS A POINTLESS EXERCISE.
LOOK AT MUSEUMS. WHO GOES TO MUSEUMS?

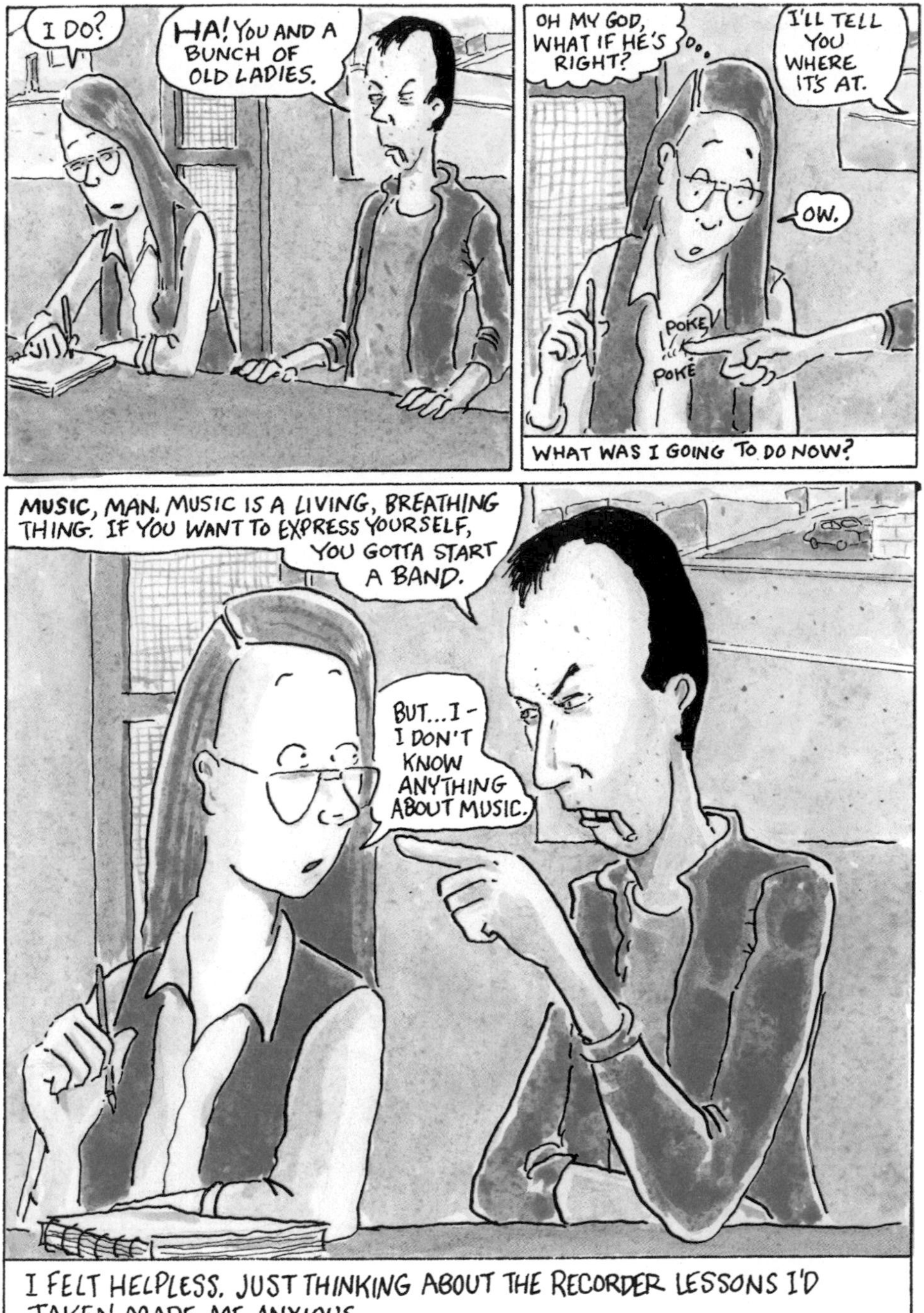
I DO?
HA! YOU AND A BUNCH OF OLD LADIES.
OH MY GOD, WHAT IF HE'S RIGHT?
I'LL TELL YOU WHERE IT'S AT.
OW.
POKE
POKE
WHAT WAS I GOING TO DO NOW?
MUSIC, MAN. MUSIC IS A LIVING, BREATHING THING. IF YOU WANT TO EXPRESS YOURSELF, YOU GOTTA START A BAND.
BUT... I - I DON'T KNOW ANYTHING ABOUT MUSIC.
I FELT HELPLESS. JUST THINKING ABOUT THE RECORDER LESSONS I'D TAKEN MADE ME ANXIOUS.

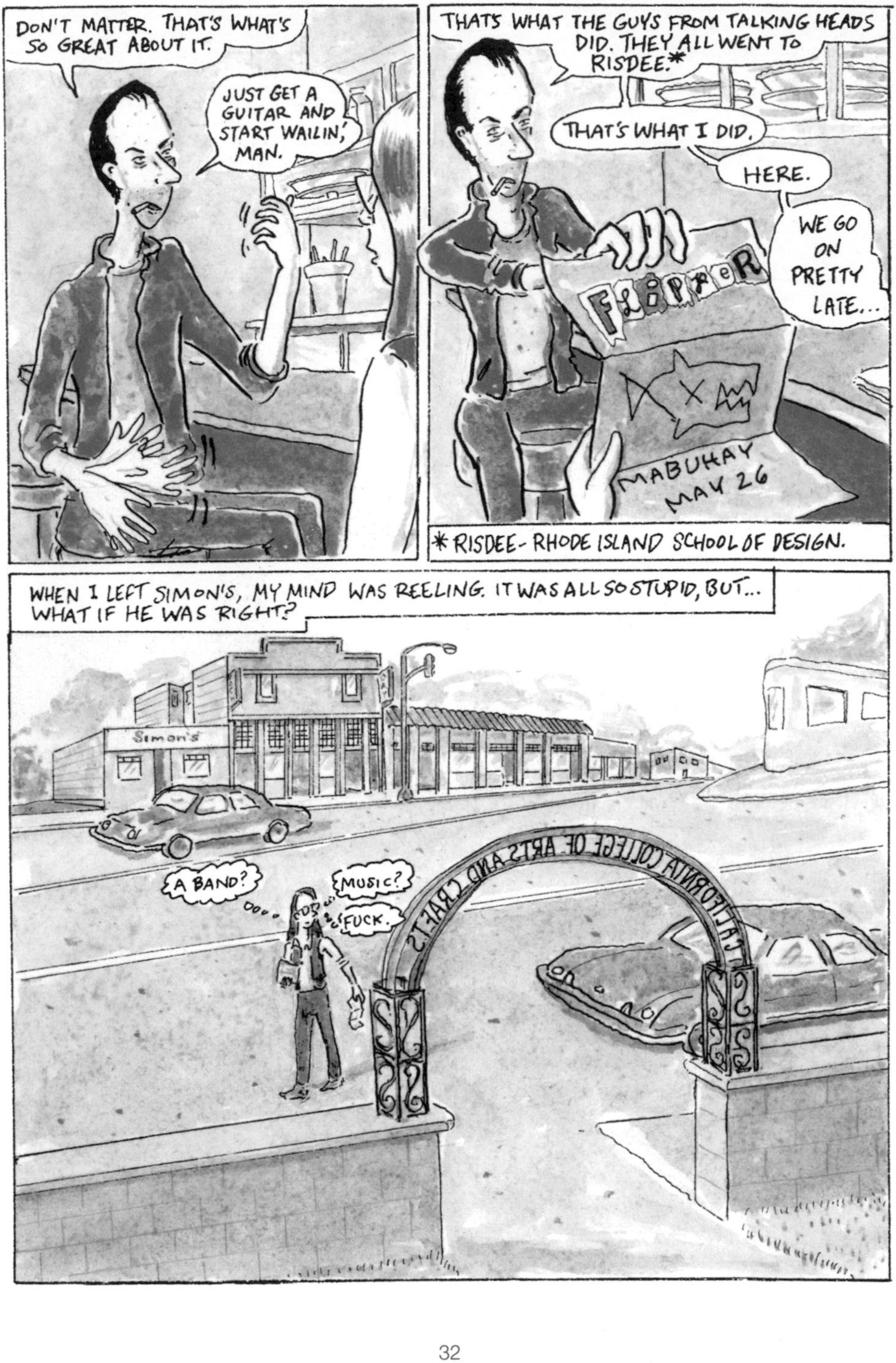

DON'T MATTER. THAT'S WHAT'S SO GREAT ABOUT IT.
JUST GET A GUITAR AND START WAILIN,' MAN.
THAT'S WHAT THE GUYS FROM TALKING HEADS DID. THEY ALL WENT TO RISDEE.*
THAT'S WHAT I DID.
HERE.
WE GO ON PRETTY LATE...
FLIPPER
MABUHAY MAY 26
* RISDEE - RHODE ISLAND SCHOOL OF DESIGN.
WHEN I LEFT SIMON'S, MY MIND WAS REELING. IT WAS ALL SO STUPID, BUT... WHAT IF HE WAS RIGHT?
Simon's
CALIFORNIA COLLEGE OF ARTS AND CRAFTS
A BAND?
MUSIC?
FUCK.

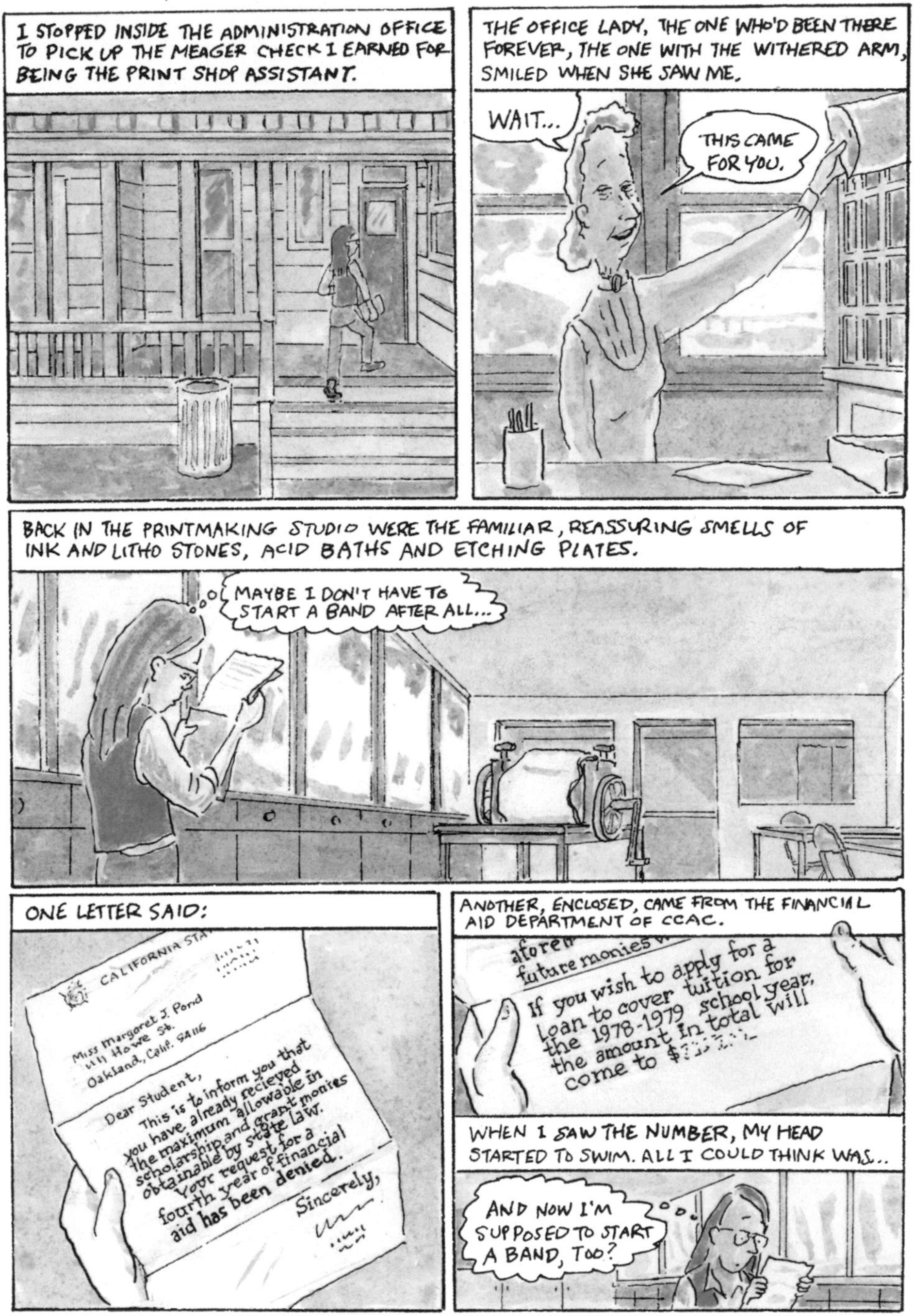
I STOPPED INSIDE THE ADMINISTRATION OFFICE TO PICK UP THE MEAGER CHECK I EARNED FOR BEING THE PRINT SHOP ASSISTANT.
THE OFFICE LADY, THE ONE WHO'D BEEN THERE FOREVER, THE ONE WITH THE WITHERED ARM, SMILED WHEN SHE SAW ME.
WAIT...
THIS CAME FOR YOU.
BACK IN THE PRINTMAKING STUDIO WERE THE FAMILIAR, REASSURING SMELLS OF INK AND LITHO STONES, ACID BATHS AND ETCHING PLATES.
MAYBE I DON'T HAVE TO START A BAND AFTER ALL...
ONE LETTER SAID:
CALIFORNIA STA
Miss Margaret J. Pond
Howe St.
Oakland, Calif. 94116
Dear Student,
This is to inform you that you have already recieved the maximum allowable in scholarship and grant monies obtainable by state law. Your request for a fourth year of financial aid has been denied.
Sincerely,
ANOTHER, ENCLOSED, CAME FROM THE FINANCIAL AID DEPARTMENT OF CCAC.
afore
future monies
If you wish to apply for a Loan to cover tuition for the 1978-1979 school year, the amount in total will come to $
WHEN I SAW THE NUMBER, MY HEAD STARTED TO SWIM. ALL I COULD THINK WAS...
AND NOW I'M SUPPOSED TO START A BAND, TOO?

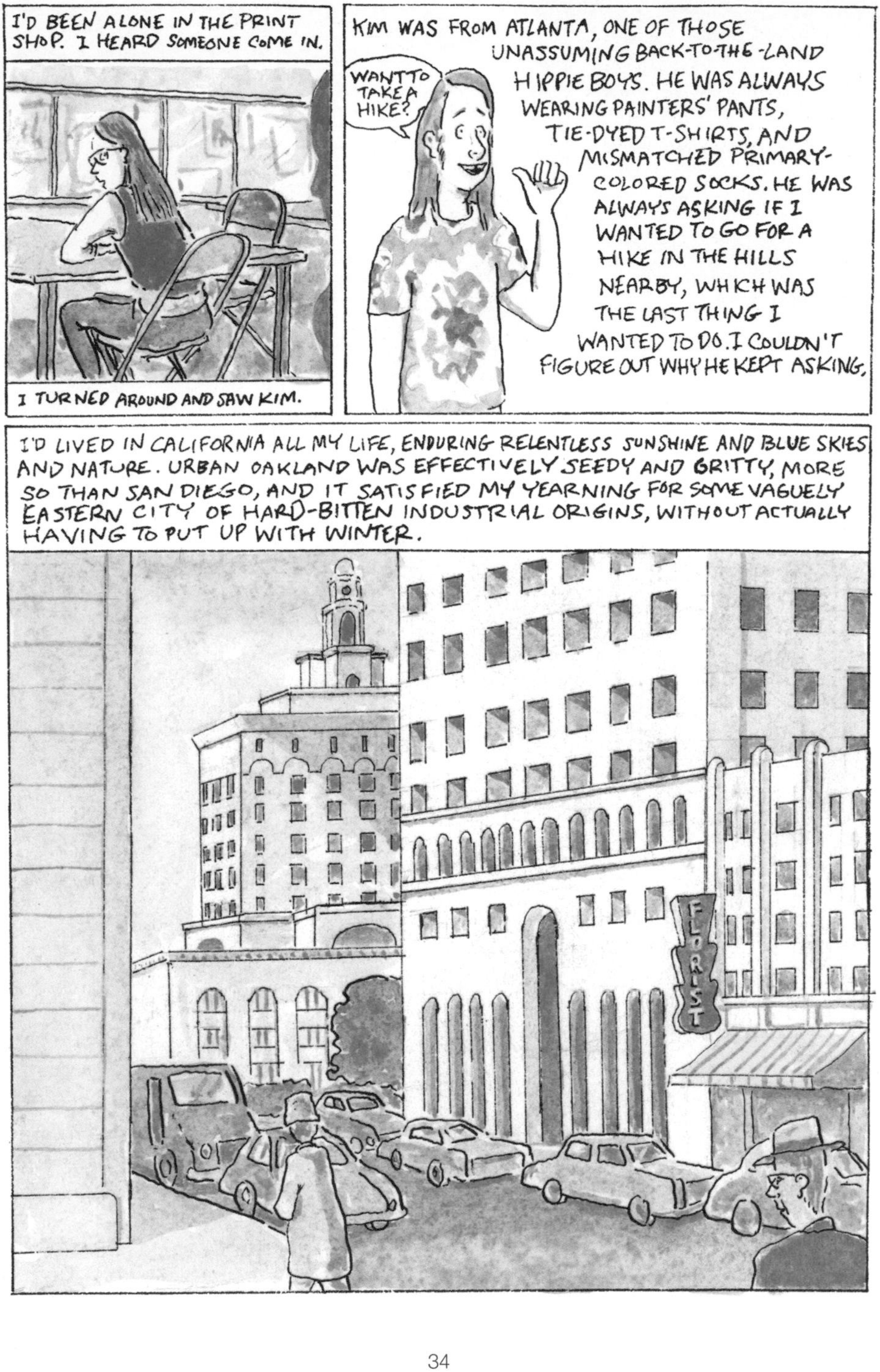
I'D BEEN ALONE IN THE PRINT SHOP. I HEARD SOMEONE COME IN.
I TURNED AROUND AND SAW KIM.
KIM WAS FROM ATLANTA, ONE OF THOSE UNASSUMING BACK-TO-THE-LAND HIPPIE BOYS. HE WAS ALWAYS WEARING PAINTERS' PANTS, TIE-DYED T-SHIRTS, AND MISMATCHED PRIMARY-COLORED SOCKS. HE WAS ALWAYS ASKING IF I WANTED TO GO FOR A HIKE IN THE HILLS NEARBY, WHICH WAS THE LAST THING I WANTED TO DO. I COULDN'T FIGURE OUT WHY HE KEPT ASKING.
WANT TO TAKE A HIKE?
I'D LIVED IN CALIFORNIA ALL MY LIFE, ENDURING RELENTLESS SUNSHINE AND BLUE SKIES AND NATURE. URBAN OAKLAND WAS EFFECTIVELY SEEDY AND GRITTY, MORE SO THAN SAN DIEGO, AND IT SATISFIED MY YEARNING FOR SOME VAGUELY EASTERN CITY OF HARD-BITTEN INDUSTRIAL ORIGINS, WITHOUT ACTUALLY HAVING TO PUT UP WITH WINTER.
FLORIST

THE FIRST THING I NOTICED
WAS THAT KIM WAS TAKING
ALL HIS HUGE WATERCOLOR
PAINTINGS- ALL OF WHICH,
DESPITE INVOLVING RAIN-
BOWS, WERE ACTUALLY
QUITE BREATHTAKING —
OUT OF HIS LOCKER AND
STUFFING THEM IN A
TRASH CAN.

THEN I SAW THAT HIS SHOULDER-LENGTH
LOCKS WERE GONE. HIS HAIR WAS NOW
SPIKEY AND SHORT, TOO, JUST LIKE
TED FALCONI'S. HE WAS WEARING A
BLACK T-SHIRT AND BLACK DENIM
JEANS. AND THE ALLMAN BROTHERS
ALBUMS KIM LISTENED TO ON THE
CRAPPY STUDIO RECORD PLAYER WERE
GONE TOO. IT WAS SOME CRAZY SONG
PLAYING NOW, SOMEONE SNEERING,
"GOD SAVE THE QUEEN."

SOMETHING WAS DEFINITELY UP. AND IT WASN'T
JUST THE CLOTHES AND THE HAIR AND THE MUSIC.
OVERNIGHT, THAT WHOLE MELLOW THING WAS
OVER. EVERYONE, SUDDENLY, WAS PISSED OFF,
AS THOUGH ALL THOSE YEARS OF BEING AGREEABLE
HAD BEEN JUST TOO MUCH. IT WAS A RELIEF,
REALLY, BUT HOW HAD I MISSED THE
ORIENTATION MEETING? I MEAN, I WAS READY
TO BE MAD TOO, BUT I COULDN'T AFFORD A
WHOLE NEW LOOK. I COULDN'T EVEN AFFORD
ART SCHOOL ANYMORE. I WAS GOING TO HAVE
TO DO SOMETHING, THOUGH, TO AVOID BEING
LEFT IN THE DUST.

I AM USED TO EATING BREAKFAST IN RESTAURANTS.

I FIND A CERTAIN COMFORT IN THE USUAL COFFEESHOP FARE...

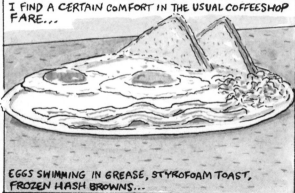

EGGS SWIMMING IN GREASE, STYROFOAM TOAST, FROZEN HASH BROWNS...

BUT WHEN I GO BACK TO THE IMPERIAL CAFE TO GET MY FREE MEAL, I FIND

FOOD HEAVEN

HERE, THEY SERVE FLUFFY PASTEL YELLOW OMELETS...

STUFFED WITH WONDERFUL FILLINGS LIKE CRAB OR CHICKEN OR ANYTHING YOU MIGHT ASK FOR...

THERE'S THAT RICH, DARK ROAST COFFEE...

WITH REAL CREAM...

ORANGE JUICE THE WAITRESS WILL SQUEEZE —RIGHT— BEFORE YOUR EYES...

THE BEST HOMEFRIES YOU'VE EVER TASTED...

ALL THIS AND STARCHED WHITE NAPKINS, TOO, I'VE NEVER SEEN QUALITY LIKE THIS BEFORE. IT'S LIKE MY LIFE.

I WAS USED TO MARGARINE, AND NOW, HERE IS BUTTER.

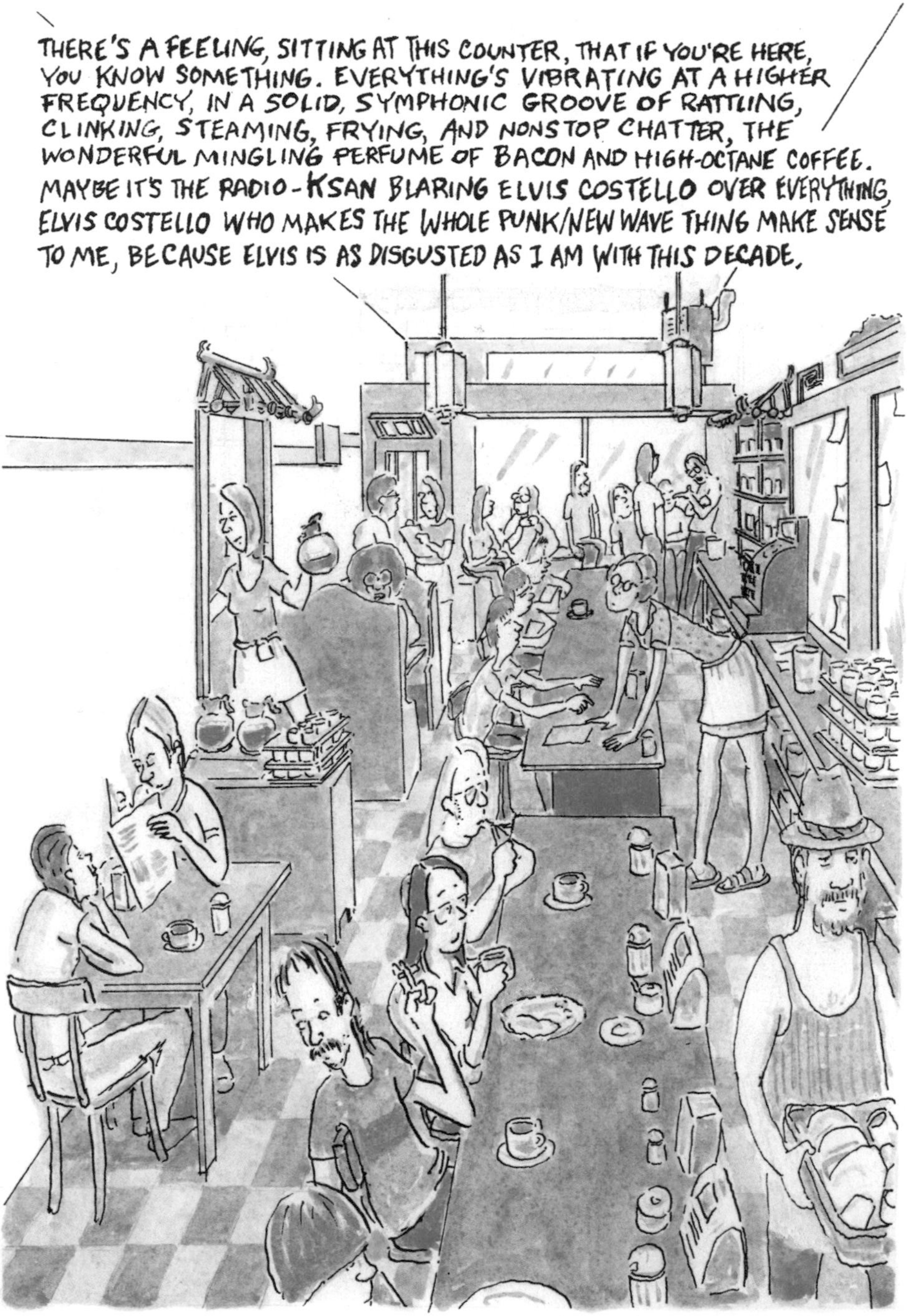
THERE'S A FEELING, SITTING AT THIS COUNTER, THAT IF YOU'RE HERE, YOU KNOW SOMETHING. EVERYTHING'S VIBRATING AT A HIGHER FREQUENCY, IN A SOLID, SYMPHONIC GROOVE OF RATTLING, CLINKING, STEAMING, FRYING, AND NONSTOP CHATTER, THE WONDERFUL MINGLING PERFUME OF BACON AND HIGH-OCTANE COFFEE. MAYBE IT'S THE RADIO-KSAN BLARING ELVIS COSTELLO OVER EVERYTHING, ELVIS COSTELLO WHO MAKES THE WHOLE PUNK/NEW WAVE THING MAKE SENSE TO ME, BECAUSE ELVIS IS AS DISGUSTED AS I AM WITH THIS DECADE.

IT'S A BUSY WEEKEND MORNING, AND IT'S VERY CROWDED. THE CROWD THAT PILES UP WAITING FOR TABLES IS A CAVALCADE OF HIPSTERS. AND IF YOU KNOW ANYTHING ABOUT HIPSTERS, YOU KNOW THAT THEIR SIGNIFIERS TELL YOU EVERYTHING.

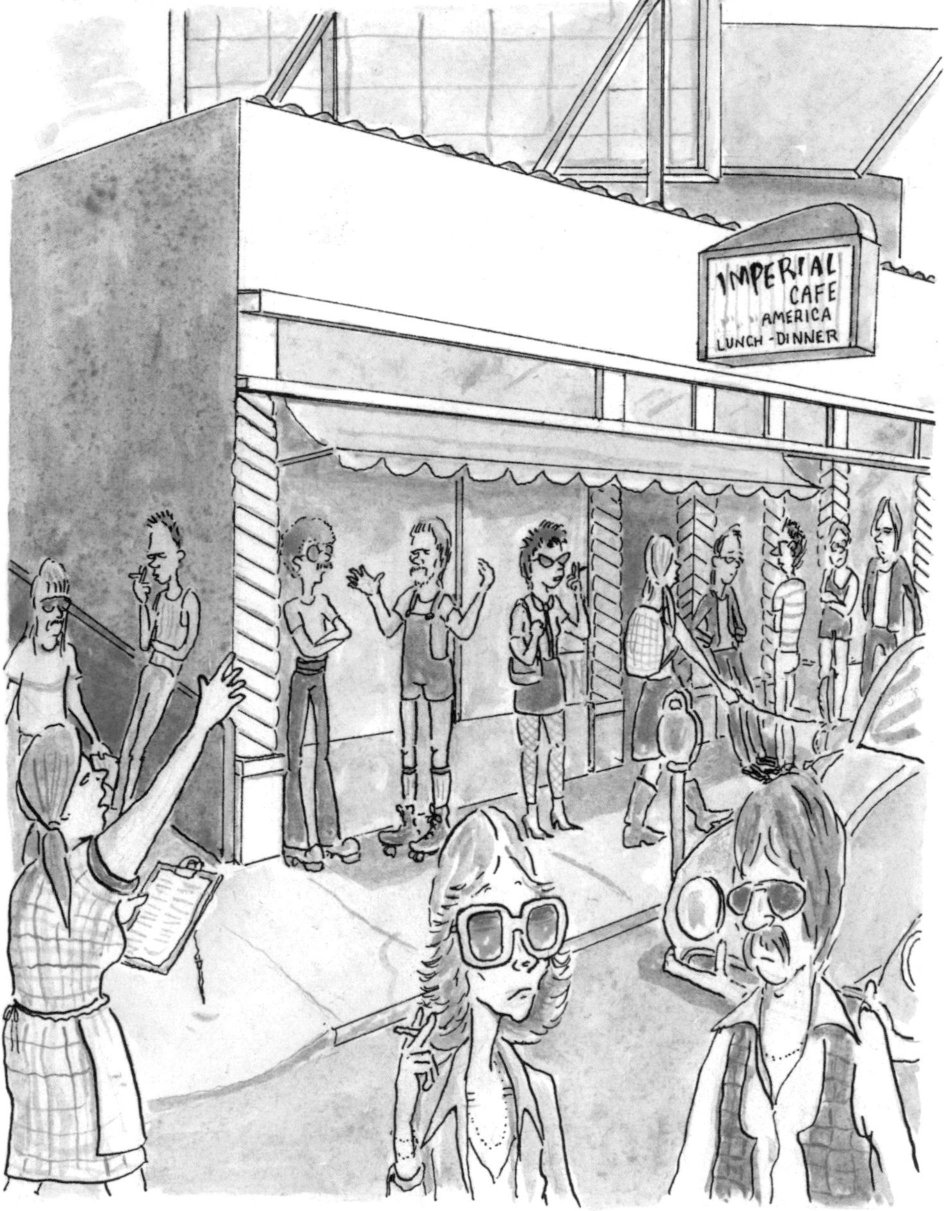
IMPERIAL
CAFE
AMERICA
LUNCH - DINNER

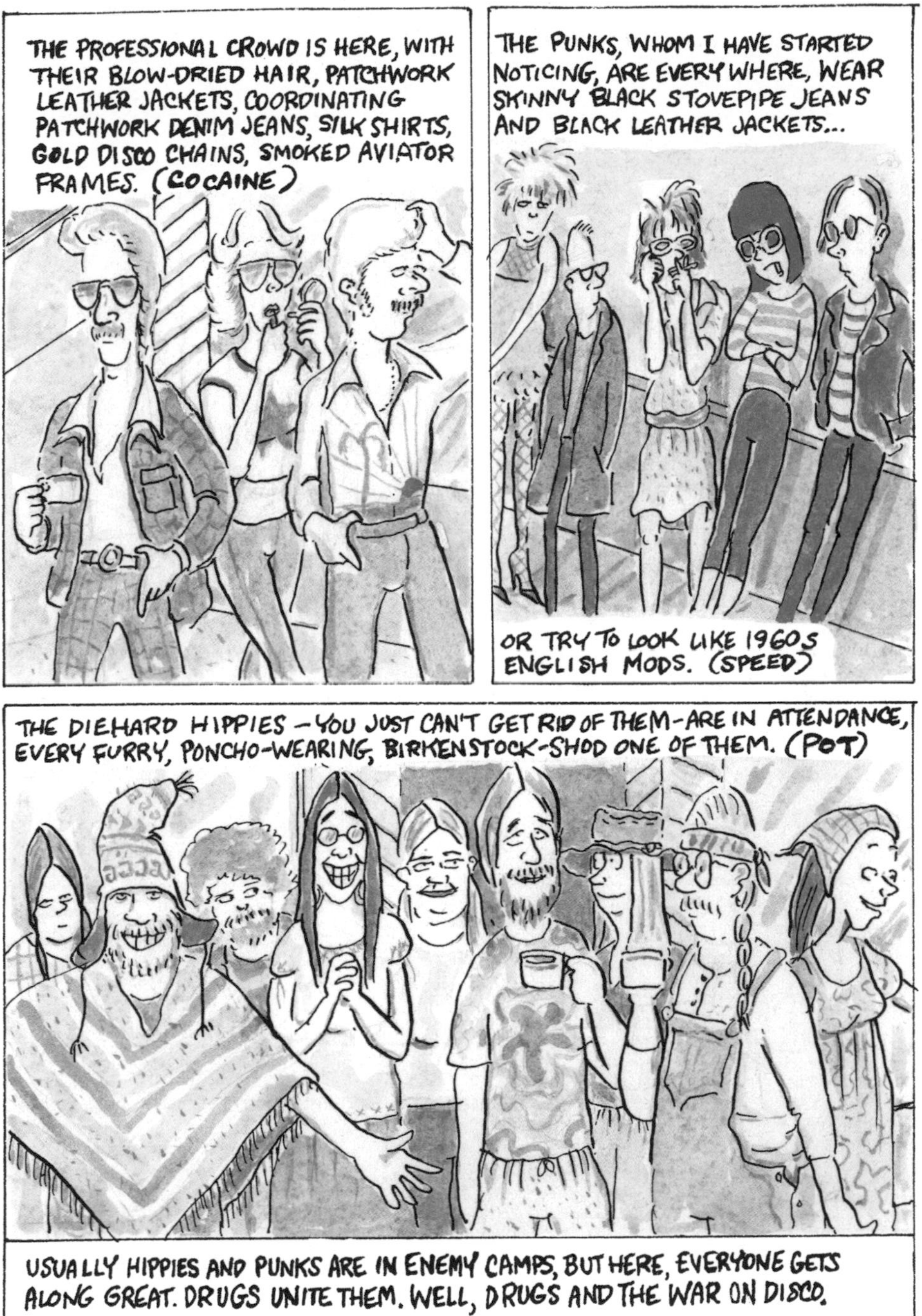
THE PROFESSIONAL CROWD IS HERE, WITH THEIR BLOW-DRIED HAIR, PATCHWORK LEATHER JACKETS, COORDINATING PATCHWORK DENIM JEANS, SILK SHIRTS, GOLD DISCO CHAINS, SMOKED AVIATOR FRAMES. (COCAINE)
THE PUNKS, WHOM I HAVE STARTED NOTICING, ARE EVERYWHERE, WEAR SKINNY BLACK STOVEPIPE JEANS AND BLACK LEATHER JACKETS...
OR TRY TO LOOK LIKE 1960S ENGLISH MODS. (SPEED)
THE DIEHARD HIPPIES – YOU JUST CAN'T GET RID OF THEM – ARE IN ATTENDANCE, EVERY FURRY, PONCHO-WEARING, BIRKENSTOCK-SHOD ONE OF THEM. (POT)
USUALLY HIPPIES AND PUNKS ARE IN ENEMY CAMPS, BUT HERE, EVERYONE GETS ALONG GREAT. DRUGS UNITE THEM. WELL, DRUGS AND THE WAR ON DISCO.

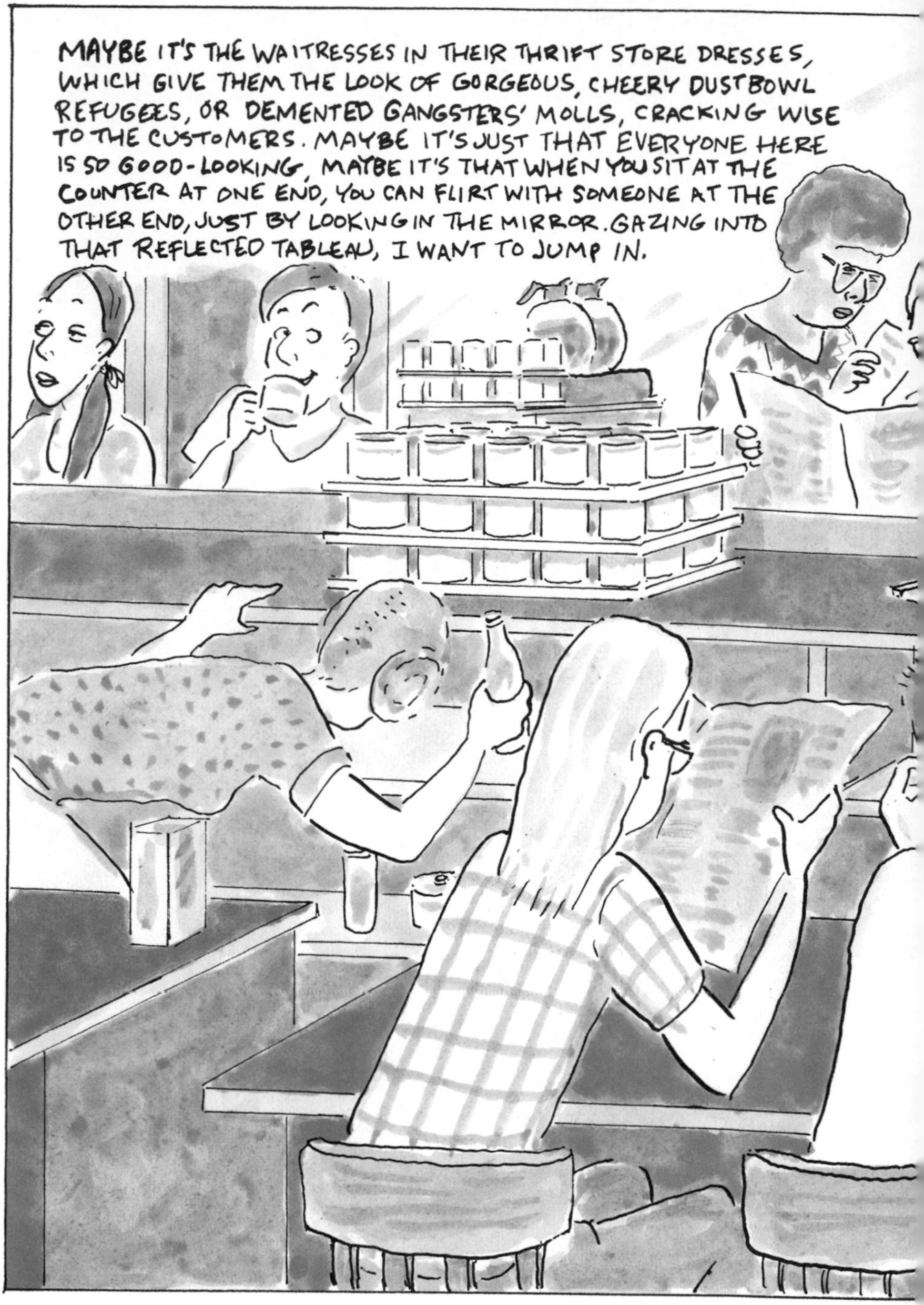
MAYBE IT'S THE WAITRESSES IN THEIR THRIFT STORE DRESSES, WHICH GIVE THEM THE LOOK OF GORGEOUS, CHEERY DUSTBOWL REFUGEES, OR DEMENTED GANGSTERS' MOLLS, CRACKING WISE TO THE CUSTOMERS. MAYBE IT'S JUST THAT EVERYONE HERE IS SO GOOD-LOOKING, MAYBE IT'S THAT WHEN YOU SIT AT THE COUNTER AT ONE END, YOU CAN FLIRT WITH SOMEONE AT THE OTHER END, JUST BY LOOKING IN THE MIRROR. GAZING INTO THAT REFLECTED TABLEAU, I WANT TO JUMP IN.

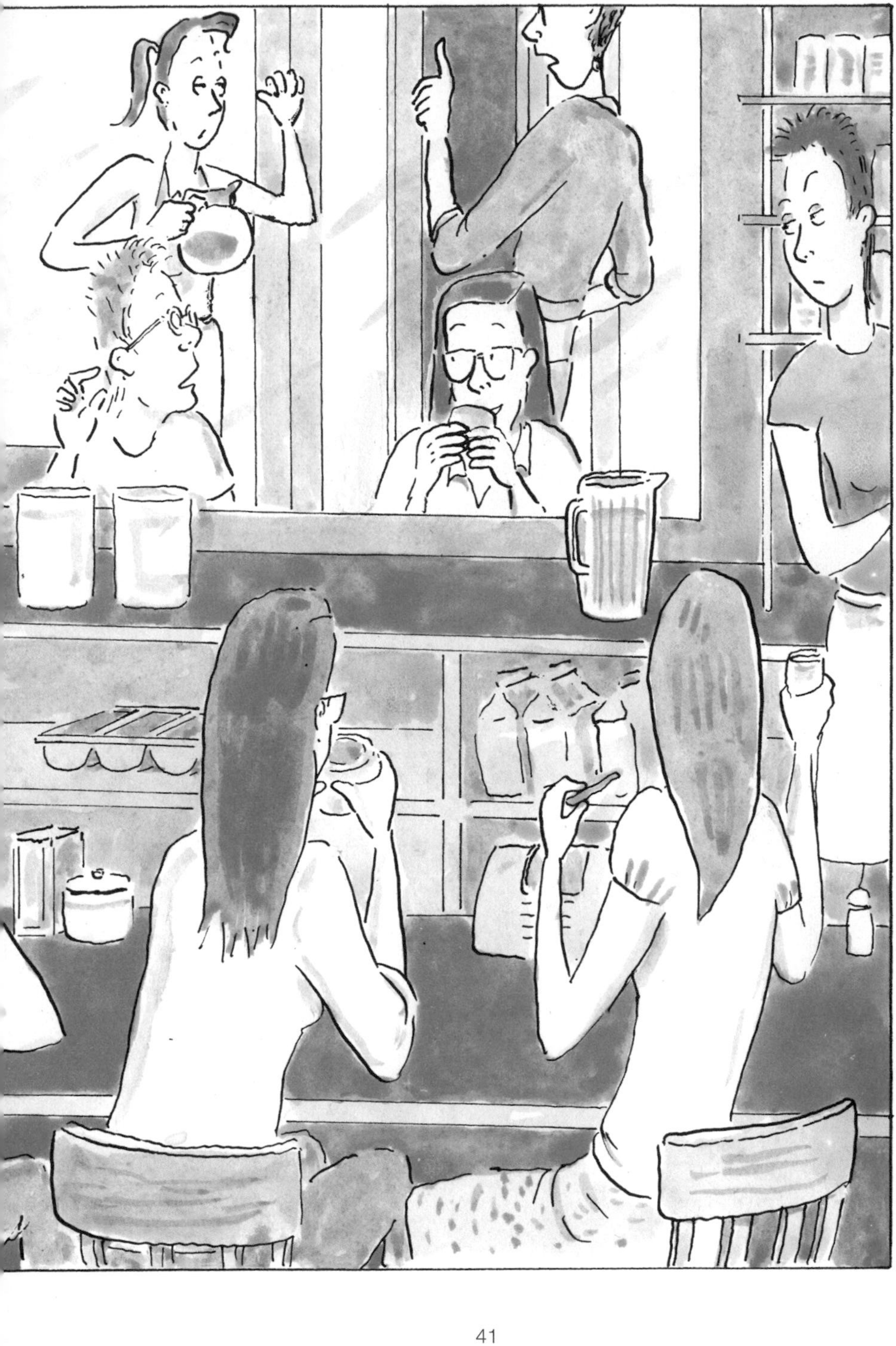

SITTING AT THE COUNTER, AFTER ABOUT SEVEN CUPS OF COFFEE, I HAVE A CRYSTALLINE MOMENT OF PURE CONSCIOUSNESS. IT COMES TO ME: I COULD WORK HERE. IT'S WHAT I AM MEANT TO DO. IT'S REAL LIFE.

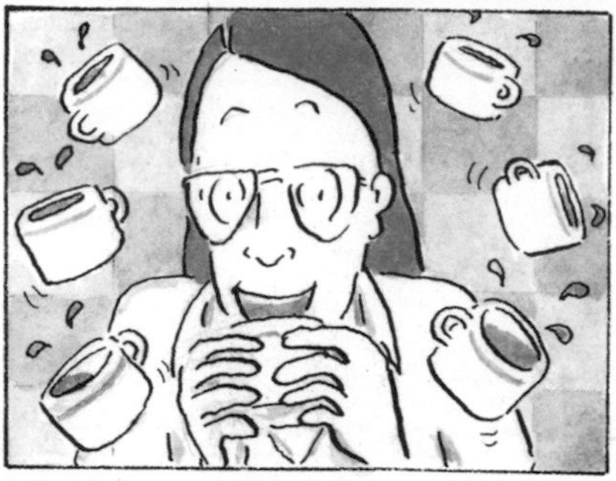

I'VE BUDDIED UP TO TINA, ONE OF THE WAITRESSES. SHE WENT TO CCAC TOO, A CERAMICS MAJOR. SHE EVEN GRADUATED, NOT LIKE ME, NOW OFFICIALLY OUT ON MY ASS.

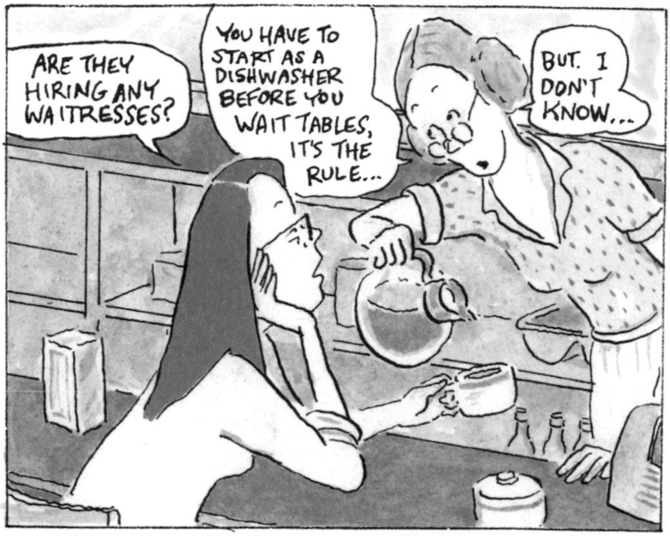
ARE THEY HIRING ANY WAITRESSES?
YOU HAVE TO START AS A DISHWASHER BEFORE YOU WAIT TABLES, IT'S THE RULE...
BUT. I DON'T KNOW...

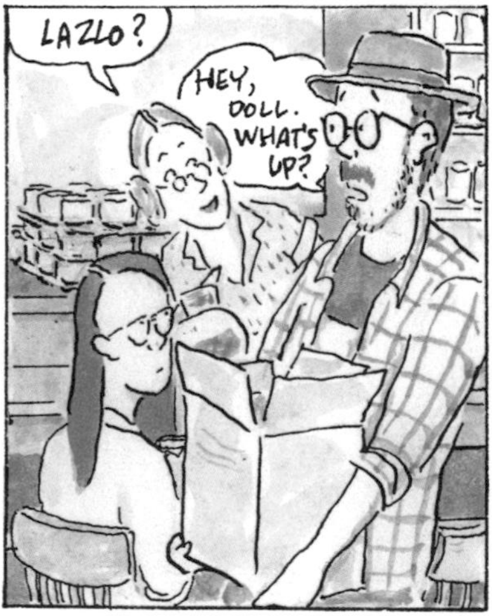
LAZLO?
HEY, DOLL. WHAT'S UP?

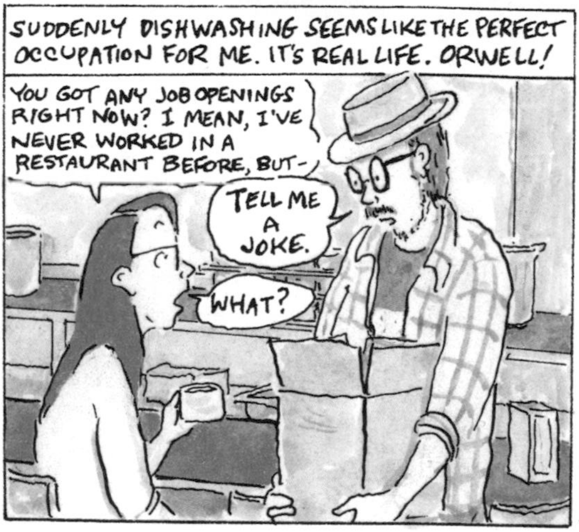
SUDDENLY DISHWASHING SEEMS LIKE THE PERFECT OCCUPATION FOR ME. IT'S REAL LIFE. ORWELL!
YOU GOT ANY JOB OPENINGS RIGHT NOW? I MEAN, I'VE NEVER WORKED IN A RESTAURANT BEFORE, BUT-
TELL ME A JOKE.
WHAT?

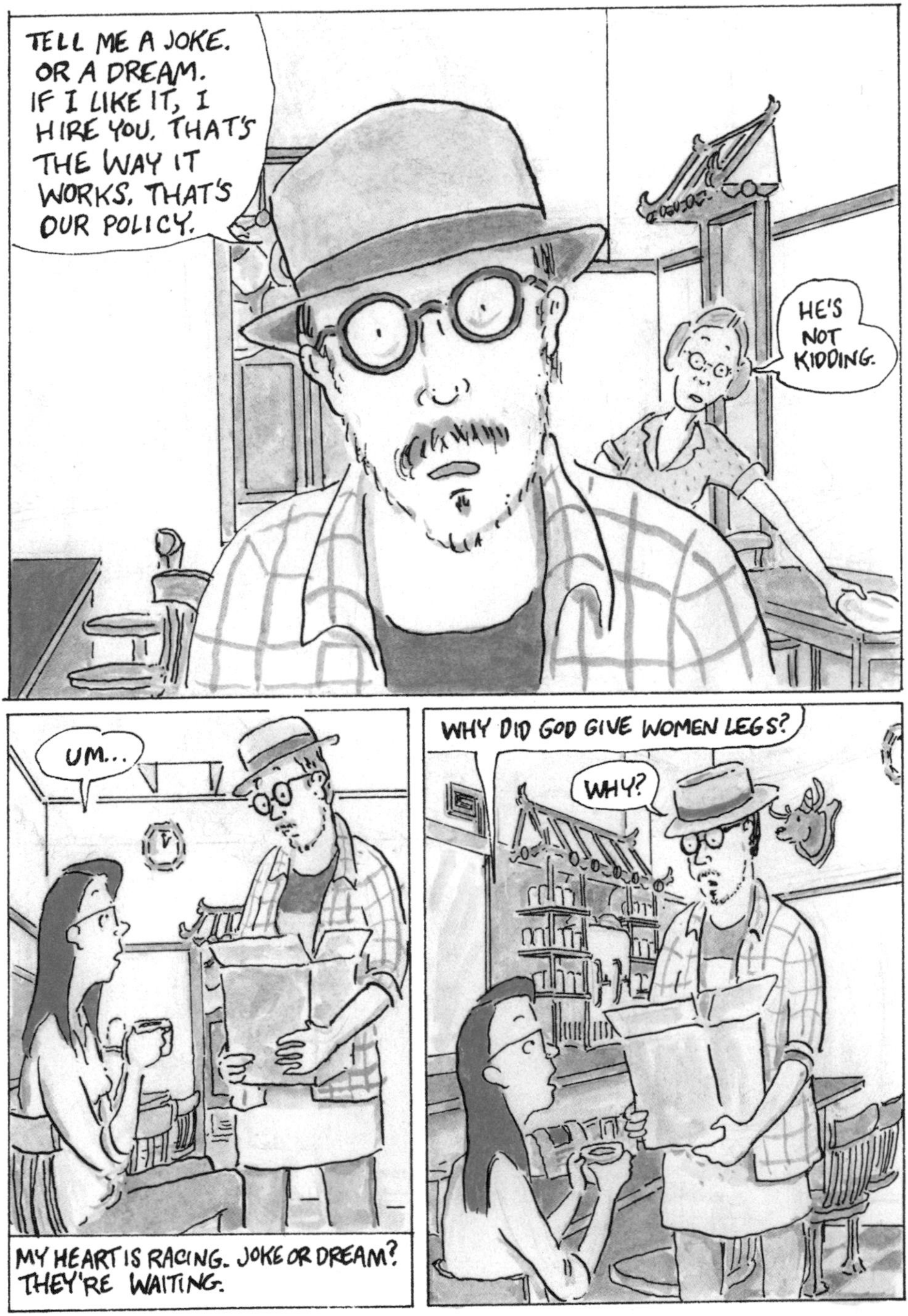
TELL ME A JOKE. OR A DREAM. IF I LIKE IT, I HIRE YOU. THAT'S THE WAY IT WORKS. THAT'S OUR POLICY.
HE'S NOT KIDDING.
UM...
MY HEART IS RACING. JOKE OR DREAM? THEY'RE WAITING.
WHY DID GOD GIVE WOMEN LEGS?
WHY?

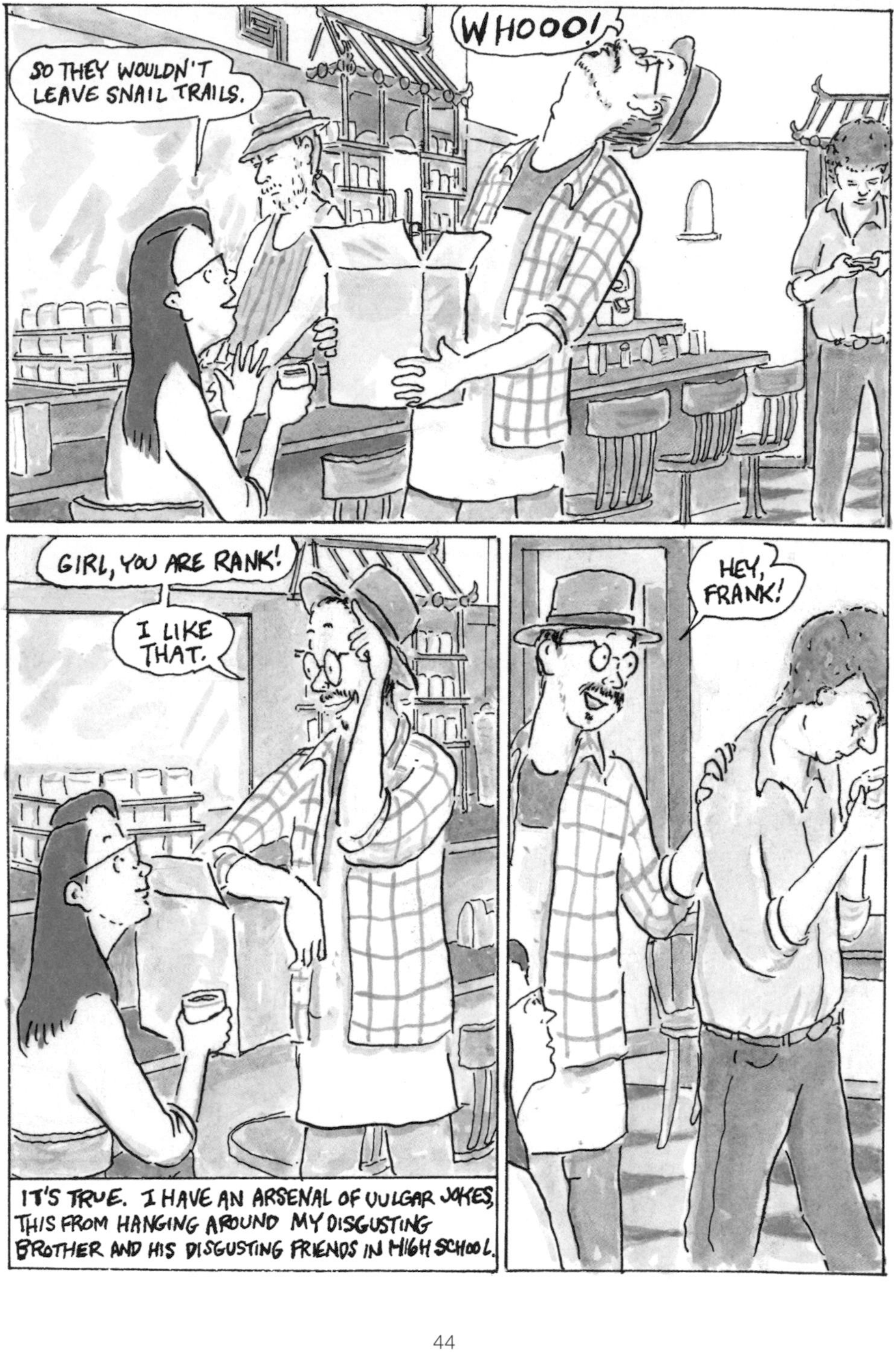
SO THEY WOULDN'T LEAVE SNAIL TRAILS.
WHOOO!
GIRL, YOU ARE RANK!
I LIKE THAT.
IT'S TRUE. I HAVE AN ARSENAL OF VULGAR JOKES, THIS FROM HANGING AROUND MY DISGUSTING BROTHER AND HIS DISGUSTING FRIENDS IN HIGH SCHOOL.
HEY, FRANK!

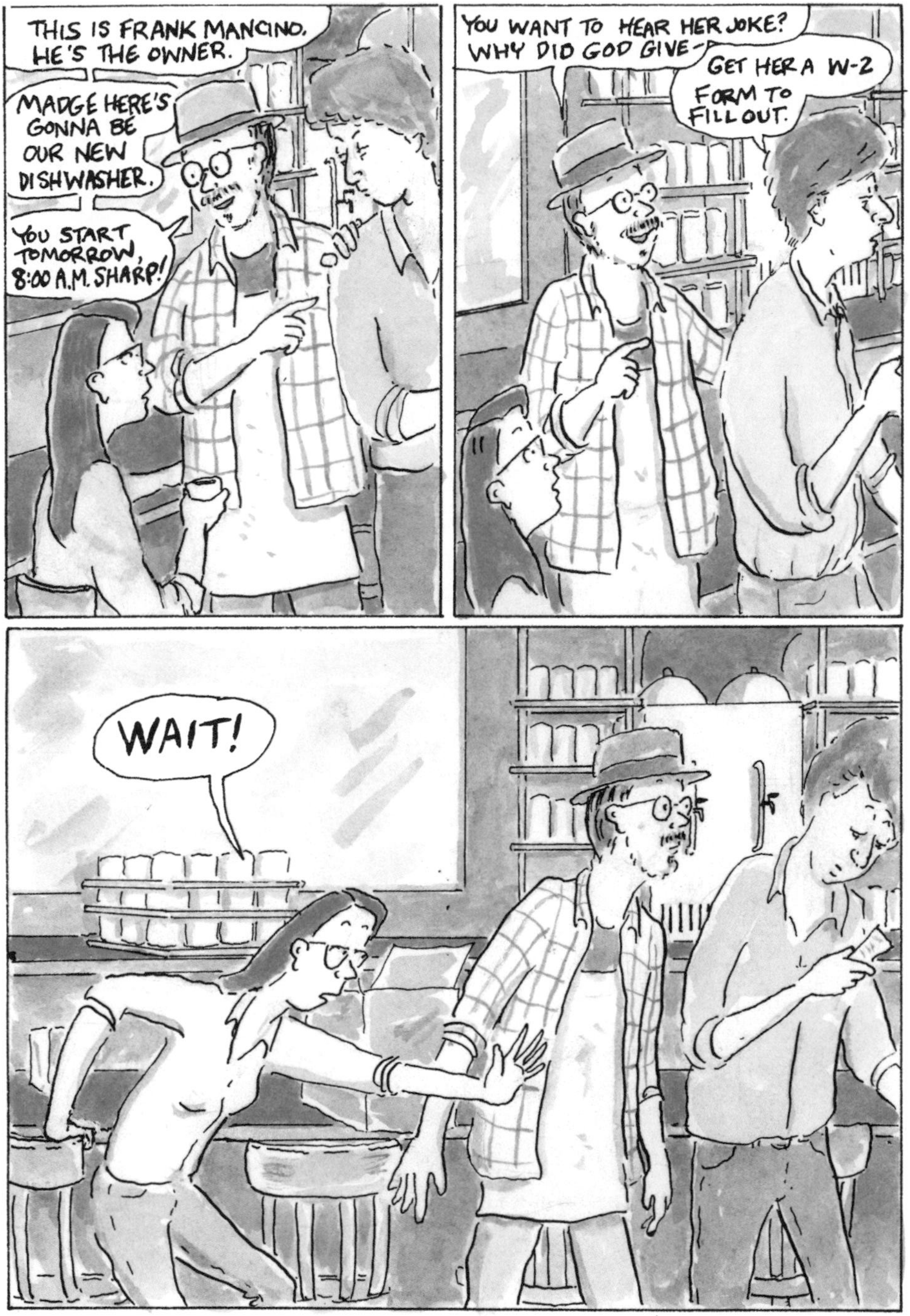
THIS IS FRANK MANCINO. HE'S THE OWNER.
MADGE HERE'S GONNA BE OUR NEW DISHWASHER.
YOU START TOMORROW, 8:00 A.M. SHARP!
YOU WANT TO HEAR HER JOKE? WHY DID GOD GIVE-
GET HER A W-2 FORM TO FILL OUT.
WAIT!

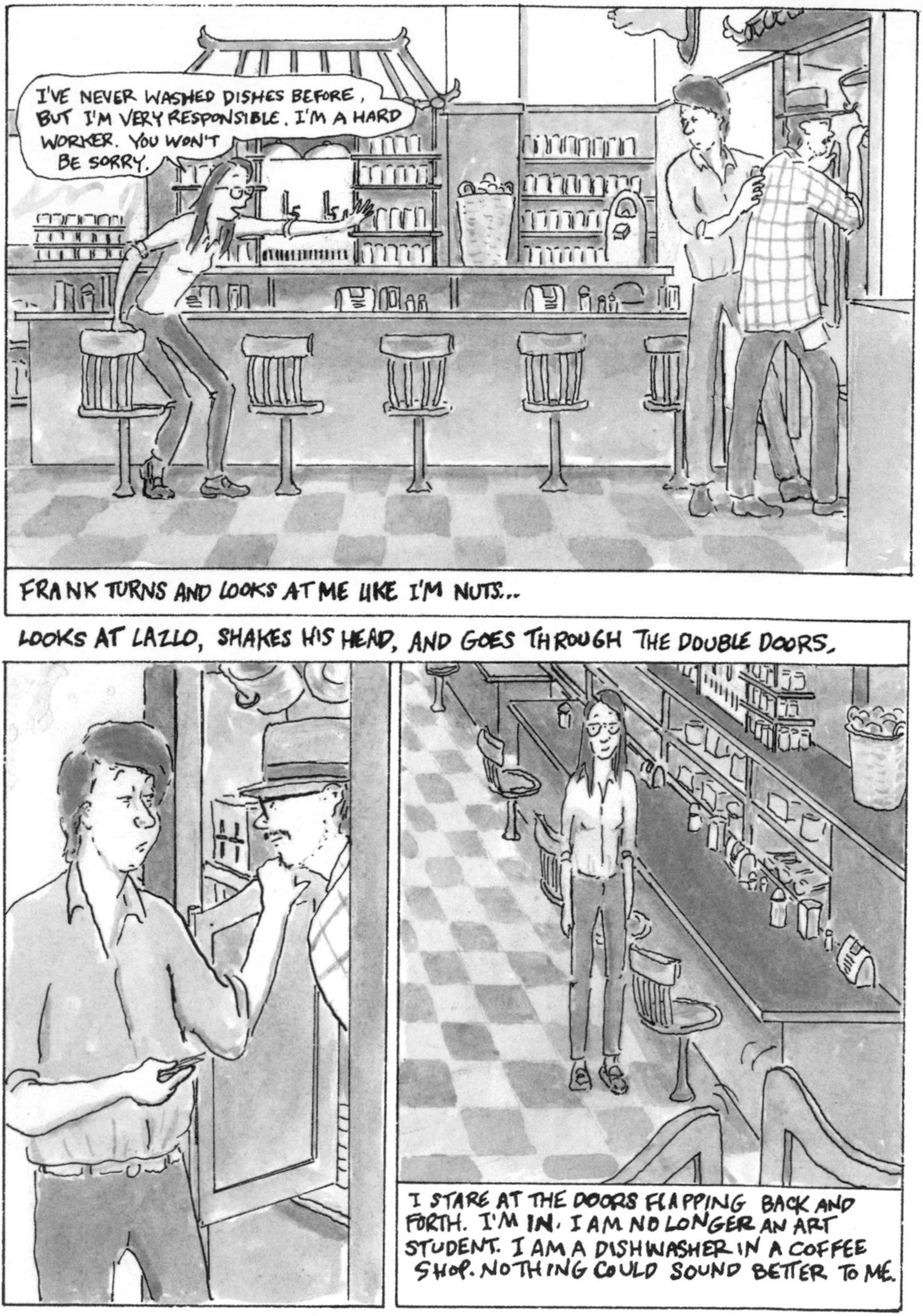
I'VE NEVER WASHED DISHES BEFORE, BUT I'M VERY RESPONSIBLE. I'M A HARD WORKER. YOU WON'T BE SORRY.
FRANK TURNS AND LOOKS AT ME LIKE I'M NUTS...
LOOKS AT LAZLO, SHAKES HIS HEAD, AND GOES THROUGH THE DOUBLE DOORS.
I STARE AT THE DOORS FLAPPING BACK AND FORTH. I'M IN. I AM NO LONGER AN ART STUDENT. I AM A DISHWASHER IN A COFFEE SHOP. NOTHING COULD SOUND BETTER TO ME.

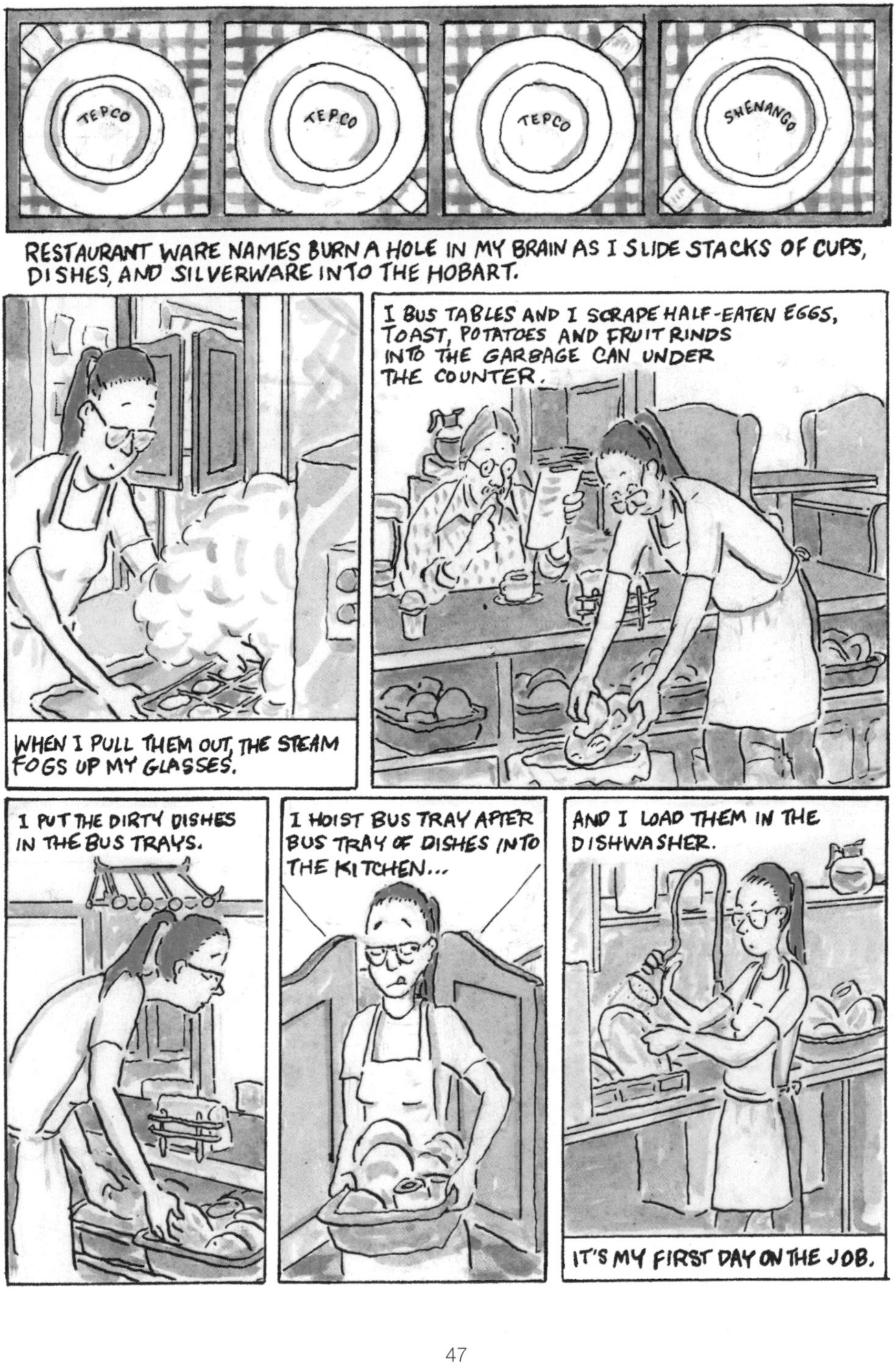
TEPCO
TEPCO
TEPCO
SHENANGO
RESTAURANT WARE NAMES BURN A HOLE IN MY BRAIN AS I SLIDE STACKS OF CUPS, DISHES, AND SILVERWARE INTO THE HOBART.
WHEN I PULL THEM OUT, THE STEAM FOGS UP MY GLASSES.
I BUS TABLES AND I SCRAPE HALF-EATEN EGGS, TOAST, POTATOES AND FRUIT RINDS INTO THE GARBAGE CAN UNDER THE COUNTER.
I PUT THE DIRTY DISHES IN THE BUS TRAYS.
I HOIST BUS TRAY AFTER BUS TRAY OF DISHES INTO THE KITCHEN...
AND I LOAD THEM IN THE DISHWASHER.
IT'S MY FIRST DAY ON THE JOB.

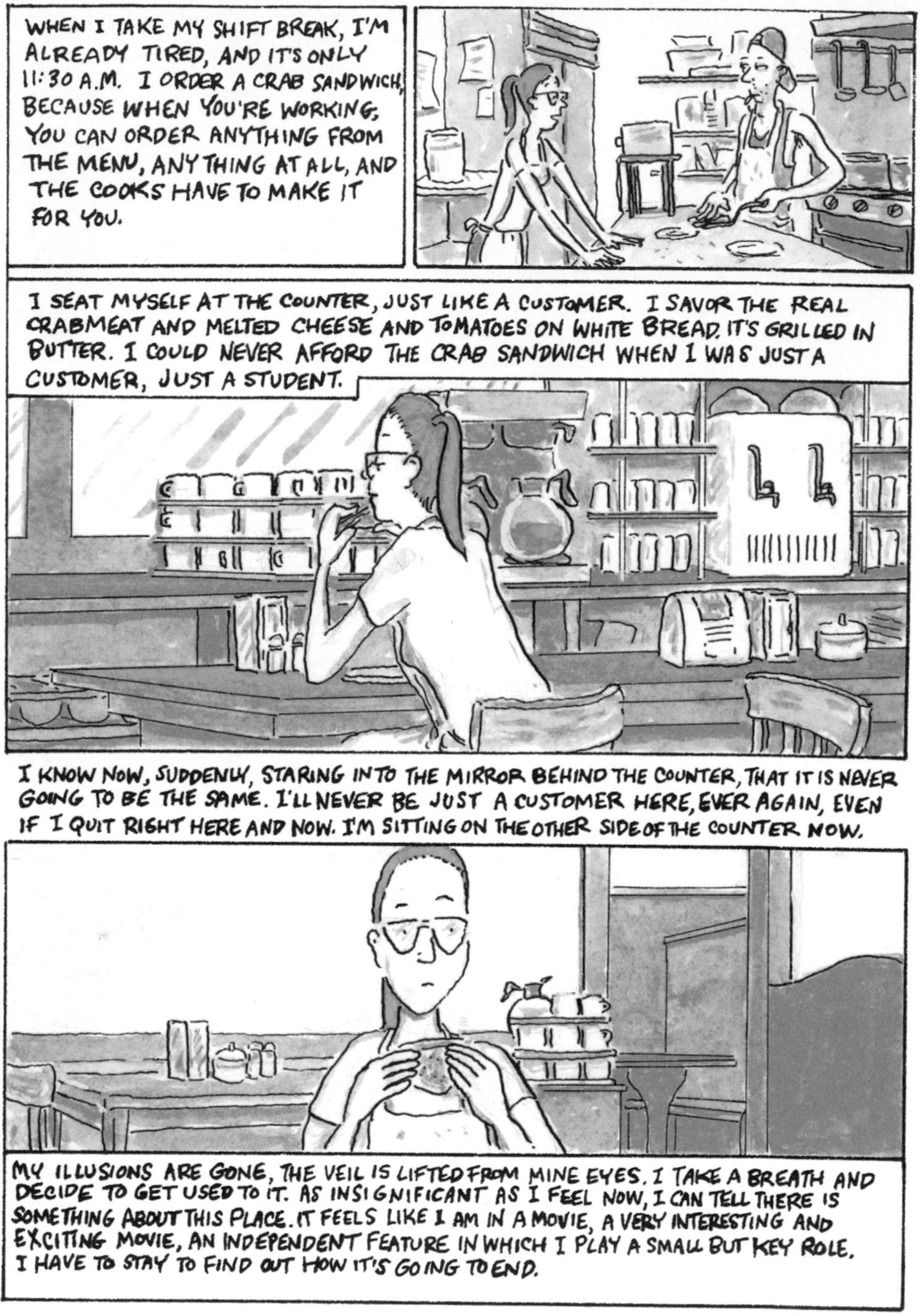
WHEN I TAKE MY SHIFT BREAK, I'M ALREADY TIRED, AND IT'S ONLY 11:30 A.M. I ORDER A CRAB SANDWICH, BECAUSE WHEN YOU'RE WORKING, YOU CAN ORDER ANYTHING FROM THE MENU, ANYTHING AT ALL, AND THE COOKS HAVE TO MAKE IT FOR YOU.
I SEAT MYSELF AT THE COUNTER, JUST LIKE A CUSTOMER. I SAVOR THE REAL CRABMEAT AND MELTED CHEESE AND TOMATOES ON WHITE BREAD. IT'S GRILLED IN BUTTER. I COULD NEVER AFFORD THE CRAB SANDWICH WHEN I WAS JUST A CUSTOMER, JUST A STUDENT.
I KNOW NOW, SUDDENLY, STARING INTO THE MIRROR BEHIND THE COUNTER, THAT IT IS NEVER GOING TO BE THE SAME. I'LL NEVER BE JUST A CUSTOMER HERE, EVER AGAIN, EVEN IF I QUIT RIGHT HERE AND NOW. I'M SITTING ON THE OTHER SIDE OF THE COUNTER NOW.
MY ILLUSIONS ARE GONE, THE VEIL IS LIFTED FROM MINE EYES. I TAKE A BREATH AND DECIDE TO GET USED TO IT. AS INSIGNIFICANT AS I FEEL NOW, I CAN TELL THERE IS SOMETHING ABOUT THIS PLACE. IT FEELS LIKE I AM IN A MOVIE, A VERY INTERESTING AND EXCITING MOVIE, AN INDEPENDENT FEATURE IN WHICH I PLAY A SMALL BUT KEY ROLE. I HAVE TO STAY TO FIND OUT HOW IT'S GOING TO END.

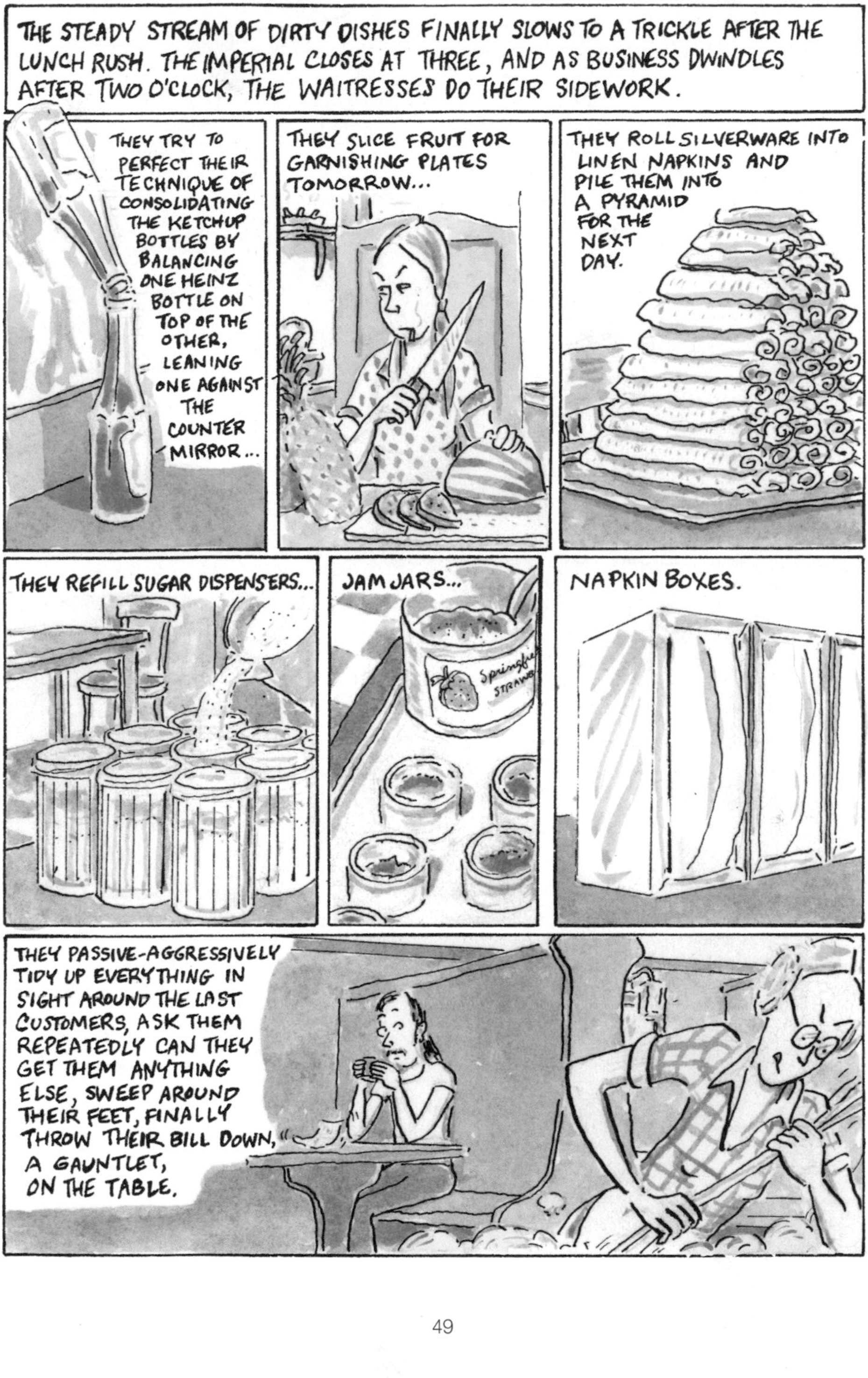
THE STEADY STREAM OF DIRTY DISHES FINALLY SLOWS TO A TRICKLE AFTER THE LUNCH RUSH. THE IMPERIAL CLOSES AT THREE, AND AS BUSINESS DWINDLES AFTER TWO O'CLOCK, THE WAITRESSES DO THEIR SIDEWORK.
THEY TRY TO PERFECT THEIR TECHNIQUE OF CONSOLIDATING THE KETCHUP BOTTLES BY BALANCING ONE HEINZ BOTTLE ON TOP OF THE OTHER, LEANING ONE AGAINST THE COUNTER MIRROR...
THEY SLICE FRUIT FOR GARNISHING PLATES TOMORROW...
THEY ROLL SILVERWARE INTO LINEN NAPKINS AND PILE THEM INTO A PYRAMID FOR THE NEXT DAY.
THEY REFILL SUGAR DISPENSERS...
JAM JARS...
NAPKIN BOXES.
THEY PASSIVE-AGGRESSIVELY TIDY UP EVERYTHING IN SIGHT AROUND THE LAST CUSTOMERS, ASK THEM REPEATEDLY CAN THEY GET THEM ANYTHING ELSE, SWEEP AROUND THEIR FEET, FINALLY THROW THEIR BILL DOWN, A GAUNTLET, ON THE TABLE.

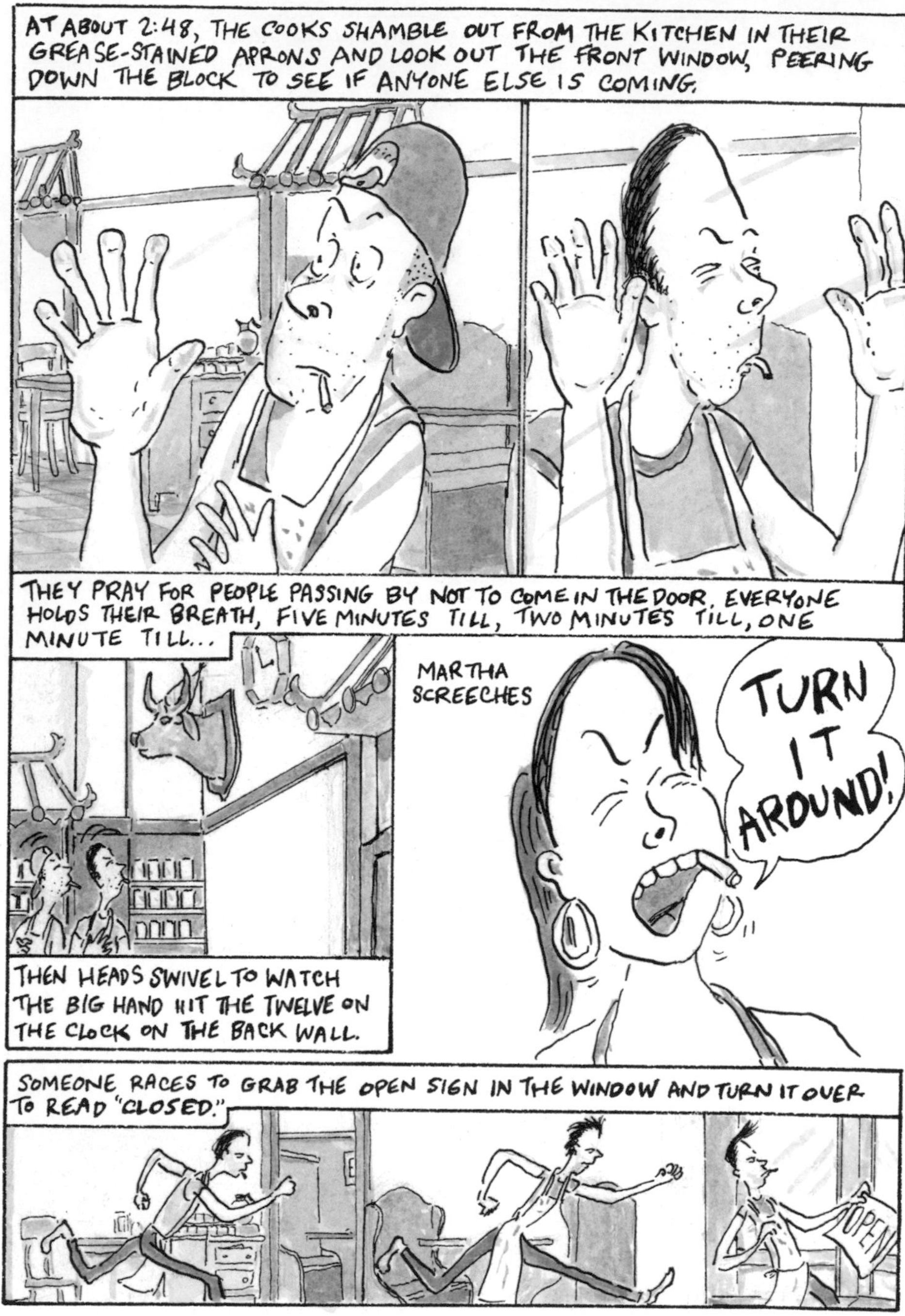
AT ABOUT 2:48, THE COOKS SHAMBLE OUT FROM THE KITCHEN IN THEIR GREASE-STAINED APRONS AND LOOK OUT THE FRONT WINDOW, PEERING DOWN THE BLOCK TO SEE IF ANYONE ELSE IS COMING.
THEY PRAY FOR PEOPLE PASSING BY NOT TO COME IN THE DOOR. EVERYONE HOLDS THEIR BREATH, FIVE MINUTES TILL, TWO MINUTES TILL, ONE MINUTE TILL...
THEN HEADS SWIVEL TO WATCH THE BIG HAND HIT THE TWELVE ON THE CLOCK ON THE BACK WALL.
MARTHA SCREECHES
TURN IT AROUND!
SOMEONE RACES TO GRAB THE OPEN SIGN IN THE WINDOW AND TURN IT OVER TO READ "CLOSED."
OPEN

THE RADIO'S VOLUME SUDDENLY GOES UP TO FULL BLAST, MICK JAGGER:

I'LL NEVER BE YOUR BEAST OF BURDEN, I'VE WALKED FOR MILES, MY FEET ARE

THE COOKS BEND OVER THE STOVE AND START TO VIGOROUSLY SCRUB THE BLACKENED GRILL WITH A POROUS BRICK THEY CALL THE FART BLOCK—BECAUSE THAT'S WHAT IT SMELLS LIKE—UNTIL THE GRILL SHINES.

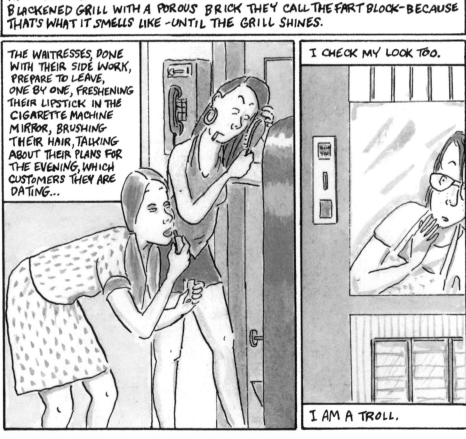

THE WAITRESSES, DONE WITH THEIR SIDE WORK, PREPARE TO LEAVE, ONE BY ONE, FRESHENING THEIR LIPSTICK IN THE CIGARETTE MACHINE MIRROR, BRUSHING THEIR HAIR, TALKING ABOUT THEIR PLANS FOR THE EVENING, WHICH CUSTOMERS THEY ARE DATING...

I CHECK MY LOOK TOO.

I AM A TROLL.

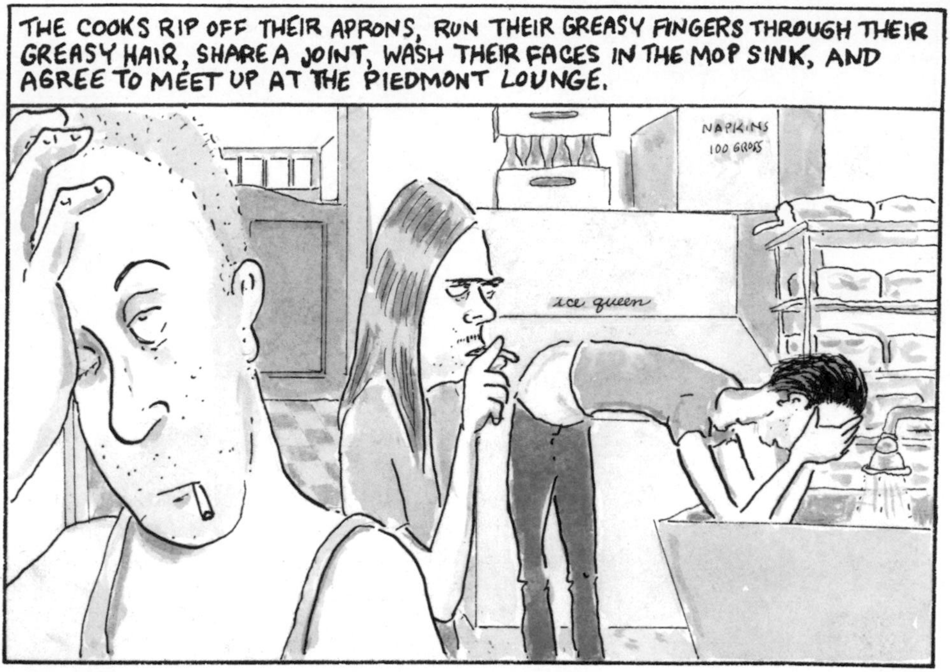
THE COOKS RIP OFF THEIR APRONS, RUN THEIR GREASY FINGERS THROUGH THEIR GREASY HAIR, SHARE A JOINT, WASH THEIR FACES IN THE MOP SINK, AND AGREE TO MEET UP AT THE PIEDMONT LOUNGE.
NAPKINS
100 GROSS
ice queen

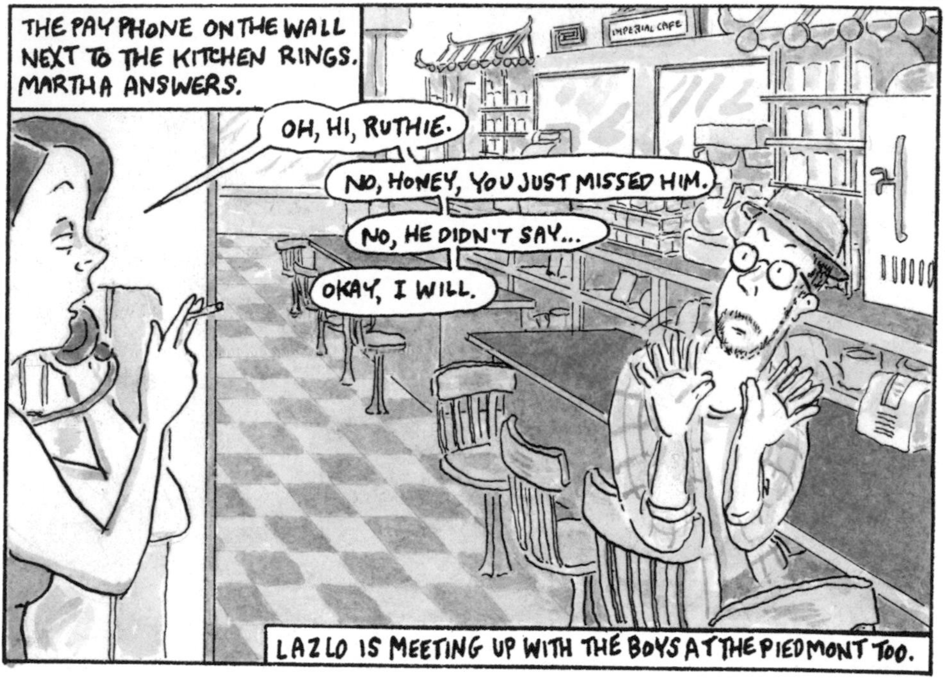
THE PAY PHONE ON THE WALL NEXT TO THE KITCHEN RINGS. MARTHA ANSWERS.
IMPERIAL CAFE
OH, HI, RUTHIE.
NO, HONEY, YOU JUST MISSED HIM.
NO, HE DIDN'T SAY...
OKAY, I WILL.
LAZLO IS MEETING UP WITH THE BOYS AT THE PIEDMONT TOO.

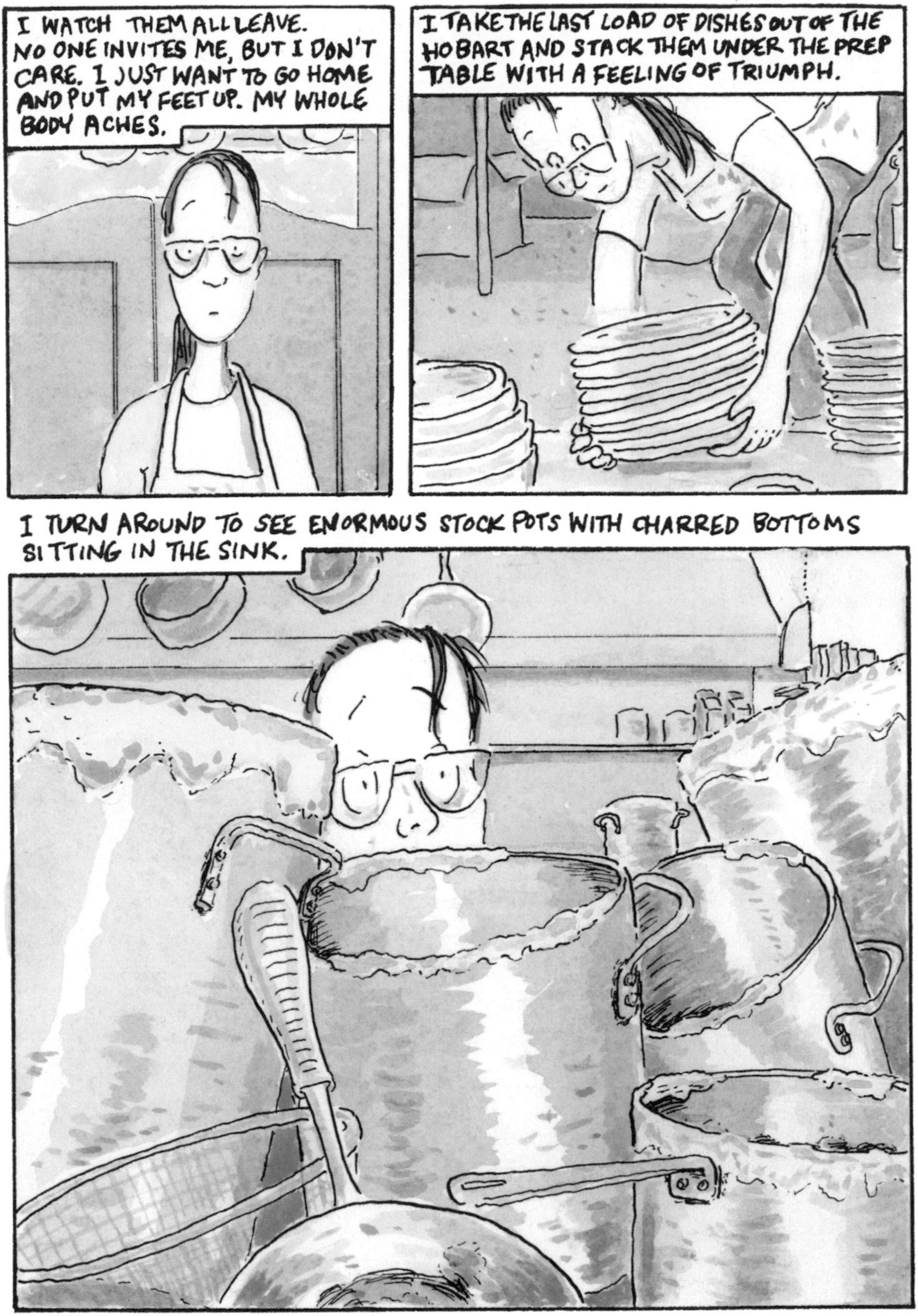
I WATCH THEM ALL LEAVE. NO ONE INVITES ME, BUT I DON'T CARE. I JUST WANT TO GO HOME AND PUT MY FEET UP. MY WHOLE BODY ACHES.
I TAKE THE LAST LOAD OF DISHES OUT OF THE HOBART AND STACK THEM UNDER THE PREP TABLE WITH A FEELING OF TRIUMPH.
I TURN AROUND TO SEE ENORMOUS STOCK POTS WITH CHARRED BOTTOMS SITTING IN THE SINK.

THEY DIDN'T TELL YOU?

IT'S BERNARDO, THE PREP COOK WITH THE BAD SKIN AND COKE BOTTLE GLASSES, WHO HAS COME IN TO CHOP STUFF FOR THE NEXT DAY.

I CAN TELL BERNARDO NEEDS TO BE KNOWING, NEEDS TO PRETEND HE'S WISE ABOUT SOMETHING, ANYTHING MORE THAN ME.

HERE...

HE GETS OUT THE STEEL WOOL AND THE AJAX FOR ME. I STUDY THE SCABS ON THE BACK OF HIS HEAD.

AFTER I'M DONE RUBBING MY FINGERS RAW OVER THE POTS, BERNARDO SHOWS ME THE MATS THE COOKS HAVE STOOD ON ALL DAY.

DISHWASHER'S 'SPOSED TO PULL UP THE MATS AND TAKE 'EM OUTSIDE, HOSE 'EM OFF.

HE SAYS THIS CASUALLY, GOING BACK TO CHOPPING. HE CAN SAY THAT BECAUSE THIS USED TO BE HIS JOB. FOR HIM, GRADUATING TO PREP COOK IS LIKE A DOCTORAL DEGREE.

I STUDY THE GREASY, HONEYCOMB-PATTERNED RUBBER AND WONDER— IS IT THE FILTHIEST THING I'VE EVER SEEN?

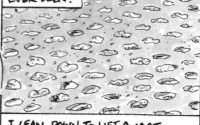

I LEAN DOWN TO LIFT A MAT, FINALLY.

I HAVE TO STICK MY FINGERS THROUGH THE HOLES TO GET A GRIP. GUNK WEDGES UNDER MY NAILS.

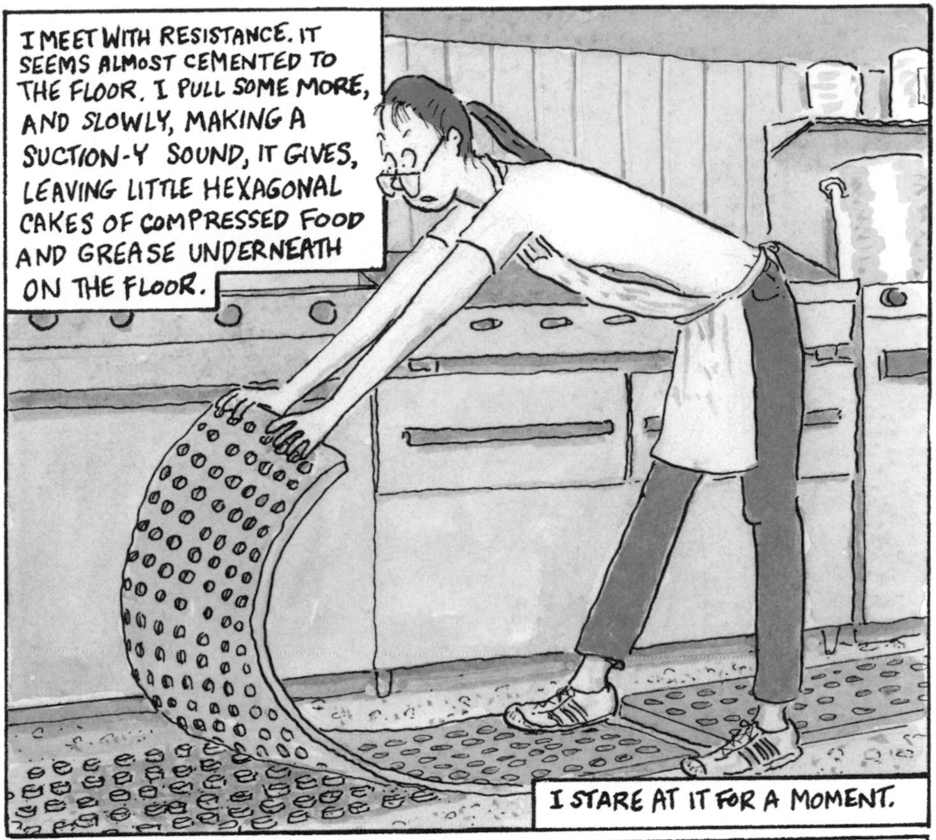
I MEET WITH RESISTANCE. IT SEEMS ALMOST CEMENTED TO THE FLOOR. I PULL SOME MORE, AND SLOWLY, MAKING A SUCTION-Y SOUND, IT GIVES, LEAVING LITTLE HEXAGONAL CAKES OF COMPRESSED FOOD AND GREASE UNDERNEATH ON THE FLOOR.
I STARE AT IT FOR A MOMENT.

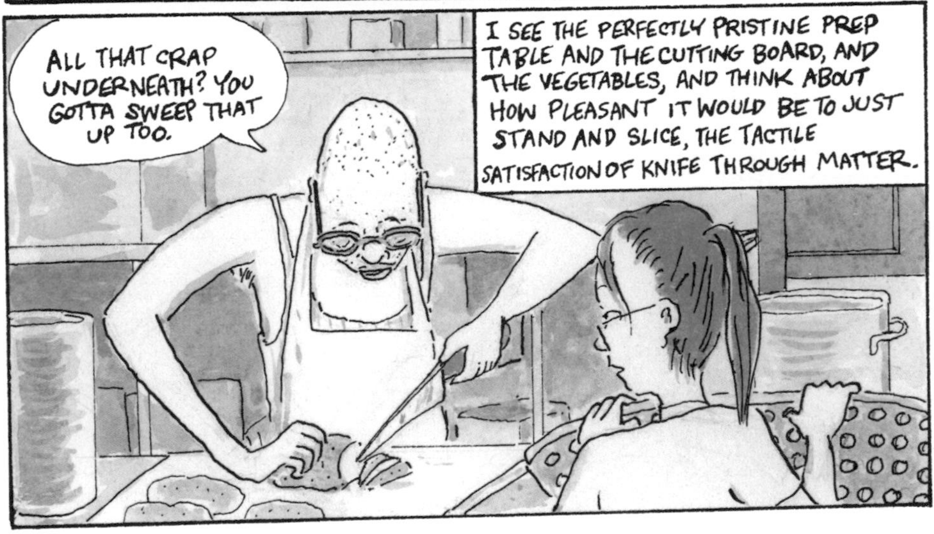
I SEE THE PERFECTLY PRISTINE PREP TABLE AND THE CUTTING BOARD, AND THE VEGETABLES, AND THINK ABOUT HOW PLEASANT IT WOULD BE TO JUST STAND AND SLICE, THE TACTILE SATISFACTION OF KNIFE THROUGH MATTER.
ALL THAT CRAP UNDERNEATH? YOU GOTTA SWEEP THAT UP TOO.

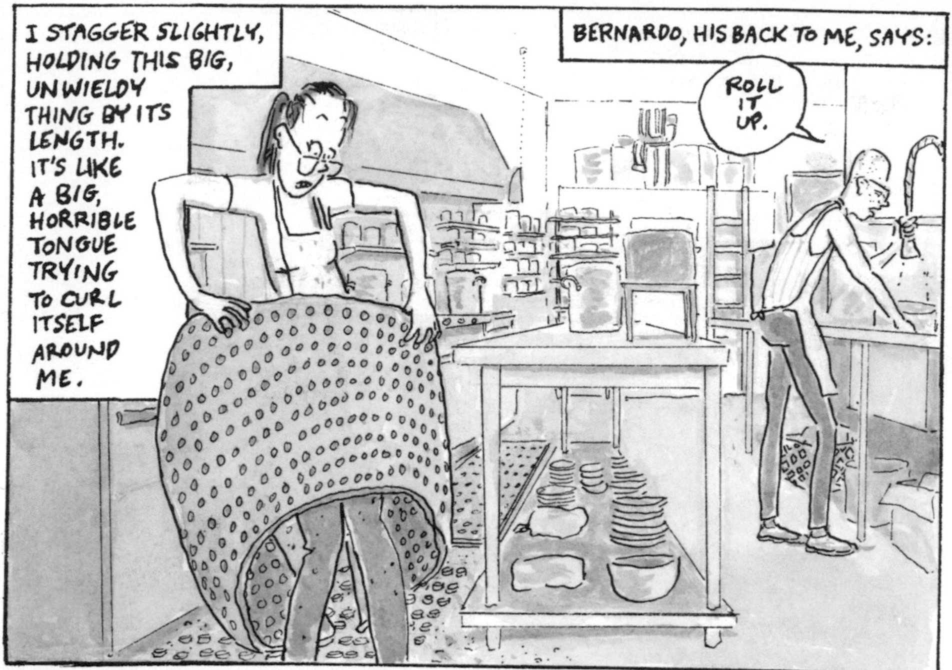
I STAGGER SLIGHTLY, HOLDING THIS BIG, UNWIELDY THING BY ITS LENGTH. IT'S LIKE A BIG, HORRIBLE TONGUE TRYING TO CURL ITSELF AROUND ME.
BERNARDO, HIS BACK TO ME, SAYS:
ROLL IT UP.

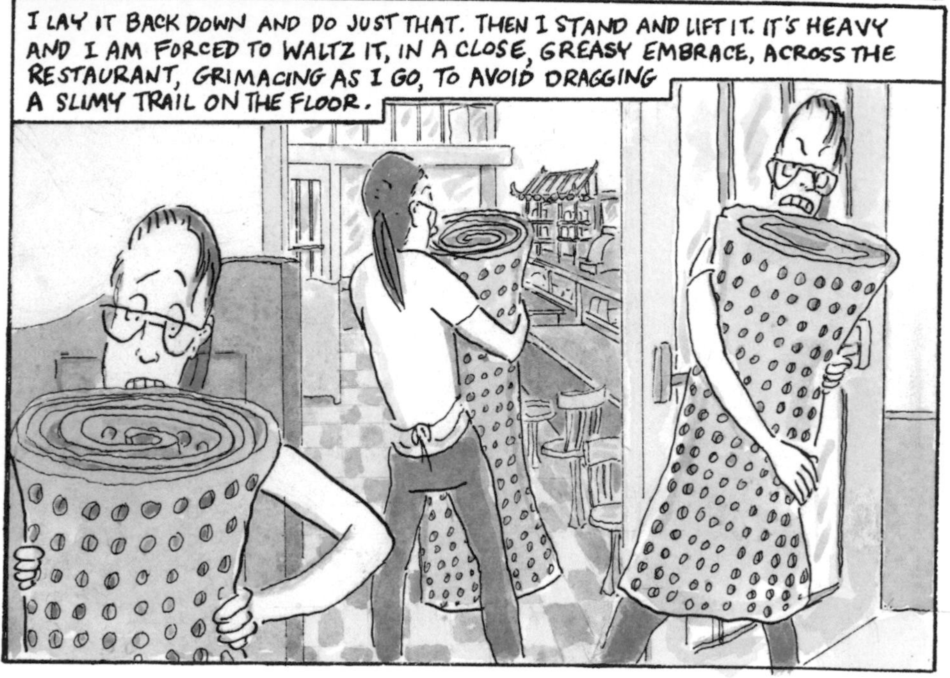
I LAY IT BACK DOWN AND DO JUST THAT. THEN I STAND AND LIFT IT. IT'S HEAVY AND I AM FORCED TO WALTZ IT, IN A CLOSE, GREASY EMBRACE, ACROSS THE RESTAURANT, GRIMACING AS I GO, TO AVOID DRAGGING A SLIMY TRAIL ON THE FLOOR.

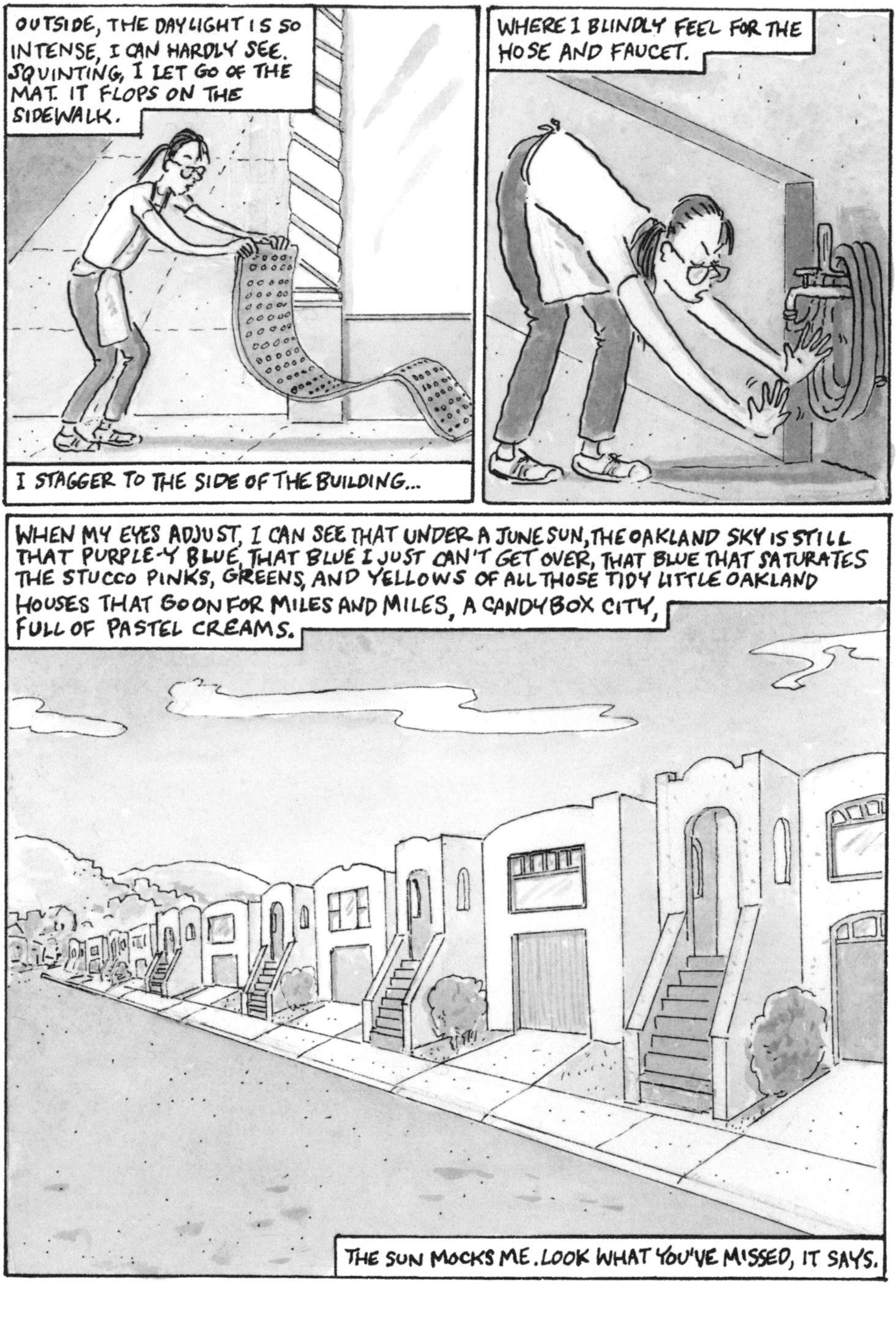
OUTSIDE, THE DAYLIGHT IS SO INTENSE, I CAN HARDLY SEE. SQUINTING, I LET GO OF THE MAT. IT FLOPS ON THE SIDEWALK.
I STAGGER TO THE SIDE OF THE BUILDING...
WHERE I BLINDLY FEEL FOR THE HOSE AND FAUCET.
WHEN MY EYES ADJUST, I CAN SEE THAT UNDER A JUNE SUN, THE OAKLAND SKY IS STILL THAT PURPLE-Y BLUE, THAT BLUE I JUST CAN'T GET OVER, THAT BLUE THAT SATURATES THE STUCCO PINKS, GREENS, AND YELLOWS OF ALL THOSE TIDY LITTLE OAKLAND HOUSES THAT GO ON FOR MILES AND MILES, A CANDYBOX CITY, FULL OF PASTEL CREAMS.
THE SUN MOCKS ME. LOOK WHAT YOU'VE MISSED, IT SAYS.

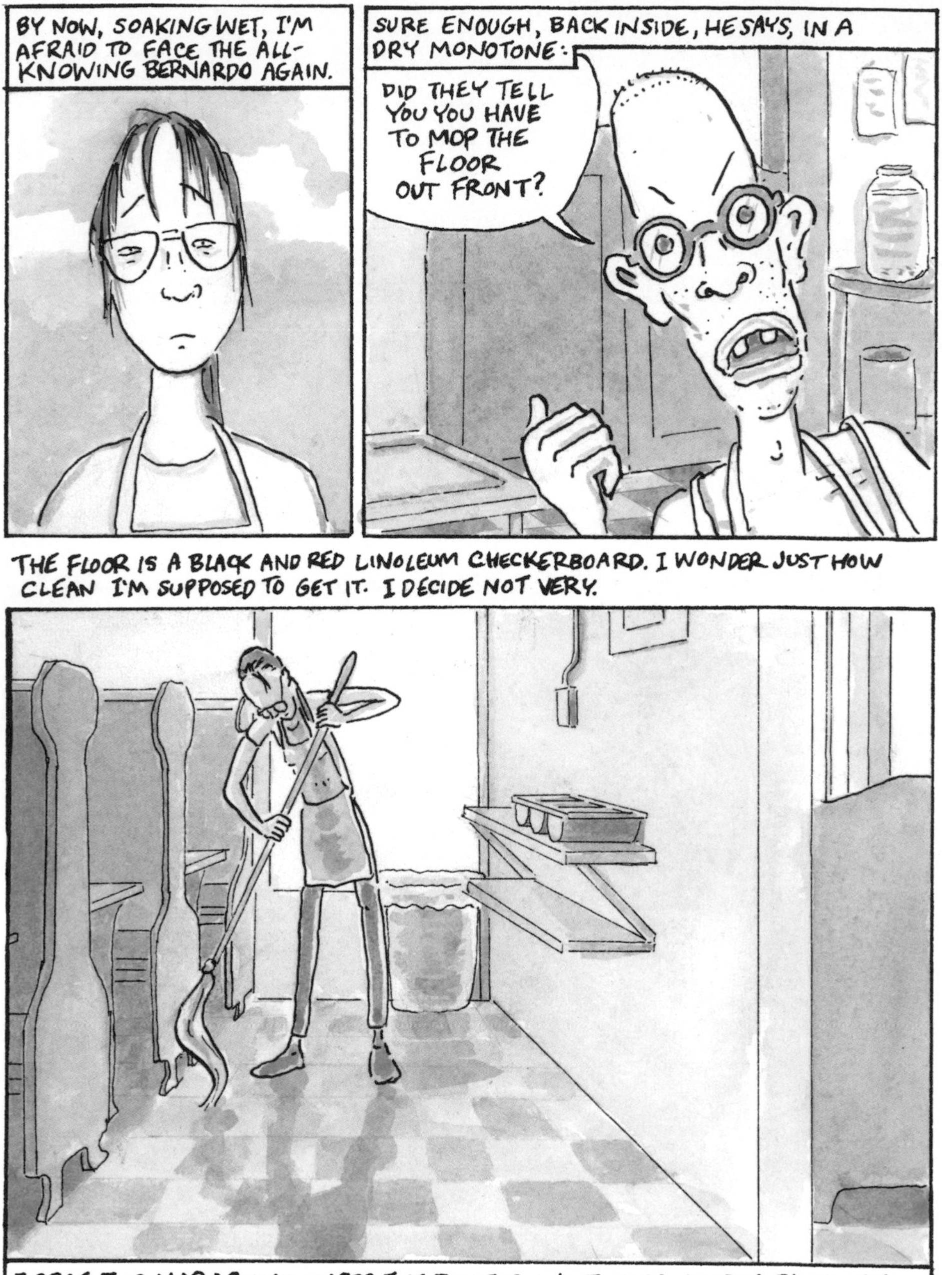
BY NOW, SOAKING WET, I'M AFRAID TO FACE THE ALL-KNOWING BERNARDO AGAIN.
SURE ENOUGH, BACK INSIDE, HE SAYS, IN A DRY MONOTONE:
DID THEY TELL YOU YOU HAVE TO MOP THE FLOOR OUT FRONT?
THE FLOOR IS A BLACK AND RED LINOLEUM CHECKERBOARD. I WONDER JUST HOW CLEAN I'M SUPPOSED TO GET IT. I DECIDE NOT VERY.
I DRAG THE MOP AROUND, UNDER THE BOOTHS AND TABLES, SLURPY. PARTS OF THE LINOLEUM ARE WORN AWAY, DOWN TO THE CEMENT.

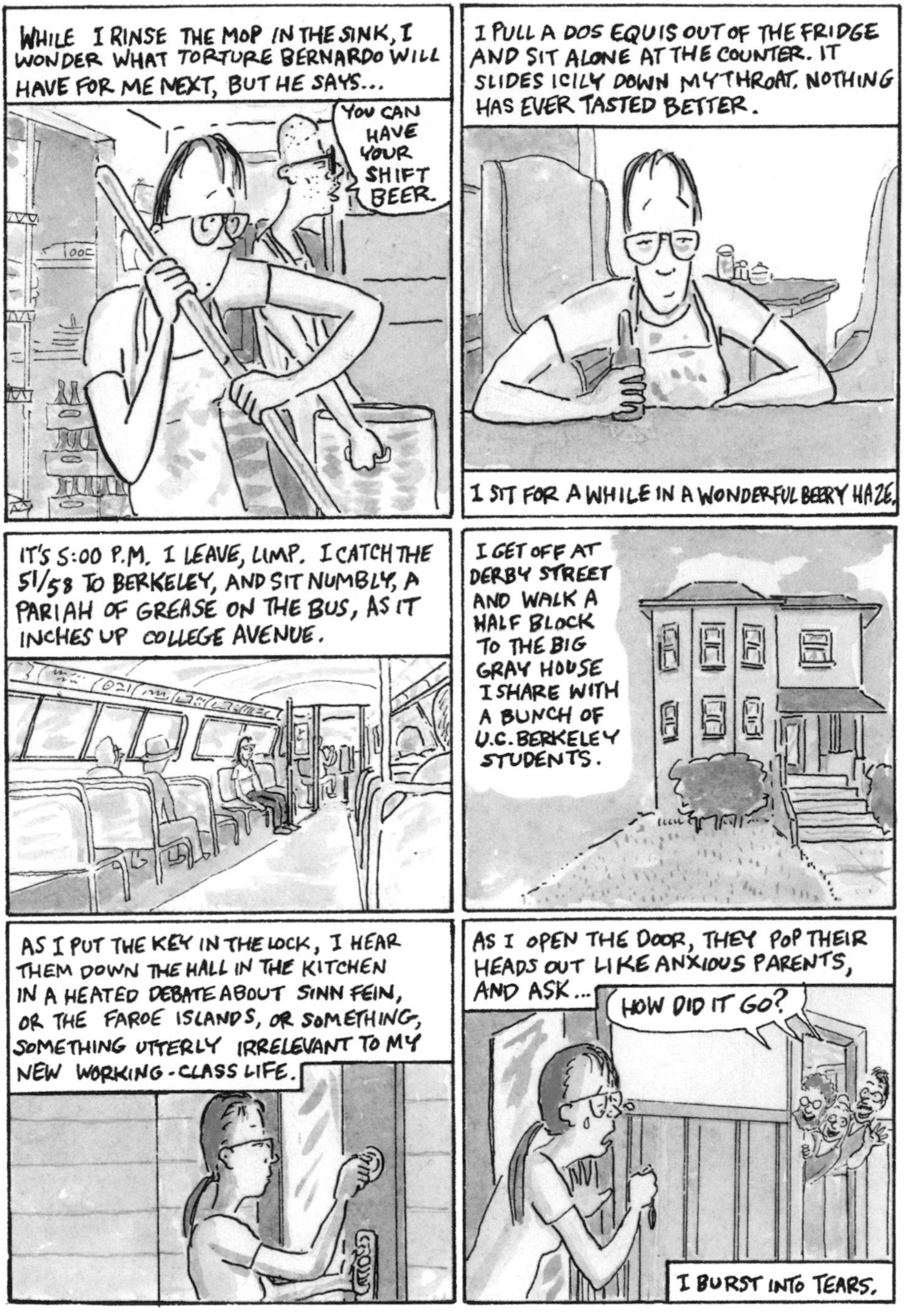
WHILE I RINSE THE MOP IN THE SINK, I WONDER WHAT TORTURE BERNARDO WILL HAVE FOR ME NEXT, BUT HE SAYS...
YOU CAN HAVE YOUR SHIFT BEER.
I PULL A DOS EQUIS OUT OF THE FRIDGE AND SIT ALONE AT THE COUNTER. IT SLIDES ICILY DOWN MY THROAT. NOTHING HAS EVER TASTED BETTER.
I SIT FOR A WHILE IN A WONDERFUL BEERY HAZE.
IT'S 5:00 P.M. I LEAVE, LIMP. I CATCH THE 51/58 TO BERKELEY, AND SIT NUMBLY, A PARIAH OF GREASE ON THE BUS, AS IT INCHES UP COLLEGE AVENUE.
I GET OFF AT DERBY STREET AND WALK A HALF BLOCK TO THE BIG GRAY HOUSE I SHARE WITH A BUNCH OF U.C. BERKELEY STUDENTS.
AS I PUT THE KEY IN THE LOCK, I HEAR THEM DOWN THE HALL IN THE KITCHEN IN A HEATED DEBATE ABOUT SINN FEIN, OR THE FAROE ISLANDS, OR SOMETHING, SOMETHING UTTERLY IRRELEVANT TO MY NEW WORKING-CLASS LIFE.
AS I OPEN THE DOOR, THEY POP THEIR HEADS OUT LIKE ANXIOUS PARENTS, AND ASK...
HOW DID IT GO?
I BURST INTO TEARS.

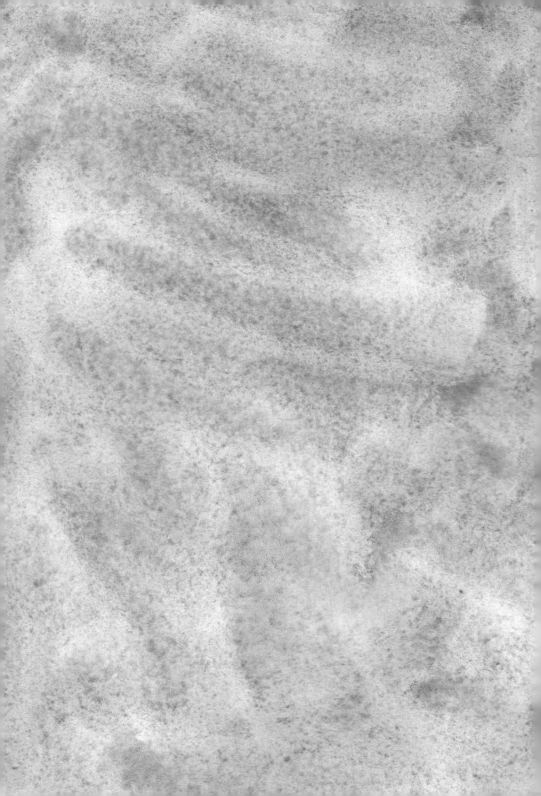

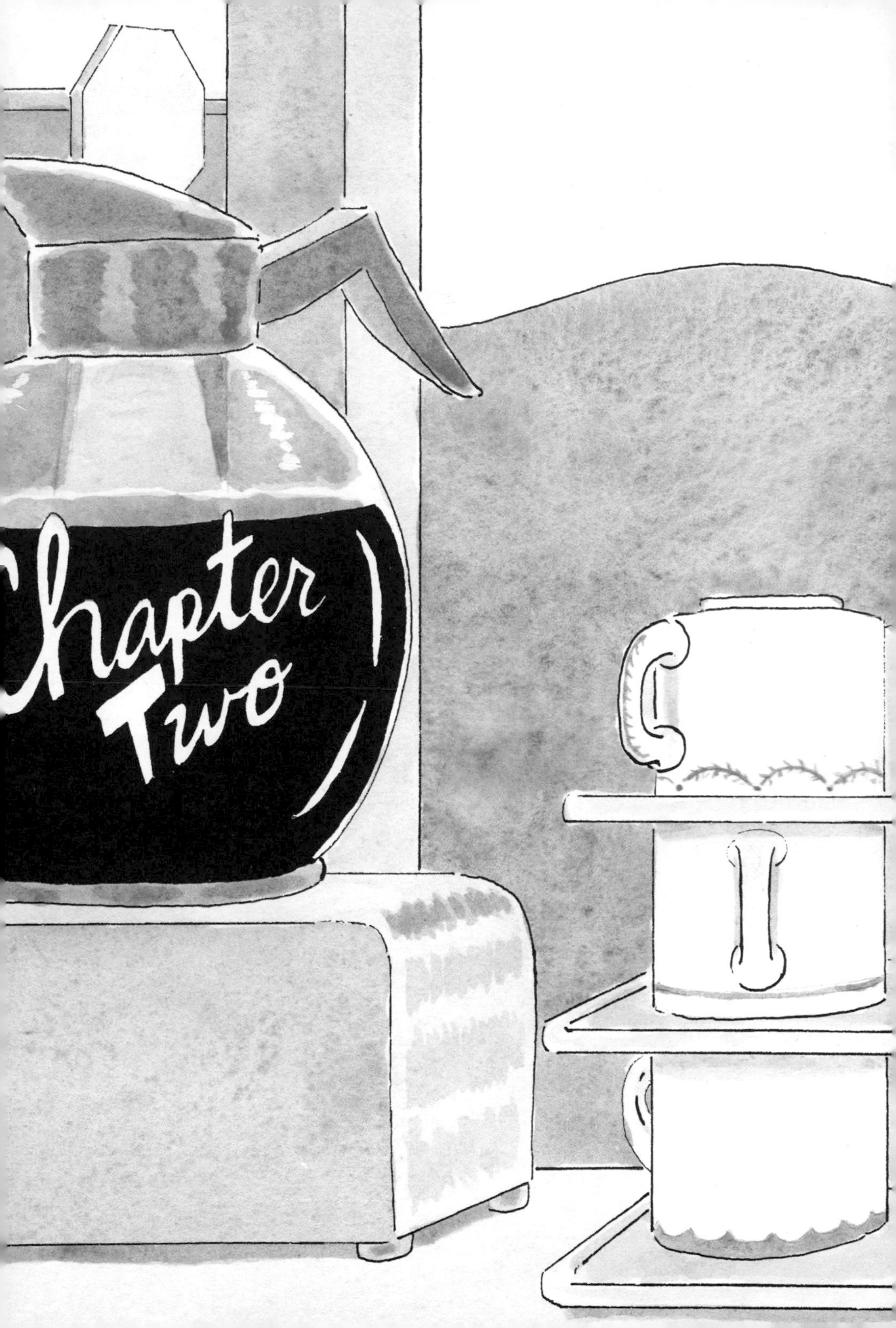
Chapter Two

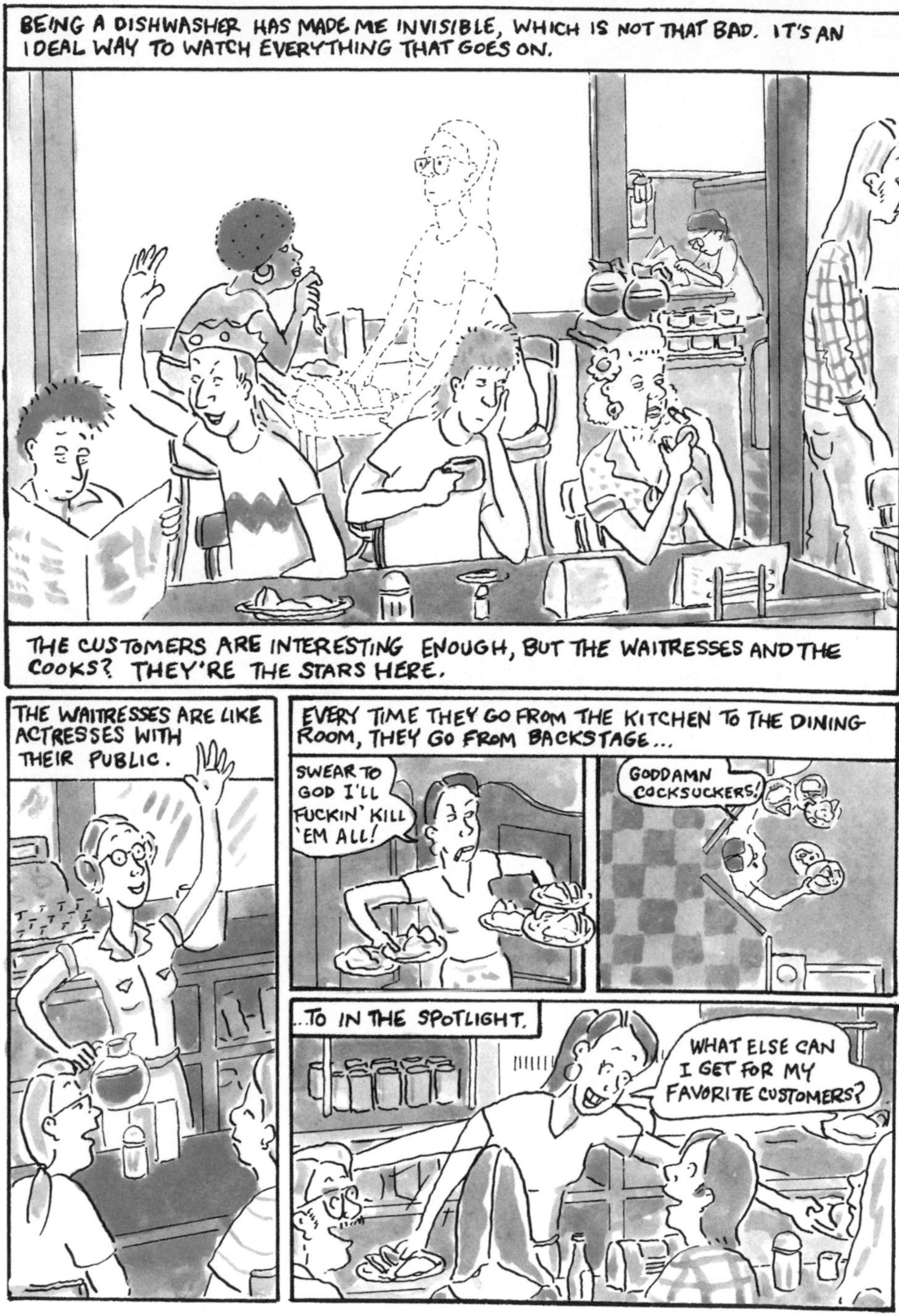
BEING A DISHWASHER HAS MADE ME INVISIBLE, WHICH IS NOT THAT BAD. IT'S AN IDEAL WAY TO WATCH EVERYTHING THAT GOES ON.
THE CUSTOMERS ARE INTERESTING ENOUGH, BUT THE WAITRESSES AND THE COOKS? THEY'RE THE STARS HERE.
THE WAITRESSES ARE LIKE ACTRESSES WITH THEIR PUBLIC.
EVERY TIME THEY GO FROM THE KITCHEN TO THE DINING-ROOM, THEY GO FROM BACKSTAGE...
SWEAR TO GOD I'LL FUCKIN' KILL 'EM ALL!
GODDAMN COCKSUCKERS!
...TO IN THE SPOTLIGHT.
WHAT ELSE CAN I GET FOR MY FAVORITE CUSTOMERS?

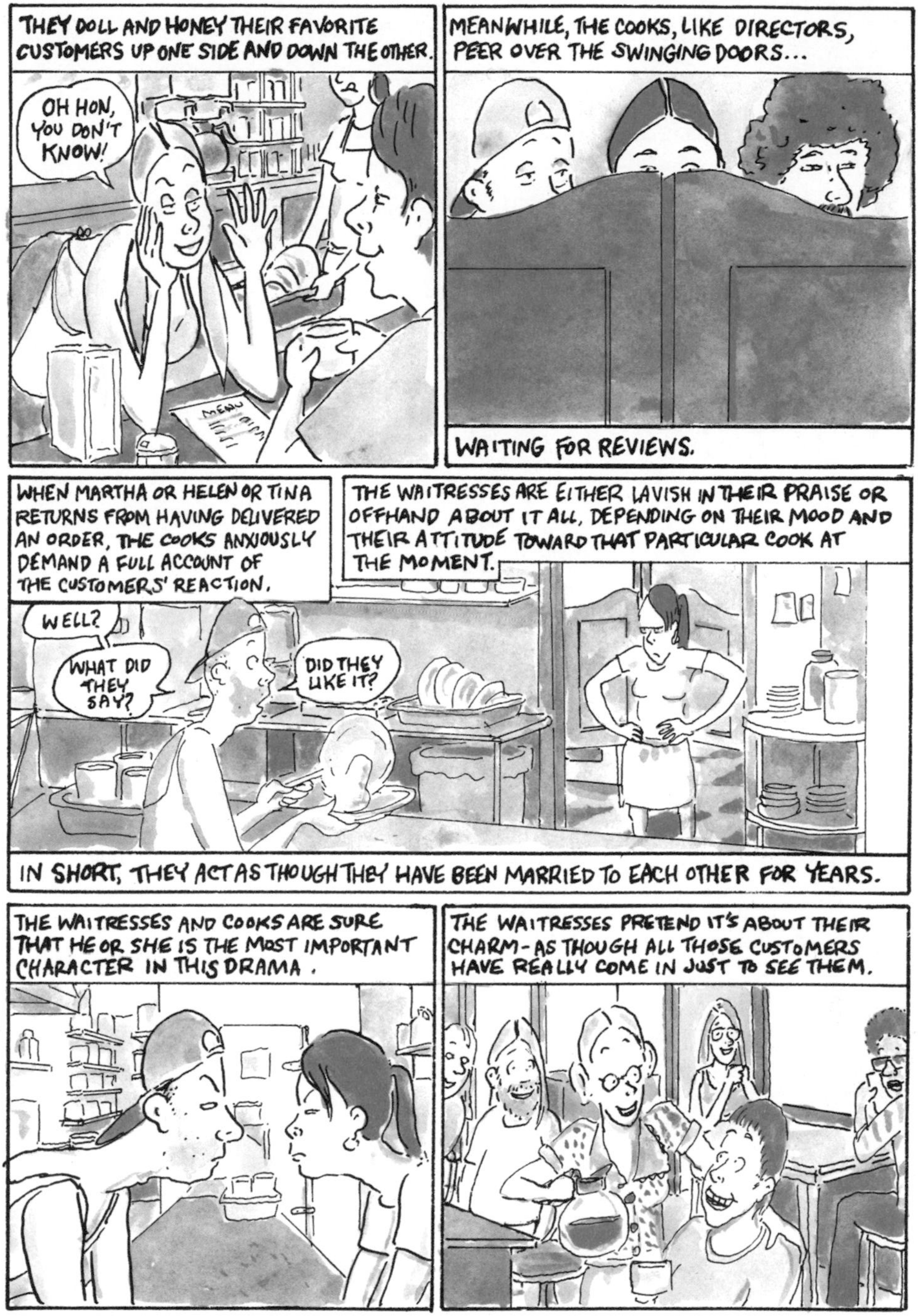

THEY DOLL AND HONEY THEIR FAVORITE CUSTOMERS UP ONE SIDE AND DOWN THE OTHER.
OH HON, YOU DON'T KNOW!
MEANWHILE, THE COOKS, LIKE DIRECTORS, PEER OVER THE SWINGING DOORS...
WAITING FOR REVIEWS.
WHEN MARTHA OR HELEN OR TINA RETURNS FROM HAVING DELIVERED AN ORDER, THE COOKS ANXIOUSLY DEMAND A FULL ACCOUNT OF THE CUSTOMERS' REACTION.
THE WAITRESSES ARE EITHER LAVISH IN THEIR PRAISE OR OFFHAND ABOUT IT ALL, DEPENDING ON THEIR MOOD AND THEIR ATTITUDE TOWARD THAT PARTICULAR COOK AT THE MOMENT.
WELL?
WHAT DID THEY SAY?
DID THEY LIKE IT?
IN SHORT, THEY ACT AS THOUGH THEY HAVE BEEN MARRIED TO EACH OTHER FOR YEARS.
THE WAITRESSES AND COOKS ARE SURE THAT HE OR SHE IS THE MOST IMPORTANT CHARACTER IN THIS DRAMA.
THE WAITRESSES PRETEND IT'S ABOUT THEIR CHARM - AS THOUGH ALL THOSE CUSTOMERS HAVE REALLY COME IN JUST TO SEE THEM.

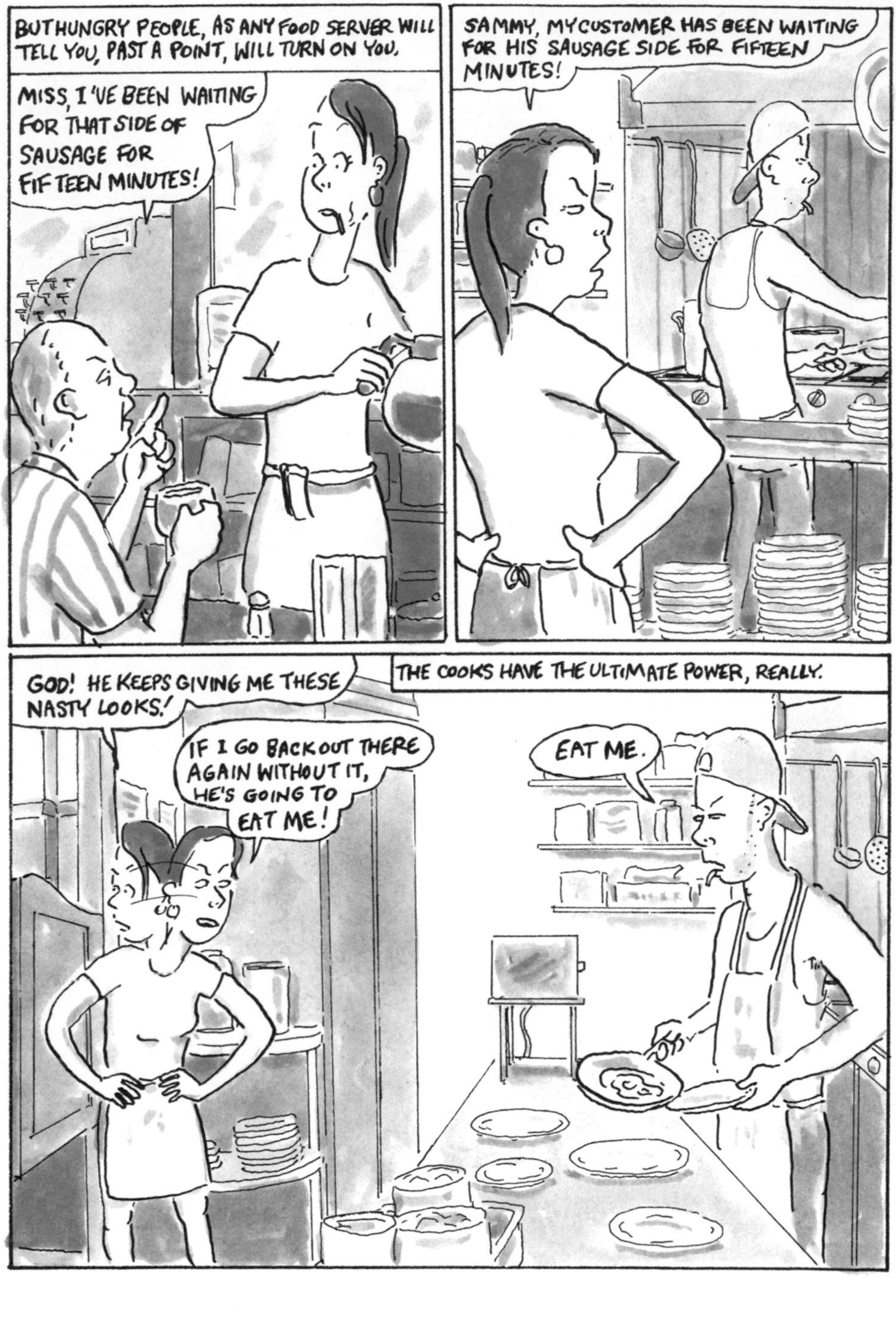
BUT HUNGRY PEOPLE, AS ANY FOOD SERVER WILL TELL YOU, PAST A POINT, WILL TURN ON YOU.
MISS, I'VE BEEN WAITING FOR THAT SIDE OF SAUSAGE FOR FIFTEEN MINUTES!
SAMMY, MY CUSTOMER HAS BEEN WAITING FOR HIS SAUSAGE SIDE FOR FIFTEEN MINUTES!
GOD! HE KEEPS GIVING ME THESE NASTY LOOKS!
IF I GO BACK OUT THERE AGAIN WITHOUT IT, HE'S GOING TO EAT ME!
THE COOKS HAVE THE ULTIMATE POWER, REALLY.
EAT ME.

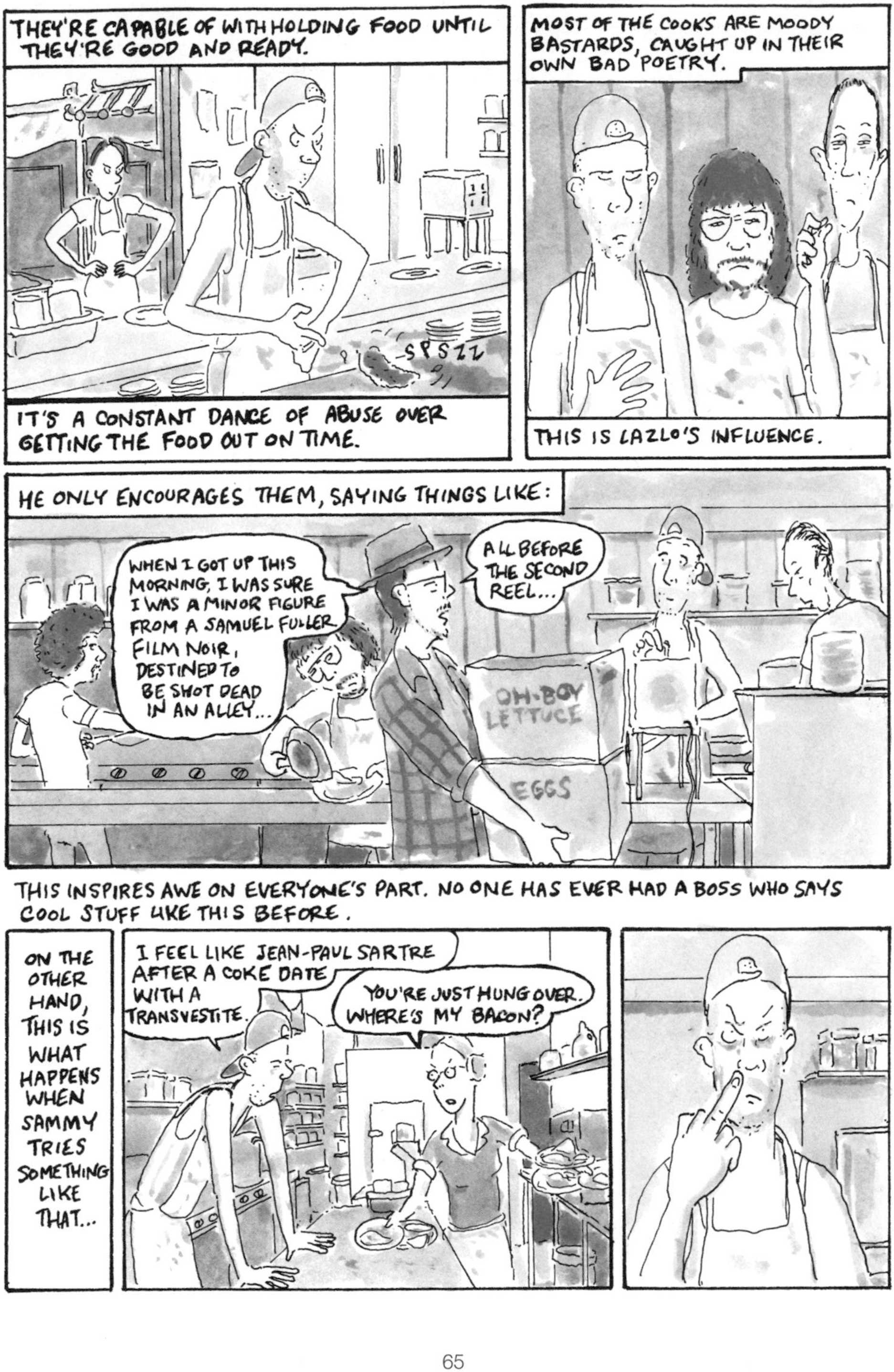
THEY'RE CAPABLE OF WITHHOLDING FOOD UNTIL THEY'RE GOOD AND READY.
-SPSZZ
IT'S A CONSTANT DANCE OF ABUSE OVER GETTING THE FOOD OUT ON TIME.
MOST OF THE COOKS ARE MOODY BASTARDS, CAUGHT UP IN THEIR OWN BAD POETRY.
THIS IS LAZLO'S INFLUENCE.
HE ONLY ENCOURAGES THEM, SAYING THINGS LIKE:
WHEN I GOT UP THIS MORNING, I WAS SURE I WAS A MINOR FIGURE FROM A SAMUEL FULLER FILM NOIR, DESTINED TO BE SHOT DEAD IN AN ALLEY...
ALL BEFORE THE SECOND REEL...
OH-BOY LETTUCE
EGGS
THIS INSPIRES AWE ON EVERYONE'S PART. NO ONE HAS EVER HAD A BOSS WHO SAYS COOL STUFF LIKE THIS BEFORE.
ON THE OTHER HAND, THIS IS WHAT HAPPENS WHEN SAMMY TRIES SOMETHING LIKE THAT...
I FEEL LIKE JEAN-PAUL SARTRE AFTER A COKE DATE WITH A TRANSVESTITE.
YOU'RE JUST HUNG OVER. WHERE'S MY BACON?

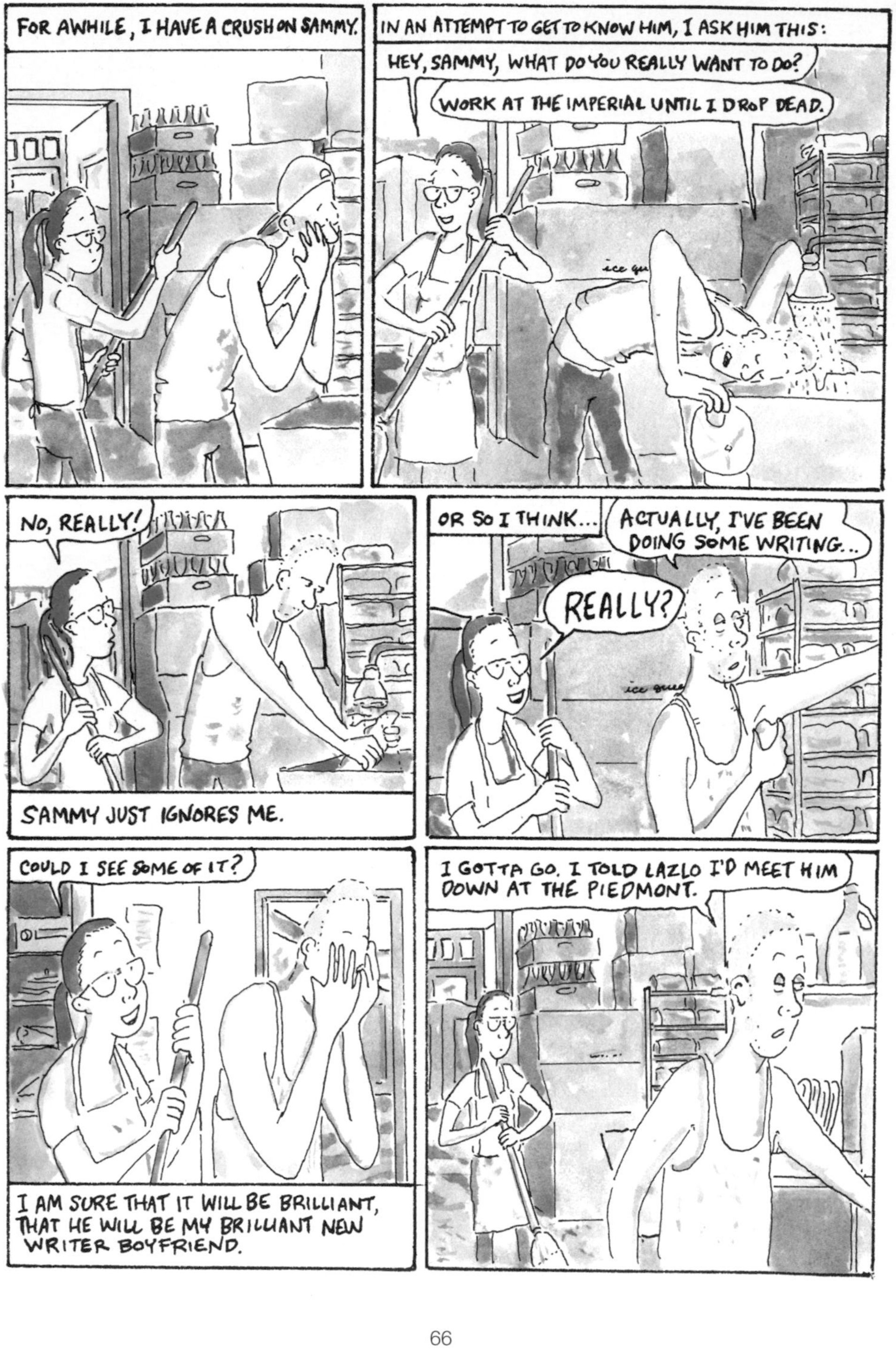
FOR AWHILE, I HAVE A CRUSH ON SAMMY.
IN AN ATTEMPT TO GET TO KNOW HIM, I ASK HIM THIS:
HEY, SAMMY, WHAT DO YOU REALLY WANT TO DO?
WORK AT THE IMPERIAL UNTIL I DROP DEAD.
NO, REALLY!
SAMMY JUST IGNORES ME.
OR SO I THINK...
ACTUALLY, I'VE BEEN DOING SOME WRITING...
REALLY?
COULD I SEE SOME OF IT?
I AM SURE THAT IT WILL BE BRILLIANT, THAT HE WILL BE MY BRILLIANT NEW WRITER BOYFRIEND.
I GOTTA GO. I TOLD LAZLO I'D MEET HIM DOWN AT THE PIEDMONT.

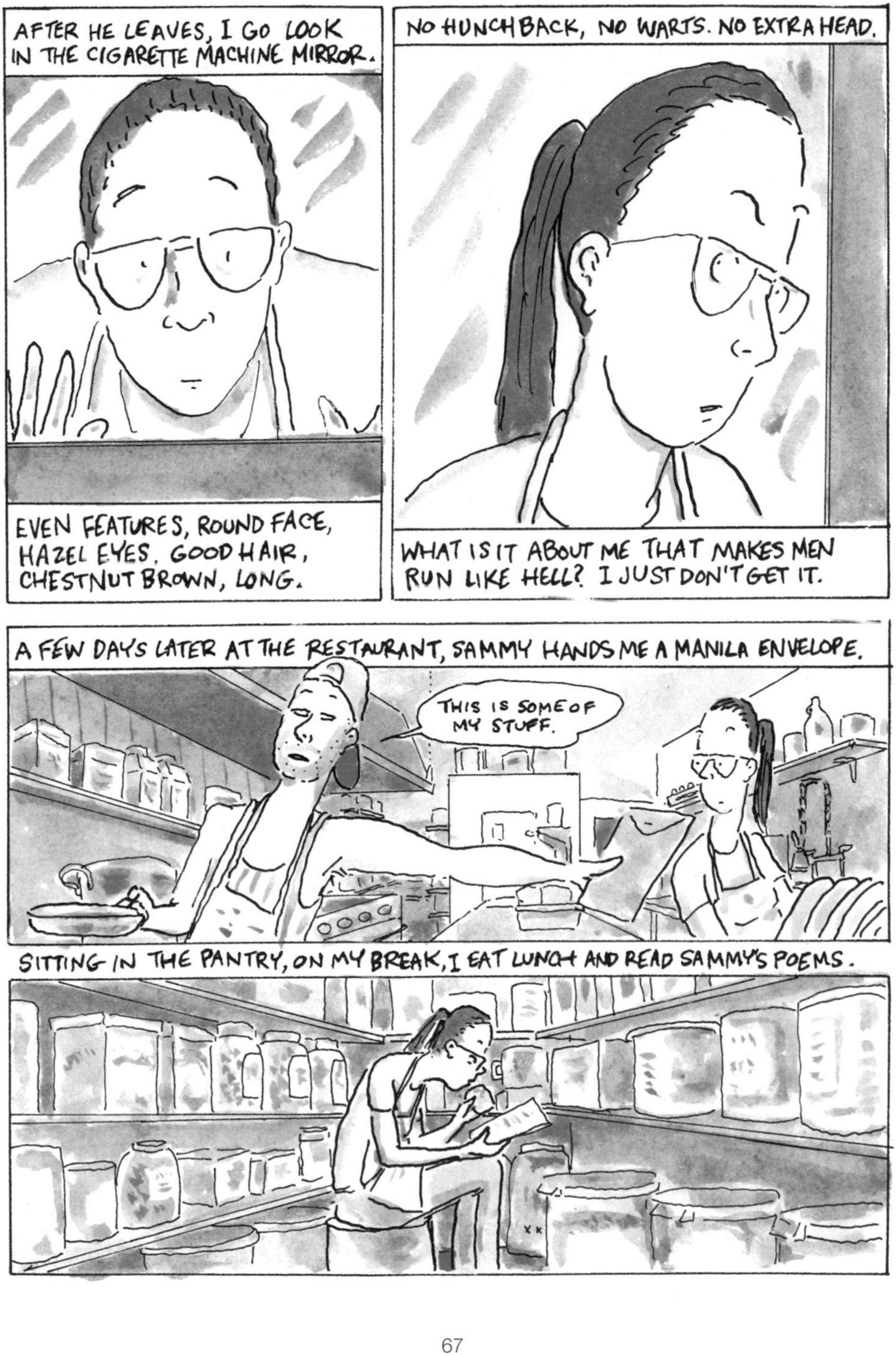
AFTER HE LEAVES, I GO LOOK IN THE CIGARETTE MACHINE MIRROR.
EVEN FEATURES, ROUND FACE, HAZEL EYES. GOOD HAIR, CHESTNUT BROWN, LONG.
NO HUNCHBACK, NO WARTS. NO EXTRA HEAD.
WHAT IS IT ABOUT ME THAT MAKES MEN RUN LIKE HELL? I JUST DON'T GET IT.
A FEW DAYS LATER AT THE RESTAURANT, SAMMY HANDS ME A MANILA ENVELOPE.
THIS IS SOME OF MY STUFF.
SITTING IN THE PANTRY, ON MY BREAK, I EAT LUNCH AND READ SAMMY'S POEMS.

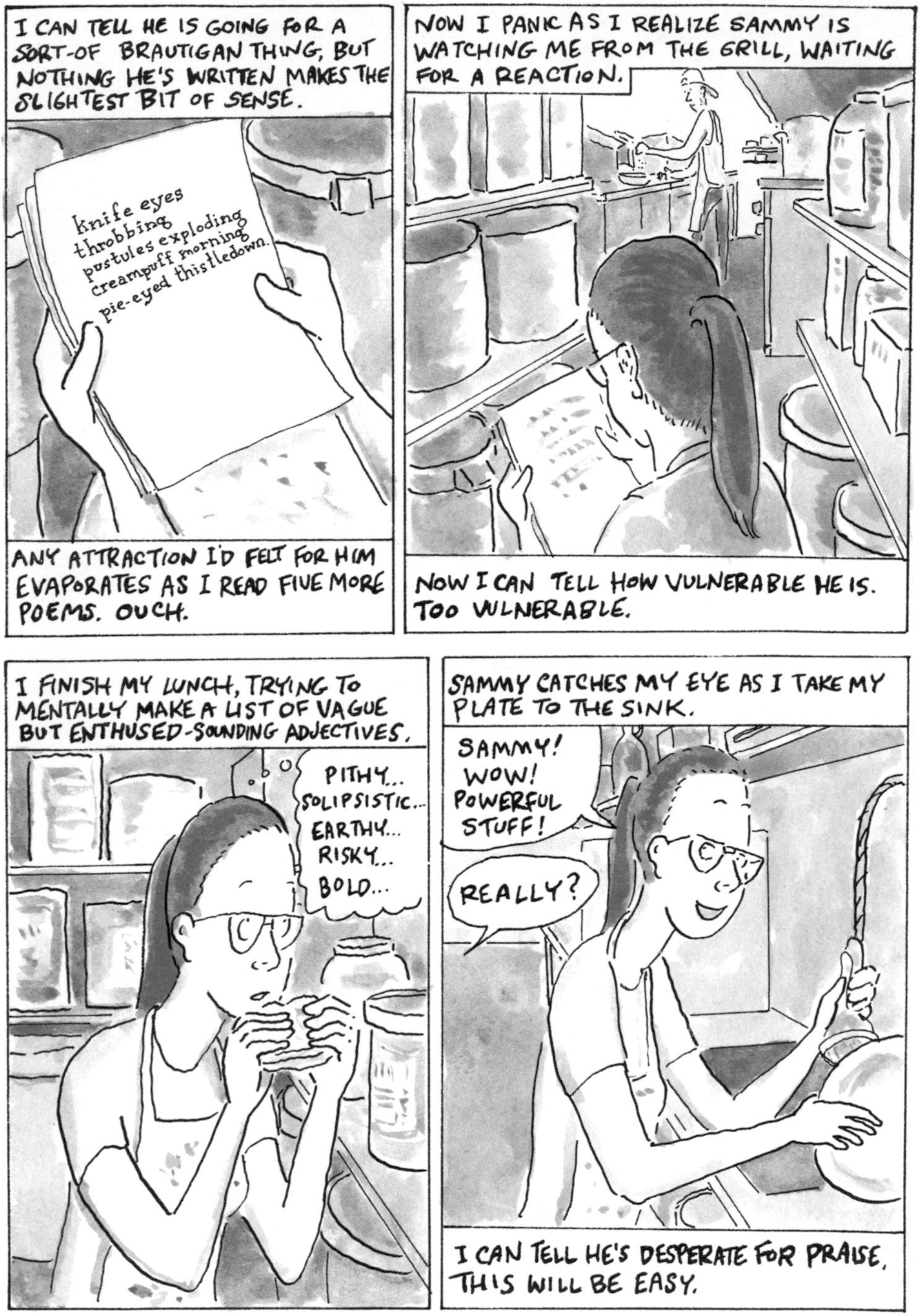
I CAN TELL HE IS GOING FOR A SORT-OF BRAUTIGAN THING, BUT NOTHING HE'S WRITTEN MAKES THE SLIGHTEST BIT OF SENSE.
knife eyes
throbbing
pustules exploding
creampuff morning
pie-eyed thistledown.
ANY ATTRACTION I'D FELT FOR HIM EVAPORATES AS I READ FIVE MORE POEMS. OUCH.
NOW I PANIC AS I REALIZE SAMMY IS WATCHING ME FROM THE GRILL, WAITING FOR A REACTION.
NOW I CAN TELL HOW VULNERABLE HE IS. TOO VULNERABLE.
I FINISH MY LUNCH, TRYING TO MENTALLY MAKE A LIST OF VAGUE BUT ENTHUSED-SOUNDING ADJECTIVES.
PITHY... SOLIPSISTIC... EARTHY... RISKY... BOLD...
SAMMY CATCHES MY EYE AS I TAKE MY PLATE TO THE SINK.
SAMMY! WOW! POWERFUL STUFF!
REALLY?
I CAN TELL HE'S DESPERATE FOR PRAISE. THIS WILL BE EASY.

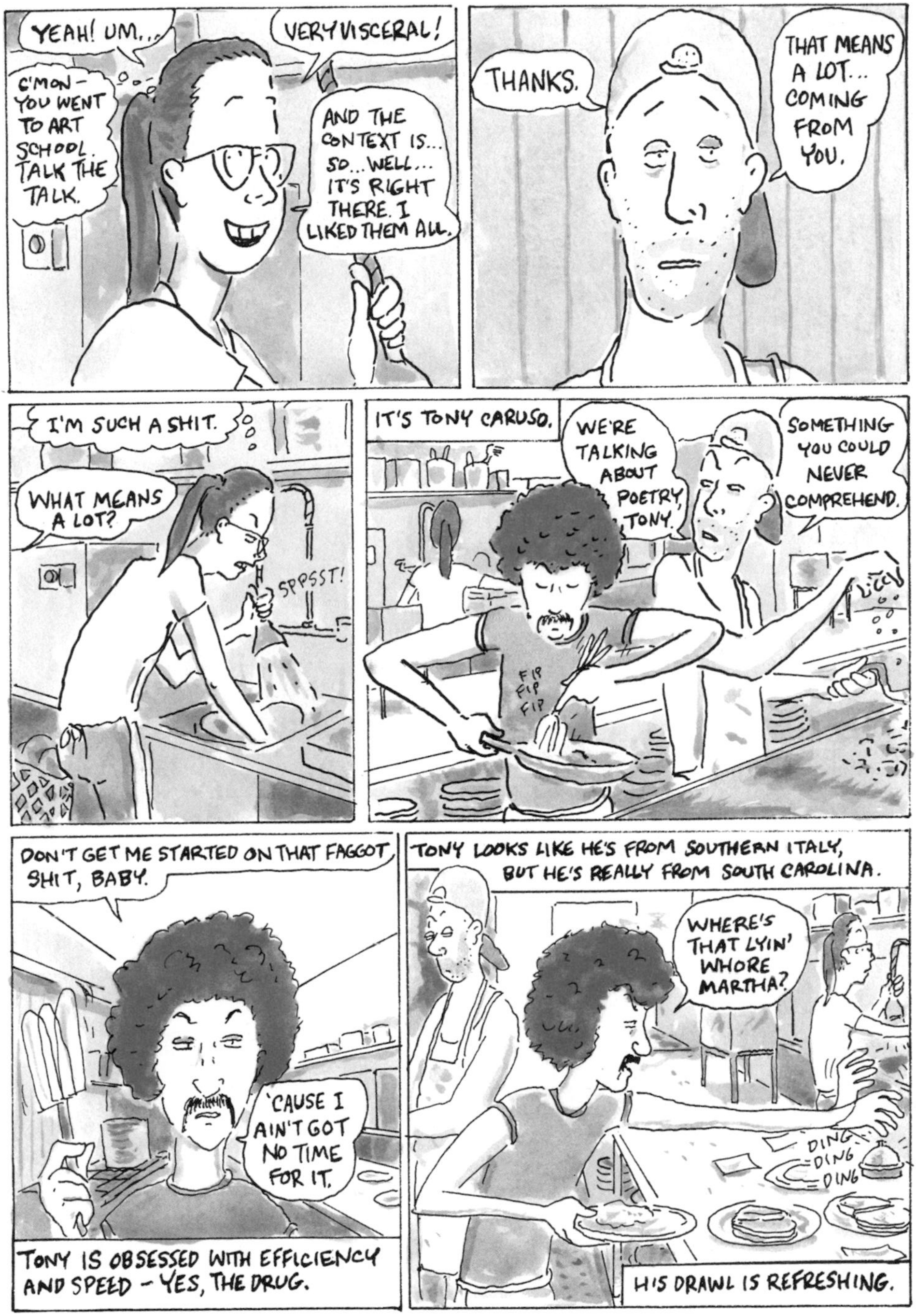
YEAH! UM...
C'MON - YOU WENT TO ART SCHOOL. TALK THE TALK.
VERY VISCERAL!
AND THE CONTEXT IS... SO... WELL... IT'S RIGHT THERE. I LIKED THEM ALL.
THANKS.
THAT MEANS A LOT... COMING FROM YOU.
I'M SUCH A SHIT.
WHAT MEANS A LOT?
SPPSST!
IT'S TONY CARUSO.
WE'RE TALKING ABOUT POETRY, TONY.
SOMETHING YOU COULD NEVER COMPREHEND.
FIP FIP FIP
DON'T GET ME STARTED ON THAT FAGGOT SHIT, BABY.
'CAUSE I AIN'T GOT NO TIME FOR IT.
TONY IS OBSESSED WITH EFFICIENCY AND SPEED - YES, THE DRUG.
TONY LOOKS LIKE HE'S FROM SOUTHERN ITALY, BUT HE'S REALLY FROM SOUTH CAROLINA.
WHERE'S THAT LYIN' WHORE MARTHA?
DING DING DING
HIS DRAWL IS REFRESHING.

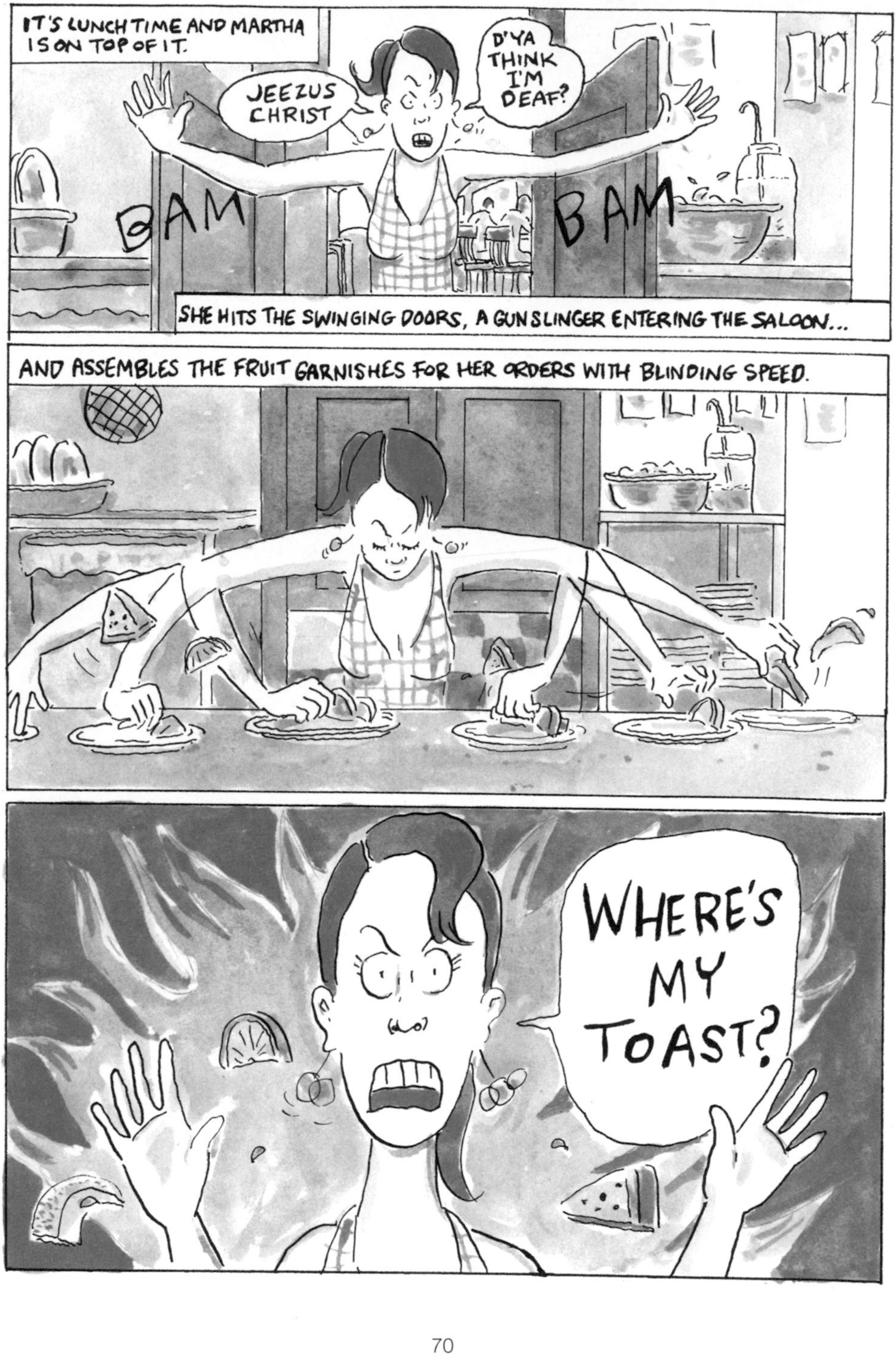
IT'S LUNCHTIME AND MARTHA IS ON TOP OF IT.
JEEZUS CHRIST
D'YA THINK I'M DEAF?
BAM
BAM
SHE HITS THE SWINGING DOORS, A GUNSLINGER ENTERING THE SALOON...
AND ASSEMBLES THE FRUIT GARNISHES FOR HER ORDERS WITH BLINDING SPEED.
WHERE'S MY TOAST?

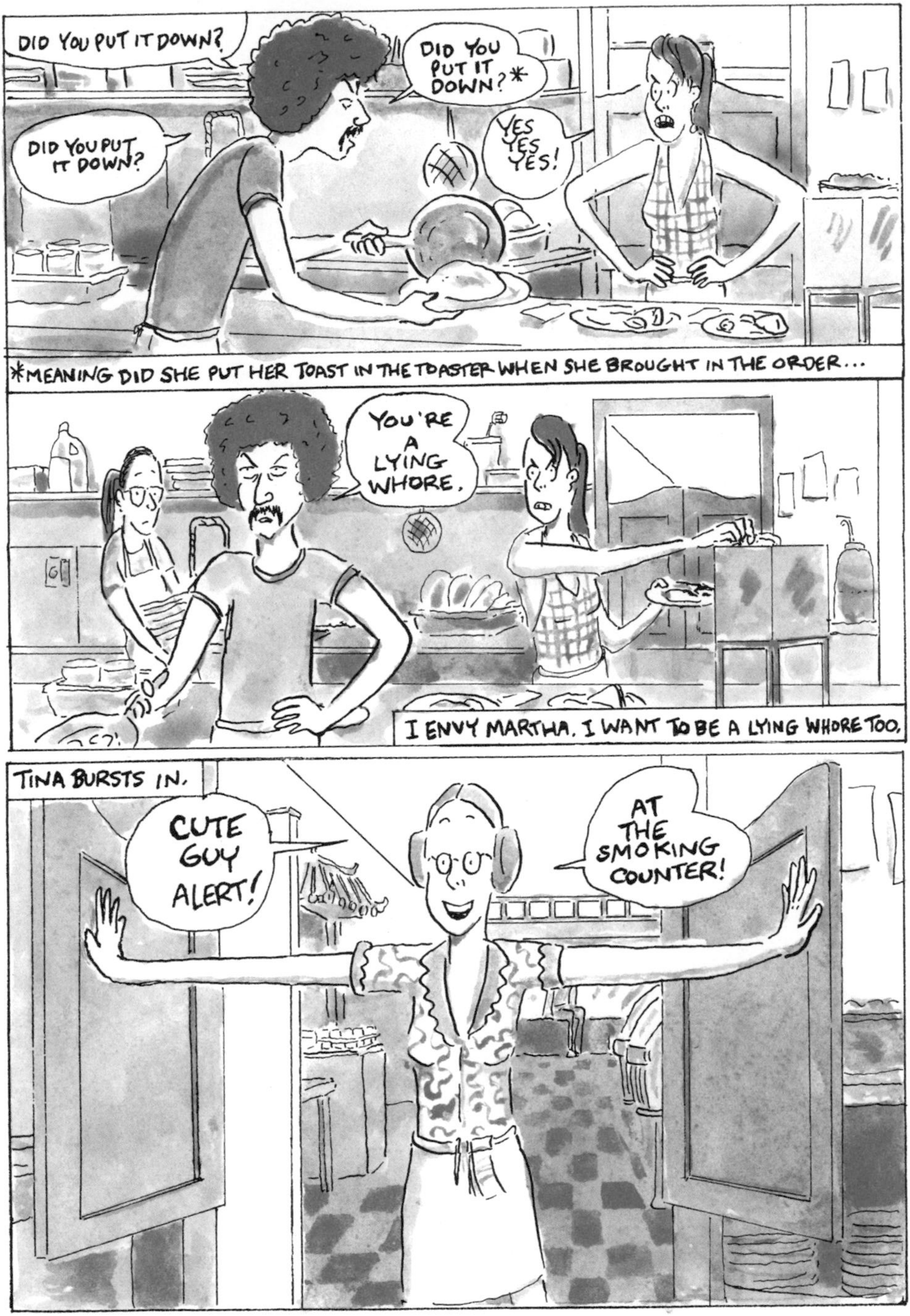
DID YOU PUT IT DOWN?
DID YOU PUT IT DOWN?
DID YOU PUT IT DOWN?*
YES YES YES!
*MEANING DID SHE PUT HER TOAST IN THE TOASTER WHEN SHE BROUGHT IN THE ORDER...
YOU'RE A LYING WHORE.
I ENVY MARTHA. I WANT TO BE A LYING WHORE TOO.
TINA BURSTS IN.
CUTE GUY ALERT!
AT THE SMOKING COUNTER!

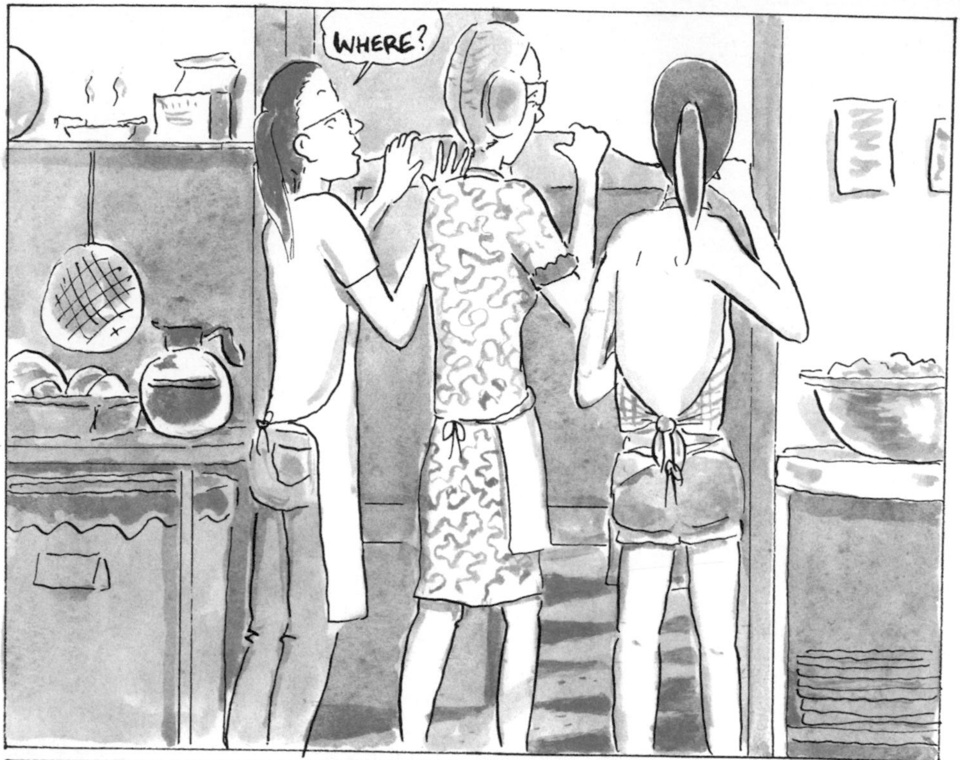
WHERE?

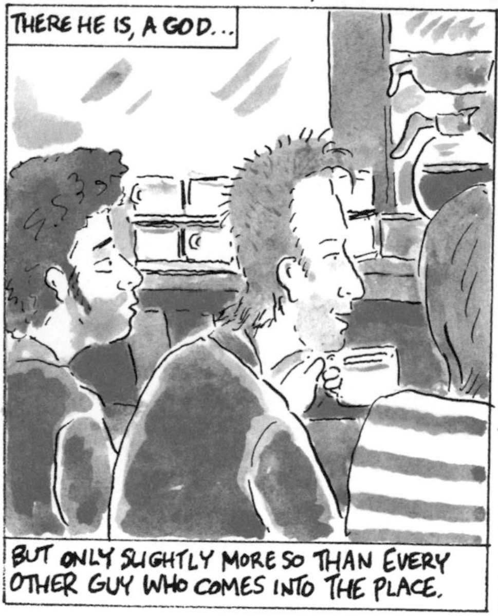
THERE HE IS, A GOD...
BUT ONLY SLIGHTLY MORE SO THAN EVERY OTHER GUY WHO COMES INTO THE PLACE.

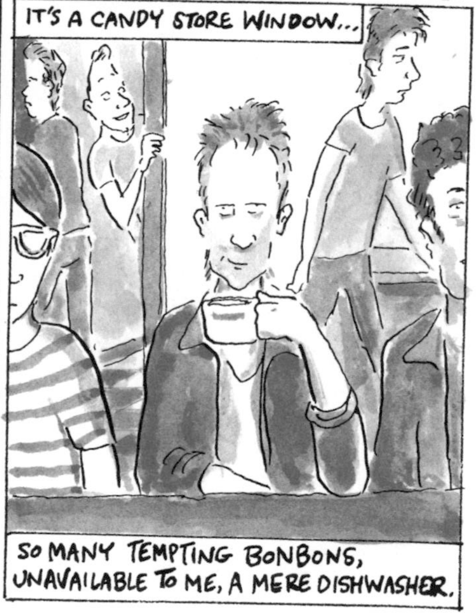
IT'S A CANDY STORE WINDOW...
SO MANY TEMPTING BONBONS, UNAVAILABLE TO ME, A MERE DISHWASHER.

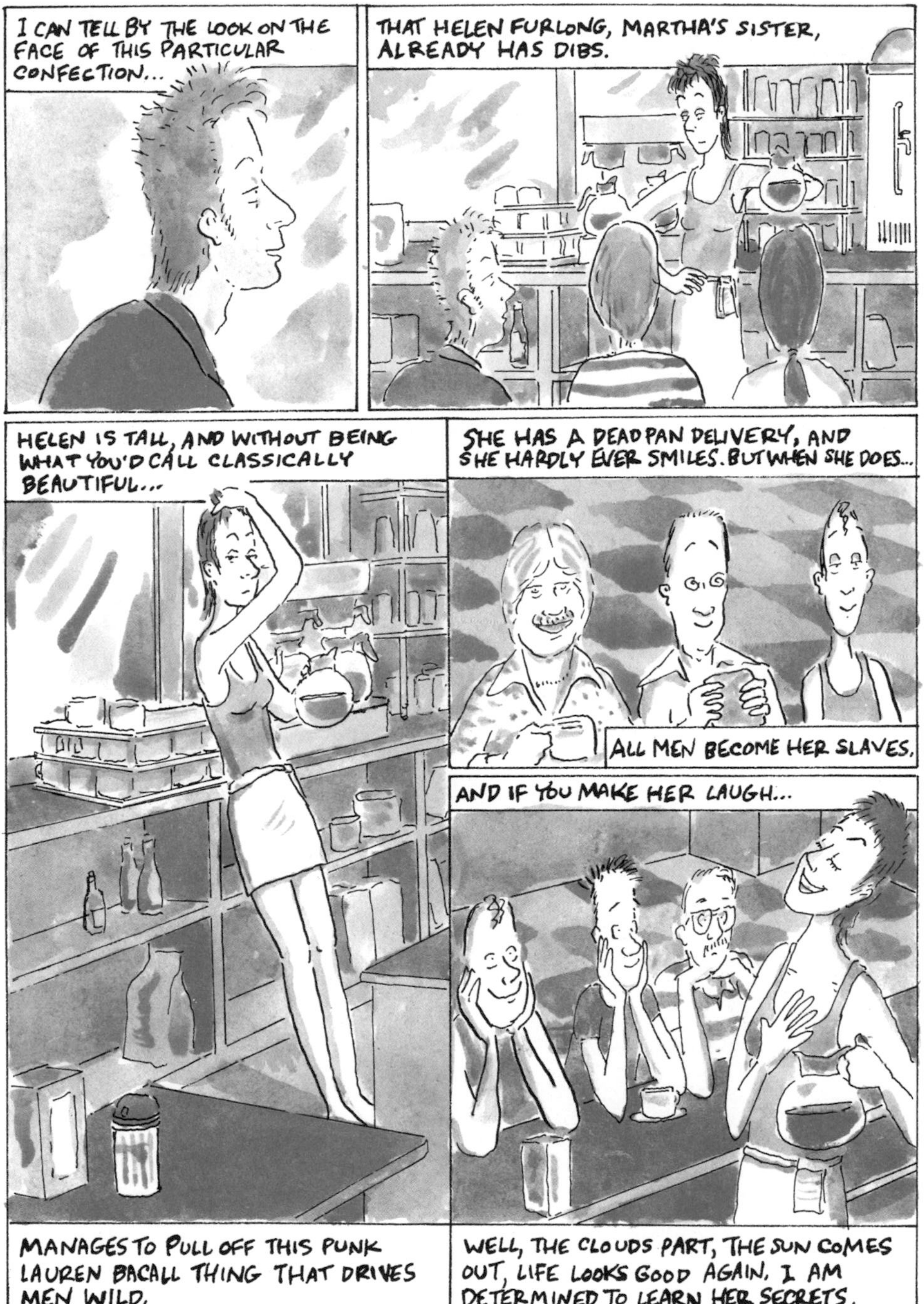
I CAN TELL BY THE LOOK ON THE FACE OF THIS PARTICULAR CONFECTION...
THAT HELEN FURLONG, MARTHA'S SISTER, ALREADY HAS DIBS.
HELEN IS TALL, AND WITHOUT BEING WHAT YOU'D CALL CLASSICALLY BEAUTIFUL...
MANAGES TO PULL OFF THIS PUNK LAUREN BACALL THING THAT DRIVES MEN WILD.
SHE HAS A DEADPAN DELIVERY, AND SHE HARDLY EVER SMILES. BUT WHEN SHE DOES...
ALL MEN BECOME HER SLAVES.
AND IF YOU MAKE HER LAUGH...
WELL, THE CLOUDS PART, THE SUN COMES OUT, LIFE LOOKS GOOD AGAIN. I AM DETERMINED TO LEARN HER SECRETS.

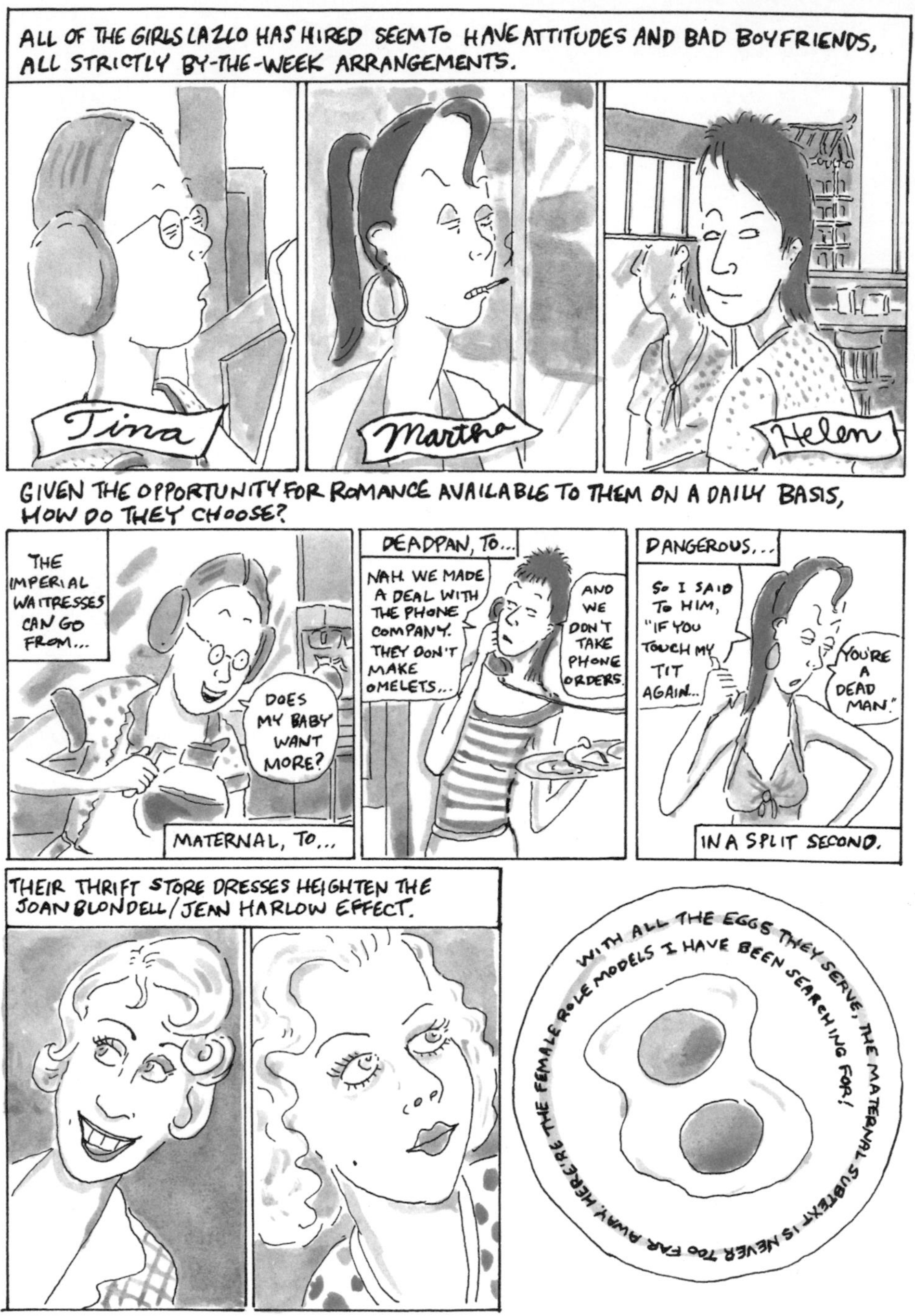

ALL OF THE GIRLS LAZLO HAS HIRED SEEM TO HAVE ATTITUDES AND BAD BOYFRIENDS, ALL STRICTLY BY-THE-WEEK ARRANGEMENTS.
Tina
Martha
Helen
GIVEN THE OPPORTUNITY FOR ROMANCE AVAILABLE TO THEM ON A DAILY BASIS, HOW DO THEY CHOOSE?
THE IMPERIAL WAITRESSES CAN GO FROM...
DOES MY BABY WANT MORE?
MATERNAL, TO...
DEADPAN, TO...
NAH. WE MADE A DEAL WITH THE PHONE COMPANY. THEY DON'T MAKE OMELETS...
AND WE DON'T TAKE PHONE ORDERS.
DANGEROUS...
SO I SAID TO HIM, "IF YOU TOUCH MY TIT AGAIN...
YOU'RE A DEAD MAN."
IN A SPLIT SECOND.
THEIR THRIFT STORE DRESSES HEIGHTEN THE JOAN BLONDELL/JEAN HARLOW EFFECT.
WITH ALL THE EGGS THEY SERVE, THE MATERNAL SUBTEXT IS NEVER TOO FAR AWAY. HERE'RE THE FEMALE ROLE MODELS I HAVE BEEN SEARCHING FOR!

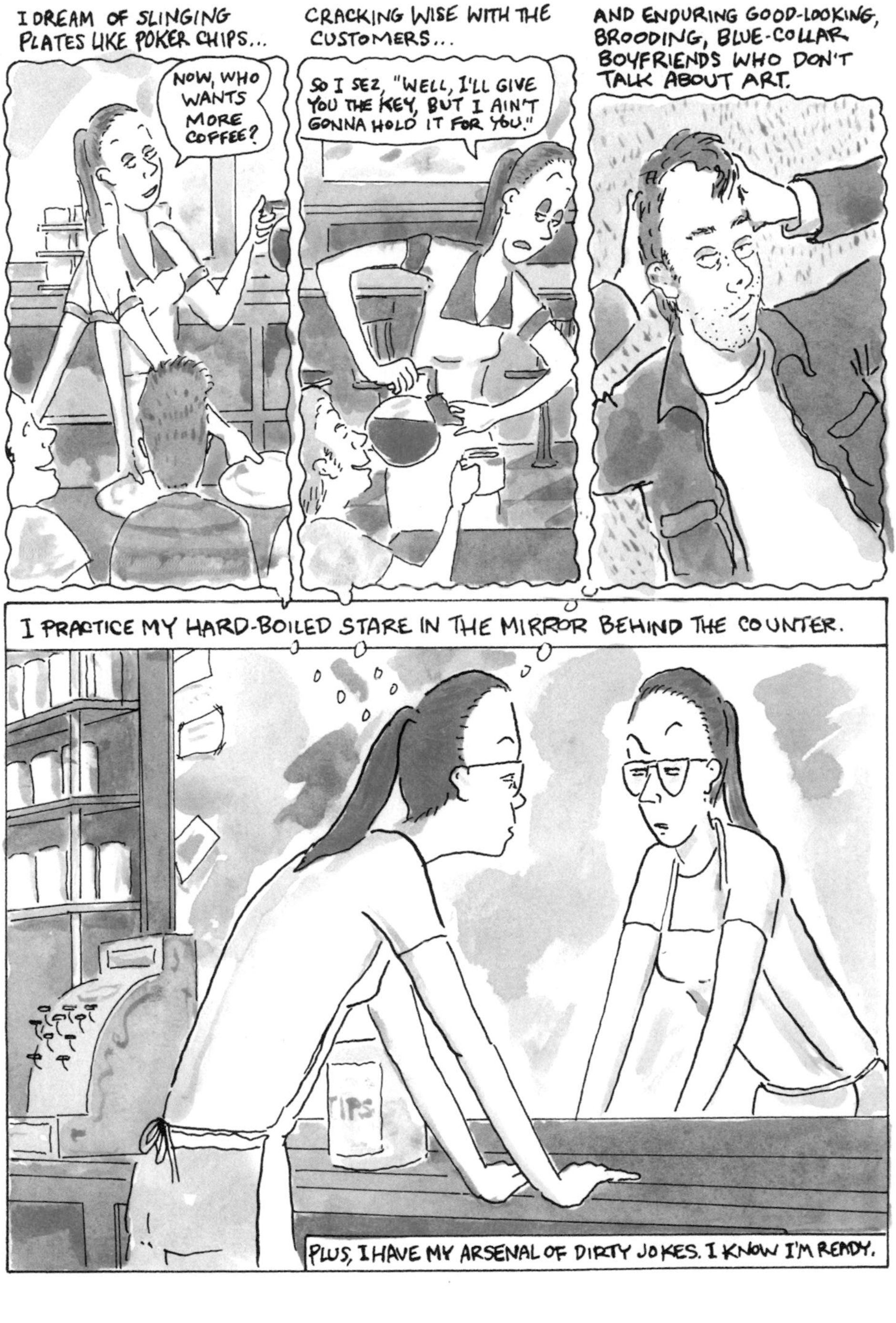
I DREAM OF SLINGING PLATES LIKE POKER CHIPS...
NOW, WHO WANTS MORE COFFEE?
CRACKING WISE WITH THE CUSTOMERS...
SO I SEZ, "WELL, I'LL GIVE YOU THE KEY, BUT I AIN'T GONNA HOLD IT FOR YOU."
AND ENDURING GOOD-LOOKING, BROODING, BLUE-COLLAR BOYFRIENDS WHO DON'T TALK ABOUT ART.
I PRACTICE MY HARD-BOILED STARE IN THE MIRROR BEHIND THE COUNTER.
TIPS
PLUS, I HAVE MY ARSENAL OF DIRTY JOKES. I KNOW I'M READY.

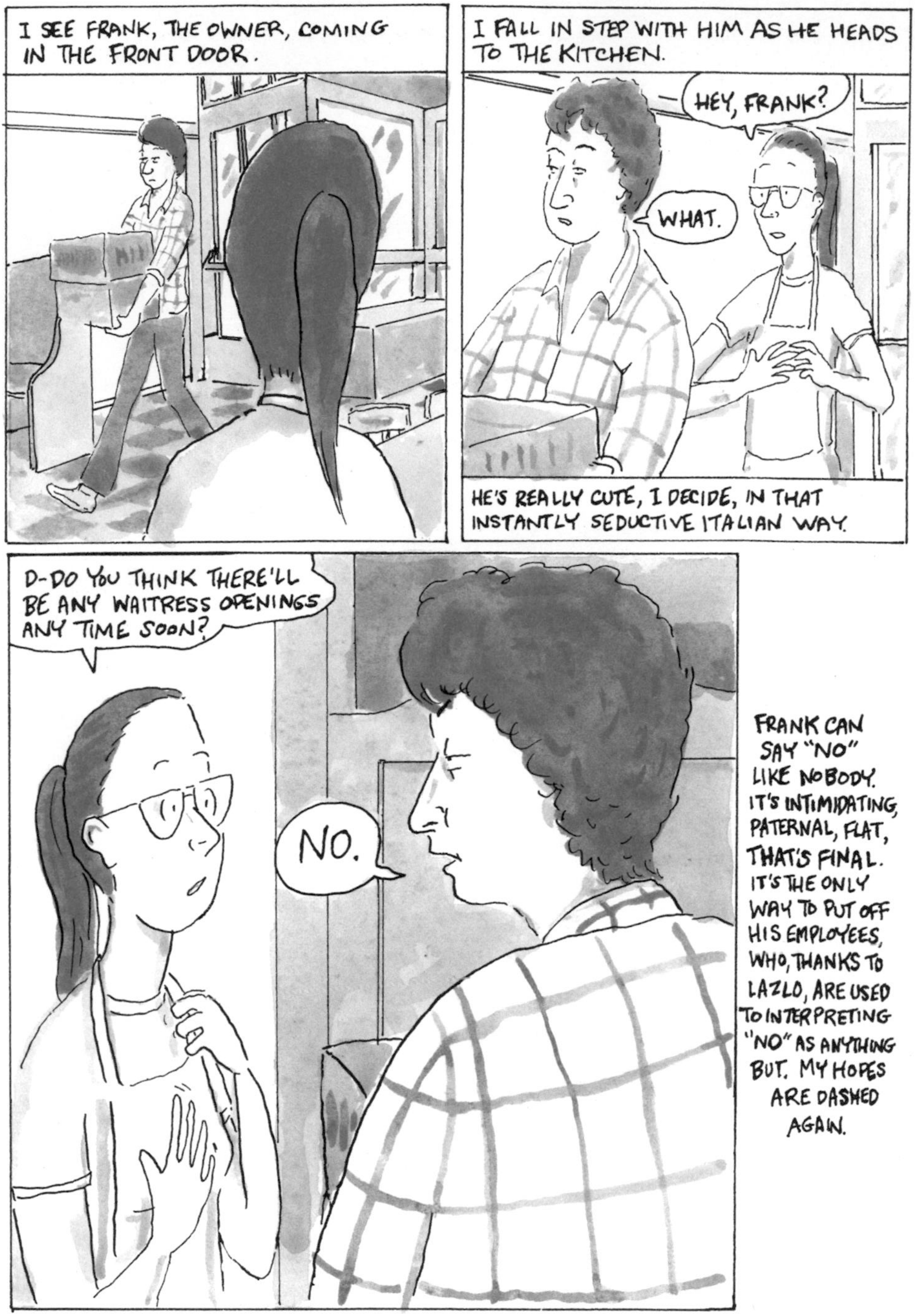
I SEE FRANK, THE OWNER, COMING IN THE FRONT DOOR.
I FALL IN STEP WITH HIM AS HE HEADS TO THE KITCHEN.
HEY, FRANK?
WHAT.
HE'S REALLY CUTE, I DECIDE, IN THAT INSTANTLY SEDUCTIVE ITALIAN WAY.
D-DO YOU THINK THERE'LL BE ANY WAITRESS OPENINGS ANY TIME SOON?
NO.
FRANK CAN SAY "NO" LIKE NOBODY. IT'S INTIMIDATING, PATERNAL, FLAT, THAT'S FINAL. IT'S THE ONLY WAY TO PUT OFF HIS EMPLOYEES, WHO, THANKS TO LAZLO, ARE USED TO INTERPRETING "NO" AS ANYTHING BUT. MY HOPES ARE DASHED AGAIN.

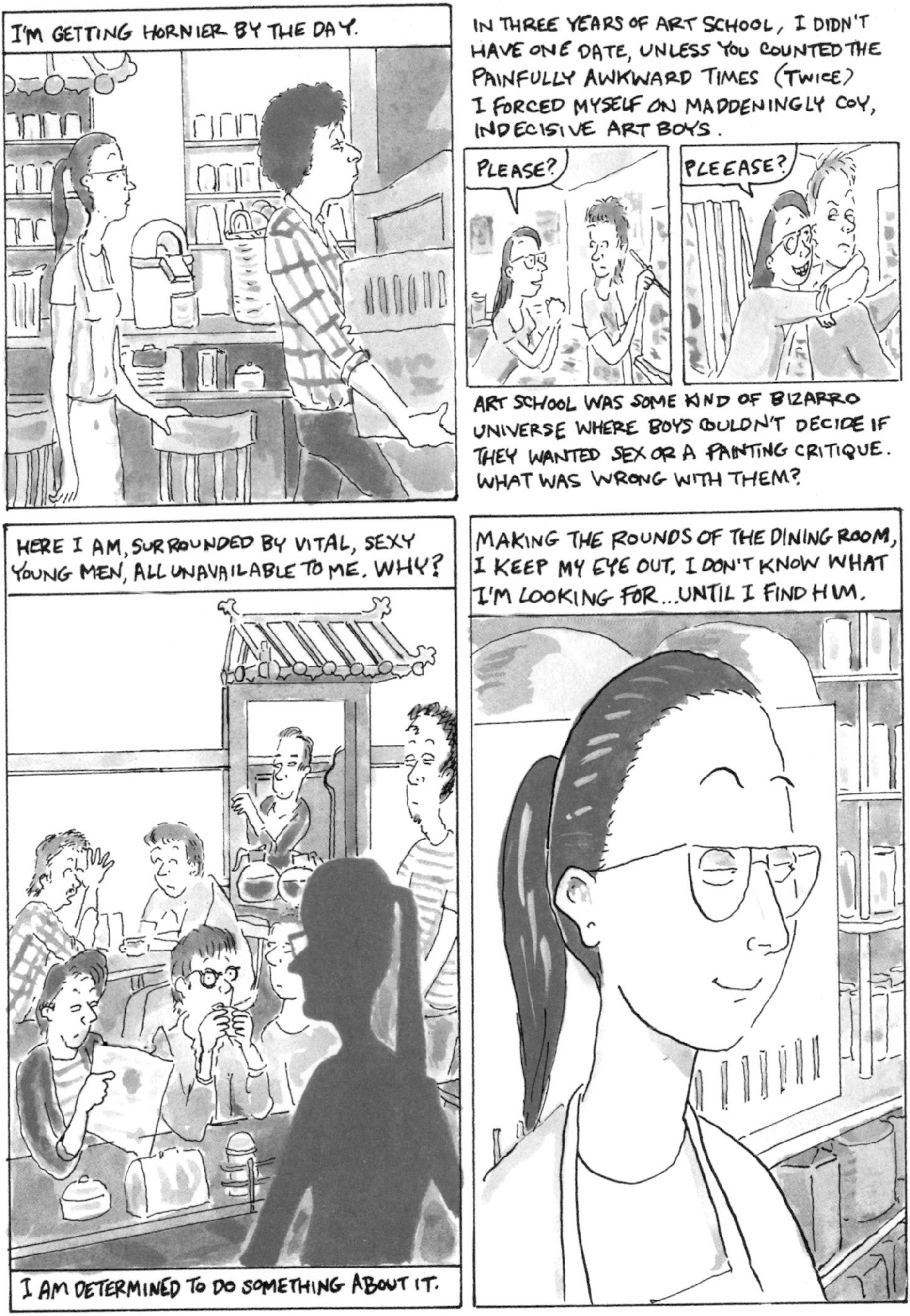
I'M GETTING HORNIER BY THE DAY.
IN THREE YEARS OF ART SCHOOL, I DIDN'T HAVE ONE DATE, UNLESS YOU COUNTED THE PAINFULLY AWKWARD TIMES (TWICE) I FORCED MYSELF ON MADDENINGLY COY, INDECISIVE ART BOYS.
PLEASE?
PLEEASE?
ART SCHOOL WAS SOME KIND OF BIZARRO UNIVERSE WHERE BOYS COULDN'T DECIDE IF THEY WANTED SEX OR A PAINTING CRITIQUE. WHAT WAS WRONG WITH THEM?
HERE I AM, SURROUNDED BY VITAL, SEXY YOUNG MEN, ALL UNAVAILABLE TO ME. WHY?
I AM DETERMINED TO DO SOMETHING ABOUT IT.
MAKING THE ROUNDS OF THE DINING ROOM, I KEEP MY EYE OUT. I DON'T KNOW WHAT I'M LOOKING FOR...UNTIL I FIND HIM.

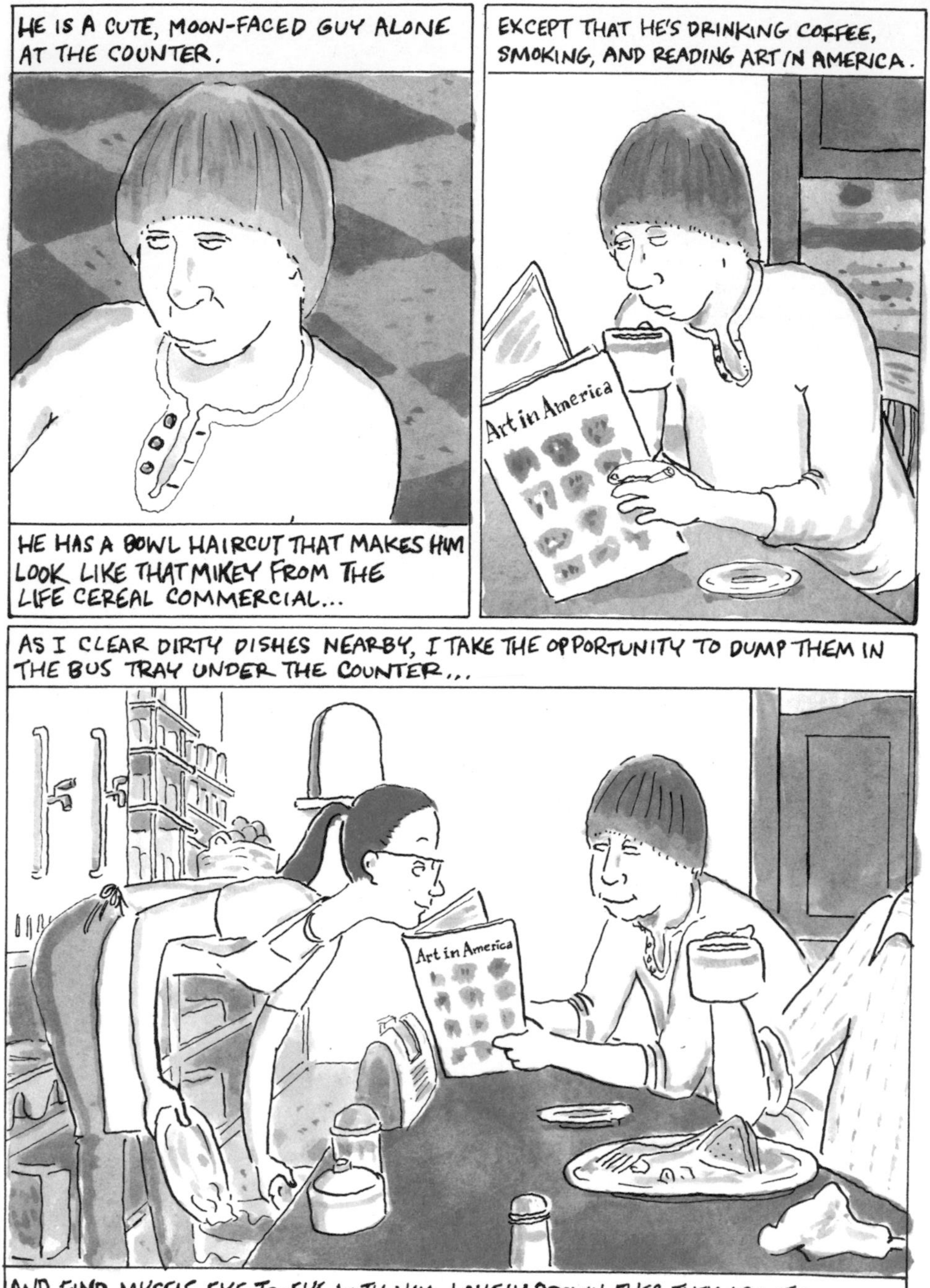
HE IS A CUTE, MOON-FACED GUY ALONE AT THE COUNTER.
HE HAS A BOWL HAIRCUT THAT MAKES HIM LOOK LIKE THAT MIKEY FROM THE LIFE CEREAL COMMERCIAL...
EXCEPT THAT HE'S DRINKING COFFEE, SMOKING, AND READING ART IN AMERICA.
Art in America
AS I CLEAR DIRTY DISHES NEARBY, I TAKE THE OPPORTUNITY TO DUMP THEM IN THE BUS TRAY UNDER THE COUNTER...
Art in America
AND FIND MYSELF EYE-TO-EYE WITH HIM. LOVELY BROWN EYES THEY ARE TOO.

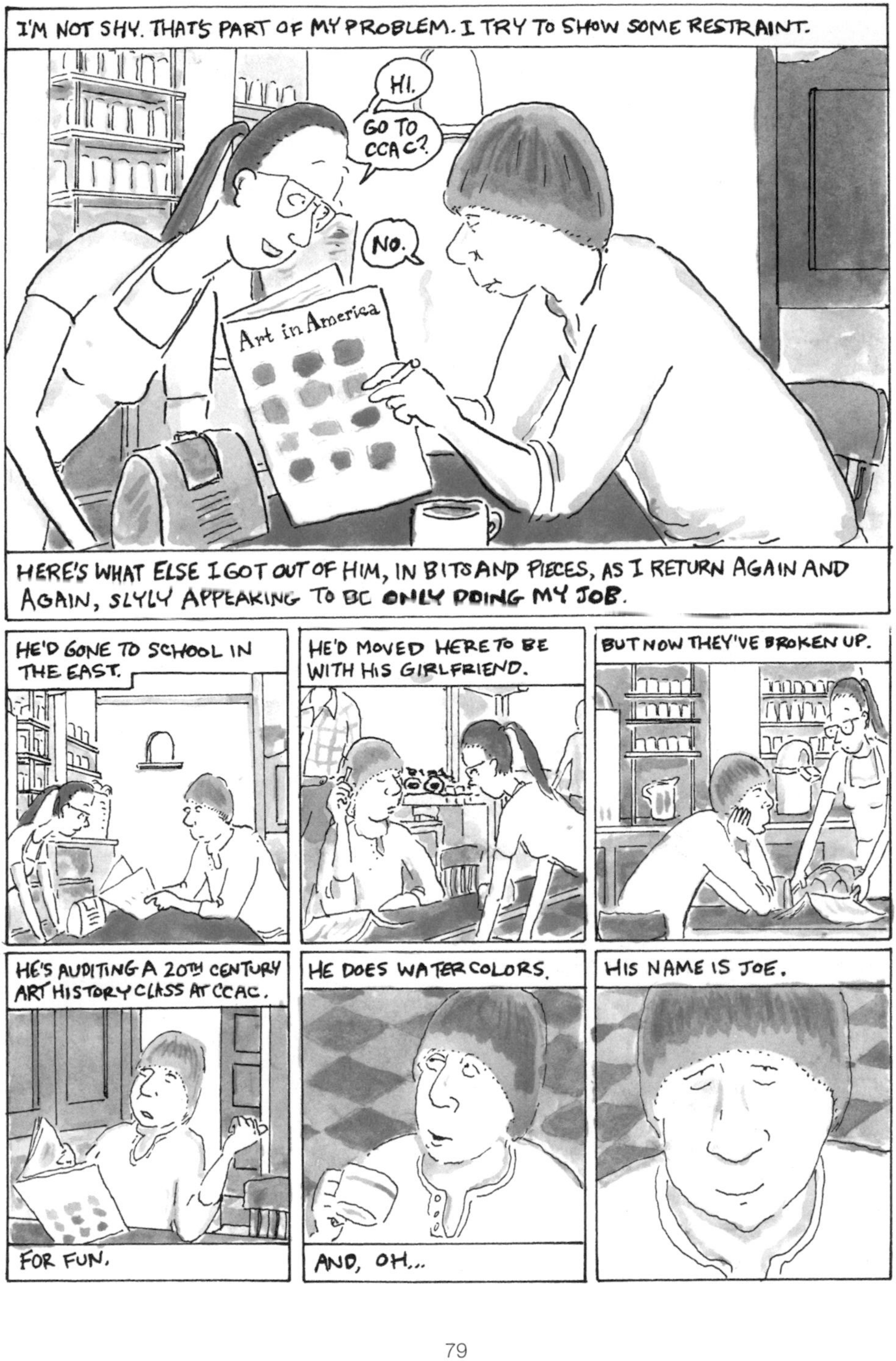
I'M NOT SHY. THAT'S PART OF MY PROBLEM. I TRY TO SHOW SOME RESTRAINT.
HI.
GO TO CCAC?
NO.
Art in America
HERE'S WHAT ELSE I GOT OUT OF HIM, IN BITS AND PIECES, AS I RETURN AGAIN AND AGAIN, SLYLY APPEARING TO BE ONLY DOING MY JOB.
HE'D GONE TO SCHOOL IN THE EAST.
HE'D MOVED HERE TO BE WITH HIS GIRLFRIEND.
BUT NOW THEY'VE BROKEN UP.
HE'S AUDITING A 20TH CENTURY ART HISTORY CLASS AT CCAC.
FOR FUN.
HE DOES WATERCOLORS.
AND, OH...
HIS NAME IS JOE.

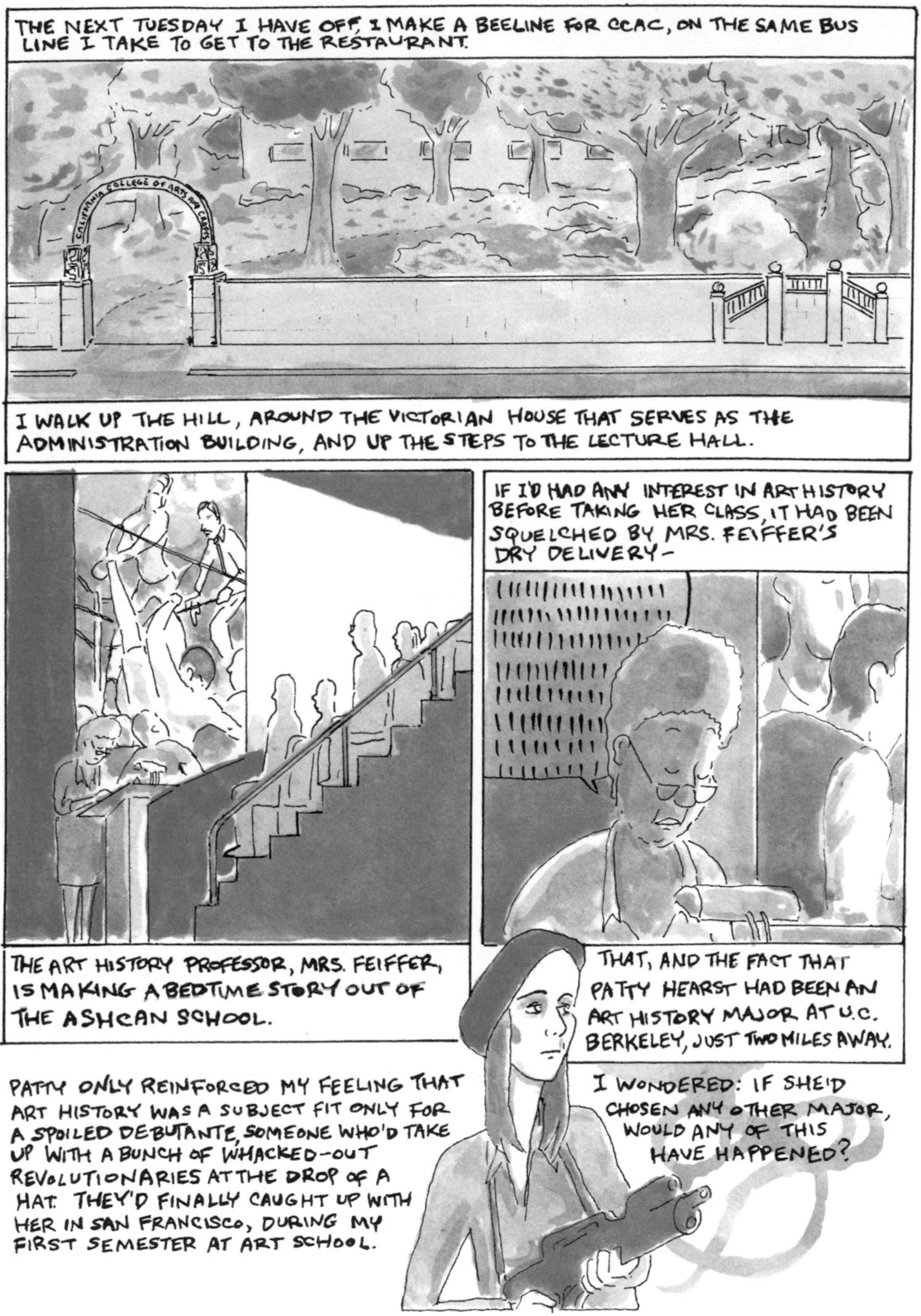
THE NEXT TUESDAY I HAVE OFF, I MAKE A BEELINE FOR CCAC, ON THE SAME BUS LINE I TAKE TO GET TO THE RESTAURANT.
I WALK UP THE HILL, AROUND THE VICTORIAN HOUSE THAT SERVES AS THE ADMINISTRATION BUILDING, AND UP THE STEPS TO THE LECTURE HALL.
THE ART HISTORY PROFESSOR, MRS. FEIFFER, IS MAKING A BEDTIME STORY OUT OF THE ASHCAN SCHOOL.
IF I'D HAD ANY INTEREST IN ART HISTORY BEFORE TAKING HER CLASS, IT HAD BEEN SQUELCHED BY MRS. FEIFFER'S DRY DELIVERY-
THAT, AND THE FACT THAT PATTY HEARST HAD BEEN AN ART HISTORY MAJOR AT U.C. BERKELEY, JUST TWO MILES AWAY.
PATTY ONLY REINFORCED MY FEELING THAT ART HISTORY WAS A SUBJECT FIT ONLY FOR A SPOILED DEBUTANTE, SOMEONE WHO'D TAKE UP WITH A BUNCH OF WHACKED-OUT REVOLUTIONARIES AT THE DROP OF A HAT. THEY'D FINALLY CAUGHT UP WITH HER IN SAN FRANCISCO, DURING MY FIRST SEMESTER AT ART SCHOOL.
I WONDERED: IF SHE'D CHOSEN ANY OTHER MAJOR, WOULD ANY OF THIS HAVE HAPPENED?

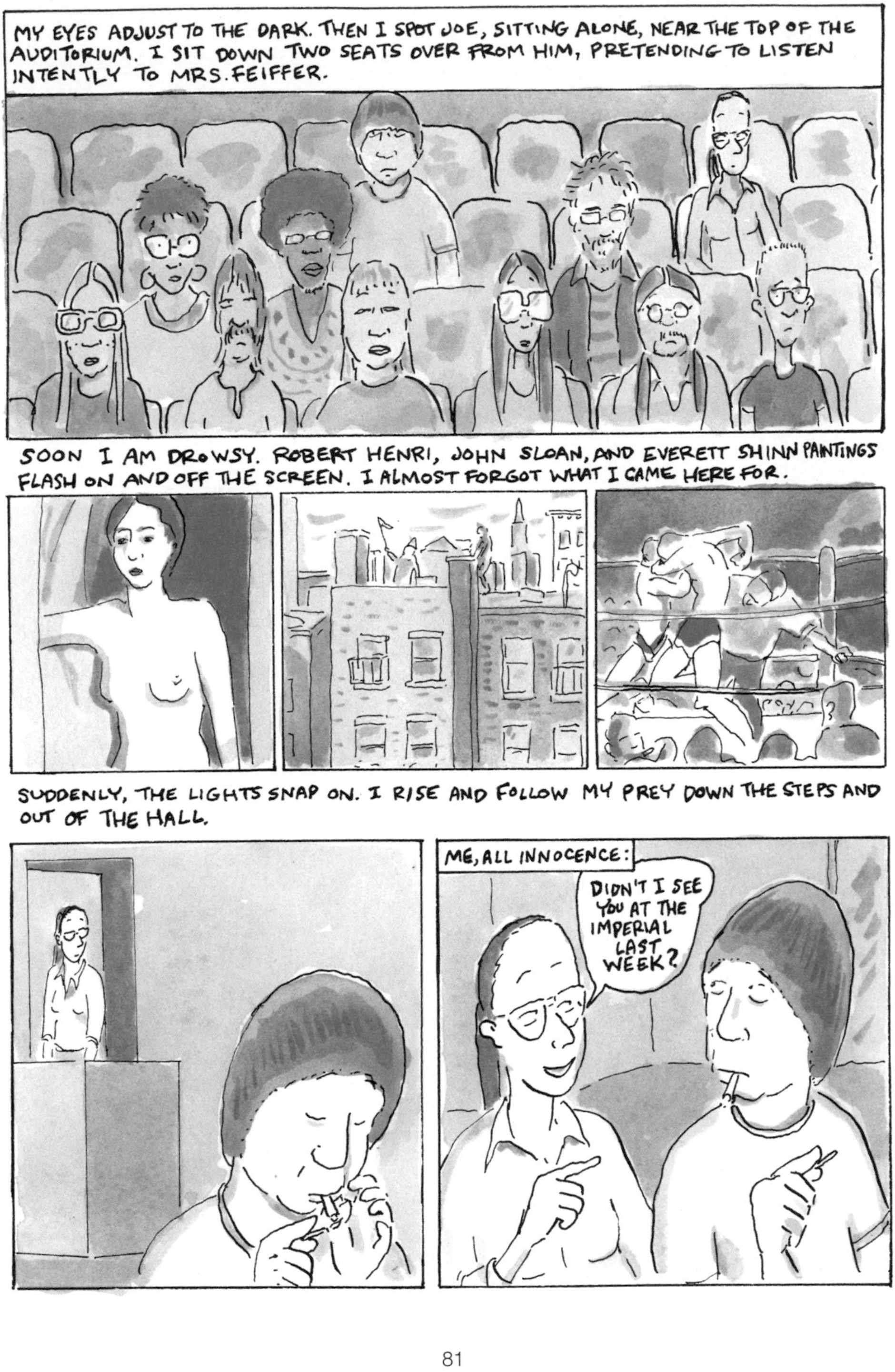
MY EYES ADJUST TO THE DARK. THEN I SPOT JOE, SITTING ALONE, NEAR THE TOP OF THE AUDITORIUM. I SIT DOWN TWO SEATS OVER FROM HIM, PRETENDING TO LISTEN INTENTLY TO MRS. FEIFFER.
SOON I AM DROWSY. ROBERT HENRI, JOHN SLOAN, AND EVERETT SHINN PAINTINGS FLASH ON AND OFF THE SCREEN. I ALMOST FORGOT WHAT I CAME HERE FOR.
SUDDENLY, THE LIGHTS SNAP ON. I RISE AND FOLLOW MY PREY DOWN THE STEPS AND OUT OF THE HALL.
ME, ALL INNOCENCE:
DIDN'T I SEE YOU AT THE IMPERIAL LAST WEEK?

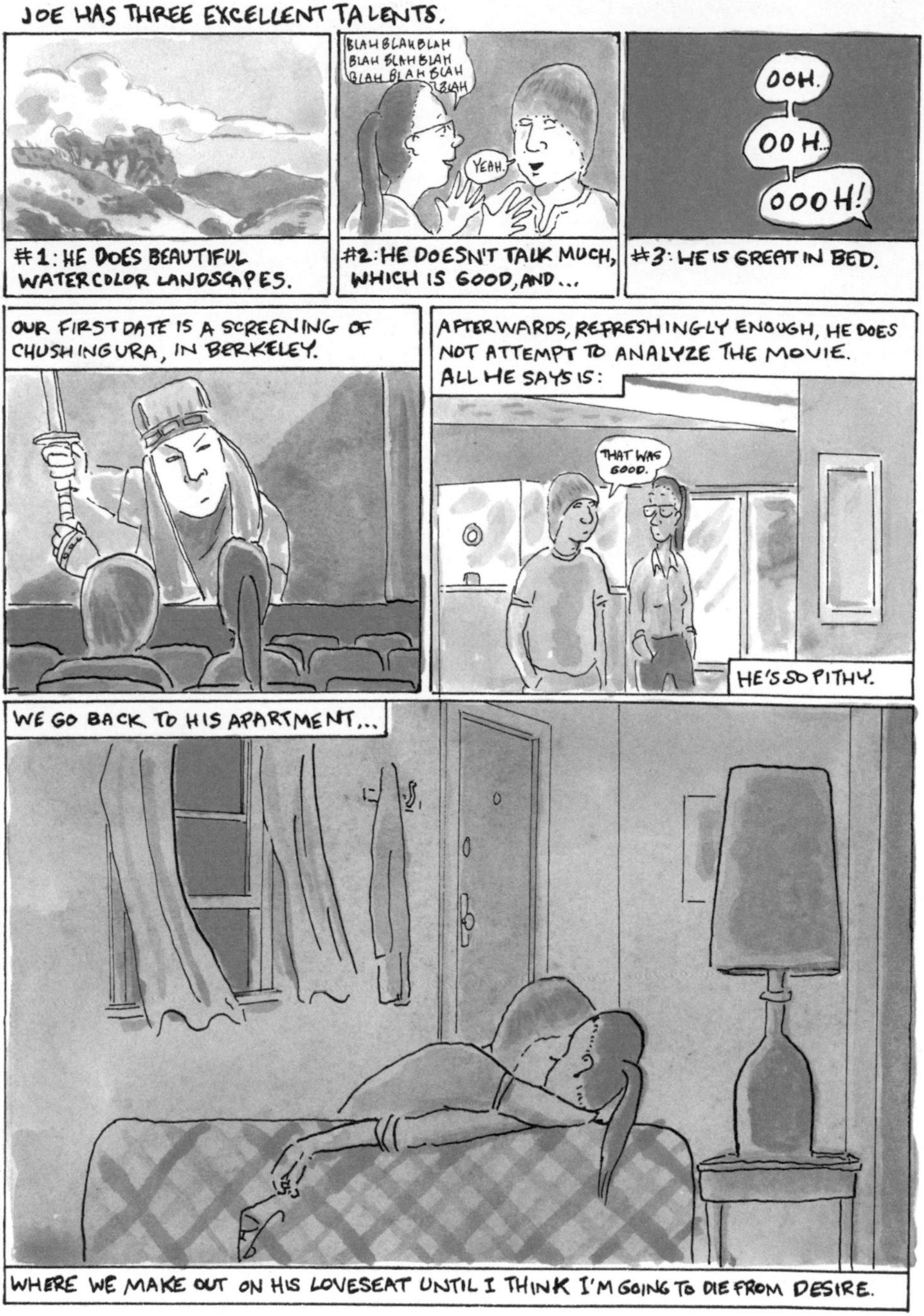
JOE HAS THREE EXCELLENT TALENTS.
#1: HE DOES BEAUTIFUL WATERCOLOR LANDSCAPES.
BLAH BLAH BLAH BLAH BLAH BLAH BLAH BLAH BLAH BLAH
YEAH.
#2: HE DOESN'T TALK MUCH, WHICH IS GOOD, AND...
OOH.
OOH...
OOOH!
#3: HE IS GREAT IN BED.
OUR FIRST DATE IS A SCREENING OF CHUSHINGURA, IN BERKELEY.
AFTERWARDS, REFRESHINGLY ENOUGH, HE DOES NOT ATTEMPT TO ANALYZE THE MOVIE. ALL HE SAYS IS:
THAT WAS GOOD.
HE'S SO PITHY.
WE GO BACK TO HIS APARTMENT...
WHERE WE MAKE OUT ON HIS LOVESEAT UNTIL I THINK I'M GOING TO DIE FROM DESIRE.

IN HIS BEDROOM, JOE HAS AN OLD BRASS BEDSTEAD.

IT STANDS HIGHER THAN MOST BEDS.

HE'S ON THE SHORT SIDE, MAYBE 5'7 OR SO.

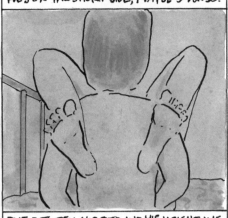

BUT BETWEEN HIS BED AND HIS HEIGHT, WE FIND THE SWEET SPOT.

I'D NEVER MADE LOVE THAT WAY BEFORE.

EVERYTHING IS MAGICALLY JUST THE RIGHT SIZE.

UNDERNEATH THAT WORKING-CLASS JERSEY GUY EXTERIOR IS A REAL SENSUALIST.

I LOVE WATCHING JOE'S FACE WHILE HE DRIVES HIMSELF INTO ME.

...LOST IN ENJOYMENT.

I AM SEXY. I AM DESIRABLE.

HERE IS THE PROOF.

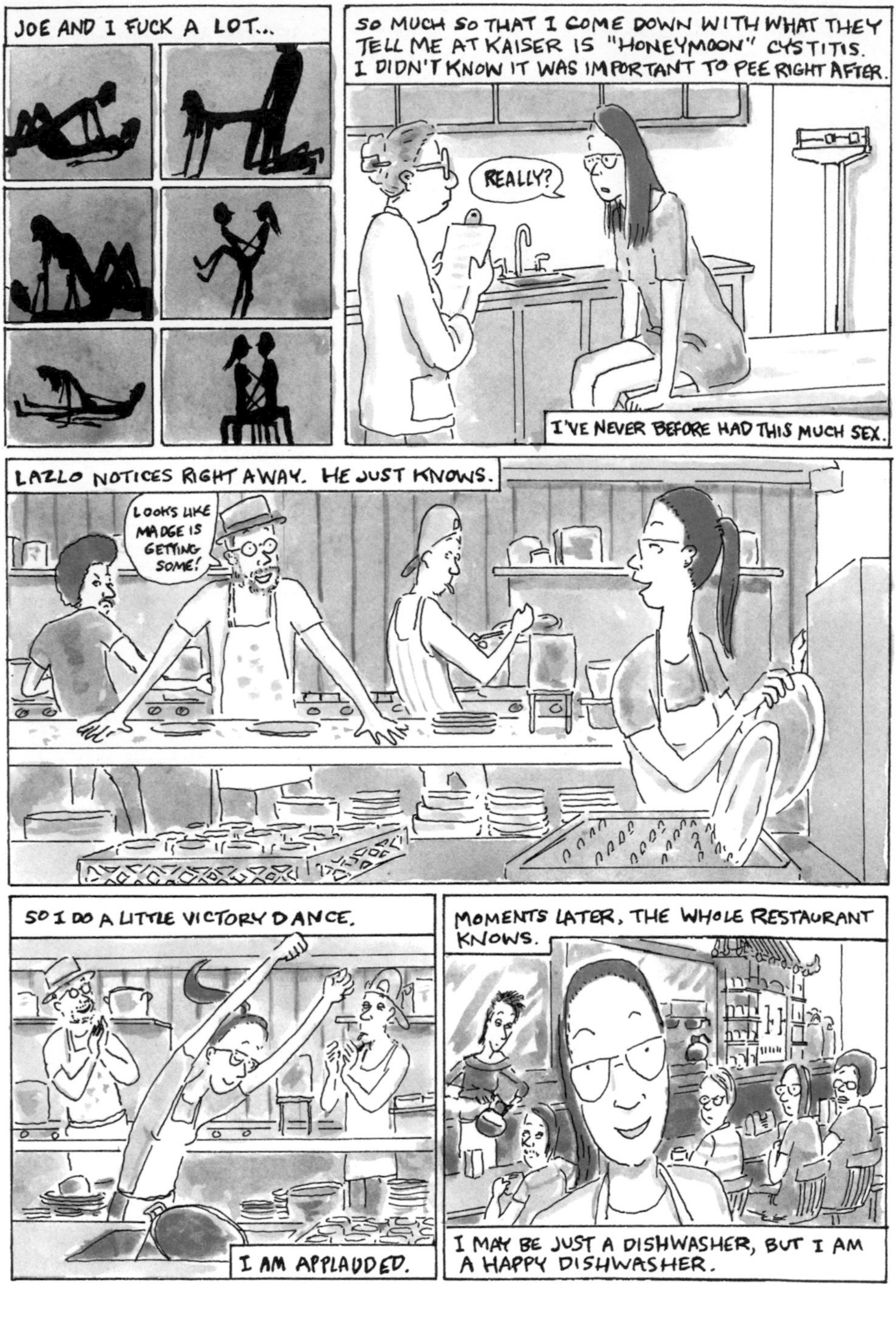
JOE AND I FUCK A LOT...
SO MUCH SO THAT I COME DOWN WITH WHAT THEY TELL ME AT KAISER IS "HONEYMOON" CYSTITIS. I DIDN'T KNOW IT WAS IMPORTANT TO PEE RIGHT AFTER.
REALLY?
I'VE NEVER BEFORE HAD THIS MUCH SEX.
LAZLO NOTICES RIGHT AWAY. HE JUST KNOWS.
LOOKS LIKE MADGE IS GETTING SOME!
SO I DO A LITTLE VICTORY DANCE.
I AM APPLAUDED.
MOMENTS LATER, THE WHOLE RESTAURANT KNOWS.
I MAY BE JUST A DISHWASHER, BUT I AM A HAPPY DISHWASHER.

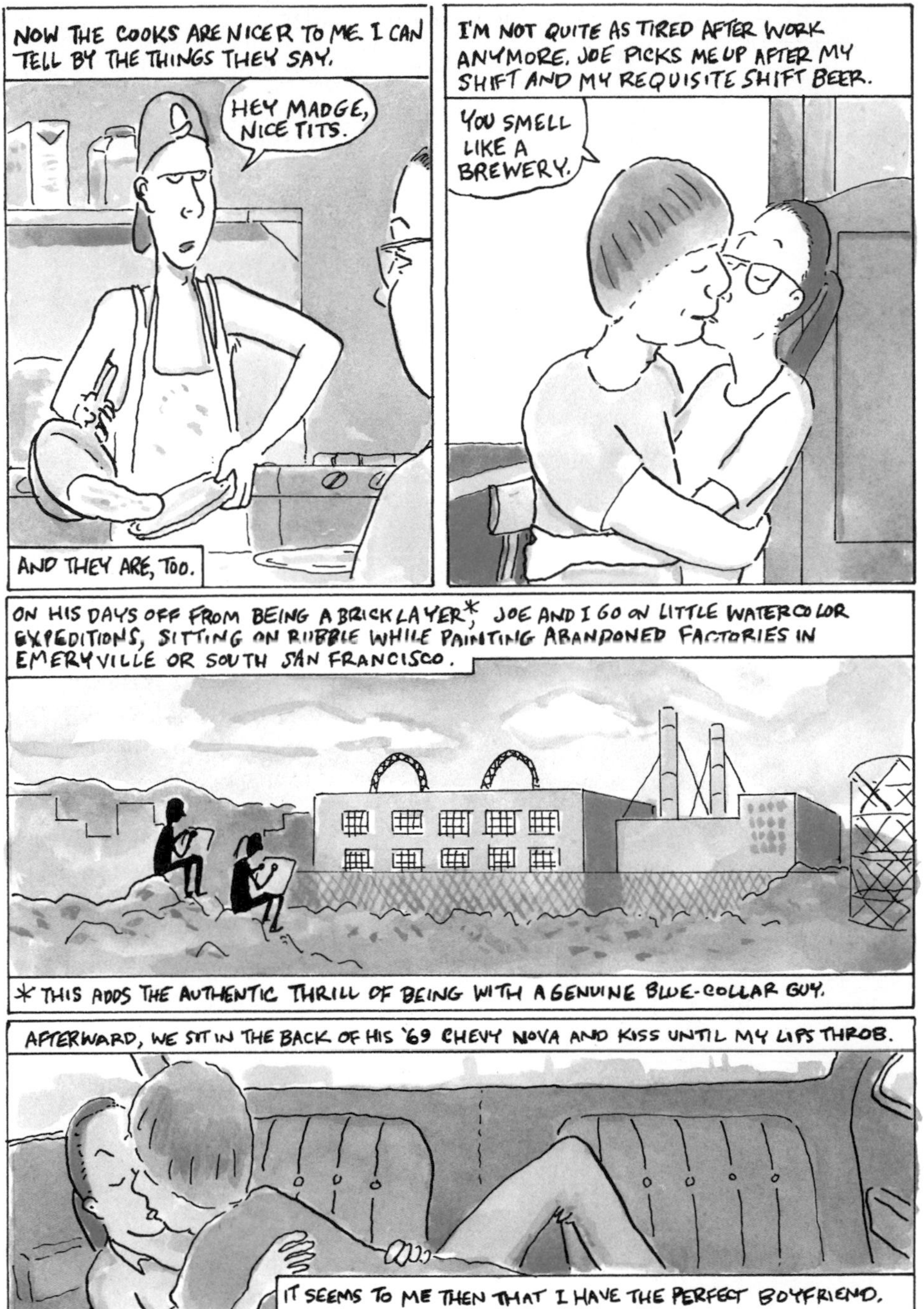
NOW THE COOKS ARE NICER TO ME. I CAN TELL BY THE THINGS THEY SAY.
HEY MADGE, NICE TITS.
AND THEY ARE, TOO.
I'M NOT QUITE AS TIRED AFTER WORK ANYMORE. JOE PICKS ME UP AFTER MY SHIFT AND MY REQUISITE SHIFT BEER.
YOU SMELL LIKE A BREWERY.
ON HIS DAYS OFF FROM BEING A BRICKLAYER* JOE AND I GO ON LITTLE WATERCOLOR EXPEDITIONS, SITTING ON RUBBLE WHILE PAINTING ABANDONED FACTORIES IN EMERYVILLE OR SOUTH SAN FRANCISCO.
* THIS ADDS THE AUTHENTIC THRILL OF BEING WITH A GENUINE BLUE-COLLAR GUY.
AFTERWARD, WE SIT IN THE BACK OF HIS '69 CHEVY NOVA AND KISS UNTIL MY LIPS THROB.
IT SEEMS TO ME THEN THAT I HAVE THE PERFECT BOYFRIEND.

ONE NIGHT, ABOUT SIX WEEKS INTO THIS ARRANGEMENT, JOE SAYS HE'LL COOK FOR ME. HE LIVES IN THE KIND OF APARTMENT YOU CAN TELL HE'S SUFFERED IN.

HIS ART SCHOOL GIRLFRIEND, SIMONE, HAD LEFT HIM TO GO FIND HERSELF.

EVEN THE WAY HE SAYS HER NAME...

SMOAN...

SOUNDS MELANCHOLY.

HE WON'T STOP TALKING ABOUT HER.

SIMONE PAINTED IN OILS.

SIMONE KNEW PEOPLE WHO KNEW JOHN WATERS.

SIMONE AND HE HAD TAKEN A TRIP TO MEXICO.

WHEN WOULD A MAN WANT TO TAKE A TRIP WITH ME? THAT POSSIBILITY SEEMS YEARS AWAY.

AT DINNER TIME, JOE TRIES TO SET THE MOOD WITH A NEW ALBUM ON THE TURNTABLE.

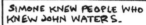

WHAT'S THIS?

A SAX SOLO SQUEALS OUT OF THE CRAPPY SPEAKERS.

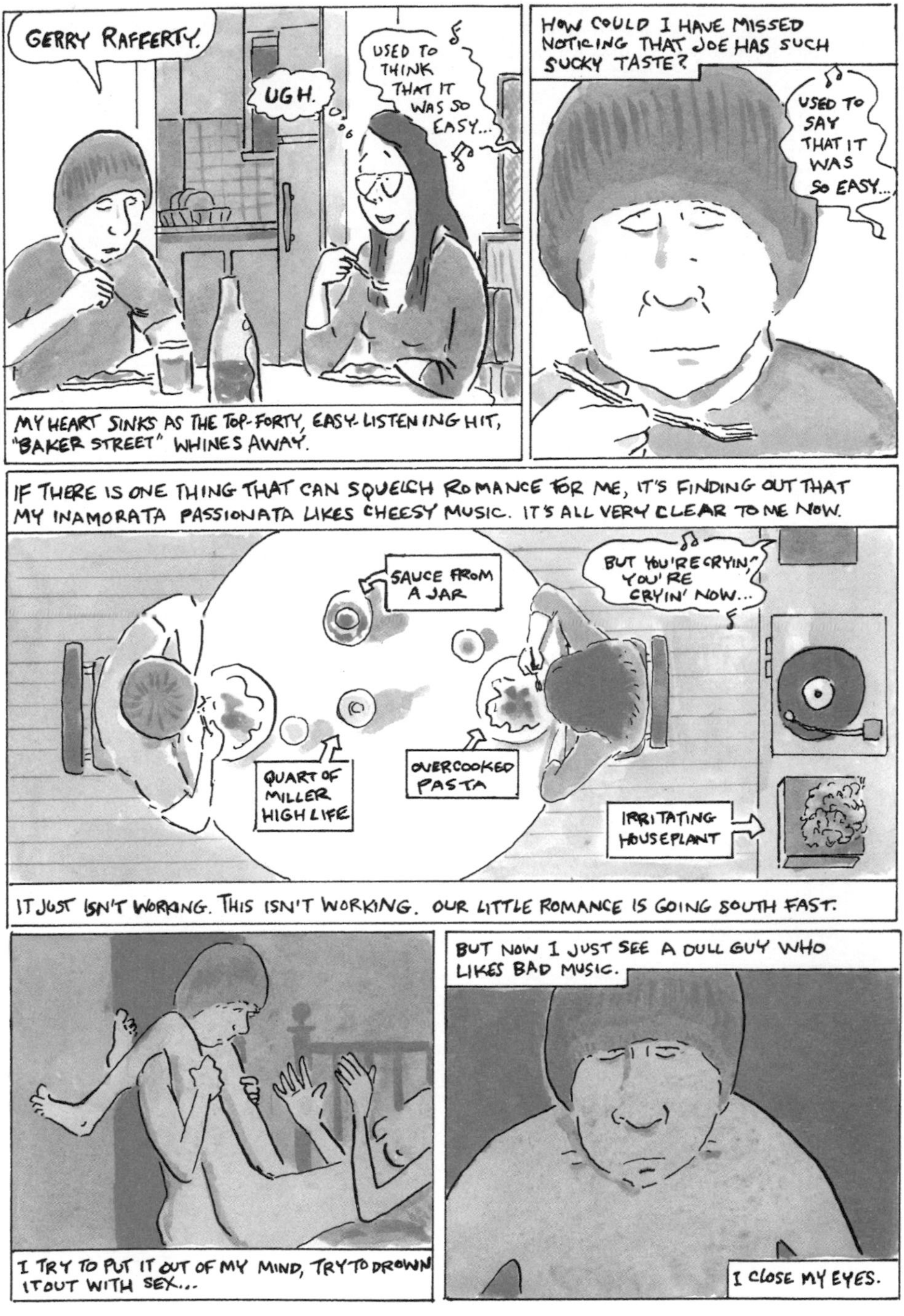
GERRY RAFFERTY.
UGH.
USED TO THINK THAT IT WAS SO EASY...
MY HEART SINKS AS THE TOP-FORTY, EASY-LISTENING HIT, "BAKER STREET" WHINES AWAY.
HOW COULD I HAVE MISSED NOTICING THAT JOE HAS SUCH SUCKY TASTE?
USED TO SAY THAT IT WAS SO EASY...
IF THERE IS ONE THING THAT CAN SQUELCH ROMANCE FOR ME, IT'S FINDING OUT THAT MY INAMORATA PASSIONATA LIKES CHEESY MUSIC. IT'S ALL VERY CLEAR TO ME NOW.
SAUCE FROM A JAR
BUT YOU'RE CRYIN', YOU'RE CRYIN' NOW...
QUART OF MILLER HIGH LIFE
OVERCOOKED PASTA
IRRITATING HOUSEPLANT
IT JUST ISN'T WORKING. THIS ISN'T WORKING. OUR LITTLE ROMANCE IS GOING SOUTH FAST.
I TRY TO PUT IT OUT OF MY MIND, TRY TO DROWN IT OUT WITH SEX...
BUT NOW I JUST SEE A DULL GUY WHO LIKES BAD MUSIC.
I CLOSE MY EYES.

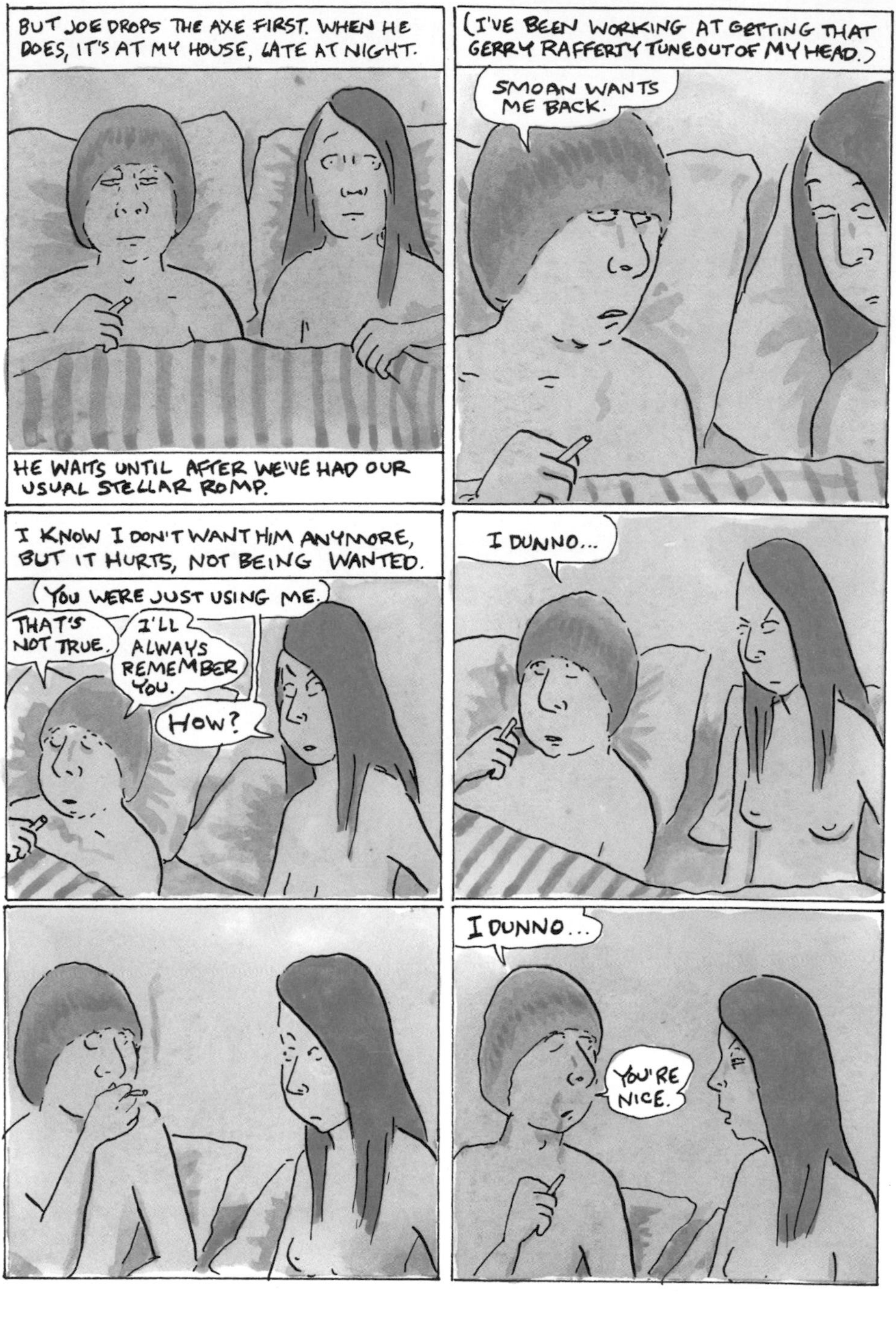

BUT JOE DROPS THE AXE FIRST. WHEN HE DOES, IT'S AT MY HOUSE, LATE AT NIGHT.
HE WAITS UNTIL AFTER WE'VE HAD OUR USUAL STELLAR ROMP.
(I'VE BEEN WORKING AT GETTING THAT GERRY RAFFERTY TUNE OUT OF MY HEAD.)
SMOAN WANTS ME BACK.
I KNOW I DON'T WANT HIM ANYMORE, BUT IT HURTS, NOT BEING WANTED.
YOU WERE JUST USING ME.
THAT'S NOT TRUE.
I'LL ALWAYS REMEMBER YOU.
HOW?
I DUNNO...
I DUNNO...
YOU'RE NICE.

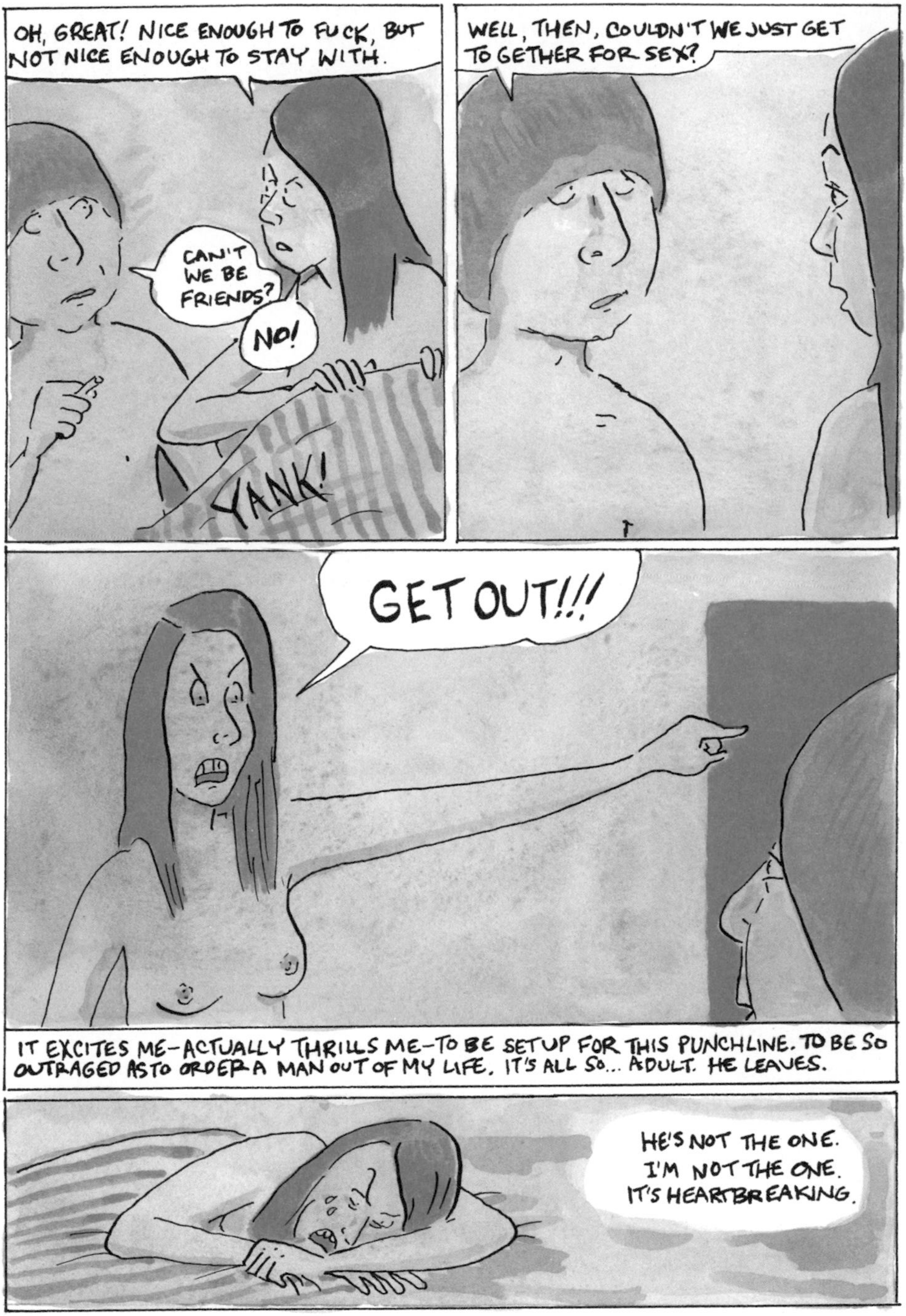
OH, GREAT! NICE ENOUGH TO FUCK, BUT NOT NICE ENOUGH TO STAY WITH.
CAN'T WE BE FRIENDS?
NO!
YANK!
WELL, THEN, COULDN'T WE JUST GET TOGETHER FOR SEX?
GET OUT!!!
IT EXCITES ME—ACTUALLY THRILLS ME—TO BE SETUP FOR THIS PUNCHLINE. TO BE SO OUTRAGED AS TO ORDER A MAN OUT OF MY LIFE. IT'S ALL SO... ADULT. HE LEAVES.
HE'S NOT THE ONE.
I'M NOT THE ONE.
IT'S HEARTBREAKING.

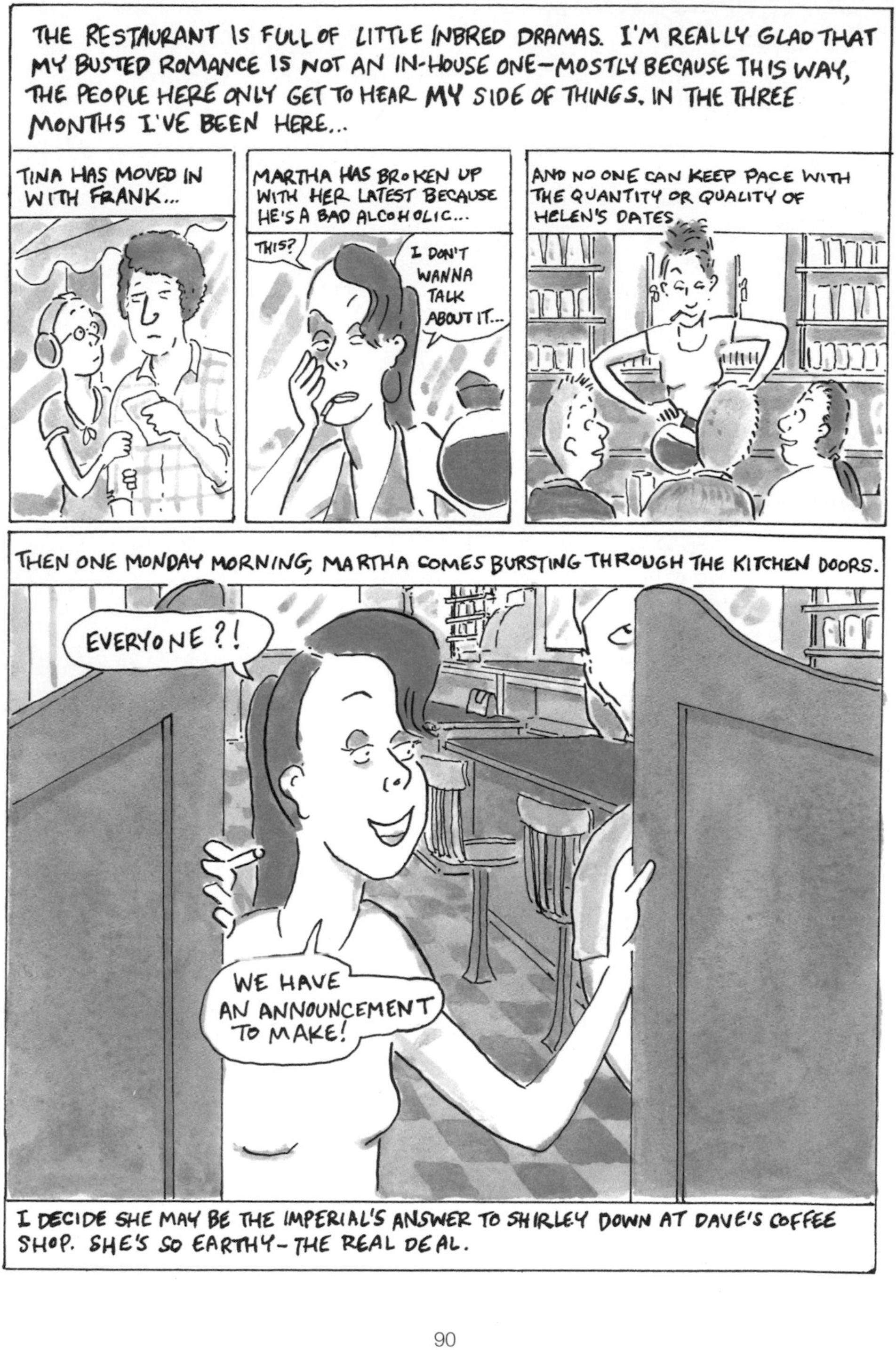
THE RESTAURANT IS FULL OF LITTLE INBRED DRAMAS. I'M REALLY GLAD THAT MY BUSTED ROMANCE IS NOT AN IN-HOUSE ONE—MOSTLY BECAUSE THIS WAY, THE PEOPLE HERE ONLY GET TO HEAR MY SIDE OF THINGS. IN THE THREE MONTHS I'VE BEEN HERE...
TINA HAS MOVED IN WITH FRANK...
MARTHA HAS BROKEN UP WITH HER LATEST BECAUSE HE'S A BAD ALCOHOLIC...
THIS?
I DON'T WANNA TALK ABOUT IT...
AND NO ONE CAN KEEP PACE WITH THE QUANTITY OR QUALITY OF HELEN'S DATES.
THEN ONE MONDAY MORNING, MARTHA COMES BURSTING THROUGH THE KITCHEN DOORS.
EVERYONE?!
WE HAVE AN ANNOUNCEMENT TO MAKE!
I DECIDE SHE MAY BE THE IMPERIAL'S ANSWER TO SHIRLEY DOWN AT DAVE'S COFFEE SHOP. SHE'S SO EARTHY—THE REAL DEAL.

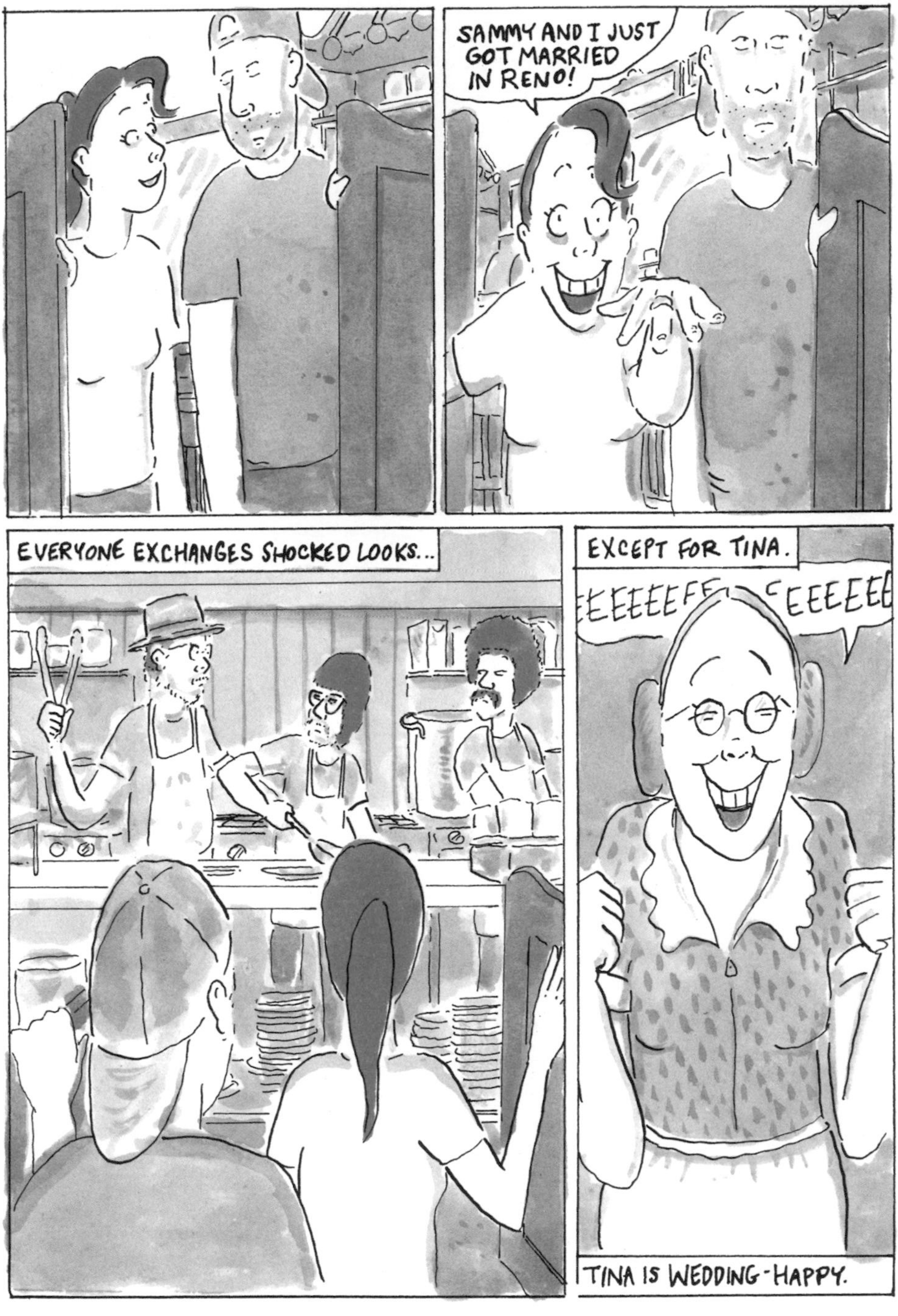
SAMMY AND I JUST GOT MARRIED IN RENO!
EVERYONE EXCHANGES SHOCKED LOOKS...
EXCEPT FOR TINA.
EEEEEEEE EEEEEE
TINA IS WEDDING-HAPPY.

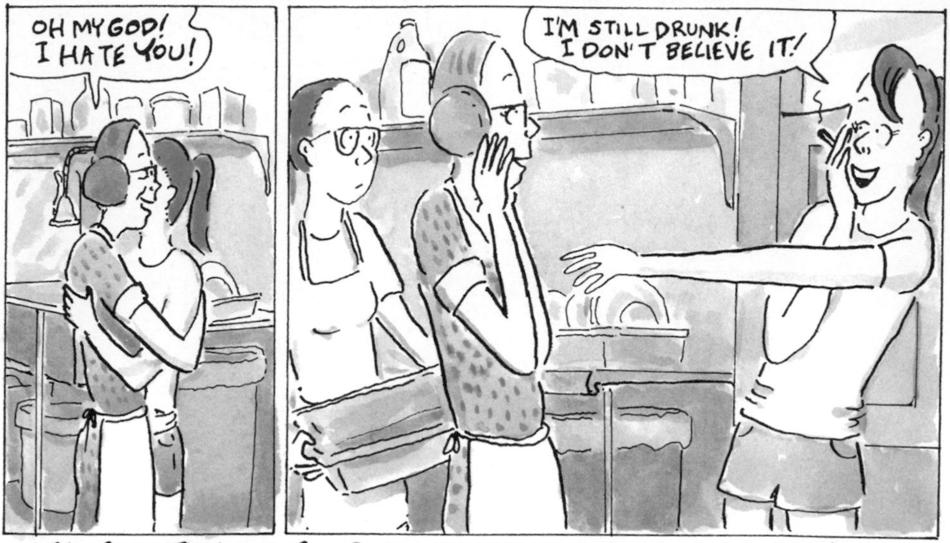
OH MY GOD! I HATE YOU!
I'M STILL DRUNK! I DON'T BELIEVE IT!

LAZLO SLIPS TONY A FIVE AND TELLS HIM TO RUN DOWN TO THE 7-ELEVEN FOR A BOTTLE OF KORBEL. LAZLO MOTIONS TINA BACK INTO THE PANTRY. THEY EMERGE, SMILING CONSPIRATORIALLY.

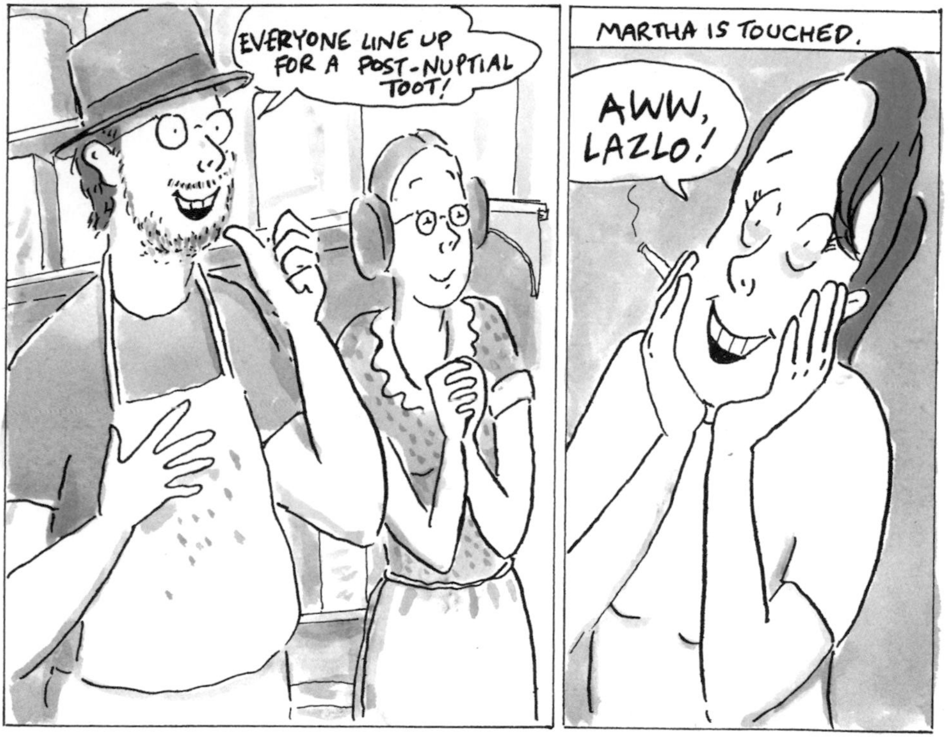
EVERYONE LINE UP FOR A POST-NUPTIAL TOOT!
MARTHA IS TOUCHED.
AWW, LAZLO!

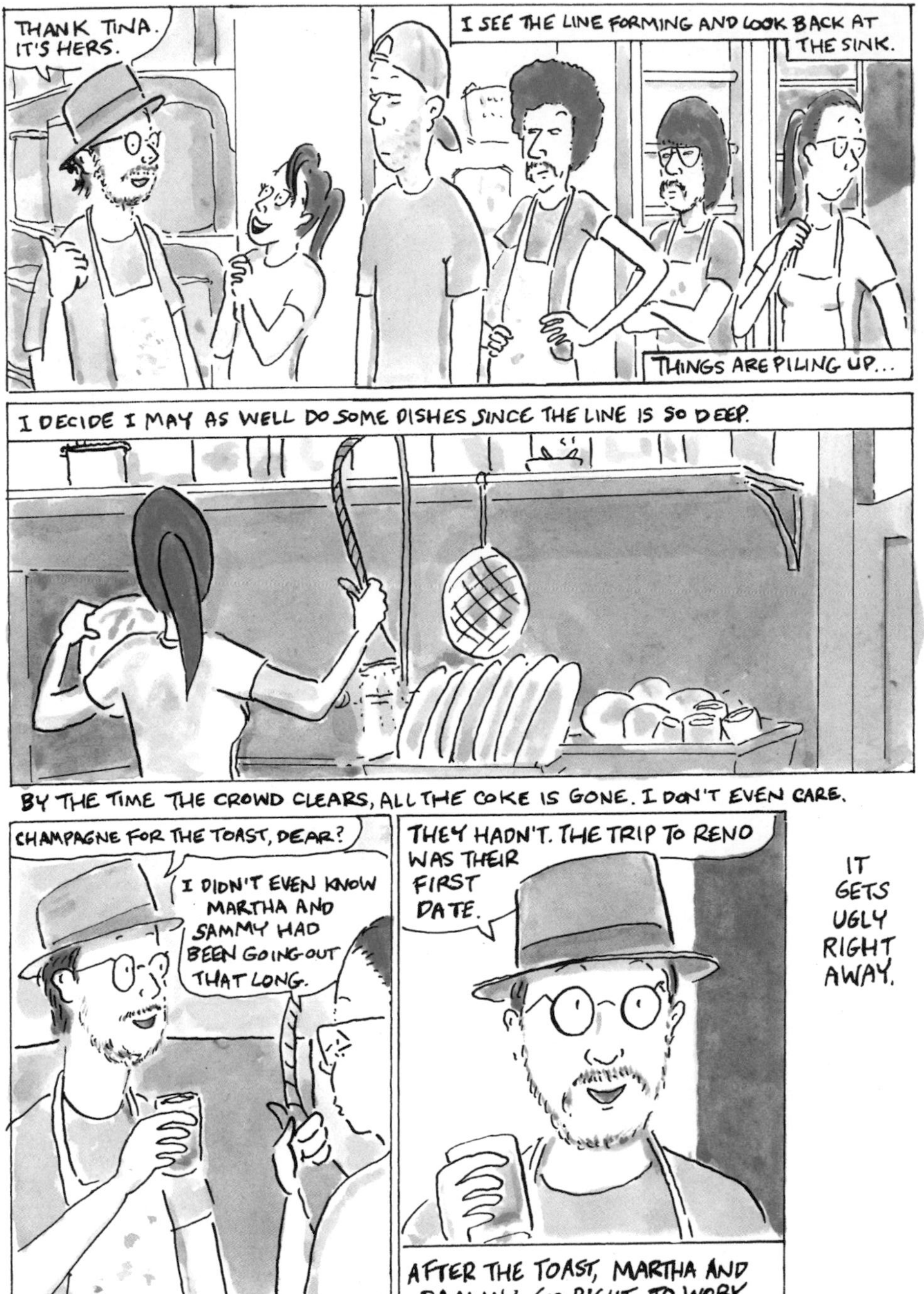
THANK TINA. IT'S HERS.
I SEE THE LINE FORMING AND LOOK BACK AT THE SINK.
THINGS ARE PILING UP...
I DECIDE I MAY AS WELL DO SOME DISHES SINCE THE LINE IS SO DEEP.
BY THE TIME THE CROWD CLEARS, ALL THE COKE IS GONE. I DON'T EVEN CARE.
CHAMPAGNE FOR THE TOAST, DEAR?
I DIDN'T EVEN KNOW MARTHA AND SAMMY HAD BEEN GOING OUT THAT LONG.
THEY HADN'T. THE TRIP TO RENO WAS THEIR FIRST DATE.
AFTER THE TOAST, MARTHA AND SAMMY GO RIGHT TO WORK.
IT GETS UGLY RIGHT AWAY.

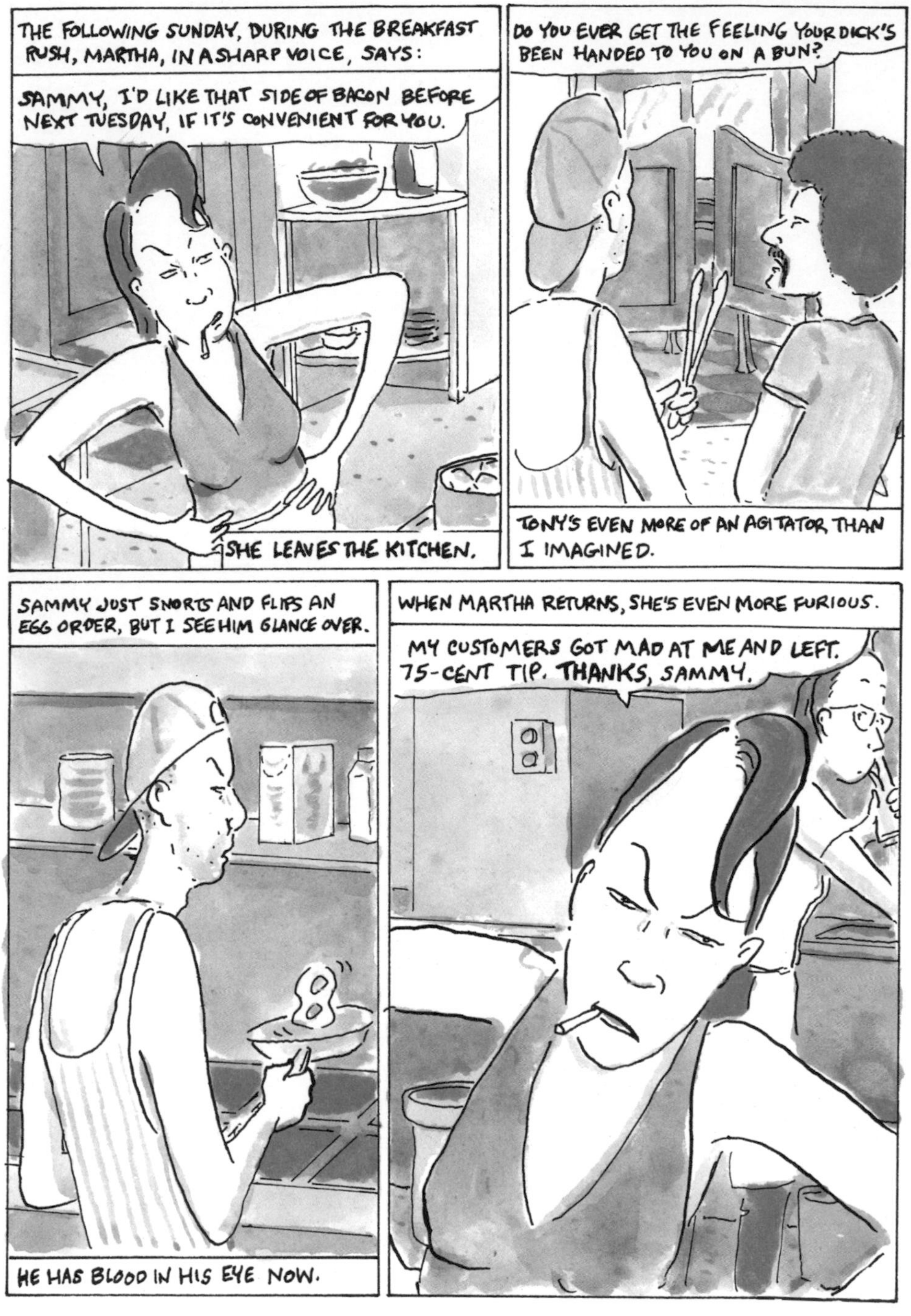

THE FOLLOWING SUNDAY, DURING THE BREAKFAST RUSH, MARTHA, IN A SHARP VOICE, SAYS:
SAMMY, I'D LIKE THAT SIDE OF BACON BEFORE NEXT TUESDAY, IF IT'S CONVENIENT FOR YOU.
SHE LEAVES THE KITCHEN.
DO YOU EVER GET THE FEELING YOUR DICK'S BEEN HANDED TO YOU ON A BUN?
TONY'S EVEN MORE OF AN AGITATOR THAN I IMAGINED.
SAMMY JUST SNORTS AND FLIPS AN EGG ORDER, BUT I SEE HIM GLANCE OVER.
HE HAS BLOOD IN HIS EYE NOW.
WHEN MARTHA RETURNS, SHE'S EVEN MORE FURIOUS.
MY CUSTOMERS GOT MAD AT ME AND LEFT. 75-CENT TIP. THANKS, SAMMY.

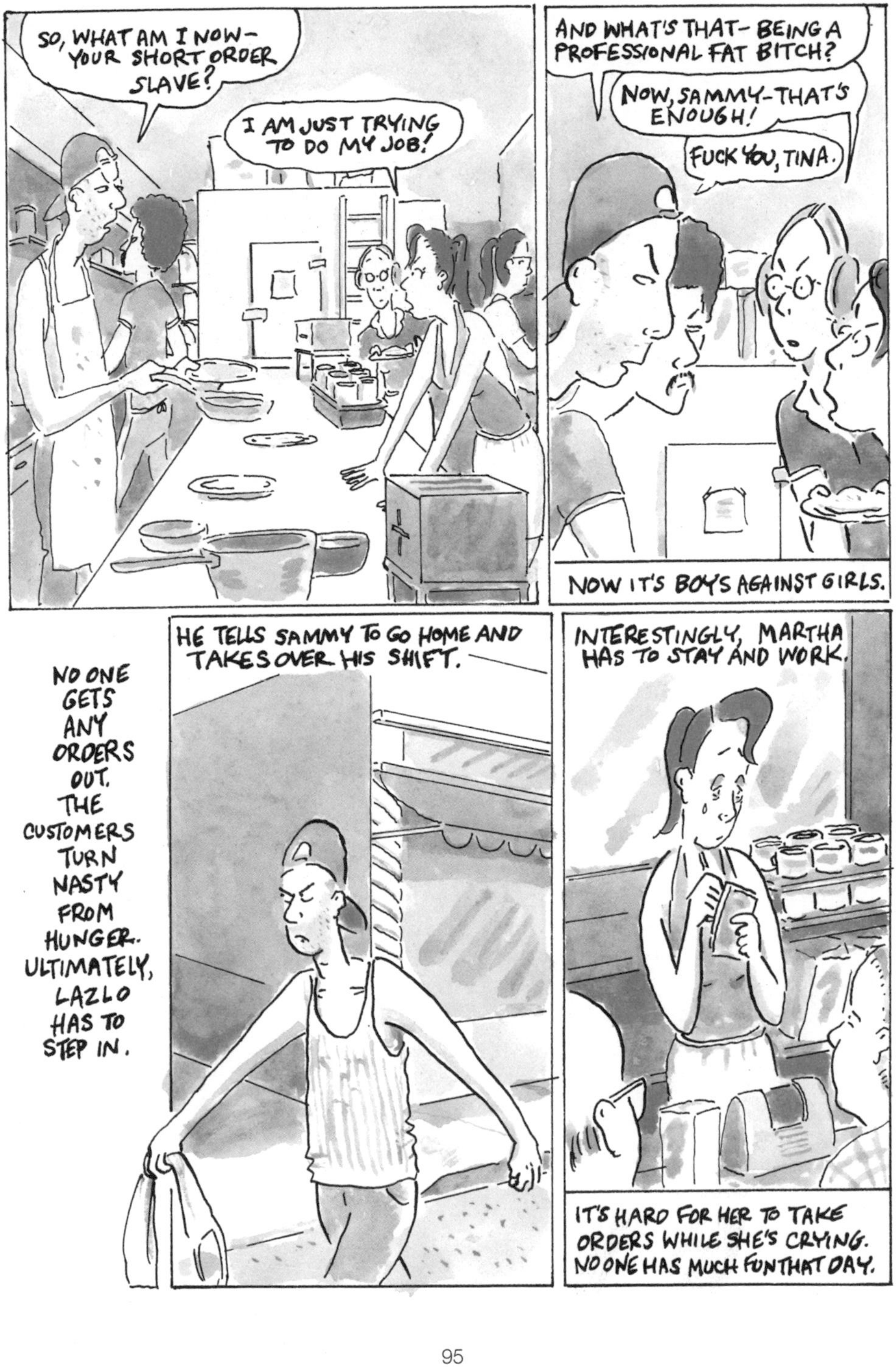
SO, WHAT AM I NOW- YOUR SHORT ORDER SLAVE?
I AM JUST TRYING TO DO MY JOB!
AND WHAT'S THAT- BEING A PROFESSIONAL FAT BITCH?
NOW, SAMMY- THAT'S ENOUGH!
FUCK YOU, TINA.
NOW IT'S BOYS AGAINST GIRLS.
NO ONE GETS ANY ORDERS OUT. THE CUSTOMERS TURN NASTY FROM HUNGER. ULTIMATELY, LAZLO HAS TO STEP IN.
HE TELLS SAMMY TO GO HOME AND TAKES OVER HIS SHIFT.
INTERESTINGLY, MARTHA HAS TO STAY AND WORK.
IT'S HARD FOR HER TO TAKE ORDERS WHILE SHE'S CRYING. NO ONE HAS MUCH FUN THAT DAY.

TUESDAY AFTERNOON, AS I'M LEAVING THE RESTAURANT, MARTHA SEES ME AND INVITES ME FOR A DRINK AT THE PIEDMONT LOUNGE. I'M FLATTERED. IT'S A FIRST FOR ME. WE WALK UP OVER 41ST STREET, TO PIEDMONT AVENUE.

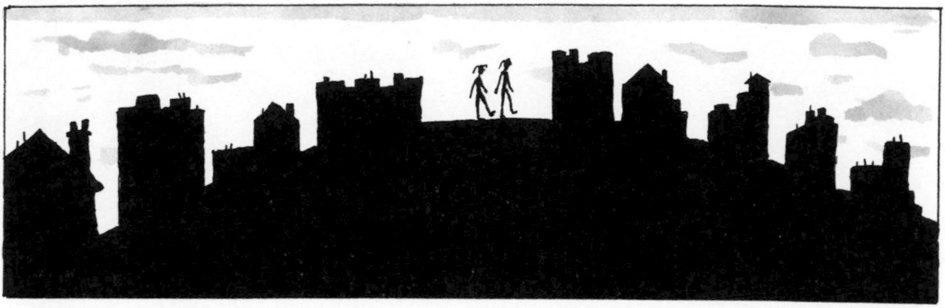

THE PIEDMONT IS YOUR QUINTESSENTIAL DIVE: PADDED WALLS, PADDED CIGARETTE-BURNED BOOTHS, STINKING, MURKY, AND LIT ONLY BY THE JUKEBOX.

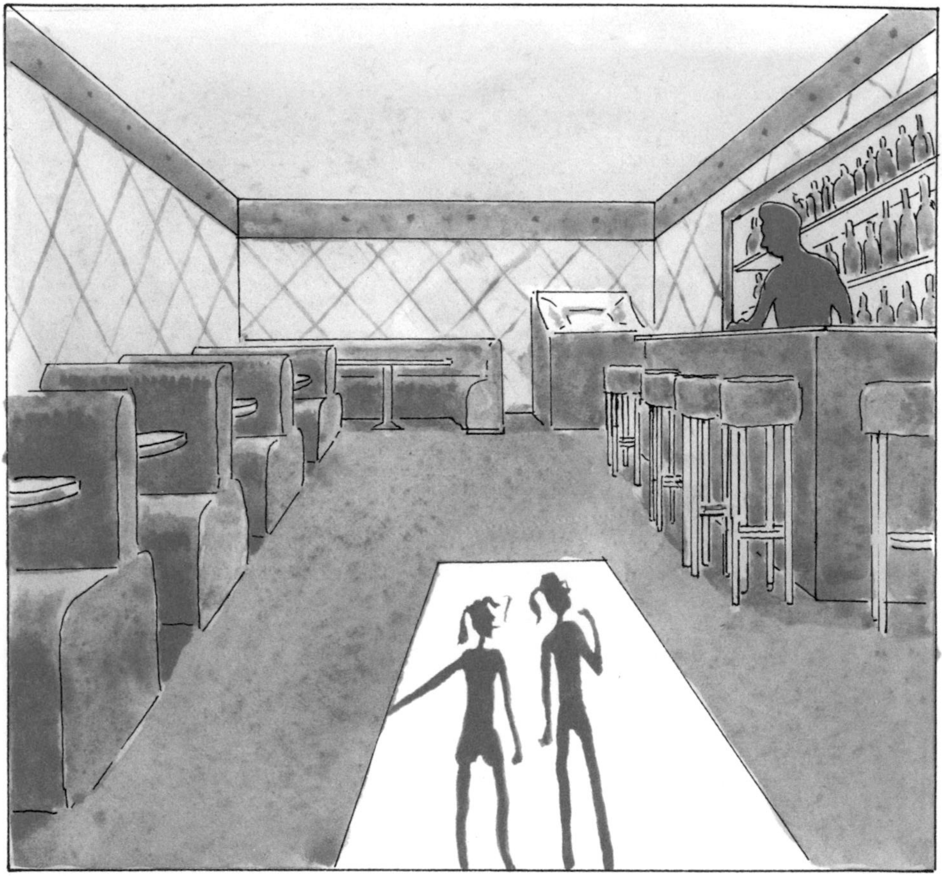

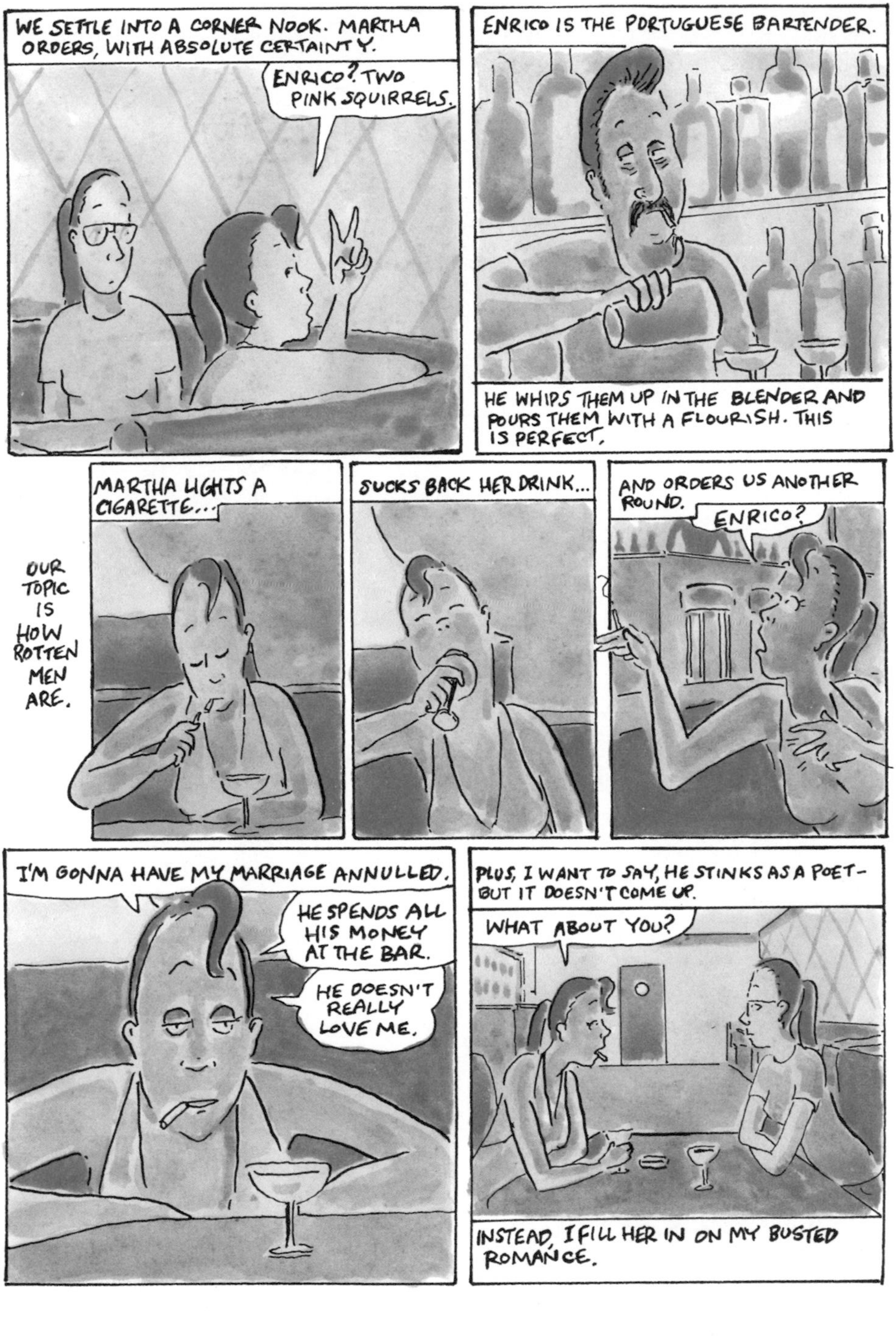
WE SETTLE INTO A CORNER NOOK. MARTHA ORDERS, WITH ABSOLUTE CERTAINTY.
ENRICO? TWO PINK SQUIRRELS.
ENRICO IS THE PORTUGUESE BARTENDER.
HE WHIPS THEM UP IN THE BLENDER AND POURS THEM WITH A FLOURISH. THIS IS PERFECT.
OUR TOPIC IS HOW ROTTEN MEN ARE.
MARTHA LIGHTS A CIGARETTE...
SUCKS BACK HER DRINK...
AND ORDERS US ANOTHER ROUND.
ENRICO?
I'M GONNA HAVE MY MARRIAGE ANNULLED.
HE SPENDS ALL HIS MONEY AT THE BAR.
HE DOESN'T REALLY LOVE ME.
PLUS, I WANT TO SAY, HE STINKS AS A POET- BUT IT DOESN'T COME UP.
WHAT ABOUT YOU?
INSTEAD, I FILL HER IN ON MY BUSTED ROMANCE.

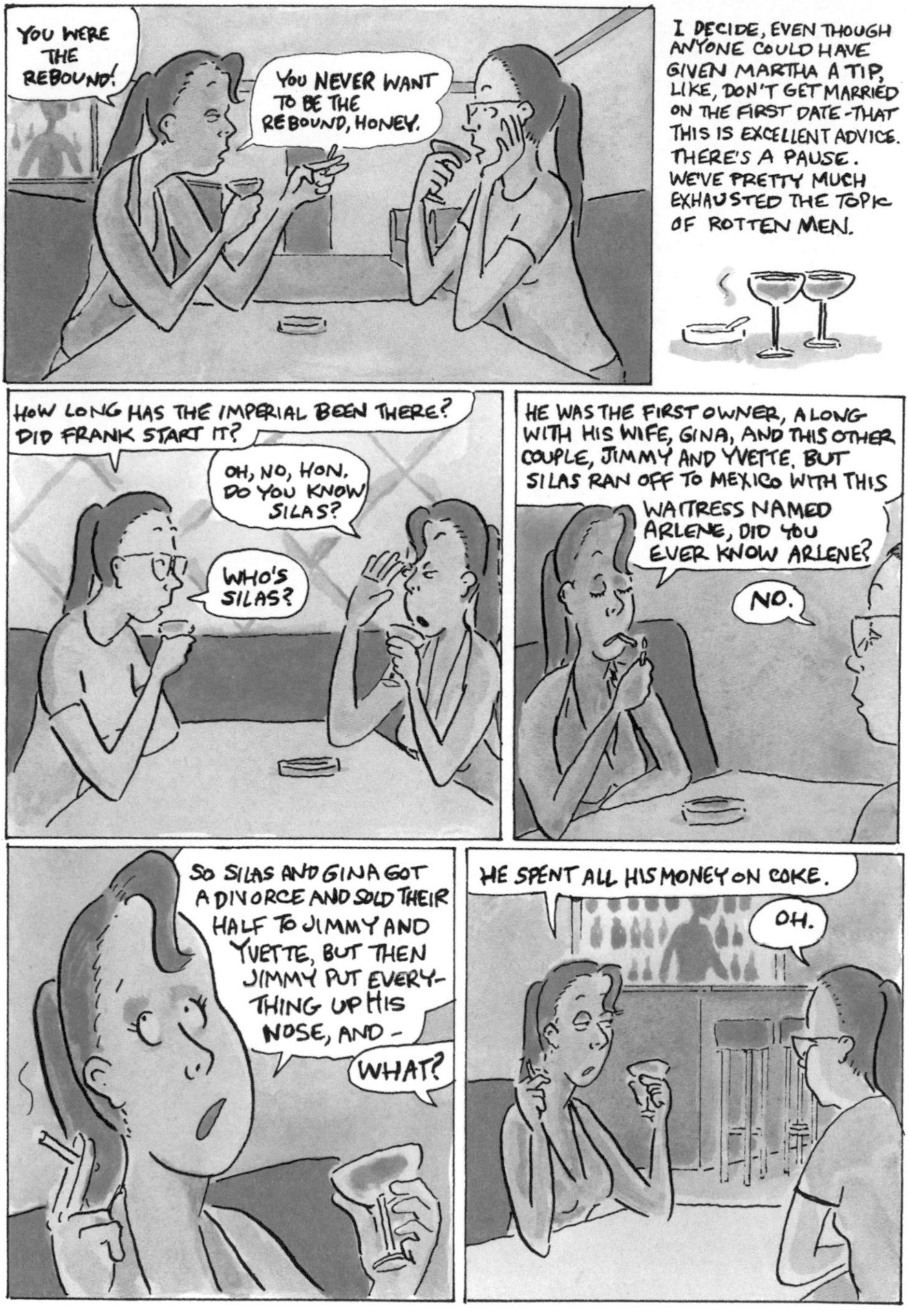
YOU WERE THE REBOUND!
YOU NEVER WANT TO BE THE REBOUND, HONEY.
I DECIDE, EVEN THOUGH ANYONE COULD HAVE GIVEN MARTHA A TIP, LIKE, DON'T GET MARRIED ON THE FIRST DATE - THAT THIS IS EXCELLENT ADVICE. THERE'S A PAUSE. WE'VE PRETTY MUCH EXHAUSTED THE TOPIC OF ROTTEN MEN.
HOW LONG HAS THE IMPERIAL BEEN THERE? DID FRANK START IT?
OH, NO, HON. DO YOU KNOW SILAS?
WHO'S SILAS?
HE WAS THE FIRST OWNER, ALONG WITH HIS WIFE, GINA, AND THIS OTHER COUPLE, JIMMY AND YVETTE. BUT SILAS RAN OFF TO MEXICO WITH THIS
WAITRESS NAMED ARLENE, DID YOU EVER KNOW ARLENE?
NO.
SO SILAS AND GINA GOT A DIVORCE AND SOLD THEIR HALF TO JIMMY AND YVETTE, BUT THEN JIMMY PUT EVERYTHING UP HIS NOSE, AND -
WHAT?
HE SPENT ALL HIS MONEY ON COKE.
OH.

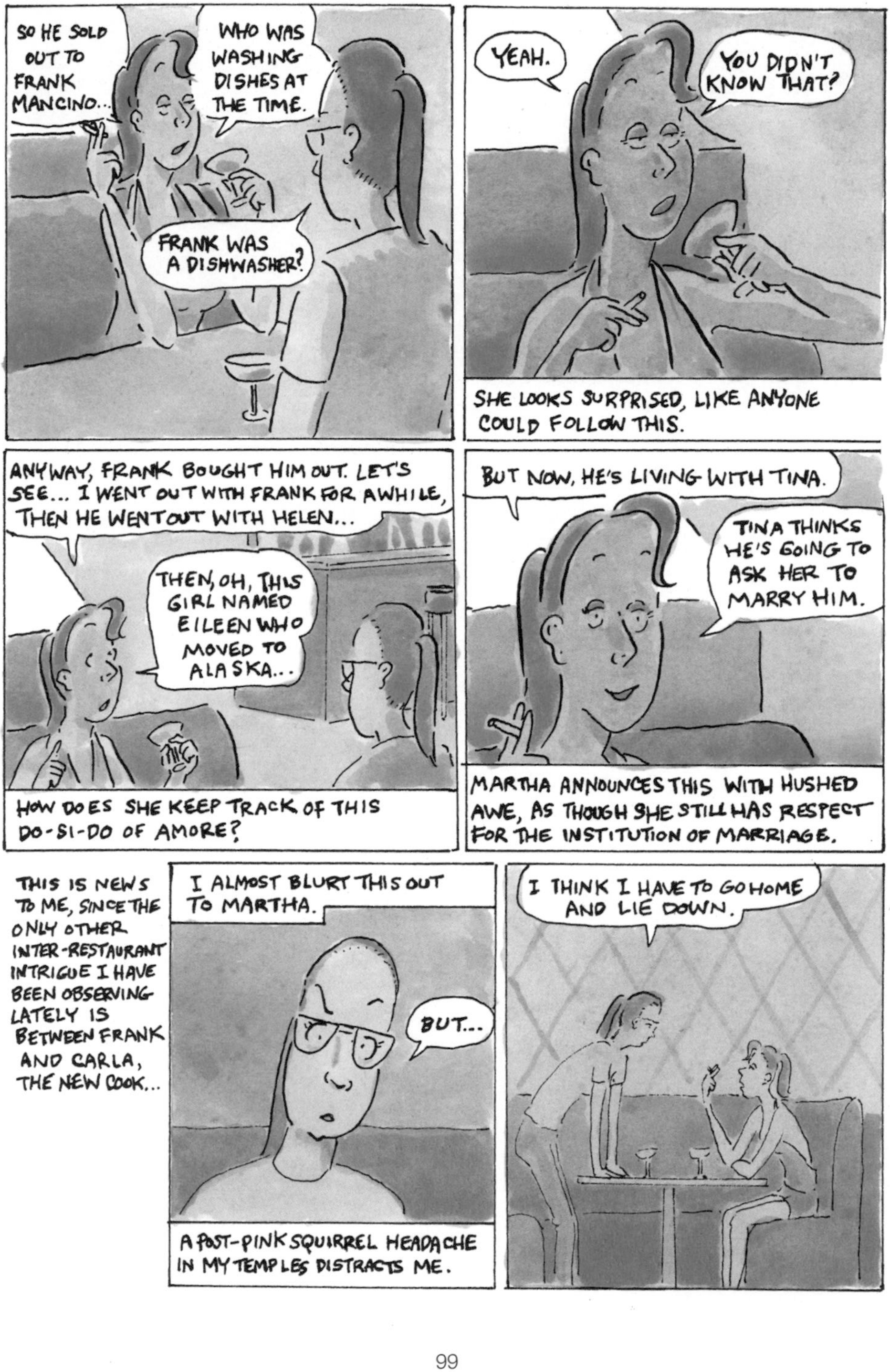

SO HE SOLD OUT TO FRANK MANCINO...
WHO WAS WASHING DISHES AT THE TIME.
FRANK WAS A DISHWASHER?
YEAH.
YOU DIDN'T KNOW THAT?
SHE LOOKS SURPRISED, LIKE ANYONE COULD FOLLOW THIS.
ANYWAY, FRANK BOUGHT HIM OUT. LET'S SEE... I WENT OUT WITH FRANK FOR AWHILE, THEN HE WENT OUT WITH HELEN...
THEN, OH, THIS GIRL NAMED EILEEN WHO MOVED TO ALASKA...
HOW DOES SHE KEEP TRACK OF THIS DO-SI-DO OF AMORE?
BUT NOW, HE'S LIVING WITH TINA.
TINA THINKS HE'S GOING TO ASK HER TO MARRY HIM.
MARTHA ANNOUNCES THIS WITH HUSHED AWE, AS THOUGH SHE STILL HAS RESPECT FOR THE INSTITUTION OF MARRIAGE.
THIS IS NEWS TO ME, SINCE THE ONLY OTHER INTER-RESTAURANT INTRIGUE I HAVE BEEN OBSERVING LATELY IS BETWEEN FRANK AND CARLA, THE NEW COOK...
I ALMOST BLURT THIS OUT TO MARTHA.
BUT...
A POST-PINK SQUIRREL HEADACHE IN MY TEMPLES DISTRACTS ME.
I THINK I HAVE TO GO HOME AND LIE DOWN.

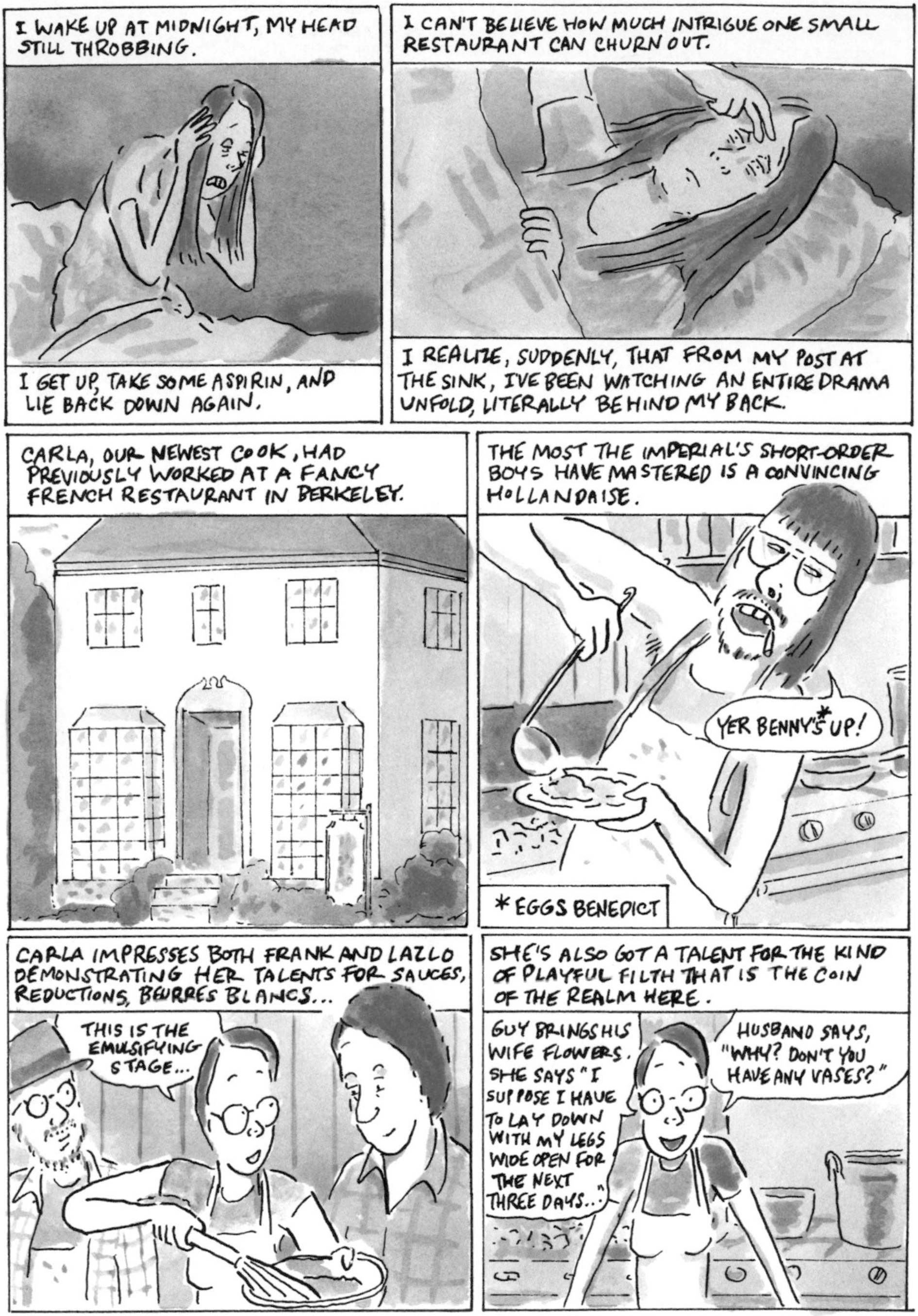
I WAKE UP AT MIDNIGHT, MY HEAD STILL THROBBING.
I GET UP, TAKE SOME ASPIRIN, AND LIE BACK DOWN AGAIN.
I CAN'T BELIEVE HOW MUCH INTRIGUE ONE SMALL RESTAURANT CAN CHURN OUT.
I REALIZE, SUDDENLY, THAT FROM MY POST AT THE SINK, I'VE BEEN WATCHING AN ENTIRE DRAMA UNFOLD, LITERALLY BEHIND MY BACK.
CARLA, OUR NEWEST COOK, HAD PREVIOUSLY WORKED AT A FANCY FRENCH RESTAURANT IN BERKELEY.
THE MOST THE IMPERIAL'S SHORT-ORDER BOYS HAVE MASTERED IS A CONVINCING HOLLANDAISE.
YER BENNY'S* UP!
* EGGS BENEDICT
CARLA IMPRESSES BOTH FRANK AND LAZLO DEMONSTRATING HER TALENTS FOR SAUCES, REDUCTIONS, BEURRES BLANCS...
THIS IS THE EMULSIFYING STAGE...
SHE'S ALSO GOT A TALENT FOR THE KIND OF PLAYFUL FILTH THAT IS THE COIN OF THE REALM HERE.
GUY BRINGS HIS WIFE FLOWERS. SHE SAYS "I SUPPOSE I HAVE TO LAY DOWN WITH MY LEGS WIDE OPEN FOR THE NEXT THREE DAYS..."
HUSBAND SAYS, "WHY? DON'T YOU HAVE ANY VASES?"

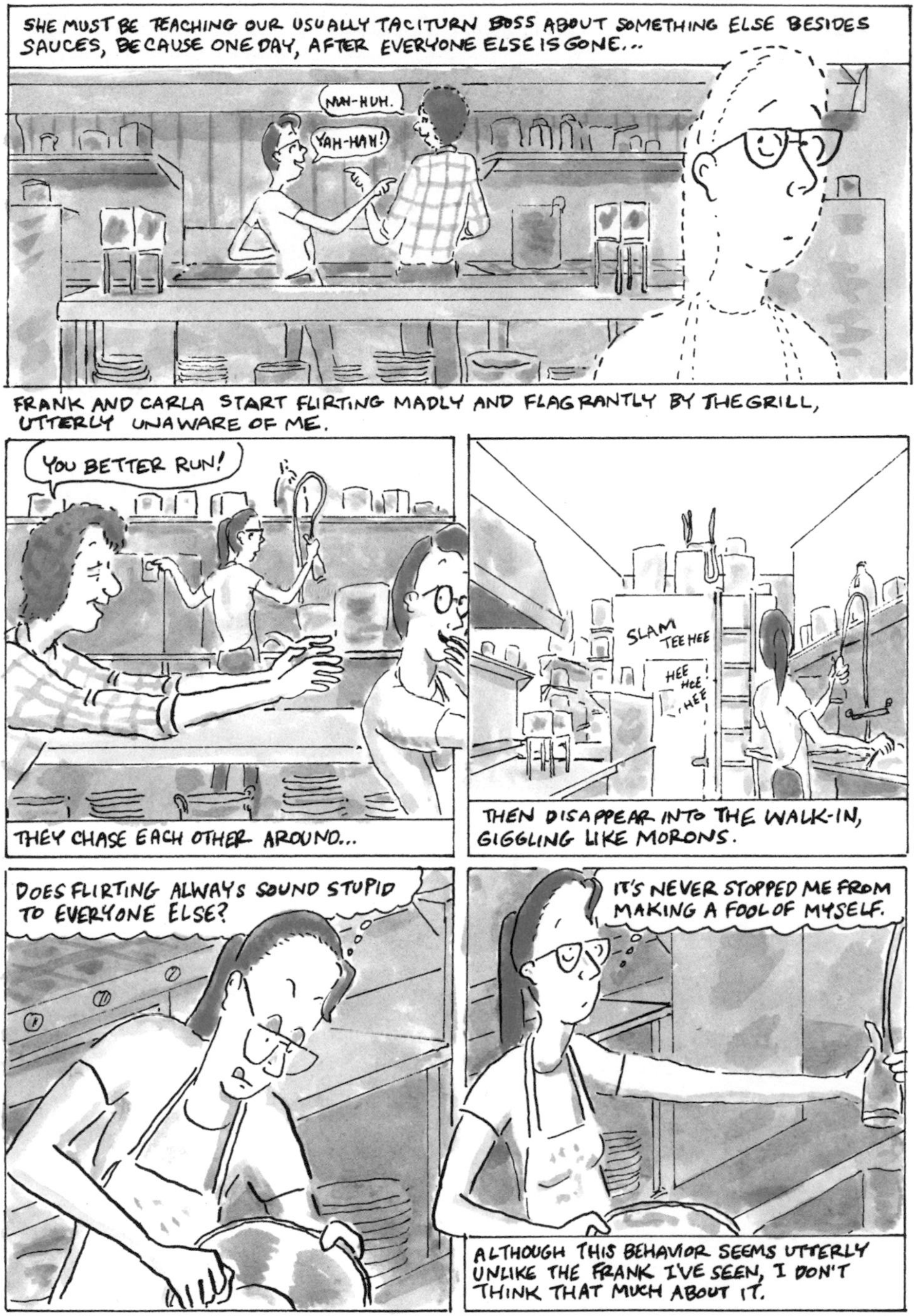
SHE MUST BE TEACHING OUR USUALLY TACITURN BOSS ABOUT SOMETHING ELSE BESIDES SAUCES, BECAUSE ONE DAY, AFTER EVERYONE ELSE IS GONE...
NAH-HUH.
YAH-HAH!
FRANK AND CARLA START FLIRTING MADLY AND FLAGRANTLY BY THE GRILL, UTTERLY UNAWARE OF ME.
YOU BETTER RUN!
THEY CHASE EACH OTHER AROUND...
SLAM
TEE HEE
HEE HEE HEE
THEN DISAPPEAR INTO THE WALK-IN, GIGGLING LIKE MORONS.
DOES FLIRTING ALWAYS SOUND STUPID TO EVERYONE ELSE?
IT'S NEVER STOPPED ME FROM MAKING A FOOL OF MYSELF.
ALTHOUGH THIS BEHAVIOR SEEMS UTTERLY UNLIKE THE FRANK I'VE SEEN, I DON'T THINK THAT MUCH ABOUT IT.

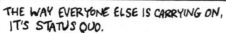

THE WAY EVERYONE ELSE IS CARRYING ON, IT'S STATUS QUO.

I LIKE TINA...

BUT WHO AM I TO RAT ON THE BOSS?

THE GOOD THING ABOUT GETTING DRUNK IN THE AFTERNOON IS THAT BY THE NEXT MORNING MY PINK SQUIRREL HANGOVER IS GONE.

I GO INTO WORK STILL WRESTLING WITH MY CONSCIENCE.

HI, LAZLO.

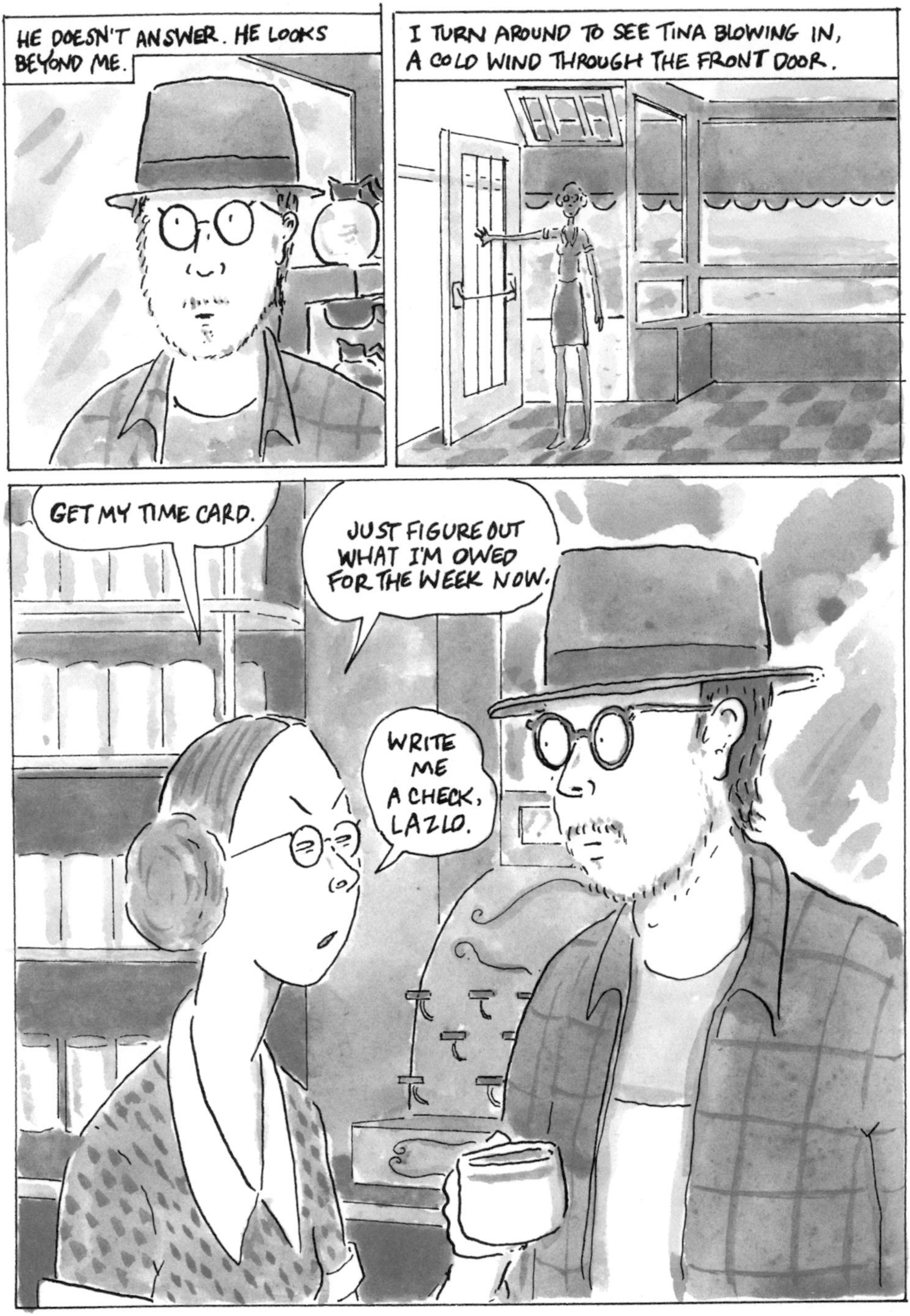
HE DOESN'T ANSWER. HE LOOKS BEYOND ME.
I TURN AROUND TO SEE TINA BLOWING IN, A COLD WIND THROUGH THE FRONT DOOR.
GET MY TIME CARD.
JUST FIGURE OUT WHAT I'M OWED FOR THE WEEK NOW.
WRITE ME A CHECK, LAZLO.

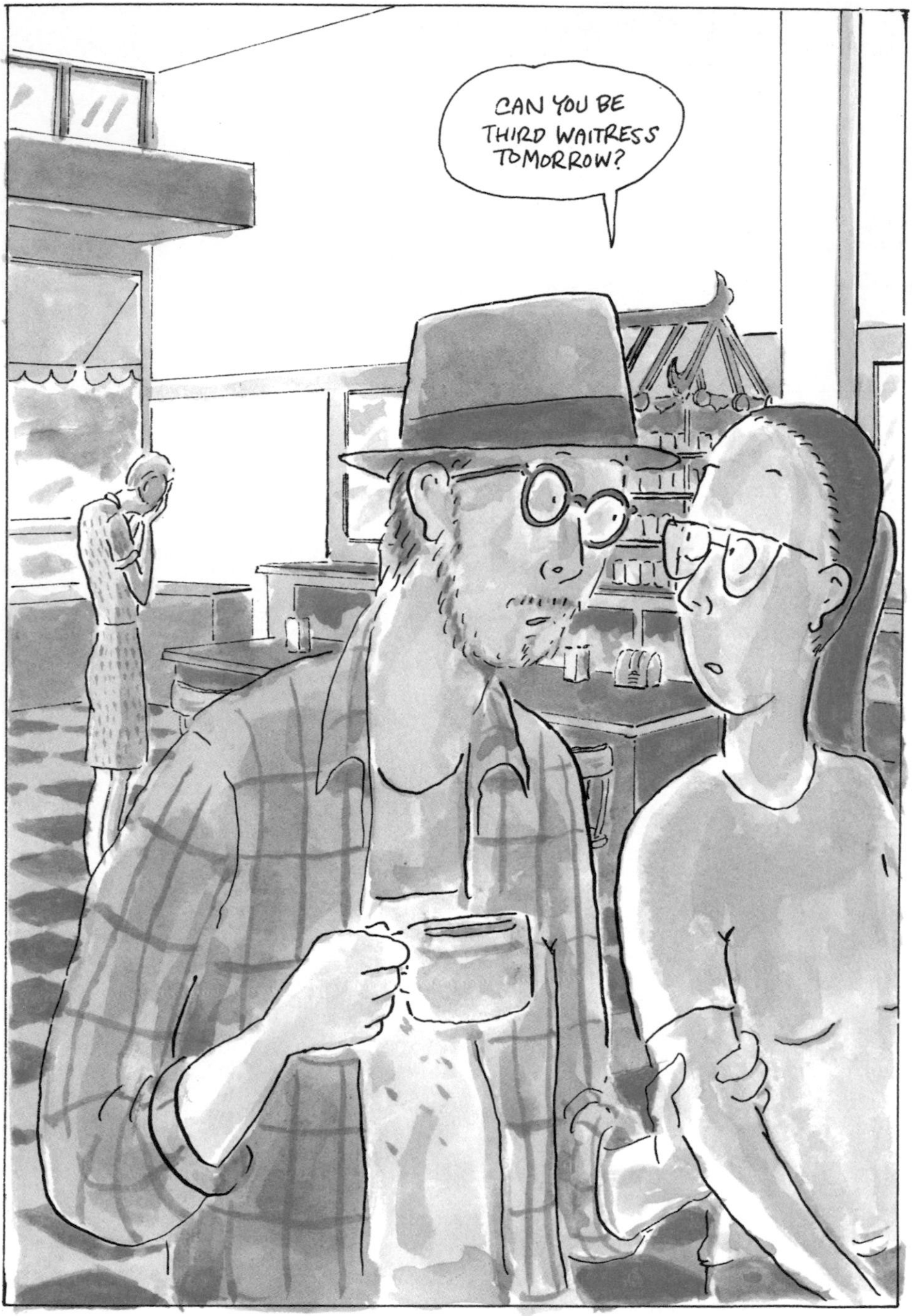
CAN YOU BE THIRD WAITRESS TOMORROW?

DESPITE THE TRAGEDY OF TINA'S LOST LOVE, I AM THRILLED AT THE PROSPECT OF MY NEW CAREER. I KNOW WHAT I'M GOING TO WEAR, HOPING FOR JUST SUCH AN EVENTUALITY. I'VE ALREADY FOUND A DRESS...

AT THE CEREBRAL PALSY THRIFT STORE ON 110TH STREET.

THE LABEL SAYS "SHELTON STROLLER." IT FITS JUST RIGHT.

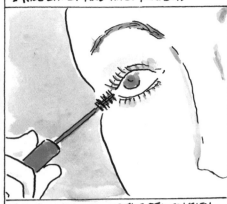
I RISE EARLY AND APPLY MAKEUP.

NOT TOO MUCH, BECAUSE I'VE STUDIED HELEN.

EYES WITH THAT SLIGHTLY BRUISED LOOK—

LIKE I'VE GOT A GANGSTER BOYFRIEND WHO SLAPS ME AROUND A LITTLE.

I DON'T PUT MY GLASSES ON.

EVEN IF I CAN'T SEE THE CUSTOMERS, I'LL FLIRT WITH THEM ANYWAY.

I'VE MADE A STARTLING TRANSFORMATION, LIKE IN THE MOVIES, WHEN THE LIBRARIAN WITH THE BUN WHIPS OFF HER SPECS AND SHAKES HER HAIR OUT.

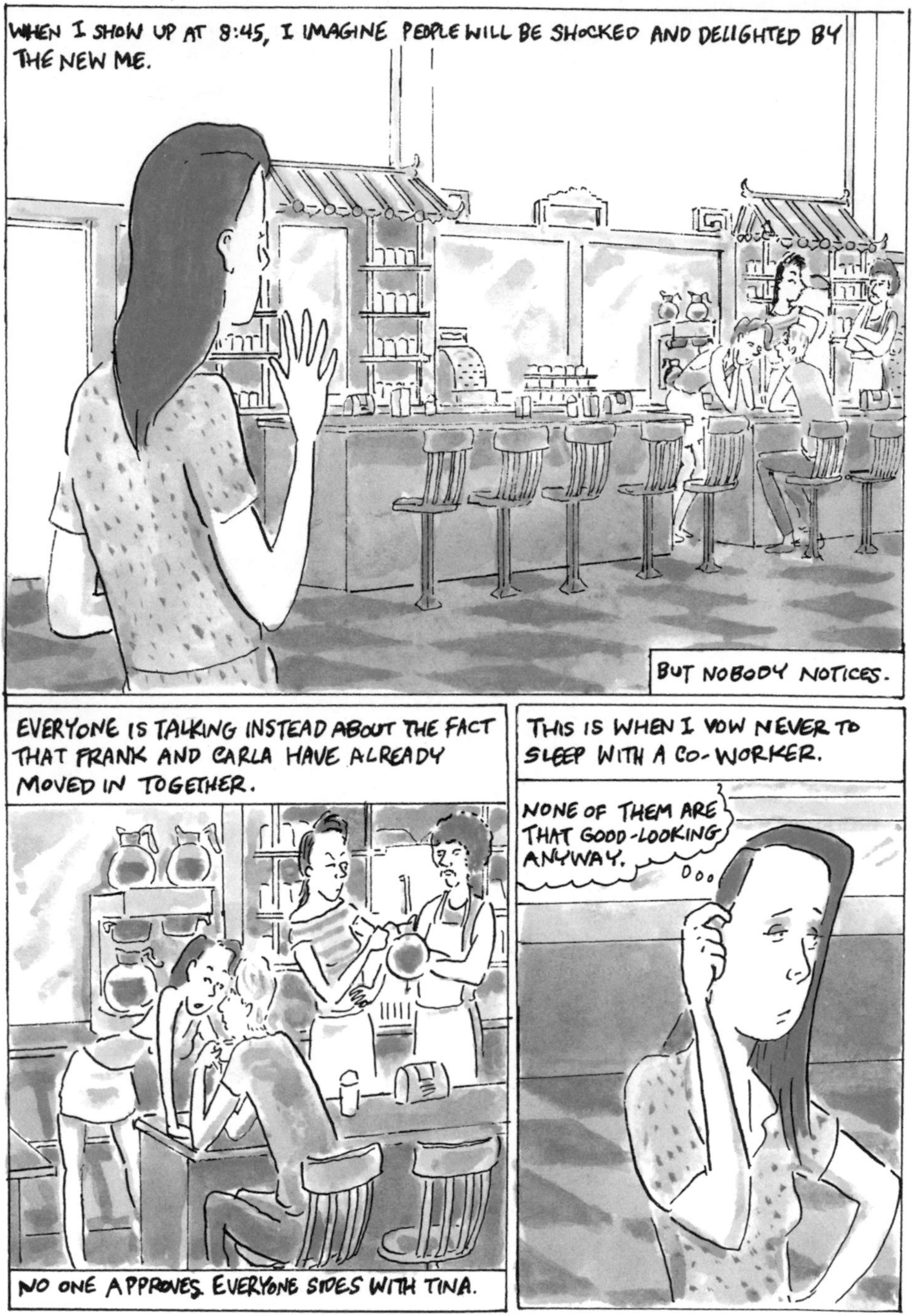
WHEN I SHOW UP AT 8:45, I IMAGINE PEOPLE WILL BE SHOCKED AND DELIGHTED BY THE NEW ME.
BUT NOBODY NOTICES.
EVERYONE IS TALKING INSTEAD ABOUT THE FACT THAT FRANK AND CARLA HAVE ALREADY MOVED IN TOGETHER.
NO ONE APPROVES. EVERYONE SIDES WITH TINA.
THIS IS WHEN I VOW NEVER TO SLEEP WITH A CO-WORKER.
NONE OF THEM ARE THAT GOOD-LOOKING ANYWAY.

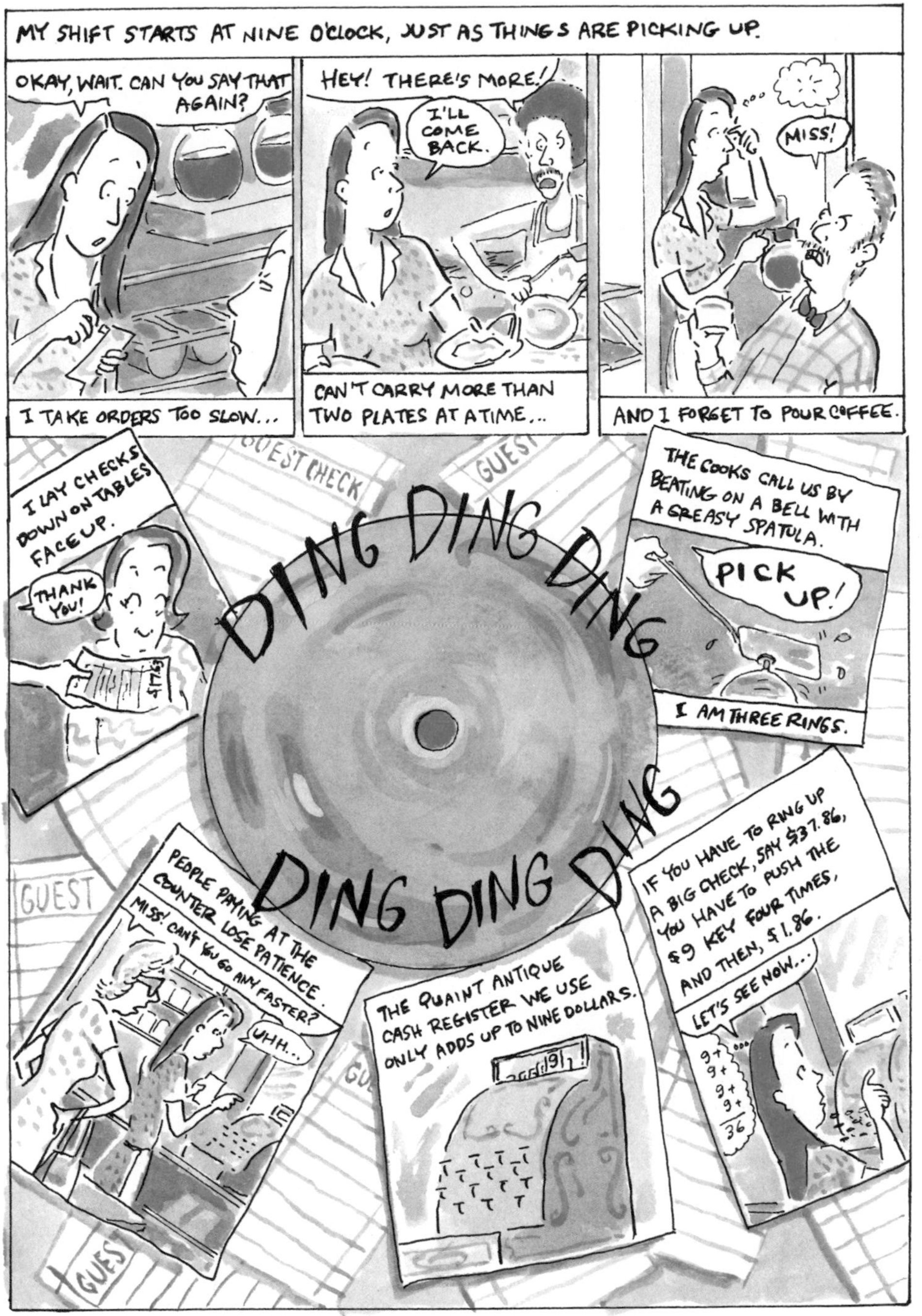
MY SHIFT STARTS AT NINE O'CLOCK, JUST AS THINGS ARE PICKING UP.
OKAY, WAIT. CAN YOU SAY THAT AGAIN?
I TAKE ORDERS TOO SLOW...
HEY! THERE'S MORE!
I'LL COME BACK.
CAN'T CARRY MORE THAN TWO PLATES AT A TIME...
MISS!
AND I FORGET TO POUR COFFEE.
I LAY CHECKS DOWN ON TABLES FACE UP.
THANK YOU!
GUEST CHECK
DING DING DING DING
THE COOKS CALL US BY BEATING ON A BELL WITH A GREASY SPATULA.
PICK UP!
I AM THREE RINGS.
DING DING DING
PEOPLE PAYING AT THE COUNTER LOSE PATIENCE.
MISS! CAN'T YOU GO ANY FASTER?
UHH...
THE QUAINT ANTIQUE CASH REGISTER WE USE ONLY ADDS UP TO NINE DOLLARS.
IF YOU HAVE TO RING UP A BIG CHECK, SAY $37.86, YOU HAVE TO PUSH THE $9 KEY FOUR TIMES, AND THEN, $1.86.
LET'S SEE NOW...
9+ 9+ 9+ 9+ 36
GUEST

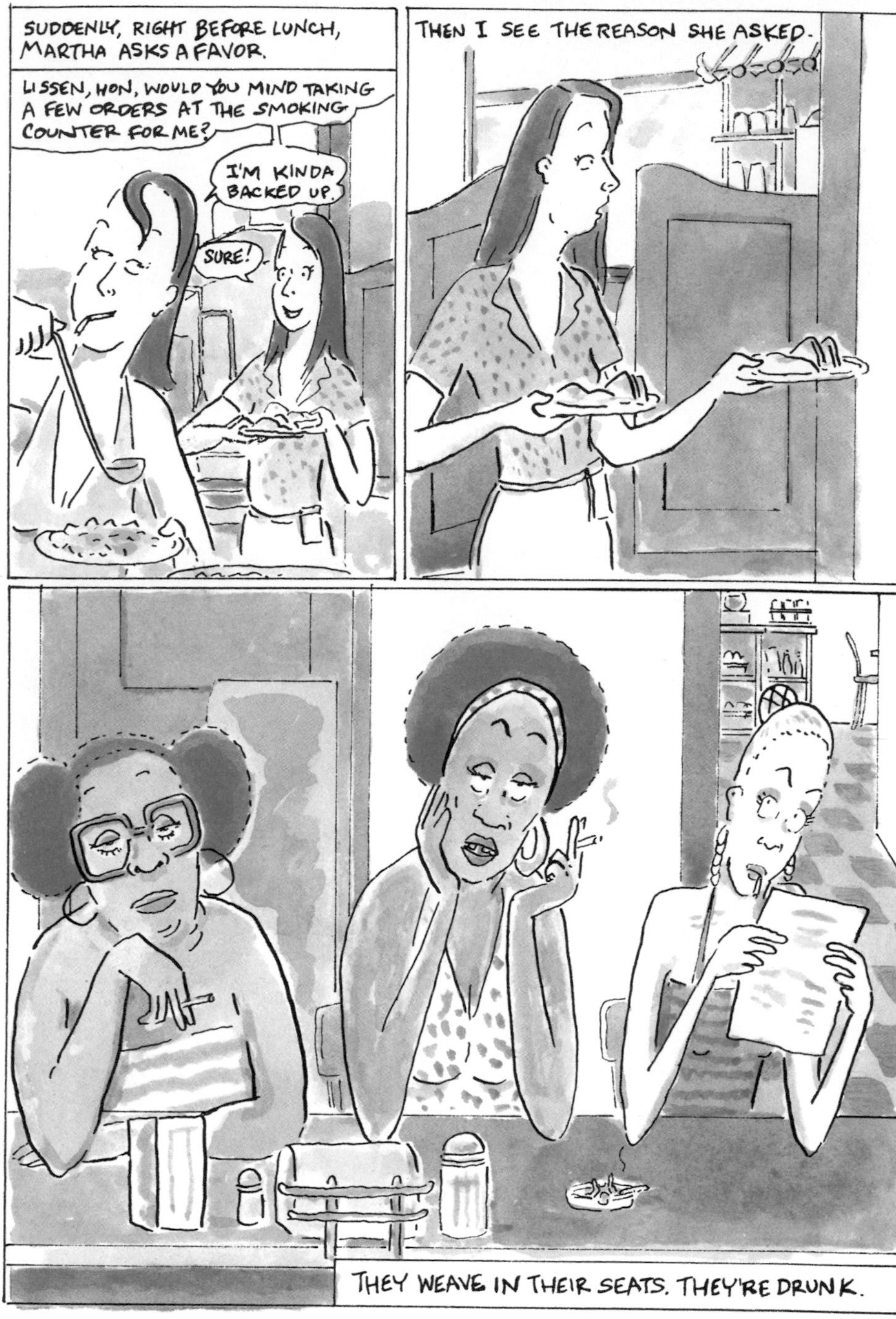
SUDDENLY, RIGHT BEFORE LUNCH, MARTHA ASKS A FAVOR.
LISSEN, HON, WOULD YOU MIND TAKING A FEW ORDERS AT THE SMOKING COUNTER FOR ME?
I'M KINDA BACKED UP.
SURE!
THEN I SEE THE REASON SHE ASKED.
THEY WEAVE IN THEIR SEATS. THEY'RE DRUNK.

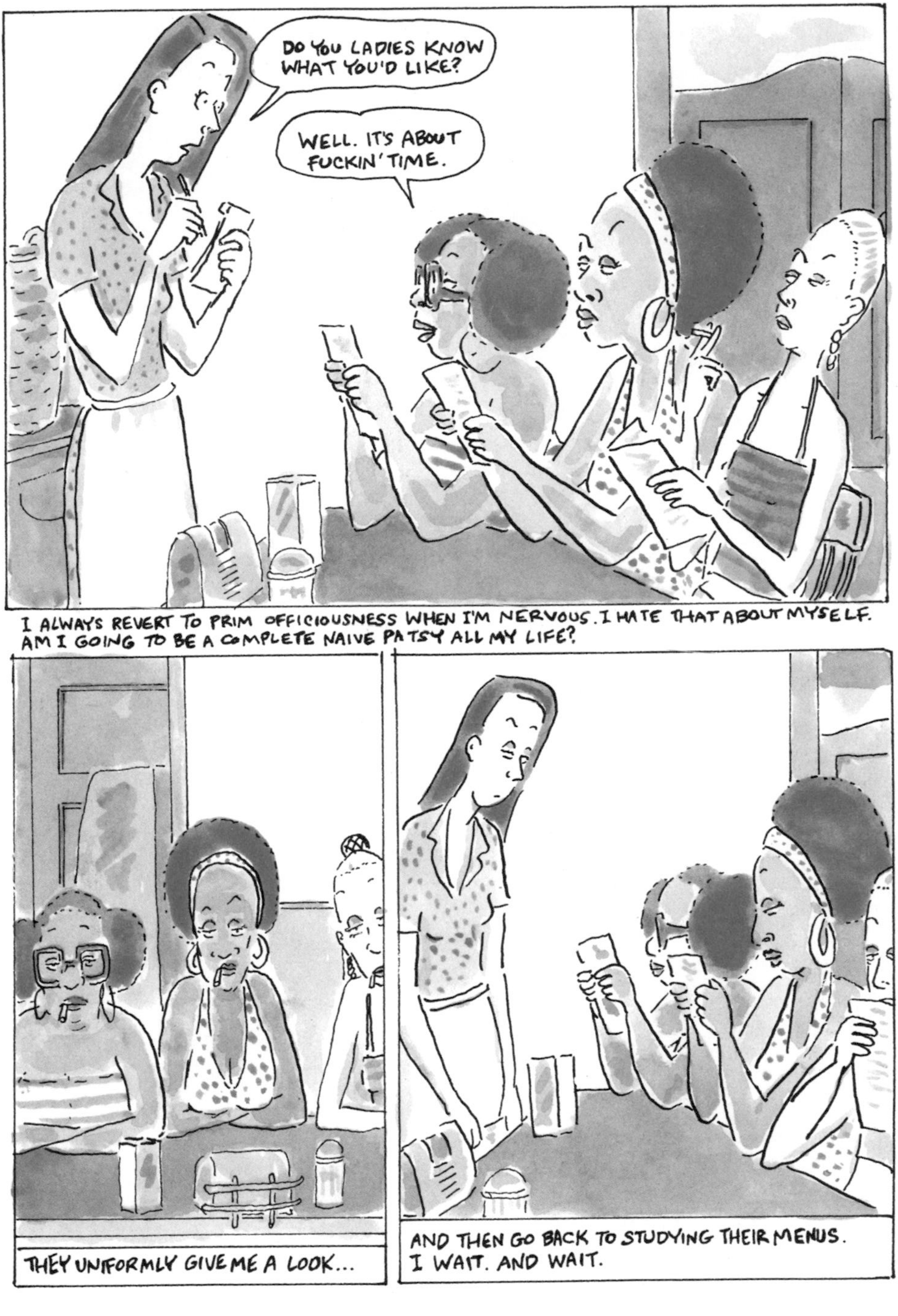
DO YOU LADIES KNOW WHAT YOU'D LIKE?
WELL. IT'S ABOUT FUCKIN' TIME.
I ALWAYS REVERT TO PRIM OFFICIOUSNESS WHEN I'M NERVOUS. I HATE THAT ABOUT MYSELF. AM I GOING TO BE A COMPLETE NAIVE PATSY ALL MY LIFE?
THEY UNIFORMLY GIVE ME A LOOK...
AND THEN GO BACK TO STUDYING THEIR MENUS. I WAIT. AND WAIT.

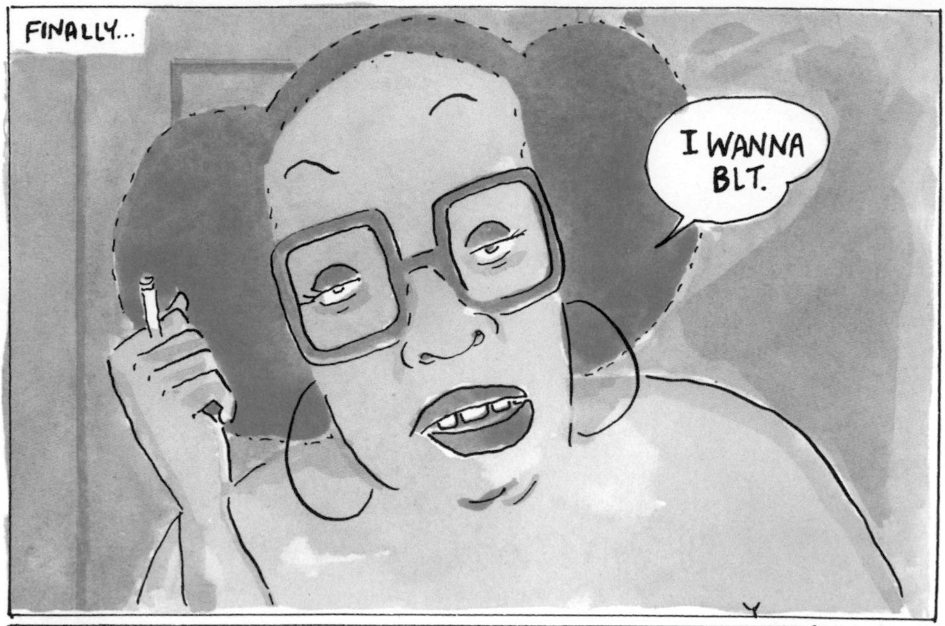
FINALLY...
I WANNA BLT.

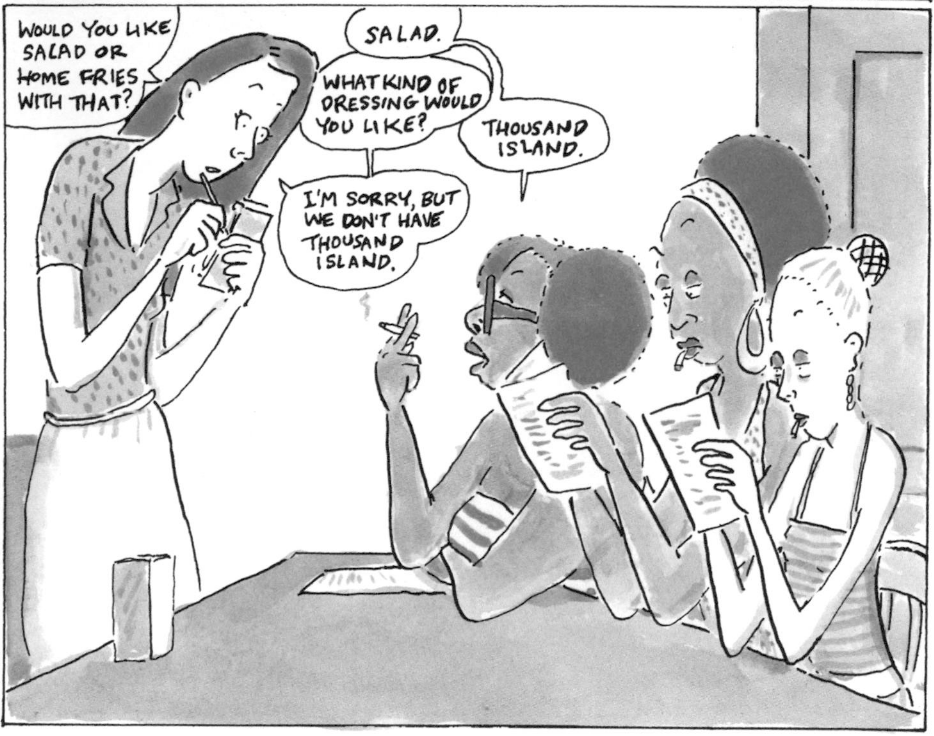
WOULD YOU LIKE SALAD OR HOME FRIES WITH THAT?
SALAD.
WHAT KIND OF DRESSING WOULD YOU LIKE?
THOUSAND ISLAND.
I'M SORRY, BUT WE DON'T HAVE THOUSAND ISLAND.

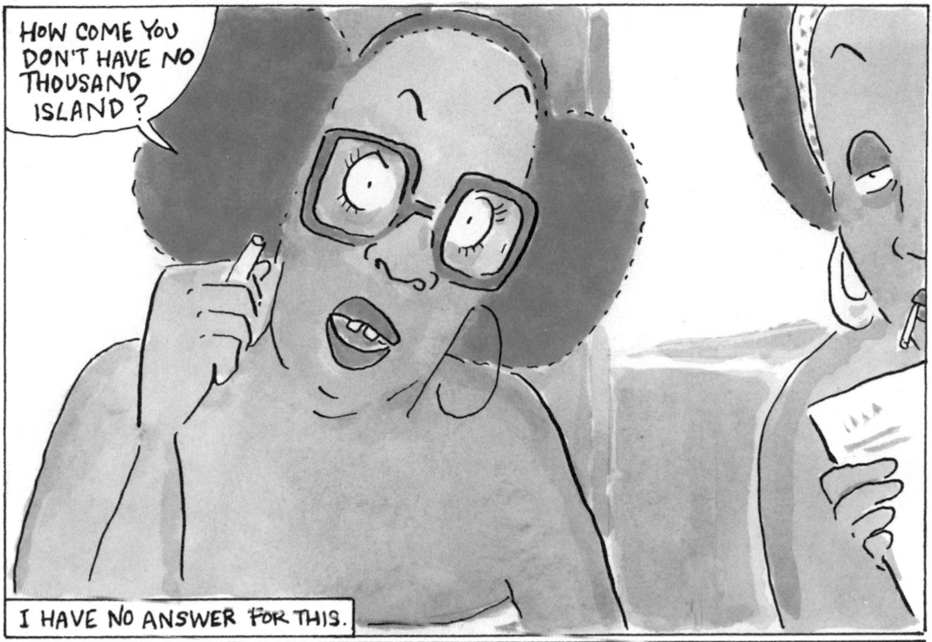
HOW COME YOU DON'T HAVE NO THOUSAND ISLAND?
I HAVE NO ANSWER FOR THIS.

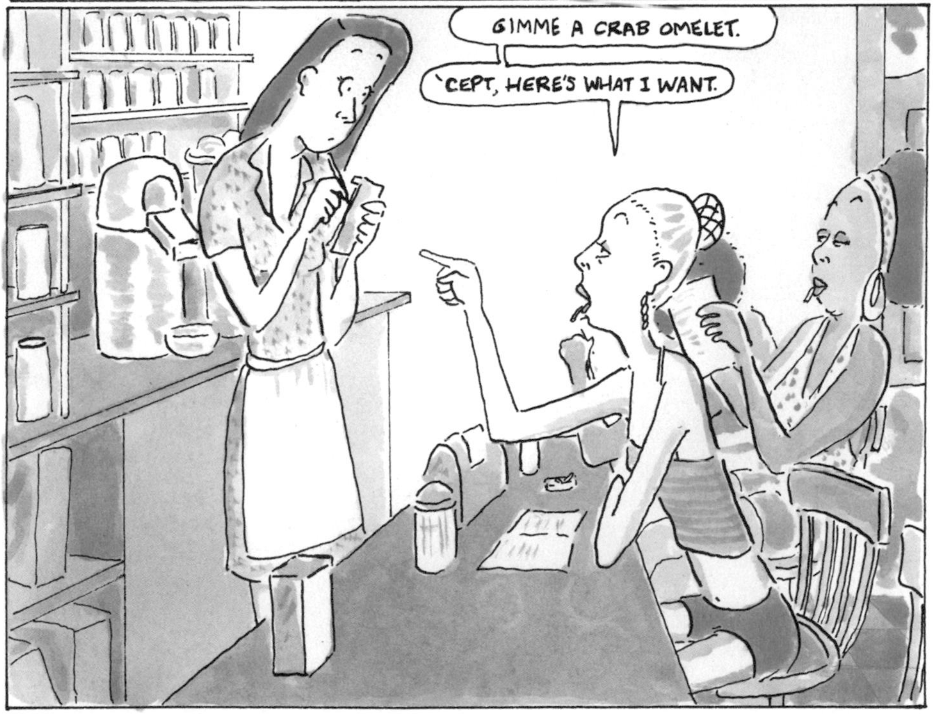
GIMME A CRAB OMELET.
'CEPT, HERE'S WHAT I WANT.

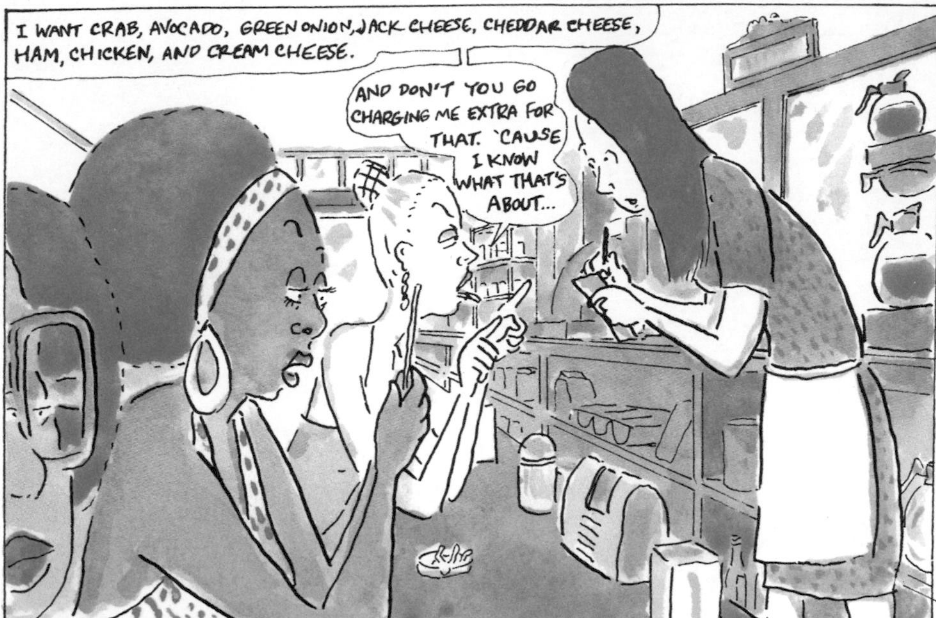
I WANT CRAB, AVOCADO, GREEN ONION, JACK CHEESE, CHEDDAR CHEESE, HAM, CHICKEN, AND CREAM CHEESE.
AND DON'T YOU GO CHARGING ME EXTRA FOR THAT. 'CAUSE I KNOW WHAT THAT'S ABOUT...

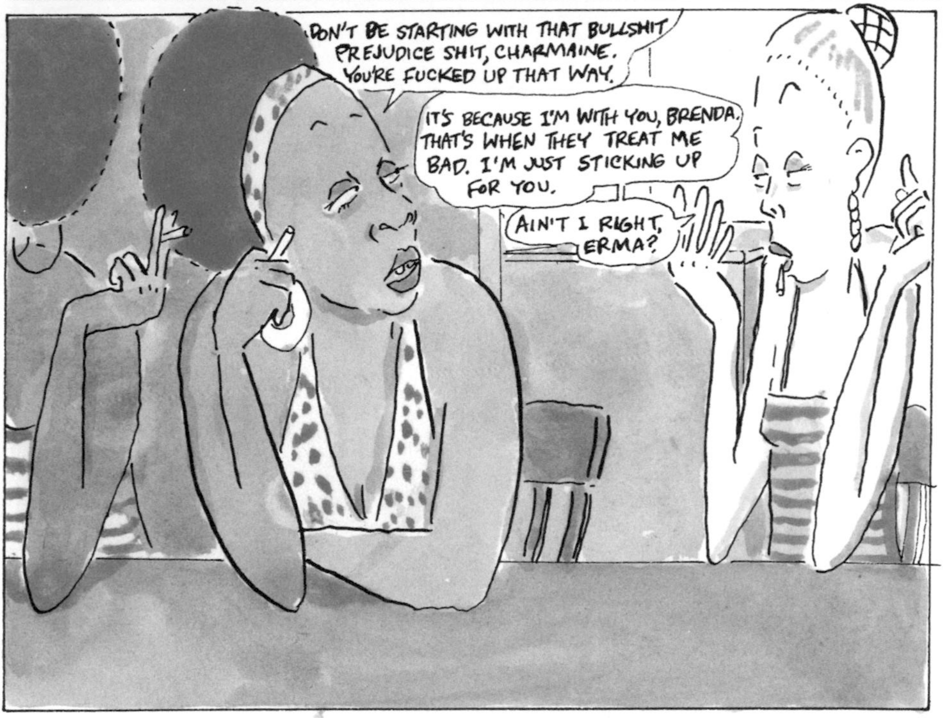
DON'T BE STARTING WITH THAT BULLSHIT PREJUDICE SHIT, CHARMAINE. YOU'RE FUCKED UP THAT WAY.
IT'S BECAUSE I'M WITH YOU, BRENDA. THAT'S WHEN THEY TREAT ME BAD. I'M JUST STICKING UP FOR YOU.
AIN'T I RIGHT, ERMA?

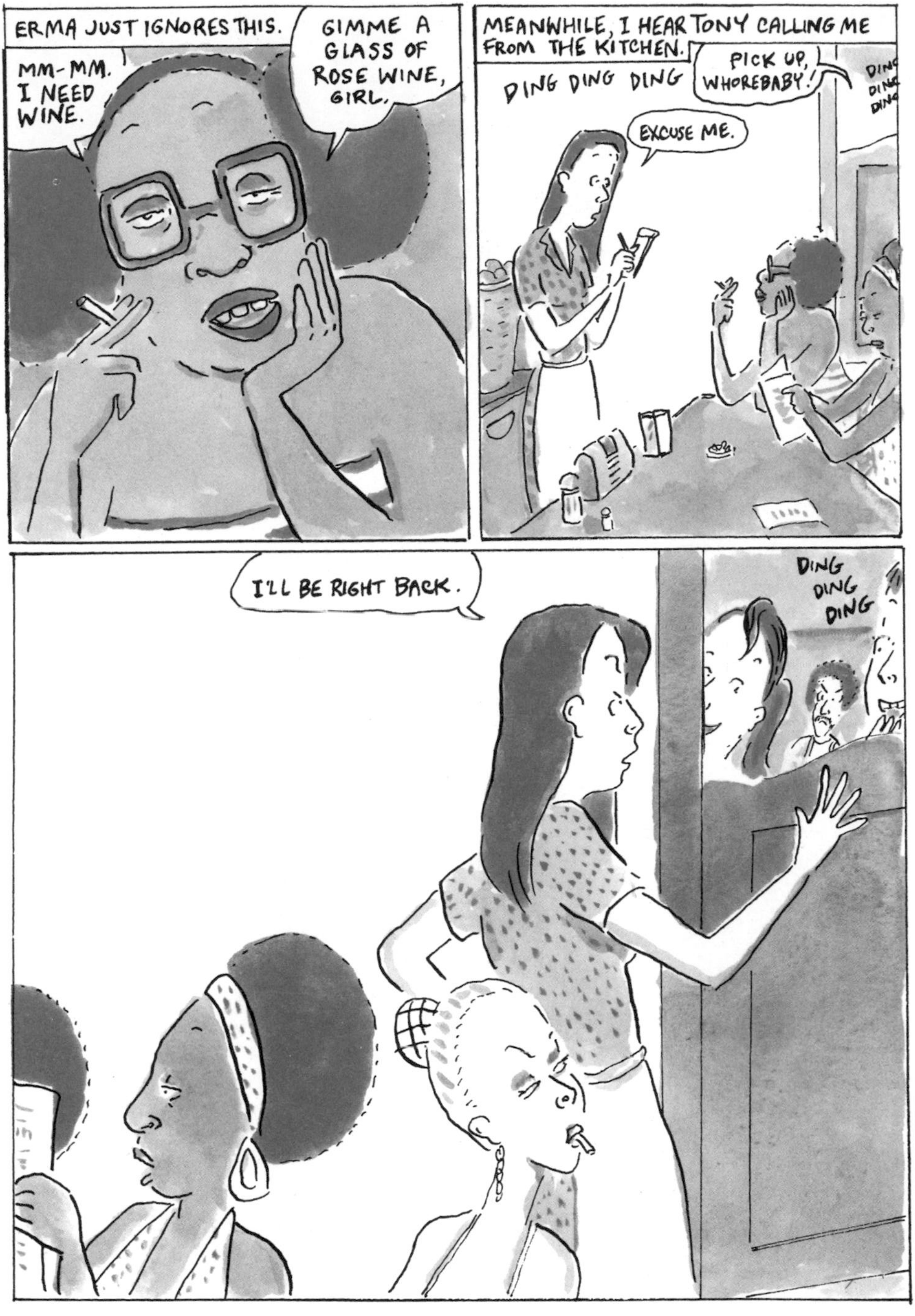
ERMA JUST IGNORES THIS.
MM-MM. I NEED WINE.
GIMME A GLASS OF ROSE WINE, GIRL.
MEANWHILE, I HEAR TONY CALLING ME FROM THE KITCHEN.
DING DING DING
PICK UP, WHOREBABY!
DING DING DING
EXCUSE ME.
I'LL BE RIGHT BACK.
DING DING DING

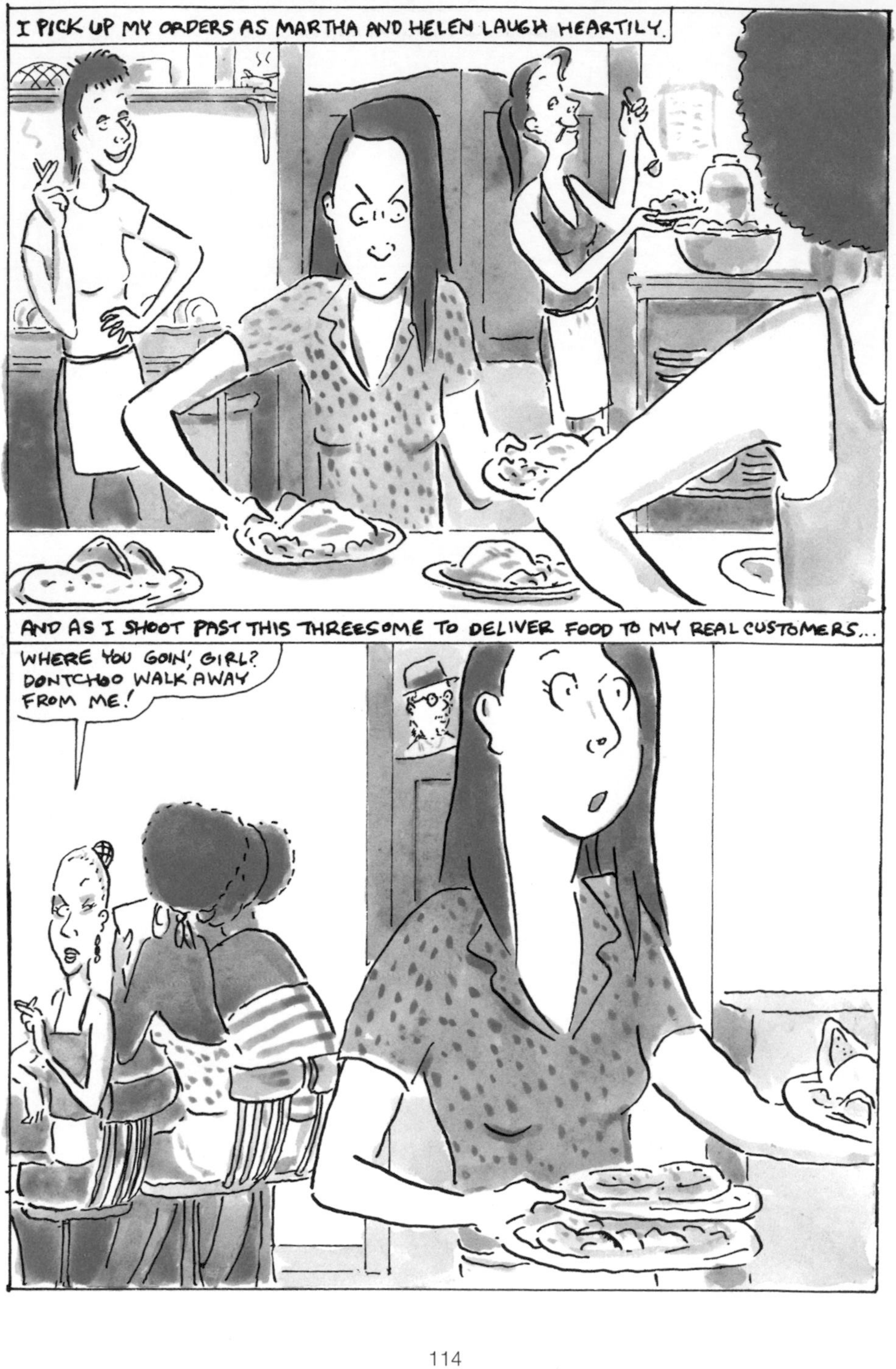
I PICK UP MY ORDERS AS MARTHA AND HELEN LAUGH HEARTILY.
AND AS I SHOOT PAST THIS THREESOME TO DELIVER FOOD TO MY REAL CUSTOMERS...
WHERE YOU GOIN', GIRL? DONTCHOO WALK AWAY FROM ME!

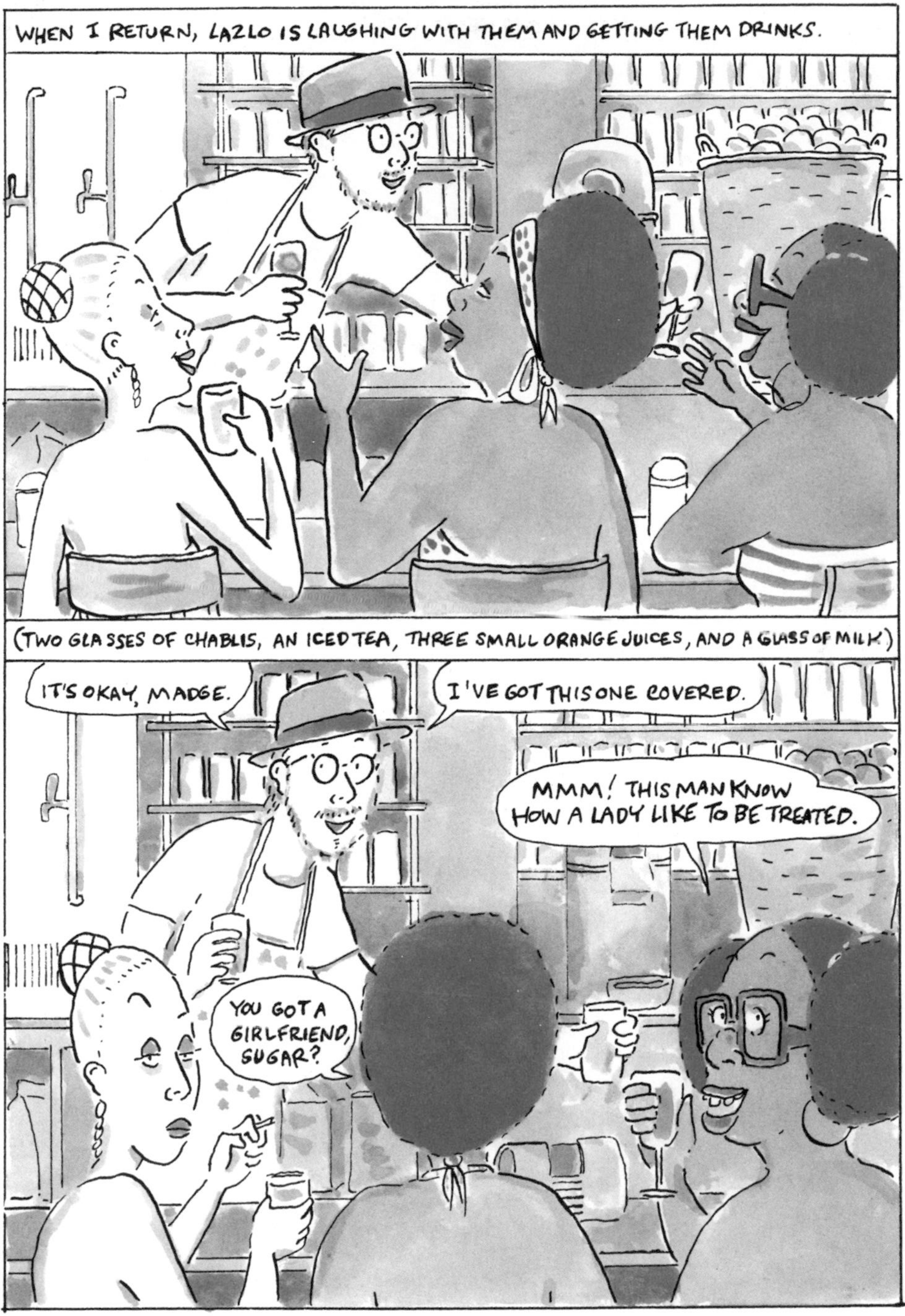
WHEN I RETURN, LAZLO IS LAUGHING WITH THEM AND GETTING THEM DRINKS.
(TWO GLASSES OF CHABLIS, AN ICED TEA, THREE SMALL ORANGE JUICES, AND A GLASS OF MILK.)
IT'S OKAY, MADGE.
I'VE GOT THIS ONE COVERED.
MMM! THIS MAN KNOW HOW A LADY LIKE TO BE TREATED.
YOU GOT A GIRLFRIEND, SUGAR?

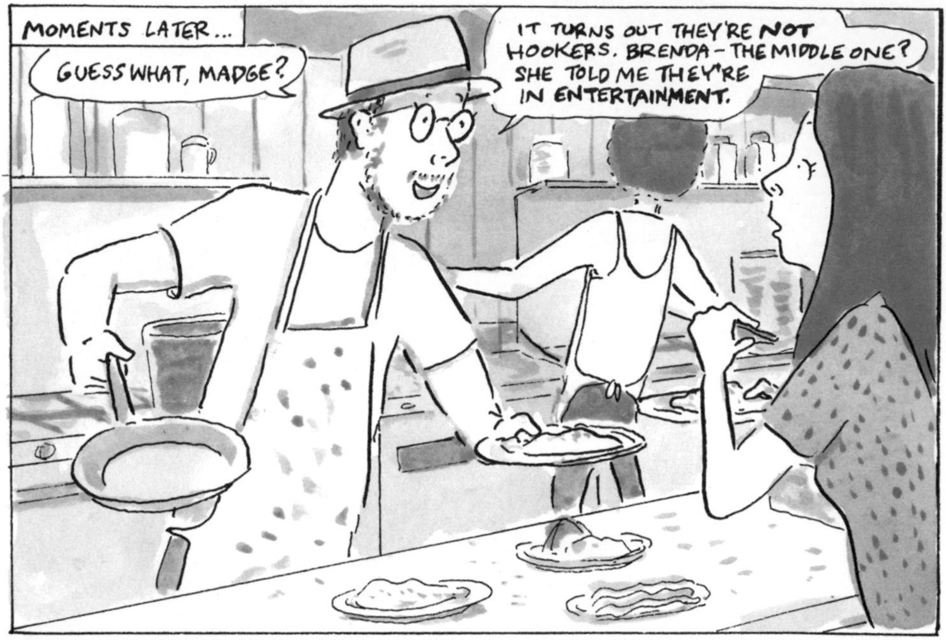
MOMENTS LATER...
GUESS WHAT, MADGE?
IT TURNS OUT THEY'RE NOT HOOKERS. BRENDA – THE MIDDLE ONE? SHE TOLD ME THEY'RE IN ENTERTAINMENT.

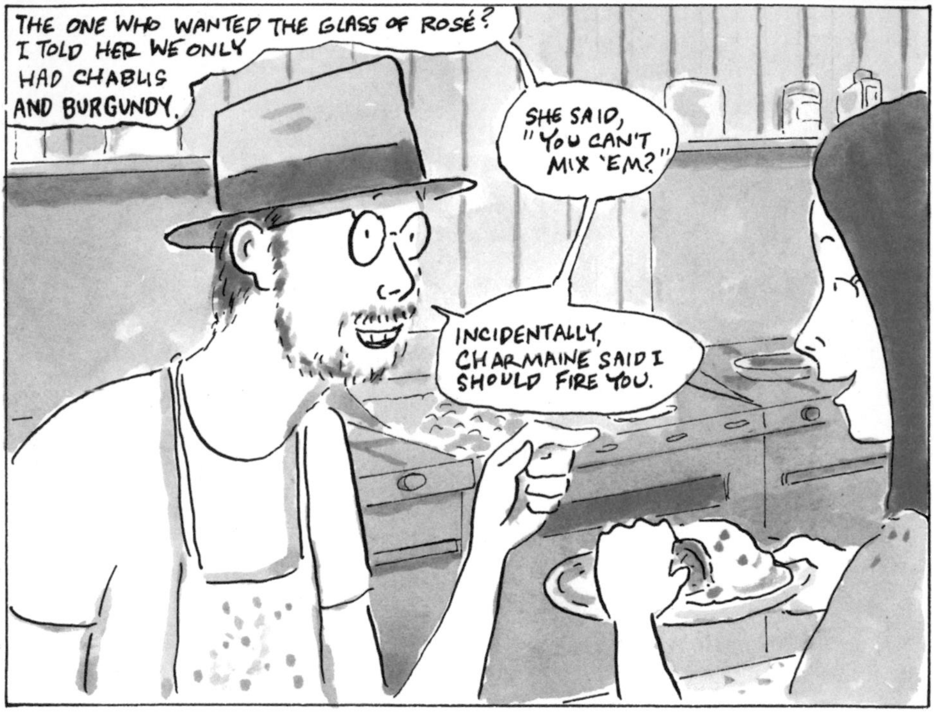
THE ONE WHO WANTED THE GLASS OF ROSÉ? I TOLD HER WE ONLY HAD CHABLIS AND BURGUNDY.
SHE SAID, "YOU CAN'T MIX 'EM?"
INCIDENTALLY, CHARMAINE SAID I SHOULD FIRE YOU.

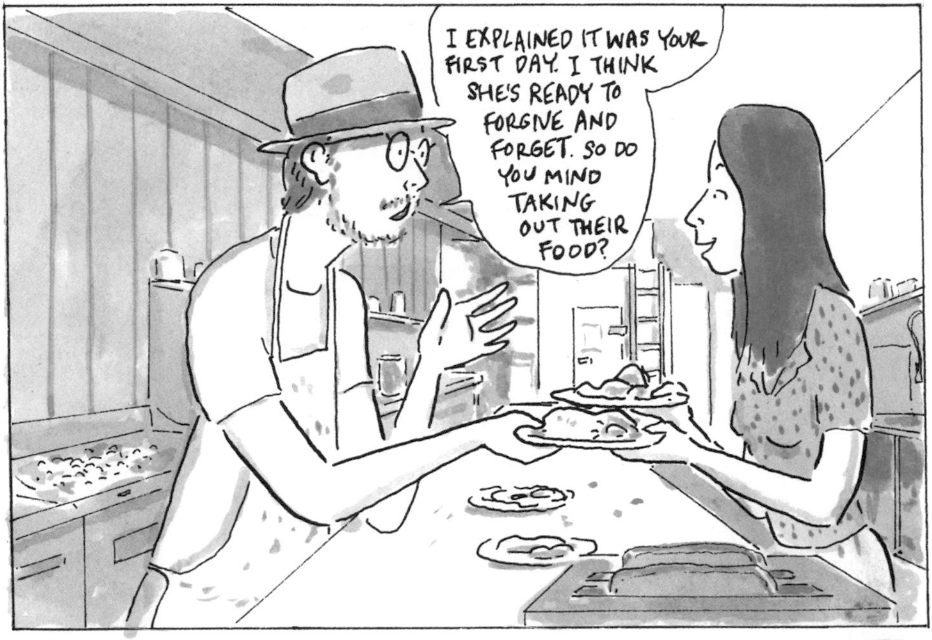
I EXPLAINED IT WAS YOUR FIRST DAY. I THINK SHE'S READY TO FORGIVE AND FORGET. SO DO YOU MIND TAKING OUT THEIR FOOD?

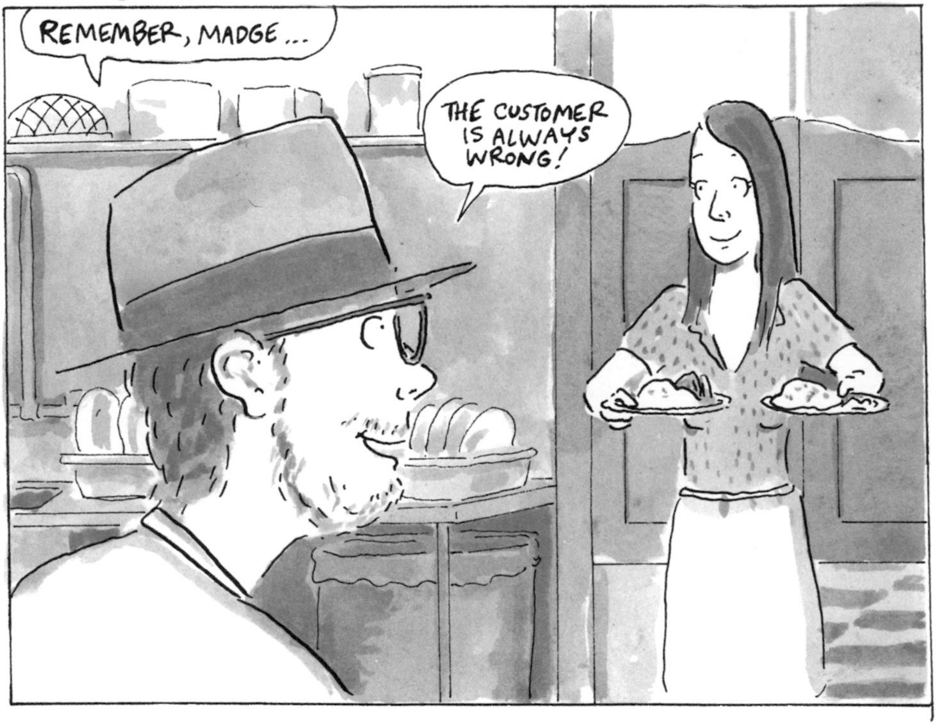
REMEMBER, MADGE...
THE CUSTOMER IS ALWAYS WRONG!

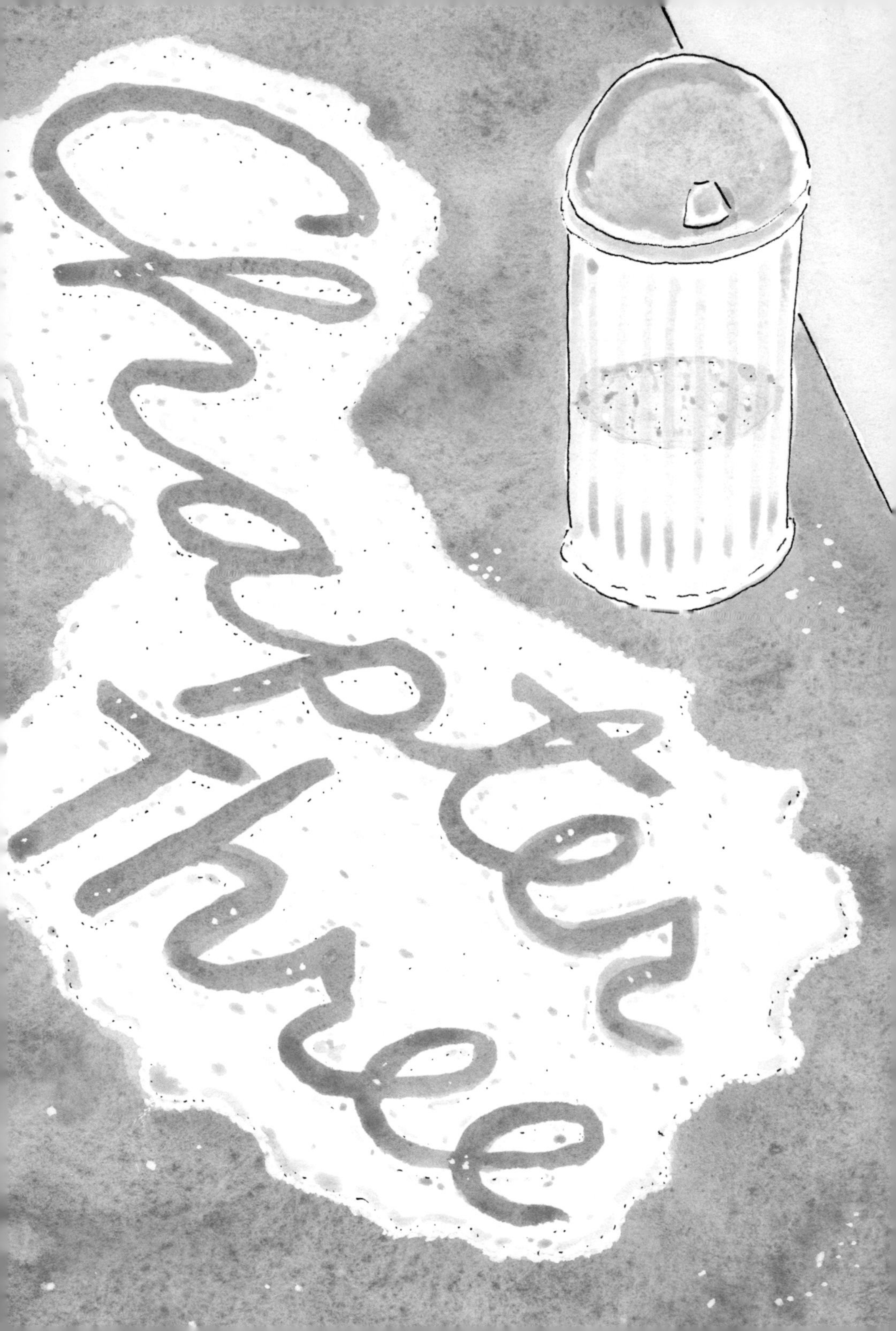
Chapter Three

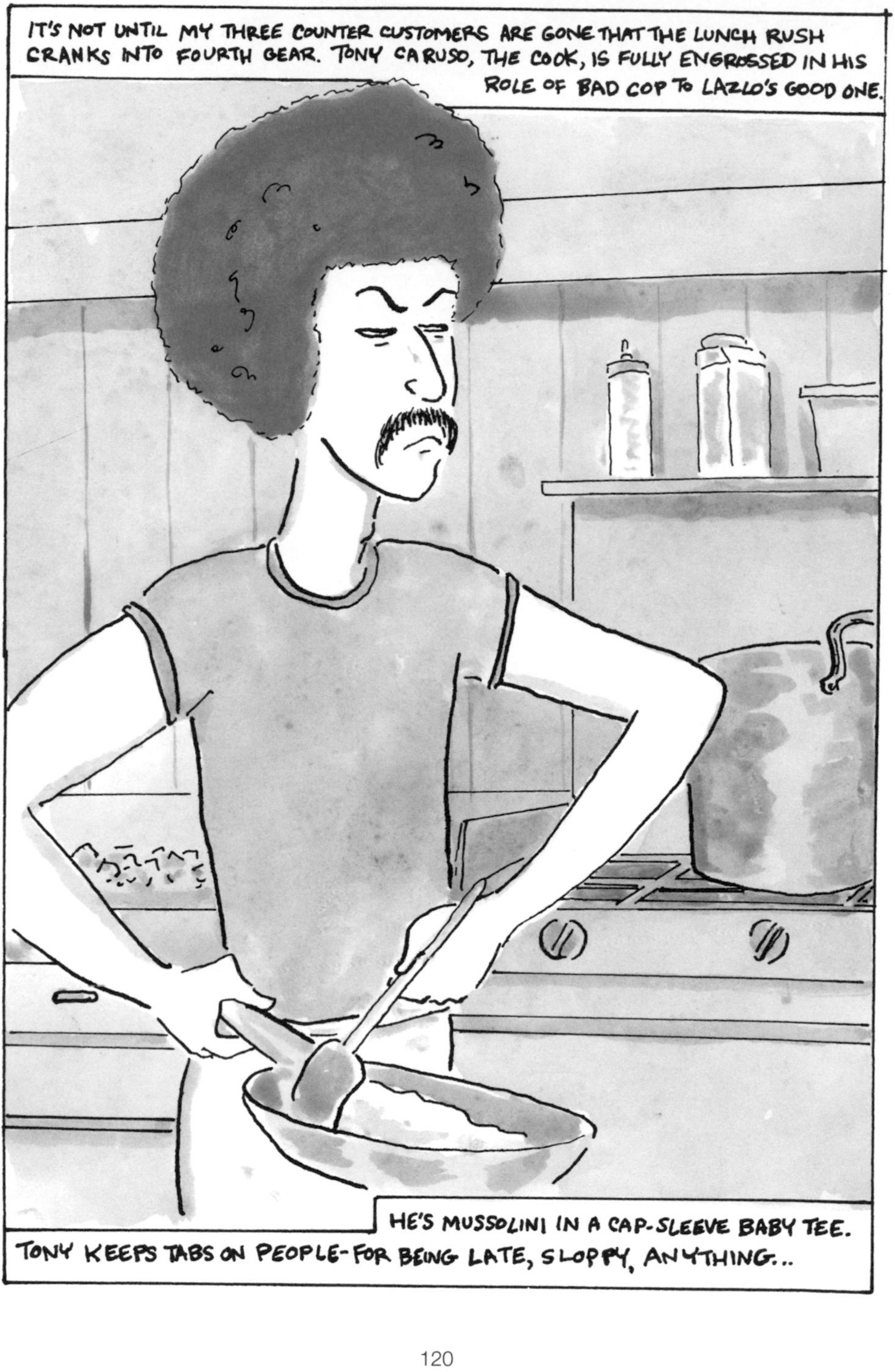
IT'S NOT UNTIL MY THREE COUNTER CUSTOMERS ARE GONE THAT THE LUNCH RUSH CRANKS INTO FOURTH GEAR. TONY CARUSO, THE COOK, IS FULLY ENGROSSED IN HIS ROLE OF BAD COP TO LAZLO'S GOOD ONE.
HE'S MUSSOLINI IN A CAP-SLEEVE BABY TEE.
TONY KEEPS TABS ON PEOPLE-FOR BEING LATE, SLOPPY, ANYTHING...

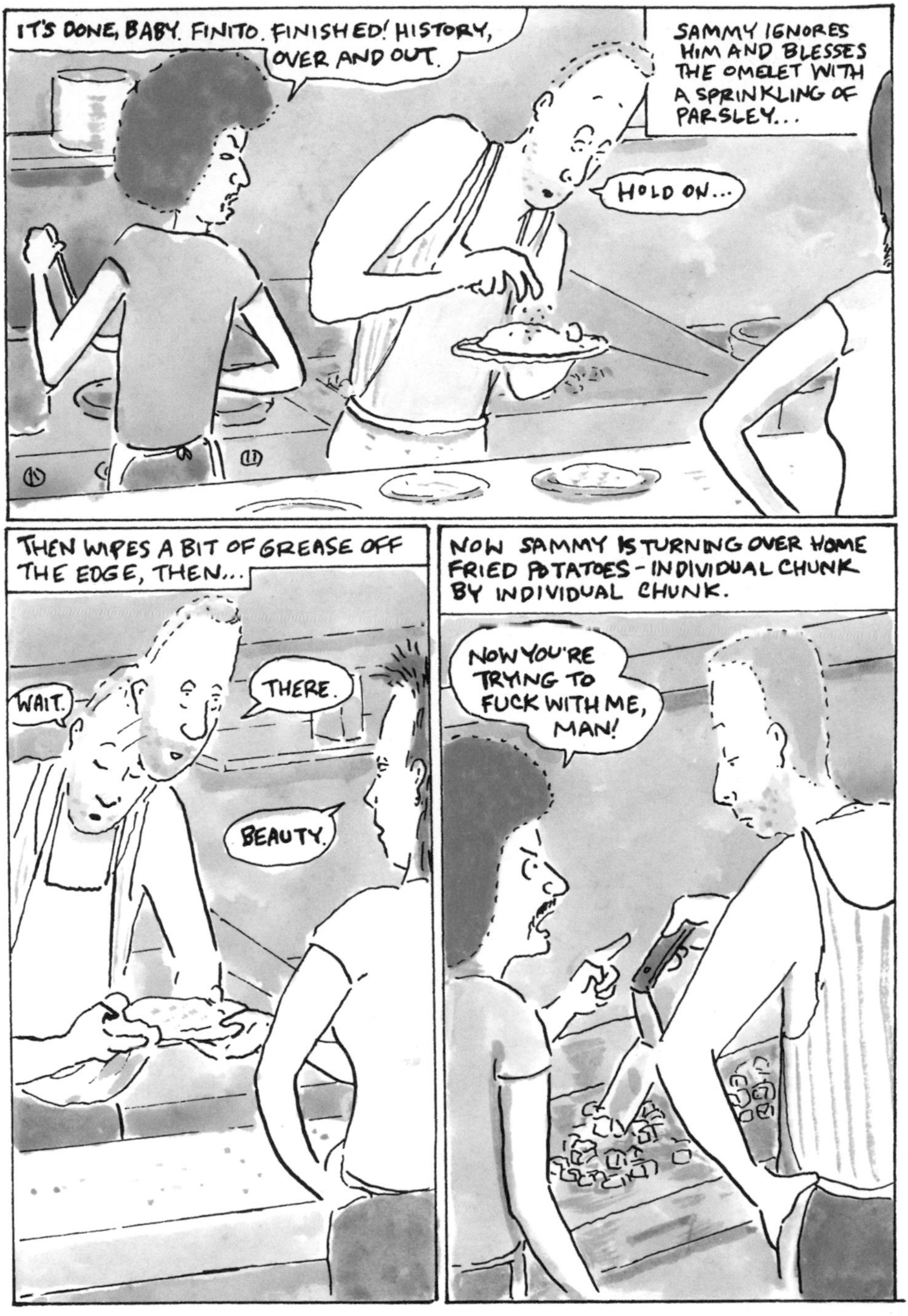
IT'S DONE, BABY. FINITO. FINISHED! HISTORY, OVER AND OUT.
SAMMY IGNORES HIM AND BLESSES THE OMELET WITH A SPRINKLING OF PARSLEY...
HOLD ON...
THEN WIPES A BIT OF GREASE OFF THE EDGE, THEN...
WAIT.
THERE.
BEAUTY.
NOW SAMMY IS TURNING OVER HOME FRIED POTATOES - INDIVIDUAL CHUNK BY INDIVIDUAL CHUNK.
NOW YOU'RE TRYING TO FUCK WITH ME, MAN!

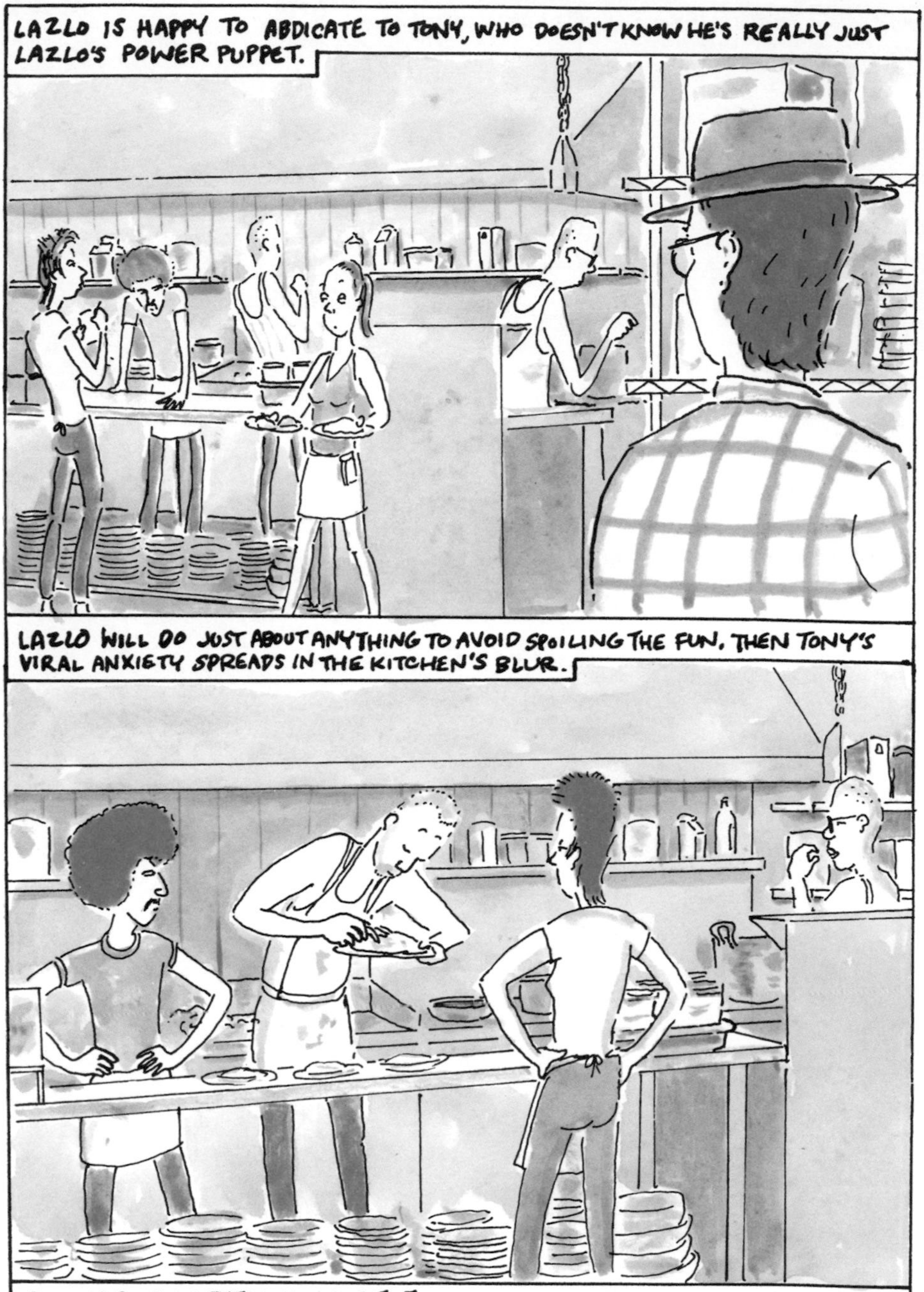
LAZLO IS HAPPY TO ABDICATE TO TONY, WHO DOESN'T KNOW HE'S REALLY JUST LAZLO'S POWER PUPPET.
LAZLO WILL DO JUST ABOUT ANYTHING TO AVOID SPOILING THE FUN. THEN TONY'S VIRAL ANXIETY SPREADS IN THE KITCHEN'S BLUR.
SAMMY TAKES AN EXTRA MOMENT TO FAN OUT AVOCADO SLICES OVER THE TOP OF AN OMELET.

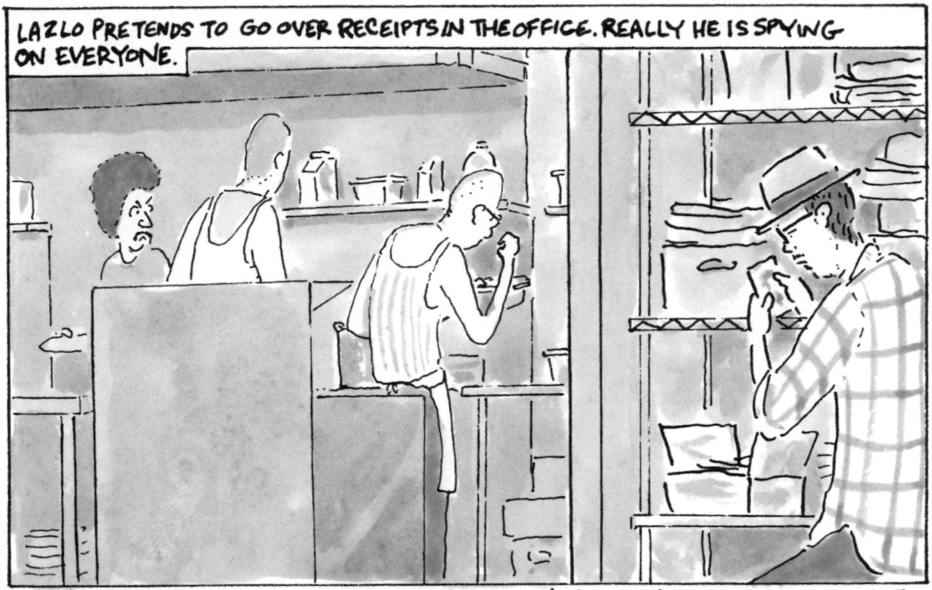
LAZLO PRETENDS TO GO OVER RECEIPTS IN THE OFFICE. REALLY HE IS SPYING ON EVERYONE.

BERNARDO IS PREPPING. NOT EVERYONE WOULD HAVE GIVEN BERNARDO A JOB THAT INVOLVED KNIVES, BUT LAZLO TRUSTS HIM. THEN IT HAPPENS.

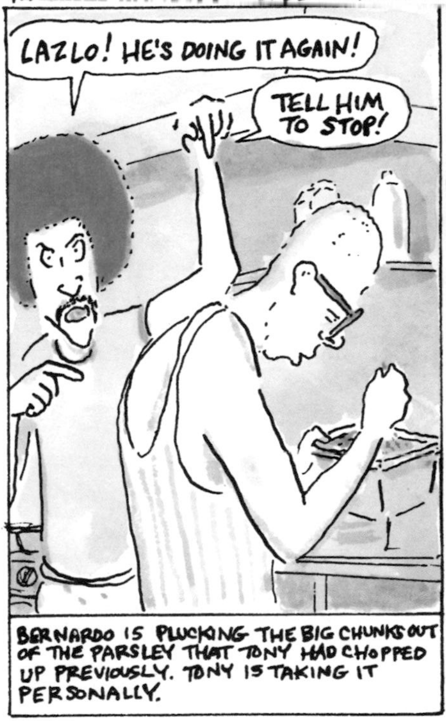
LAZLO! HE'S DOING IT AGAIN!
TELL HIM TO STOP!
BERNARDO IS PLUCKING THE BIG CHUNKS OUT OF THE PARSLEY THAT TONY HAD CHOPPED UP PREVIOUSLY. TONY IS TAKING IT PERSONALLY.

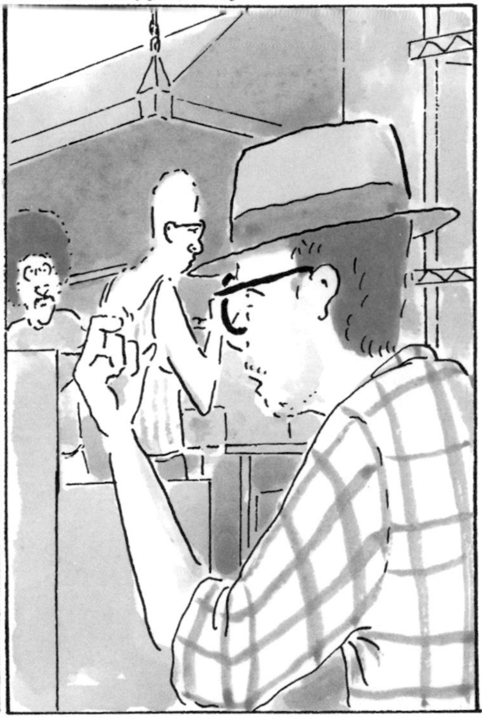

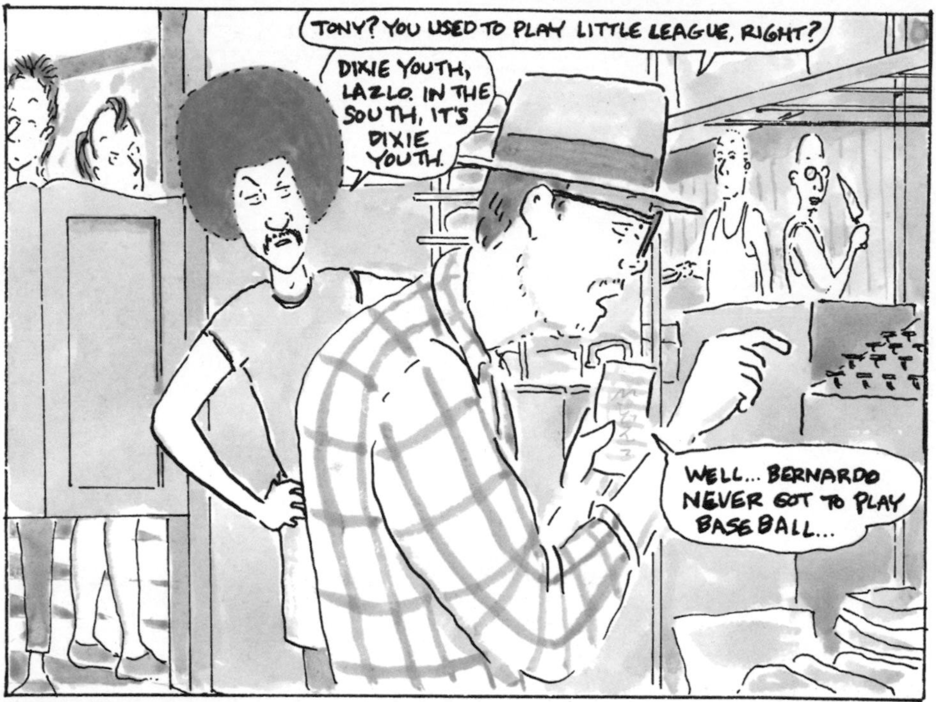
TONY? YOU USED TO PLAY LITTLE LEAGUE, RIGHT?
DIXIE YOUTH, LAZLO. IN THE SOUTH, IT'S DIXIE YOUTH.
WELL... BERNARDO NEVER GOT TO PLAY BASEBALL...

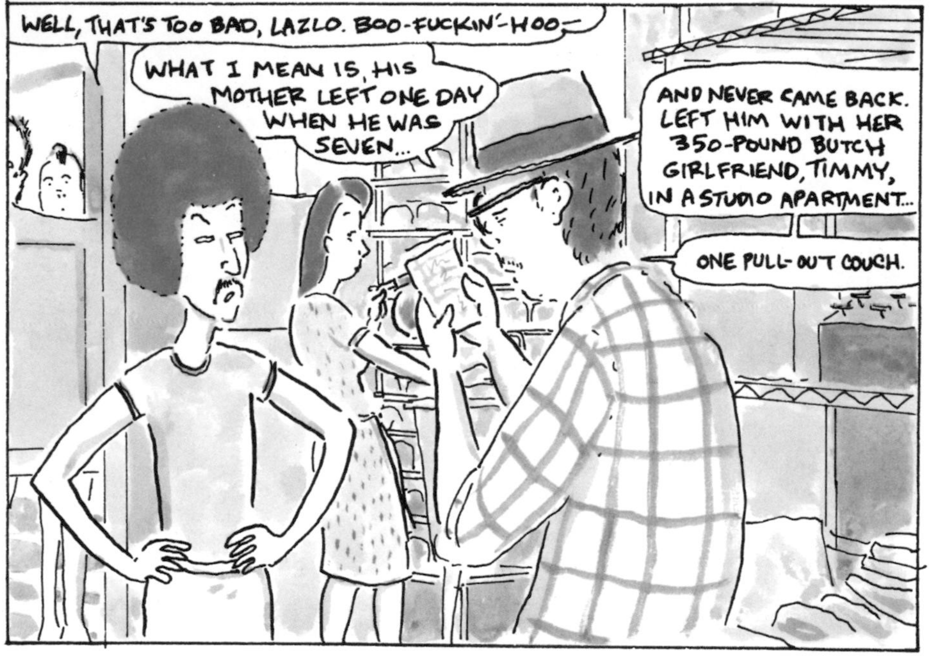
WELL, THAT'S TOO BAD, LAZLO. BOO-FUCKIN'-HOO-
WHAT I MEAN IS, HIS MOTHER LEFT ONE DAY WHEN HE WAS SEVEN...
AND NEVER CAME BACK. LEFT HIM WITH HER 350-POUND BUTCH GIRLFRIEND, TIMMY, IN A STUDIO APARTMENT...
ONE PULL-OUT COUCH.

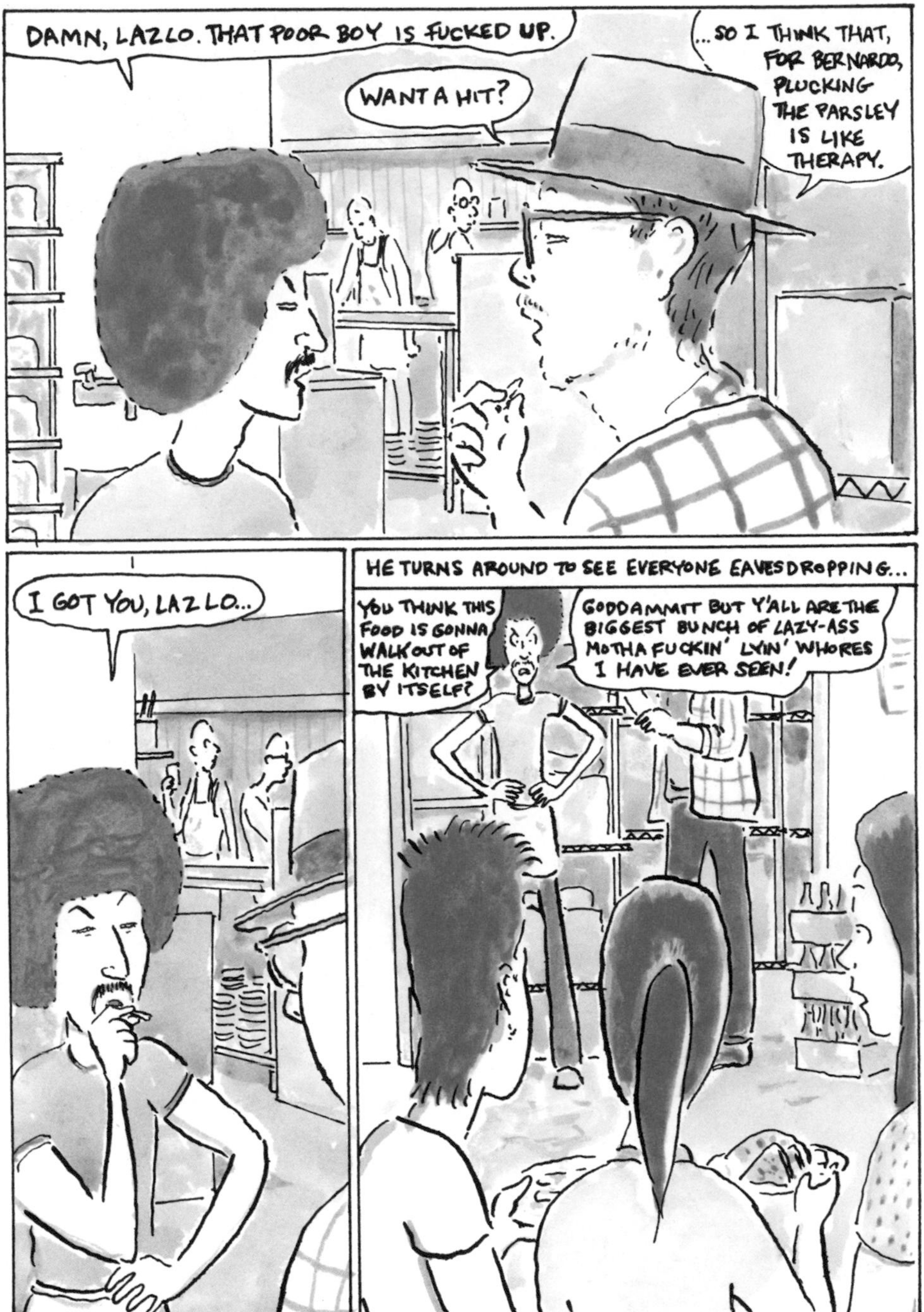
DAMN, LAZLO. THAT POOR BOY IS FUCKED UP.
WANT A HIT?
...SO I THINK THAT, FOR BERNARDO, PLUCKING THE PARSLEY IS LIKE THERAPY.
I GOT YOU, LAZLO...
HE TURNS AROUND TO SEE EVERYONE EAVESDROPPING...
YOU THINK THIS FOOD IS GONNA WALK OUT OF THE KITCHEN BY ITSELF?
GODDAMMIT BUT Y'ALL ARE THE BIGGEST BUNCH OF LAZY-ASS MOTHA FUCKIN' LYIN' WHORES I HAVE EVER SEEN!

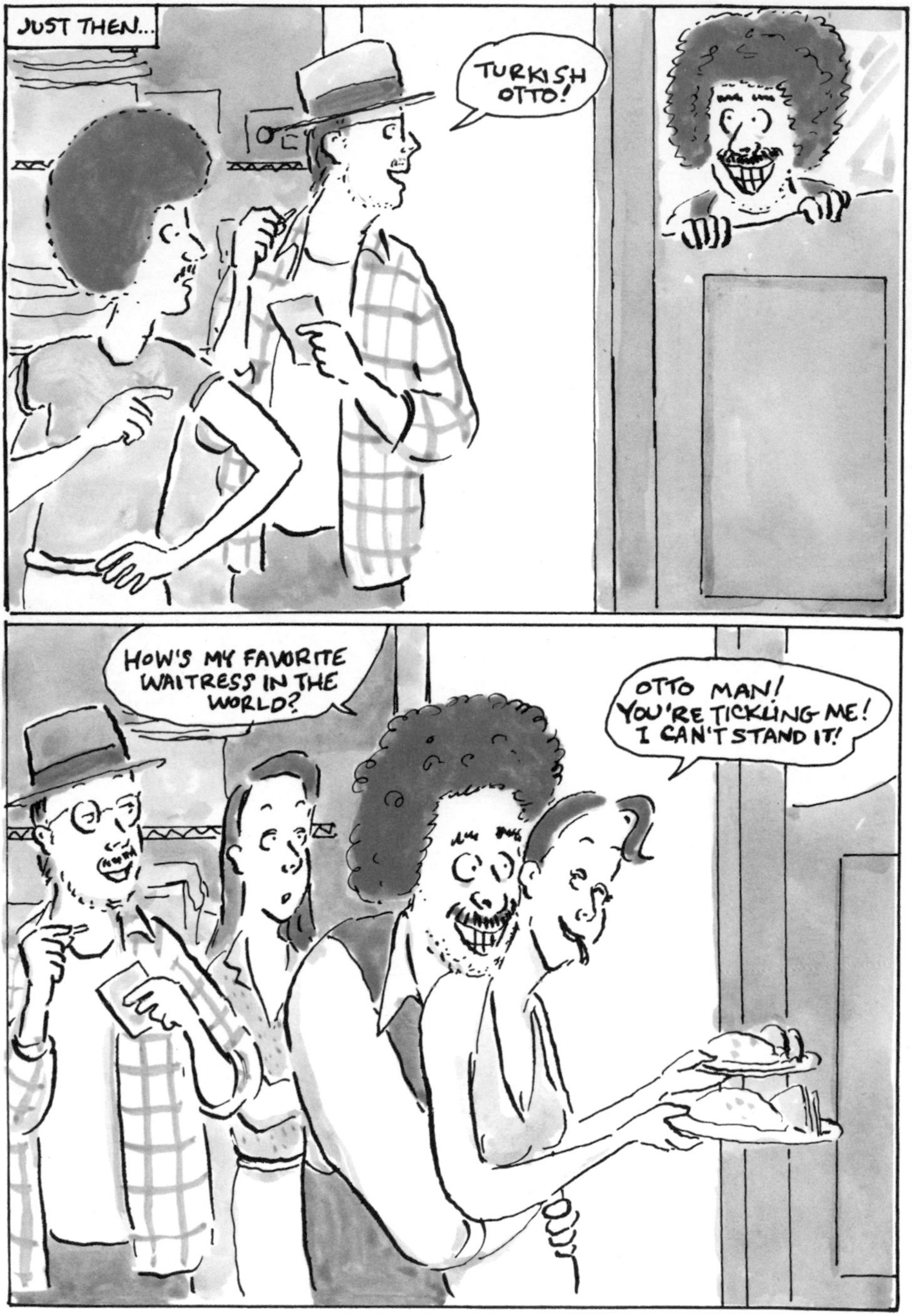
JUST THEN...
TURKISH OTTO!
HOW'S MY FAVORITE WAITRESS IN THE WORLD?
OTTO MAN! YOU'RE TICKLING ME! I CAN'T STAND IT!

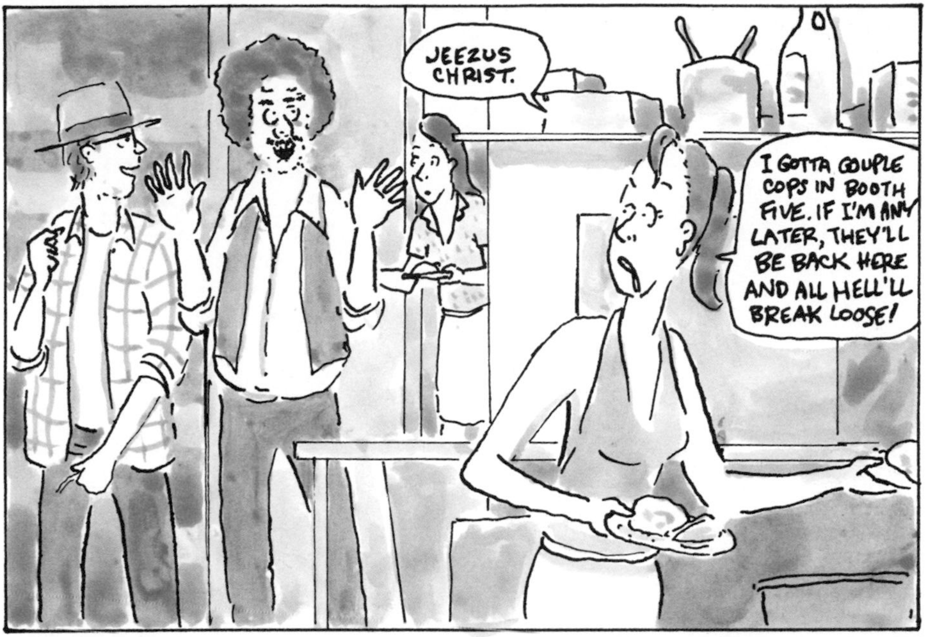
JEEZUS CHRIST.
I GOTTA COUPLE COPS IN BOOTH FIVE. IF I'M ANY LATER, THEY'LL BE BACK HERE AND ALL HELL'LL BREAK LOOSE!

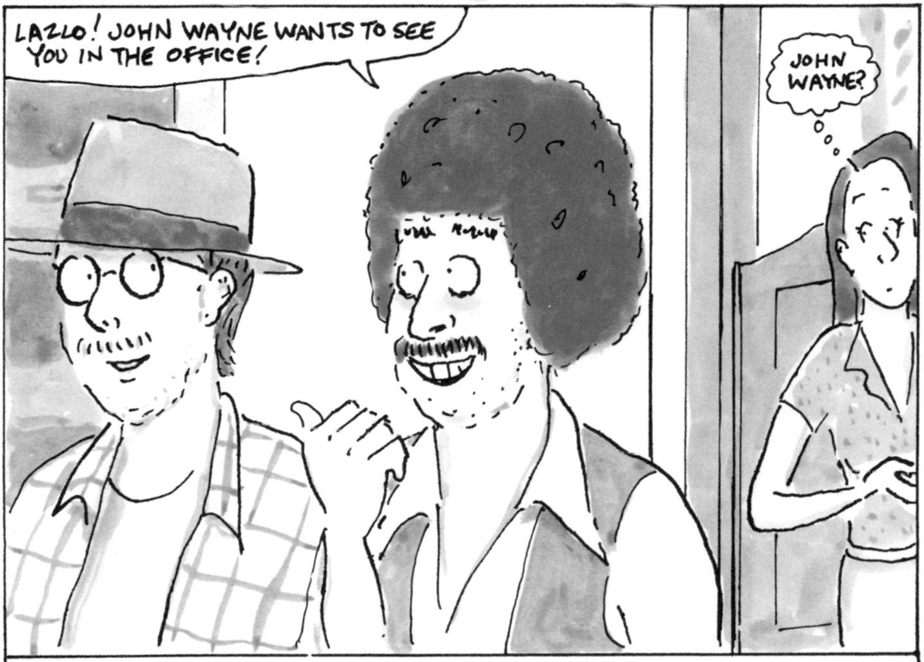
LAZLO! JOHN WAYNE WANTS TO SEE YOU IN THE OFFICE!
JOHN WAYNE?

OTTO HAS A VOICE LIKE TIN CANS SMASHED UNDER CAR WHEELS.

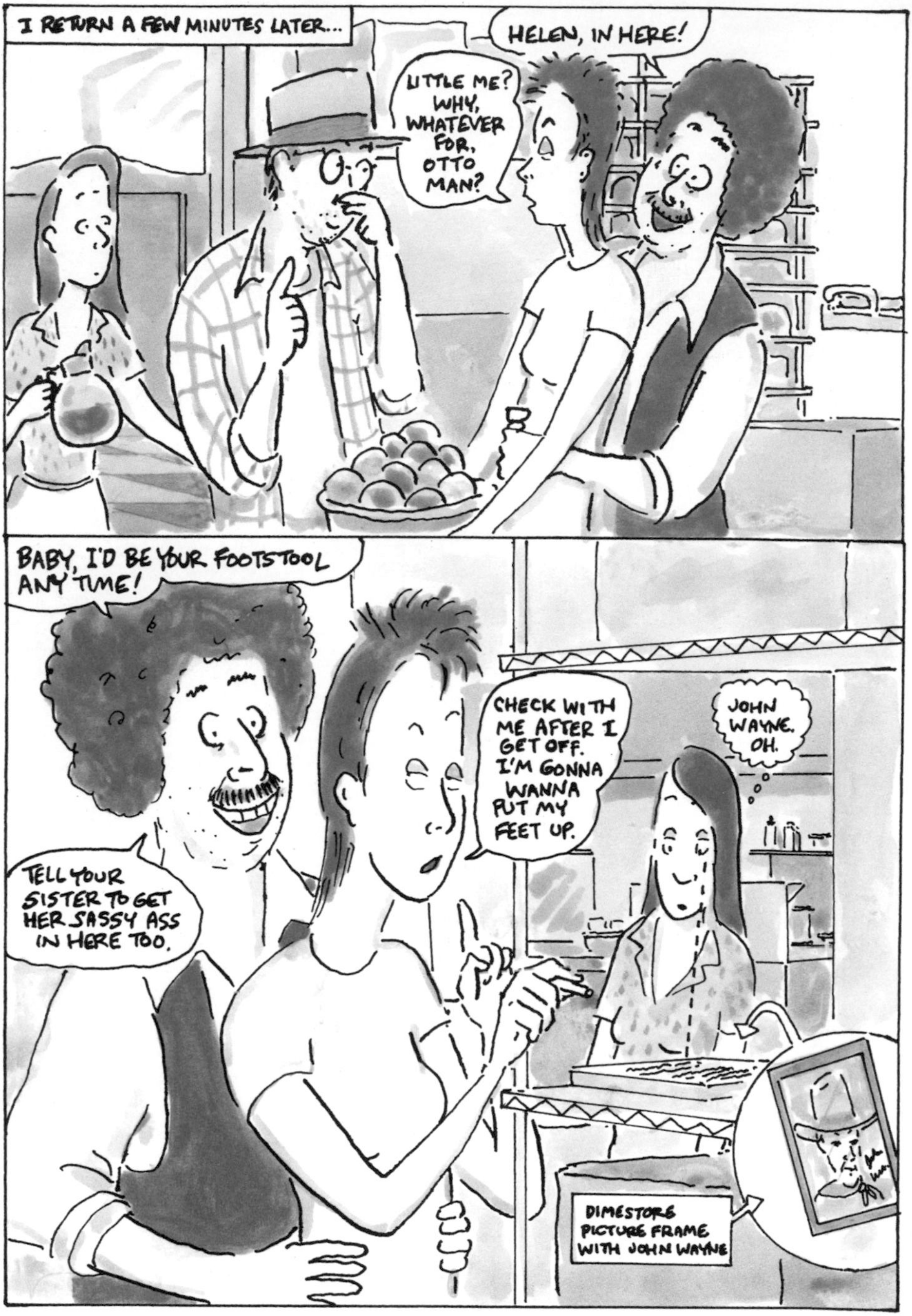
I RETURN A FEW MINUTES LATER...
HELEN, IN HERE!
LITTLE ME? WHY, WHATEVER FOR, OTTO MAN?
BABY, I'D BE YOUR FOOTSTOOL ANY TIME!
CHECK WITH ME AFTER I GET OFF. I'M GONNA WANNA PUT MY FEET UP.
JOHN WAYNE. OH.
TELL YOUR SISTER TO GET HER SASSY ASS IN HERE TOO.
DIMESTORE PICTURE FRAME WITH JOHN WAYNE

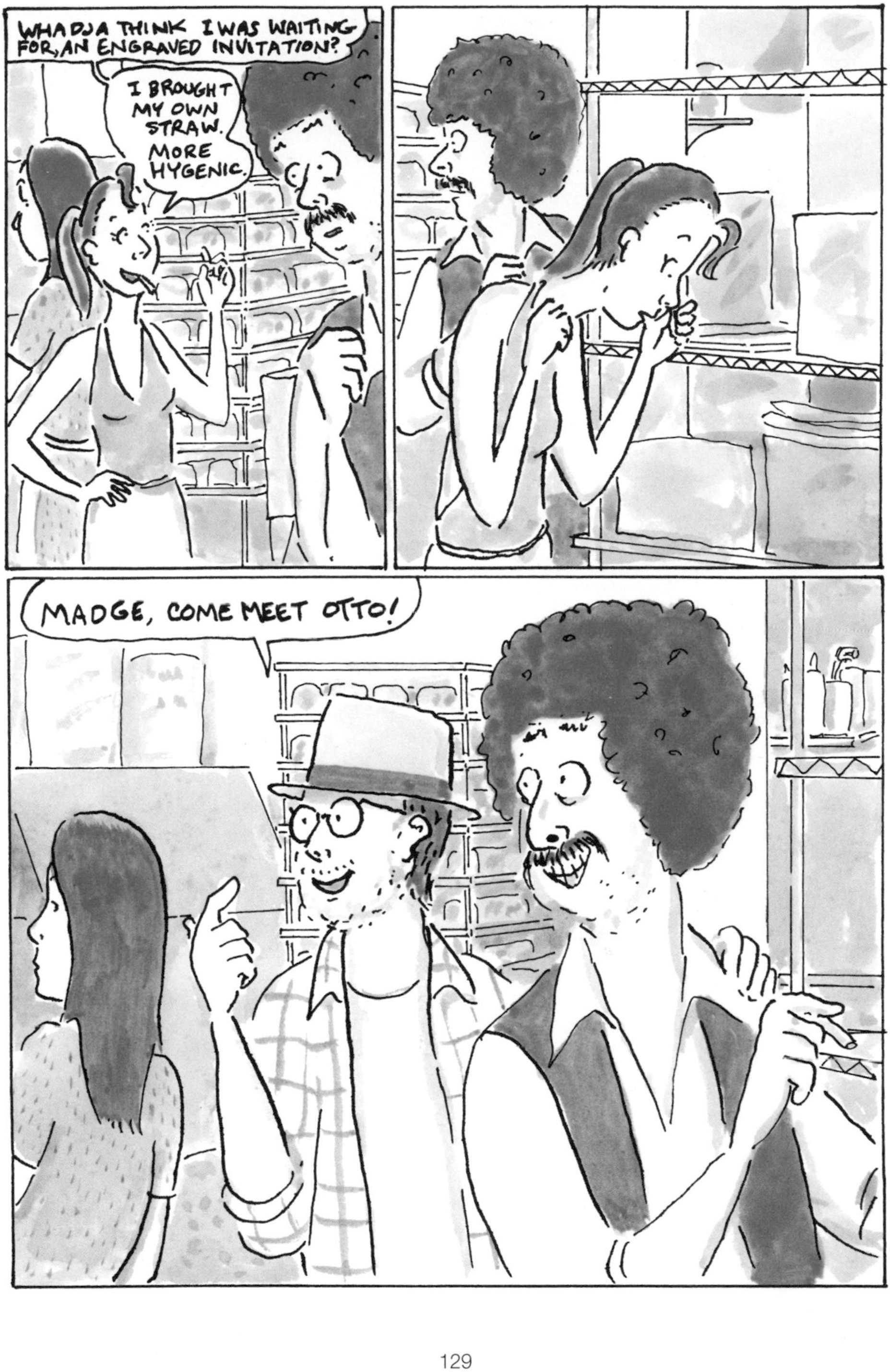
WHADJA THINK I WAS WAITING FOR, AN ENGRAVED INVITATION?
I BROUGHT MY OWN STRAW. MORE HYGENIC.
MADGE, COME MEET OTTO!

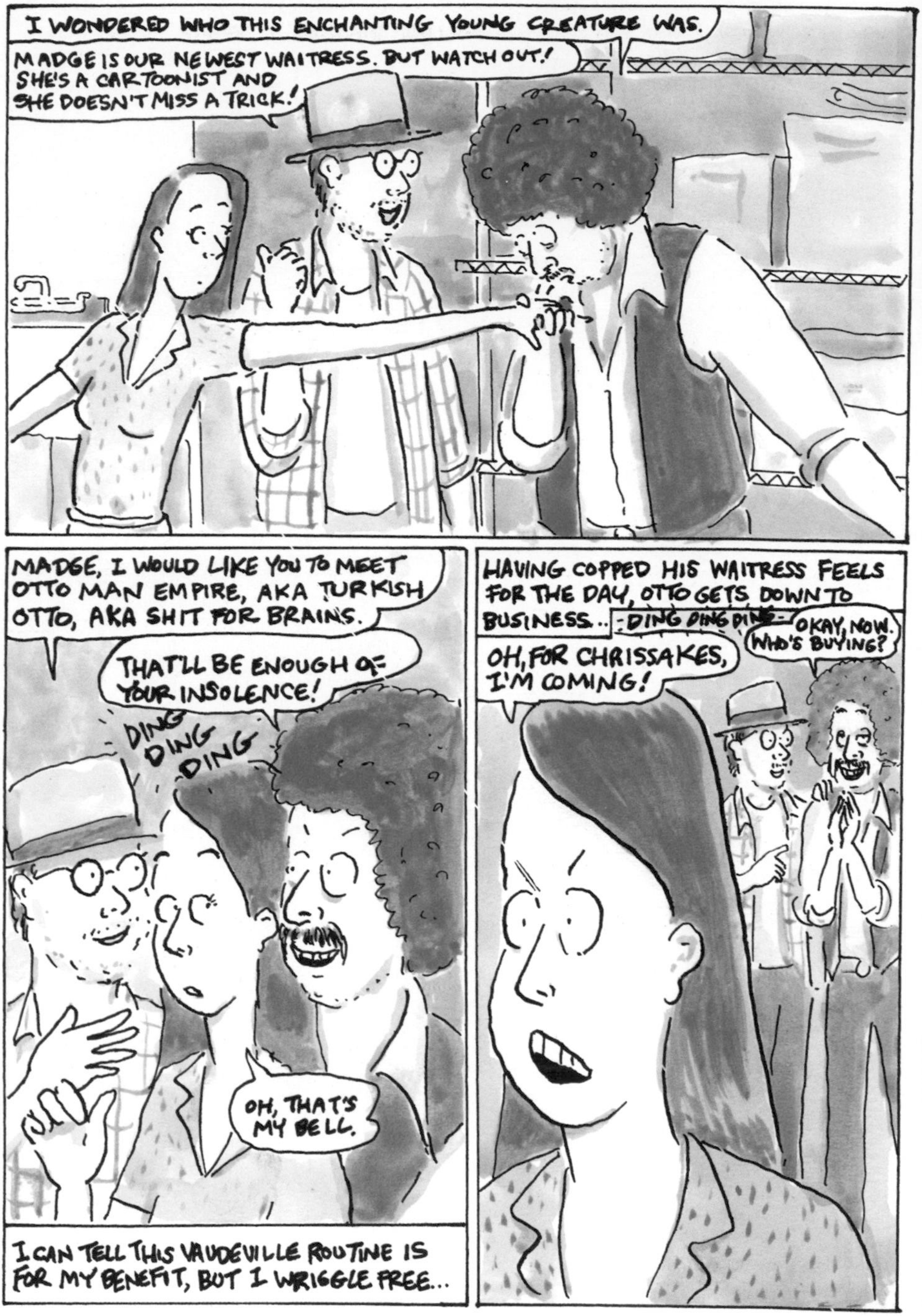
I WONDERED WHO THIS ENCHANTING YOUNG CREATURE WAS.
MADGE IS OUR NEWEST WAITRESS. BUT WATCH OUT! SHE'S A CARTOONIST AND SHE DOESN'T MISS A TRICK!
MADGE, I WOULD LIKE YOU TO MEET OTTO MAN EMPIRE, AKA TURKISH OTTO, AKA SHIT FOR BRAINS.
THAT'LL BE ENOUGH OF YOUR INSOLENCE!
DING DING DING
OH, THAT'S MY BELL.
I CAN TELL THIS VAUDEVILLE ROUTINE IS FOR MY BENEFIT, BUT I WRIGGLE FREE...
HAVING COPPED HIS WAITRESS FEELS FOR THE DAY, OTTO GETS DOWN TO BUSINESS...
DING DING DING
OKAY, NOW. WHO'S BUYING?
OH, FOR CHRISSAKES, I'M COMING!

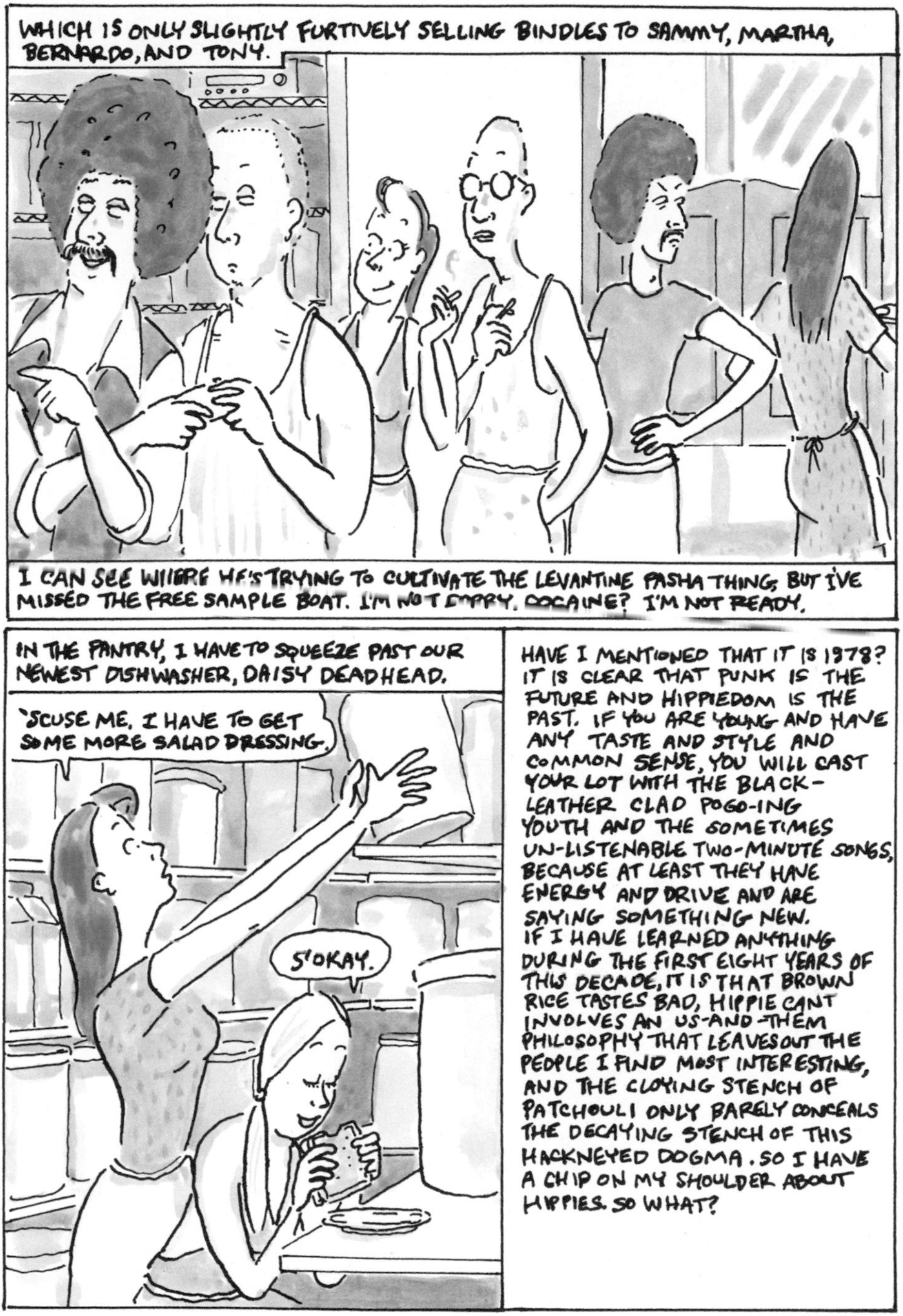
WHICH IS ONLY SLIGHTLY FURTIVELY SELLING BINDLES TO SAMMY, MARTHA, BERNARDO, AND TONY.
I CAN SEE WHERE HE'S TRYING TO CULTIVATE THE LEVANTINE PASHA THING, BUT I'VE MISSED THE FREE SAMPLE BOAT. I'M NOT SORRY. COCAINE? I'M NOT READY.
IN THE PANTRY, I HAVE TO SQUEEZE PAST OUR NEWEST DISHWASHER, DAISY DEADHEAD.
'SCUSE ME. I HAVE TO GET SOME MORE SALAD DRESSING.
S'OKAY.
HAVE I MENTIONED THAT IT IS 1978? IT IS CLEAR THAT PUNK IS THE FUTURE AND HIPPIEDOM IS THE PAST. IF YOU ARE YOUNG AND HAVE ANY TASTE AND STYLE AND COMMON SENSE, YOU WILL CAST YOUR LOT WITH THE BLACK-LEATHER CLAD POGO-ING YOUTH AND THE SOMETIMES UN-LISTENABLE TWO-MINUTE SONGS, BECAUSE AT LEAST THEY HAVE ENERGY AND DRIVE AND ARE SAYING SOMETHING NEW.
IF I HAVE LEARNED ANYTHING DURING THE FIRST EIGHT YEARS OF THIS DECADE, IT IS THAT BROWN RICE TASTES BAD, HIPPIE CANT INVOLVES AN US-AND-THEM PHILOSOPHY THAT LEAVES OUT THE PEOPLE I FIND MOST INTERESTING, AND THE CLOYING STENCH OF PATCHOULI ONLY BARELY CONCEALS THE DECAYING STENCH OF THIS HACKNEYED DOGMA. SO I HAVE A CHIP ON MY SHOULDER ABOUT HIPPIES. SO WHAT?

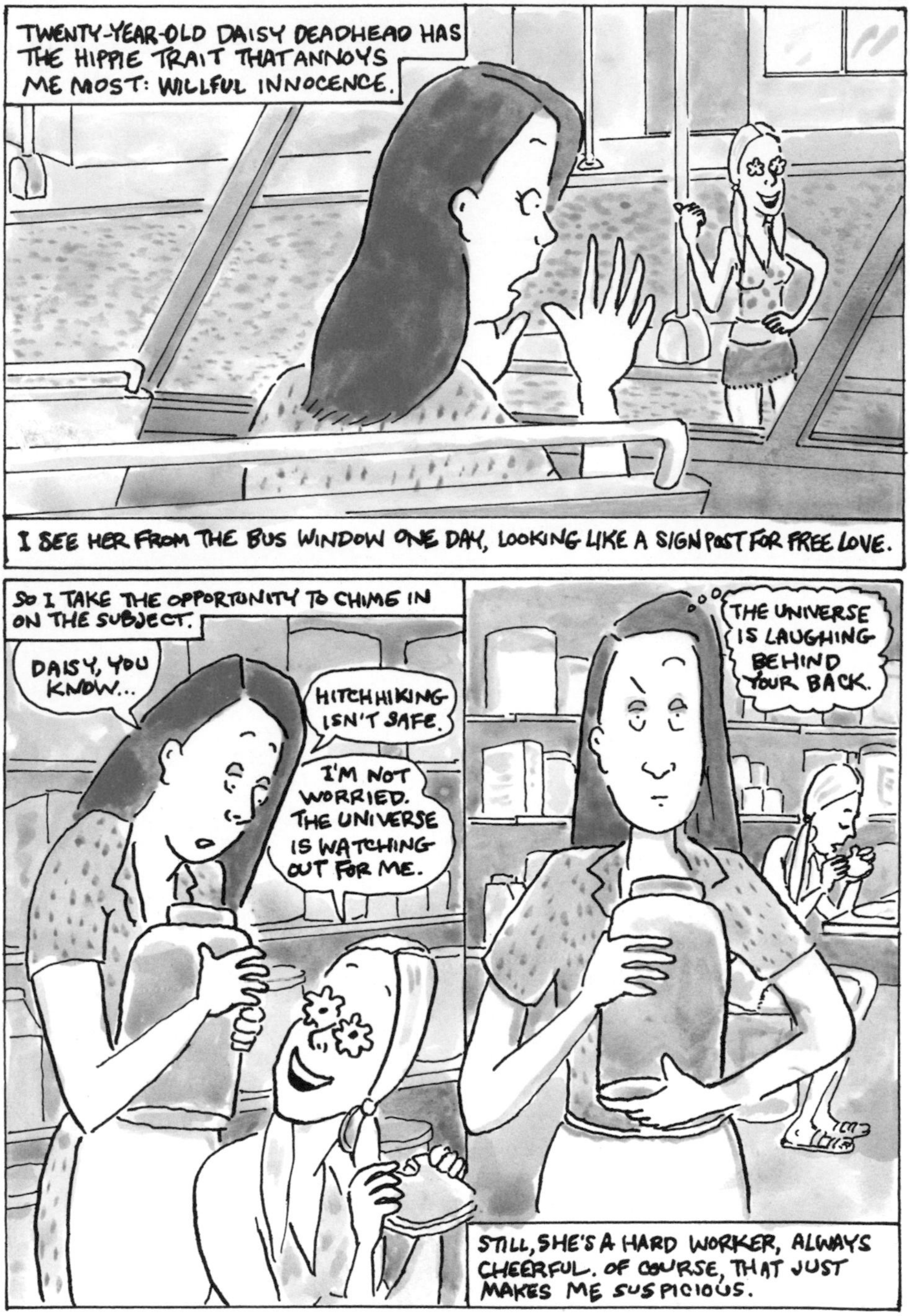
TWENTY-YEAR-OLD DAISY DEADHEAD HAS THE HIPPIE TRAIT THAT ANNOYS ME MOST: WILLFUL INNOCENCE.
I SEE HER FROM THE BUS WINDOW ONE DAY, LOOKING LIKE A SIGNPOST FOR FREE LOVE.
SO I TAKE THE OPPORTUNITY TO CHIME IN ON THE SUBJECT.
DAISY, YOU KNOW...
HITCHHIKING ISN'T SAFE.
I'M NOT WORRIED. THE UNIVERSE IS WATCHING OUT FOR ME.
THE UNIVERSE IS LAUGHING BEHIND YOUR BACK.
STILL, SHE'S A HARD WORKER, ALWAYS CHEERFUL. OF COURSE, THAT JUST MAKES ME SUSPICIOUS.

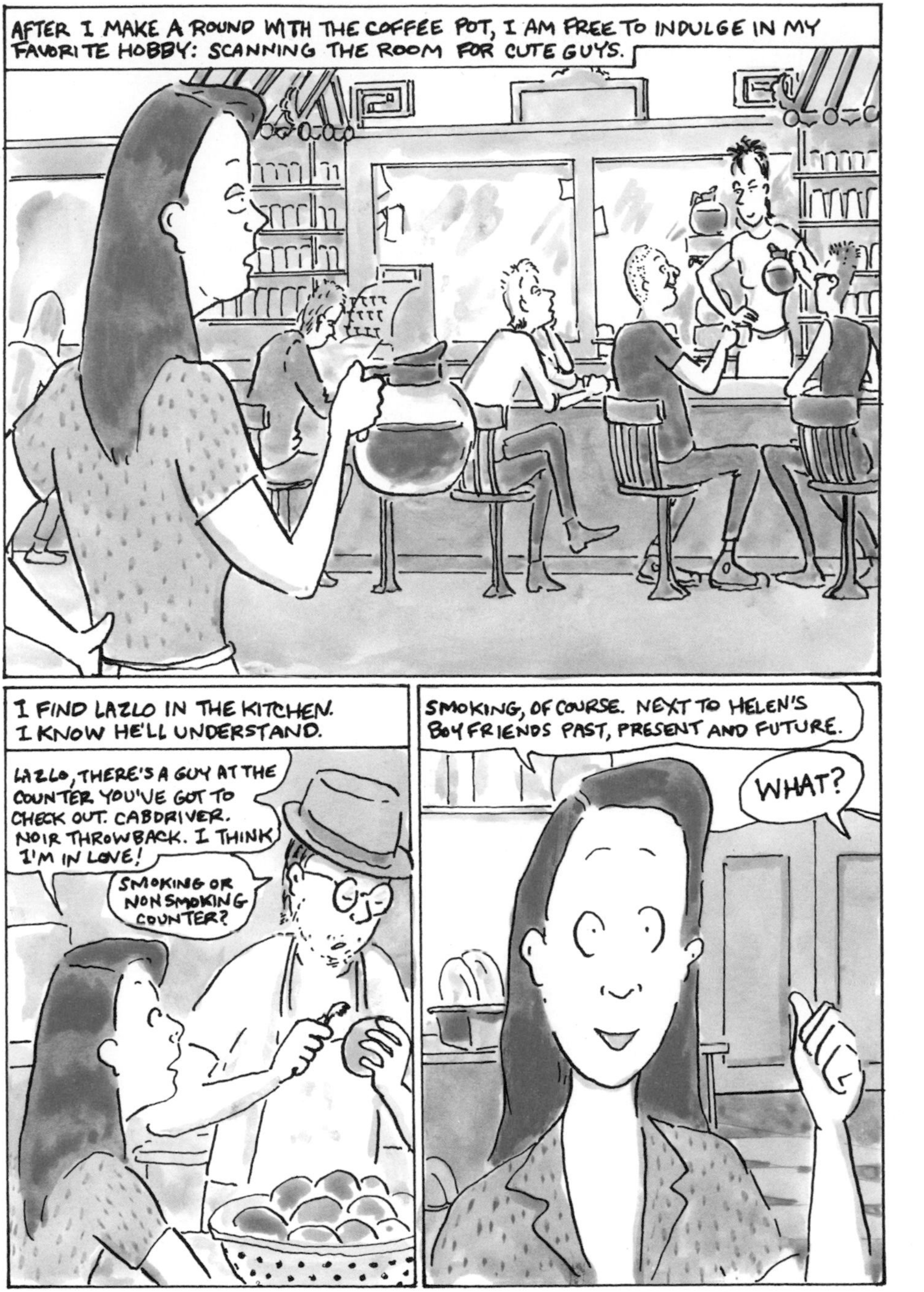

AFTER I MAKE A ROUND WITH THE COFFEE POT, I AM FREE TO INDULGE IN MY FAVORITE HOBBY: SCANNING THE ROOM FOR CUTE GUYS.
I FIND LAZLO IN THE KITCHEN. I KNOW HE'LL UNDERSTAND.
LAZLO, THERE'S A GUY AT THE COUNTER YOU'VE GOT TO CHECK OUT. CABDRIVER. NOIR THROWBACK. I THINK I'M IN LOVE!
SMOKING OR NONSMOKING COUNTER?
SMOKING, OF COURSE. NEXT TO HELEN'S BOYFRIENDS PAST, PRESENT AND FUTURE.
WHAT?

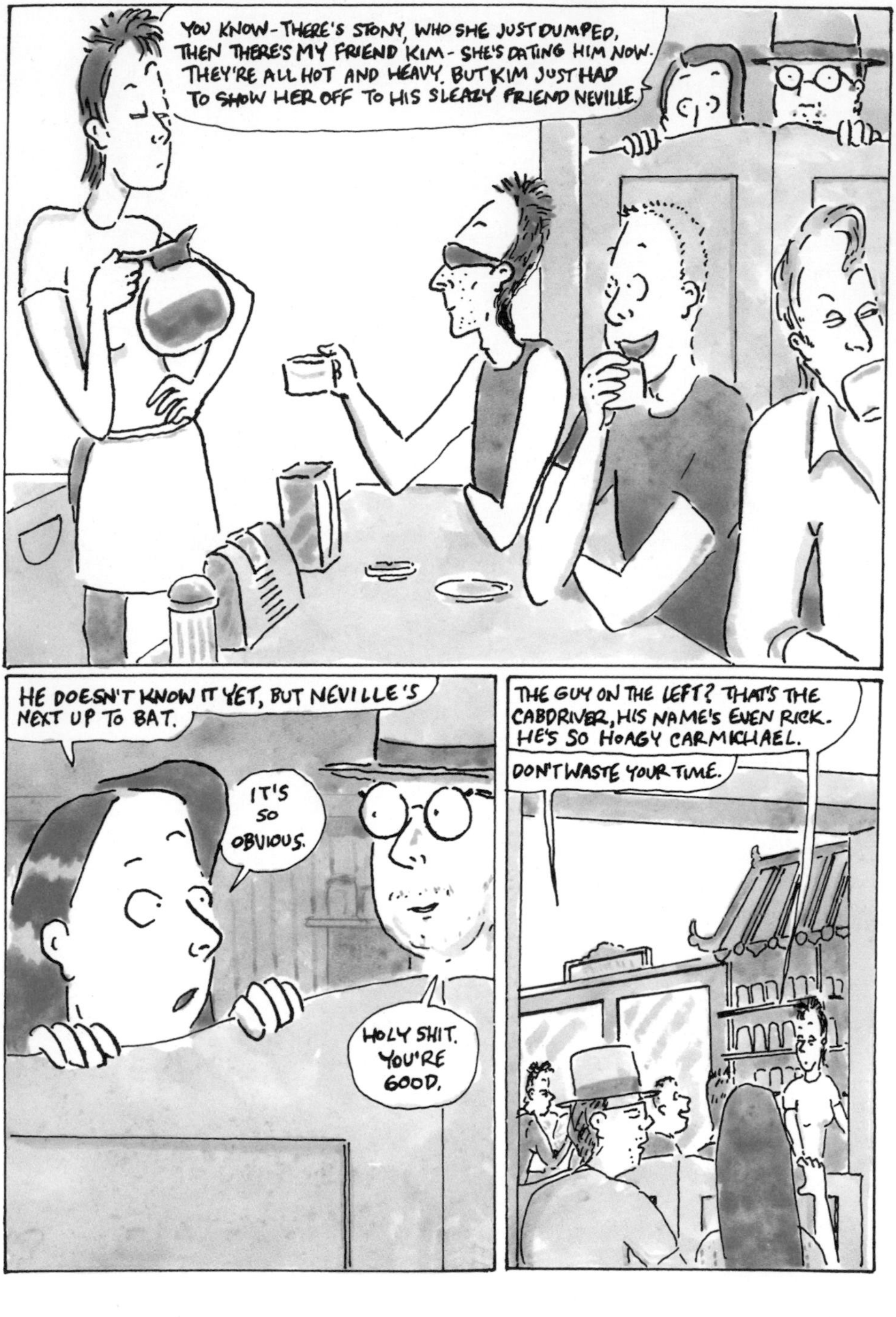
YOU KNOW - THERE'S STONY, WHO SHE JUST DUMPED, THEN THERE'S MY FRIEND KIM - SHE'S DATING HIM NOW. THEY'RE ALL HOT AND HEAVY. BUT KIM JUST HAD TO SHOW HER OFF TO HIS SLEAZY FRIEND NEVILLE.
HE DOESN'T KNOW IT YET, BUT NEVILLE'S NEXT UP TO BAT.
IT'S SO OBVIOUS.
HOLY SHIT. YOU'RE GOOD.
THE GUY ON THE LEFT? THAT'S THE CABDRIVER, HIS NAME'S EVEN RICK. HE'S SO HOAGY CARMICHAEL.
DON'T WASTE YOUR TIME.

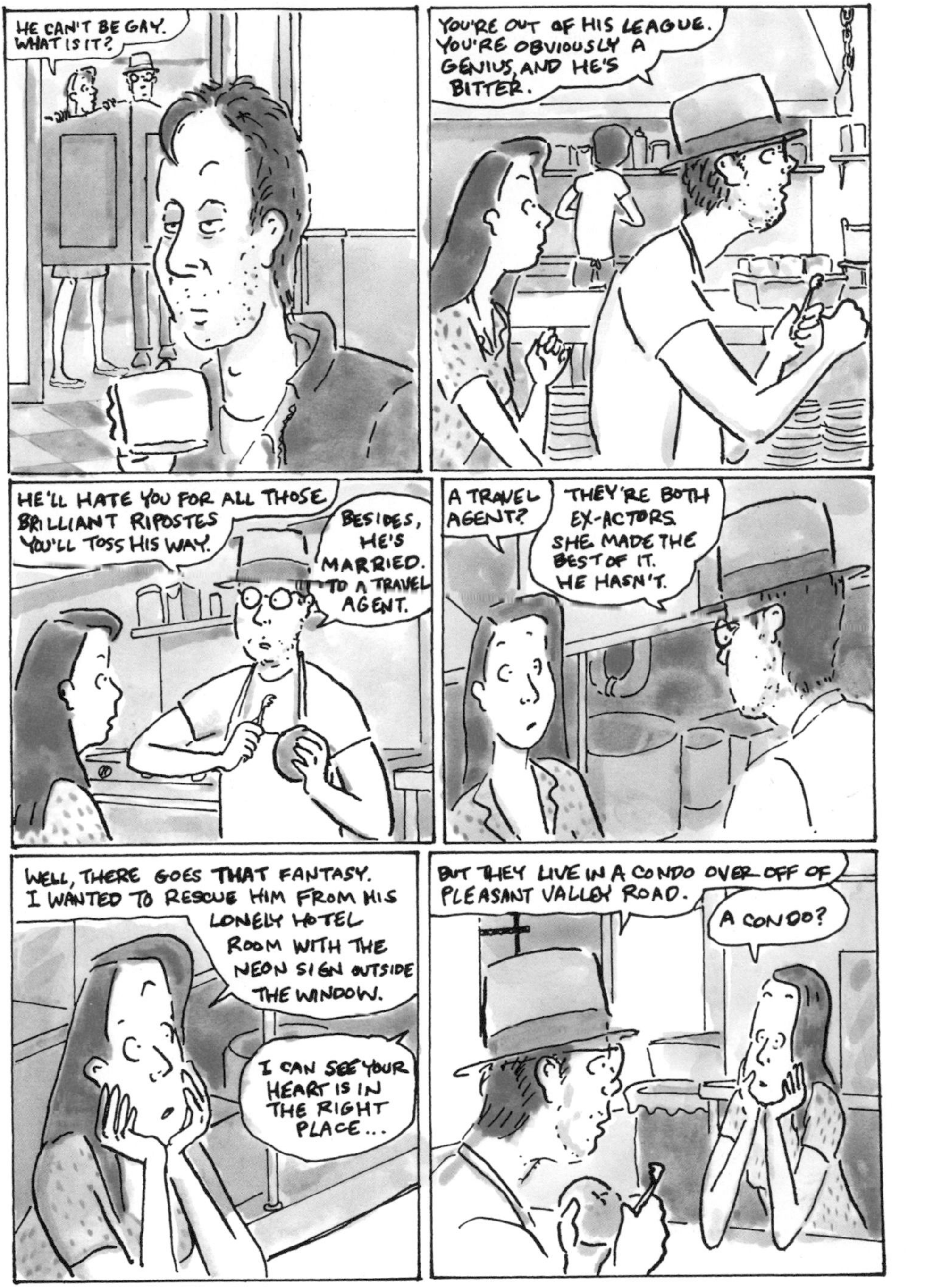
HE CAN'T BE GAY. WHAT IS IT?
YOU'RE OUT OF HIS LEAGUE. YOU'RE OBVIOUSLY A GENIUS, AND HE'S BITTER.
HE'LL HATE YOU FOR ALL THOSE BRILLIANT RIPOSTES YOU'LL TOSS HIS WAY.
BESIDES, HE'S MARRIED. TO A TRAVEL AGENT.
A TRAVEL AGENT?
THEY'RE BOTH EX-ACTORS. SHE MADE THE BEST OF IT. HE HASN'T.
WELL, THERE GOES THAT FANTASY. I WANTED TO RESCUE HIM FROM HIS LONELY HOTEL ROOM WITH THE NEON SIGN OUTSIDE THE WINDOW.
I CAN SEE YOUR HEART IS IN THE RIGHT PLACE...
BUT THEY LIVE IN A CONDO OVER OFF OF PLEASANT VALLEY ROAD.
A CONDO?

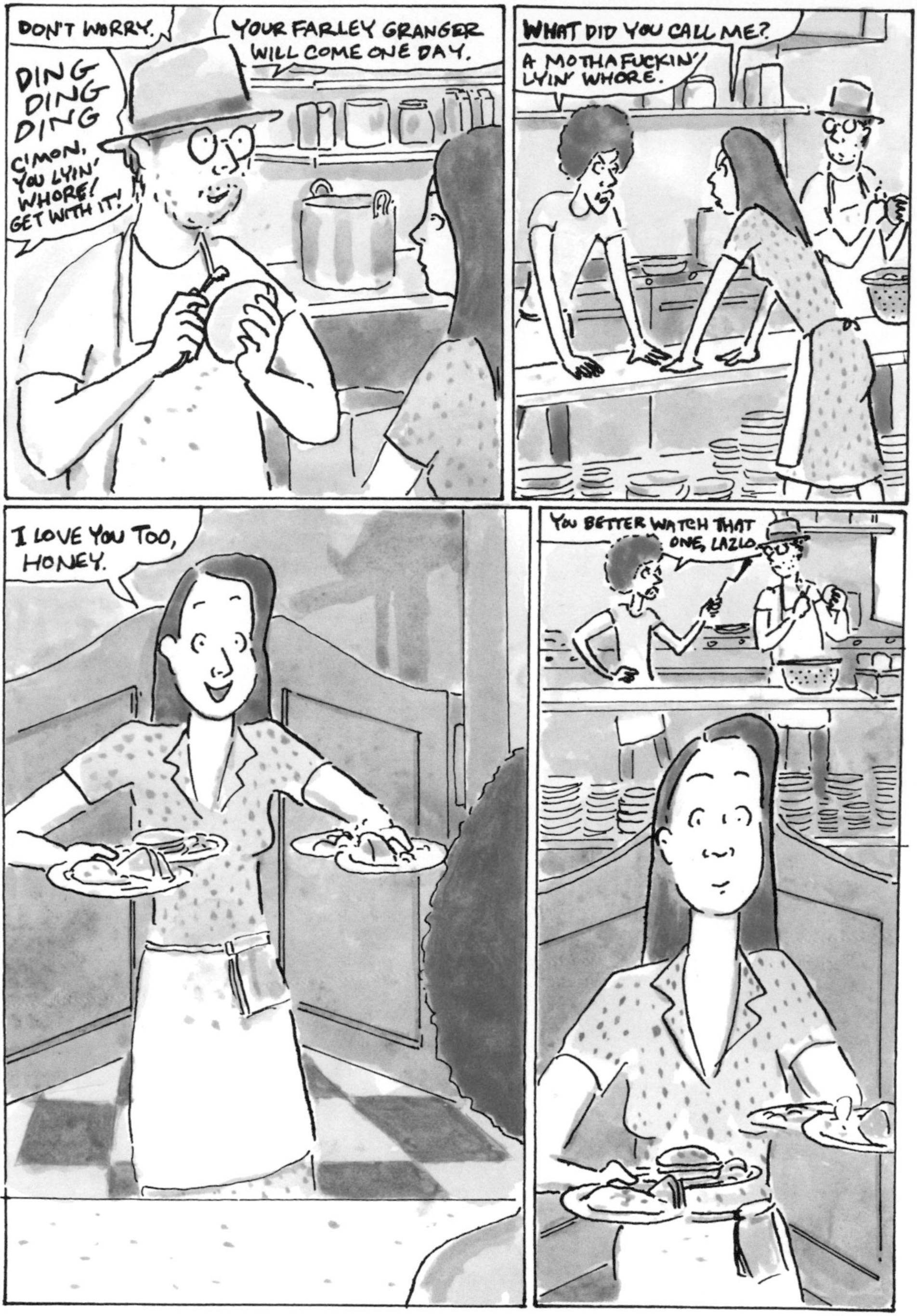
DON'T WORRY.
YOUR FARLEY GRANGER WILL COME ONE DAY.
DING DING DING C'MON, YOU LYIN' WHORE! GET WITH IT!
WHAT DID YOU CALL ME?
A MOTHAFUCKIN' LYIN' WHORE.
I LOVE YOU TOO, HONEY.
YOU BETTER WATCH THAT ONE, LAZLO.

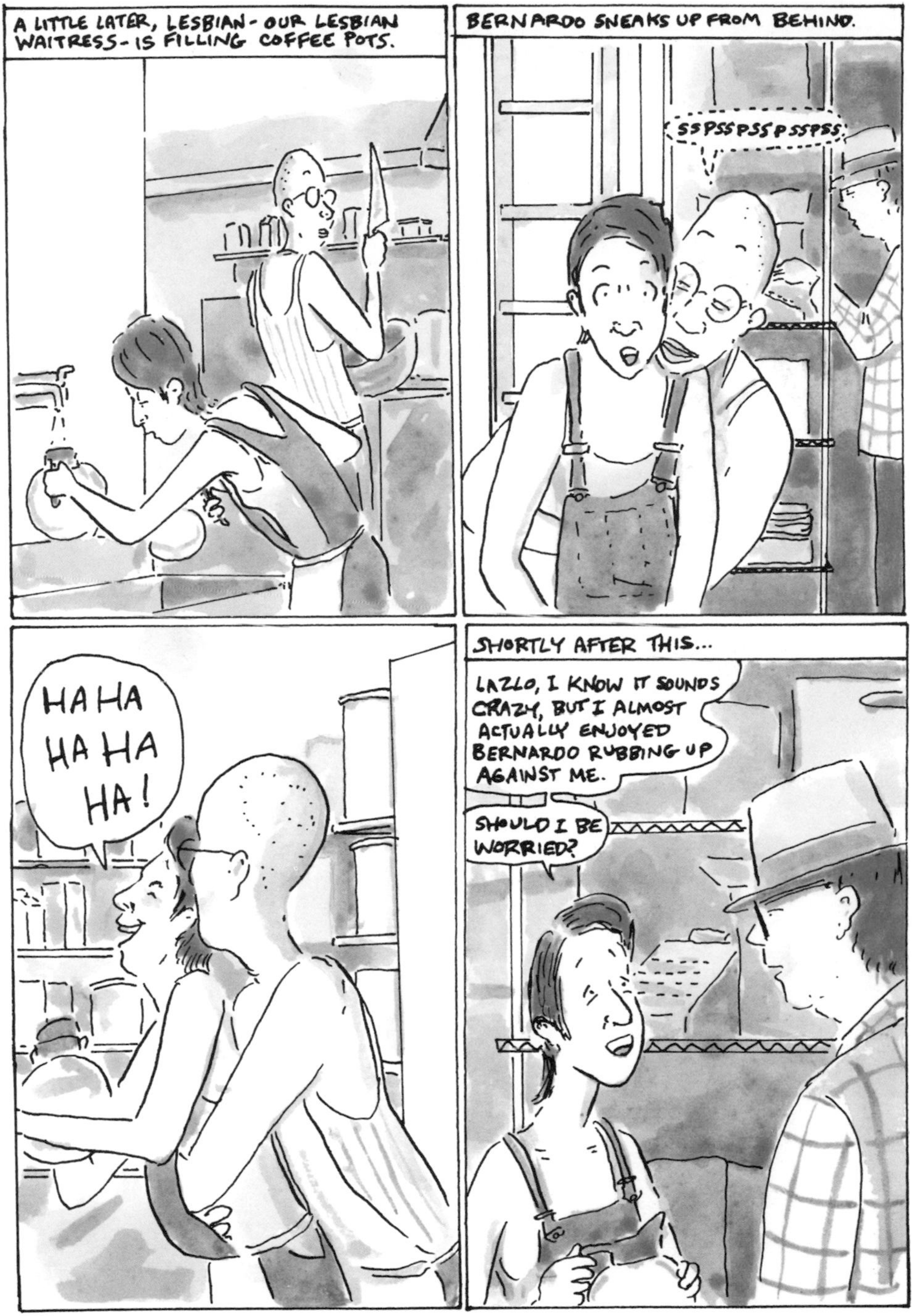
A LITTLE LATER, LESBIAN- OUR LESBIAN WAITRESS- IS FILLING COFFEE POTS.
BERNARDO SNEAKS UP FROM BEHIND.
SSPSSPSSPSSPSS
HA HA HA HA HA!
SHORTLY AFTER THIS...
LAZLO, I KNOW IT SOUNDS CRAZY, BUT I ALMOST ACTUALLY ENJOYED BERNARDO RUBBING UP AGAINST ME.
SHOULD I BE WORRIED?

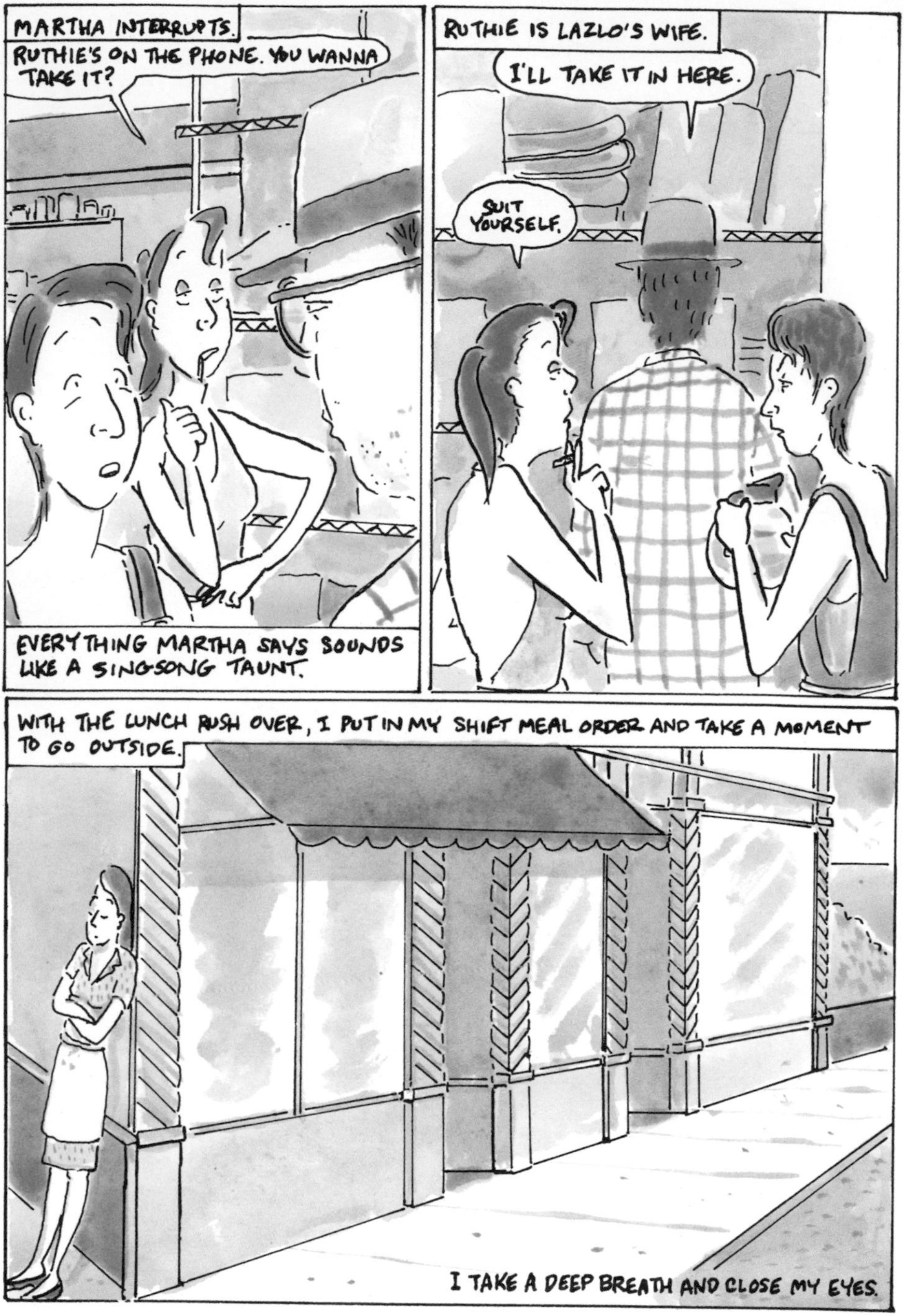
MARTHA INTERRUPTS.
RUTHIE'S ON THE PHONE. YOU WANNA TAKE IT?
EVERYTHING MARTHA SAYS SOUNDS LIKE A SINGSONG TAUNT.
RUTHIE IS LAZLO'S WIFE.
I'LL TAKE IT IN HERE.
SUIT YOURSELF.
WITH THE LUNCH RUSH OVER, I PUT IN MY SHIFT MEAL ORDER AND TAKE A MOMENT TO GO OUTSIDE.
I TAKE A DEEP BREATH AND CLOSE MY EYES.

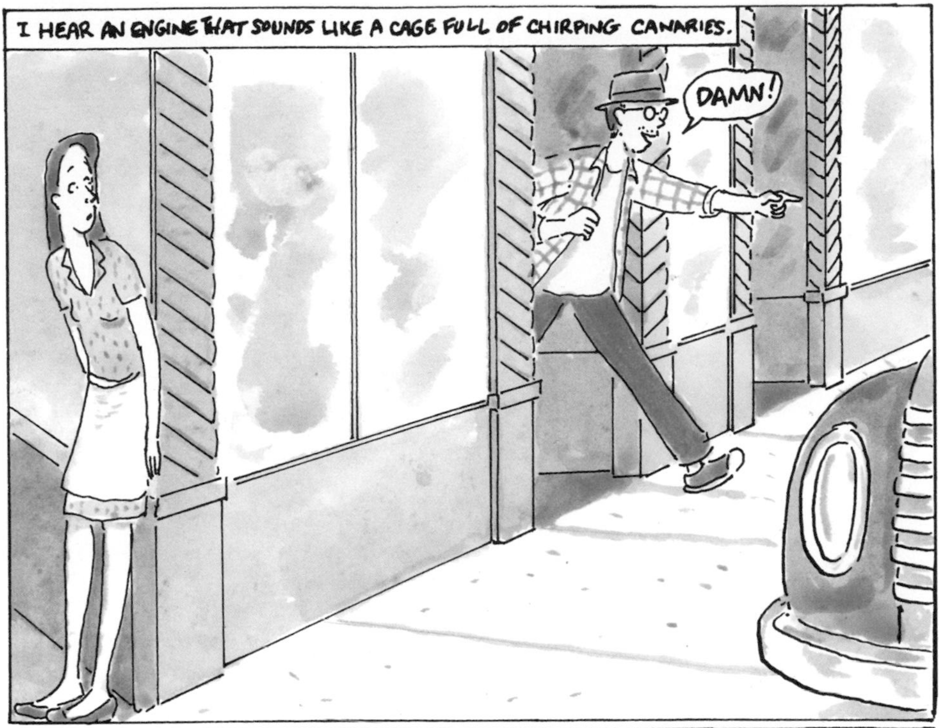
I HEAR AN ENGINE THAT SOUNDS LIKE A CAGE FULL OF CHIRPING CANARIES.
DAMN!

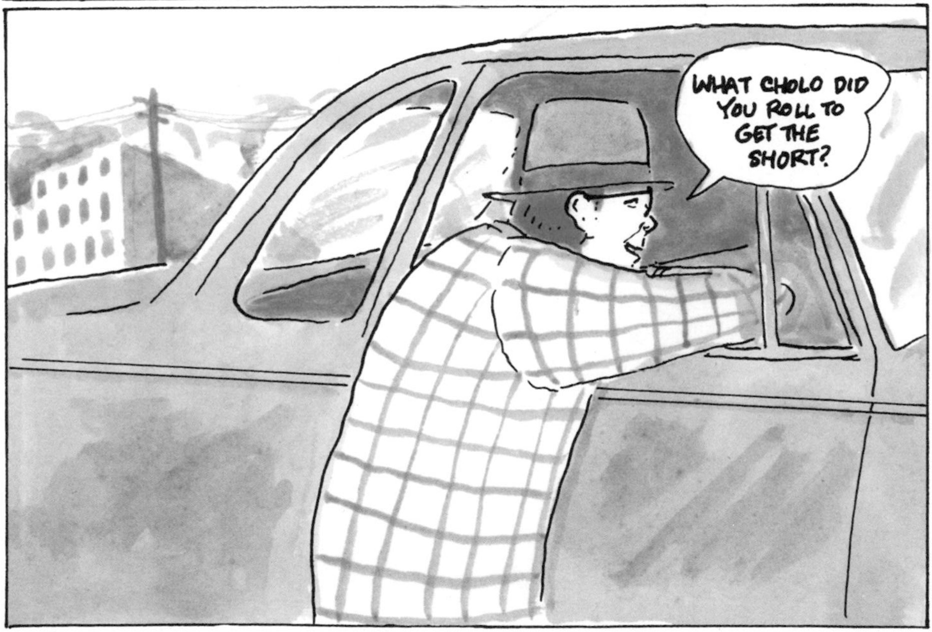
WHAT CHOLO DID YOU ROLL TO GET THE SHORT?

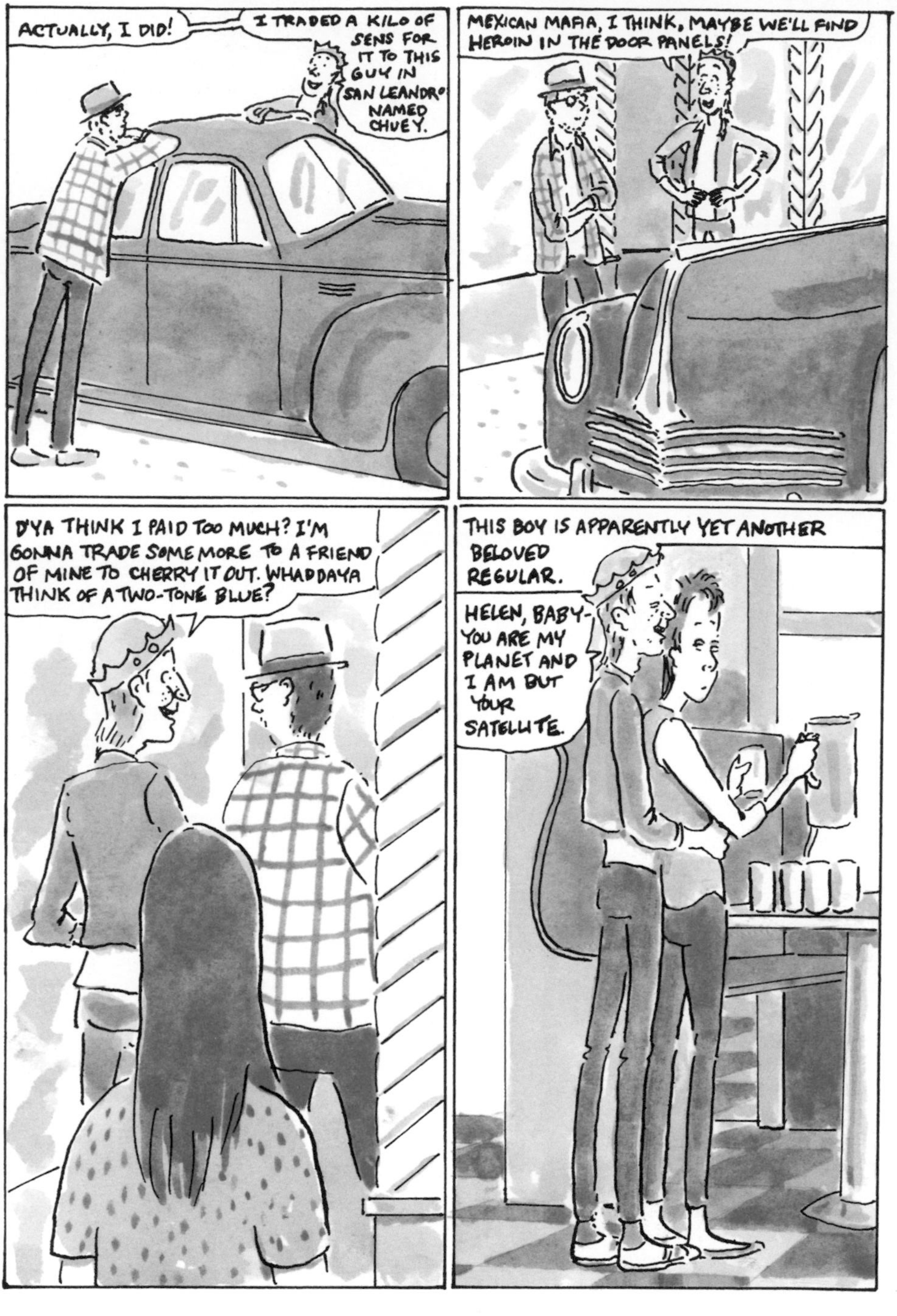
ACTUALLY, I DID!
I TRADED A KILO OF SENS FOR IT TO THIS GUY IN SAN LEANDRO NAMED CHUEY.
MEXICAN MAFIA, I THINK, MAYBE WE'LL FIND HEROIN IN THE DOOR PANELS!
D'YA THINK I PAID TOO MUCH? I'M GONNA TRADE SOME MORE TO A FRIEND OF MINE TO CHERRY IT OUT. WHADDAYA THINK OF A TWO-TONE BLUE?
THIS BOY IS APPARENTLY YET ANOTHER BELOVED REGULAR.
HELEN, BABY-YOU ARE MY PLANET AND I AM BUT YOUR SATELLITE.

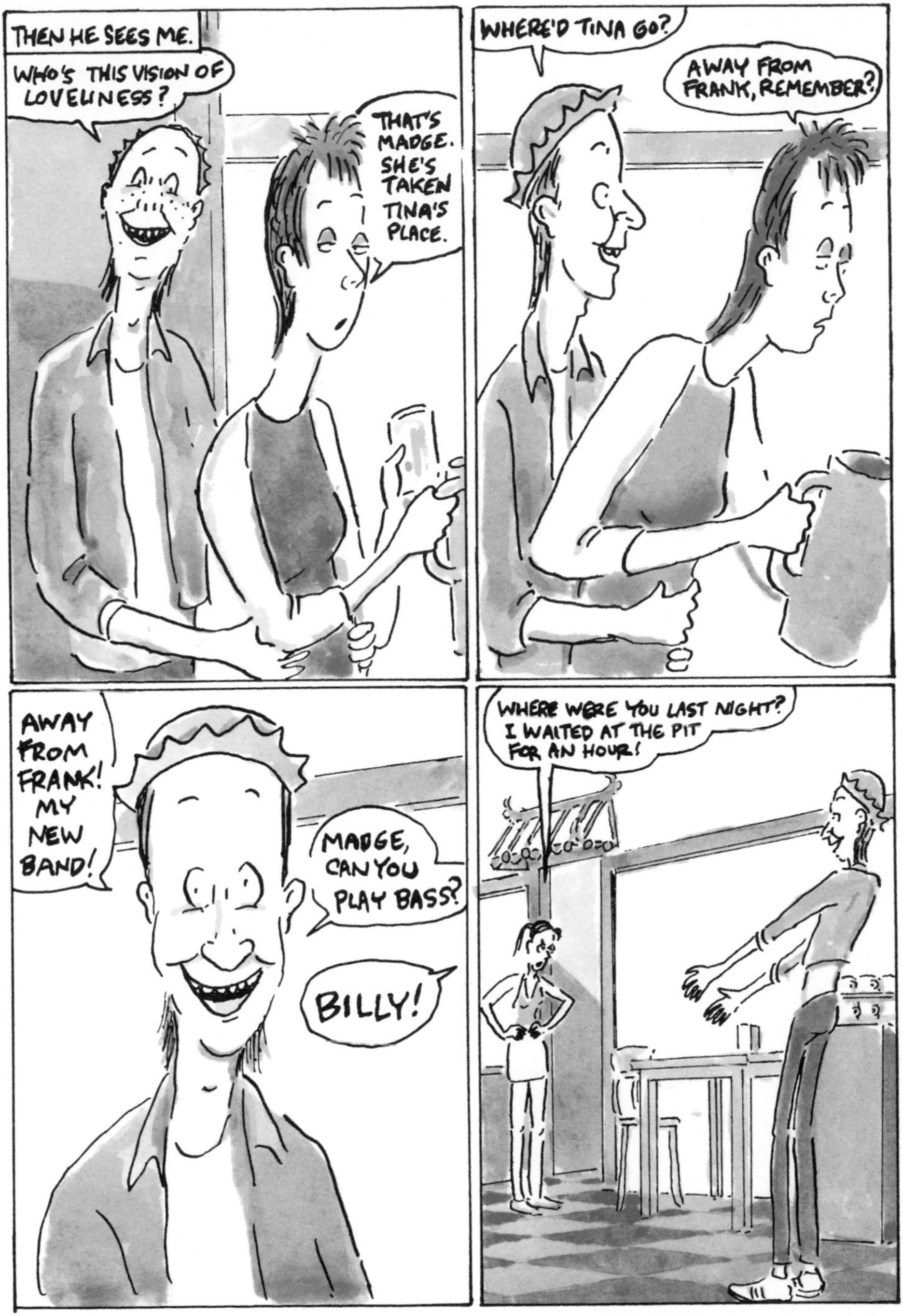
THEN HE SEES ME.
WHO'S THIS VISION OF LOVELINESS?
THAT'S MADGE. SHE'S TAKEN TINA'S PLACE.
WHERE'D TINA GO?
AWAY FROM FRANK, REMEMBER?
AWAY FROM FRANK! MY NEW BAND!
MADGE, CAN YOU PLAY BASS?
BILLY!
WHERE WERE YOU LAST NIGHT? I WAITED AT THE PIT FOR AN HOUR!

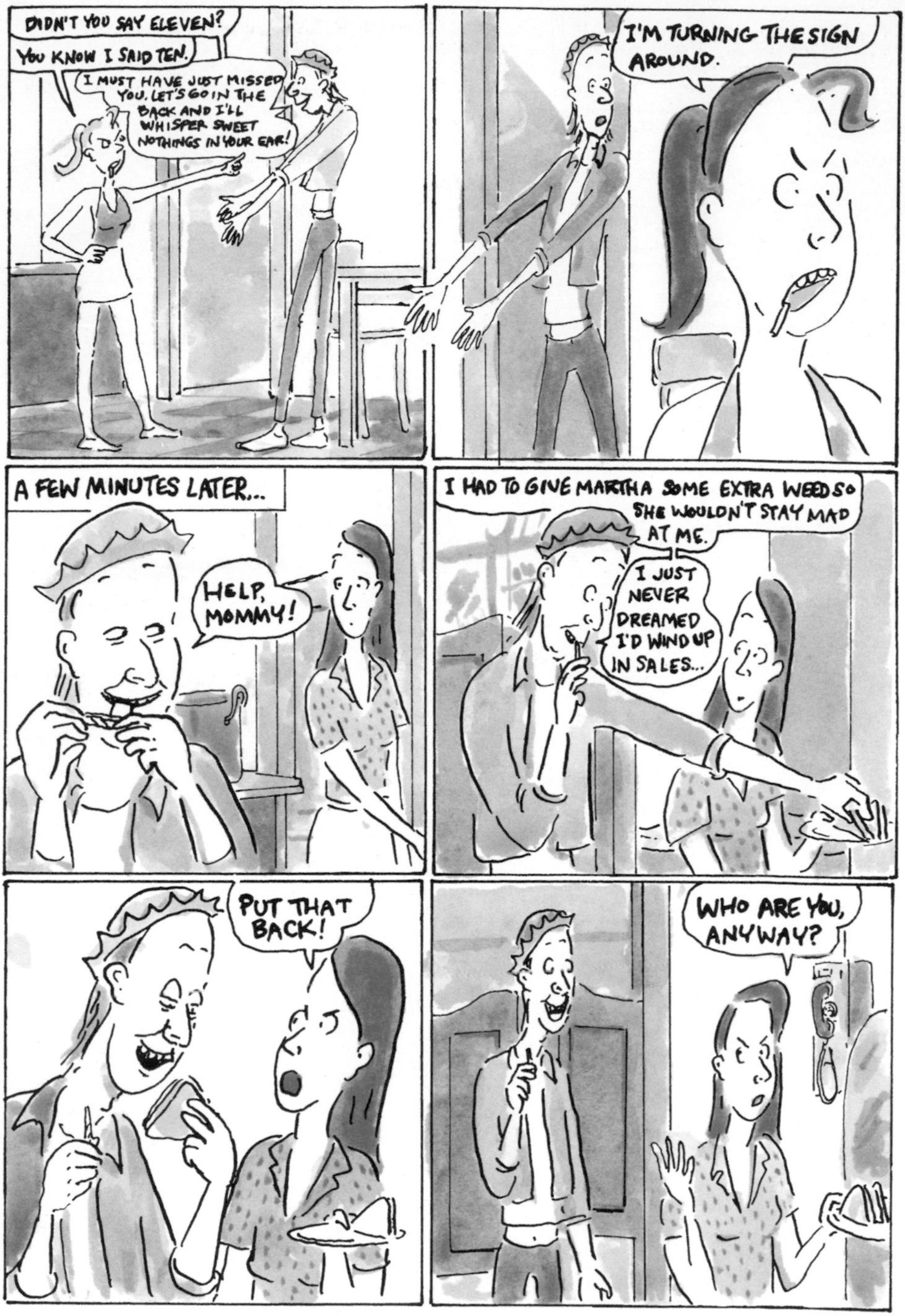

DIDN'T YOU SAY ELEVEN?
YOU KNOW I SAID TEN.
I MUST HAVE JUST MISSED YOU. LET'S GO IN THE BACK AND I'LL WHISPER SWEET NOTHINGS IN YOUR EAR!
I'M TURNING THE SIGN AROUND.
A FEW MINUTES LATER...
HELP, MOMMY!
I HAD TO GIVE MARTHA SOME EXTRA WEED SO SHE WOULDN'T STAY MAD AT ME.
I JUST NEVER DREAMED I'D WIND UP IN SALES...
PUT THAT BACK!
WHO ARE YOU, ANYWAY?

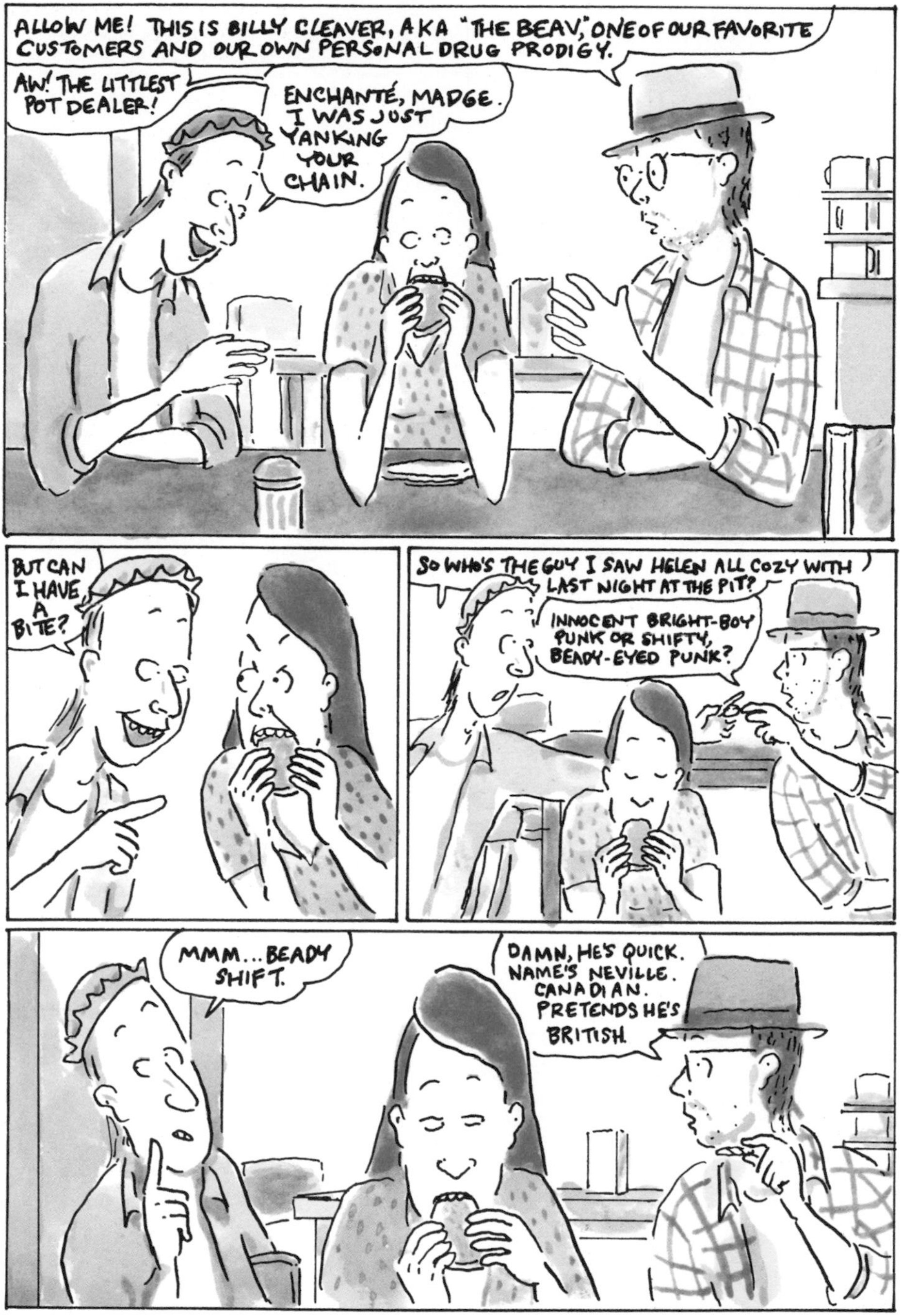
ALLOW ME! THIS IS BILLY CLEAVER, AKA "THE BEAV," ONE OF OUR FAVORITE CUSTOMERS AND OUR OWN PERSONAL DRUG PRODIGY.
AW! THE LITTLEST POT DEALER!
ENCHANTÉ, MADGE. I WAS JUST YANKING YOUR CHAIN.
BUT CAN I HAVE A BITE?
SO WHO'S THE GUY I SAW HELEN ALL COZY WITH LAST NIGHT AT THE PIT?
INNOCENT BRIGHT-BOY PUNK OR SHIFTY, BEADY-EYED PUNK?
MMM... BEADY SHIFT.
DAMN, HE'S QUICK. NAME'S NEVILLE. CANADIAN. PRETENDS HE'S BRITISH.

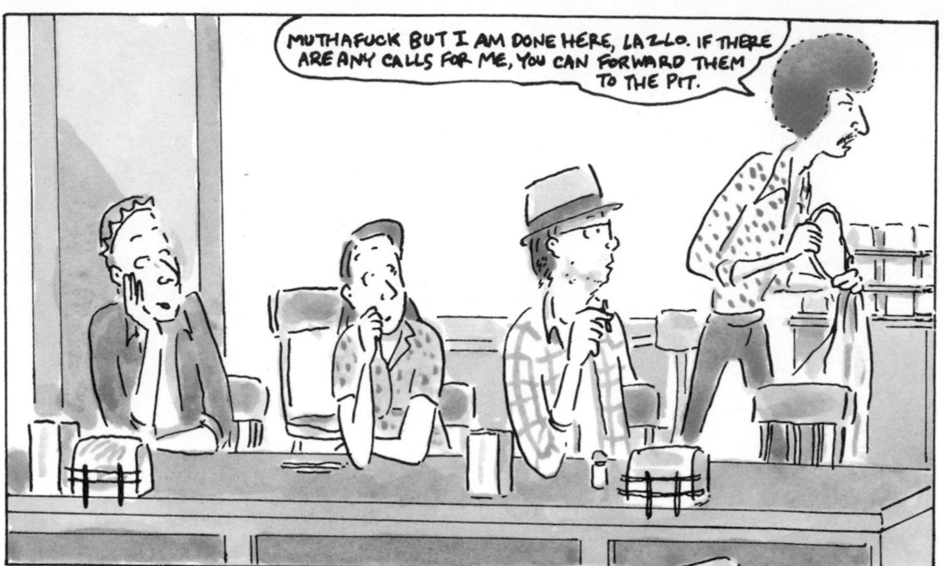
MUTHAFUCK BUT I AM DONE HERE, LAZLO. IF THERE ARE ANY CALLS FOR ME, YOU CAN FORWARD THEM TO THE PIT.

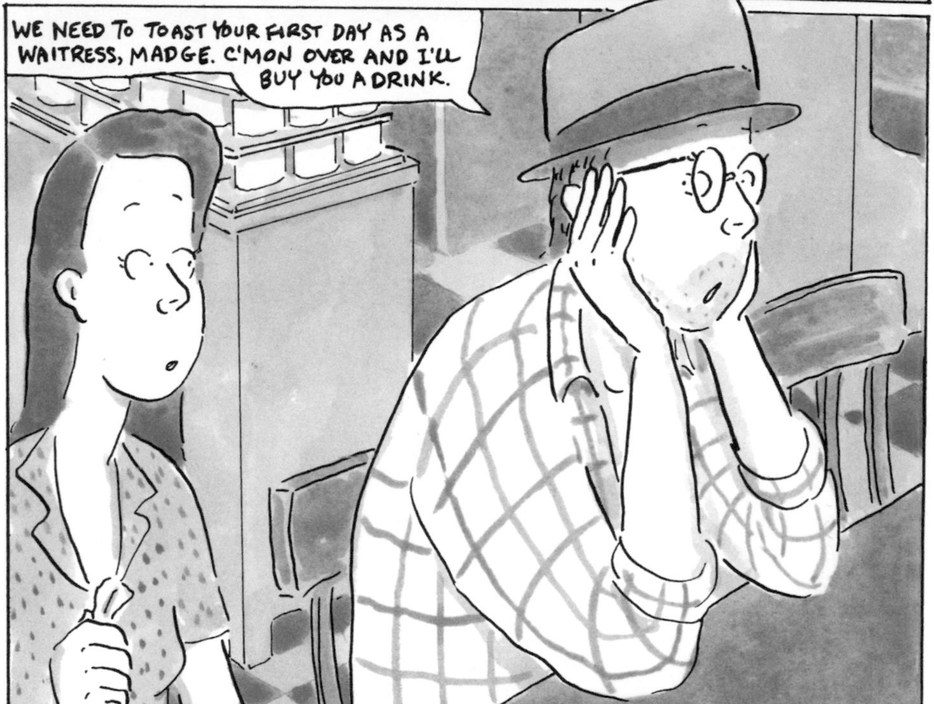
WE NEED TO TOAST YOUR FIRST DAY AS A WAITRESS, MADGE. C'MON OVER AND I'LL BUY YOU A DRINK.

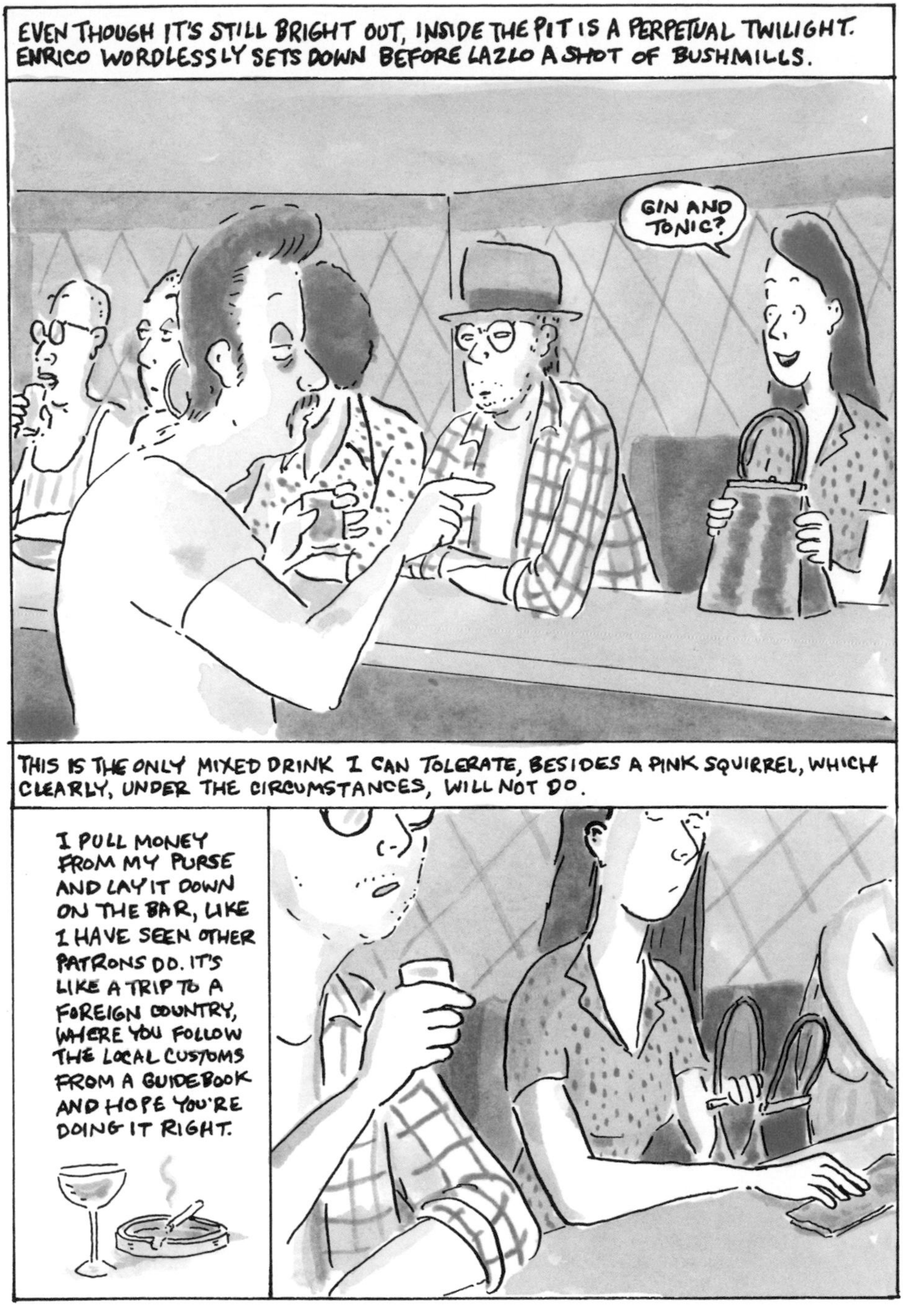
EVEN THOUGH IT'S STILL BRIGHT OUT, INSIDE THE PIT IS A PERPETUAL TWILIGHT. ENRICO WORDLESSLY SETS DOWN BEFORE LAZLO A SHOT OF BUSHMILLS.
GIN AND TONIC?
THIS IS THE ONLY MIXED DRINK I CAN TOLERATE, BESIDES A PINK SQUIRREL, WHICH CLEARLY, UNDER THE CIRCUMSTANCES, WILL NOT DO.
I PULL MONEY FROM MY PURSE AND LAY IT DOWN ON THE BAR, LIKE I HAVE SEEN OTHER PATRONS DO. IT'S LIKE A TRIP TO A FOREIGN COUNTRY, WHERE YOU FOLLOW THE LOCAL CUSTOMS FROM A GUIDEBOOK AND HOPE YOU'RE DOING IT RIGHT.

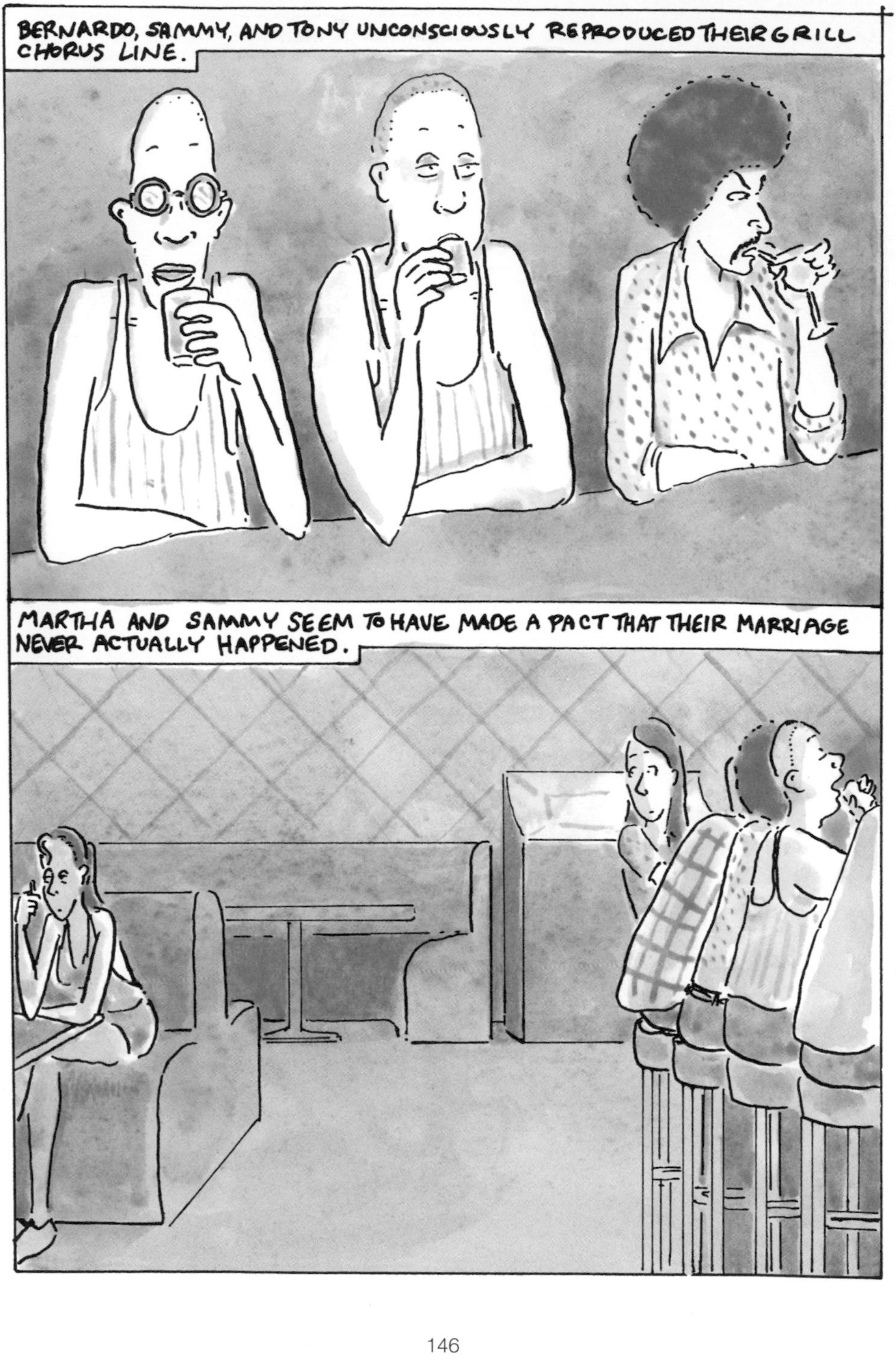
BERNARDO, SAMMY, AND TONY UNCONSCIOUSLY REPRODUCED THEIR GRILL CHORUS LINE.
MARTHA AND SAMMY SEEM TO HAVE MADE A PACT THAT THEIR MARRIAGE NEVER ACTUALLY HAPPENED.

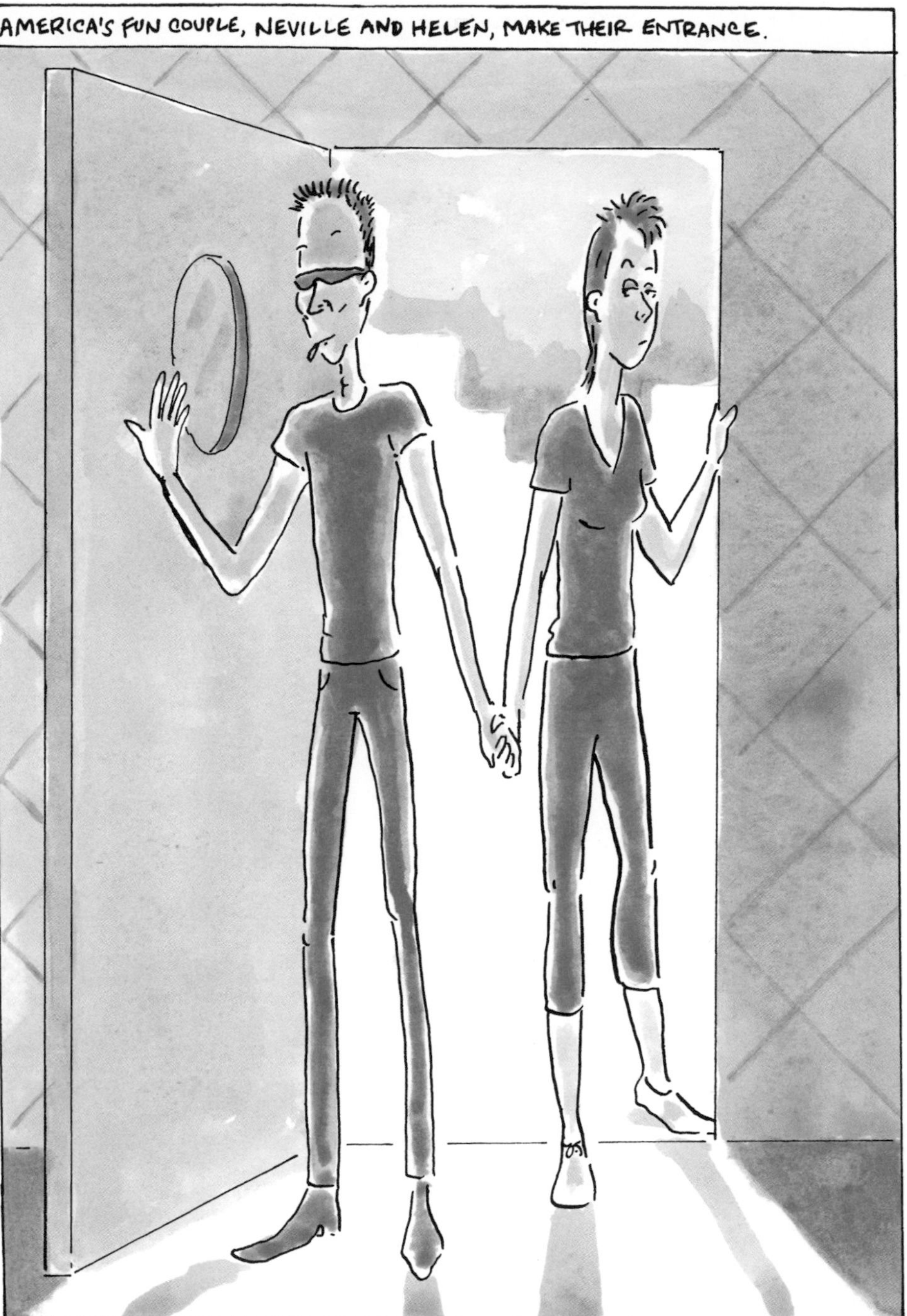
AMERICA'S FUN COUPLE, NEVILLE AND HELEN, MAKE THEIR ENTRANCE.

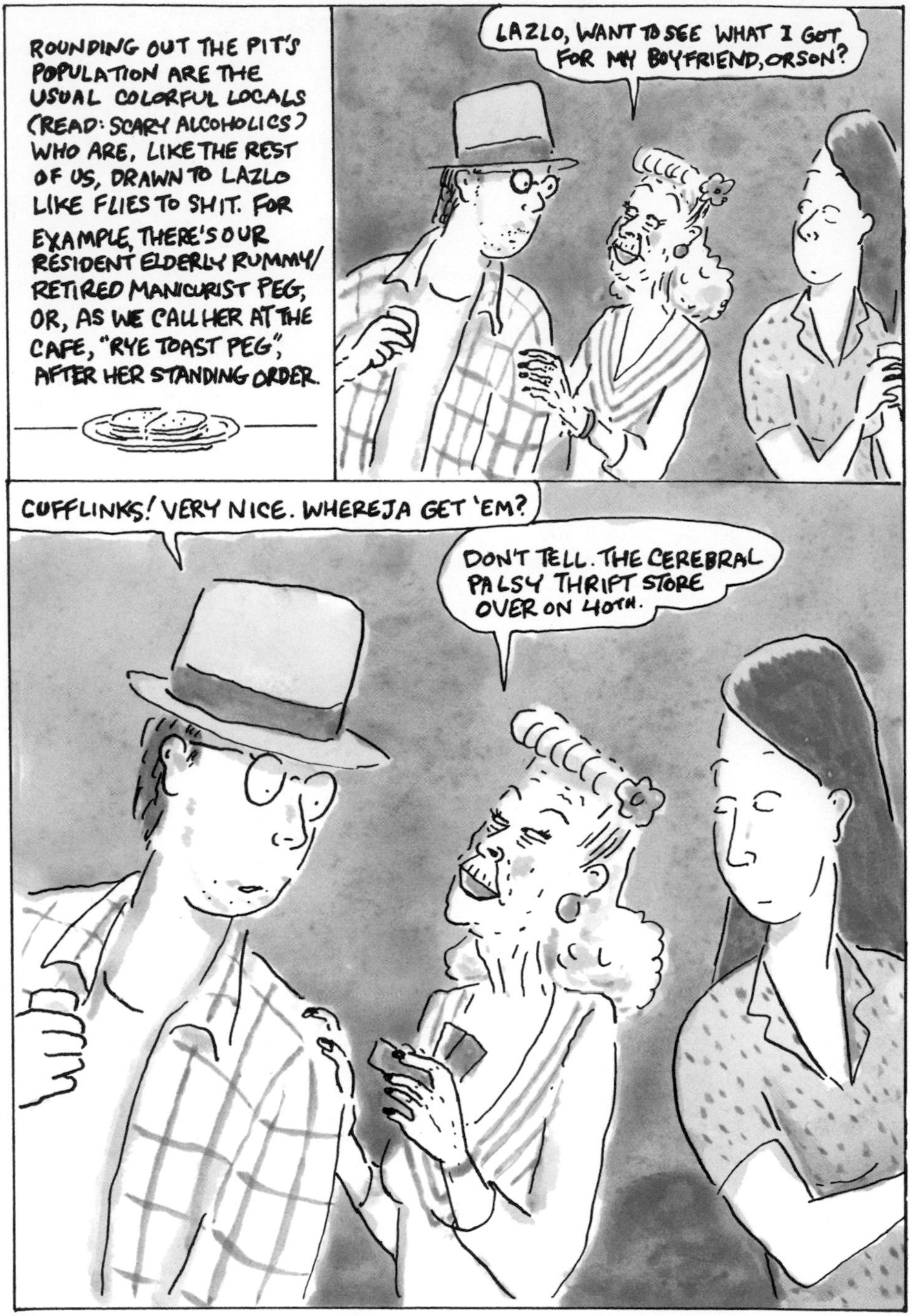
ROUNDING OUT THE PIT'S POPULATION ARE THE USUAL COLORFUL LOCALS (READ: SCARY ALCOHOLICS) WHO ARE, LIKE THE REST OF US, DRAWN TO LAZLO LIKE FLIES TO SHIT. FOR EXAMPLE, THERE'S OUR RESIDENT ELDERLY RUMMY/ RETIRED MANICURIST PEG, OR, AS WE CALL HER AT THE CAFE, "RYE TOAST PEG", AFTER HER STANDING ORDER.
LAZLO, WANT TO SEE WHAT I GOT FOR MY BOYFRIEND, ORSON?
CUFFLINKS! VERY NICE. WHEREJA GET 'EM?
DON'T TELL. THE CEREBRAL PALSY THRIFT STORE OVER ON 40TH.

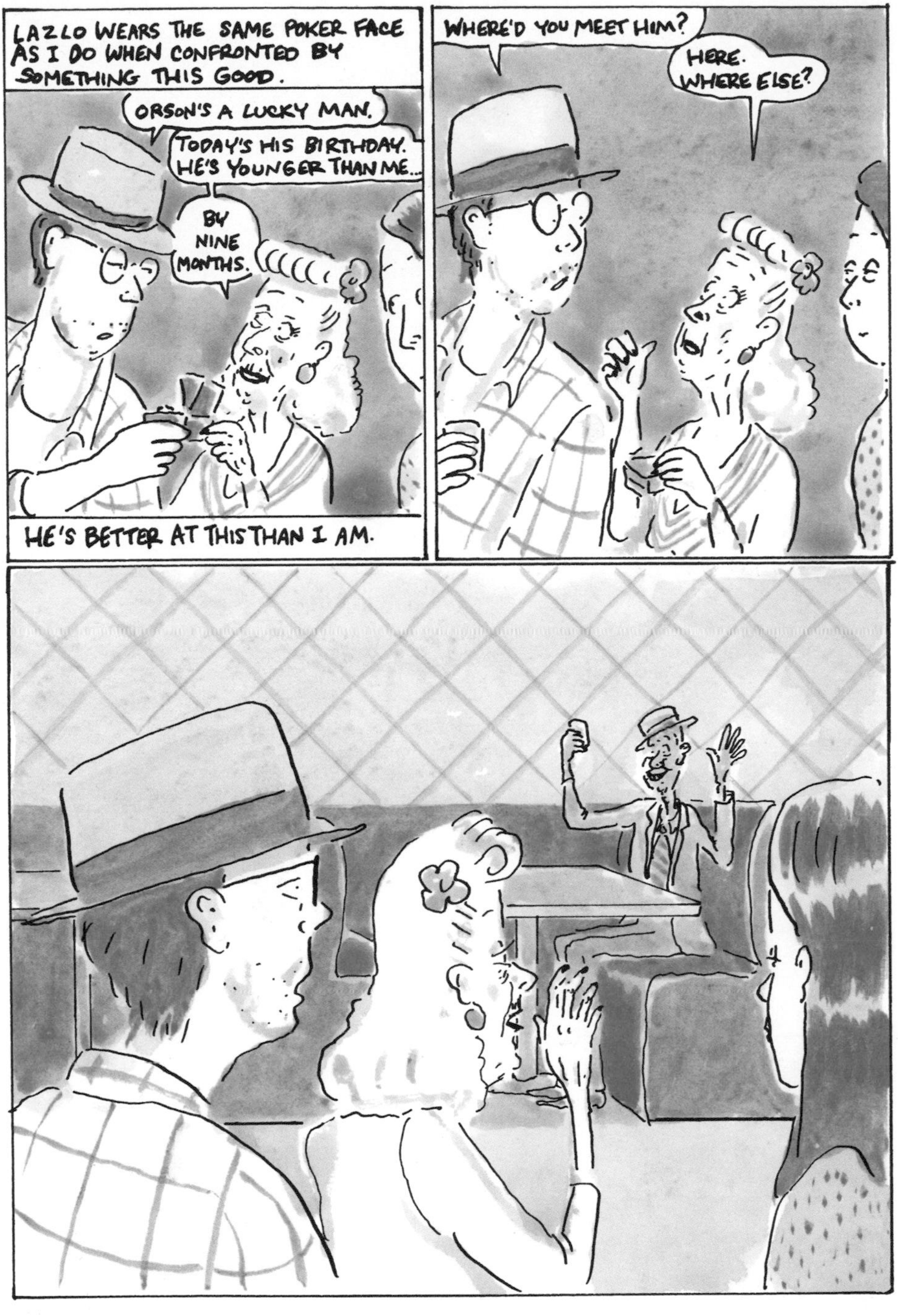
LAZLO WEARS THE SAME POKER FACE AS I DO WHEN CONFRONTED BY SOMETHING THIS GOOD.
ORSON'S A LUCKY MAN.
TODAY'S HIS BIRTHDAY. HE'S YOUNGER THAN ME...
BY NINE MONTHS.
HE'S BETTER AT THIS THAN I AM.
WHERE'D YOU MEET HIM?
HERE. WHERE ELSE?

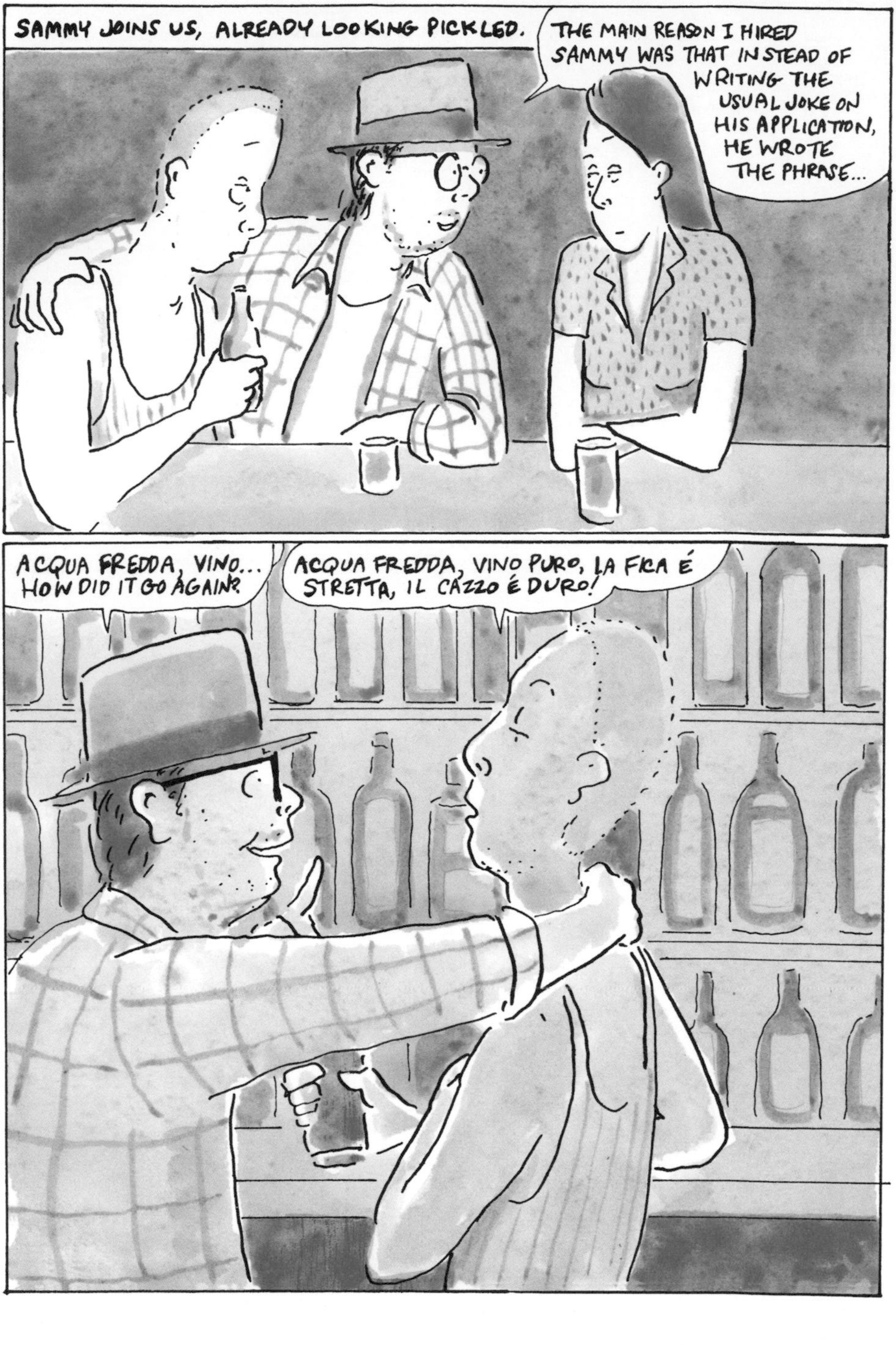
SAMMY JOINS US, ALREADY LOOKING PICKLED.
THE MAIN REASON I HIRED SAMMY WAS THAT INSTEAD OF WRITING THE USUAL JOKE ON HIS APPLICATION, HE WROTE THE PHRASE...
ACQUA FREDDA, VINO... HOW DID IT GO AGAIN?
ACQUA FREDDA, VINO PURO, LA FICA É STRETTA, IL CAZZO É DURO!

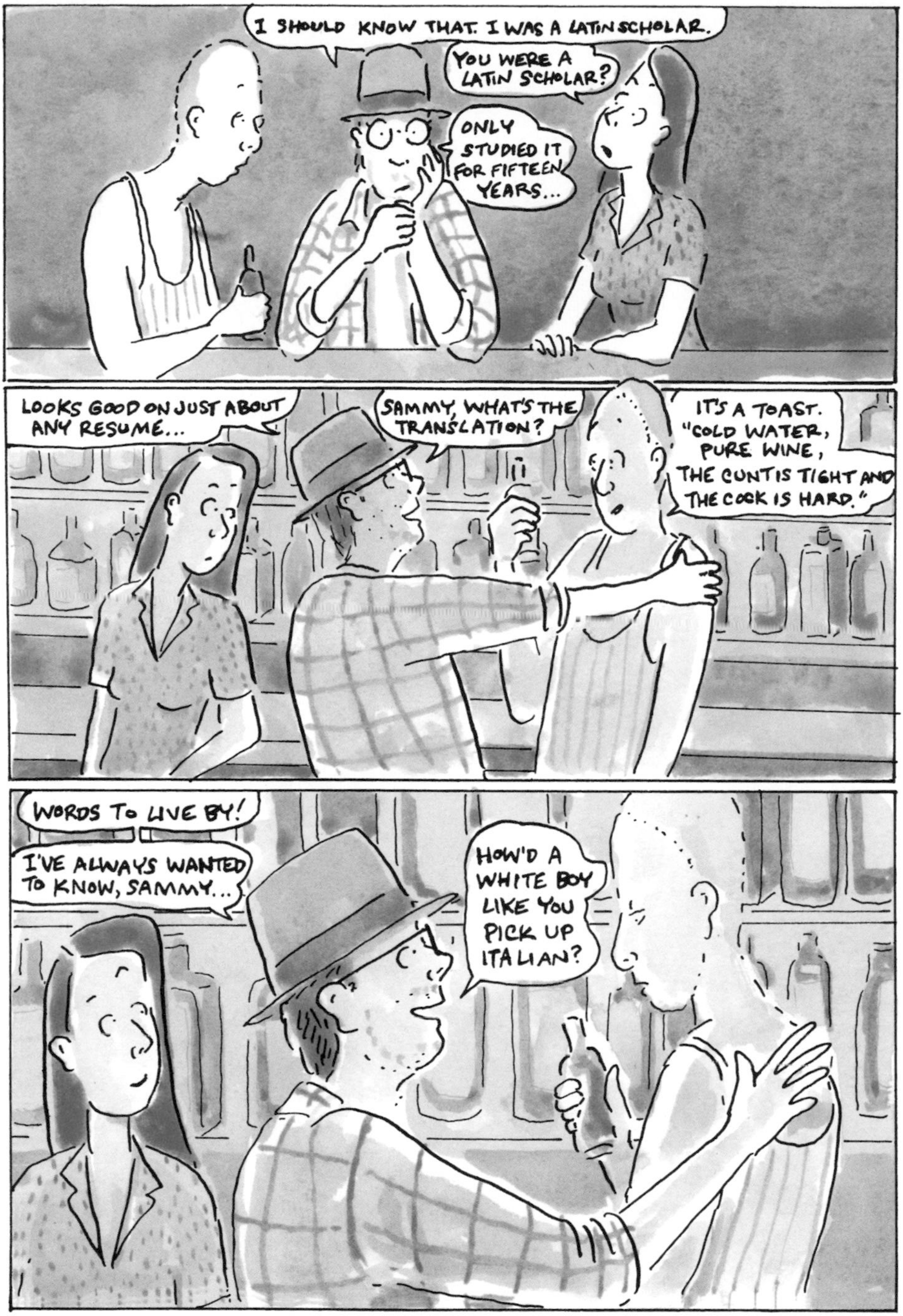
I SHOULD KNOW THAT. I WAS A LATIN SCHOLAR.
YOU WERE A LATIN SCHOLAR?
ONLY STUDIED IT FOR FIFTEEN YEARS...
LOOKS GOOD ON JUST ABOUT ANY RESUME...
SAMMY, WHAT'S THE TRANSLATION?
IT'S A TOAST. "COLD WATER, PURE WINE, THE CUNT IS TIGHT AND THE COCK IS HARD."
WORDS TO LIVE BY!
I'VE ALWAYS WANTED TO KNOW, SAMMY...
HOW'D A WHITE BOY LIKE YOU PICK UP ITALIAN?

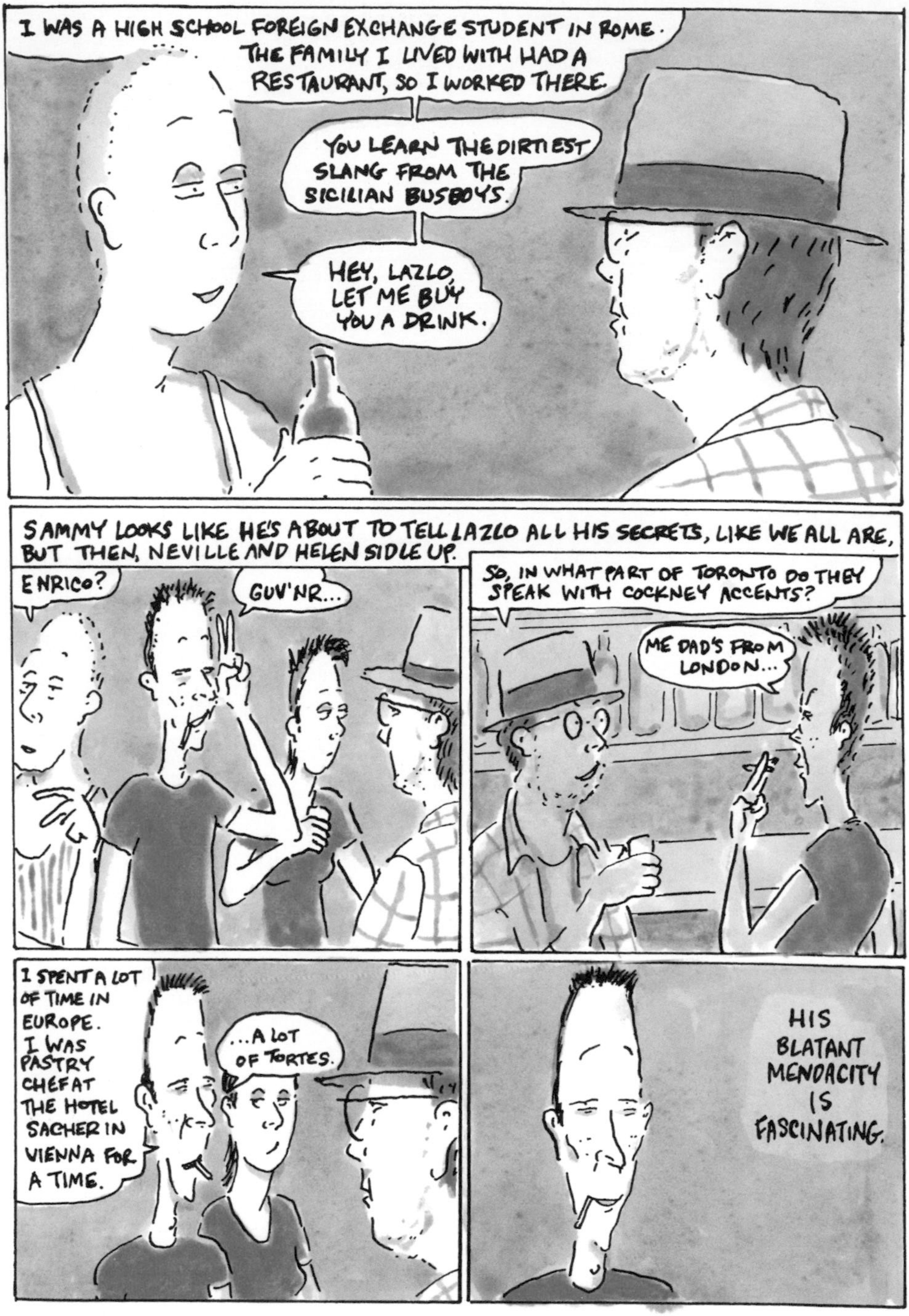
I WAS A HIGH SCHOOL FOREIGN EXCHANGE STUDENT IN ROME.
THE FAMILY I LIVED WITH HAD A RESTAURANT, SO I WORKED THERE.
YOU LEARN THE DIRTIEST SLANG FROM THE SICILIAN BUSBOYS.
HEY, LAZLO, LET ME BUY YOU A DRINK.
SAMMY LOOKS LIKE HE'S ABOUT TO TELL LAZLO ALL HIS SECRETS, LIKE WE ALL ARE, BUT THEN, NEVILLE AND HELEN SIDLE UP.
ENRICO?
GUV'NR...
SO, IN WHAT PART OF TORONTO DO THEY SPEAK WITH COCKNEY ACCENTS?
ME DAD'S FROM LONDON...
I SPENT A LOT OF TIME IN EUROPE. I WAS PASTRY CHEF AT THE HOTEL SACHER IN VIENNA FOR A TIME.
...A LOT OF TORTES.
HIS BLATANT MENDACITY IS FASCINATING.

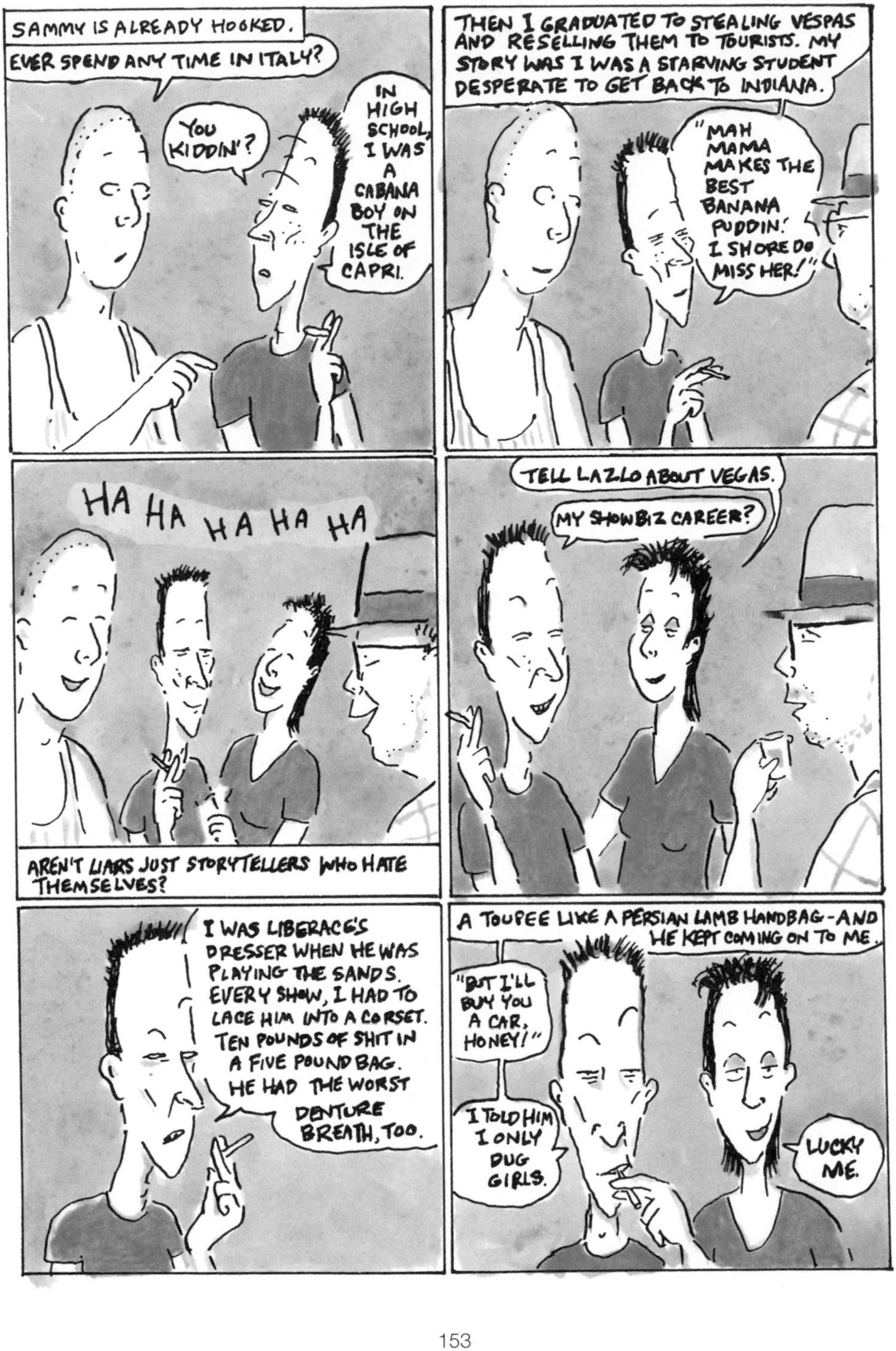
SAMMY IS ALREADY HOOKED.
EVER SPEND ANY TIME IN ITALY?
YOU KIDDIN'?
IN HIGH SCHOOL, I WAS A CABANA BOY ON THE ISLE OF CAPRI.
THEN I GRADUATED TO STEALING VESPAS AND RESELLING THEM TO TOURISTS. MY STORY WAS I WAS A STARVING STUDENT DESPERATE TO GET BACK TO INDIANA.
"MAH MAMA MAKES THE BEST BANANA PUDDIN'. I SHORE DO MISS HER!"
HA HA HA HA HA
AREN'T LIARS JUST STORYTELLERS WHO HATE THEMSELVES?
TELL LAZLO ABOUT VEGAS.
MY SHOWBIZ CAREER?
I WAS LIBERACE'S DRESSER WHEN HE WAS PLAYING THE SANDS. EVERY SHOW, I HAD TO LACE HIM INTO A CORSET. TEN POUNDS OF SHIT IN A FIVE POUND BAG. HE HAD THE WORST DENTURE BREATH, TOO.
A TOUPEE LIKE A PERSIAN LAMB HANDBAG - AND HE KEPT COMING ON TO ME.
"BUT I'LL BUY YOU A CAR, HONEY!"
I TOLD HIM I ONLY DUG GIRLS.
LUCKY ME.

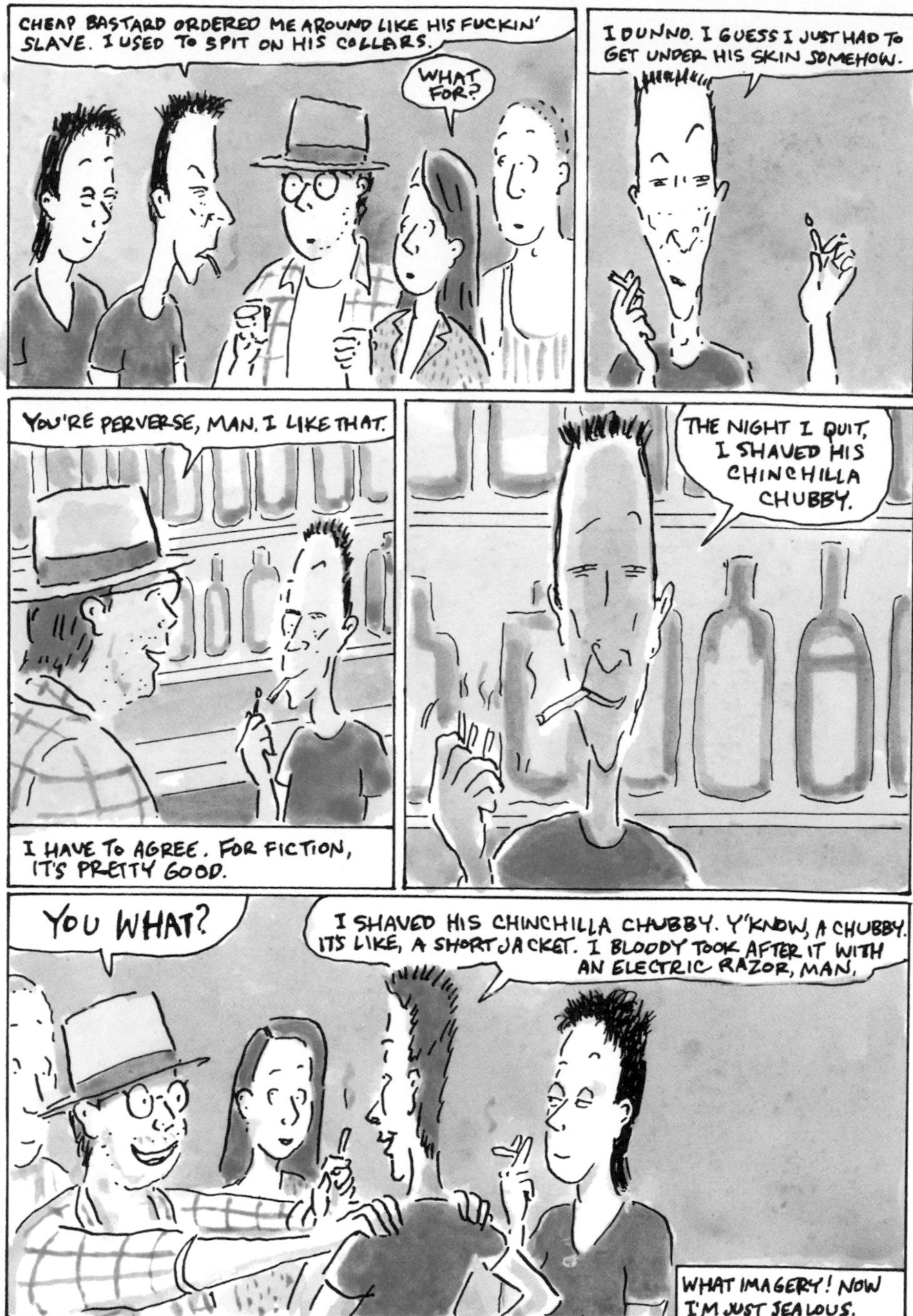
CHEAP BASTARD ORDERED ME AROUND LIKE HIS FUCKIN' SLAVE. I USED TO SPIT ON HIS COLLARS.
WHAT FOR?
I DUNNO. I GUESS I JUST HAD TO GET UNDER HIS SKIN SOMEHOW.
YOU'RE PERVERSE, MAN. I LIKE THAT.
I HAVE TO AGREE. FOR FICTION, IT'S PRETTY GOOD.
THE NIGHT I QUIT, I SHAVED HIS CHINCHILLA CHUBBY.
YOU WHAT?
I SHAVED HIS CHINCHILLA CHUBBY. Y'KNOW, A CHUBBY. IT'S LIKE, A SHORT JACKET. I BLOODY TOOK AFTER IT WITH AN ELECTRIC RAZOR, MAN.
WHAT IMAGERY! NOW I'M JUST JEALOUS.

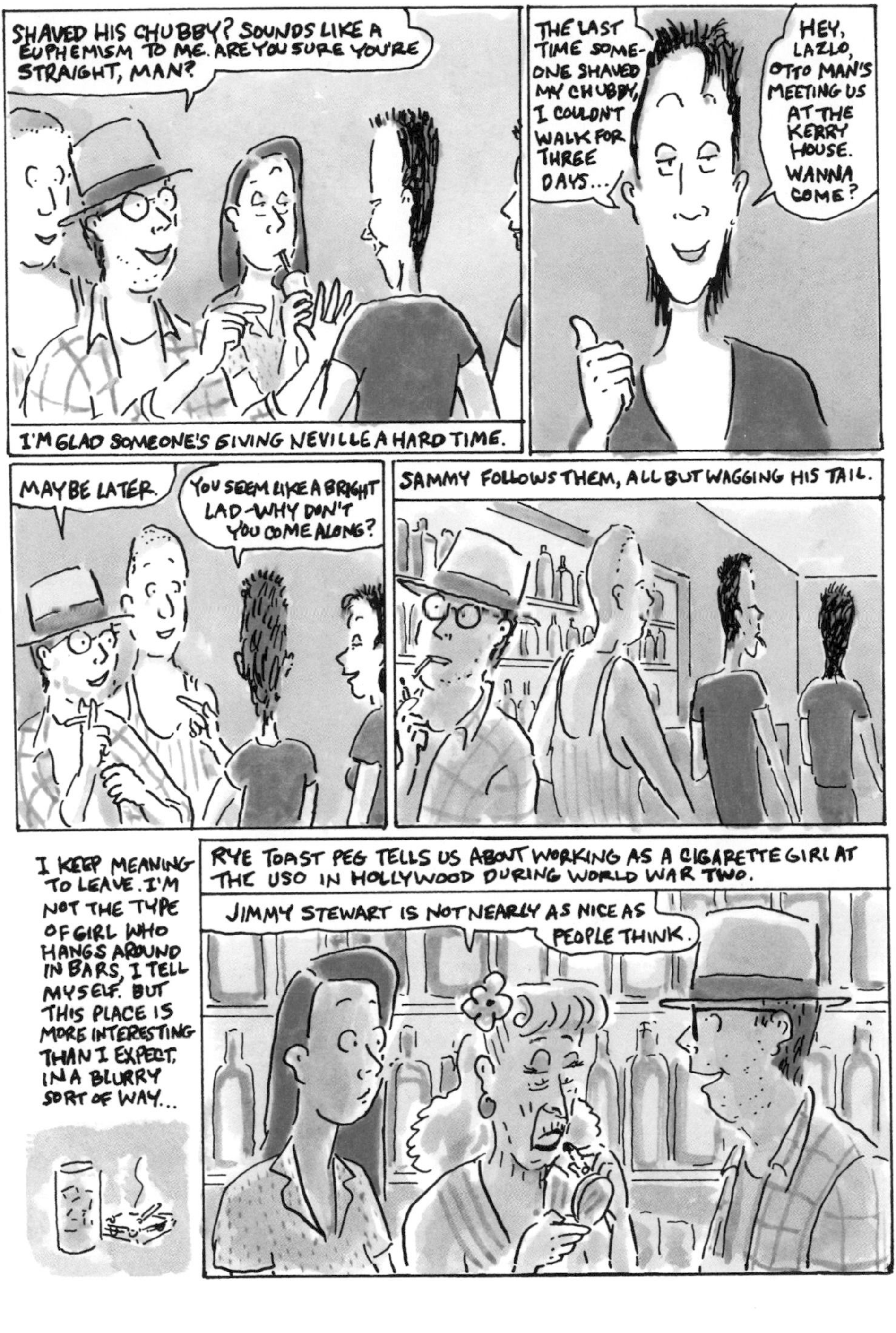
SHAVED HIS CHUBBY? SOUNDS LIKE A EUPHEMISM TO ME. ARE YOU SURE YOU'RE STRAIGHT, MAN?
I'M GLAD SOMEONE'S GIVING NEVILLE A HARD TIME.
THE LAST TIME SOMEONE SHAVED MY CHUBBY, I COULDN'T WALK FOR THREE DAYS...
HEY, LAZLO, OTTO MAN'S MEETING US AT THE KERRY HOUSE. WANNA COME?
MAYBE LATER.
YOU SEEM LIKE A BRIGHT LAD—WHY DON'T YOU COME ALONG?
SAMMY FOLLOWS THEM, ALL BUT WAGGING HIS TAIL.
I KEEP MEANING TO LEAVE. I'M NOT THE TYPE OF GIRL WHO HANGS AROUND IN BARS, I TELL MYSELF. BUT THIS PLACE IS MORE INTERESTING THAN I EXPECT, IN A BLURRY SORT OF WAY...
RYE TOAST PEG TELLS US ABOUT WORKING AS A CIGARETTE GIRL AT THE USO IN HOLLYWOOD DURING WORLD WAR TWO.
JIMMY STEWART IS NOT NEARLY AS NICE AS PEOPLE THINK.

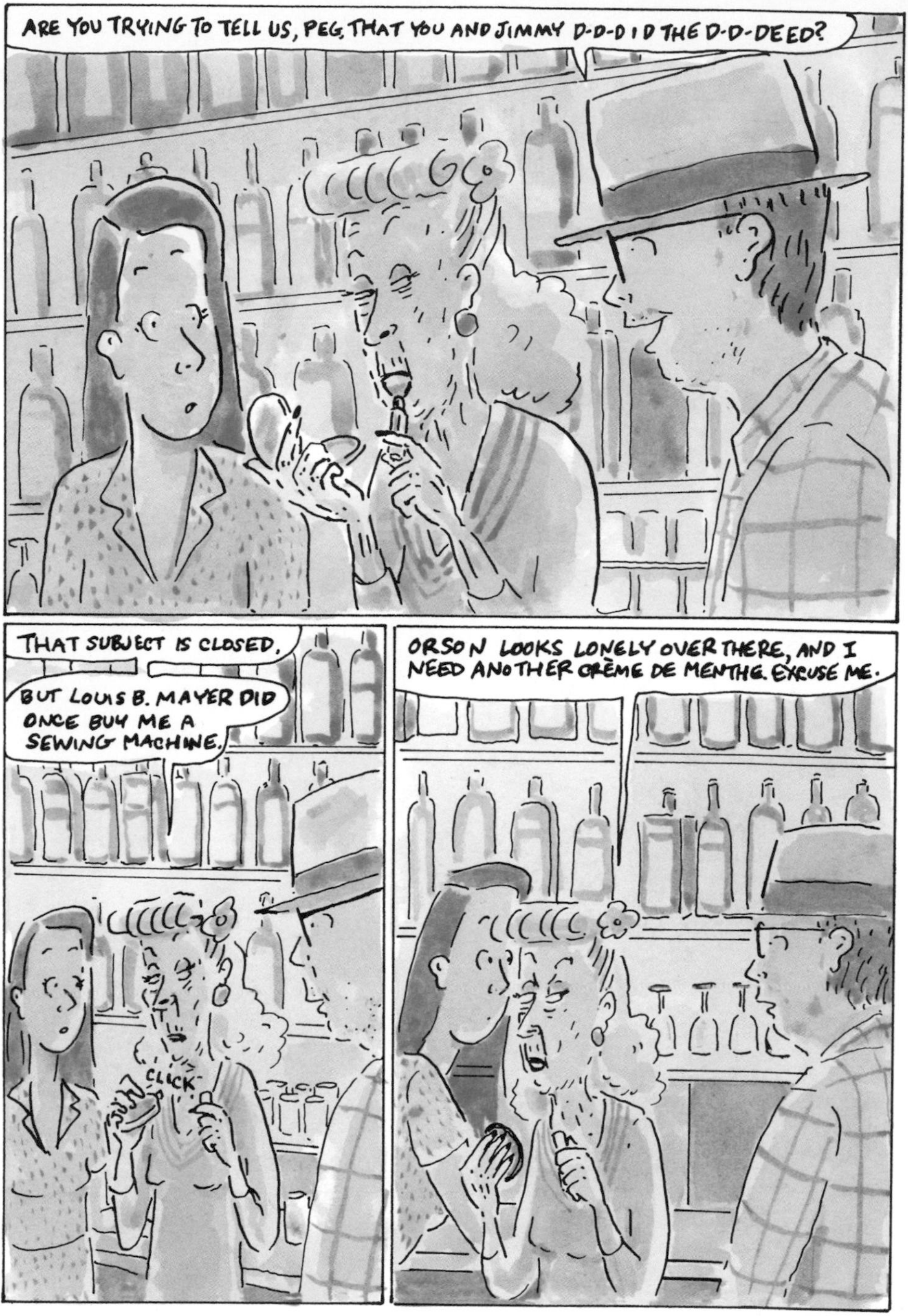
ARE YOU TRYING TO TELL US, PEG, THAT YOU AND JIMMY D-D-DID THE D-D-DEED?
THAT SUBJECT IS CLOSED.
BUT LOUIS B. MAYER DID ONCE BUY ME A SEWING MACHINE.
CLICK
ORSON LOOKS LONELY OVER THERE, AND I NEED ANOTHER CRÈME DE MENTHE. EXCUSE ME.

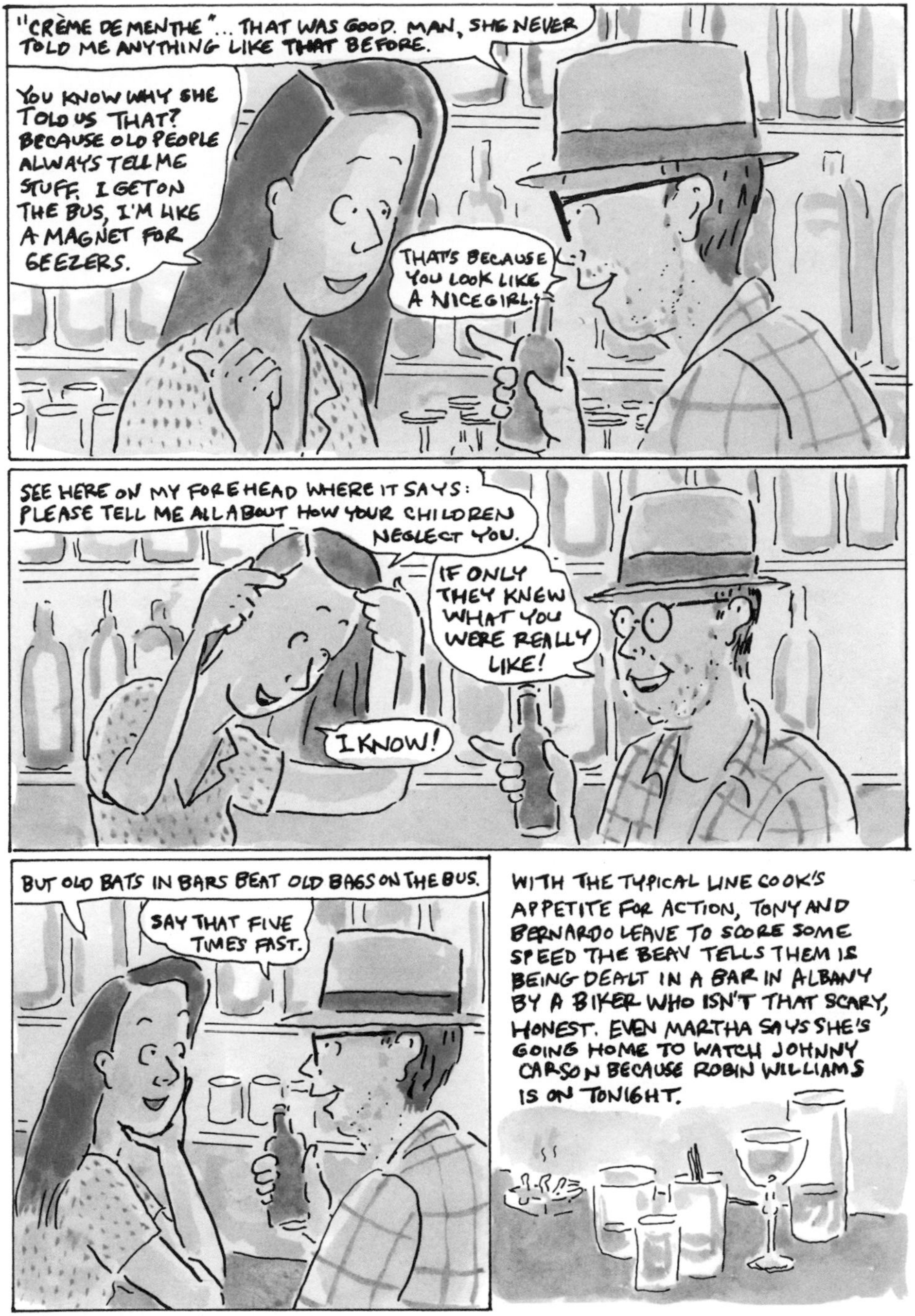
"CRÈME DE MENTHE"... THAT WAS GOOD. MAN, SHE NEVER TOLD ME ANYTHING LIKE THAT BEFORE.
YOU KNOW WHY SHE TOLD US THAT? BECAUSE OLD PEOPLE ALWAYS TELL ME STUFF. I GET ON THE BUS, I'M LIKE A MAGNET FOR GEEZERS.
THAT'S BECAUSE YOU LOOK LIKE A NICE GIRL.
SEE HERE ON MY FOREHEAD WHERE IT SAYS: PLEASE TELL ME ALL ABOUT HOW YOUR CHILDREN NEGLECT YOU.
IF ONLY THEY KNEW WHAT YOU WERE REALLY LIKE!
I KNOW!
BUT OLD BATS IN BARS BEAT OLD BAGS ON THE BUS.
SAY THAT FIVE TIMES FAST.
WITH THE TYPICAL LINE COOK'S APPETITE FOR ACTION, TONY AND BERNARDO LEAVE TO SCORE SOME SPEED THE BEAV TELLS THEM IS BEING DEALT IN A BAR IN ALBANY BY A BIKER WHO ISN'T THAT SCARY, HONEST. EVEN MARTHA SAYS SHE'S GOING HOME TO WATCH JOHNNY CARSON BECAUSE ROBIN WILLIAMS IS ON TONIGHT.

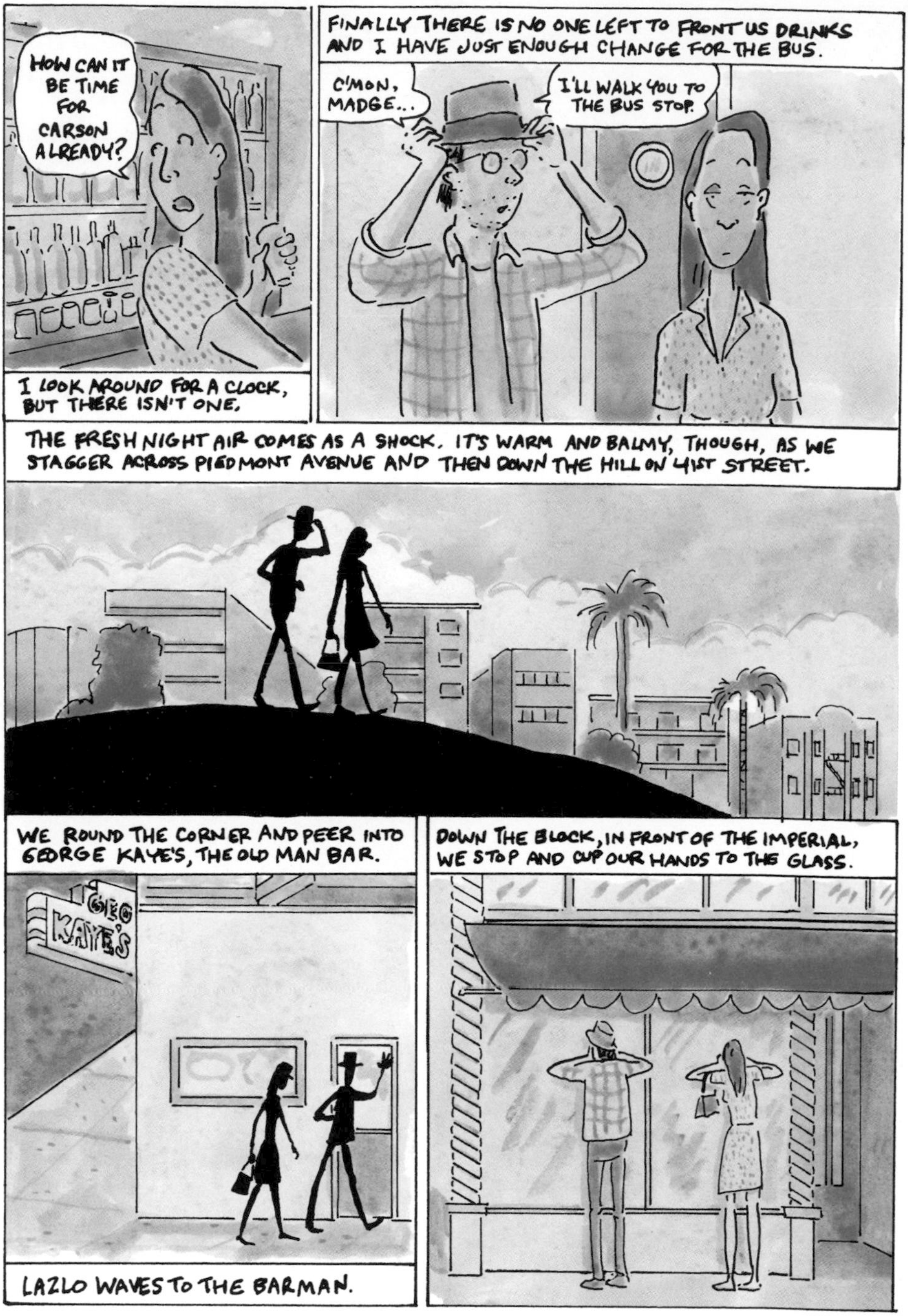
HOW CAN IT BE TIME FOR CARSON ALREADY?
I LOOK AROUND FOR A CLOCK, BUT THERE ISN'T ONE.
FINALLY THERE IS NO ONE LEFT TO FRONT US DRINKS AND I HAVE JUST ENOUGH CHANGE FOR THE BUS.
C'MON, MADGE...
I'LL WALK YOU TO THE BUS STOP.
THE FRESH NIGHT AIR COMES AS A SHOCK. IT'S WARM AND BALMY, THOUGH, AS WE STAGGER ACROSS PIEDMONT AVENUE AND THEN DOWN THE HILL ON 41ST STREET.
WE ROUND THE CORNER AND PEER INTO GEORGE KAYE'S, THE OLD MAN BAR.
GEO KAYE'S
LAZLO WAVES TO THE BARMAN.
DOWN THE BLOCK, IN FRONT OF THE IMPERIAL, WE STOP AND CUP OUR HANDS TO THE GLASS.

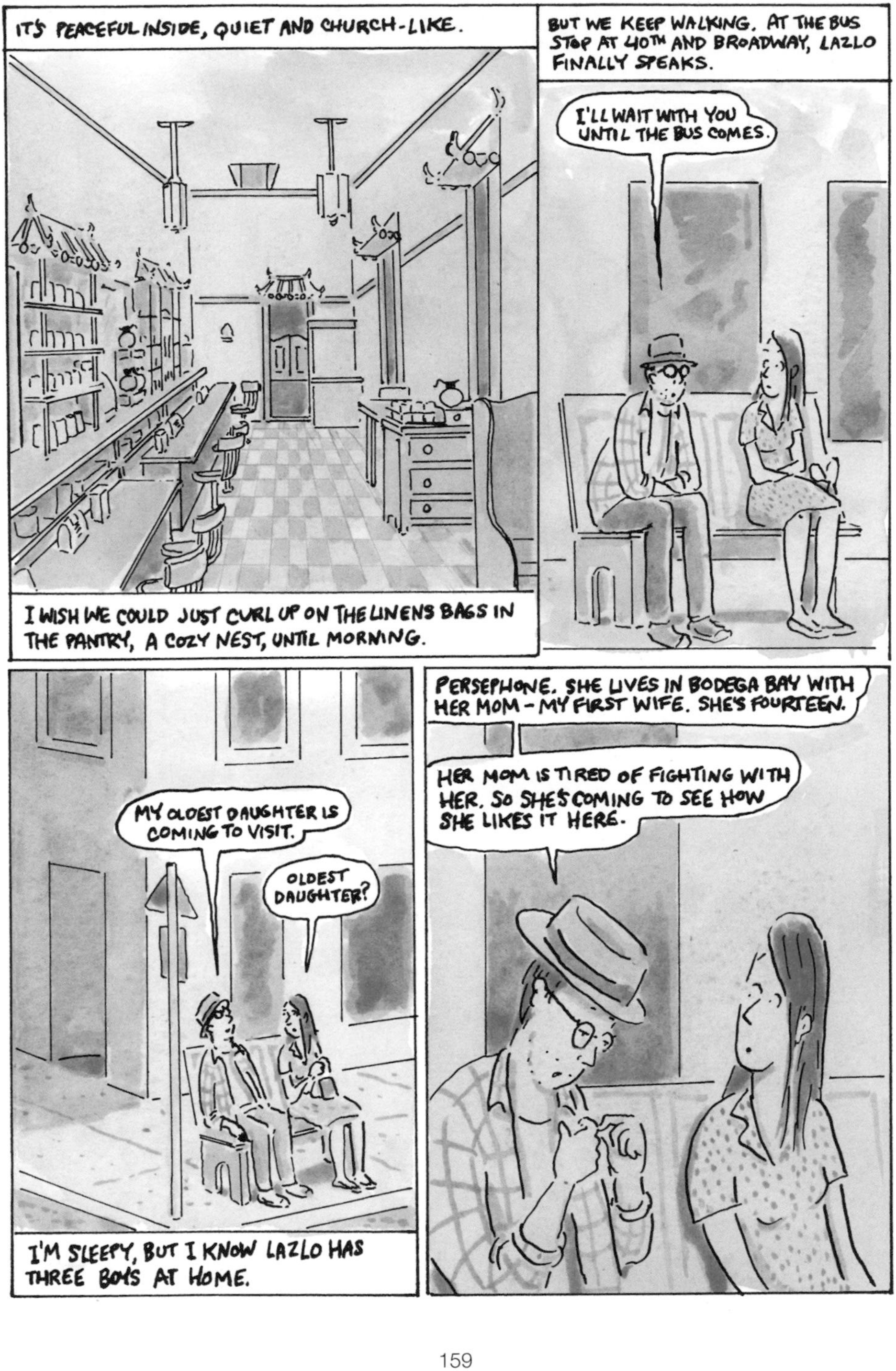
IT'S PEACEFUL INSIDE, QUIET AND CHURCH-LIKE.
I WISH WE COULD JUST CURL UP ON THE LINENS BAGS IN THE PANTRY, A COZY NEST, UNTIL MORNING.
BUT WE KEEP WALKING. AT THE BUS STOP AT 40TH AND BROADWAY, LAZLO FINALLY SPEAKS.
I'LL WAIT WITH YOU UNTIL THE BUS COMES.
MY OLDEST DAUGHTER IS COMING TO VISIT.
OLDEST DAUGHTER?
I'M SLEEPY, BUT I KNOW LAZLO HAS THREE BOYS AT HOME.
PERSEPHONE. SHE LIVES IN BODEGA BAY WITH HER MOM - MY FIRST WIFE. SHE'S FOURTEEN.
HER MOM IS TIRED OF FIGHTING WITH HER. SO SHE'S COMING TO SEE HOW SHE LIKES IT HERE.

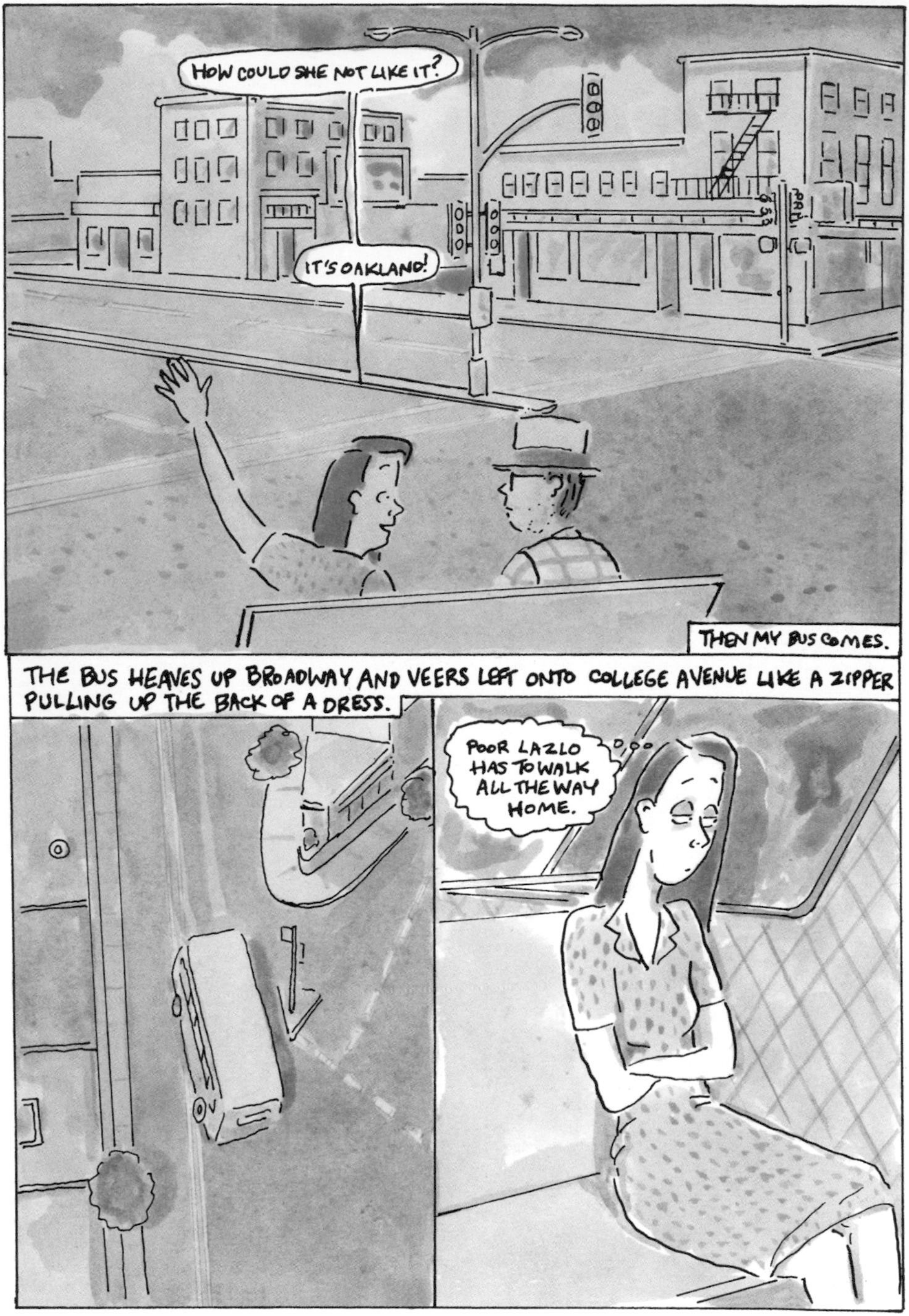
HOW COULD SHE NOT LIKE IT?
IT'S OAKLAND!
THEN MY BUS COMES.
THE BUS HEAVES UP BROADWAY AND VEERS LEFT ONTO COLLEGE AVENUE LIKE A ZIPPER PULLING UP THE BACK OF A DRESS.
POOR LAZLO HAS TO WALK ALL THE WAY HOME.

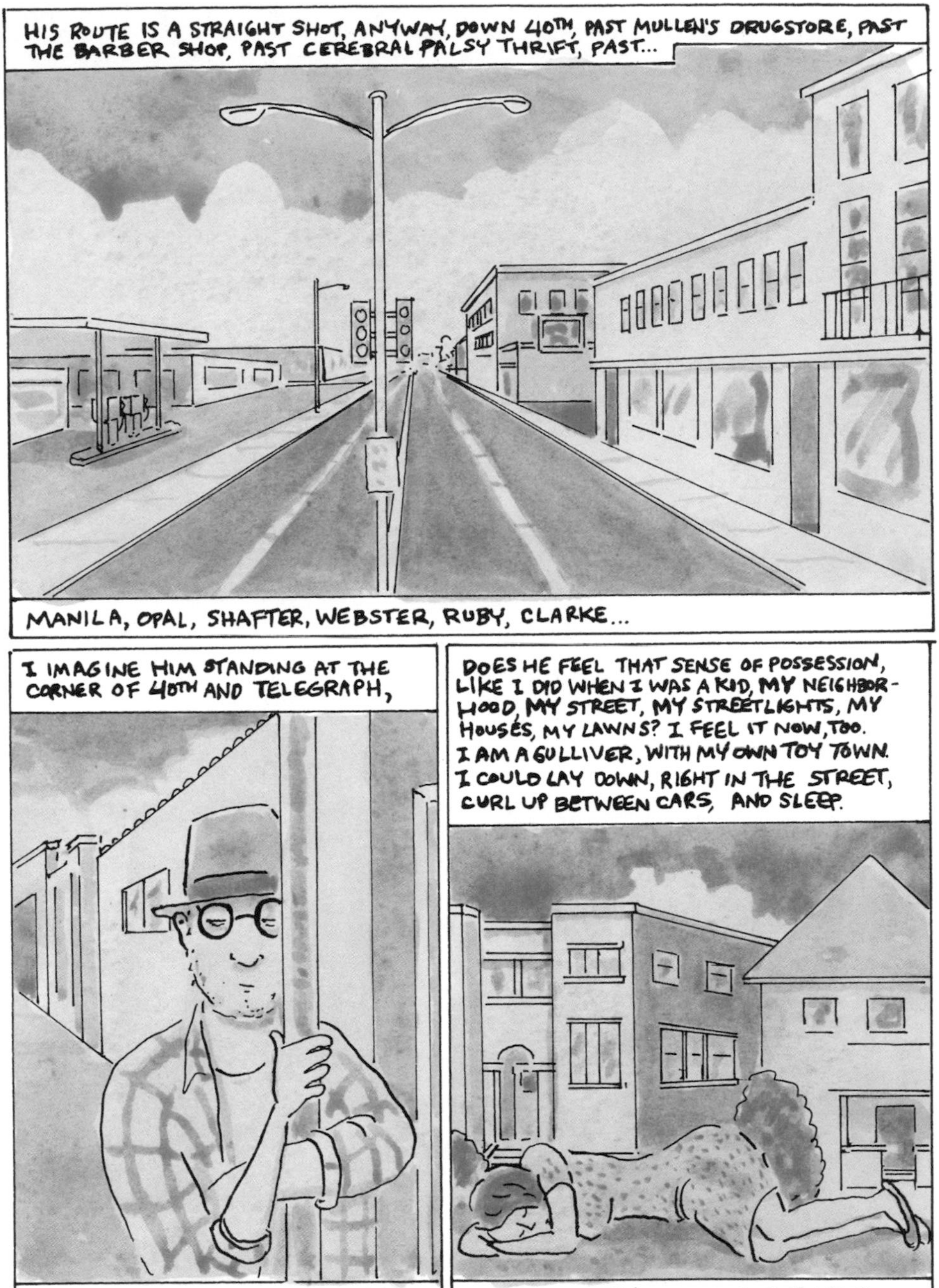
HIS ROUTE IS A STRAIGHT SHOT, ANYWAY, DOWN 40TH, PAST MULLEN'S DRUGSTORE, PAST THE BARBER SHOP, PAST CEREBRAL PALSY THRIFT, PAST...
MANILA, OPAL, SHAFTER, WEBSTER, RUBY, CLARKE...
I IMAGINE HIM STANDING AT THE CORNER OF 40TH AND TELEGRAPH,
EMBRACING THE COOL TRAFFIC POST AS HE WAITS FOR THE LIGHT.
DOES HE FEEL THAT SENSE OF POSSESSION, LIKE I DID WHEN I WAS A KID, MY NEIGHBORHOOD, MY STREET, MY STREETLIGHTS, MY HOUSES, MY LAWNS? I FEEL IT NOW, TOO. I AM A GULLIVER, WITH MY OWN TOY TOWN. I COULD LAY DOWN, RIGHT IN THE STREET, CURL UP BETWEEN CARS, AND SLEEP.
I FIGHT TO STAY AWAKE. GOT TO KEEP LAZLO WALKING.

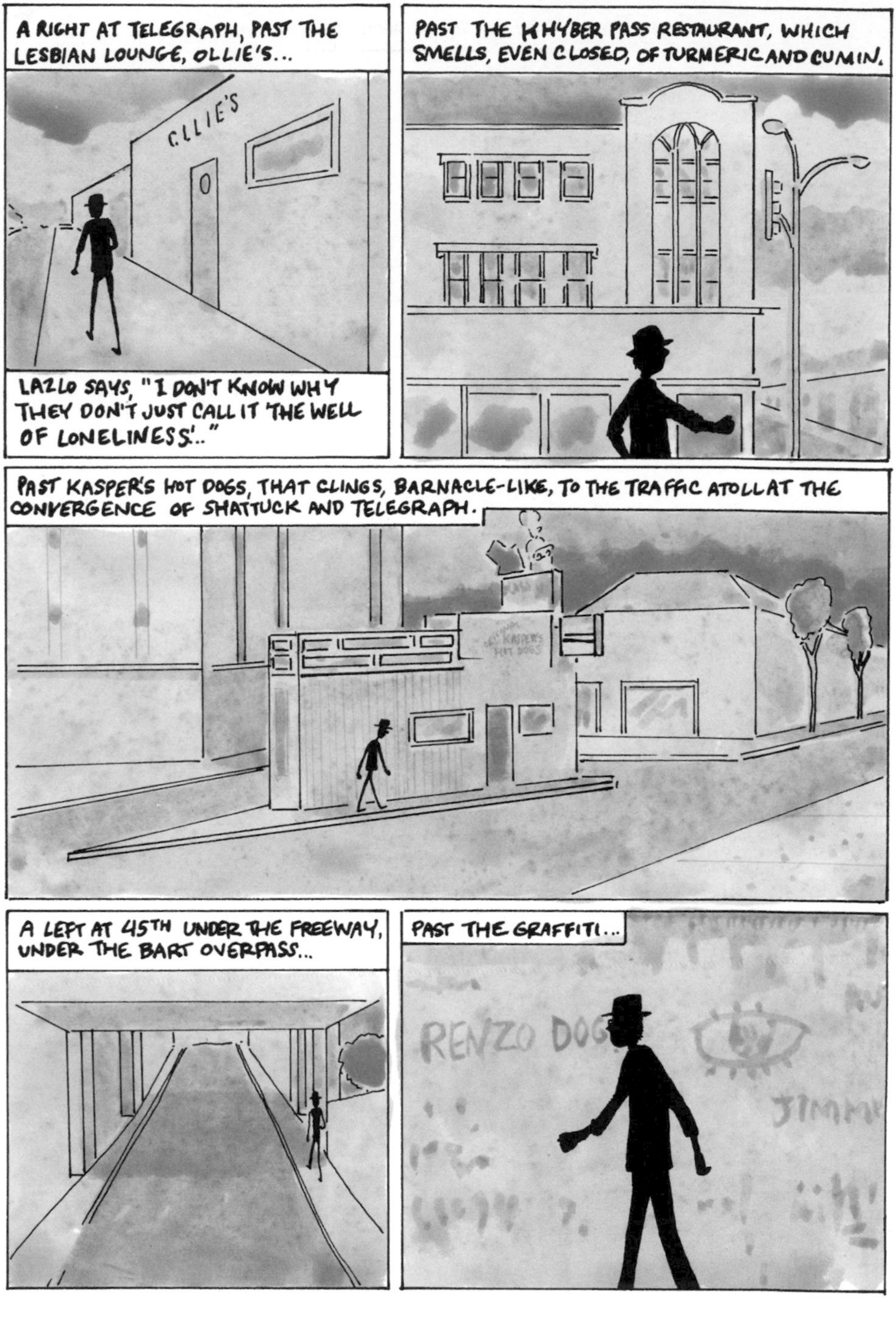
A RIGHT AT TELEGRAPH, PAST THE LESBIAN LOUNGE, OLLIE'S...
OLLIE'S
LAZLO SAYS, "I DON'T KNOW WHY THEY DON'T JUST CALL IT 'THE WELL OF LONELINESS'..."
PAST THE KHYBER PASS RESTAURANT, WHICH SMELLS, EVEN CLOSED, OF TURMERIC AND CUMIN.
PAST KASPER'S HOT DOGS, THAT CLINGS, BARNACLE-LIKE, TO THE TRAFFIC ATOLL AT THE CONVERGENCE OF SHATTUCK AND TELEGRAPH.
A LEFT AT 45TH UNDER THE FREEWAY, UNDER THE BART OVERPASS...
PAST THE GRAFFITI...
RENZO DOG

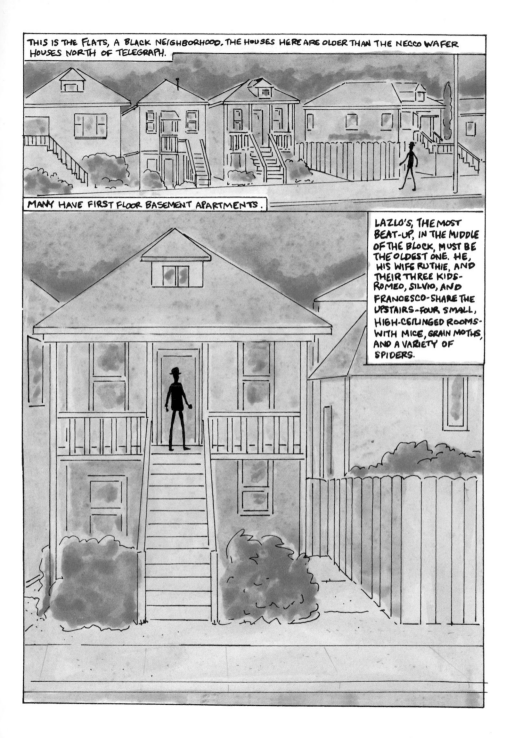

THIS IS THE FLATS, A BLACK NEIGHBORHOOD. THE HOUSES HERE ARE OLDER THAN THE NECCO WAFER HOUSES NORTH OF TELEGRAPH.

MANY HAVE FIRST FLOOR BASEMENT APARTMENTS.

LAZLO'S, THE MOST BEAT-UP, IN THE MIDDLE OF THE BLOCK, MUST BE THE OLDEST ONE. HE, HIS WIFE RUTHIE, AND THEIR THREE KIDS—ROMEO, SILVIO, AND FRANCESCO—SHARE THE UPSTAIRS—FOUR SMALL, HIGH-CEILINGED ROOMS—WITH MICE, GRAIN MOTHS, AND A VARIETY OF SPIDERS.

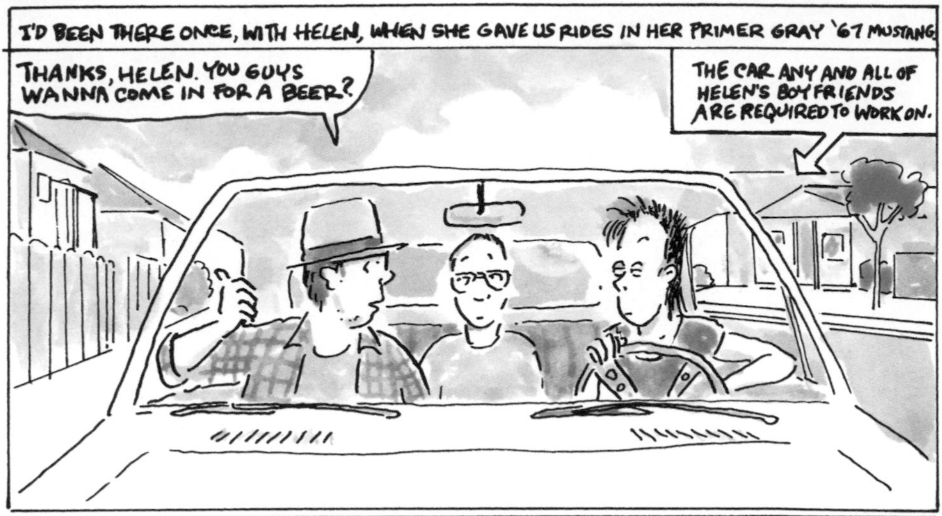
I'D BEEN THERE ONCE, WITH HELEN, WHEN SHE GAVE US RIDES IN HER PRIMER GRAY '67 MUSTANG.
THANKS, HELEN. YOU GUYS WANNA COME IN FOR A BEER?
THE CAR ANY AND ALL OF HELEN'S BOYFRIENDS ARE REQUIRED TO WORK ON.

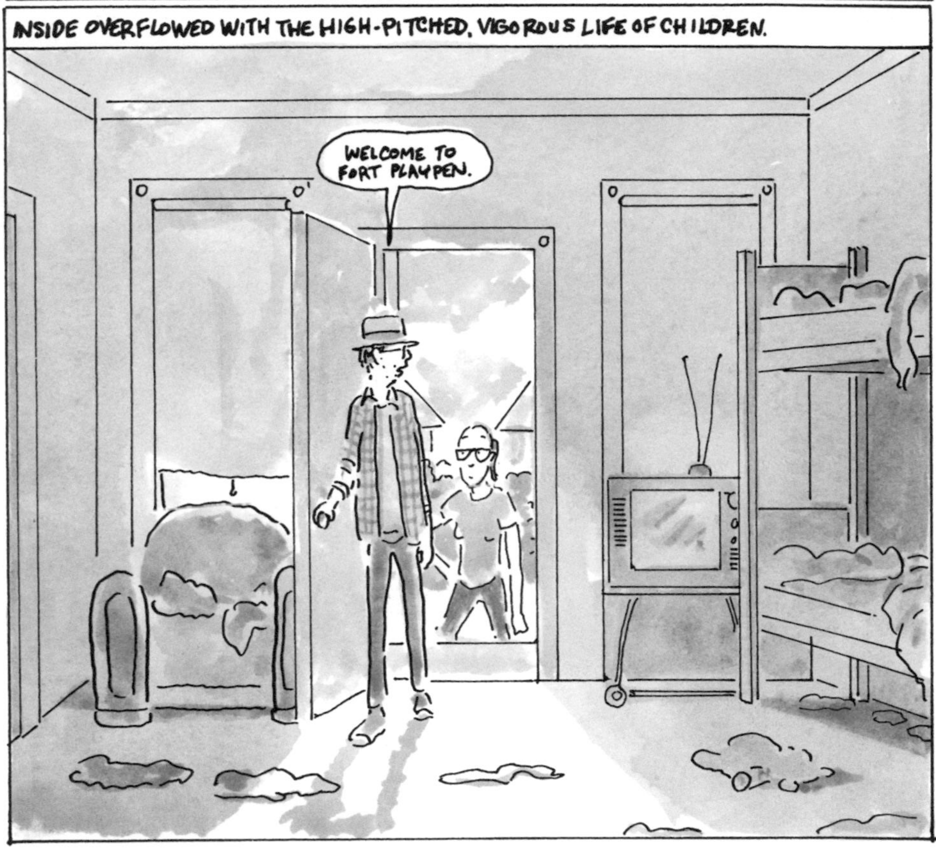
INSIDE OVERFLOWED WITH THE HIGH-PITCHED, VIGOROUS LIFE OF CHILDREN.
WELCOME TO FORT PLAYPEN.

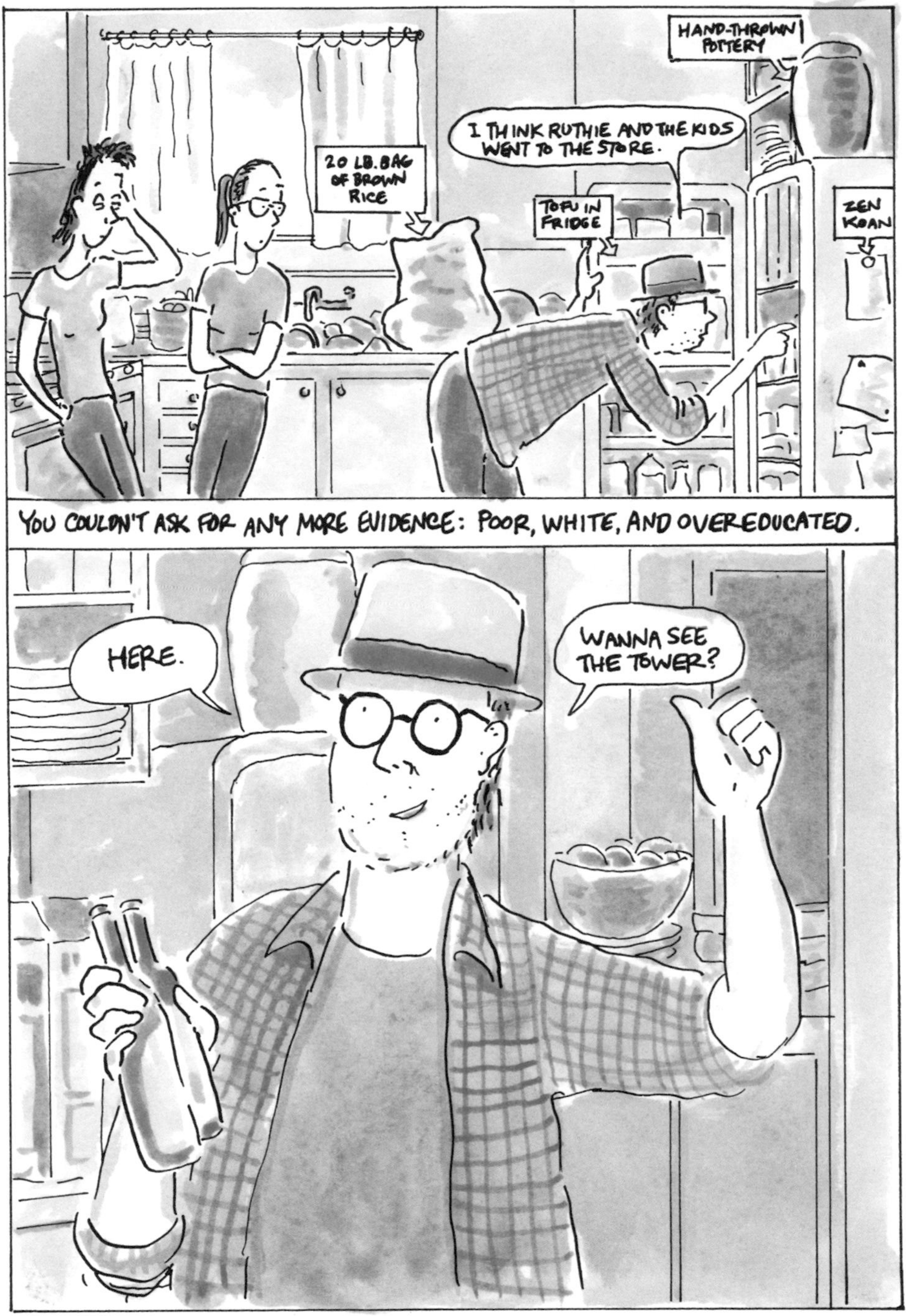
HAND-THROWN POTTERY
20 LB. BAG OF BROWN RICE
I THINK RUTHIE AND THE KIDS WENT TO THE STORE.
TOFU IN FRIDGE
ZEN KOAN
YOU COULDN'T ASK FOR ANY MORE EVIDENCE: POOR, WHITE, AND OVEREDUCATED.
HERE.
WANNA SEE THE TOWER?

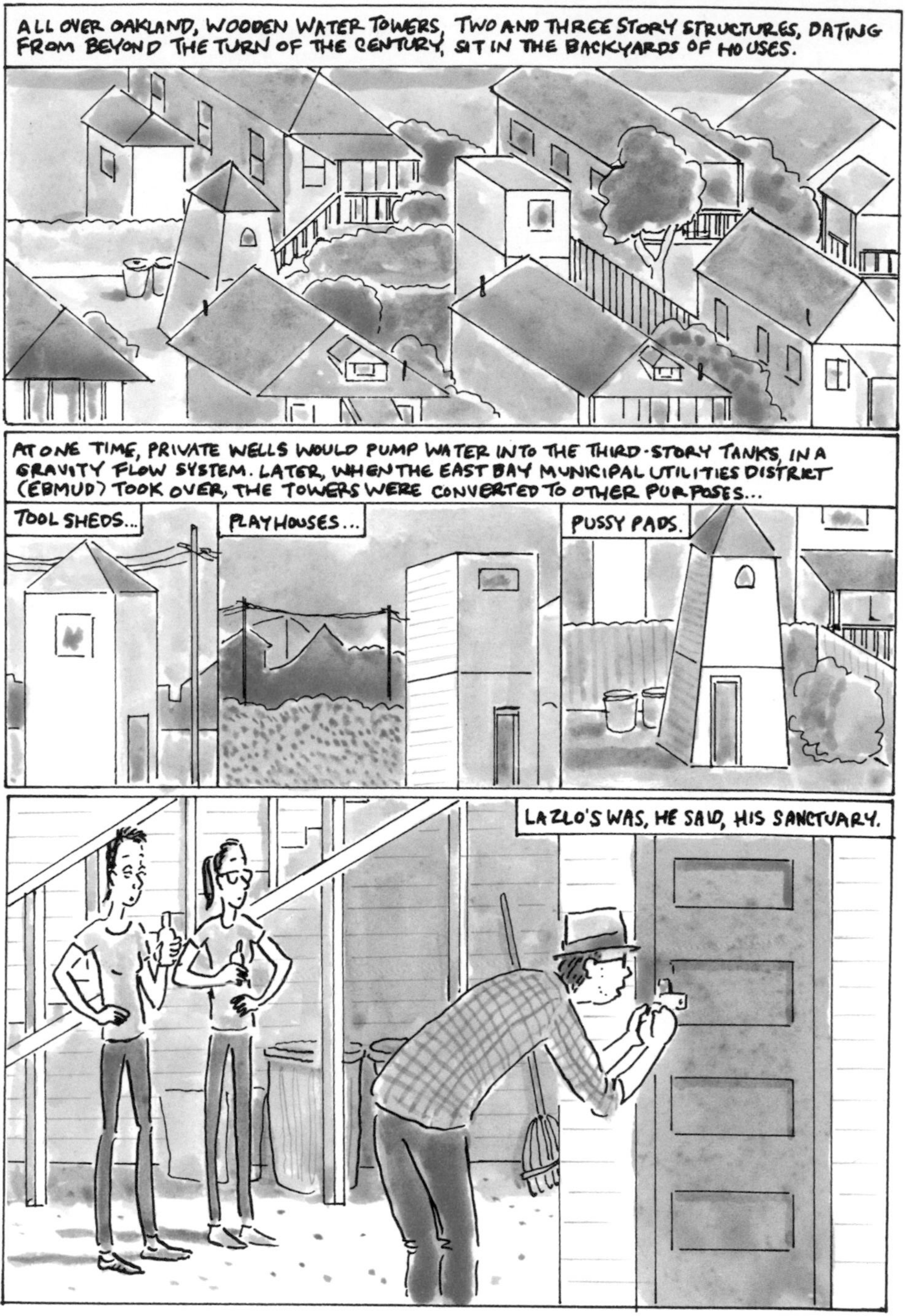
ALL OVER OAKLAND, WOODEN WATER TOWERS, TWO AND THREE STORY STRUCTURES, DATING FROM BEYOND THE TURN OF THE CENTURY, SIT IN THE BACKYARDS OF HOUSES.
AT ONE TIME, PRIVATE WELLS WOULD PUMP WATER INTO THE THIRD-STORY TANKS, IN A GRAVITY FLOW SYSTEM. LATER, WHEN THE EAST BAY MUNICIPAL UTILITIES DISTRICT (EBMUD) TOOK OVER, THE TOWERS WERE CONVERTED TO OTHER PURPOSES...
TOOL SHEDS...
PLAYHOUSES...
PUSSY PADS.
LAZLO'S WAS, HE SAID, HIS SANCTUARY.

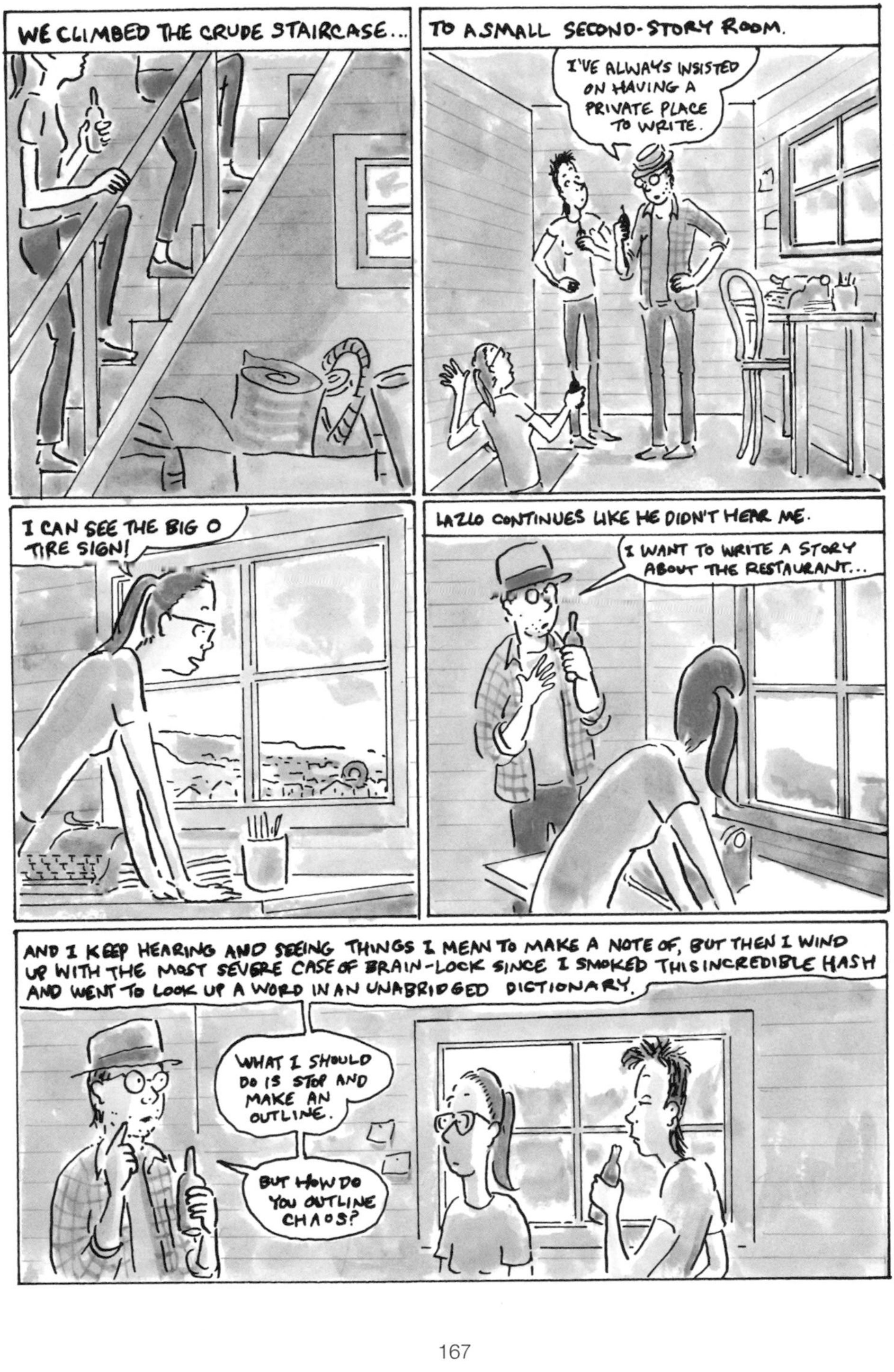
WE CLIMBED THE CRUDE STAIRCASE...
TO A SMALL SECOND-STORY ROOM.
I'VE ALWAYS INSISTED ON HAVING A PRIVATE PLACE TO WRITE.
I CAN SEE THE BIG O TIRE SIGN!
LAZLO CONTINUES LIKE HE DIDN'T HEAR ME.
I WANT TO WRITE A STORY ABOUT THE RESTAURANT...
AND I KEEP HEARING AND SEEING THINGS I MEAN TO MAKE A NOTE OF, BUT THEN I WIND UP WITH THE MOST SEVERE CASE OF BRAIN-LOCK SINCE I SMOKED THIS INCREDIBLE HASH AND WENT TO LOOK UP A WORD IN AN UNABRIDGED DICTIONARY.
WHAT I SHOULD DO IS STOP AND MAKE AN OUTLINE.
BUT HOW DO YOU OUTLINE CHAOS?

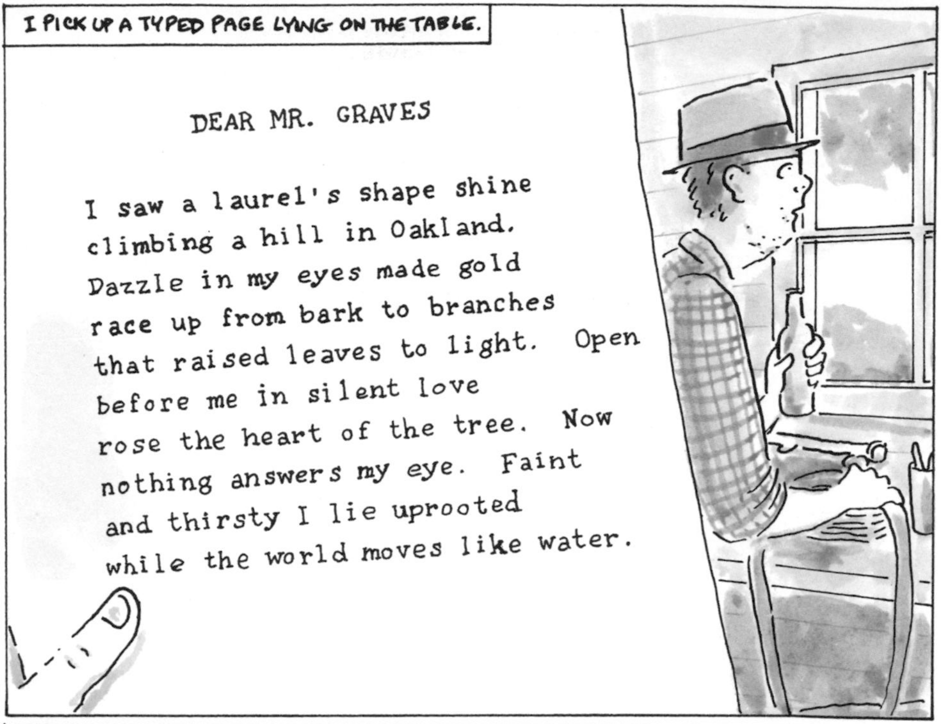
I PICK UP A TYPED PAGE LYING ON THE TABLE.
DEAR MR. GRAVES
I saw a laurel's shape shine
climbing a hill in Oakland.
Dazzle in my eyes made gold
race up from bark to branches
that raised leaves to light. Open
before me in silent love
rose the heart of the tree. Now
nothing answers my eye. Faint
and thirsty I lie uprooted
while the world moves like water.

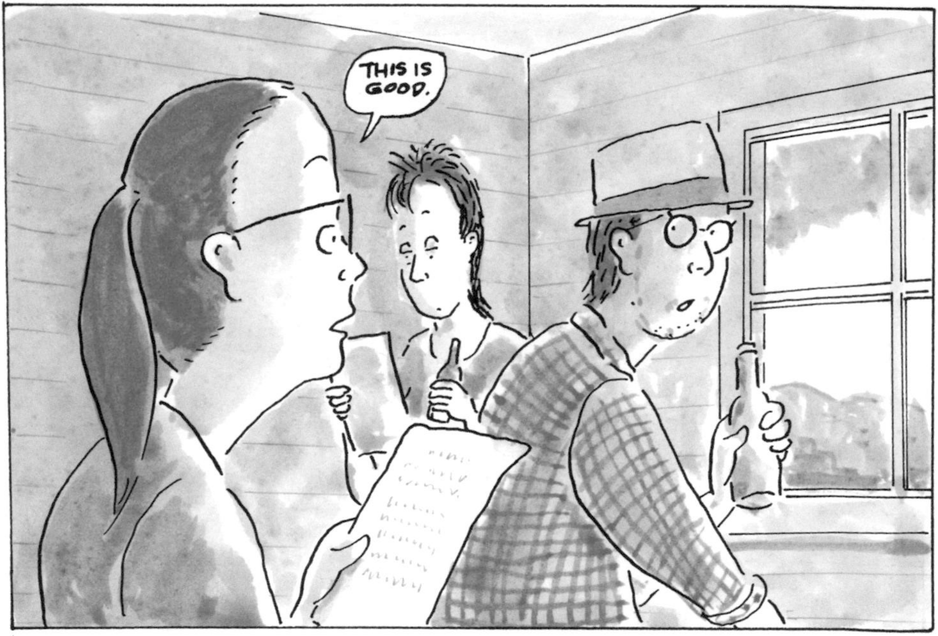
THIS IS GOOD.

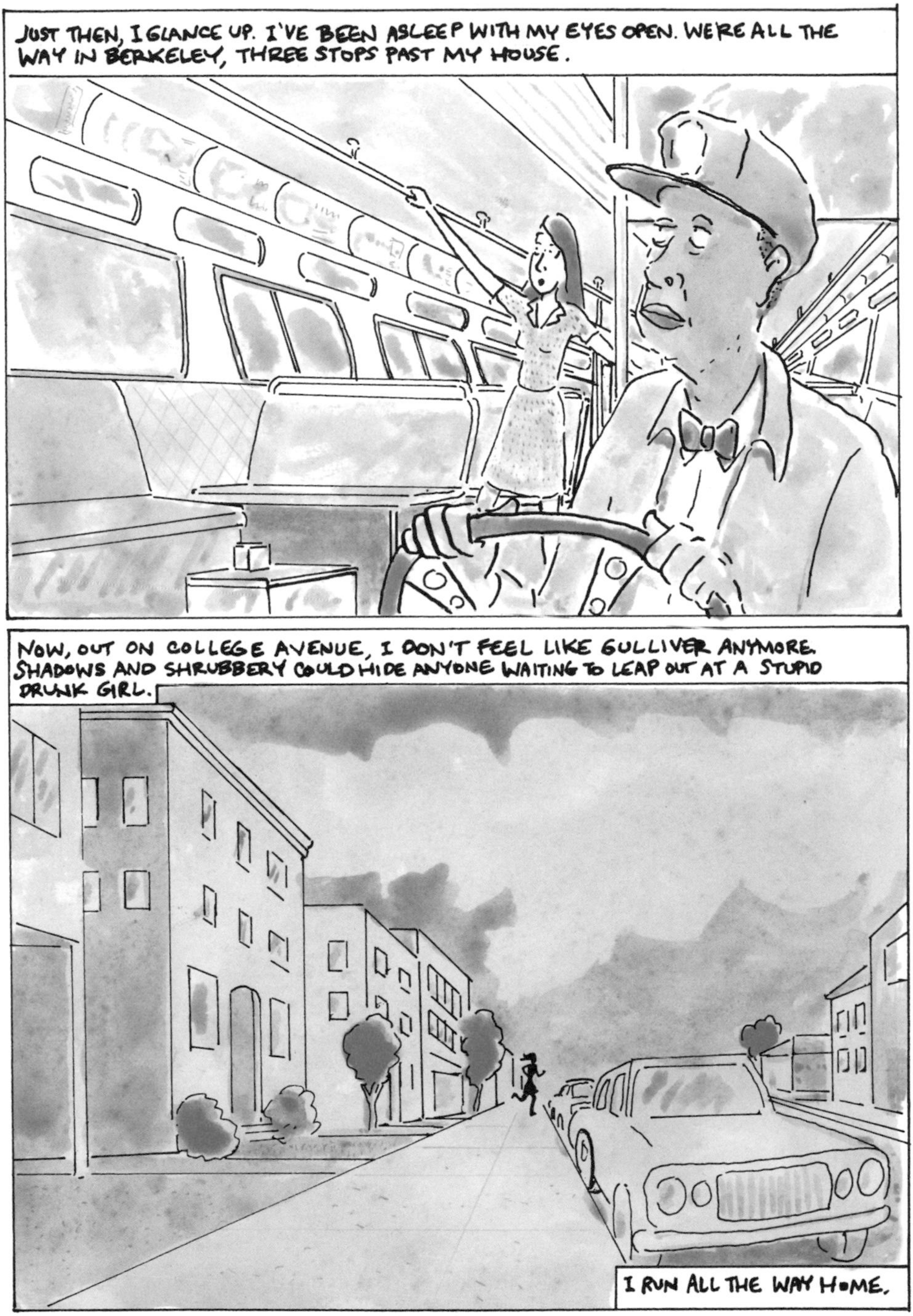
JUST THEN, I GLANCE UP. I'VE BEEN ASLEEP WITH MY EYES OPEN. WE'RE ALL THE WAY IN BERKELEY, THREE STOPS PAST MY HOUSE.
NOW, OUT ON COLLEGE AVENUE, I DON'T FEEL LIKE GULLIVER ANYMORE. SHADOWS AND SHRUBBERY COULD HIDE ANYONE WAITING TO LEAP OUT AT A STUPID DRUNK GIRL.
I RUN ALL THE WAY HOME.

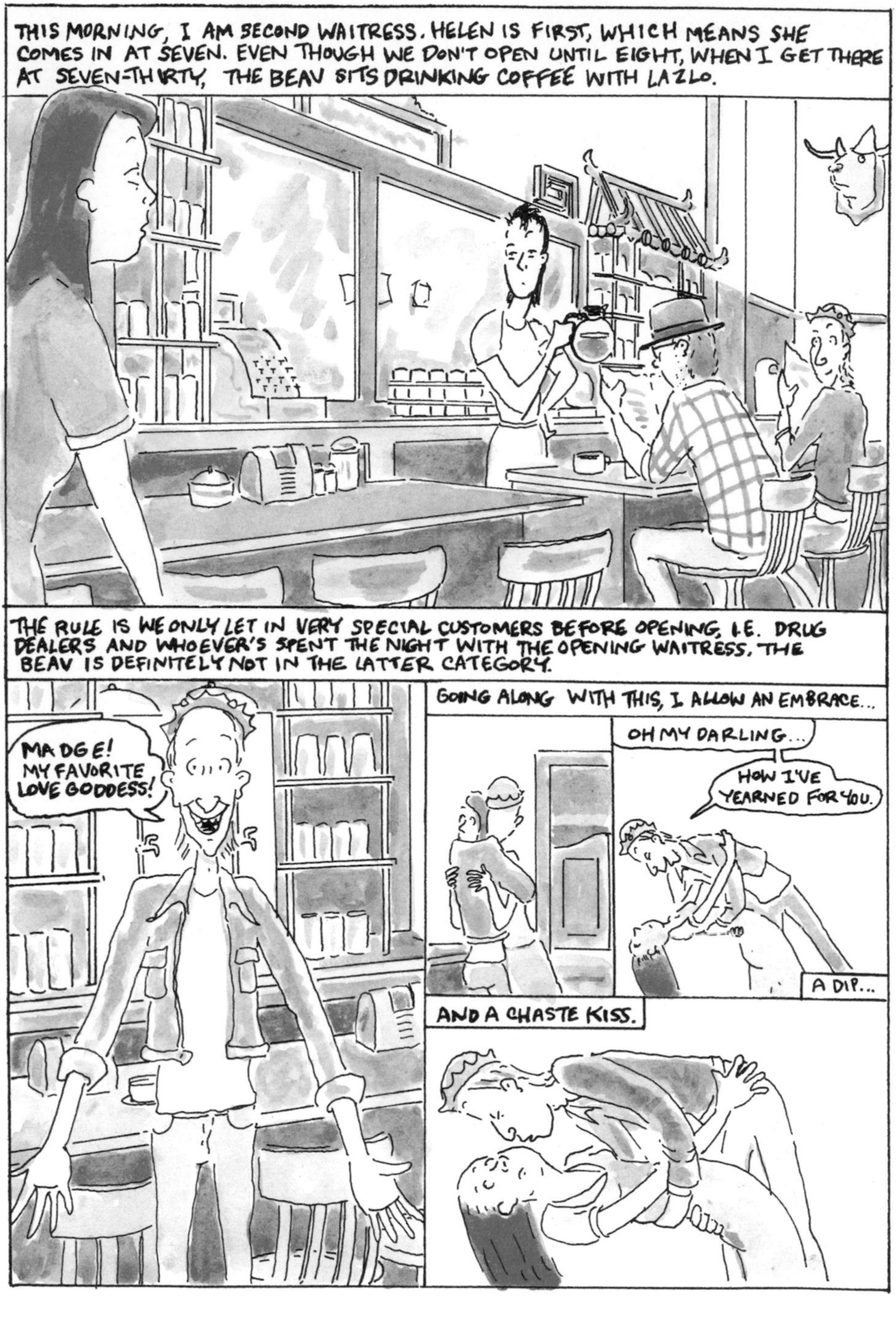
THIS MORNING, I AM SECOND WAITRESS. HELEN IS FIRST, WHICH MEANS SHE COMES IN AT SEVEN. EVEN THOUGH WE DON'T OPEN UNTIL EIGHT, WHEN I GET THERE AT SEVEN-THIRTY, THE BEAV SITS DRINKING COFFEE WITH LAZLO.
THE RULE IS WE ONLY LET IN VERY SPECIAL CUSTOMERS BEFORE OPENING, I.E. DRUG DEALERS AND WHOEVER'S SPENT THE NIGHT WITH THE OPENING WAITRESS. THE BEAV IS DEFINITELY NOT IN THE LATTER CATEGORY.
MADGE! MY FAVORITE LOVE GODDESS!
GOING ALONG WITH THIS, I ALLOW AN EMBRACE...
OH MY DARLING...
HOW I'VE YEARNED FOR YOU.
A DIP...
AND A CHASTE KISS.

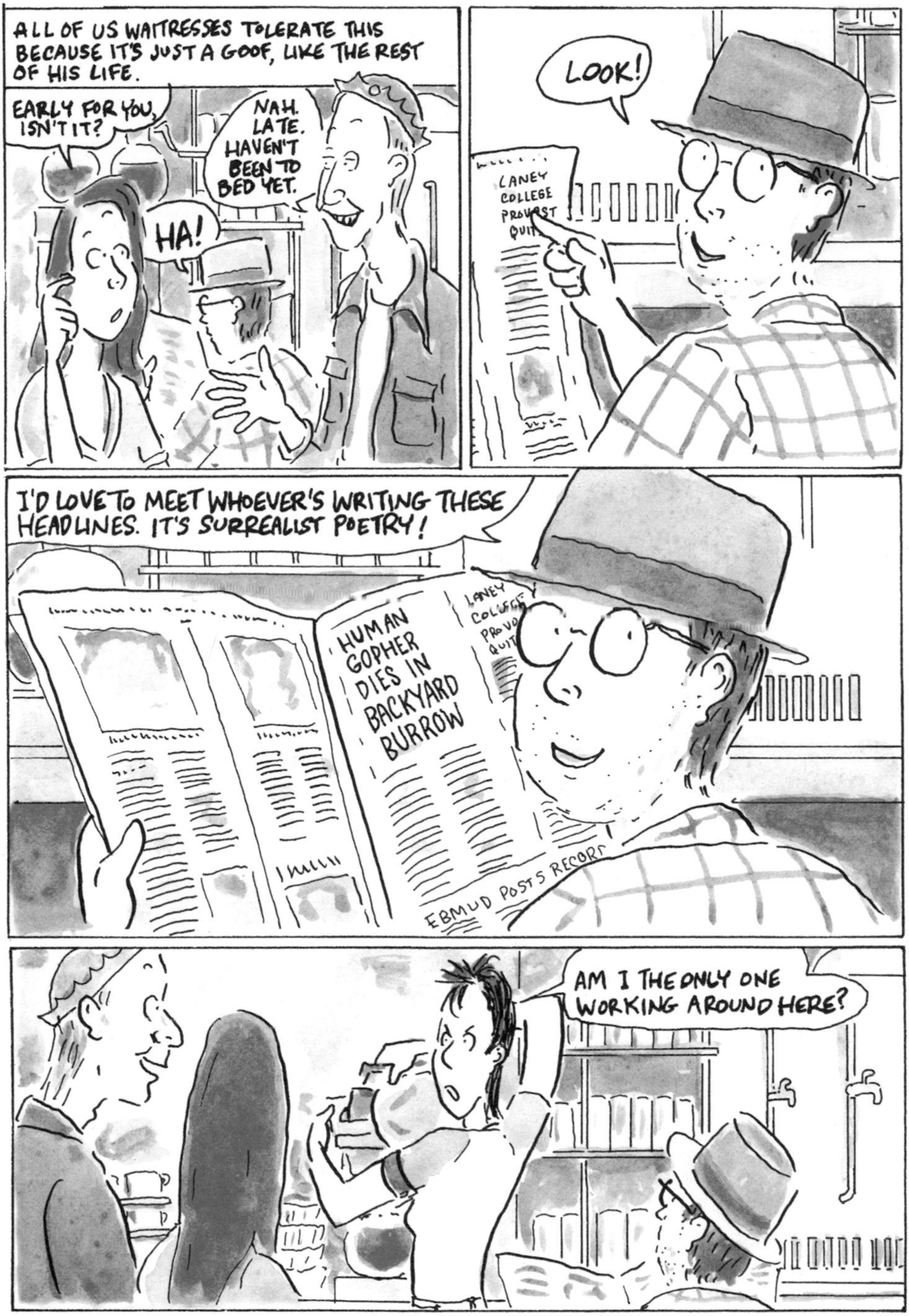
ALL OF US WAITRESSES TOLERATE THIS BECAUSE IT'S JUST A GOOF, LIKE THE REST OF HIS LIFE.
EARLY FOR YOU, ISN'T IT?
NAH. LATE. HAVEN'T BEEN TO BED YET.
HA!
LANEY COLLEGE PROVOST QUITS
LOOK!
I'D LOVE TO MEET WHOEVER'S WRITING THESE HEADLINES. IT'S SURREALIST POETRY!
HUMAN GOPHER DIES IN BACKYARD BURROW
EBMUD POSTS RECORD
AM I THE ONLY ONE WORKING AROUND HERE?

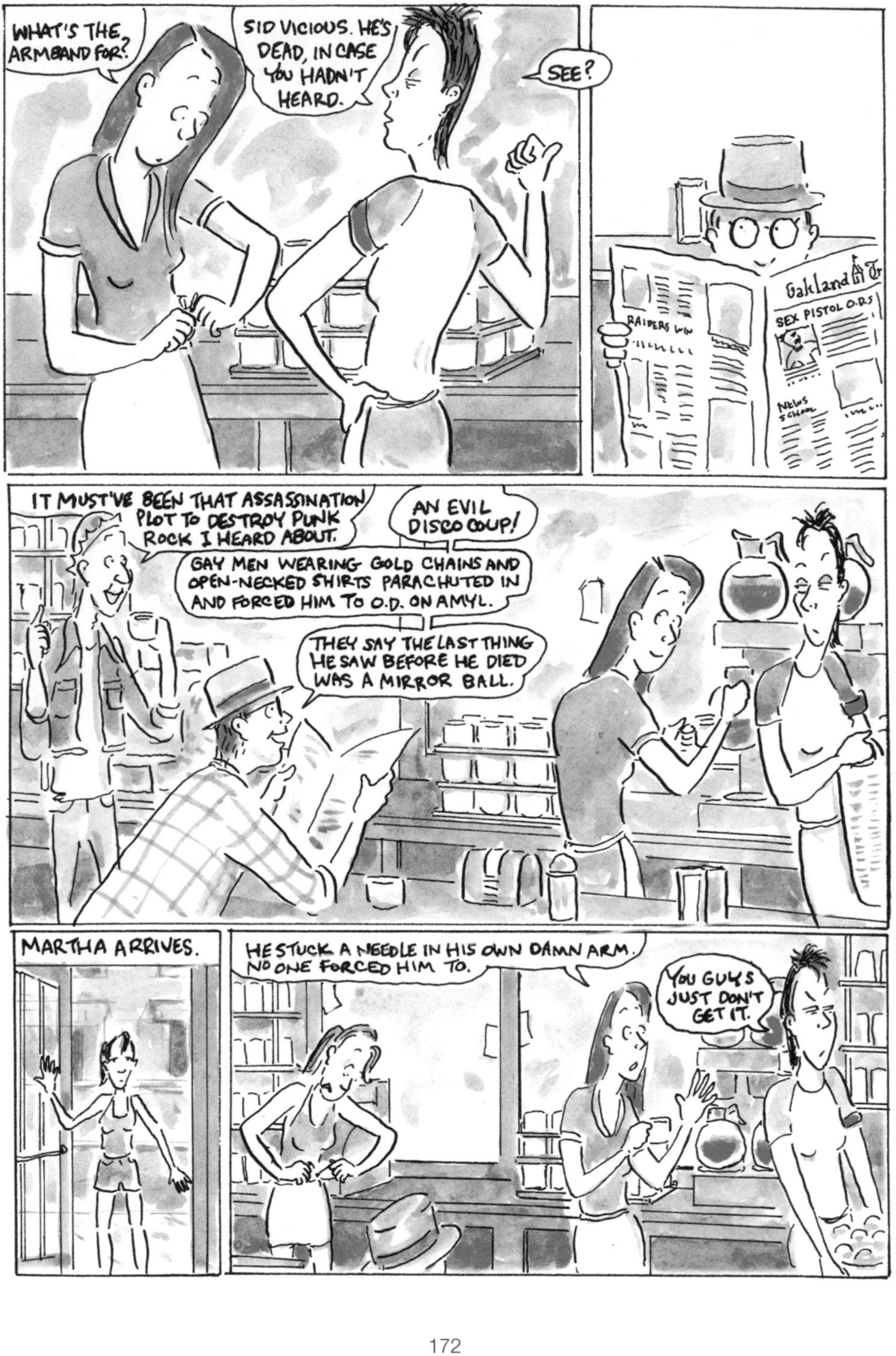
WHAT'S THE ARMBAND FOR?
SID VICIOUS. HE'S DEAD, IN CASE YOU HADN'T HEARD.
SEE?
Oakland Tr
RAIDERS WIN
SEX PISTOL O.D.S
NEWS SCHOOL
IT MUST'VE BEEN THAT ASSASSINATION PLOT TO DESTROY PUNK ROCK I HEARD ABOUT.
AN EVIL DISCO COUP!
GAY MEN WEARING GOLD CHAINS AND OPEN-NECKED SHIRTS PARACHUTED IN AND FORCED HIM TO O.D. ON AMYL.
THEY SAY THE LAST THING HE SAW BEFORE HE DIED WAS A MIRROR BALL.
MARTHA ARRIVES.
HE STUCK A NEEDLE IN HIS OWN DAMN ARM. NO ONE FORCED HIM TO.
YOU GUYS JUST DON'T GET IT.

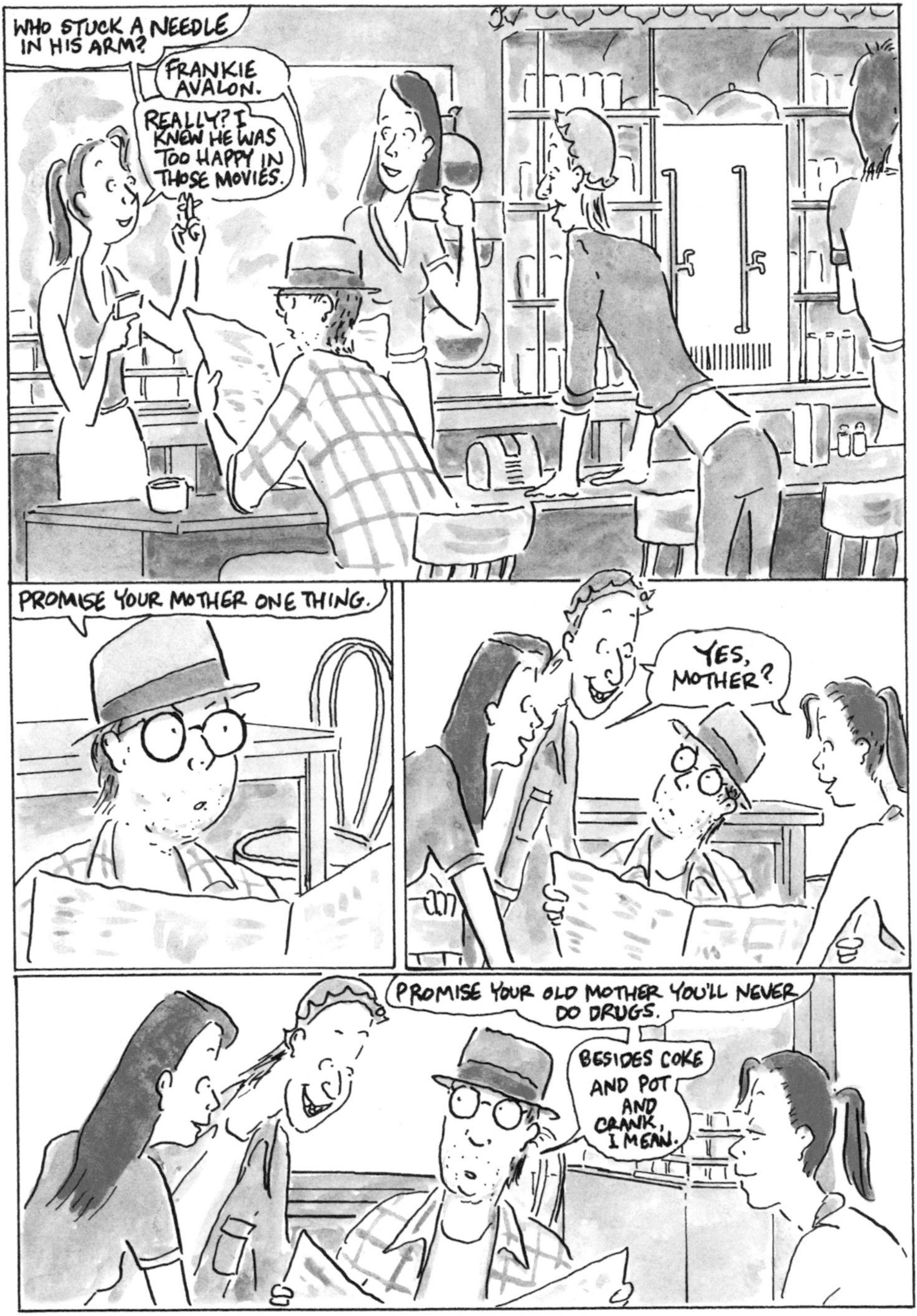
WHO STUCK A NEEDLE IN HIS ARM?
FRANKIE AVALON.
REALLY? I KNEW HE WAS TOO HAPPY IN THOSE MOVIES.
PROMISE YOUR MOTHER ONE THING.
YES, MOTHER?
PROMISE YOUR OLD MOTHER YOU'LL NEVER DO DRUGS.
BESIDES COKE AND POT AND CRANK, I MEAN.

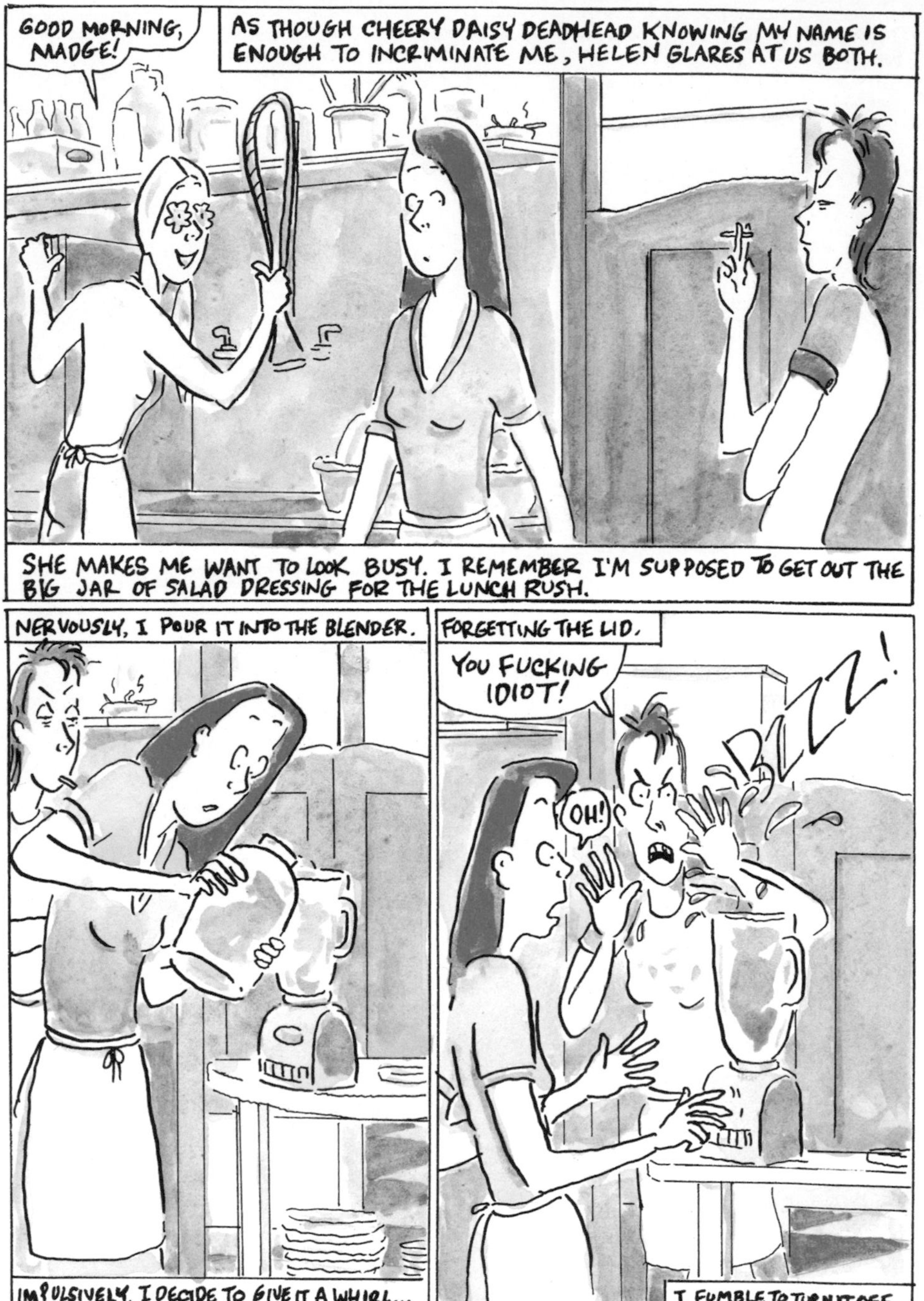
GOOD MORNING, MADGE!
AS THOUGH CHEERY DAISY DEADHEAD KNOWING MY NAME IS ENOUGH TO INCRIMINATE ME, HELEN GLARES AT US BOTH.
SHE MAKES ME WANT TO LOOK BUSY. I REMEMBER I'M SUPPOSED TO GET OUT THE BIG JAR OF SALAD DRESSING FOR THE LUNCH RUSH.
NERVOUSLY, I POUR IT INTO THE BLENDER.
IMPULSIVELY, I DECIDE TO GIVE IT A WHIRL...
FORGETTING THE LID.
YOU FUCKING IDIOT!
BZZZ!
OH!
I FUMBLE TO TURN IT OFF.

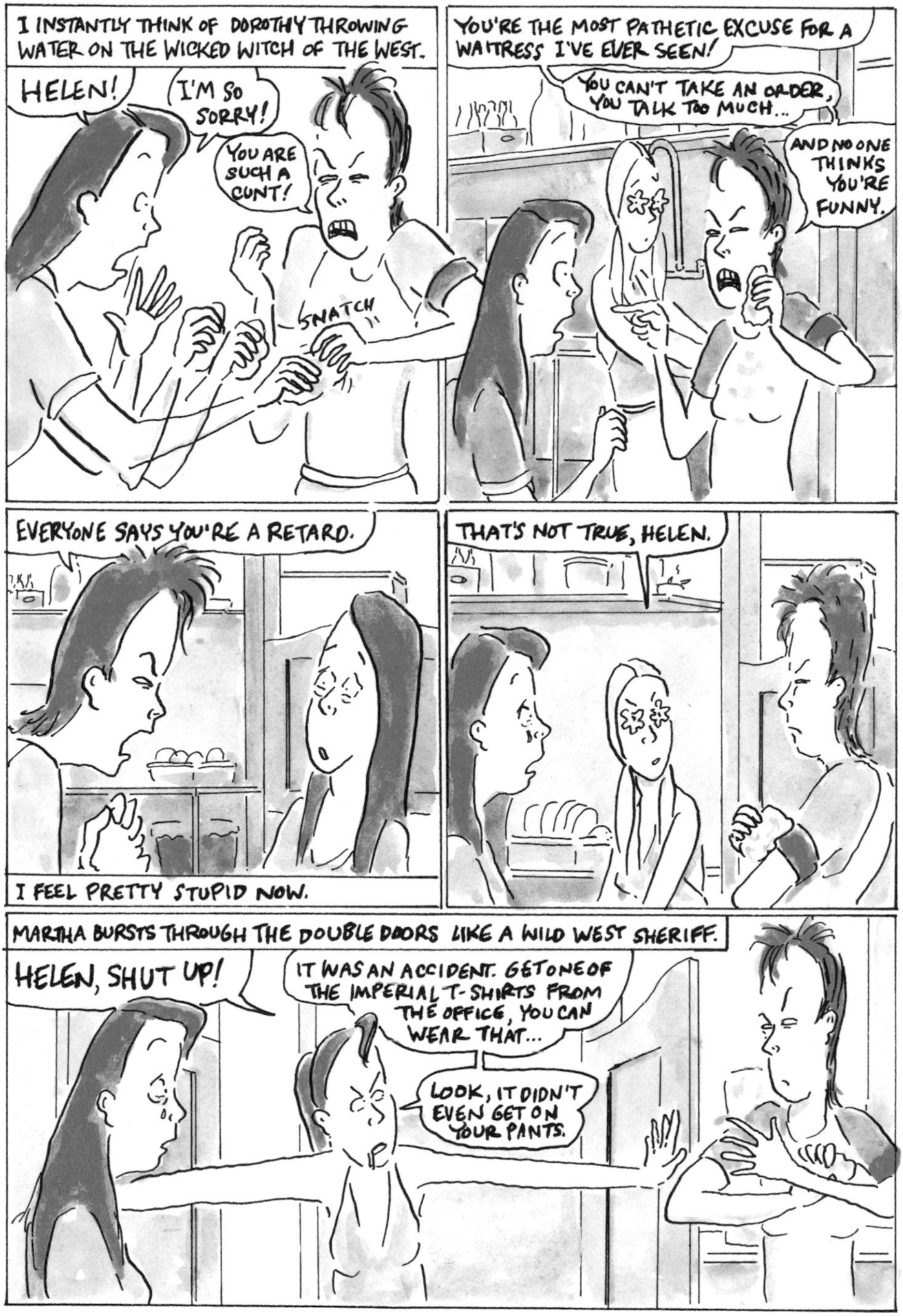
I INSTANTLY THINK OF DOROTHY THROWING WATER ON THE WICKED WITCH OF THE WEST.
HELEN!
I'M SO SORRY!
YOU ARE SUCH A CUNT!
SNATCH
YOU'RE THE MOST PATHETIC EXCUSE FOR A WAITRESS I'VE EVER SEEN!
YOU CAN'T TAKE AN ORDER, YOU TALK TOO MUCH...
AND NO ONE THINKS YOU'RE FUNNY.
EVERYONE SAYS YOU'RE A RETARD.
I FEEL PRETTY STUPID NOW.
THAT'S NOT TRUE, HELEN.
MARTHA BURSTS THROUGH THE DOUBLE DOORS LIKE A WILD WEST SHERIFF.
HELEN, SHUT UP!
IT WAS AN ACCIDENT. GET ONE OF THE IMPERIAL T-SHIRTS FROM THE OFFICE, YOU CAN WEAR THAT...
LOOK, IT DIDN'T EVEN GET ON YOUR PANTS.

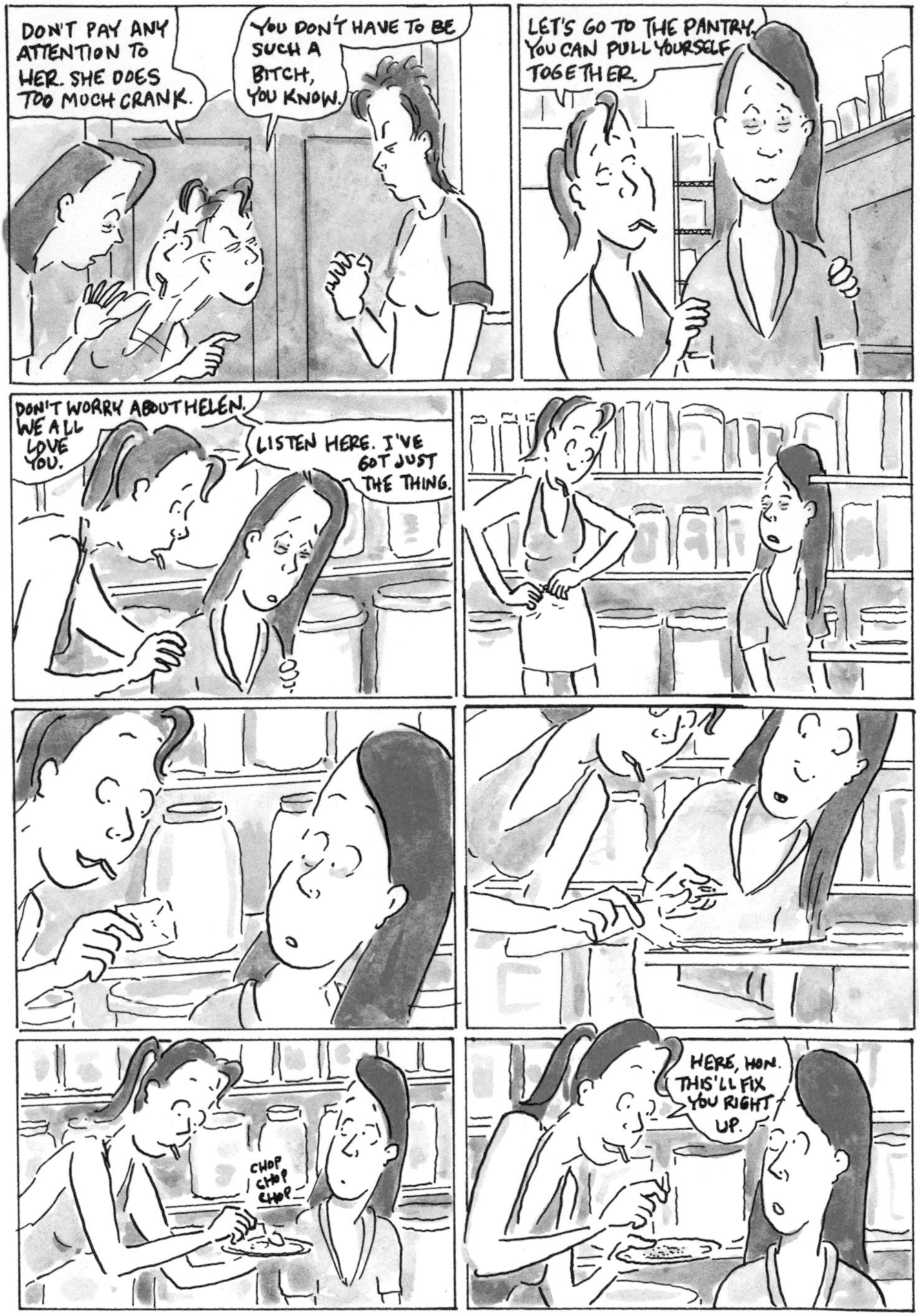
DON'T PAY ANY ATTENTION TO HER. SHE DOES TOO MUCH CRANK.
YOU DON'T HAVE TO BE SUCH A BITCH, YOU KNOW.
LET'S GO TO THE PANTRY. YOU CAN PULL YOURSELF TOGETHER.
DON'T WORRY ABOUT HELEN. WE ALL LOVE YOU.
LISTEN HERE. I'VE GOT JUST THE THING.
CHOP CHOP CHOP
HERE, HON. THIS'LL FIX YOU RIGHT UP.

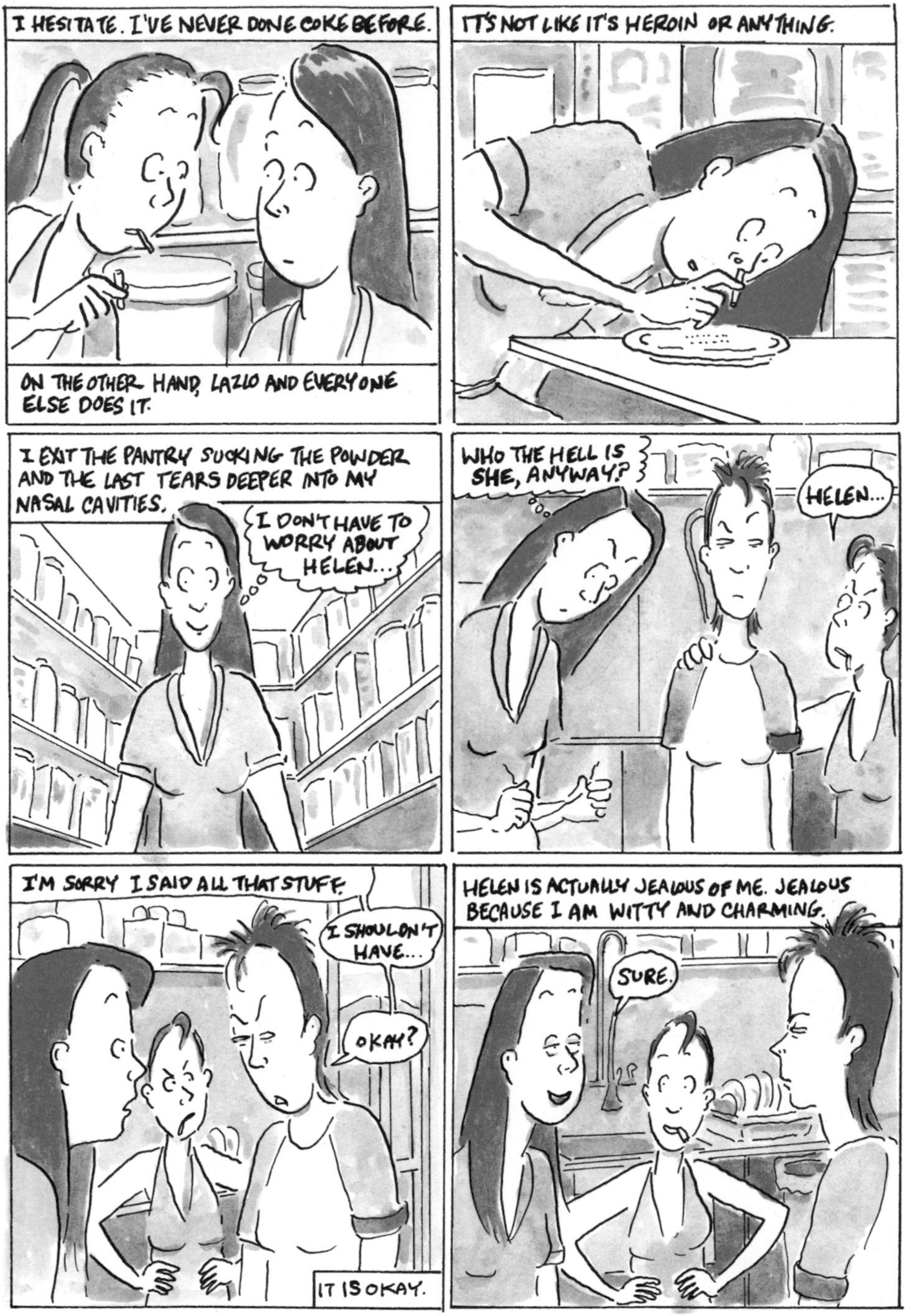
I HESITATE. I'VE NEVER DONE COKE BEFORE.
ON THE OTHER HAND, LAZLO AND EVERYONE ELSE DOES IT.
IT'S NOT LIKE IT'S HEROIN OR ANYTHING.
I EXIT THE PANTRY SUCKING THE POWDER AND THE LAST TEARS DEEPER INTO MY NASAL CAVITIES.
I DON'T HAVE TO WORRY ABOUT HELEN...
WHO THE HELL IS SHE, ANYWAY?
HELEN...
I'M SORRY I SAID ALL THAT STUFF.
I SHOULDN'T HAVE...
OKAY?
IT IS OKAY.
HELEN IS ACTUALLY JEALOUS OF ME. JEALOUS BECAUSE I AM WITTY AND CHARMING.
SURE.

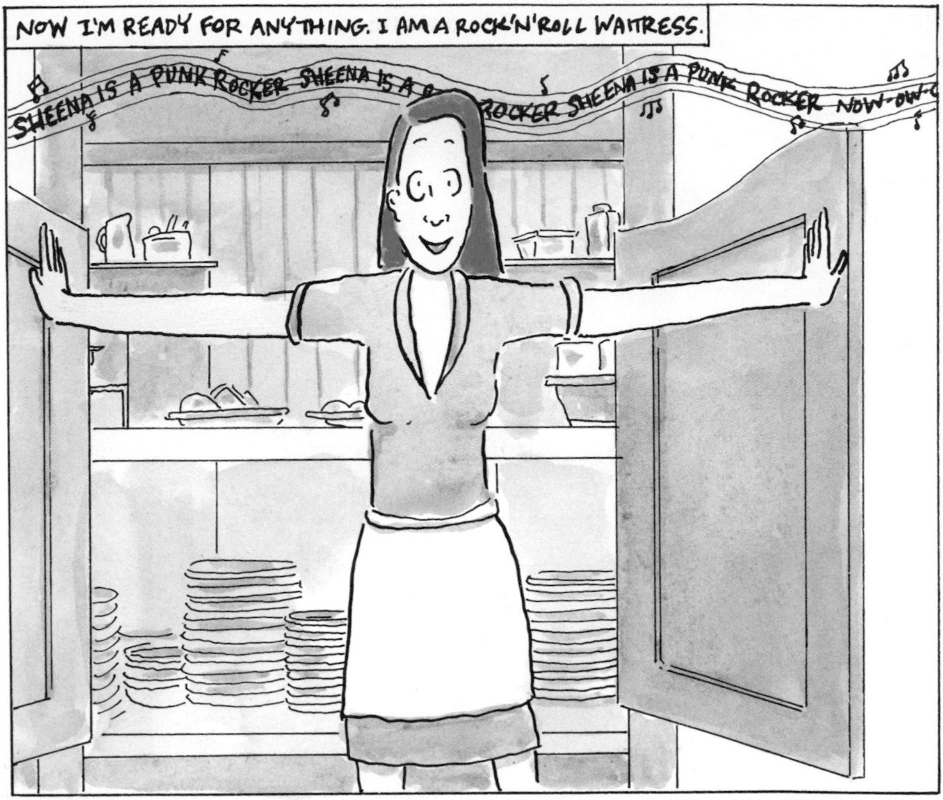
NOW I'M READY FOR ANYTHING. I AM A ROCK'N'ROLL WAITRESS.
SHEENA IS A PUNK ROCKER SHEENA IS A

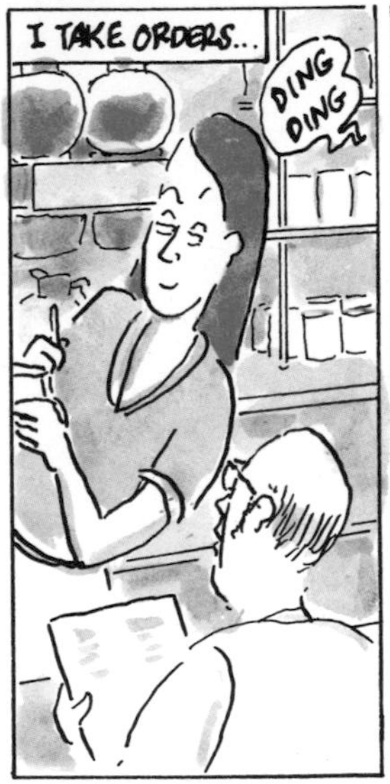
I TAKE ORDERS...
DING DING

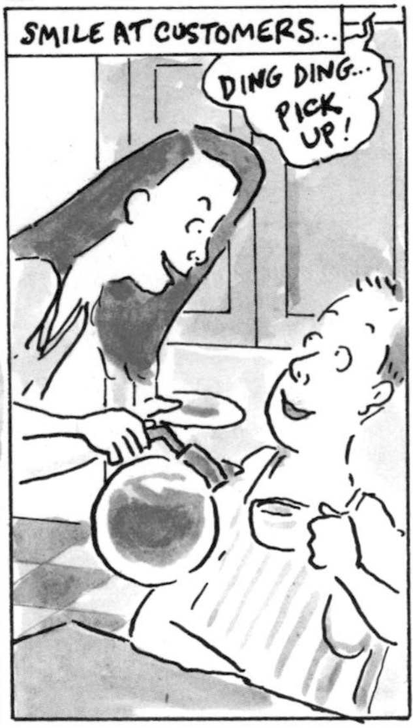
SMILE AT CUSTOMERS...
DING DING... PICK UP!

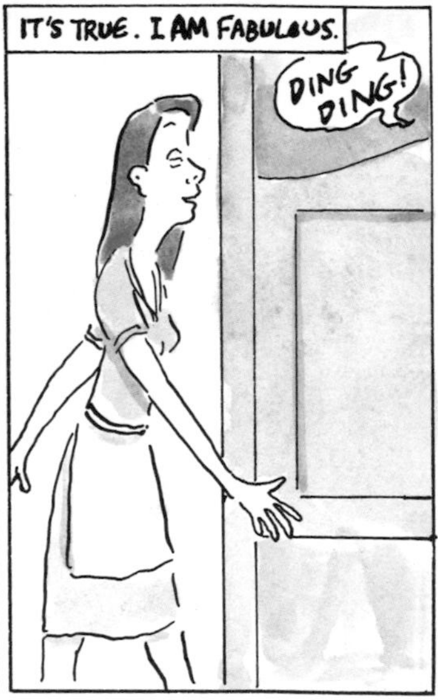
IT'S TRUE. I AM FABULOUS.
DING DING!

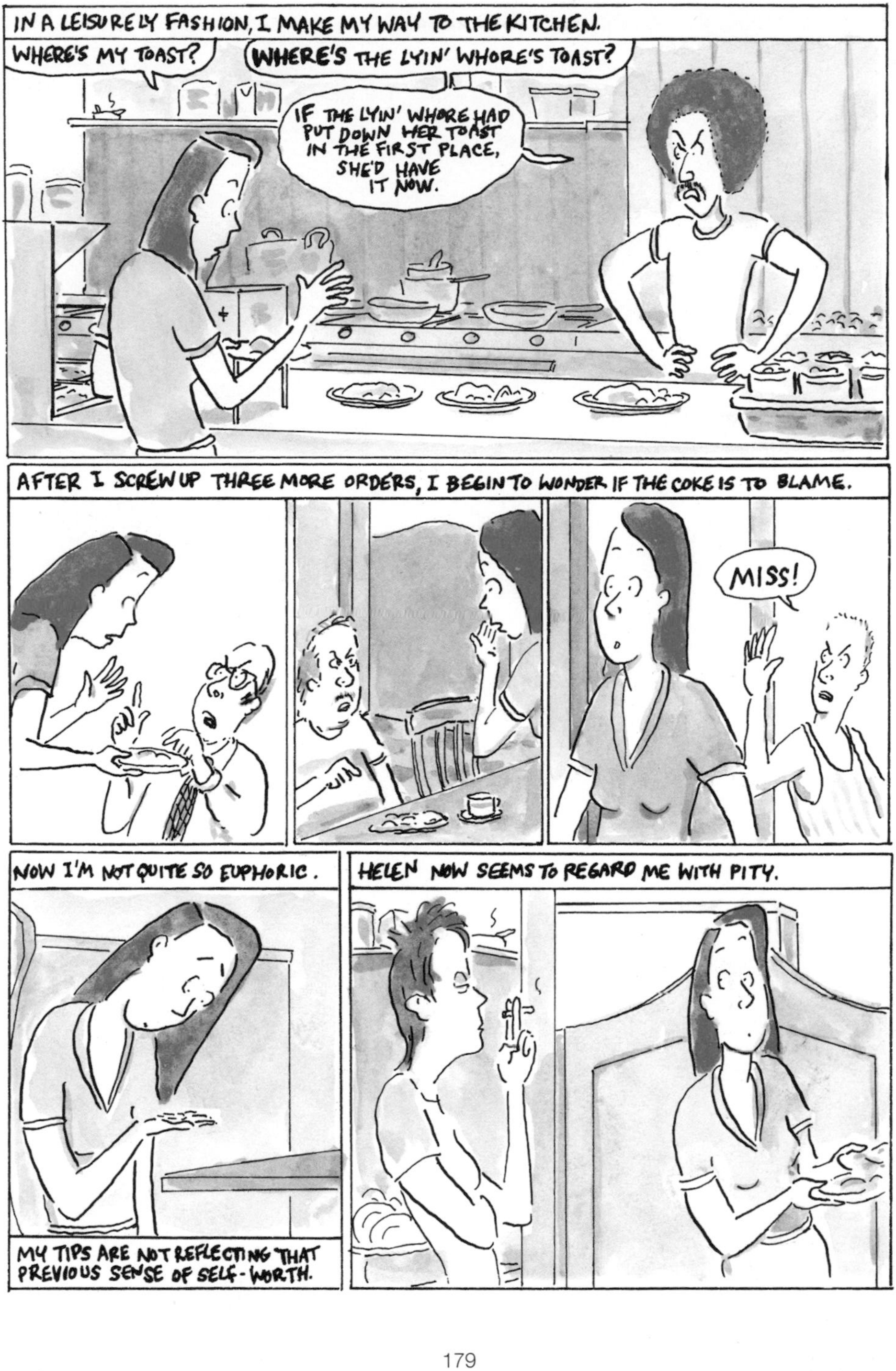
IN A LEISURELY FASHION, I MAKE MY WAY TO THE KITCHEN.
WHERE'S MY TOAST?
WHERE'S THE LYIN' WHORE'S TOAST?
IF THE LYIN' WHORE HAD PUT DOWN HER TOAST IN THE FIRST PLACE, SHE'D HAVE IT NOW.
AFTER I SCREW UP THREE MORE ORDERS, I BEGIN TO WONDER IF THE COKE IS TO BLAME.
MISS!
NOW I'M NOT QUITE SO EUPHORIC.
MY TIPS ARE NOT REFLECTING THAT PREVIOUS SENSE OF SELF-WORTH.
HELEN NOW SEEMS TO REGARD ME WITH PITY.

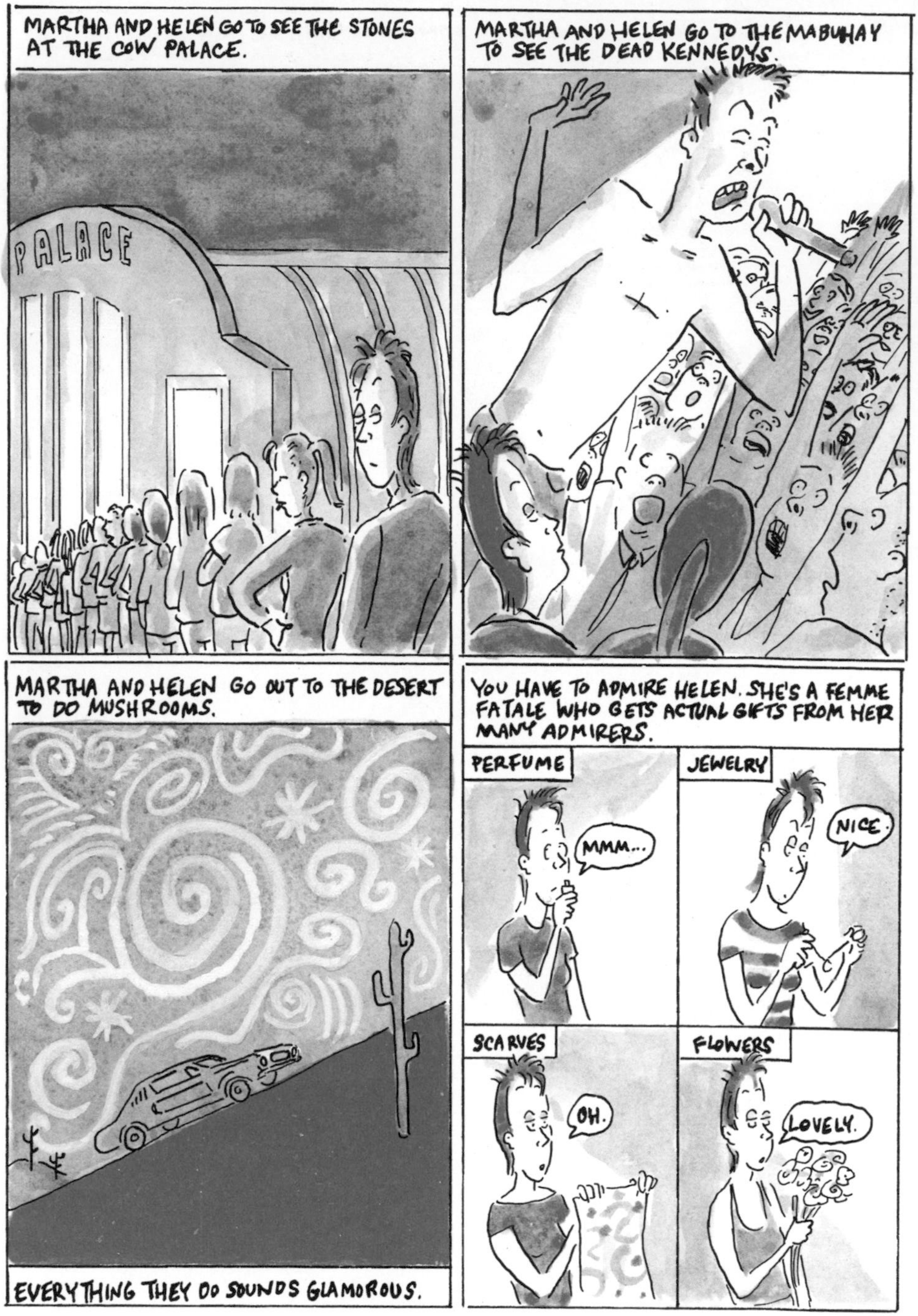
MARTHA AND HELEN GO TO SEE THE STONES AT THE COW PALACE.
PALACE
MARTHA AND HELEN GO TO THE MABUHAY TO SEE THE DEAD KENNEDYS.
MARTHA AND HELEN GO OUT TO THE DESERT TO DO MUSHROOMS.
EVERYTHING THEY DO SOUNDS GLAMOROUS.
YOU HAVE TO ADMIRE HELEN. SHE'S A FEMME FATALE WHO GETS ACTUAL GIFTS FROM HER MANY ADMIRERS.
PERFUME
MMM...
JEWELRY
NICE.
SCARVES
OH.
FLOWERS
LOVELY.

I'M CLEARLY DOING SOMETHING WRONG, BECAUSE HERE'S WHAT I GET FROM THE RARE BOYFRIEND WHO COMES ACROSS WITH THE GOODS:

YES, I CAN READ. HOW DID YOU KNOW?

OH, A BOOK!

FOR ME?

HELEN'S BOYFRIENDS ALWAYS HAVE CLASS.

ON TOP OF THAT, THE REGULAR CUSTOMERS HERE STILL AREN'T SURE ABOUT ME — LIKE THIS ONE, MURRAY:

WHO'S THE NEW GAL?

SHE AIN'T MUCH TO LOOK AT, BUT SHE'S GOT PERSONALITY PLUS!

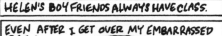

EVEN AFTER I GET OVER MY EMBARRASSED RAGE...

PERSONALITY PLUS!

GRRR!!!

HE'S A PATHETIC LOSER WHO RUNS A PET DETECTIVE AGENCY...

CALLED "BARNABY BONES" FOR GOD'S SAKE.

IDIOT!

SCRAPE SCRAPE SCRAPE

EVEN AFTER I EXACT MY REVENGE...

HEY! SMALL O.J. FOR PERSONALITY PLUS!

BY GIVING HIM A NICKNAME HE IS FOREVER STUCK WITH...

I DECIDE I'M TIRED OF MY PERSONALITY.

I JUST WANT TO BE GORGEOUS, MYSTERIOUS, AND DESIRABLE.

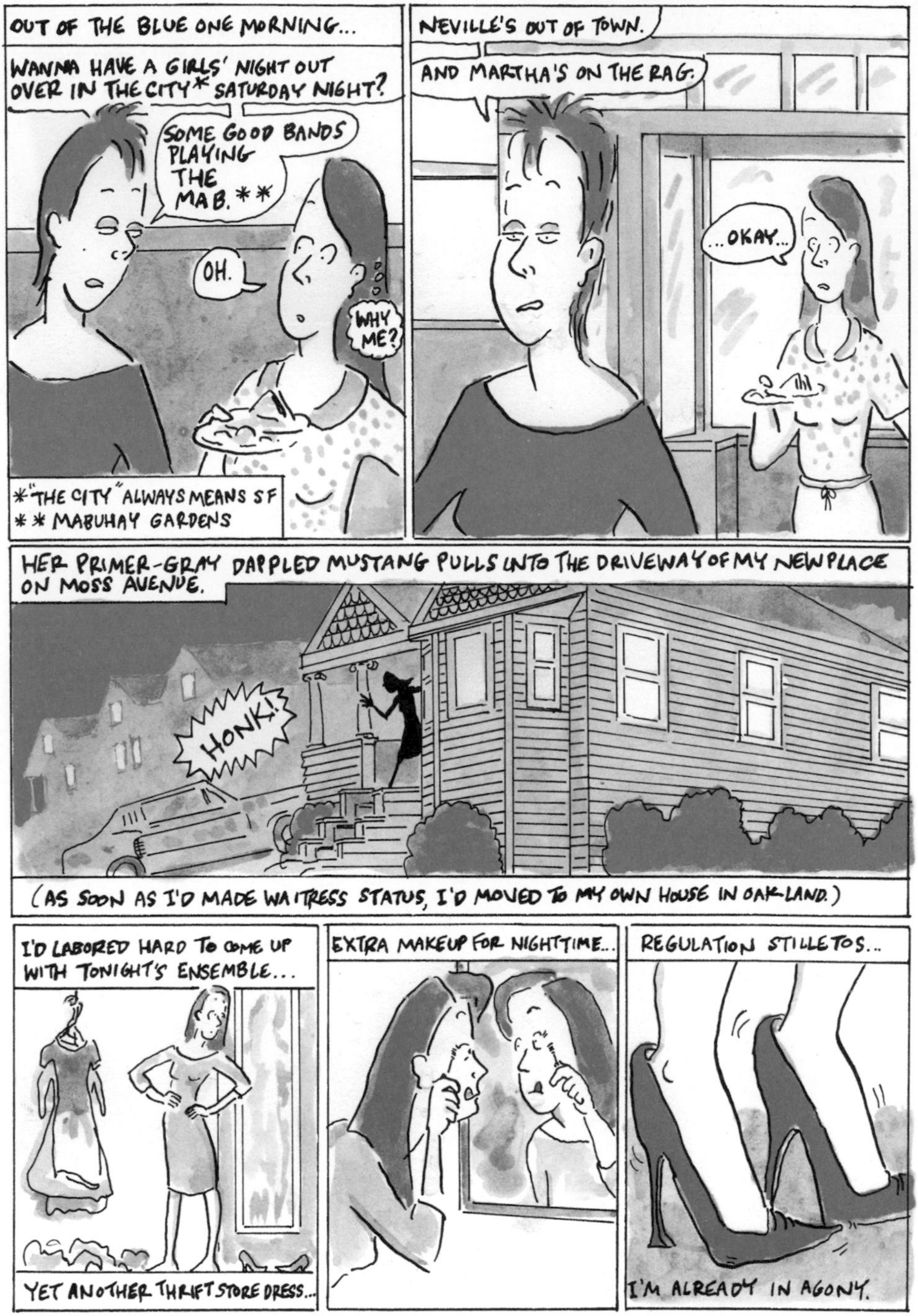

OUT OF THE BLUE ONE MORNING...
WANNA HAVE A GIRLS' NIGHT OUT OVER IN THE CITY* SATURDAY NIGHT?
SOME GOOD BANDS PLAYING THE MAB.**
OH.
WHY ME?
*"THE CITY" ALWAYS MEANS SF
** MABUHAY GARDENS
NEVILLE'S OUT OF TOWN.
AND MARTHA'S ON THE RAG.
...OKAY...
HER PRIMER-GRAY DAPPLED MUSTANG PULLS INTO THE DRIVEWAY OF MY NEW PLACE ON MOSS AVENUE.
HONK!
(AS SOON AS I'D MADE WAITRESS STATUS, I'D MOVED TO MY OWN HOUSE IN OAKLAND.)
I'D LABORED HARD TO COME UP WITH TONIGHT'S ENSEMBLE...
YET ANOTHER THRIFT STORE DRESS...
EXTRA MAKEUP FOR NIGHTTIME...
REGULATION STILLETOS...
I'M ALREADY IN AGONY.

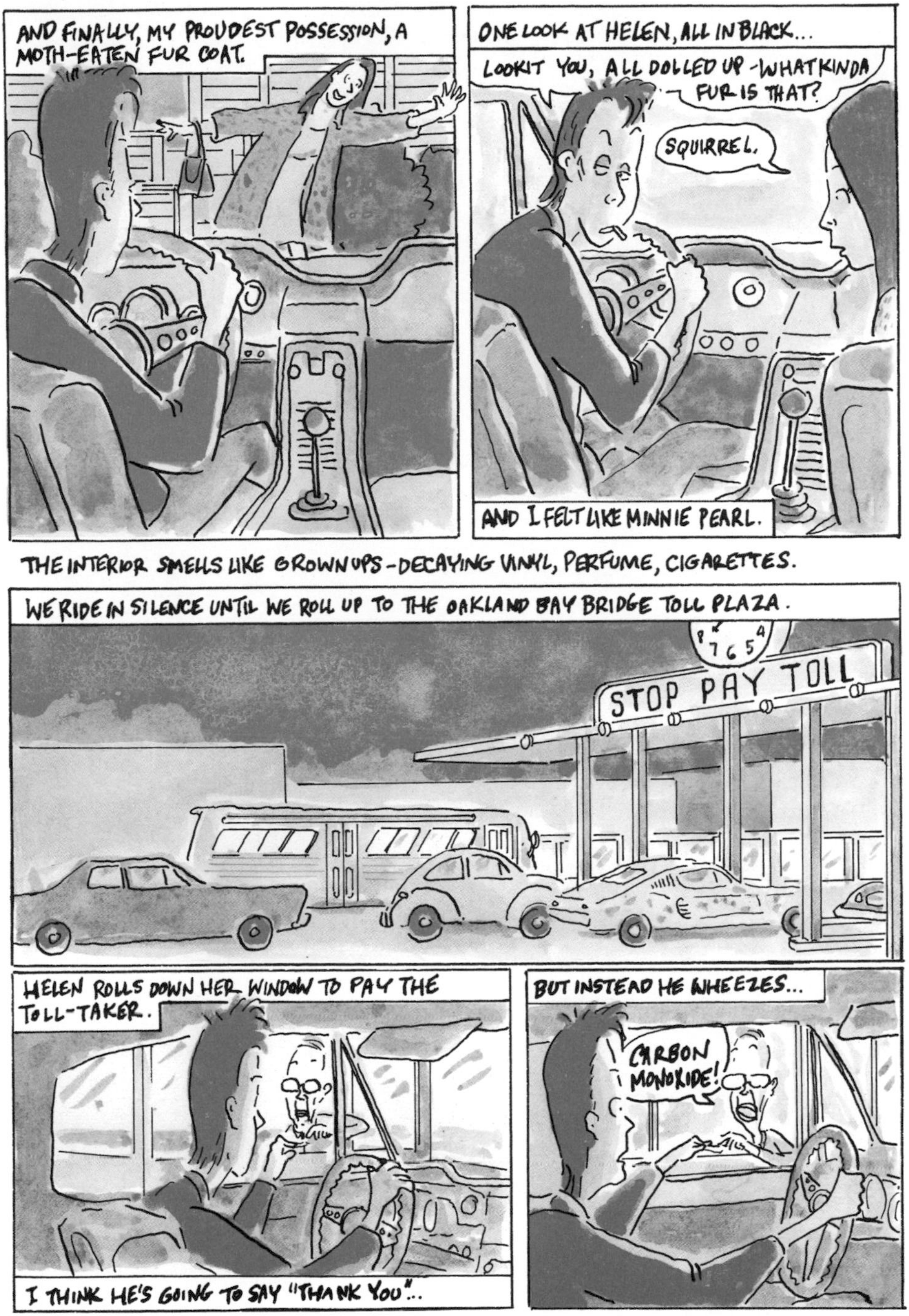
AND FINALLY, MY PROUDEST POSSESSION, A MOTH-EATEN FUR COAT.
ONE LOOK AT HELEN, ALL IN BLACK...
LOOKIT YOU, ALL DOLLED UP - WHATKINDA FUR IS THAT?
SQUIRREL.
AND I FELT LIKE MINNIE PEARL.
THE INTERIOR SMELLS LIKE GROWNUPS - DECAYING VINYL, PERFUME, CIGARETTES.
WE RIDE IN SILENCE UNTIL WE ROLL UP TO THE OAKLAND BAY BRIDGE TOLL PLAZA.
STOP PAY TOLL
HELEN ROLLS DOWN HER WINDOW TO PAY THE TOLL-TAKER.
I THINK HE'S GOING TO SAY "THANK YOU"...
BUT INSTEAD HE WHEEZES...
CARBON MONOXIDE!

AS WE PULL AWAY...

HA HA HA HA!

THE ICE IS BROKEN.

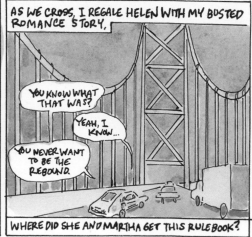

AS WE CROSS, I REGALE HELEN WITH MY BUSTED ROMANCE STORY.

YOU KNOW WHAT THAT WAS?

YEAH, I KNOW...

YOU NEVER WANT TO BE THE REBOUND.

WHERE DID SHE AND MARTHA GET THIS RULEBOOK?

WE ARE LUCKY AND FIND A PARKING PLACE IN CHINATOWN, ONLY SIX BLOCKS FROM THE CLUB.

CAROL DODA TOPLESS LIVE ACT

BIG AL'S

ADULT BOOK STORE

WE PASS PEEPSHOWS AND FLOPHOUSES AND OLD MAN BARS. WINOS STAGGER TOWARD US. I WALK FASTER BUT HELEN JUST LAUGHS, AMUSED, FEARLESS.

INSIDE THE MABUHAY, THE WALLS THROB.

FUCK ME

FUCK YOU

KILL ME KILL YOU

AS ALWAYS, CHECKING THE GENERAL FASHION SENSE OF THE CROWD...

DIE MOMMY DIE MOMMY-DIE MOMMY DIE

I DECIDE YOU CAN'T GO WRONG WITH SPIKE HEELS AND A RATTY FUR COAT.

I CAN'T FIGURE OUT HOW ANYONE MEETS IN THESE PLACES,

SLASH AND BURN SLASH AND BURN SLASH SLASH SLAS

HELEN WANTS TO STAY UNTIL 1:00 A.M., BECAUSE SHE KNOWS THE BASS PLAYER.

I'M EXHAUSTED ALREADY.

HATE MY LIFE

YOU CAN'T HEAR YOURSELF THINK.

WHCH BND YUCUMSEE?

WHAT?

KNE MY WIF

WHICH BAND DID YOU COME TO SEE?

LIVE TO DIE

GET A KN

NONE OF THEM.

STINKING PU

ROTTEN

WE STARE AT EACH OTHER A TAD TOO LONG.

GRAB MY DICK

DICK

I FEEL COMPELLED TO SAY SOMETHING.

ARE YOU A MUSICIAN?

STICKS

YEAH.

DIE DIE DIE

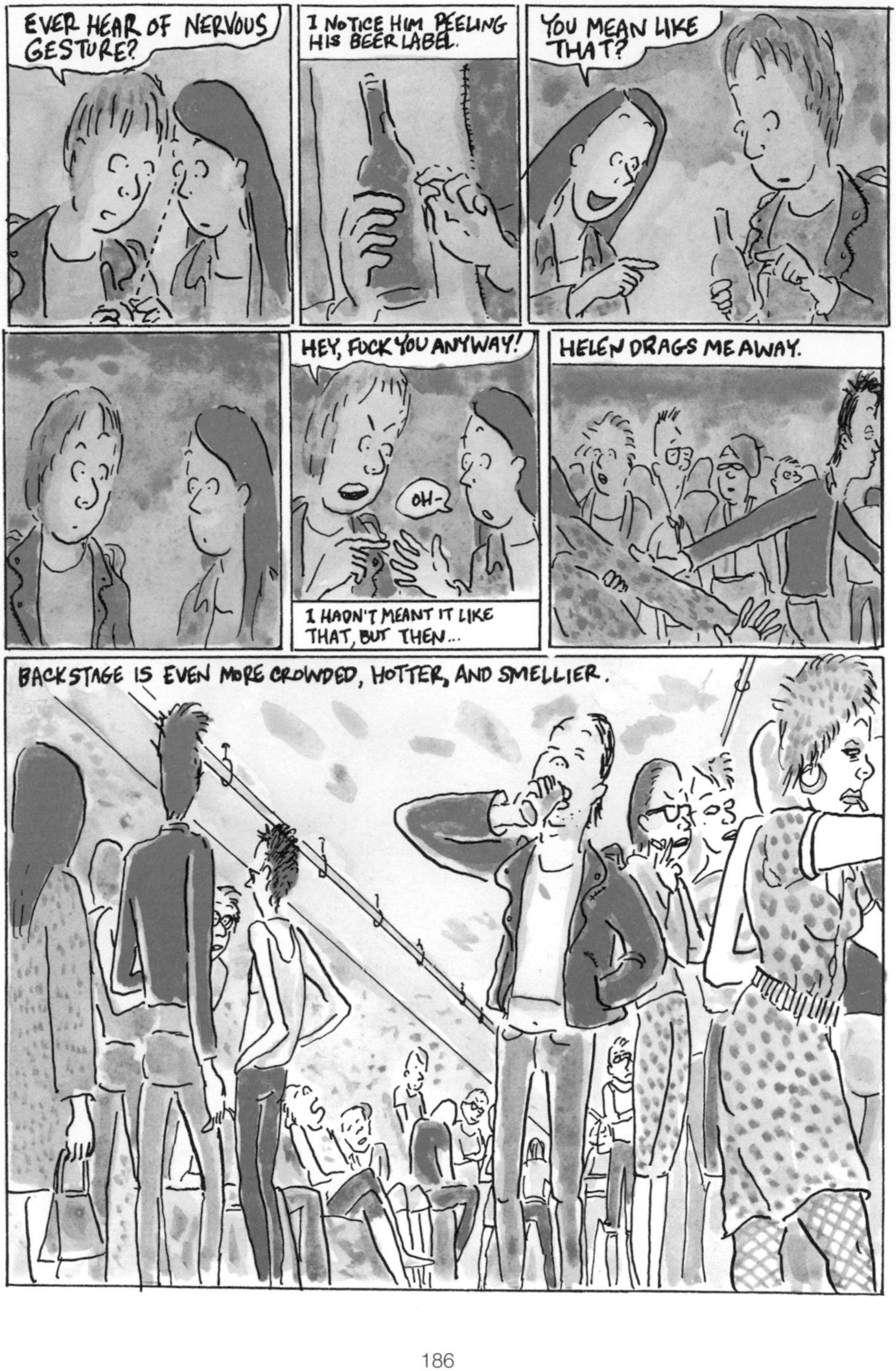
EVER HEAR OF NERVOUS GESTURE?
I NOTICE HIM PEELING HIS BEER LABEL.
YOU MEAN LIKE THAT?
HEY, FUCK YOU ANYWAY!
OH-
I HADN'T MEANT IT LIKE THAT, BUT THEN...
HELEN DRAGS ME AWAY.
BACKSTAGE IS EVEN MORE CROWDED, HOTTER, AND SMELLIER.

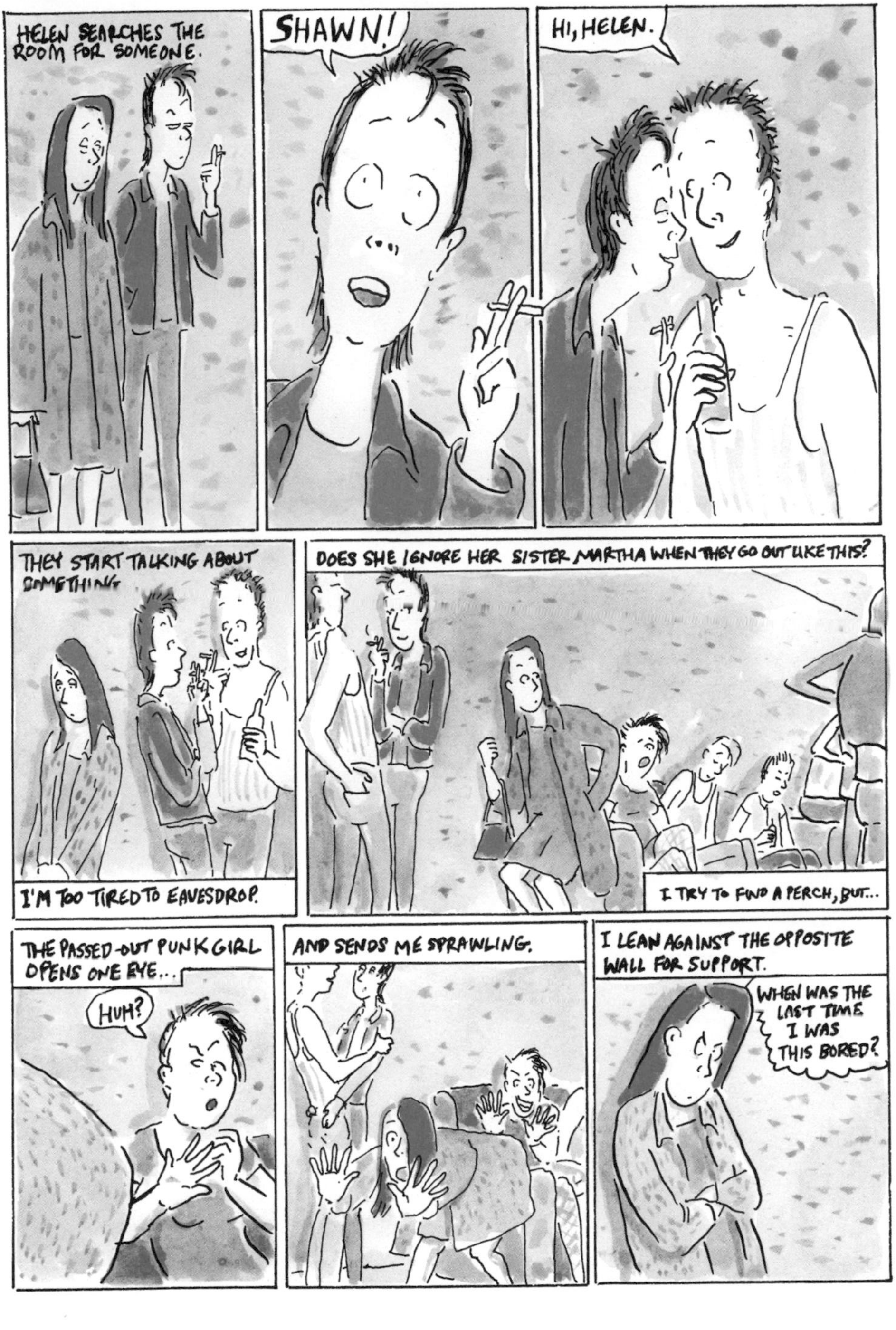
HELEN SEARCHES THE ROOM FOR SOMEONE.
SHAWN!
HI, HELEN.
THEY START TALKING ABOUT SOMETHING.
I'M TOO TIRED TO EAVESDROP.
DOES SHE IGNORE HER SISTER MARTHA WHEN THEY GO OUT LIKE THIS?
I TRY TO FIND A PERCH, BUT...
THE PASSED-OUT PUNK GIRL OPENS ONE EYE...
HUH?
AND SENDS ME SPRAWLING.
I LEAN AGAINST THE OPPOSITE WALL FOR SUPPORT.
WHEN WAS THE LAST TIME I WAS THIS BORED?

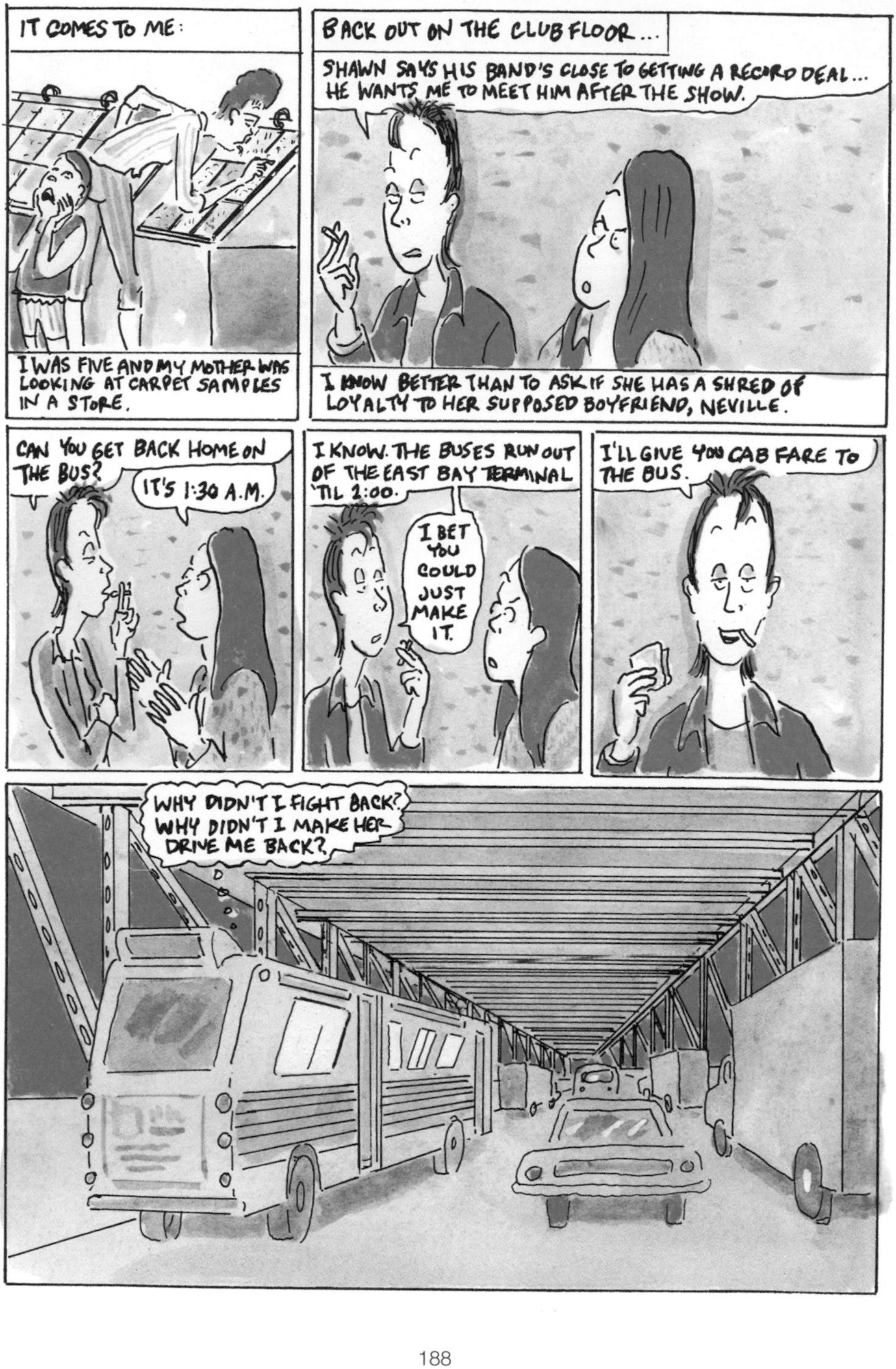
IT COMES TO ME:
I WAS FIVE AND MY MOTHER WAS LOOKING AT CARPET SAMPLES IN A STORE.
BACK OUT ON THE CLUB FLOOR...
SHAWN SAYS HIS BAND'S CLOSE TO GETTING A RECORD DEAL... HE WANTS ME TO MEET HIM AFTER THE SHOW.
I KNOW BETTER THAN TO ASK IF SHE HAS A SHRED OF LOYALTY TO HER SUPPOSED BOYFRIEND, NEVILLE.
CAN YOU GET BACK HOME ON THE BUS?
IT'S 1:30 A.M.
I KNOW. THE BUSES RUN OUT OF THE EAST BAY TERMINAL 'TIL 2:00.
I BET YOU COULD JUST MAKE IT.
I'LL GIVE YOU CAB FARE TO THE BUS.
WHY DIDN'T I FIGHT BACK? WHY DIDN'T I MAKE HER DRIVE ME BACK?

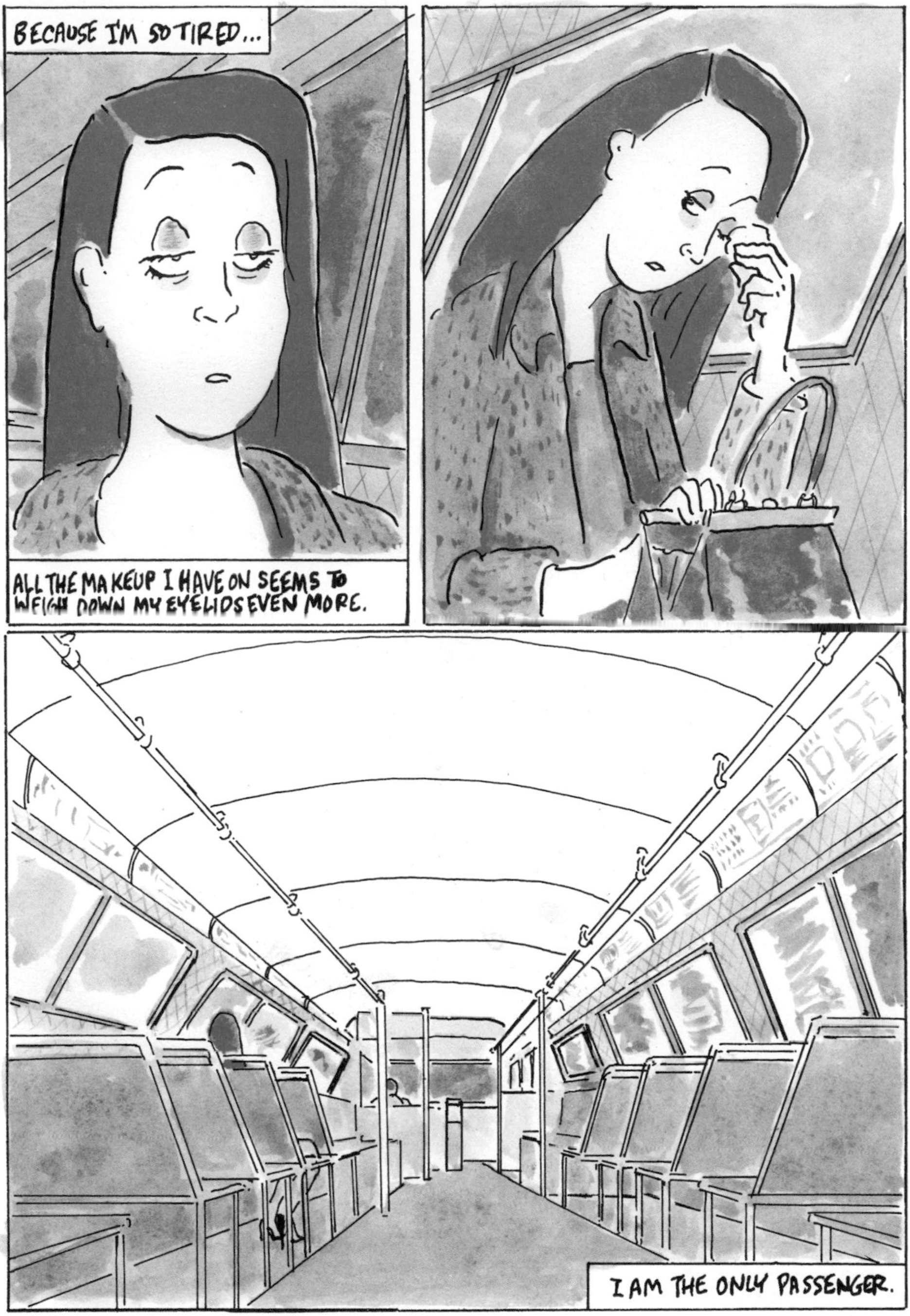
BECAUSE I'M SO TIRED...
ALL THE MAKEUP I HAVE ON SEEMS TO WEIGH DOWN MY EYELIDS EVEN MORE.
I AM THE ONLY PASSENGER.

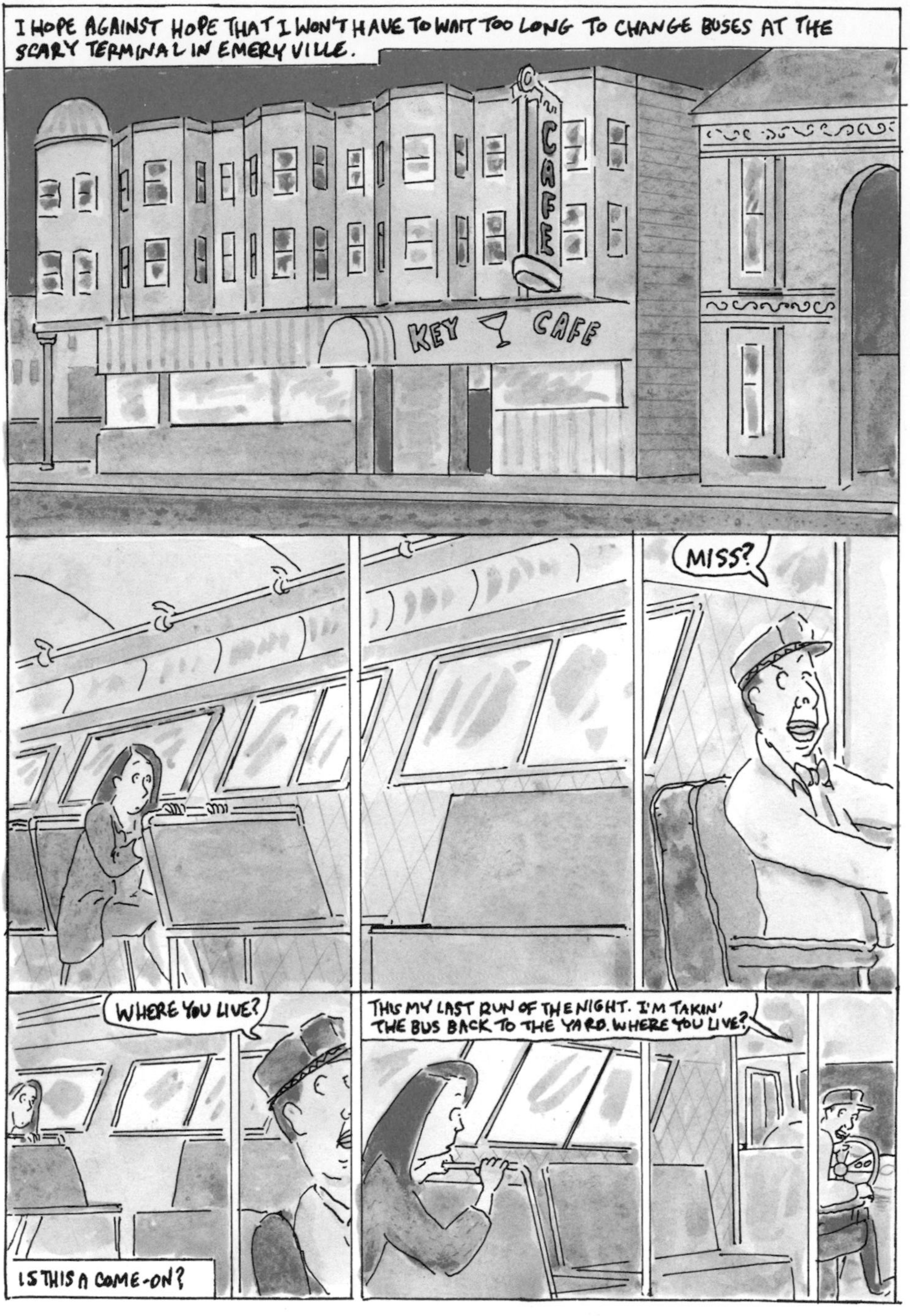
I HOPE AGAINST HOPE THAT I WON'T HAVE TO WAIT TOO LONG TO CHANGE BUSES AT THE SCARY TERMINAL IN EMERYVILLE.
KEY CAFE
CAFE
MISS?
WHERE YOU LIVE?
IS THIS A COME-ON?
THIS MY LAST RUN OF THE NIGHT. I'M TAKIN' THE BUS BACK TO THE YARD. WHERE YOU LIVE?

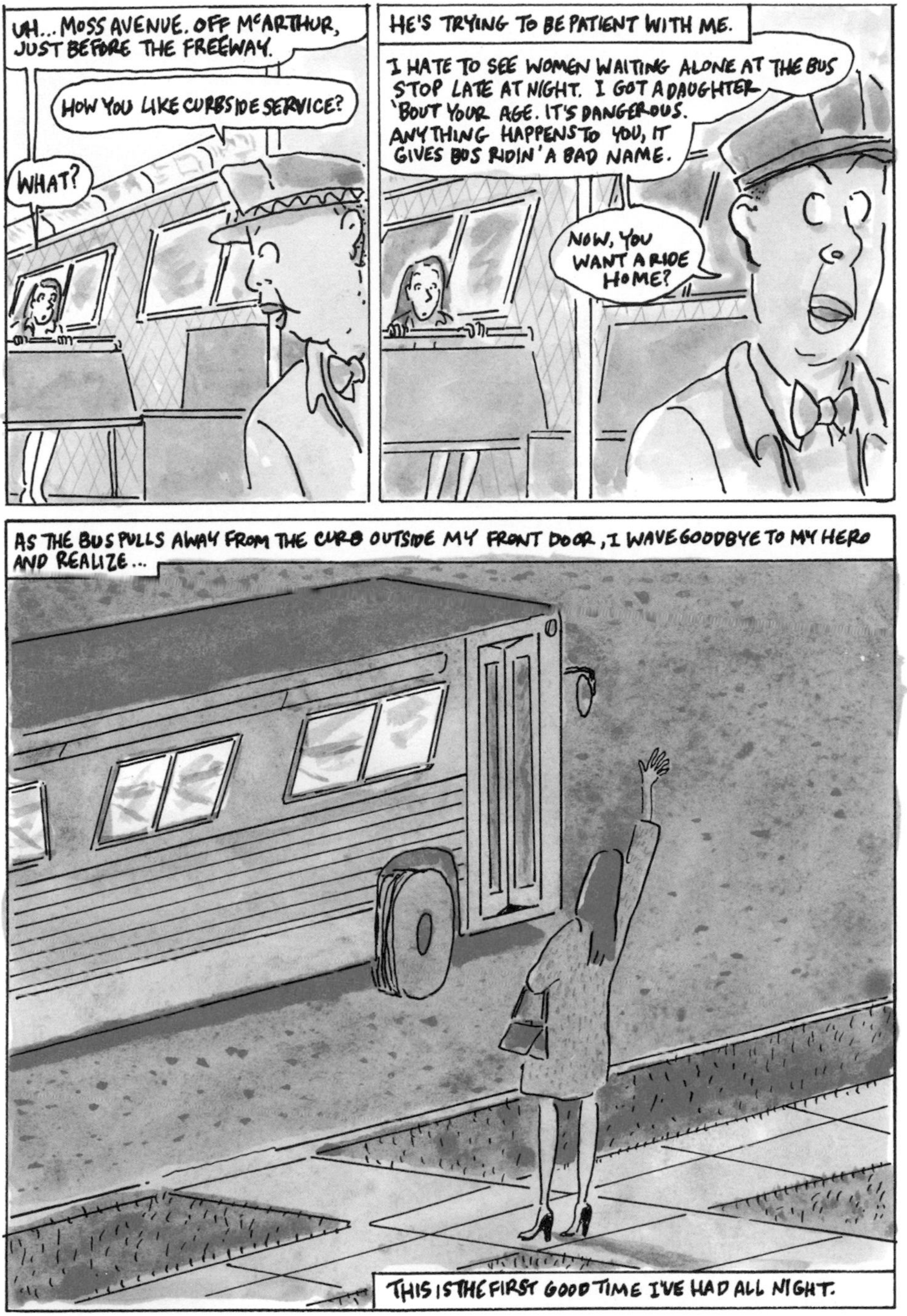

UH... MOSS AVENUE. OFF McARTHUR, JUST BEFORE THE FREEWAY.
HOW YOU LIKE CURBSIDE SERVICE?
WHAT?
HE'S TRYING TO BE PATIENT WITH ME.
I HATE TO SEE WOMEN WAITING ALONE AT THE BUS STOP LATE AT NIGHT. I GOT A DAUGHTER 'BOUT YOUR AGE. IT'S DANGEROUS. ANYTHING HAPPENS TO YOU, IT GIVES BUS RIDIN' A BAD NAME.
NOW, YOU WANT A RIDE HOME?
AS THE BUS PULLS AWAY FROM THE CURB OUTSIDE MY FRONT DOOR, I WAVE GOODBYE TO MY HERO AND REALIZE...
THIS IS THE FIRST GOOD TIME I'VE HAD ALL NIGHT.

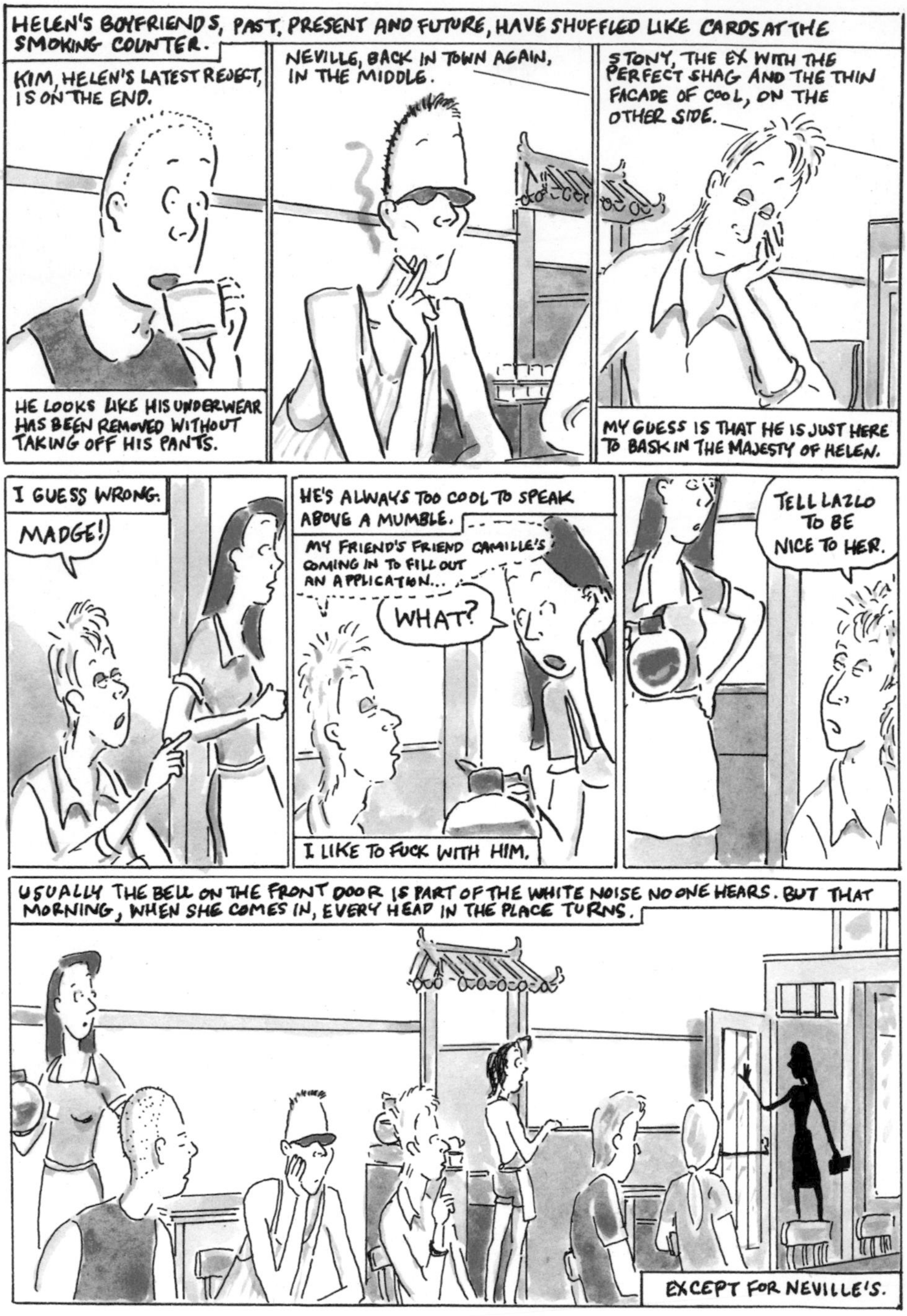
HELEN'S BOYFRIENDS, PAST, PRESENT AND FUTURE, HAVE SHUFFLED LIKE CARDS AT THE SMOKING COUNTER.
KIM, HELEN'S LATEST REJECT, IS ON THE END.
HE LOOKS LIKE HIS UNDERWEAR HAS BEEN REMOVED WITHOUT TAKING OFF HIS PANTS.
NEVILLE, BACK IN TOWN AGAIN, IN THE MIDDLE.
STONY, THE EX WITH THE PERFECT SHAG AND THE THIN FACADE OF COOL, ON THE OTHER SIDE.
MY GUESS IS THAT HE IS JUST HERE TO BASK IN THE MAJESTY OF HELEN.
I GUESS WRONG.
MADGE!
HE'S ALWAYS TOO COOL TO SPEAK ABOVE A MUMBLE.
MY FRIEND'S FRIEND CAMILLE'S COMING IN TO FILL OUT AN APPLICATION...
WHAT?
I LIKE TO FUCK WITH HIM.
TELL LAZLO TO BE NICE TO HER.
USUALLY THE BELL ON THE FRONT DOOR IS PART OF THE WHITE NOISE NO ONE HEARS. BUT THAT MORNING, WHEN SHE COMES IN, EVERY HEAD IN THE PLACE TURNS.
EXCEPT FOR NEVILLE'S.

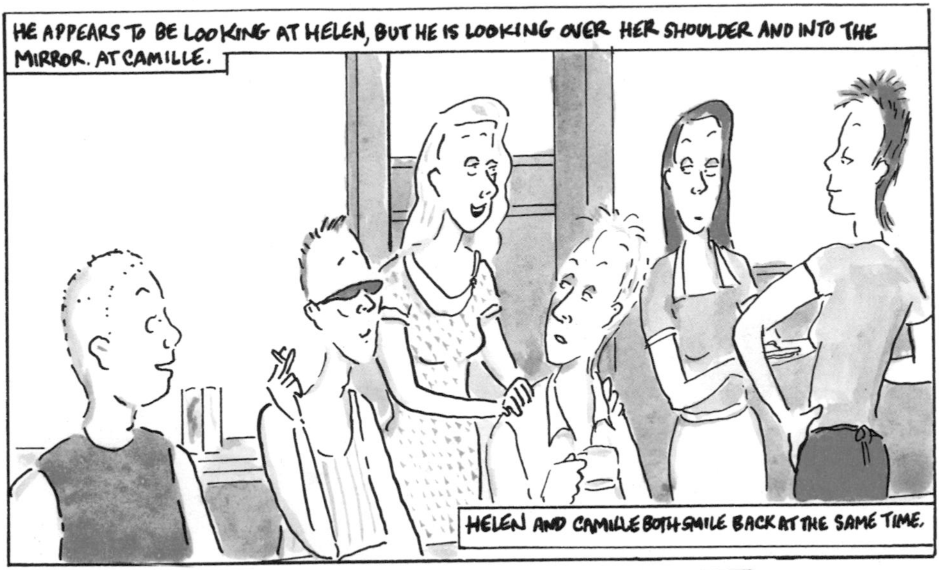
HE APPEARS TO BE LOOKING AT HELEN, BUT HE IS LOOKING OVER HER SHOULDER AND INTO THE MIRROR. AT CAMILLE.
HELEN AND CAMILLE BOTH SMILE BACK AT THE SAME TIME.

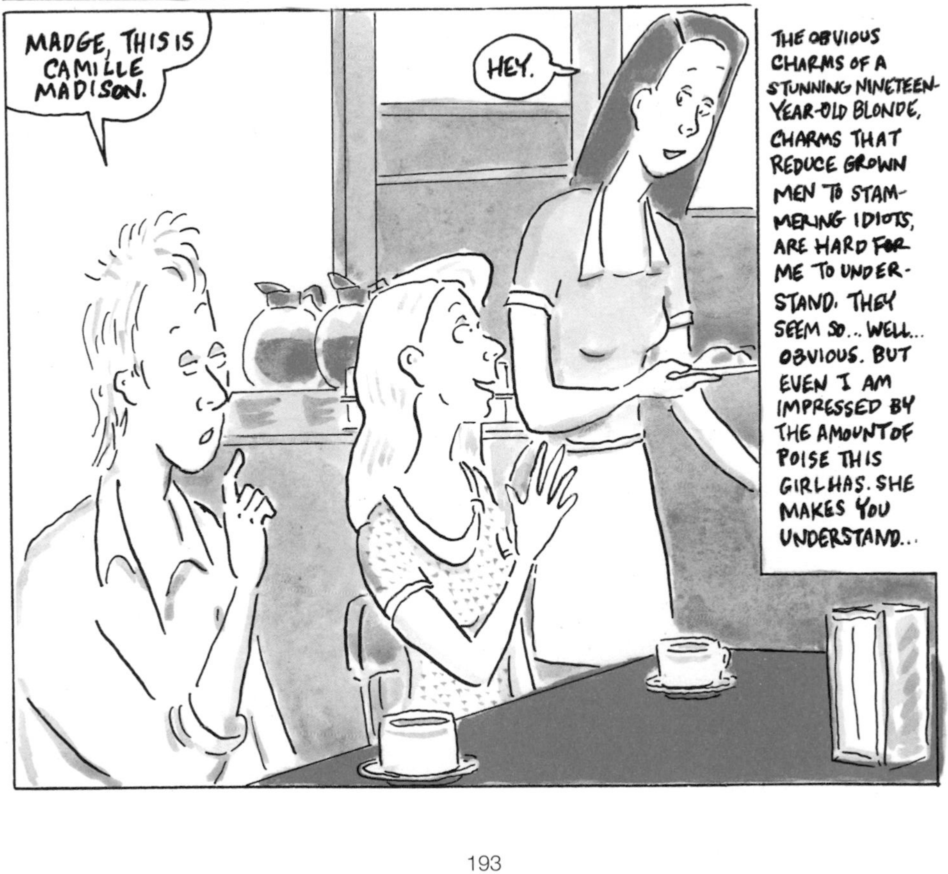
MADGE, THIS IS CAMILLE MADISON.
HEY.
THE OBVIOUS CHARMS OF A STUNNING NINETEEN-YEAR-OLD BLONDE, CHARMS THAT REDUCE GROWN MEN TO STAMMERING IDIOTS, ARE HARD FOR ME TO UNDERSTAND. THEY SEEM SO... WELL... OBVIOUS. BUT EVEN I AM IMPRESSED BY THE AMOUNT OF POISE THIS GIRL HAS. SHE MAKES YOU UNDERSTAND...

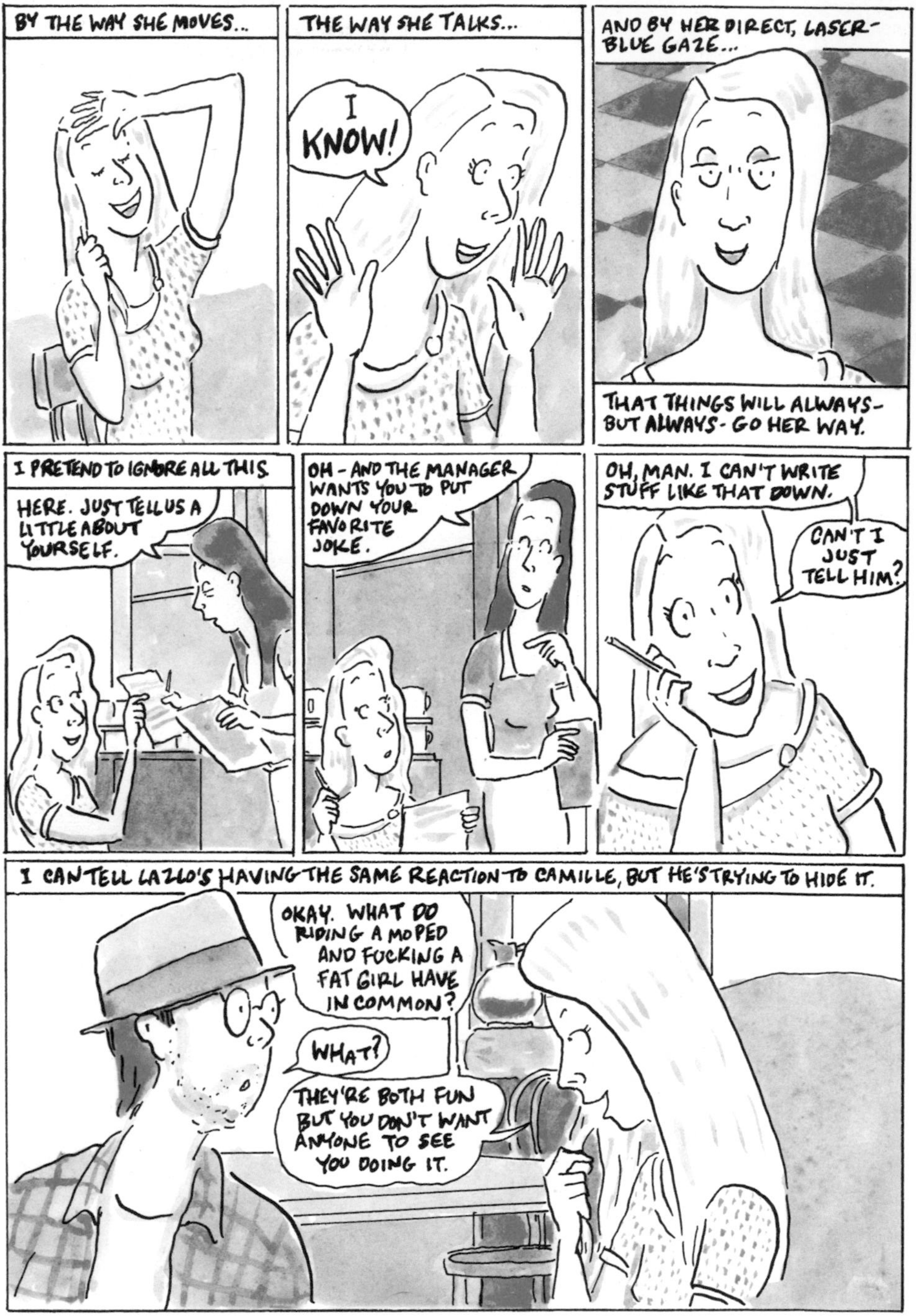
BY THE WAY SHE MOVES...
THE WAY SHE TALKS...
I KNOW!
AND BY HER DIRECT, LASER-BLUE GAZE...
THAT THINGS WILL ALWAYS- BUT ALWAYS- GO HER WAY.
I PRETEND TO IGNORE ALL THIS.
HERE. JUST TELL US A LITTLE ABOUT YOURSELF.
OH - AND THE MANAGER WANTS YOU TO PUT DOWN YOUR FAVORITE JOKE.
OH, MAN. I CAN'T WRITE STUFF LIKE THAT DOWN.
CAN'T I JUST TELL HIM?
I CAN TELL LAZLO'S HAVING THE SAME REACTION TO CAMILLE, BUT HE'S TRYING TO HIDE IT.
OKAY. WHAT DO RIDING A MOPED AND FUCKING A FAT GIRL HAVE IN COMMON?
WHAT?
THEY'RE BOTH FUN BUT YOU DON'T WANT ANYONE TO SEE YOU DOING IT.

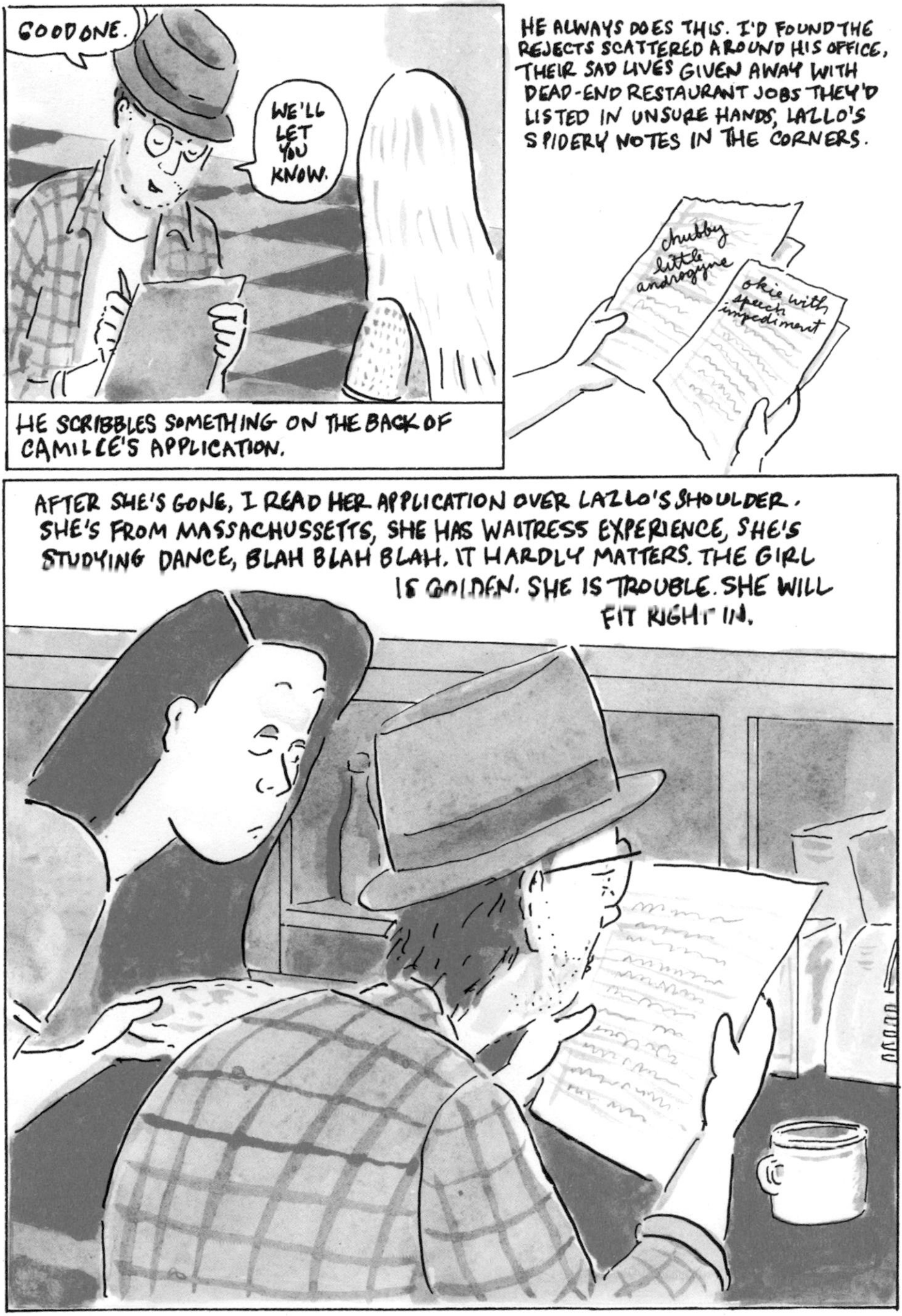
GOOD ONE.
WE'LL LET YOU KNOW.
HE SCRIBBLES SOMETHING ON THE BACK OF CAMILLE'S APPLICATION.
HE ALWAYS DOES THIS. I'D FOUND THE REJECTS SCATTERED AROUND HIS OFFICE, THEIR SAD LIVES GIVEN AWAY WITH DEAD-END RESTAURANT JOBS THEY'D LISTED IN UNSURE HANDS, LAZLO'S SPIDERY NOTES IN THE CORNERS.
chubby little androgyne
okie with speech impediment
AFTER SHE'S GONE, I READ HER APPLICATION OVER LAZLO'S SHOULDER. SHE'S FROM MASSACHUSSETTS, SHE HAS WAITRESS EXPERIENCE, SHE'S STUDYING DANCE, BLAH BLAH BLAH. IT HARDLY MATTERS. THE GIRL IS GOLDEN. SHE IS TROUBLE. SHE WILL FIT RIGHT IN.

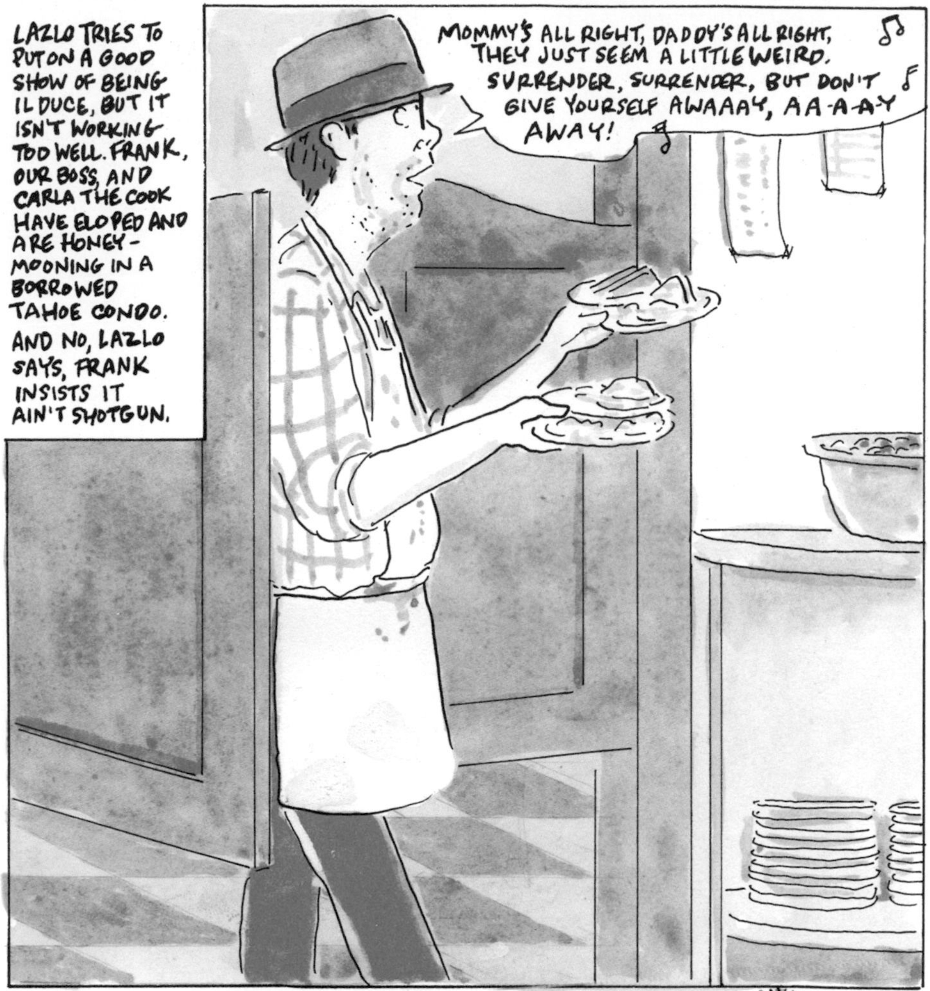
LAZLO TRIES TO PUT ON A GOOD SHOW OF BEING IL DUCE, BUT IT ISN'T WORKING TOO WELL. FRANK, OUR BOSS, AND CARLA THE COOK HAVE ELOPED AND ARE HONEY-MOONING IN A BORROWED TAHOE CONDO.
AND NO, LAZLO SAYS, FRANK INSISTS IT AIN'T SHOTGUN.
MOMMY'S ALL RIGHT, DADDY'S ALL RIGHT, THEY JUST SEEM A LITTLE WEIRD. SURRENDER, SURRENDER, BUT DON'T GIVE YOURSELF AWAAAY, AA-A-A-Y AWAY!

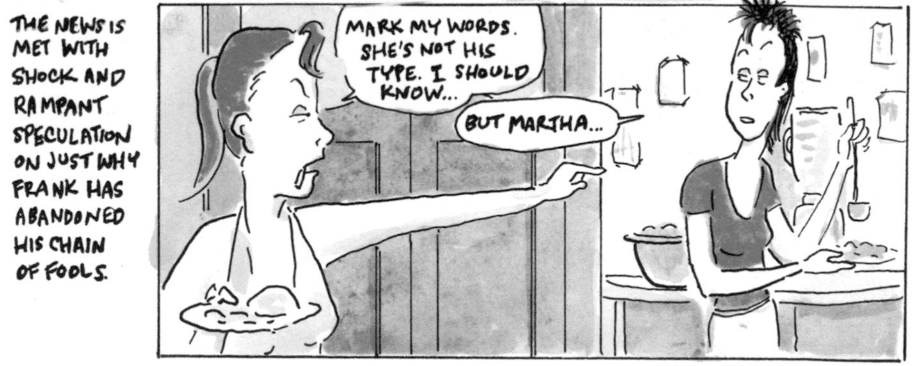
THE NEWS IS MET WITH SHOCK AND RAMPANT SPECULATION ON JUST WHY FRANK HAS ABANDONED HIS CHAIN OF FOOLS.
MARK MY WORDS. SHE'S NOT HIS TYPE. I SHOULD KNOW...
BUT MARTHA...

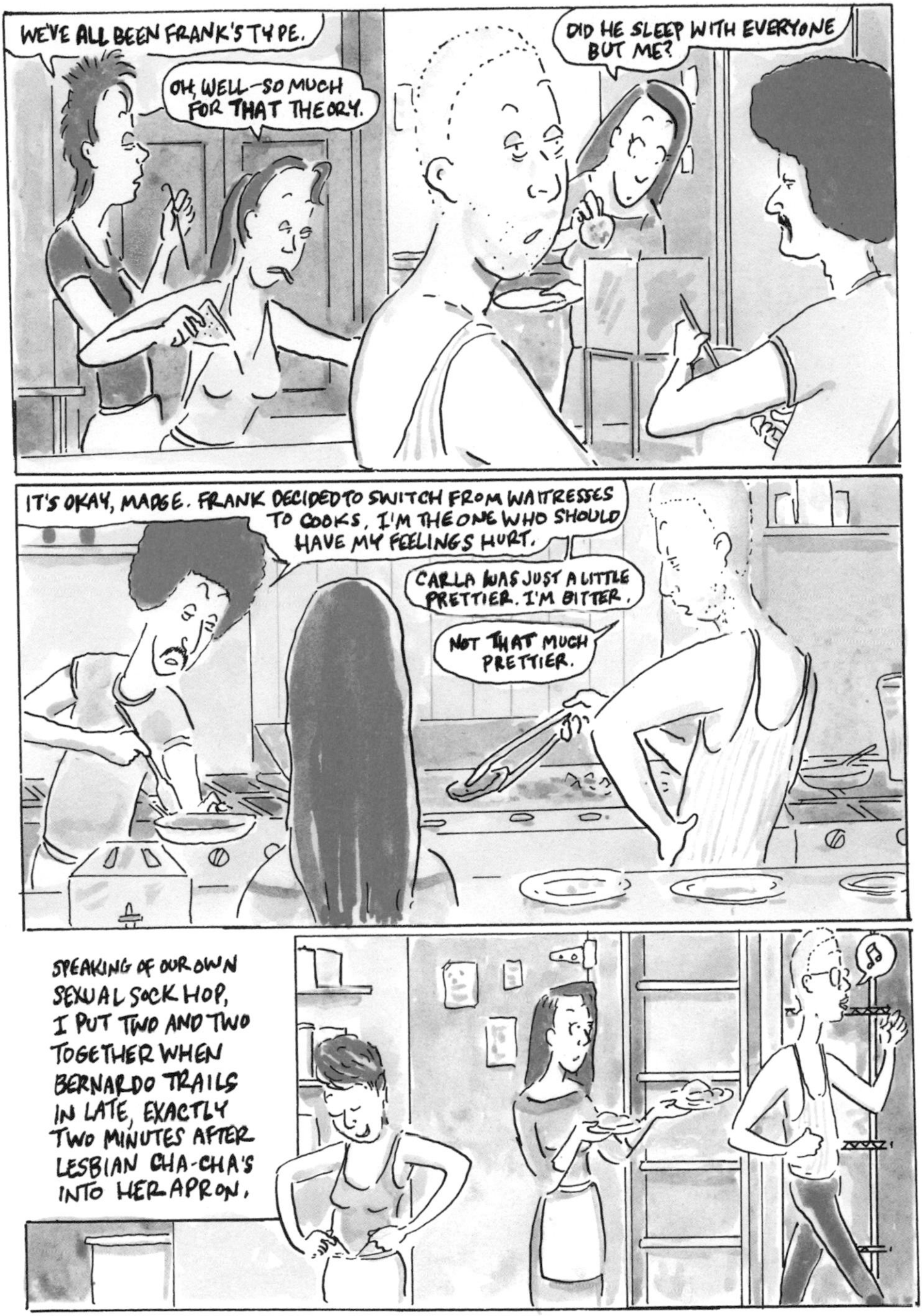
WE'VE ALL BEEN FRANK'S TYPE.
OH, WELL—SO MUCH FOR THAT THEORY.
DID HE SLEEP WITH EVERYONE BUT ME?
IT'S OKAY, MADGE. FRANK DECIDED TO SWITCH FROM WAITRESSES TO COOKS. I'M THE ONE WHO SHOULD HAVE MY FEELINGS HURT.
CARLA WAS JUST A LITTLE PRETTIER. I'M BITTER.
NOT THAT MUCH PRETTIER.
SPEAKING OF OUR OWN SEXUAL SOCK HOP, I PUT TWO AND TWO TOGETHER WHEN BERNARDO TRAILS IN LATE, EXACTLY TWO MINUTES AFTER LESBIAN CHA-CHA'S INTO HER APRON.

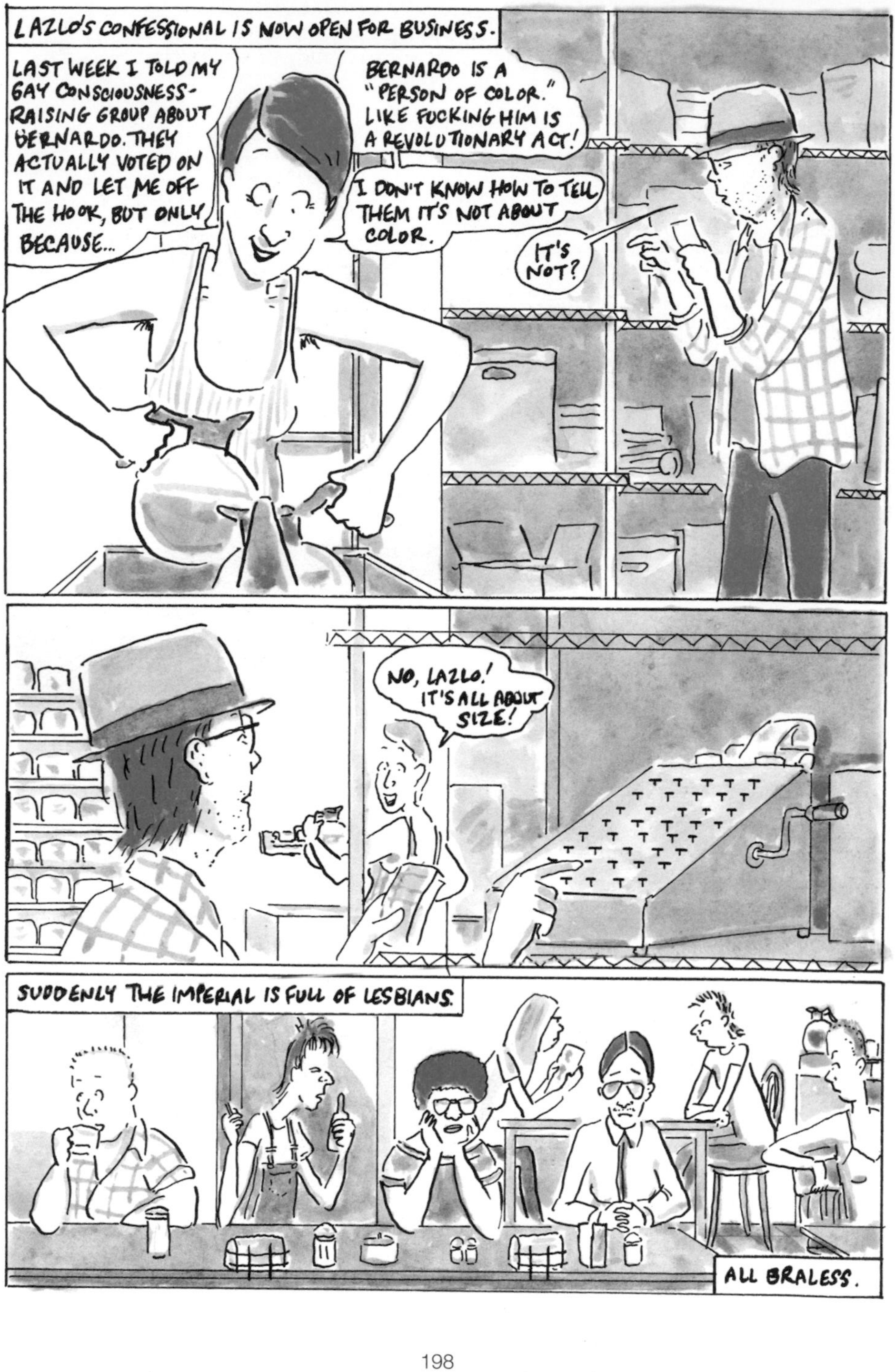
LAZLO'S CONFESSIONAL IS NOW OPEN FOR BUSINESS.
LAST WEEK I TOLD MY GAY CONSCIOUSNESS-RAISING GROUP ABOUT BERNARDO. THEY ACTUALLY VOTED ON IT AND LET ME OFF THE HOOK, BUT ONLY BECAUSE...
BERNARDO IS A "PERSON OF COLOR." LIKE FUCKING HIM IS A REVOLUTIONARY ACT!
I DON'T KNOW HOW TO TELL THEM IT'S NOT ABOUT COLOR.
IT'S NOT?
NO, LAZLO! IT'S ALL ABOUT SIZE!
SUDDENLY THE IMPERIAL IS FULL OF LESBIANS.
ALL BRALESS.

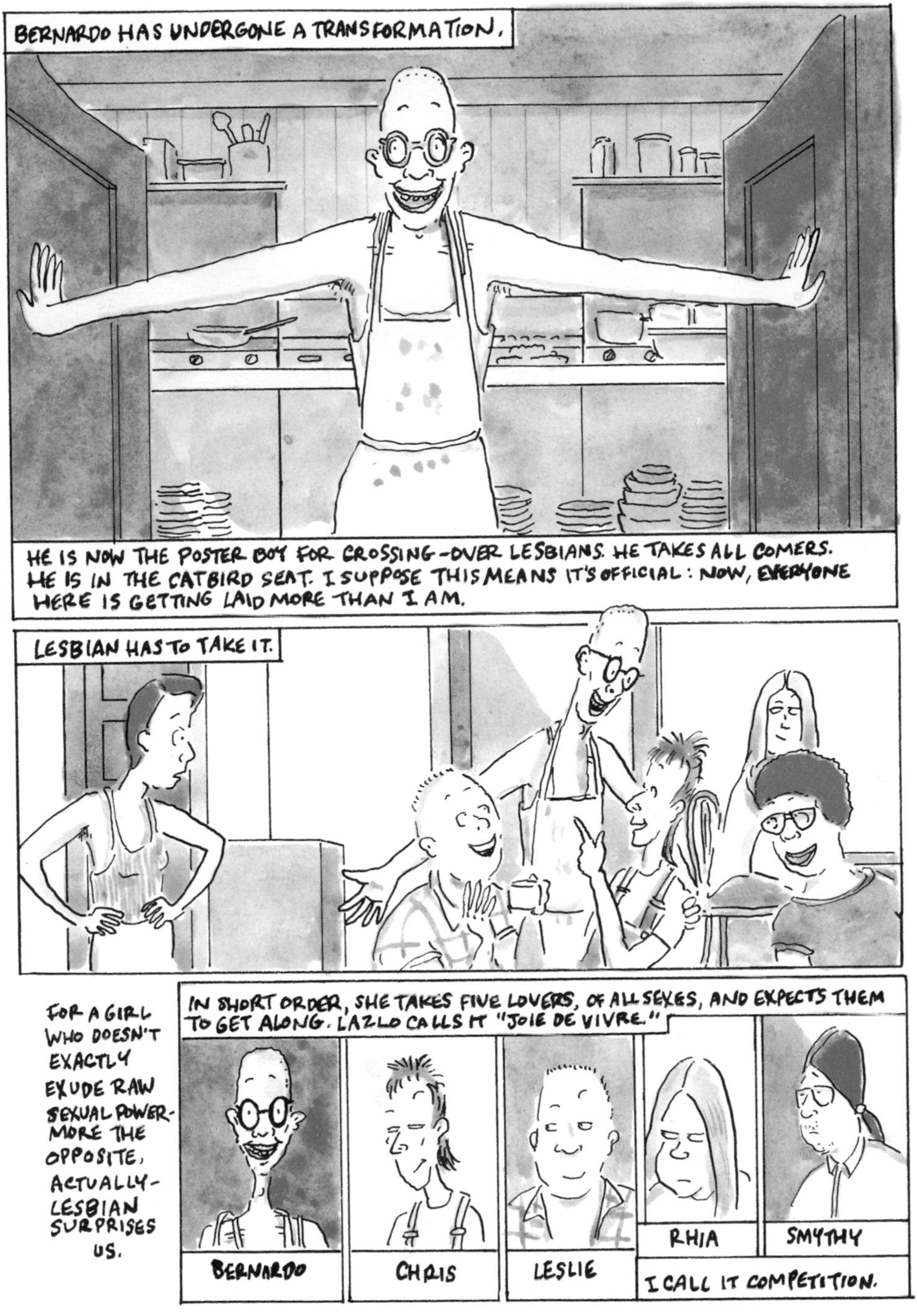
BERNARDO HAS UNDERGONE A TRANSFORMATION.
HE IS NOW THE POSTER BOY FOR CROSSING-OVER LESBIANS. HE TAKES ALL COMERS. HE IS IN THE CATBIRD SEAT. I SUPPOSE THIS MEANS IT'S OFFICIAL: NOW, EVERYONE HERE IS GETTING LAID MORE THAN I AM.
LESBIAN HAS TO TAKE IT.
FOR A GIRL WHO DOESN'T EXACTLY EXUDE RAW SEXUAL POWER- MORE THE OPPOSITE, ACTUALLY- LESBIAN SURPRISES US.
IN SHORT ORDER, SHE TAKES FIVE LOVERS, OF ALL SEXES, AND EXPECTS THEM TO GET ALONG. LAZLO CALLS IT "JOIE DE VIVRE."
BERNARDO
CHRIS
LESLIE
RHIA
SMYTHY
I CALL IT COMPETITION.

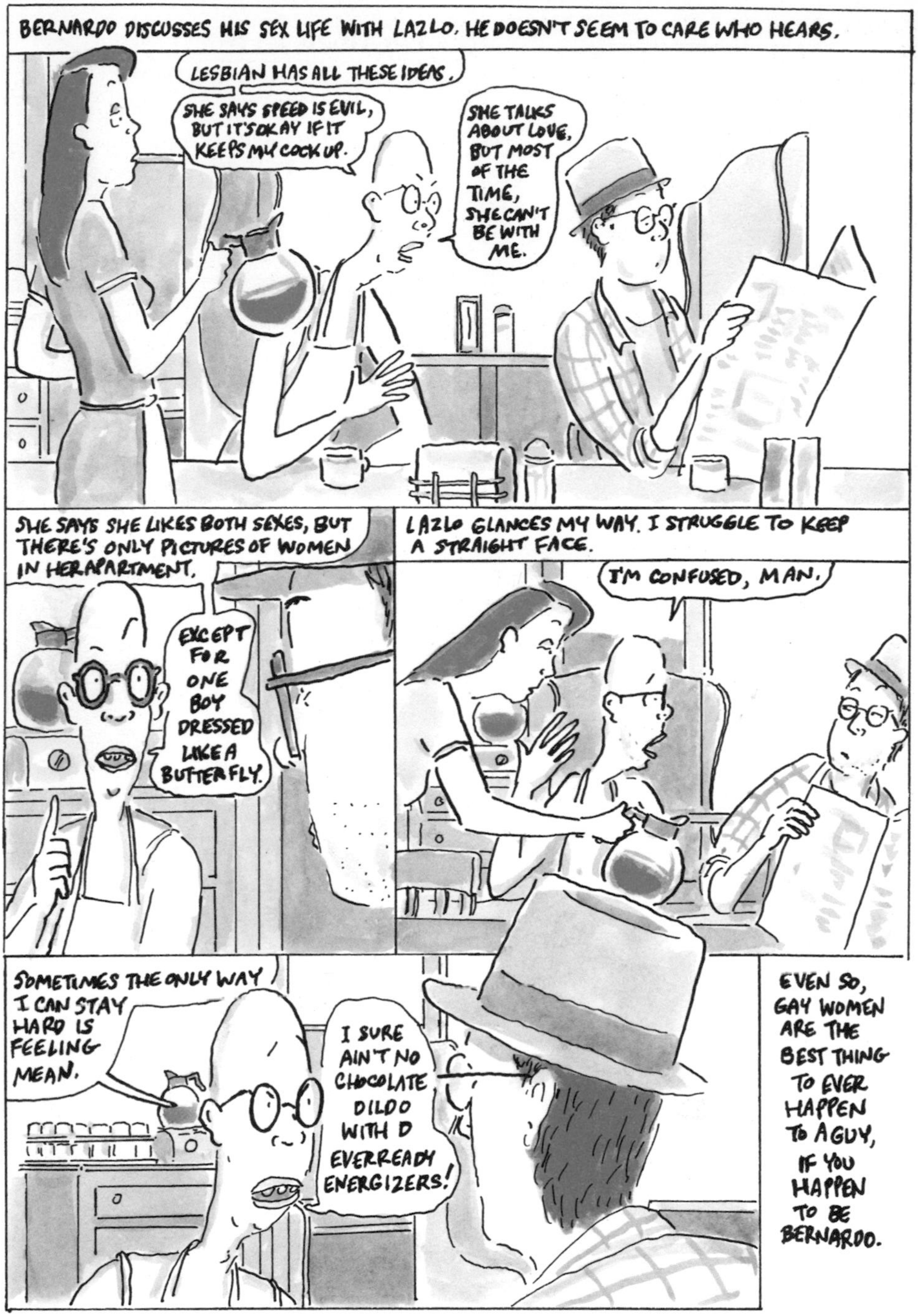
BERNARDO DISCUSSES HIS SEX LIFE WITH LAZLO. HE DOESN'T SEEM TO CARE WHO HEARS.
LESBIAN HAS ALL THESE IDEAS.
SHE SAYS SPEED IS EVIL, BUT IT'S OKAY IF IT KEEPS MY COCK UP.
SHE TALKS ABOUT LOVE, BUT MOST OF THE TIME, SHE CAN'T BE WITH ME.
SHE SAYS SHE LIKES BOTH SEXES, BUT THERE'S ONLY PICTURES OF WOMEN IN HER APARTMENT.
EXCEPT FOR ONE BOY DRESSED LIKE A BUTTERFLY.
LAZLO GLANCES MY WAY. I STRUGGLE TO KEEP A STRAIGHT FACE.
I'M CONFUSED, MAN.
SOMETIMES THE ONLY WAY I CAN STAY HARD IS FEELING MEAN.
I SURE AIN'T NO CHOCOLATE DILDO WITH D EVERREADY ENERGIZERS!
EVEN SO, GAY WOMEN ARE THE BEST THING TO EVER HAPPEN TO A GUY, IF YOU HAPPEN TO BE BERNARDO.

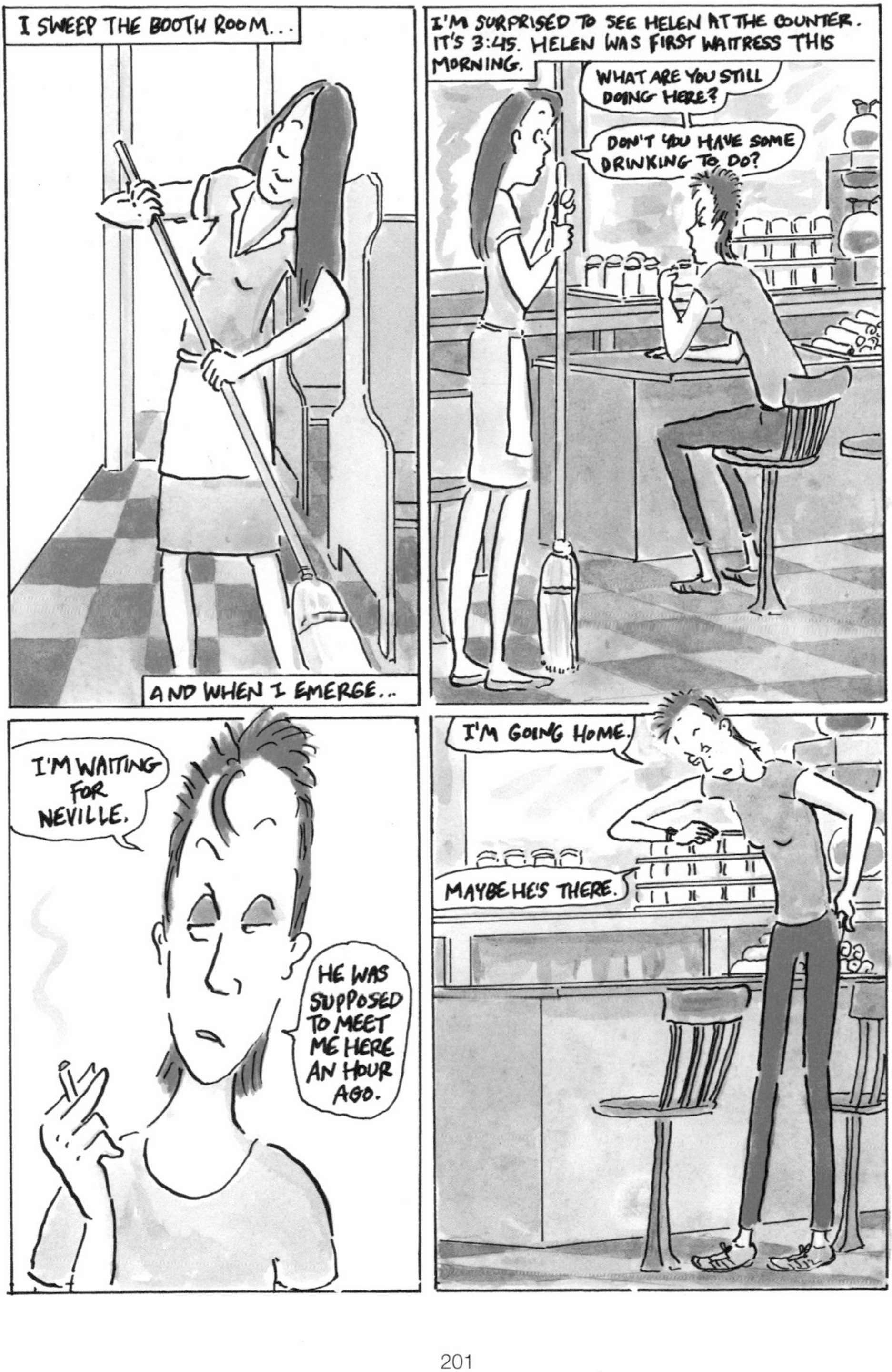
I SWEEP THE BOOTH ROOM...
AND WHEN I EMERGE...
I'M SURPRISED TO SEE HELEN AT THE COUNTER. IT'S 3:45. HELEN WAS FIRST WAITRESS THIS MORNING.
WHAT ARE YOU STILL DOING HERE?
DON'T YOU HAVE SOME DRINKING TO DO?
I'M WAITING FOR NEVILLE.
HE WAS SUPPOSED TO MEET ME HERE AN HOUR AGO.
I'M GOING HOME.
MAYBE HE'S THERE.

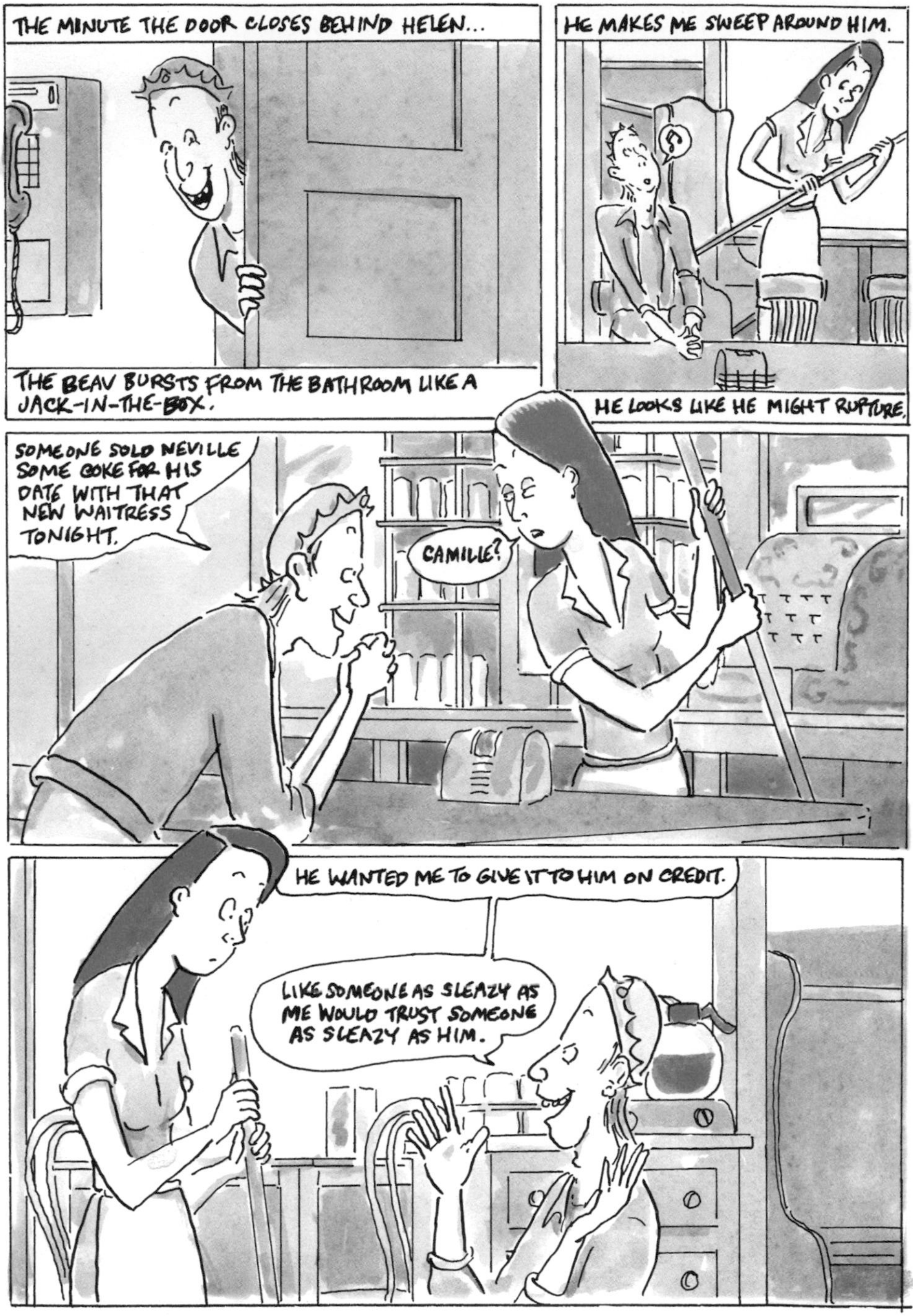
THE MINUTE THE DOOR CLOSES BEHIND HELEN...
THE BEAV BURSTS FROM THE BATHROOM LIKE A JACK-IN-THE-BOX.
HE MAKES ME SWEEP AROUND HIM.
HE LOOKS LIKE HE MIGHT RUPTURE.
SOMEONE SOLD NEVILLE SOME COKE FOR HIS DATE WITH THAT NEW WAITRESS TONIGHT.
CAMILLE?
HE WANTED ME TO GIVE IT TO HIM ON CREDIT.
LIKE SOMEONE AS SLEAZY AS ME WOULD TRUST SOMEONE AS SLEAZY AS HIM.

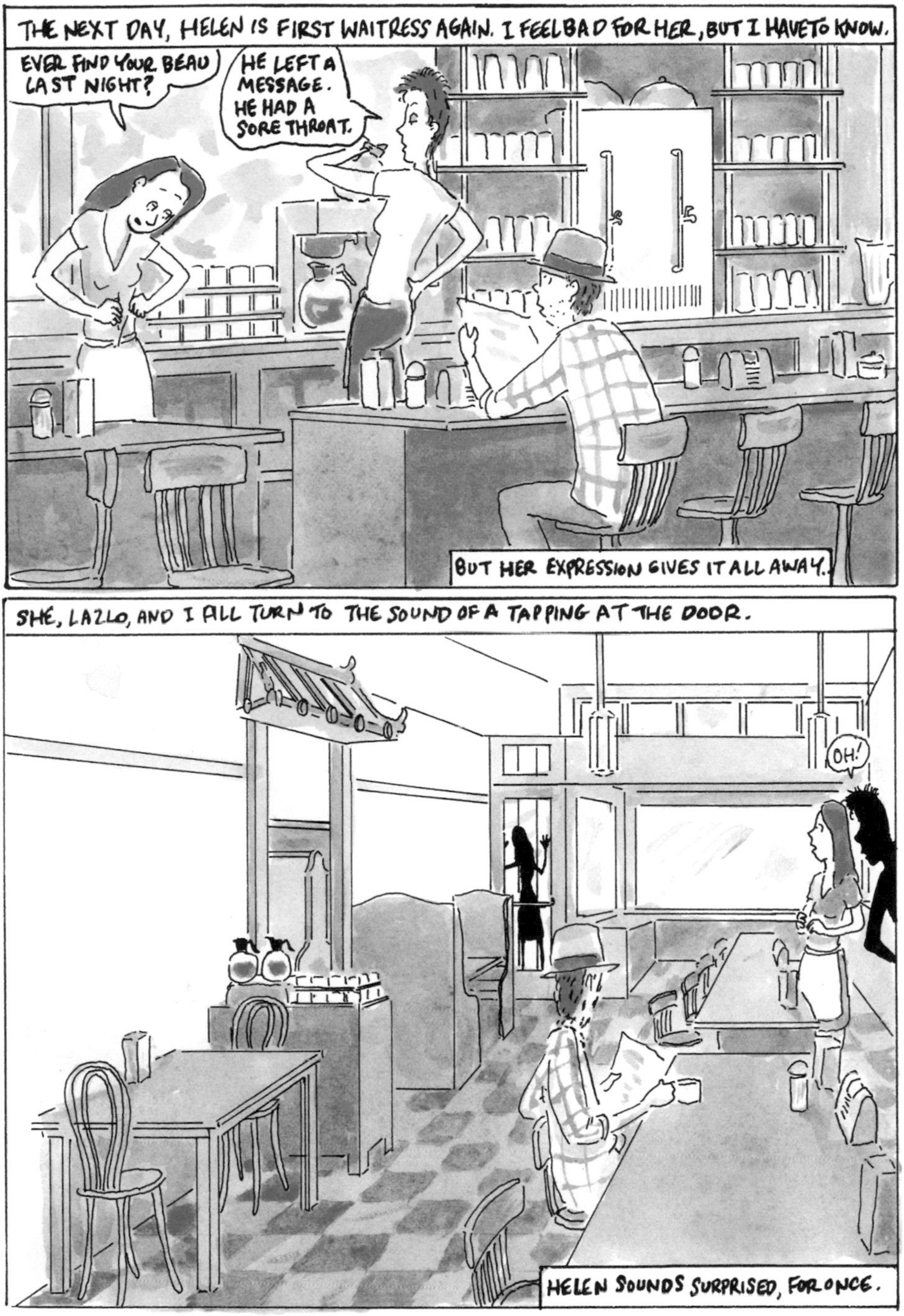
THE NEXT DAY, HELEN IS FIRST WAITRESS AGAIN. I FEEL BAD FOR HER, BUT I HAVE TO KNOW.
EVER FIND YOUR BEAU LAST NIGHT?
HE LEFT A MESSAGE. HE HAD A SORE THROAT.
BUT HER EXPRESSION GIVES IT ALL AWAY.
SHE, LAZLO, AND I ALL TURN TO THE SOUND OF A TAPPING AT THE DOOR.
OH!
HELEN SOUNDS SURPRISED, FOR ONCE.

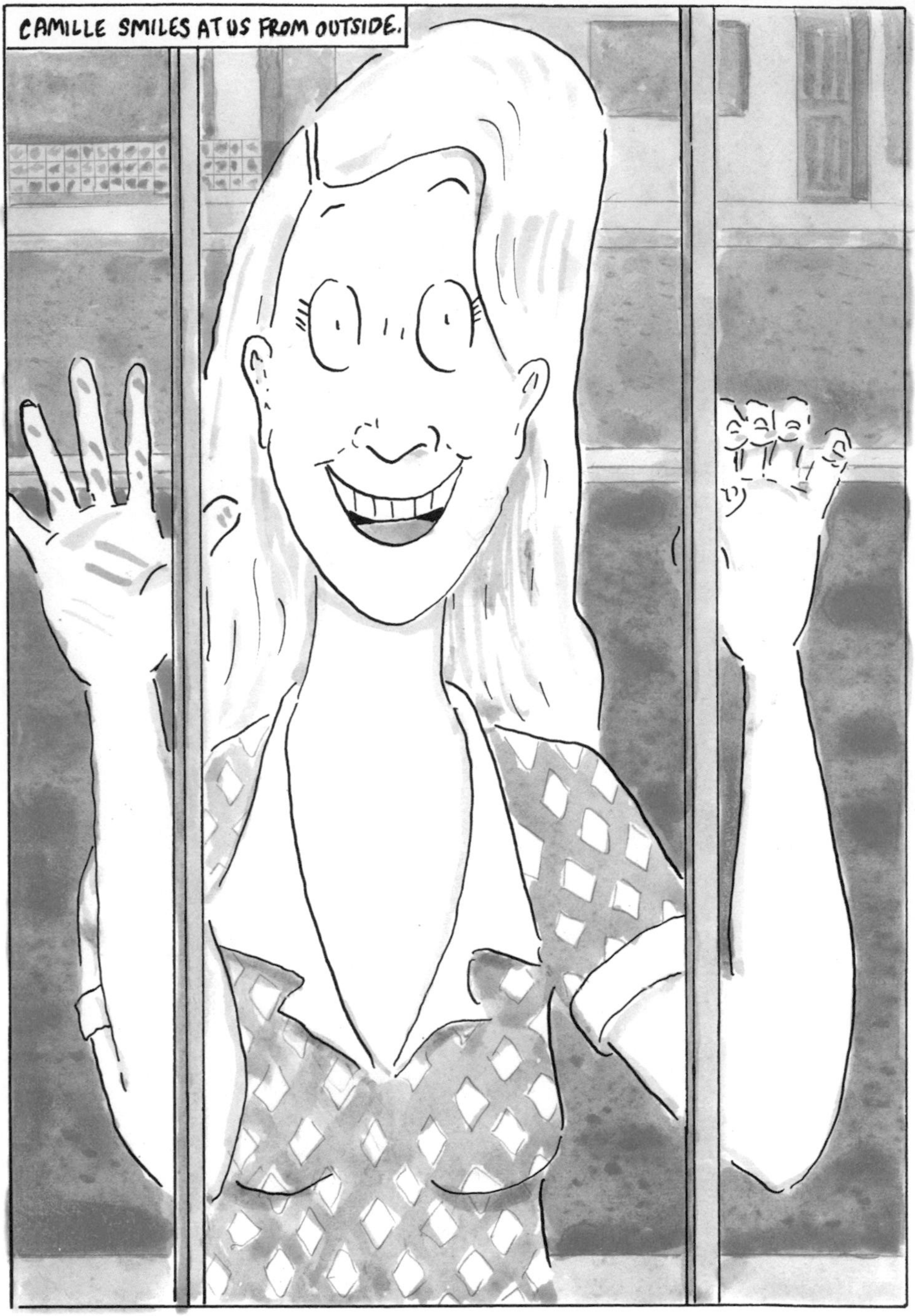
CAMILLE SMILES AT US FROM OUTSIDE.

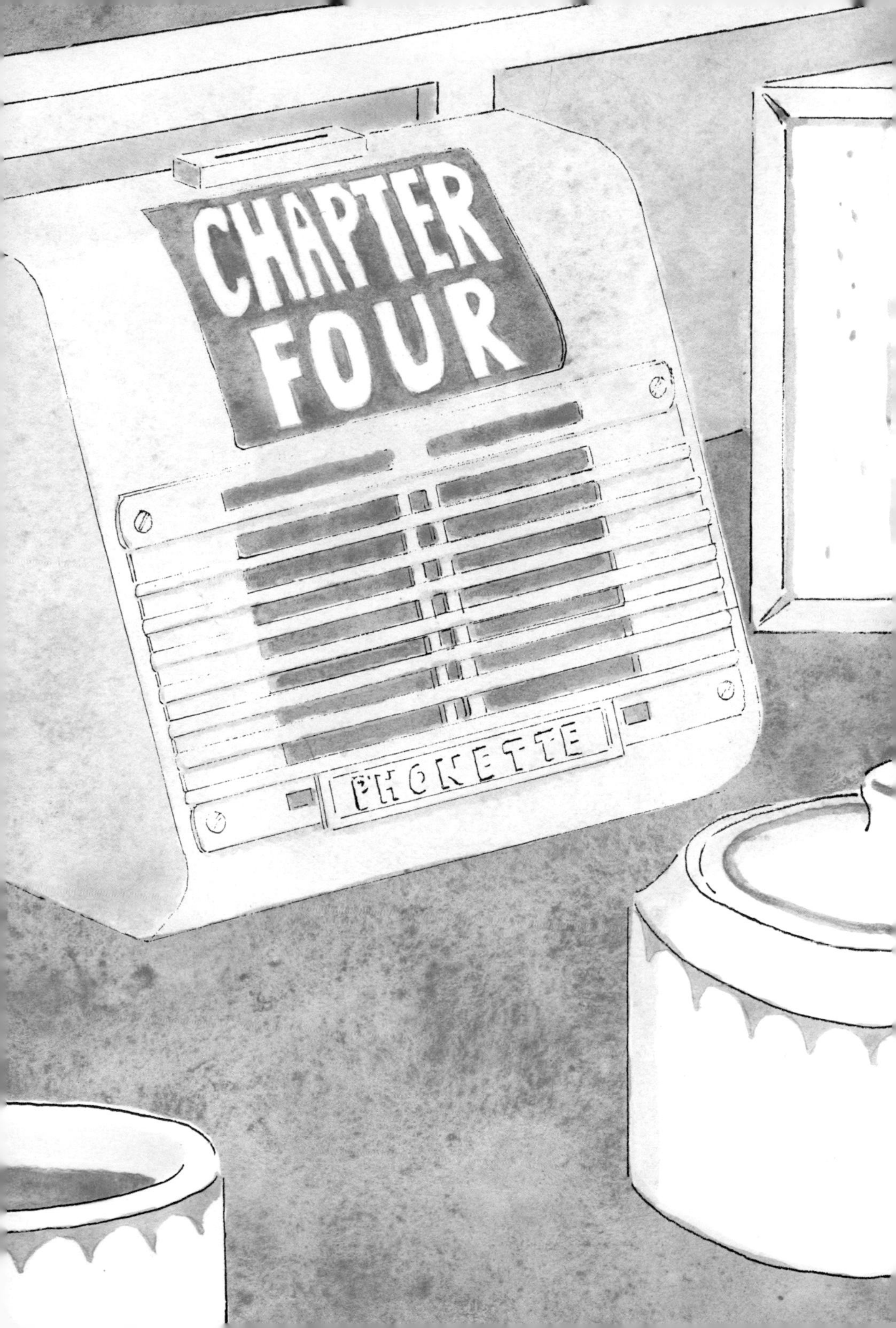
CHAPTER FOUR
PHONETTE

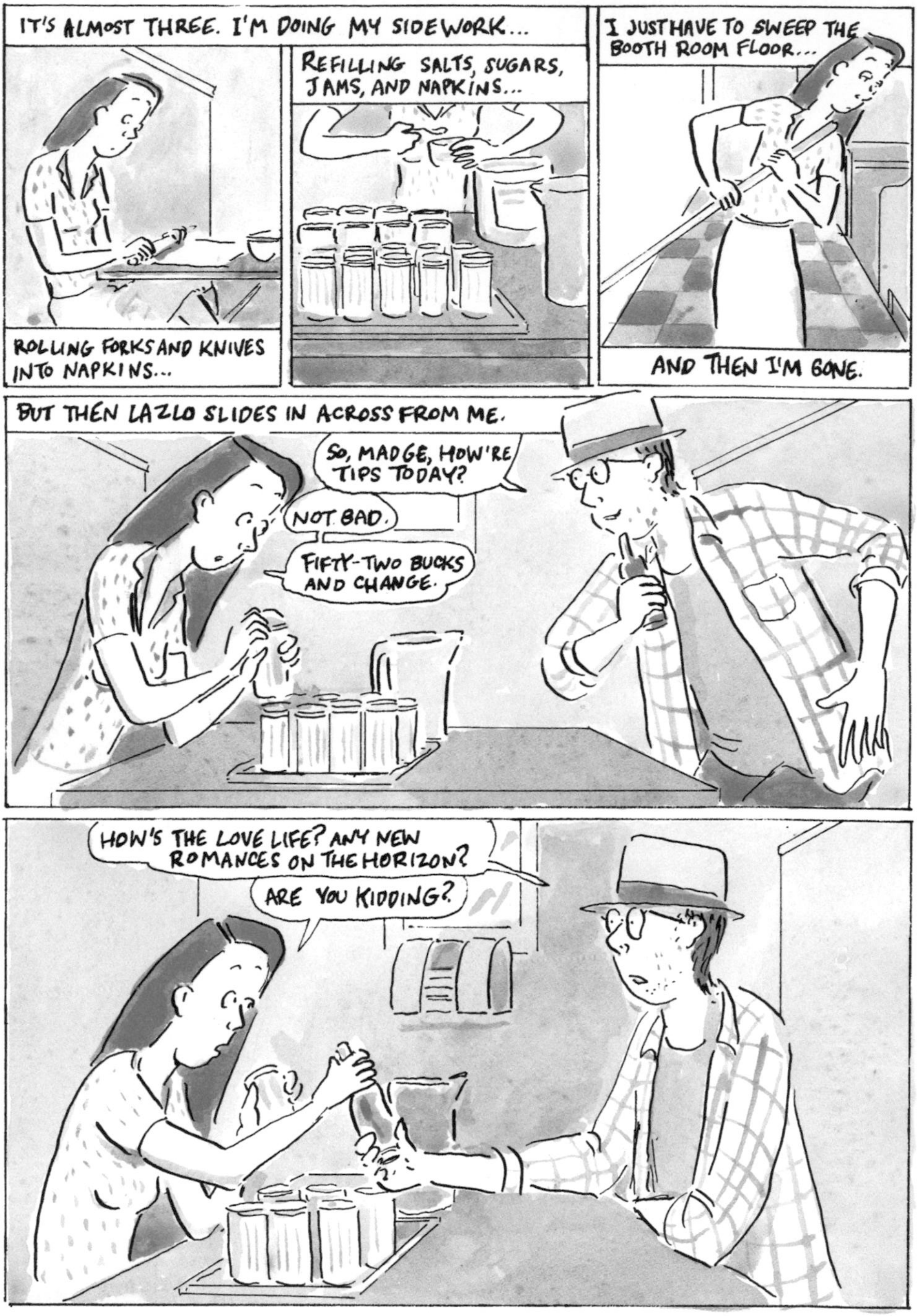
IT'S ALMOST THREE. I'M DOING MY SIDEWORK...
ROLLING FORKS AND KNIVES INTO NAPKINS...
REFILLING SALTS, SUGARS, JAMS, AND NAPKINS...
I JUST HAVE TO SWEEP THE BOOTH ROOM FLOOR...
AND THEN I'M GONE.
BUT THEN LAZLO SLIDES IN ACROSS FROM ME.
SO, MADGE, HOW'RE TIPS TODAY?
NOT BAD.
FIFTY-TWO BUCKS AND CHANGE.
HOW'S THE LOVE LIFE? ANY NEW ROMANCES ON THE HORIZON?
ARE YOU KIDDING?

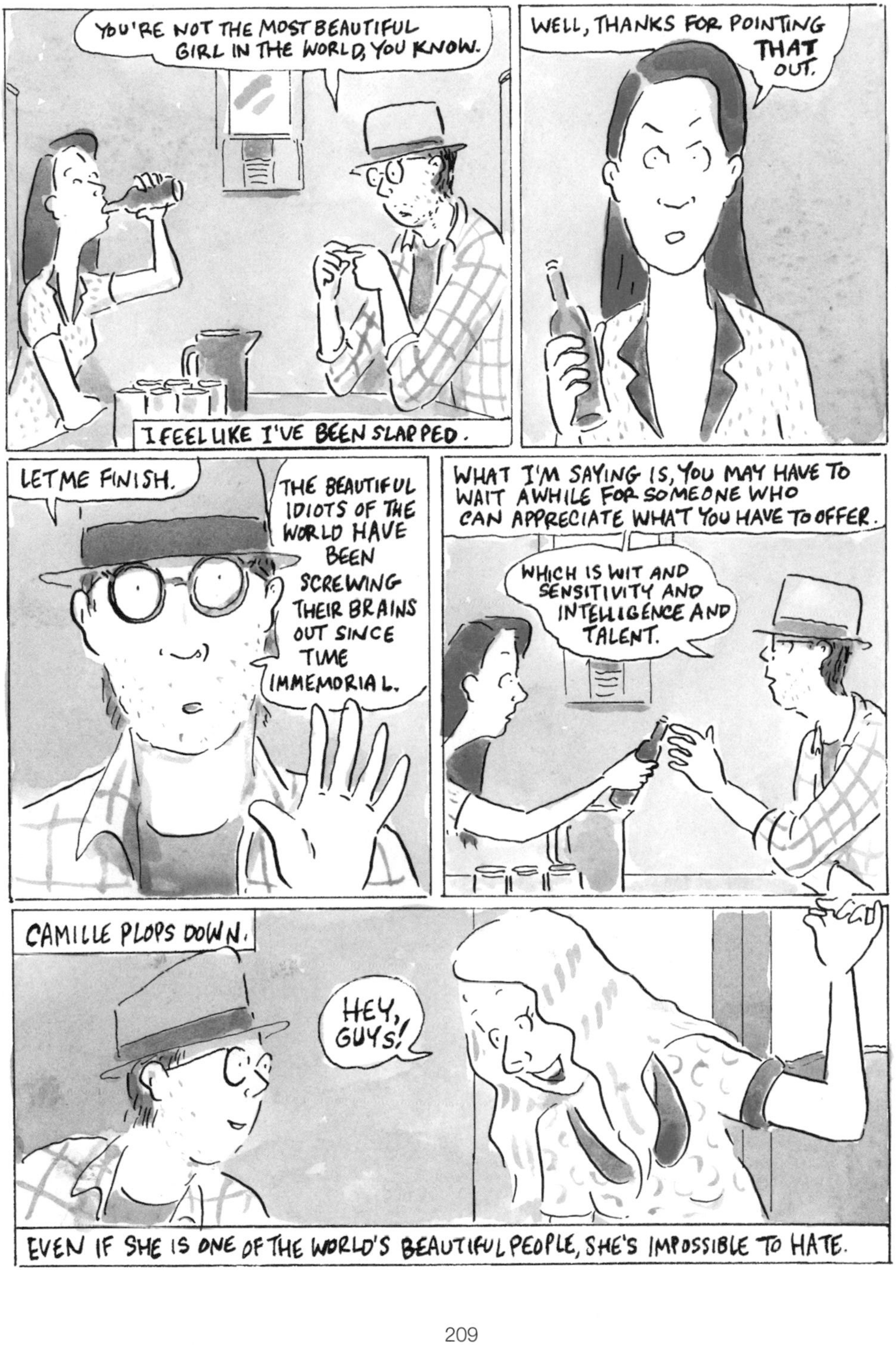
YOU'RE NOT THE MOST BEAUTIFUL GIRL IN THE WORLD, YOU KNOW.
I FEEL LIKE I'VE BEEN SLAPPED.
WELL, THANKS FOR POINTING THAT OUT.
LET ME FINISH.
THE BEAUTIFUL IDIOTS OF THE WORLD HAVE BEEN SCREWING THEIR BRAINS OUT SINCE TIME IMMEMORIAL.
WHAT I'M SAYING IS, YOU MAY HAVE TO WAIT AWHILE FOR SOMEONE WHO CAN APPRECIATE WHAT YOU HAVE TO OFFER.
WHICH IS WIT AND SENSITIVITY AND INTELLIGENCE AND TALENT.
CAMILLE PLOPS DOWN.
HEY, GUYS!
EVEN IF SHE IS ONE OF THE WORLD'S BEAUTIFUL PEOPLE, SHE'S IMPOSSIBLE TO HATE.

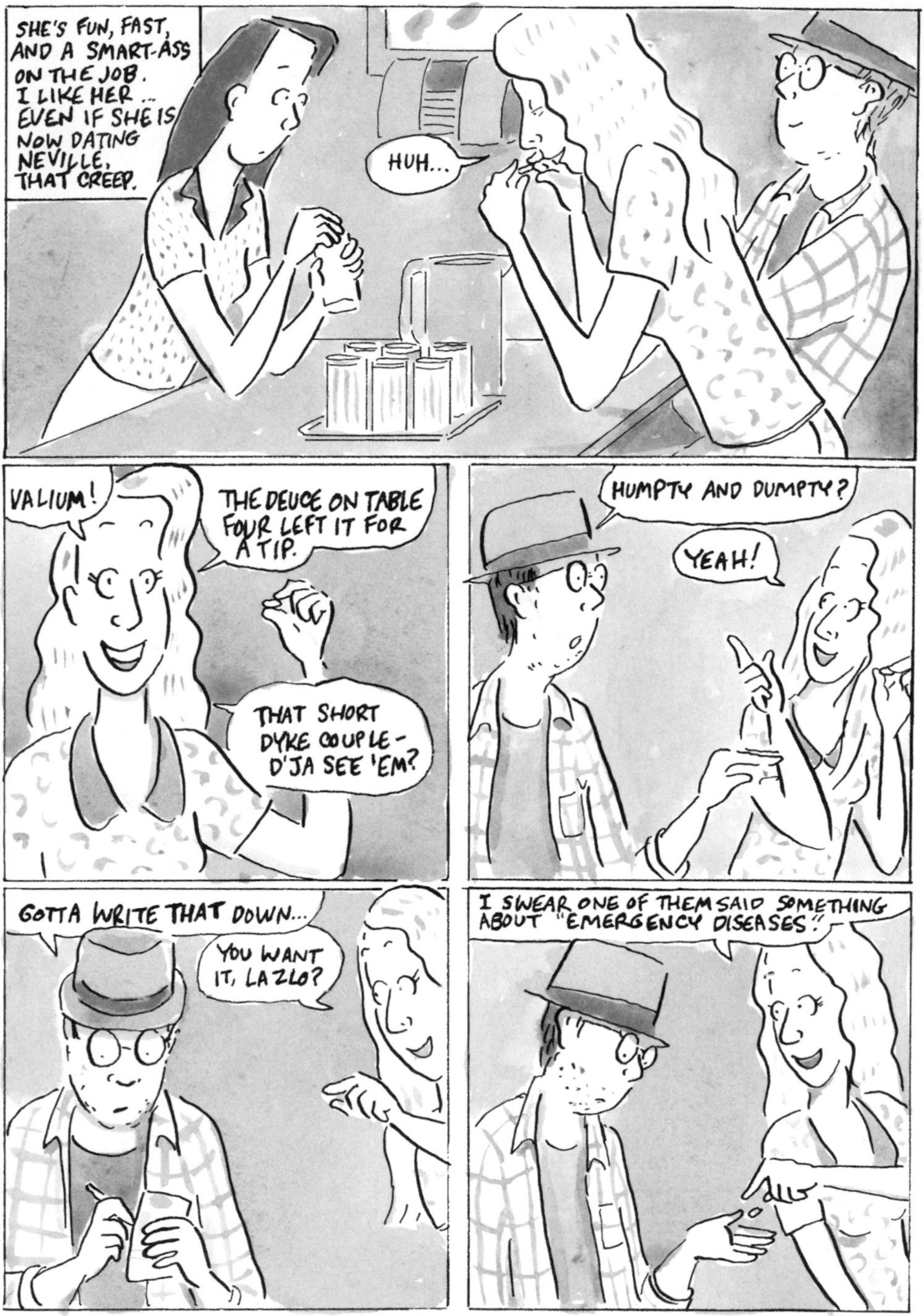

SHE'S FUN, FAST, AND A SMART-ASS ON THE JOB. I LIKE HER... EVEN IF SHE IS NOW DATING NEVILLE, THAT CREEP.
HUH...
VALIUM!
THE DEUCE ON TABLE FOUR LEFT IT FOR A TIP.
THAT SHORT DYKE COUPLE - D'JA SEE 'EM?
HUMPTY AND DUMPTY?
YEAH!
GOTTA WRITE THAT DOWN...
YOU WANT IT, LAZLO?
I SWEAR ONE OF THEM SAID SOMETHING ABOUT "EMERGENCY DISEASES"!

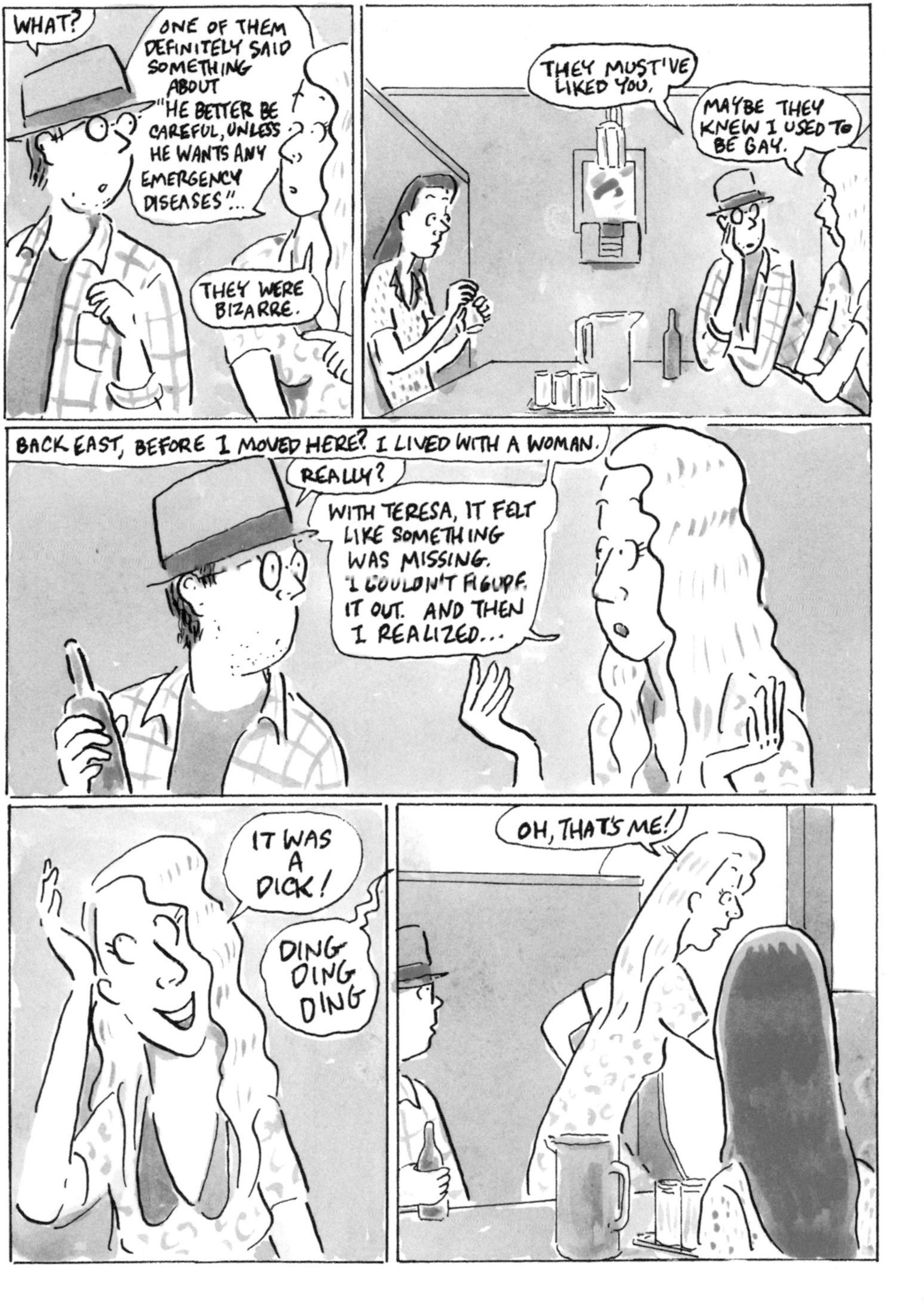
WHAT?
ONE OF THEM DEFINITELY SAID SOMETHING ABOUT "HE BETTER BE CAREFUL, UNLESS HE WANTS ANY EMERGENCY DISEASES"...
THEY WERE BIZARRE.
THEY MUST'VE LIKED YOU.
MAYBE THEY KNEW I USED TO BE GAY.
BACK EAST, BEFORE I MOVED HERE? I LIVED WITH A WOMAN.
REALLY?
WITH TERESA, IT FELT LIKE SOMETHING WAS MISSING. I COULDN'T FIGURE IT OUT. AND THEN I REALIZED...
IT WAS A DICK!
DING DING DING
OH, THAT'S ME!

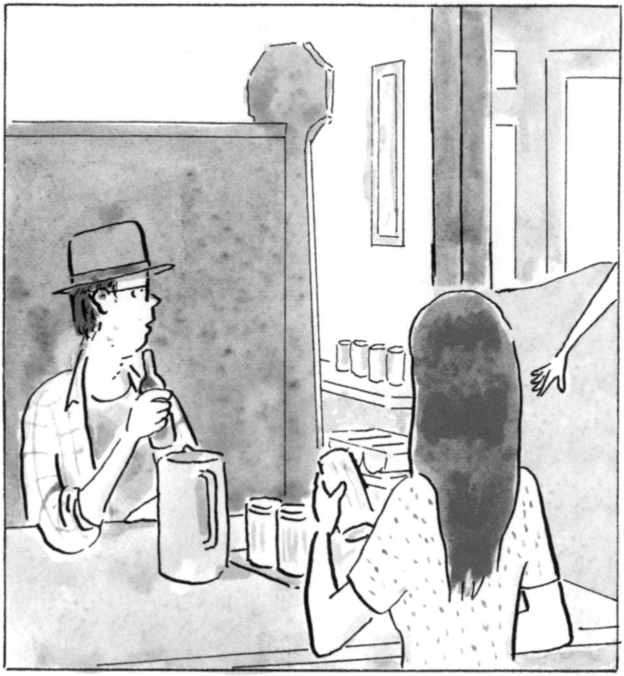

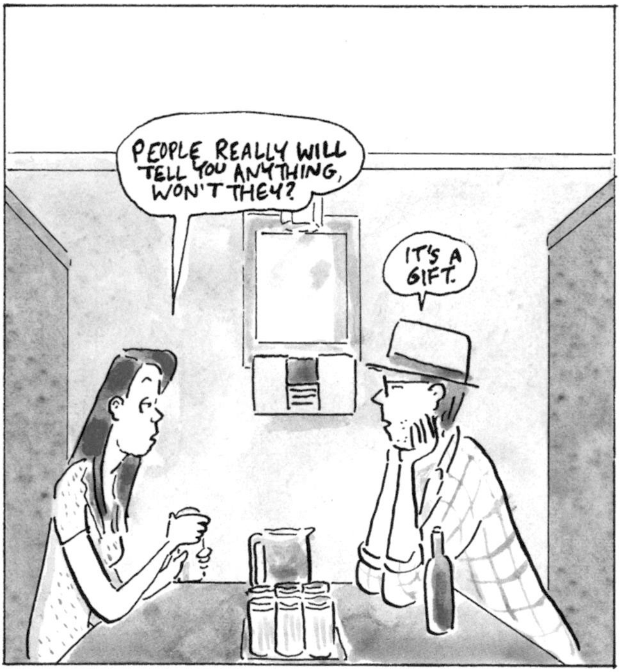
PEOPLE REALLY WILL TELL YOU ANYTHING, WON'T THEY?
IT'S A GIFT.

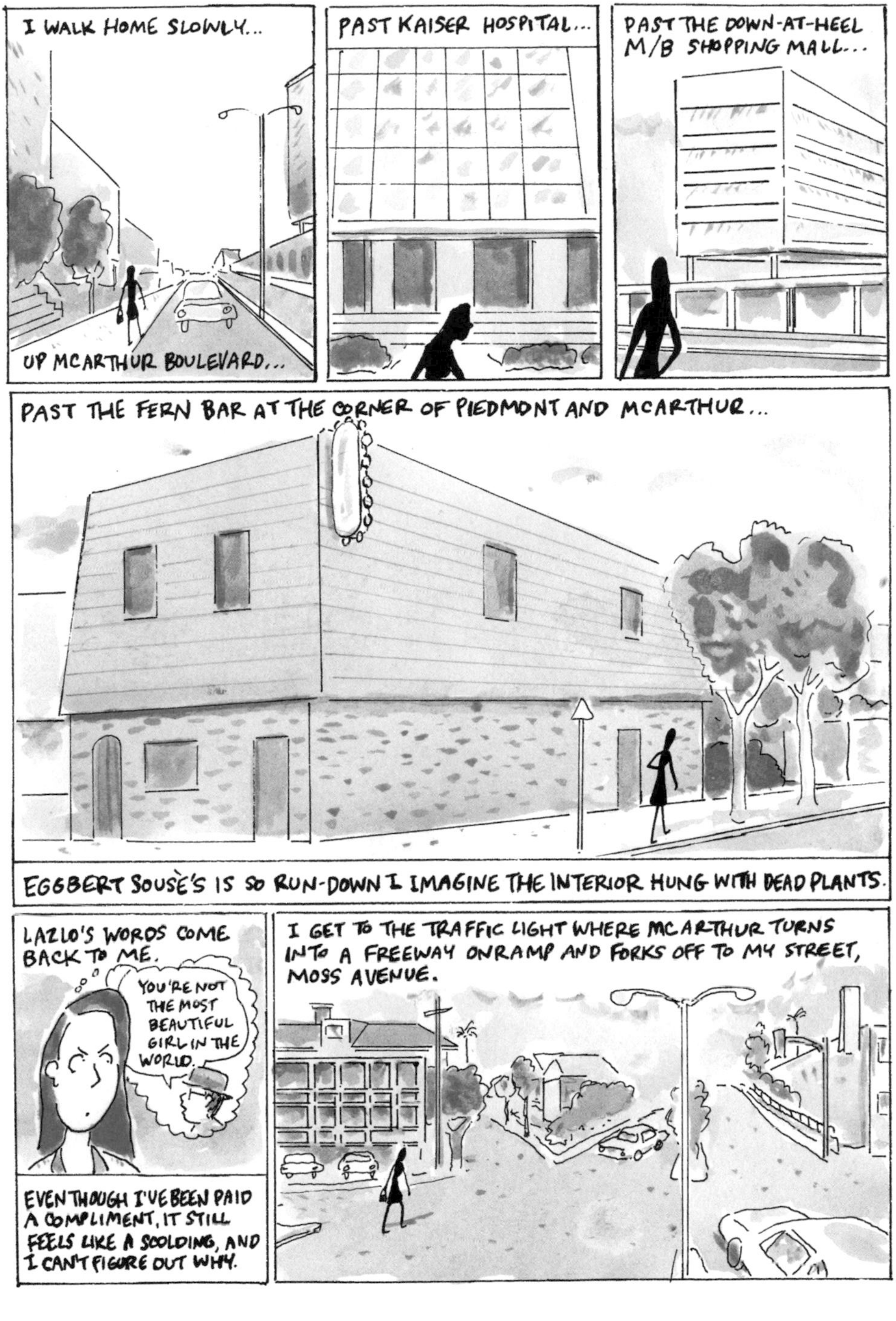

I WALK HOME SLOWLY...
UP MCARTHUR BOULEVARD...
PAST KAISER HOSPITAL...
PAST THE DOWN-AT-HEEL M/B SHOPPING MALL...
PAST THE FERN BAR AT THE CORNER OF PIEDMONT AND MCARTHUR...
EGGBERT SOUSÈ'S IS SO RUN-DOWN I IMAGINE THE INTERIOR HUNG WITH DEAD PLANTS.
LAZLO'S WORDS COME BACK TO ME.
YOU'RE NOT THE MOST BEAUTIFUL GIRL IN THE WORLD.
EVEN THOUGH I'VE BEEN PAID A COMPLIMENT, IT STILL FEELS LIKE A SCOLDING, AND I CAN'T FIGURE OUT WHY.
I GET TO THE TRAFFIC LIGHT WHERE MCARTHUR TURNS INTO A FREEWAY ONRAMP AND FORKS OFF TO MY STREET, MOSS AVENUE.

MINE IS THE SECOND FALLING-DOWN VICTORIAN BUNGALOW FROM THE CORNER.

THE HOUSE IS IN A *STATE OF DECAY* THAT IS STILL ROMANTIC, BEFORE IT HITS DESPERATION. ALMOST EVERYONE I KNOW LIVES IN A HOUSE LIKE THIS.

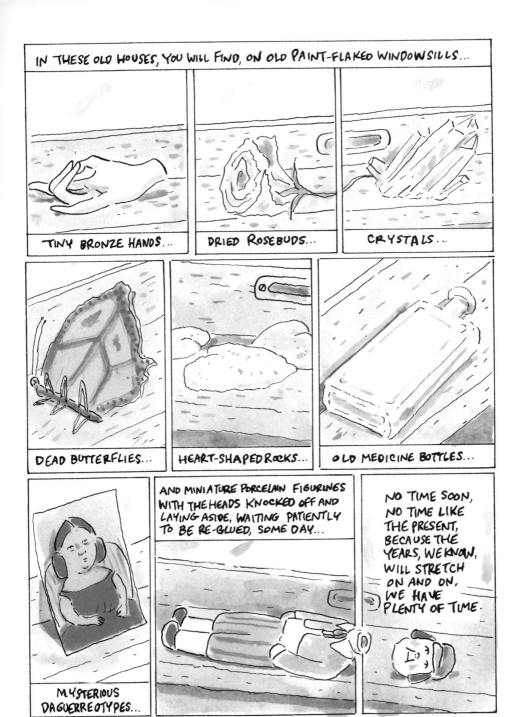

IN THESE OLD HOUSES, YOU WILL FIND, ON OLD PAINT-FLAKED WINDOWSILLS...

TINY BRONZE HANDS...

DRIED ROSEBUDS...

CRYSTALS...

DEAD BUTTERFLIES...

HEART-SHAPED ROCKS...

OLD MEDICINE BOTTLES...

AND MINIATURE PORCELAIN FIGURINES WITH THE HEADS KNOCKED OFF AND LAYING ASIDE, WAITING PATIENTLY TO BE RE-GLUED, SOME DAY...

NO TIME SOON, NO TIME LIKE THE PRESENT, BECAUSE THE YEARS, WE KNOW, WILL STRETCH ON AND ON, WE HAVE PLENTY OF TIME.

MYSTERIOUS DAGUERREOTYPES...

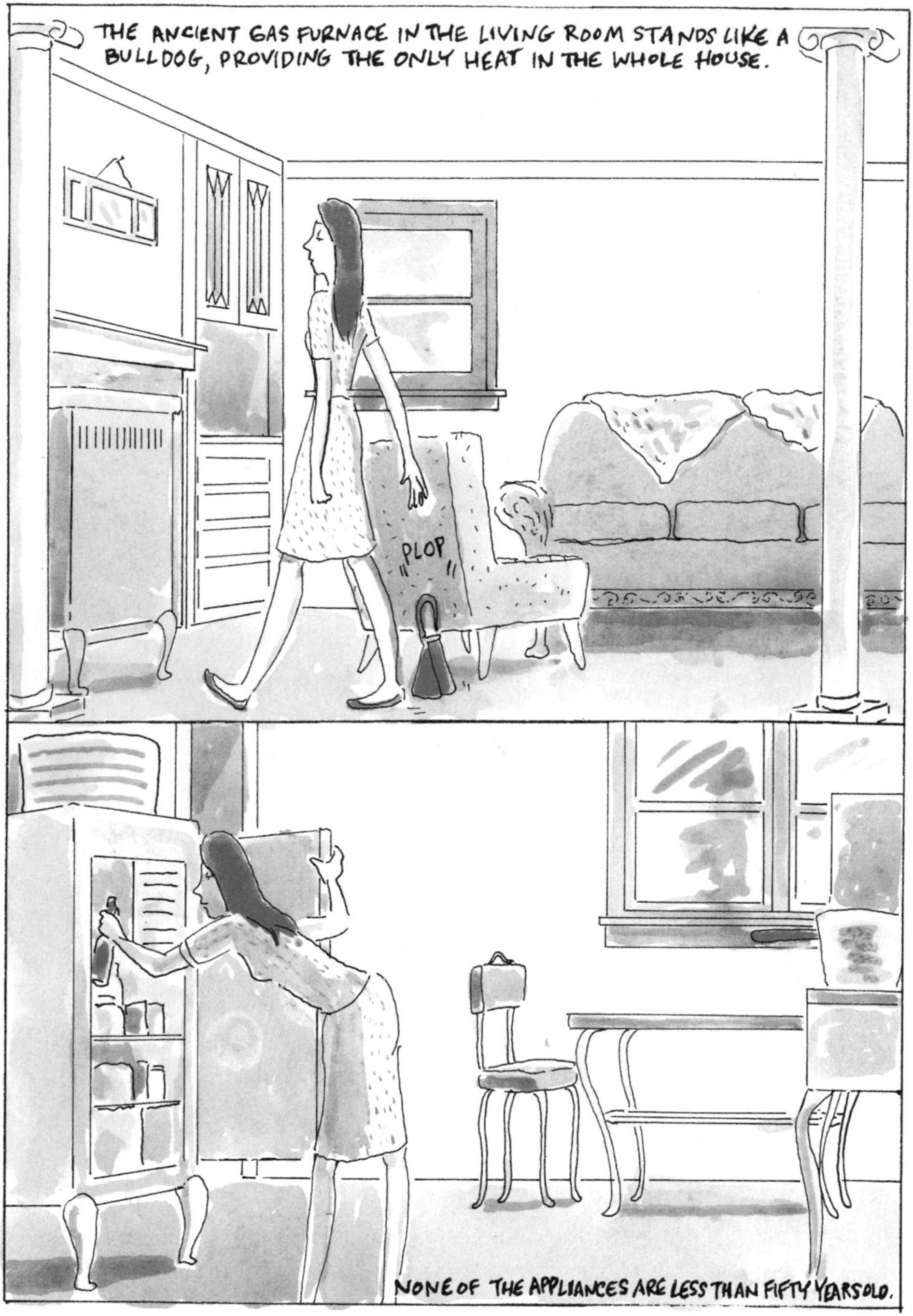
THE ANCIENT GAS FURNACE IN THE LIVING ROOM STANDS LIKE A BULLDOG, PROVIDING THE ONLY HEAT IN THE WHOLE HOUSE.
PLOP
NONE OF THE APPLIANCES ARE LESS THAN FIFTY YEARS OLD.

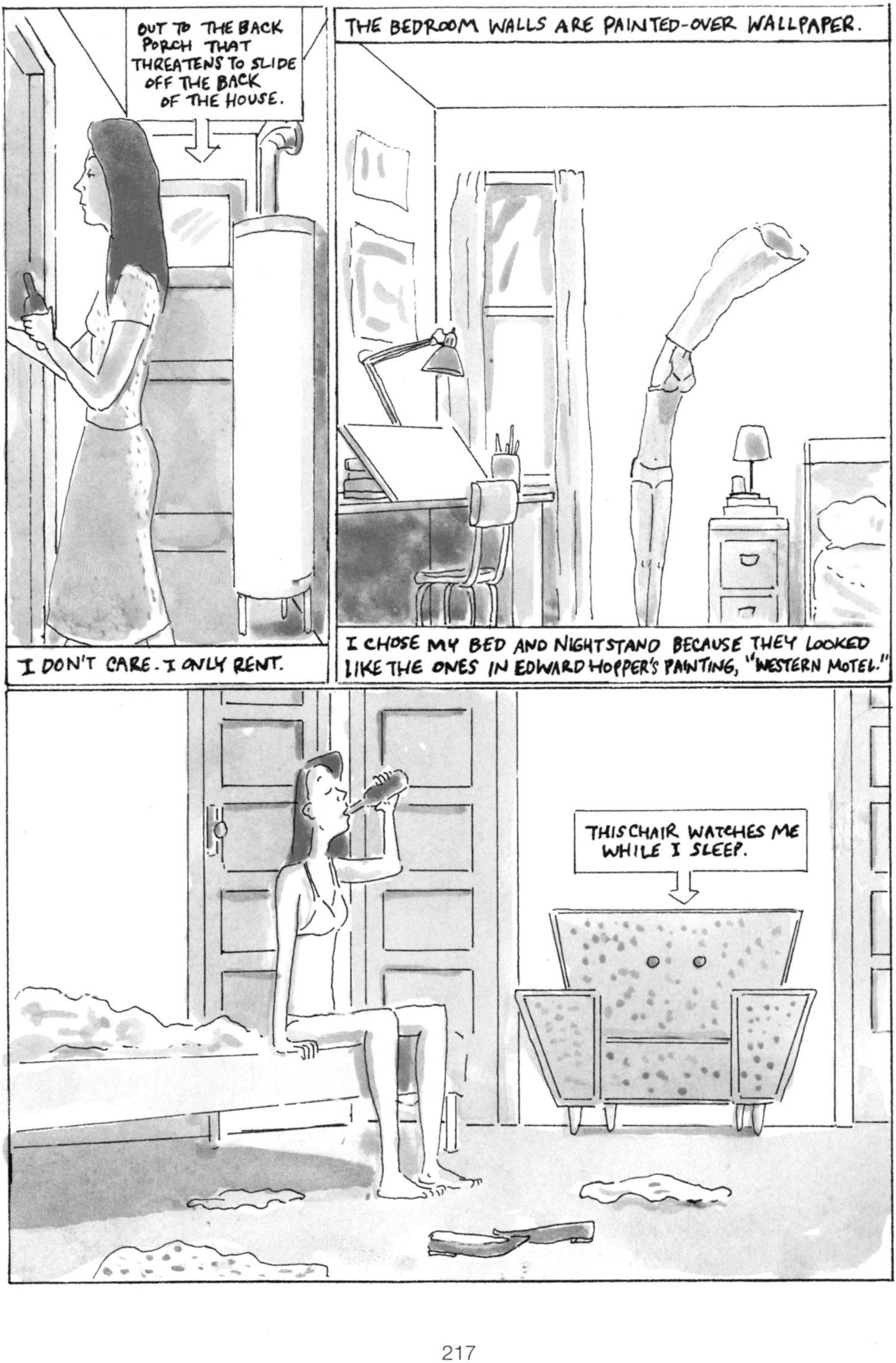
OUT TO THE BACK PORCH THAT THREATENS TO SLIDE OFF THE BACK OF THE HOUSE.
I DON'T CARE. I ONLY RENT.
THE BEDROOM WALLS ARE PAINTED-OVER WALLPAPER.
I CHOSE MY BED AND NIGHTSTAND BECAUSE THEY LOOKED LIKE THE ONES IN EDWARD HOPPER'S PAINTING, "WESTERN MOTEL."
THIS CHAIR WATCHES ME WHILE I SLEEP.

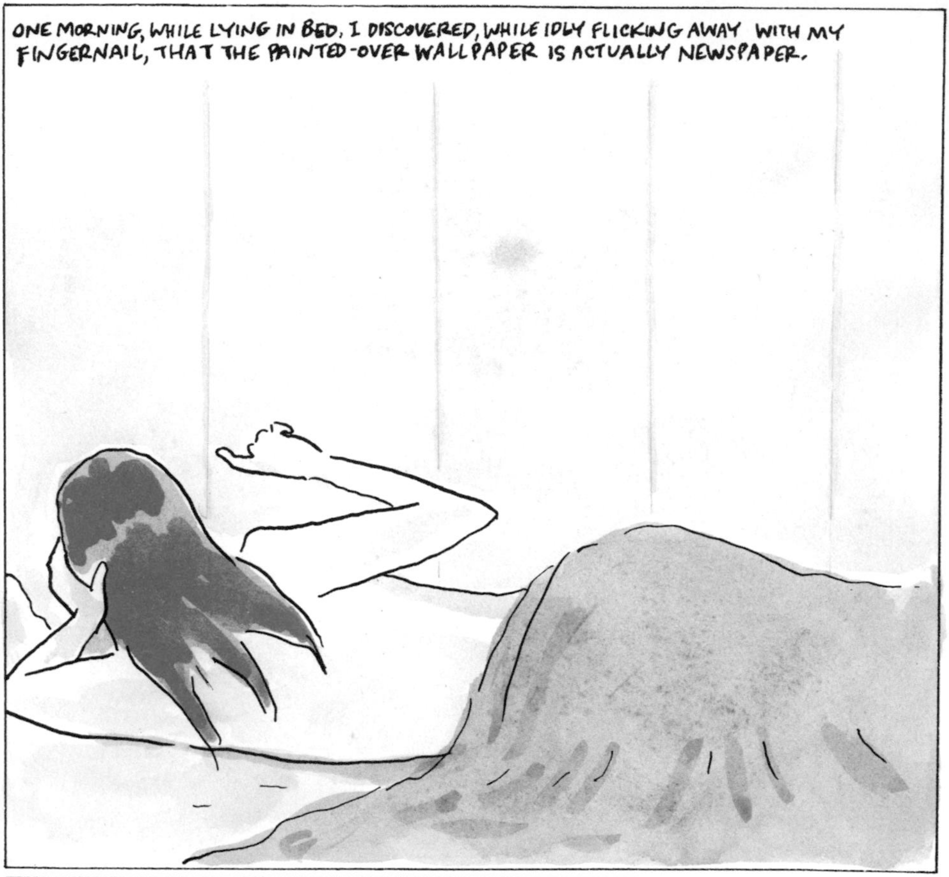
ONE MORNING, WHILE LYING IN BED, I DISCOVERED, WHILE IDLY FLICKING AWAY WITH MY FINGERNAIL, THAT THE PAINTED-OVER WALLPAPER IS ACTUALLY NEWSPAPER.

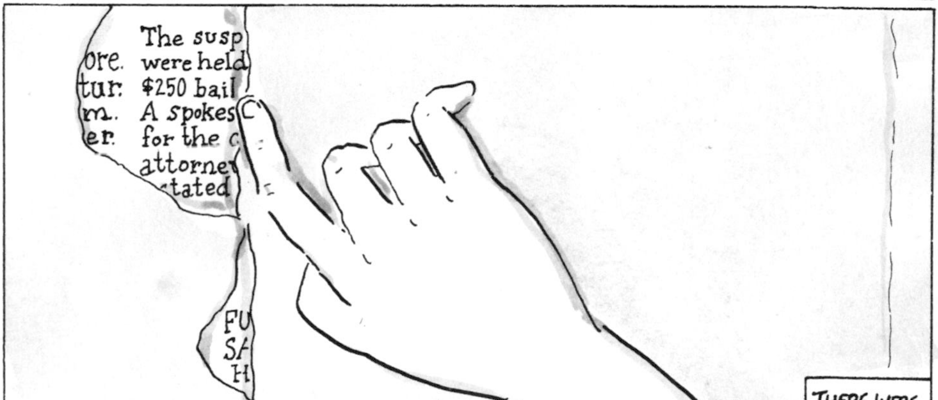
The susp
ore. were held
tur. $250 bail
m. A spokes
er. for the
attorne
tated
FU
SA
H
THERE WERE WORDS UNDER THE PAINT.

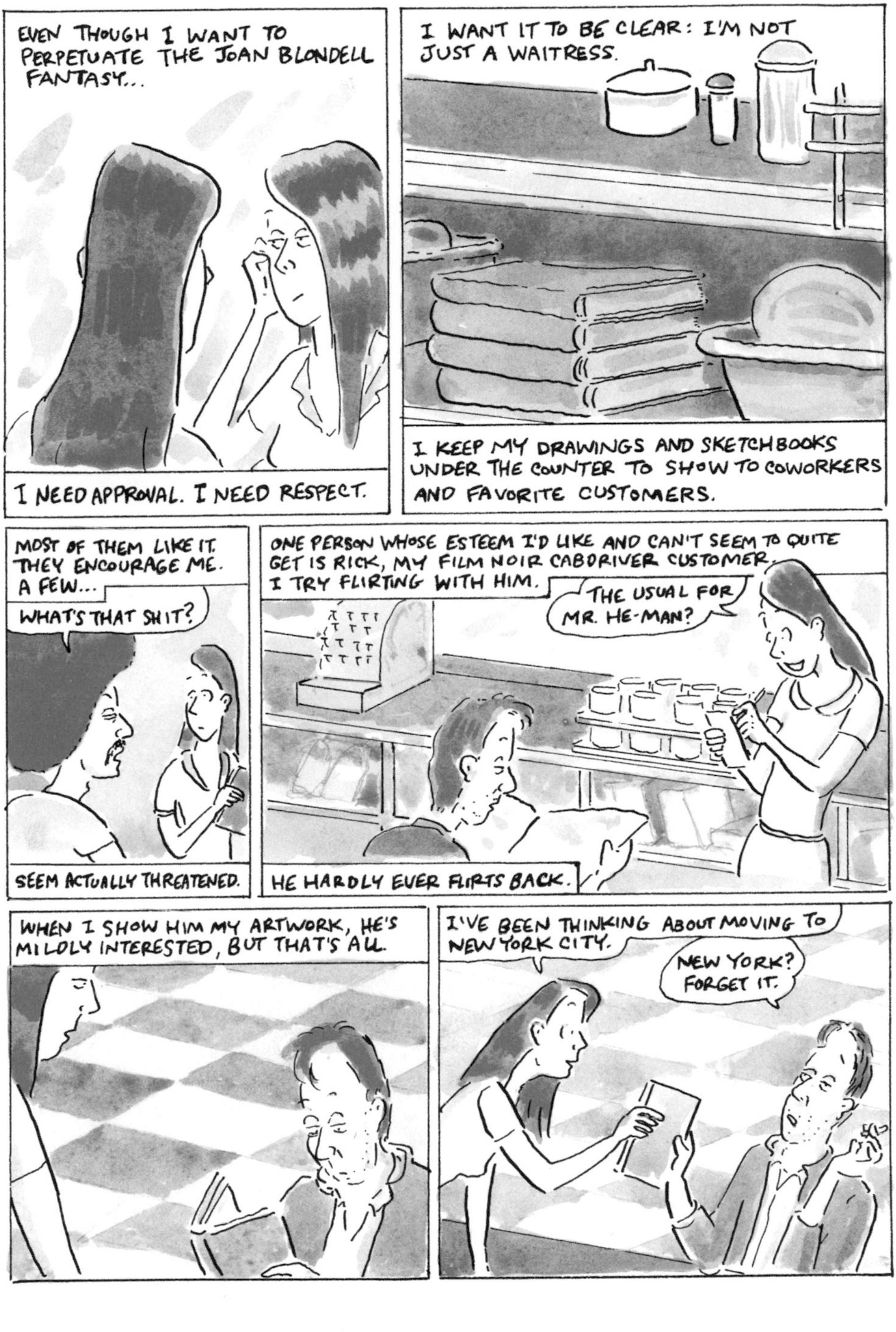
EVEN THOUGH I WANT TO PERPETUATE THE JOAN BLONDELL FANTASY...
I NEED APPROVAL. I NEED RESPECT.
I WANT IT TO BE CLEAR: I'M NOT JUST A WAITRESS.
I KEEP MY DRAWINGS AND SKETCHBOOKS UNDER THE COUNTER TO SHOW TO COWORKERS AND FAVORITE CUSTOMERS.
MOST OF THEM LIKE IT. THEY ENCOURAGE ME. A FEW...
WHAT'S THAT SHIT?
SEEM ACTUALLY THREATENED.
ONE PERSON WHOSE ESTEEM I'D LIKE AND CAN'T SEEM TO QUITE GET IS RICK, MY FILM NOIR CABDRIVER CUSTOMER. I TRY FLIRTING WITH HIM.
THE USUAL FOR MR. HE-MAN?
HE HARDLY EVER FLIRTS BACK.
WHEN I SHOW HIM MY ARTWORK, HE'S MILDLY INTERESTED, BUT THAT'S ALL.
I'VE BEEN THINKING ABOUT MOVING TO NEW YORK CITY.
NEW YORK? FORGET IT.

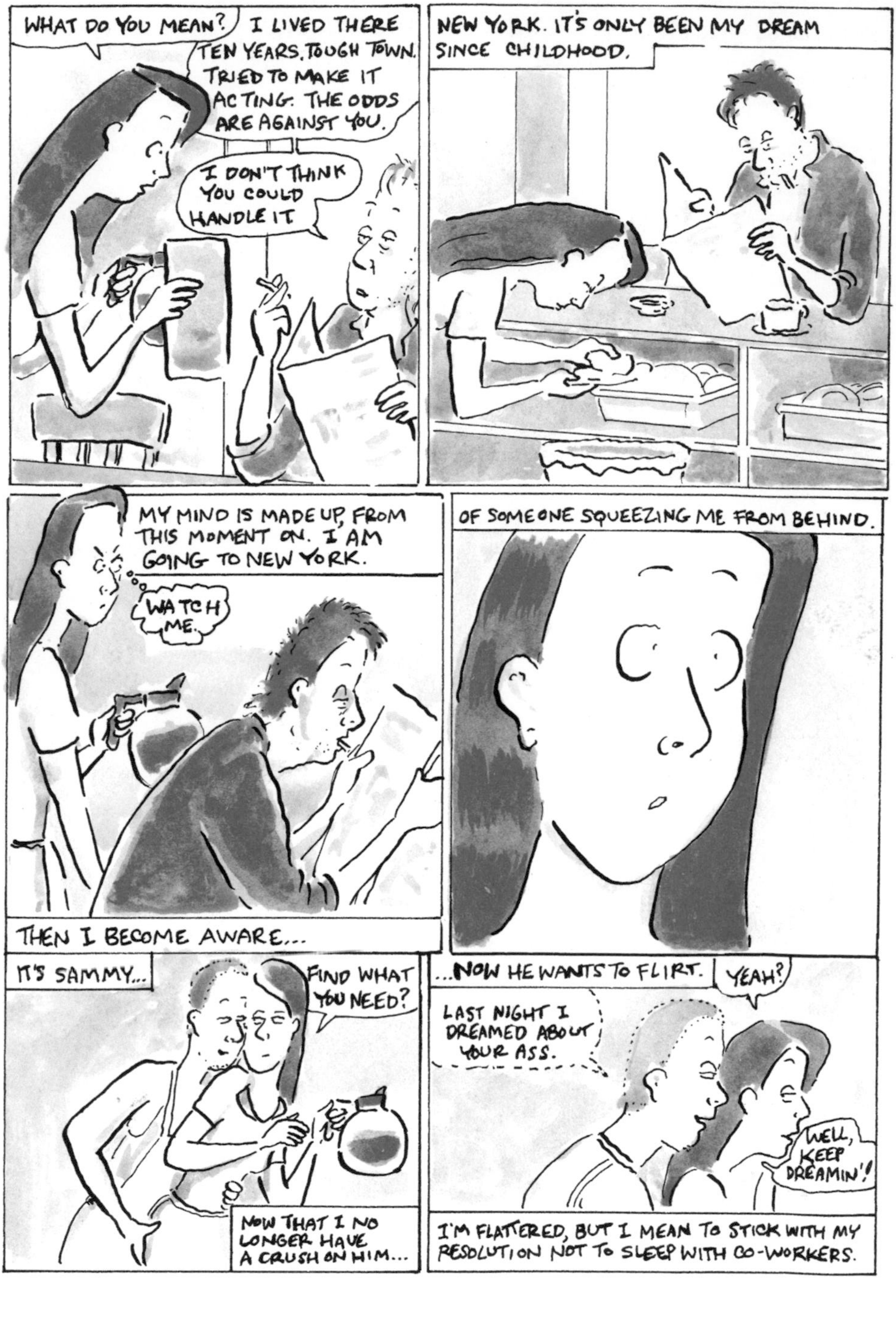
WHAT DO YOU MEAN?
I LIVED THERE TEN YEARS. TOUGH TOWN. TRIED TO MAKE IT ACTING. THE ODDS ARE AGAINST YOU.
I DON'T THINK YOU COULD HANDLE IT.
NEW YORK. IT'S ONLY BEEN MY DREAM SINCE CHILDHOOD.
MY MIND IS MADE UP, FROM THIS MOMENT ON. I AM GOING TO NEW YORK.
WATCH ME.
THEN I BECOME AWARE...
OF SOMEONE SQUEEZING ME FROM BEHIND.
IT'S SAMMY...
FIND WHAT YOU NEED?
NOW THAT I NO LONGER HAVE A CRUSH ON HIM...
...NOW HE WANTS TO FLIRT.
YEAH?
LAST NIGHT I DREAMED ABOUT YOUR ASS.
WELL, KEEP DREAMIN'!
I'M FLATTERED, BUT I MEAN TO STICK WITH MY RESOLUTION NOT TO SLEEP WITH CO-WORKERS.

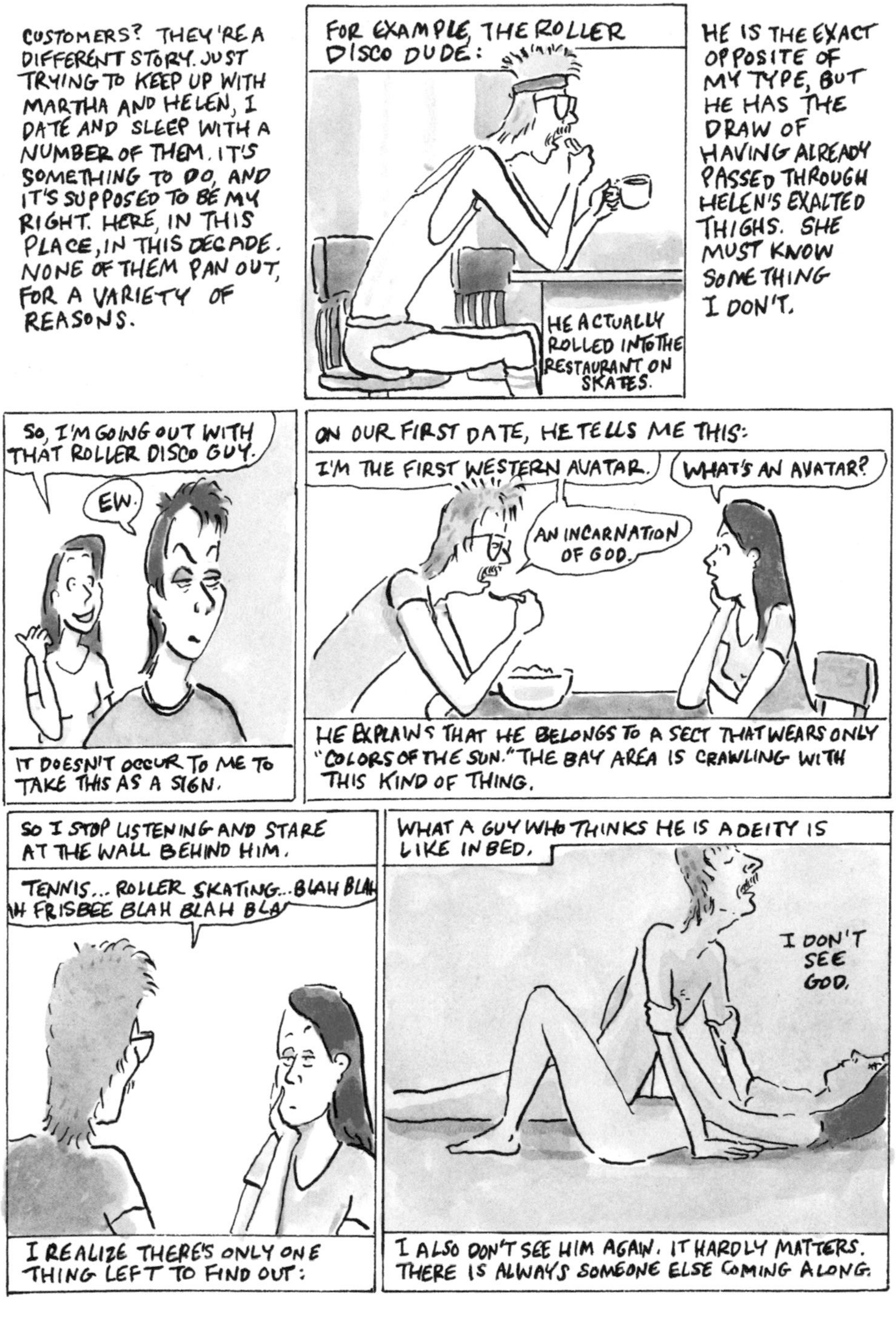
CUSTOMERS? THEY'RE A DIFFERENT STORY. JUST TRYING TO KEEP UP WITH MARTHA AND HELEN, I DATE AND SLEEP WITH A NUMBER OF THEM. IT'S SOMETHING TO DO, AND IT'S SUPPOSED TO BE MY RIGHT. HERE, IN THIS PLACE, IN THIS DECADE. NONE OF THEM PAN OUT, FOR A VARIETY OF REASONS.
FOR EXAMPLE, THE ROLLER DISCO DUDE:
HE ACTUALLY ROLLED INTO THE RESTAURANT ON SKATES.
HE IS THE EXACT OPPOSITE OF MY TYPE, BUT HE HAS THE DRAW OF HAVING ALREADY PASSED THROUGH HELEN'S EXALTED THIGHS. SHE MUST KNOW SOMETHING I DON'T.
SO, I'M GOING OUT WITH THAT ROLLER DISCO GUY.
EW.
IT DOESN'T OCCUR TO ME TO TAKE THIS AS A SIGN.
ON OUR FIRST DATE, HE TELLS ME THIS:
I'M THE FIRST WESTERN AVATAR.
WHAT'S AN AVATAR?
AN INCARNATION OF GOD.
HE EXPLAINS THAT HE BELONGS TO A SECT THAT WEARS ONLY "COLORS OF THE SUN." THE BAY AREA IS CRAWLING WITH THIS KIND OF THING.
SO I STOP LISTENING AND STARE AT THE WALL BEHIND HIM.
TENNIS... ROLLER SKATING... BLAH BLAH
AH FRISBEE BLAH BLAH BLA
I REALIZE THERE'S ONLY ONE THING LEFT TO FIND OUT:
WHAT A GUY WHO THINKS HE IS A DEITY IS LIKE IN BED.
I DON'T SEE GOD.
I ALSO DON'T SEE HIM AGAIN. IT HARDLY MATTERS. THERE IS ALWAYS SOMEONE ELSE COMING ALONG.

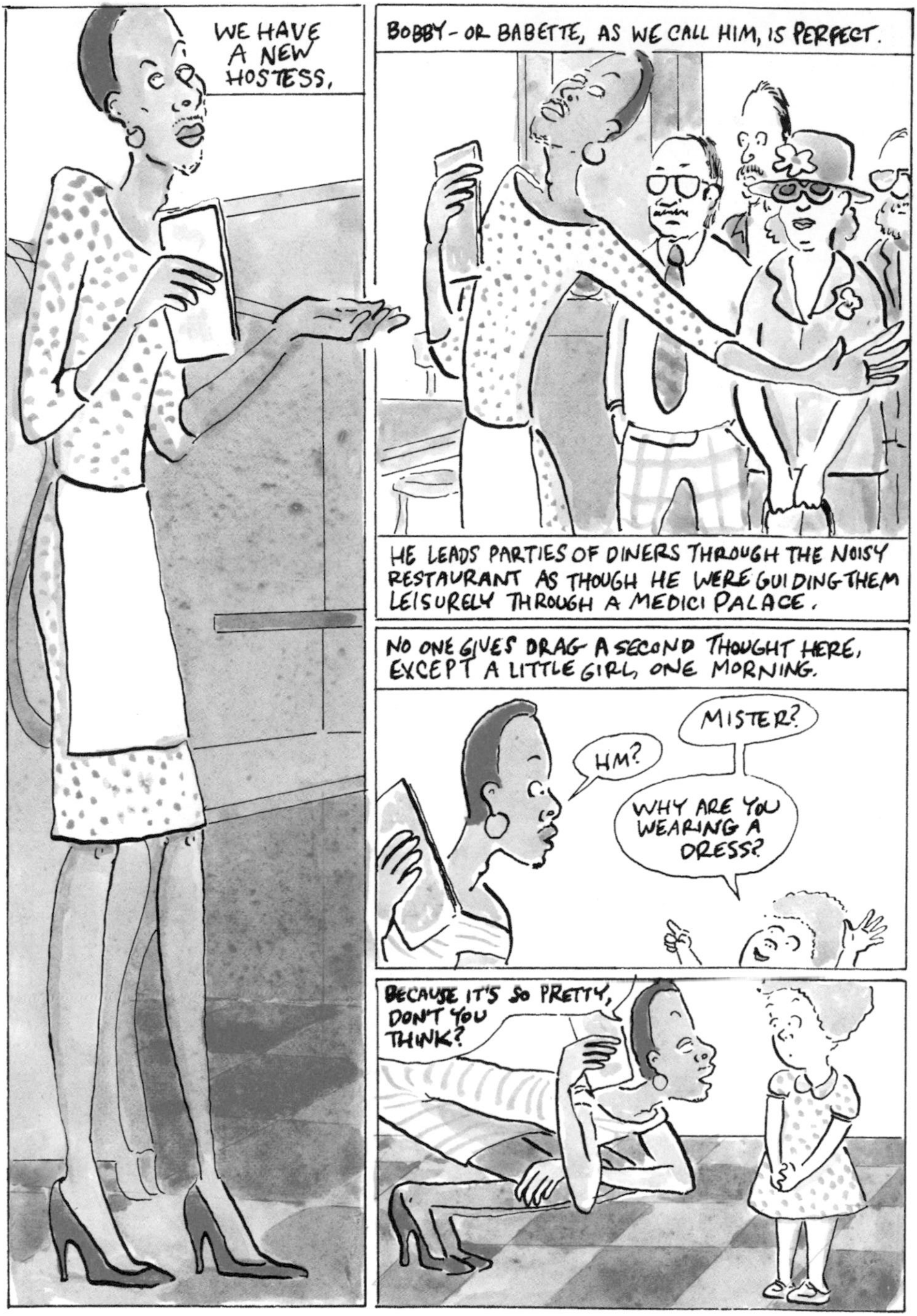
WE HAVE A NEW HOSTESS.
BOBBY- OR BABETTE, AS WE CALL HIM, IS PERFECT.
HE LEADS PARTIES OF DINERS THROUGH THE NOISY RESTAURANT AS THOUGH HE WERE GUIDING THEM LEISURELY THROUGH A MEDICI PALACE.
NO ONE GIVES DRAG A SECOND THOUGHT HERE, EXCEPT A LITTLE GIRL, ONE MORNING.
MISTER?
HM?
WHY ARE YOU WEARING A DRESS?
BECAUSE IT'S SO PRETTY, DON'T YOU THINK?

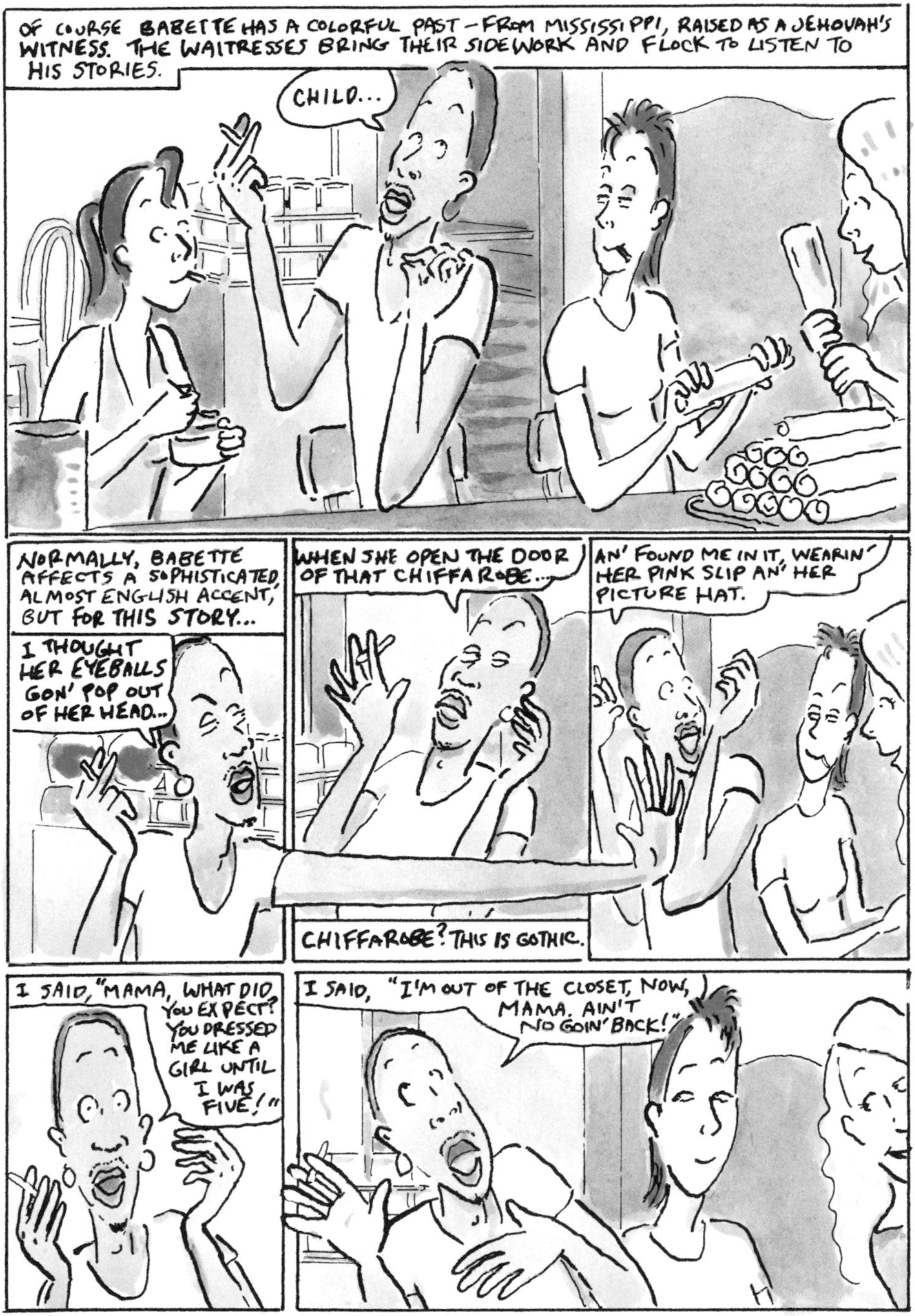
OF COURSE BABETTE HAS A COLORFUL PAST—FROM MISSISSIPPI, RAISED AS A JEHOVAH'S WITNESS. THE WAITRESSES BRING THEIR SIDEWORK AND FLOCK TO LISTEN TO HIS STORIES.
CHILD...
NORMALLY, BABETTE AFFECTS A SOPHISTICATED, ALMOST ENGLISH ACCENT, BUT FOR THIS STORY...
I THOUGHT HER EYEBALLS GON' POP OUT OF HER HEAD...
WHEN SHE OPEN THE DOOR OF THAT CHIFFAROBE...
CHIFFAROBE? THIS IS GOTHIC.
AN' FOUND ME IN IT, WEARIN' HER PINK SLIP AN' HER PICTURE HAT.
I SAID, "MAMA, WHAT DID YOU EXPECT? YOU DRESSED ME LIKE A GIRL UNTIL I WAS FIVE!"
I SAID, "I'M OUT OF THE CLOSET, NOW, MAMA. AIN'T NO GOIN' BACK!"

HE SHEDS HIS SOUTHERN PATOIS AND GOES BACK TO BEING NOEL COWARD.

BLESS MAMA'S HEART. SHE LOVED HER JESUS BUT SHE LOVED HER BOBBY MORE. SHE'D BEEN SAVING HER MONEY FOR A TRIP TO A J W CONVENTION BUT SHE BOUGHT ME A ONE-WAY TICKET OUT HERE INSTEAD.

SHE KNEW I'D NEVER SURVIVE IN TUNICA, MISSISSIPPI.

MY AUNT REGINA SAID, "BOBBY, WHY CAN'T YOU JUST GO TO NAWLINS?"

MAMA SAID, "GINA, BOBBY TOO QUEER FO' NAWLINS!"

IN THIS TOUCHING TABLEAU, EVERYONE IS SPEECHLESS FOR ONCE. THEY REGARD BOBBY AS THOUGH HE IS THE BUDDHA, A REPOSITORY FOR ALL THE WORLD'S SUFFERING AND WISDOM.

I CATCH LAZLO'S EYE. HE'S BEEN LISTENING TOO.

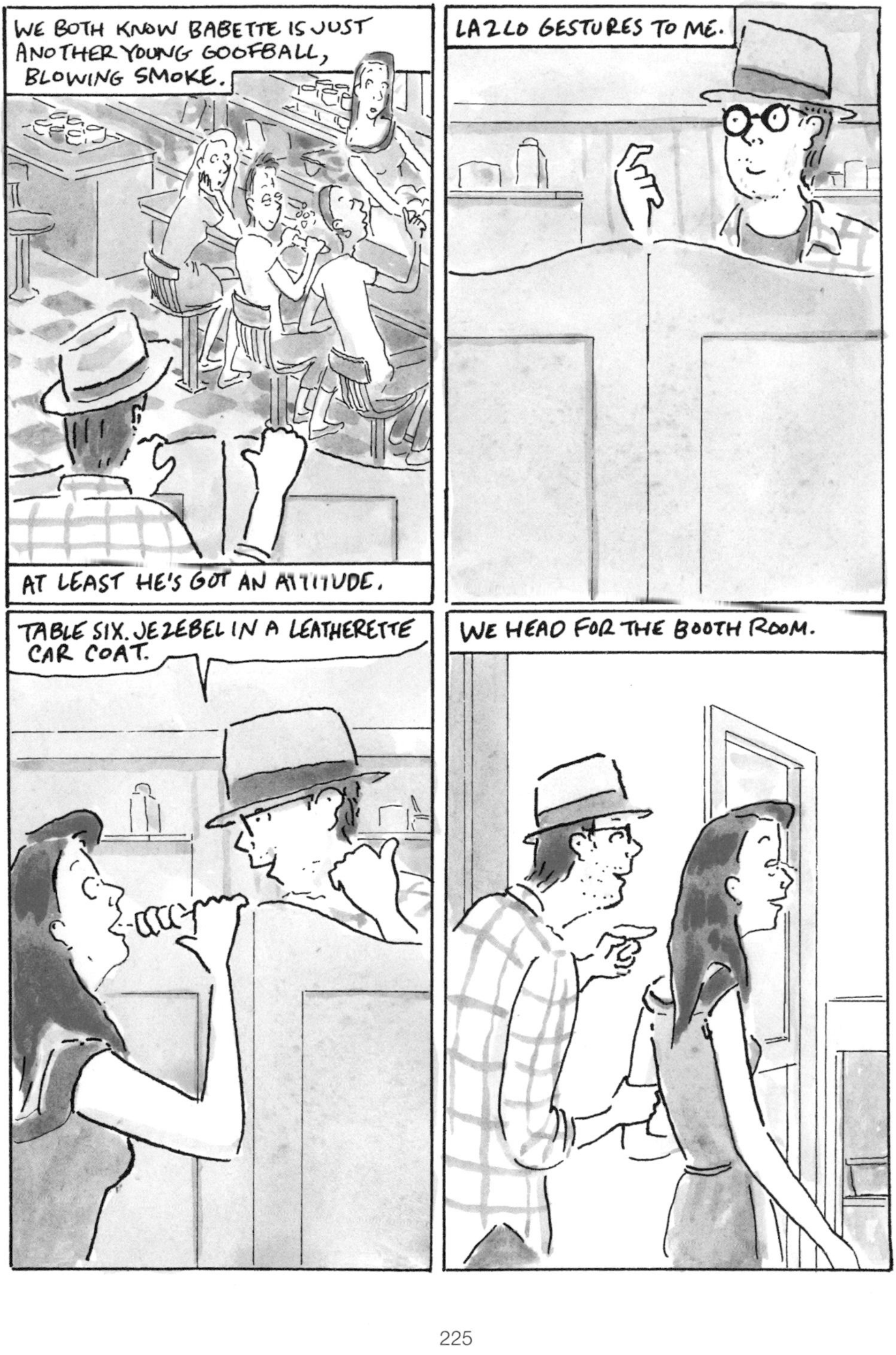
WE BOTH KNOW BABETTE IS JUST ANOTHER YOUNG GOOFBALL, BLOWING SMOKE.
AT LEAST HE'S GOT AN ATTITUDE.
LAZLO GESTURES TO ME.
TABLE SIX. JEZEBEL IN A LEATHERETTE CAR COAT.
WE HEAD FOR THE BOOTH ROOM.

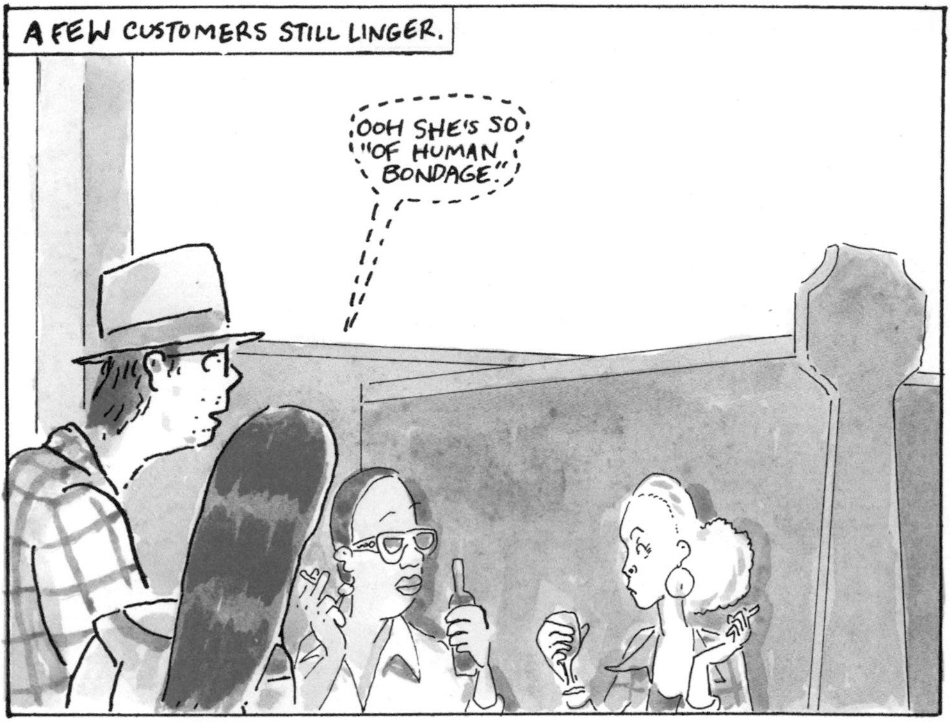
A FEW CUSTOMERS STILL LINGER.
OOH SHE'S SO "OF HUMAN BONDAGE."

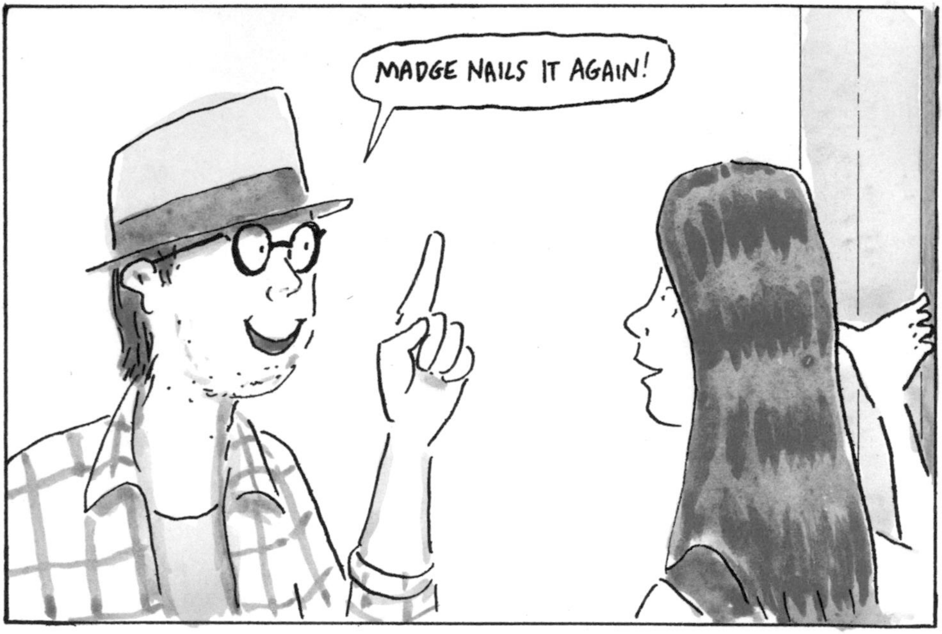
MADGE NAILS IT AGAIN!

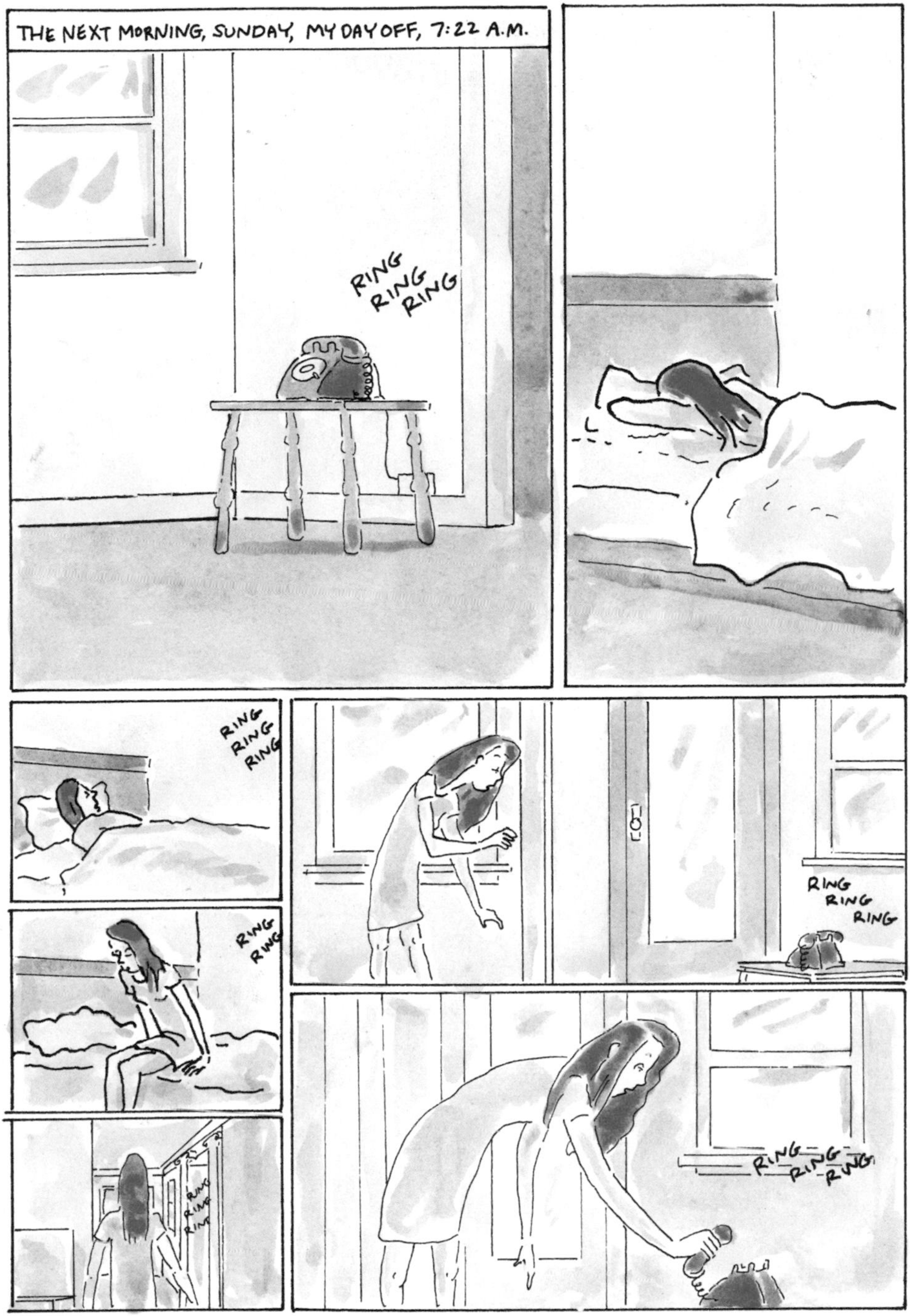
THE NEXT MORNING, SUNDAY, MY DAY OFF, 7:22 A.M.
RING RING RING
RING RING RING
RING RING
RING RING RING
RING RING RING
RING RING RING

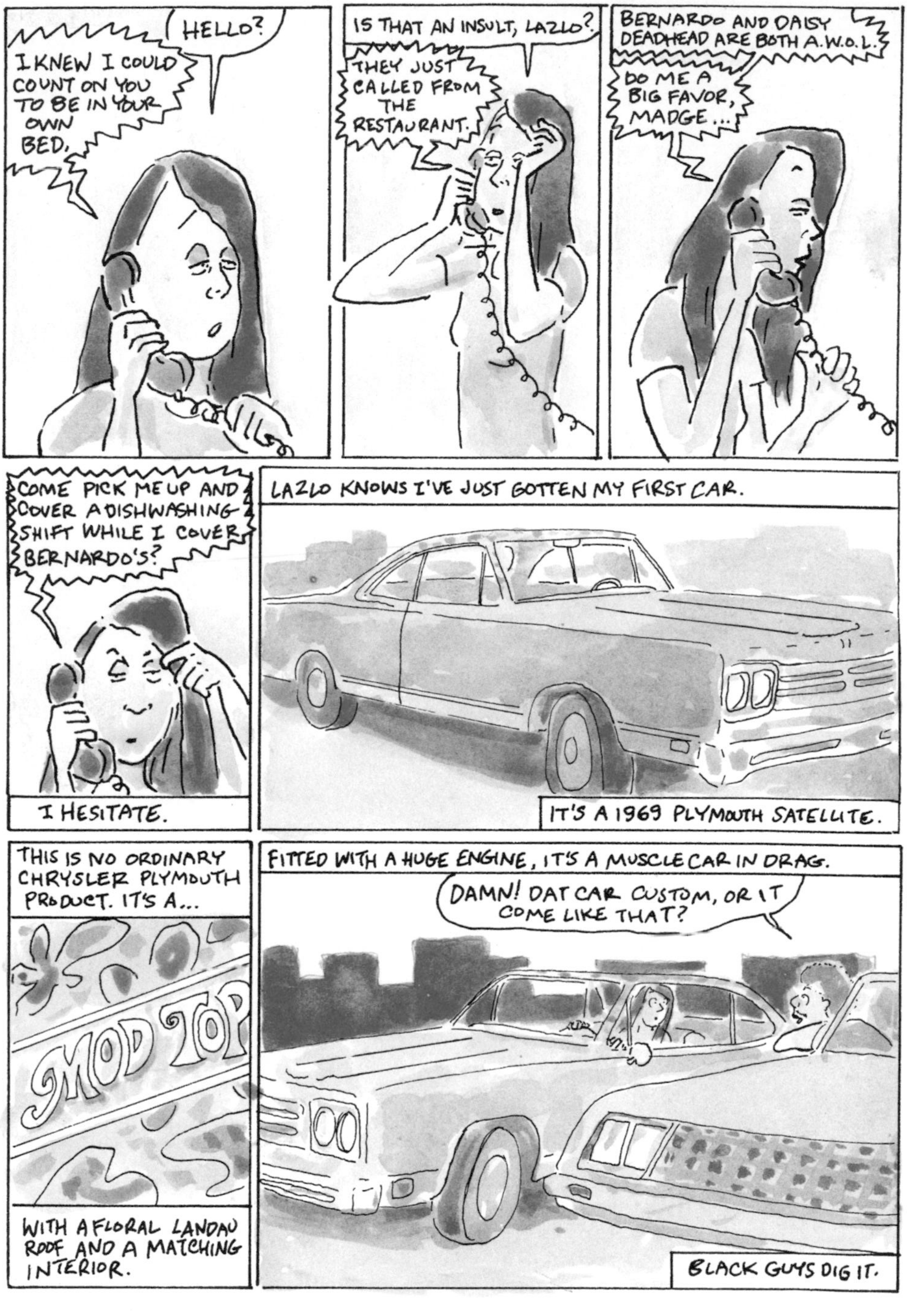
HELLO?
I KNEW I COULD COUNT ON YOU TO BE IN YOUR OWN BED.
IS THAT AN INSULT, LAZLO?
THEY JUST CALLED FROM THE RESTAURANT.
BERNARDO AND DAISY DEADHEAD ARE BOTH A.W.O.L.
DO ME A BIG FAVOR, MADGE...
COME PICK ME UP AND COVER A DISHWASHING SHIFT WHILE I COVER BERNARDO'S?
I HESITATE.
LAZLO KNOWS I'VE JUST GOTTEN MY FIRST CAR.
IT'S A 1969 PLYMOUTH SATELLITE.
THIS IS NO ORDINARY CHRYSLER PLYMOUTH PRODUCT. IT'S A...
MOD TOP
WITH A FLORAL LANDAU ROOF AND A MATCHING INTERIOR.
FITTED WITH A HUGE ENGINE, IT'S A MUSCLE CAR IN DRAG.
DAMN! DAT CAR CUSTOM, OR IT COME LIKE THAT?
BLACK GUYS DIG IT.

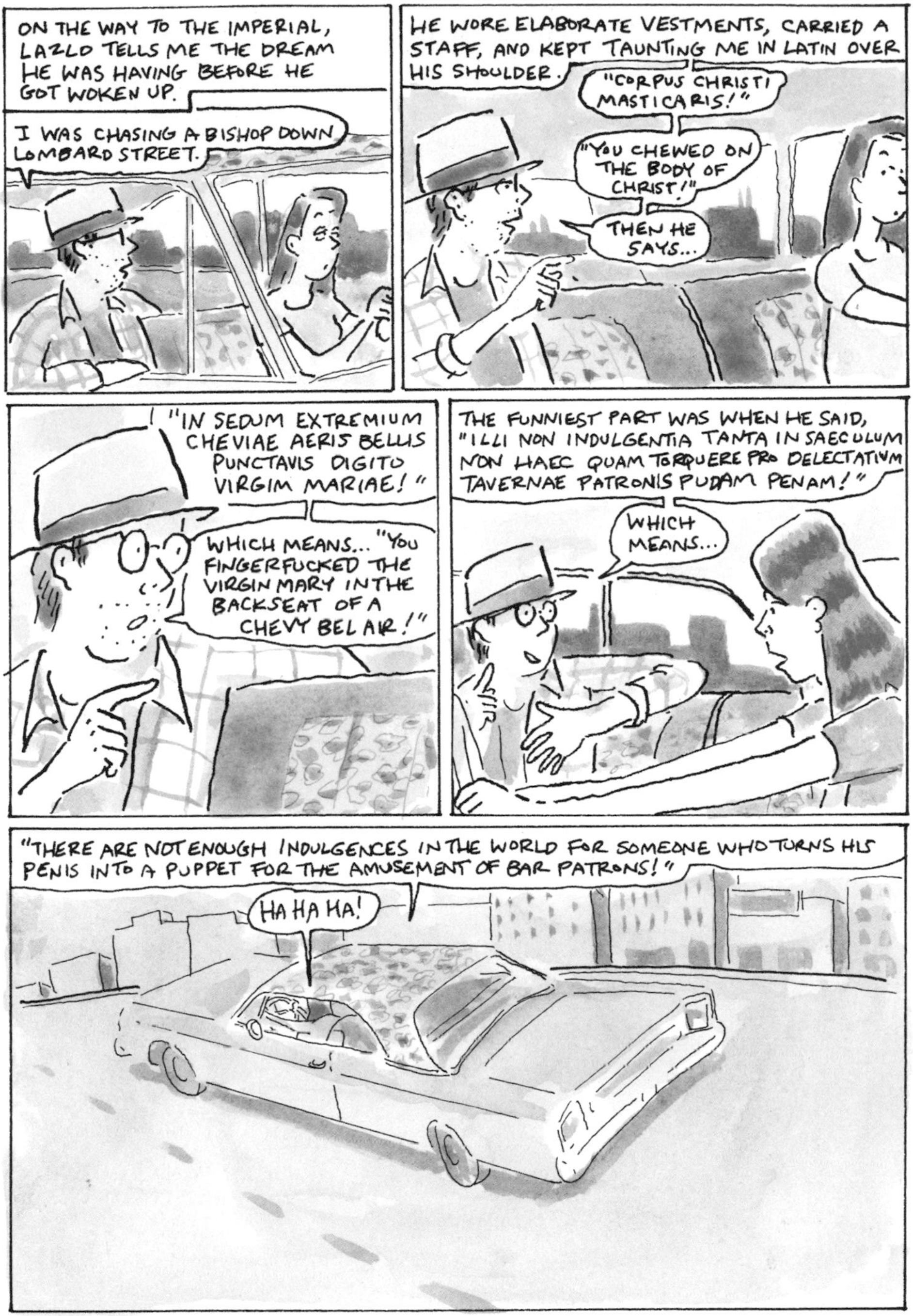
ON THE WAY TO THE IMPERIAL, LAZLO TELLS ME THE DREAM HE WAS HAVING BEFORE HE GOT WOKEN UP.
I WAS CHASING A BISHOP DOWN LOMBARD STREET.
HE WORE ELABORATE VESTMENTS, CARRIED A STAFF, AND KEPT TAUNTING ME IN LATIN OVER HIS SHOULDER.
"CORPUS CHRISTI MASTICARIS!"
"YOU CHEWED ON THE BODY OF CHRIST!"
THEN HE SAYS...
"IN SEDUM EXTREMIUM CHEVIAE AERIS BELLIS PUNCTAVIS DIGITO VIRGIM MARIAE!"
WHICH MEANS... "YOU FINGERFUCKED THE VIRGIN MARY IN THE BACKSEAT OF A CHEVY BEL AIR!"
THE FUNNIEST PART WAS WHEN HE SAID, "ILLI NON INDULGENTIA TANTA IN SAECULUM NON HAEC QUAM TORQUERE PRO DELECTATIVM TAVERNAE PATRONIS PUDAM PENAM!"
WHICH MEANS...
"THERE ARE NOT ENOUGH INDULGENCES IN THE WORLD FOR SOMEONE WHO TURNS HIS PENIS INTO A PUPPET FOR THE AMUSEMENT OF BAR PATRONS!"
HA HA HA!

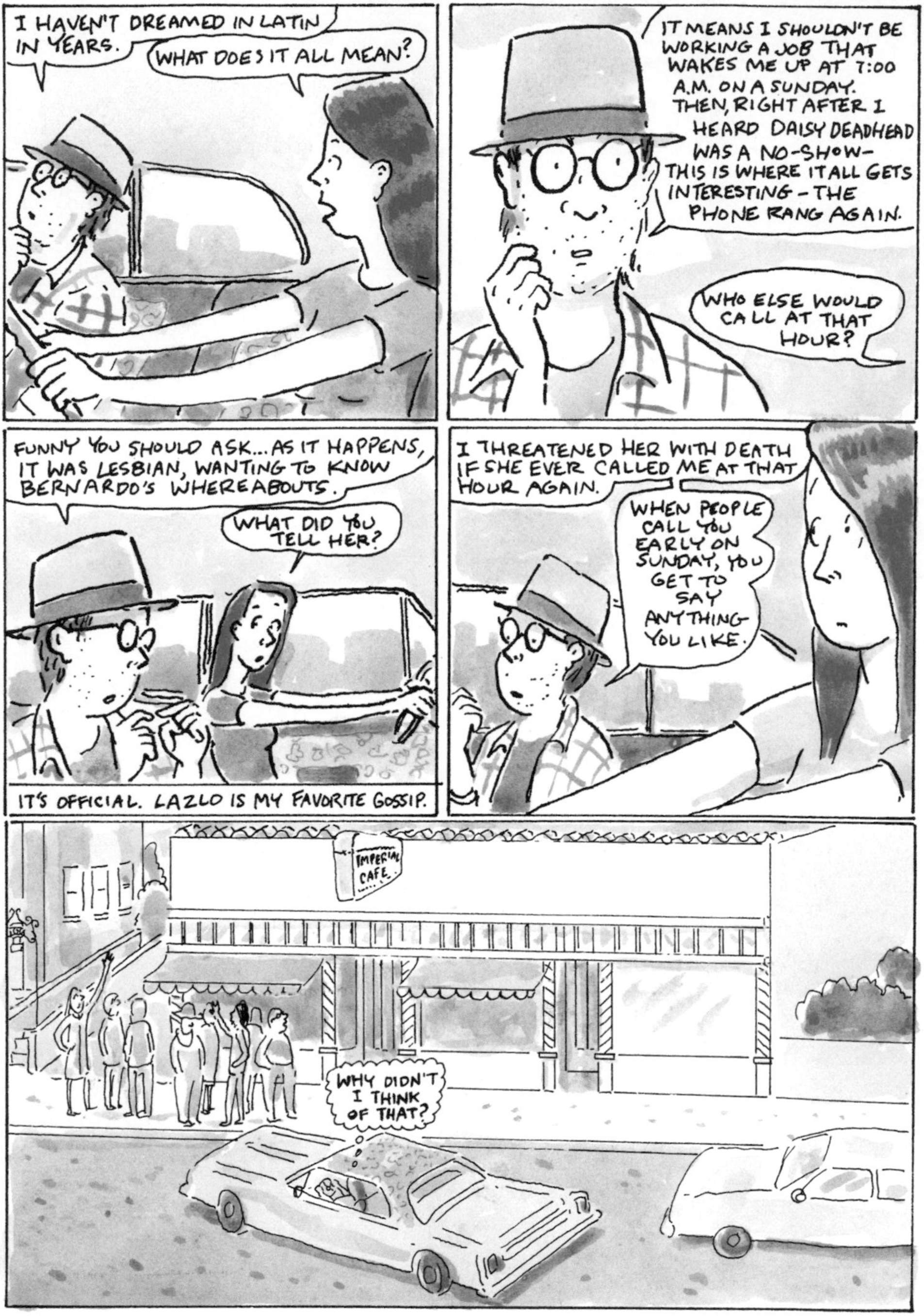
I HAVEN'T DREAMED IN LATIN IN YEARS.
WHAT DOES IT ALL MEAN?
IT MEANS I SHOULDN'T BE WORKING A JOB THAT WAKES ME UP AT 7:00 A.M. ON A SUNDAY. THEN, RIGHT AFTER I HEARD DAISY DEADHEAD WAS A NO-SHOW- THIS IS WHERE IT ALL GETS INTERESTING - THE PHONE RANG AGAIN.
WHO ELSE WOULD CALL AT THAT HOUR?
FUNNY YOU SHOULD ASK... AS IT HAPPENS, IT WAS LESBIAN, WANTING TO KNOW BERNARDO'S WHEREABOUTS.
WHAT DID YOU TELL HER?
IT'S OFFICIAL. LAZLO IS MY FAVORITE GOSSIP.
I THREATENED HER WITH DEATH IF SHE EVER CALLED ME AT THAT HOUR AGAIN.
WHEN PEOPLE CALL YOU EARLY ON SUNDAY, YOU GET TO SAY ANYTHING YOU LIKE.
IMPERIAL CAFE
WHY DIDN'T I THINK OF THAT?

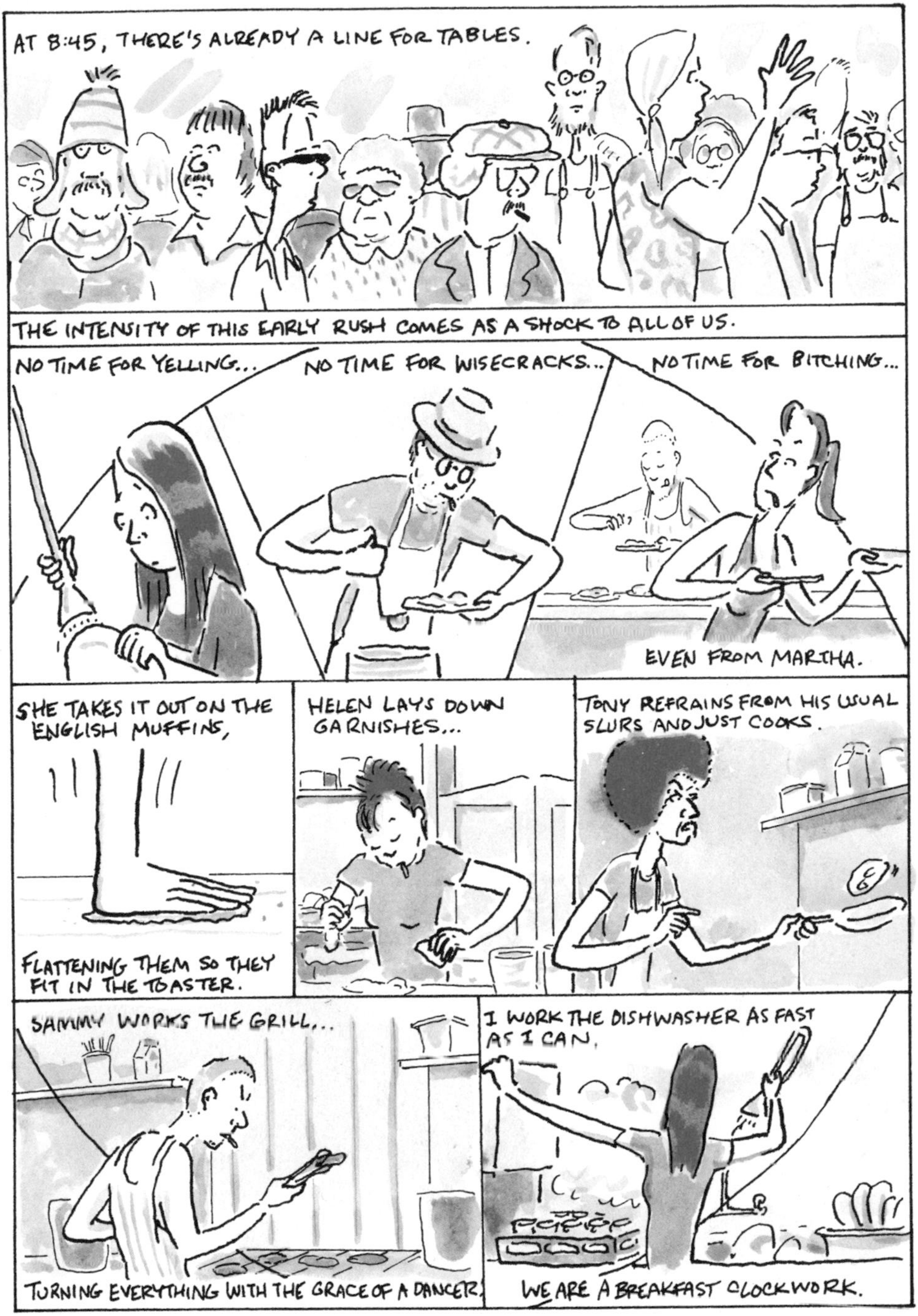
AT 8:45, THERE'S ALREADY A LINE FOR TABLES.
THE INTENSITY OF THIS EARLY RUSH COMES AS A SHOCK TO ALL OF US.
NO TIME FOR YELLING...
NO TIME FOR WISECRACKS...
NO TIME FOR BITCHING...
EVEN FROM MARTHA.
SHE TAKES IT OUT ON THE ENGLISH MUFFINS,
FLATTENING THEM SO THEY FIT IN THE TOASTER.
HELEN LAYS DOWN GARNISHES...
TONY REFRAINS FROM HIS USUAL SLURS AND JUST COOKS.
SAMMY WORKS THE GRILL,...
TURNING EVERYTHING WITH THE GRACE OF A DANCER.
I WORK THE DISHWASHER AS FAST AS I CAN.
WE ARE A BREAKFAST CLOCKWORK.

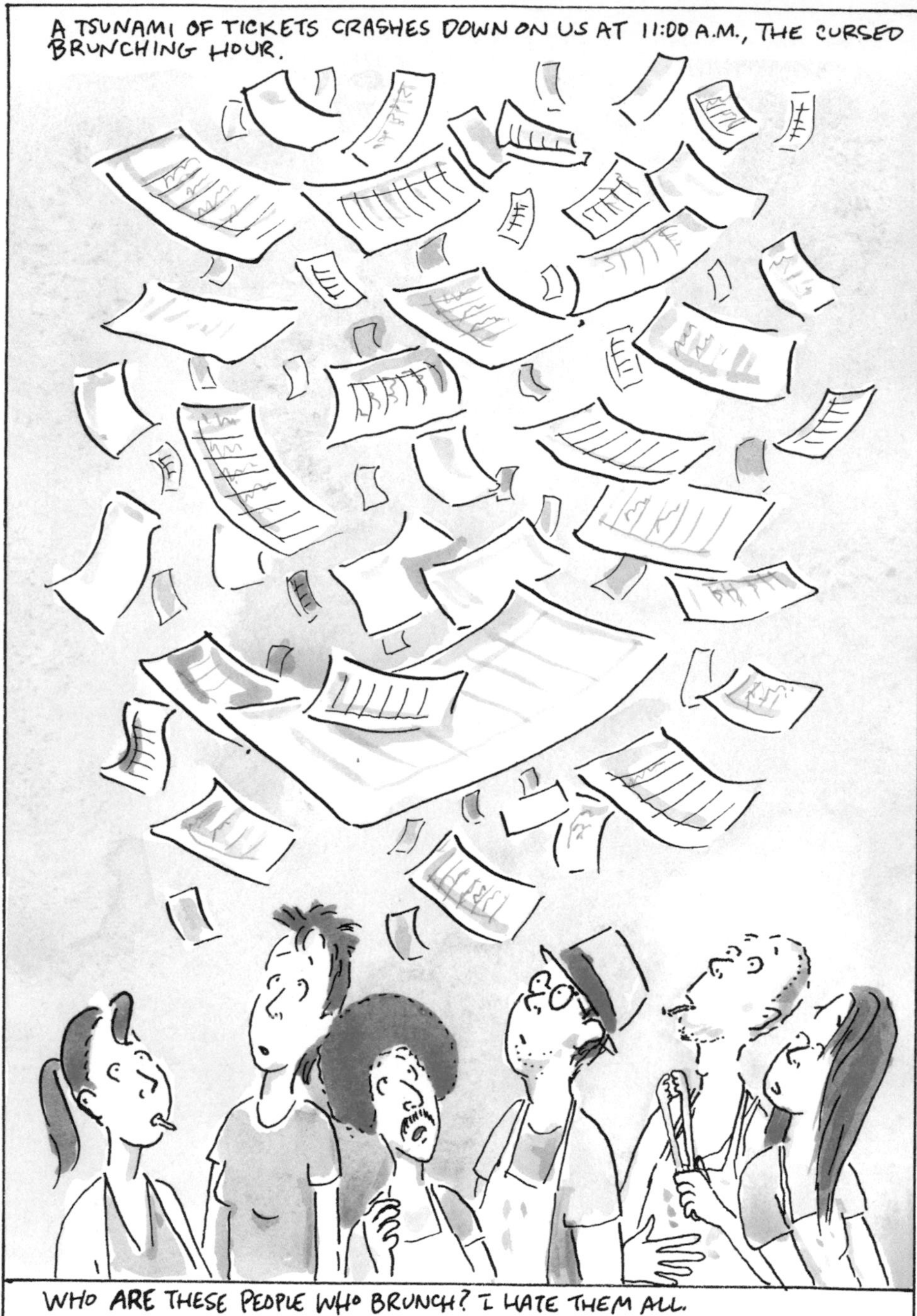
A TSUNAMI OF TICKETS CRASHES DOWN ON US AT 11:00 A.M., THE CURSED BRUNCHING HOUR.
WHO ARE THESE PEOPLE WHO BRUNCH? I HATE THEM ALL.

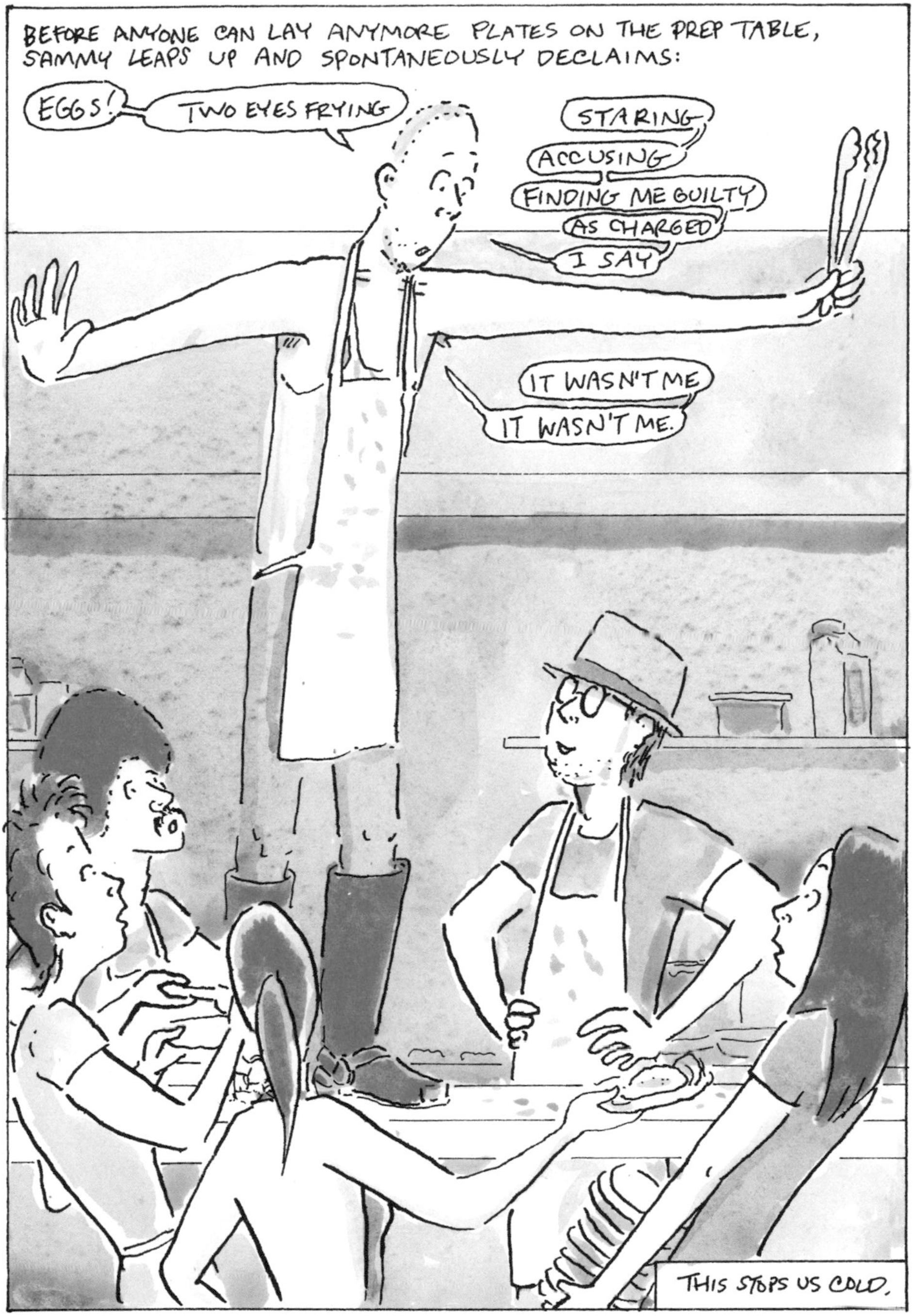
BEFORE ANYONE CAN LAY ANYMORE PLATES ON THE PREP TABLE, SAMMY LEAPS UP AND SPONTANEOUSLY DECLAIMS:
EGGS!
TWO EYES FRYING
STARING
ACCUSING
FINDING ME GUILTY
AS CHARGED
I SAY
IT WASN'T ME
IT WASN'T ME.
THIS STOPS US COLD.

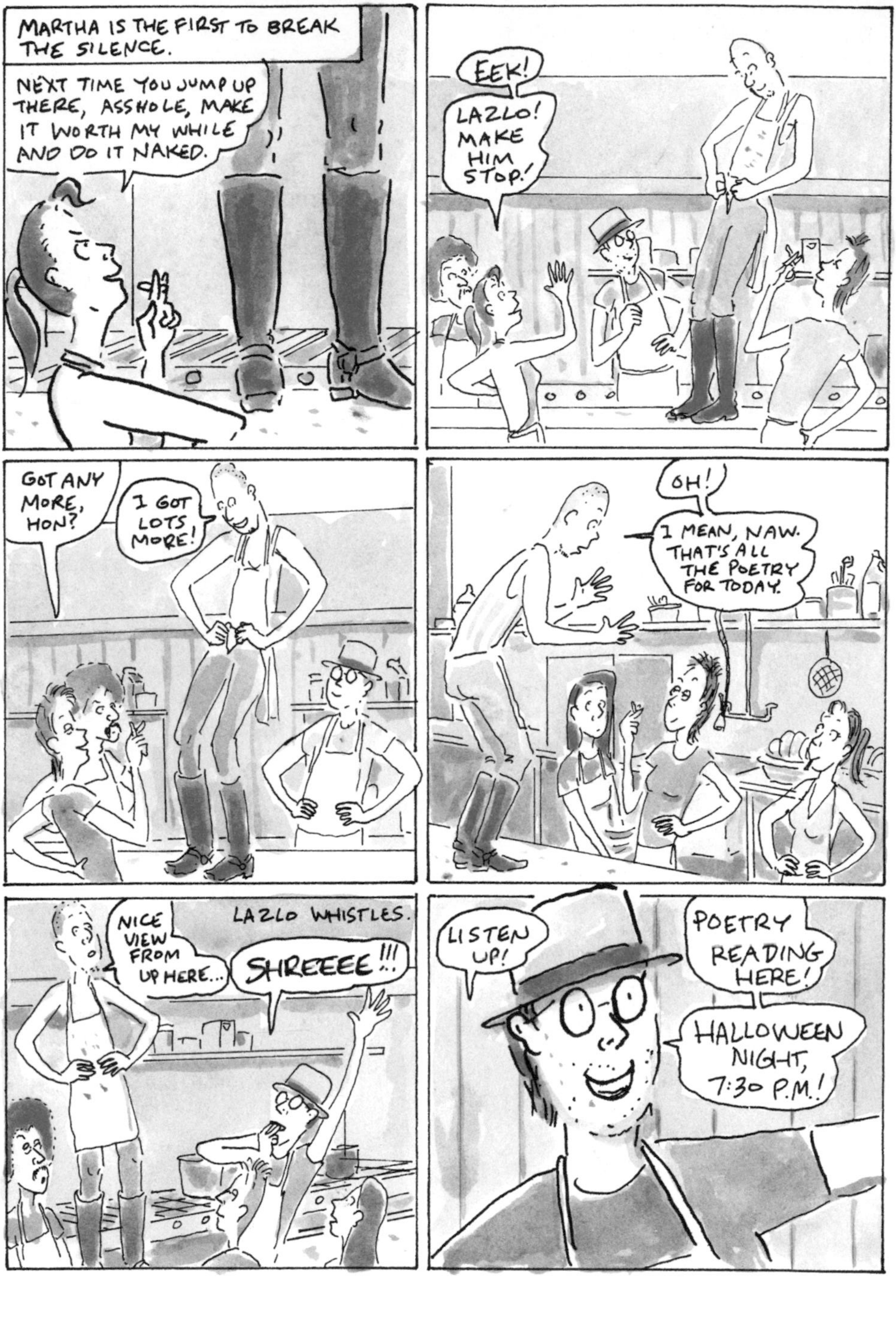
MARTHA IS THE FIRST TO BREAK THE SILENCE.
NEXT TIME YOU JUMP UP THERE, ASSHOLE, MAKE IT WORTH MY WHILE AND DO IT NAKED.
EEK!
LAZLO! MAKE HIM STOP!
GOT ANY MORE, HON?
I GOT LOTS MORE!
OH!
I MEAN, NAW. THAT'S ALL THE POETRY FOR TODAY.
NICE VIEW FROM UP HERE...
LAZLO WHISTLES.
SHREEEE!!!
LISTEN UP!
POETRY READING HERE!
HALLOWEEN NIGHT, 7:30 P.M.!

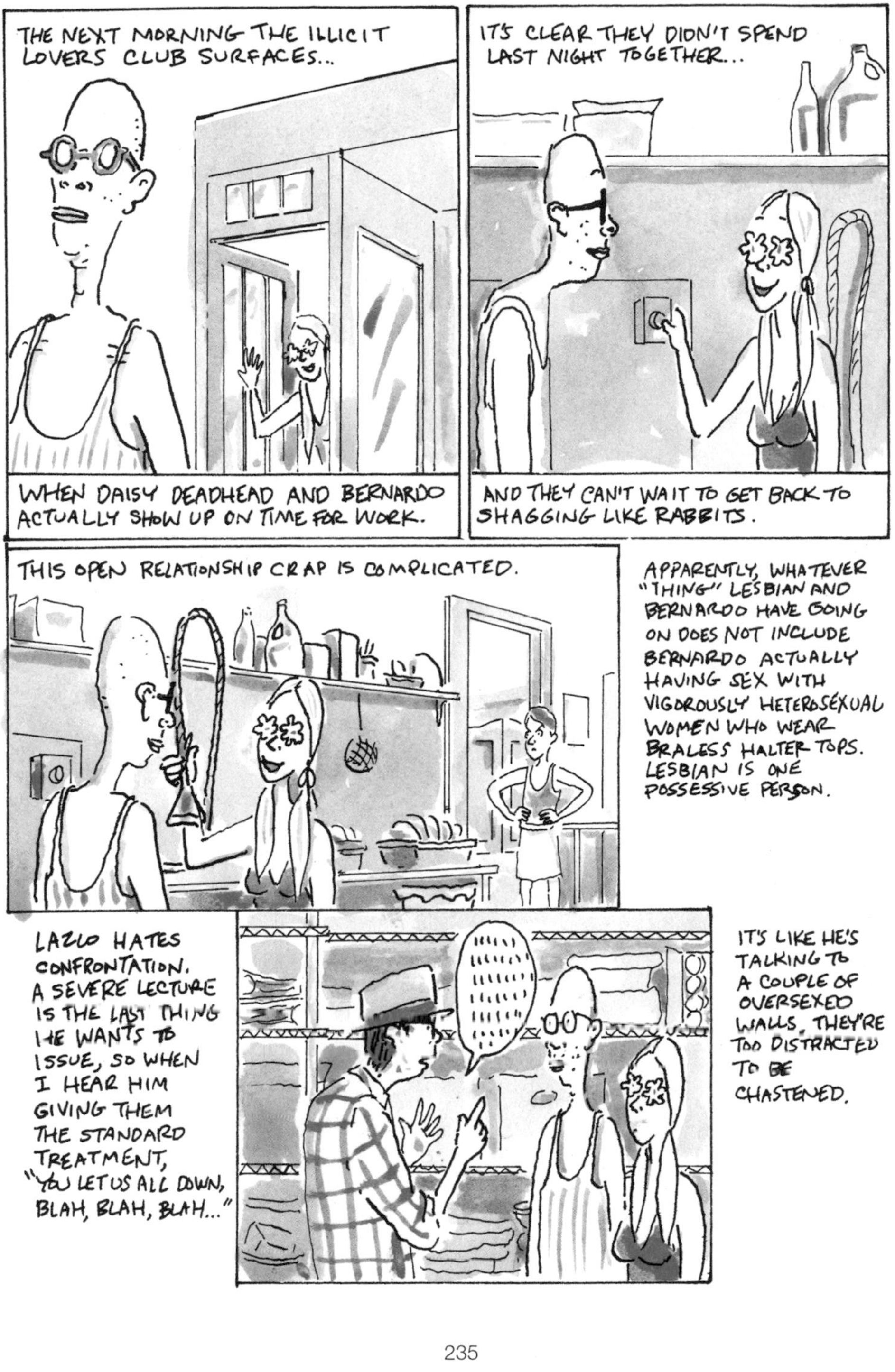
THE NEXT MORNING THE ILLICIT LOVERS CLUB SURFACES...
WHEN DAISY DEADHEAD AND BERNARDO ACTUALLY SHOW UP ON TIME FOR WORK.
IT'S CLEAR THEY DIDN'T SPEND LAST NIGHT TOGETHER...
AND THEY CAN'T WAIT TO GET BACK TO SHAGGING LIKE RABBITS.
THIS OPEN RELATIONSHIP CRAP IS COMPLICATED.
APPARENTLY, WHATEVER "THING" LESBIAN AND BERNARDO HAVE GOING ON DOES NOT INCLUDE BERNARDO ACTUALLY HAVING SEX WITH VIGOROUSLY HETEROSEXUAL WOMEN WHO WEAR BRALESS HALTER TOPS. LESBIAN IS ONE POSSESSIVE PERSON.
LAZLO HATES CONFRONTATION. A SEVERE LECTURE IS THE LAST THING HE WANTS TO ISSUE, SO WHEN I HEAR HIM GIVING THEM THE STANDARD TREATMENT, "YOU LET US ALL DOWN, BLAH, BLAH, BLAH..."
IT'S LIKE HE'S TALKING TO A COUPLE OF OVERSEXED WALLS. THEY'RE TOO DISTRACTED TO BE CHASTENED.

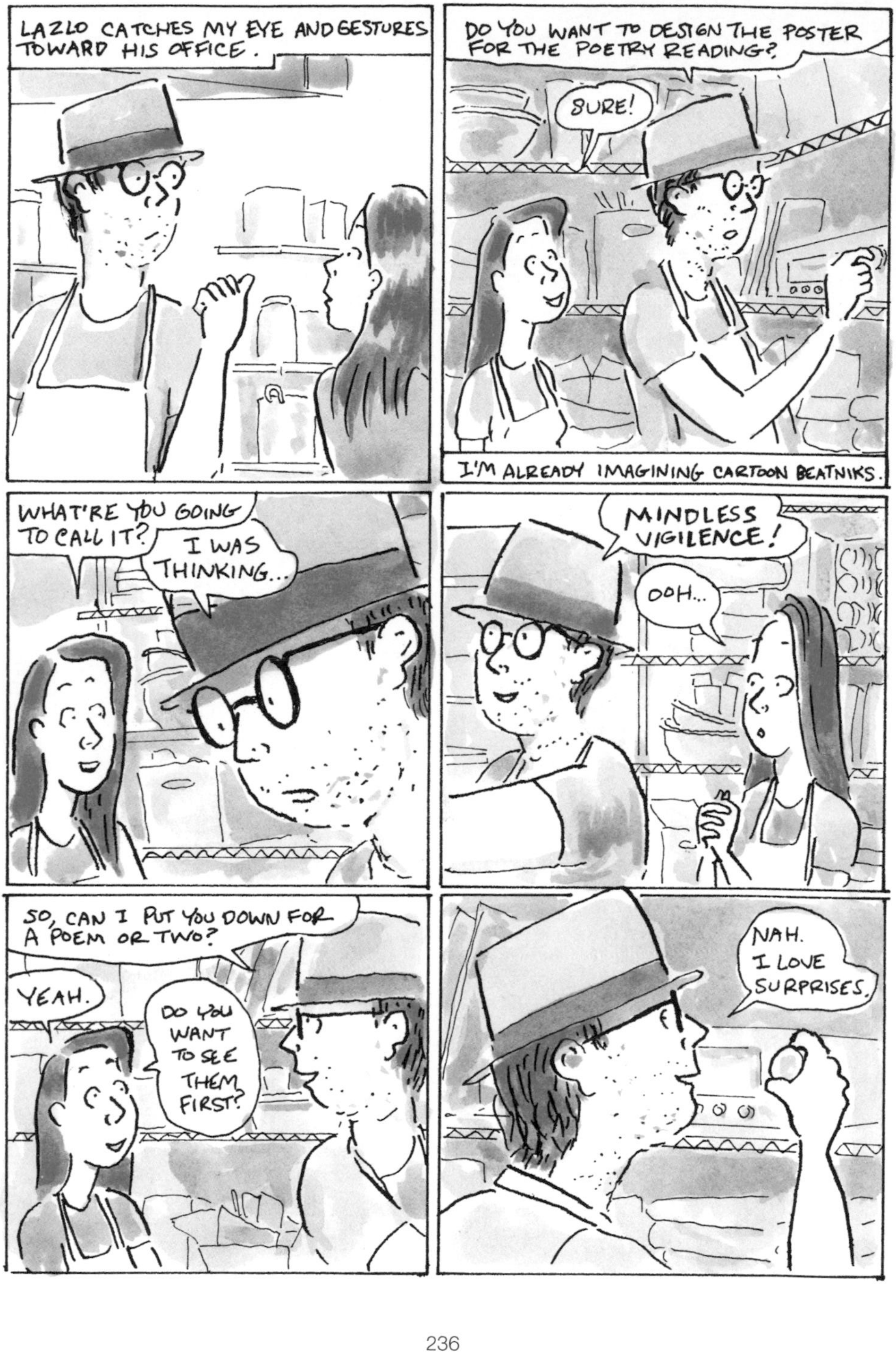
LAZLO CATCHES MY EYE AND GESTURES TOWARD HIS OFFICE.
DO YOU WANT TO DESIGN THE POSTER FOR THE POETRY READING?
SURE!
I'M ALREADY IMAGINING CARTOON BEATNIKS.
WHAT'RE YOU GOING TO CALL IT?
I WAS THINKING...
MINDLESS VIGILENCE!
OOH...
SO, CAN I PUT YOU DOWN FOR A POEM OR TWO?
YEAH.
DO YOU WANT TO SEE THEM FIRST?
NAH. I LOVE SURPRISES.

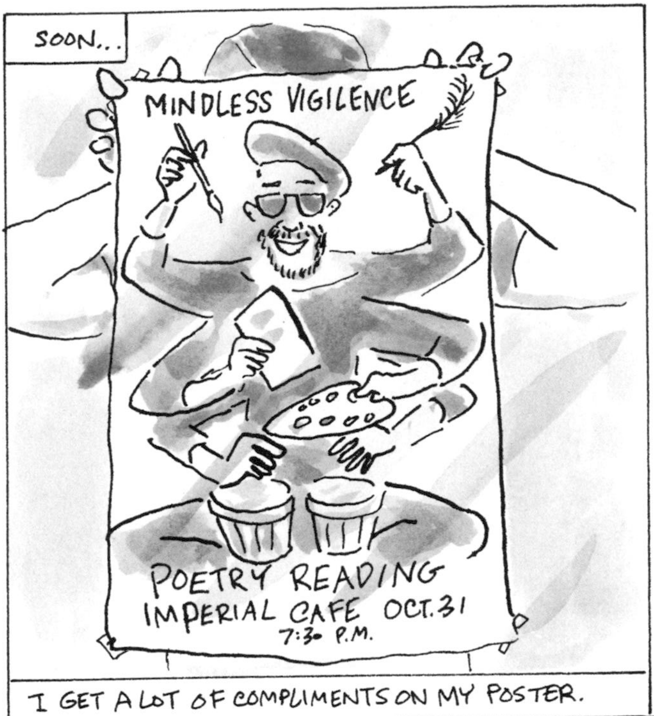
SOON...
MINDLESS VIGILENCE
POETRY READING
IMPERIAL CAFE OCT. 31
7:30 P.M.
I GET A LOT OF COMPLIMENTS ON MY POSTER.

BUT BEST OF ALL, SOMEONE SUGGESTS I SHOW MY WORK TO THE EDITOR OF THE BERKELEY BARB. BY NOW, THE BARB IS NO LONGER THE ROILING HOTBED OF RADICAL CHIC IT ONCE WAS. IT'S MORE OF A LEFTIST VERSION OF THE NATIONAL ENQUIRER. I DON'T CARE. I JUST WANT TO GET PUBLISHED.

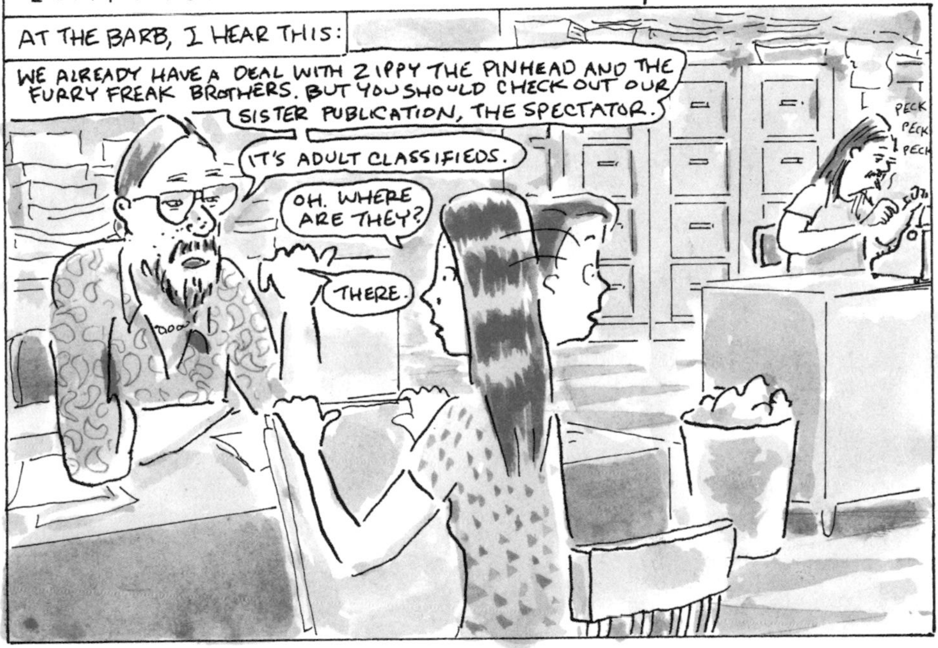
AT THE BARB, I HEAR THIS:
WE ALREADY HAVE A DEAL WITH ZIPPY THE PINHEAD AND THE FURRY FREAK BROTHERS. BUT YOU SHOULD CHECK OUT OUR SISTER PUBLICATION, THE SPECTATOR.
IT'S ADULT CLASSIFIEDS.
OH. WHERE ARE THEY?
THERE.
PECK
PECK
PECK

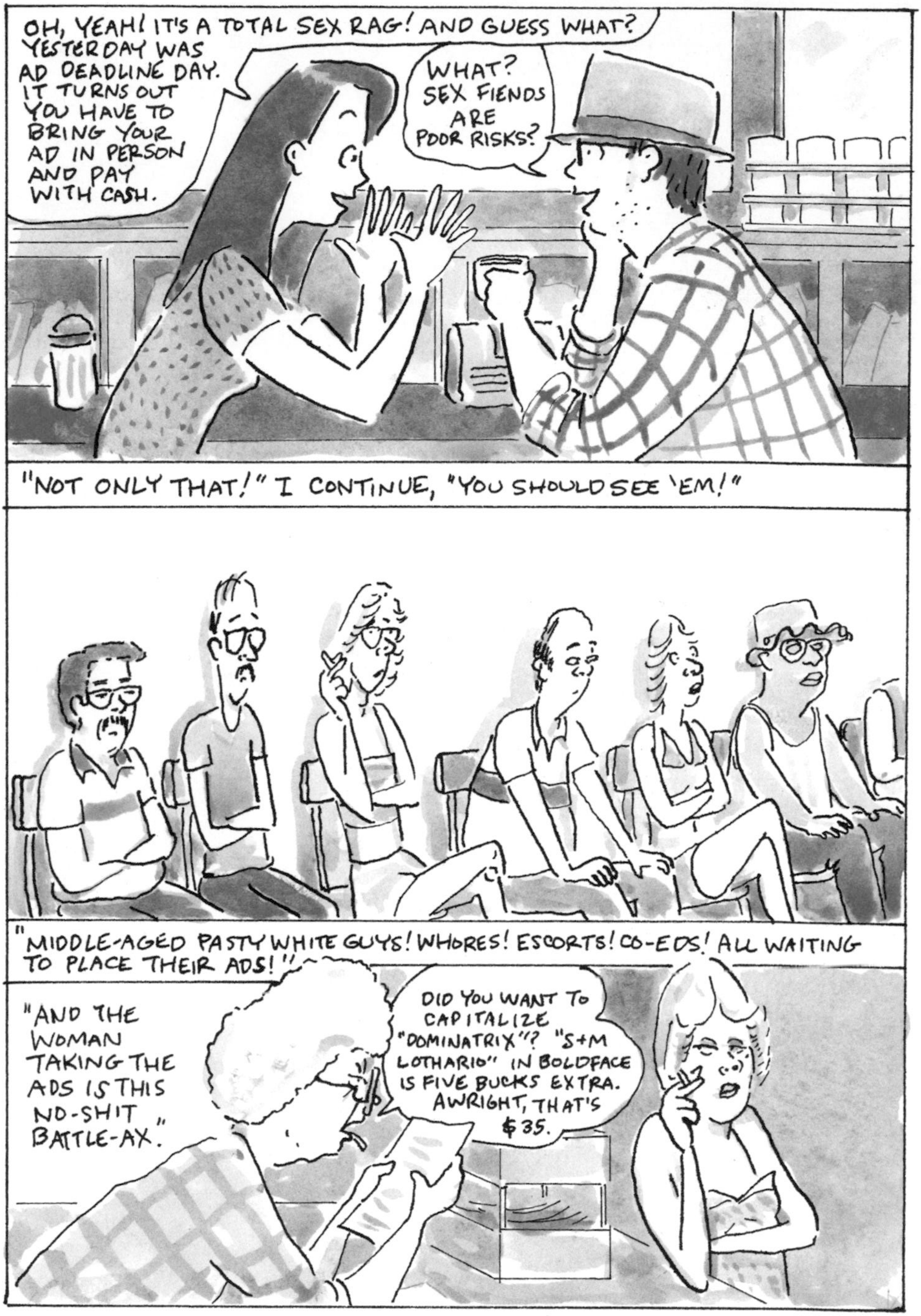

OH, YEAH! IT'S A TOTAL SEX RAG! AND GUESS WHAT? YESTERDAY WAS AD DEADLINE DAY. IT TURNS OUT YOU HAVE TO BRING YOUR AD IN PERSON AND PAY WITH CASH.
WHAT? SEX FIENDS ARE POOR RISKS?
"NOT ONLY THAT!" I CONTINUE, "YOU SHOULD SEE 'EM!"
"MIDDLE-AGED PASTY WHITE GUYS! WHORES! ESCORTS! CO-EDS! ALL WAITING TO PLACE THEIR ADS!"
"AND THE WOMAN TAKING THE ADS IS THIS NO-SHIT BATTLE-AX."
DID YOU WANT TO CAPITALIZE "DOMINATRIX"? "S+M LOTHARIO" IN BOLDFACE IS FIVE BUCKS EXTRA. AWRIGHT, THAT'S $35.

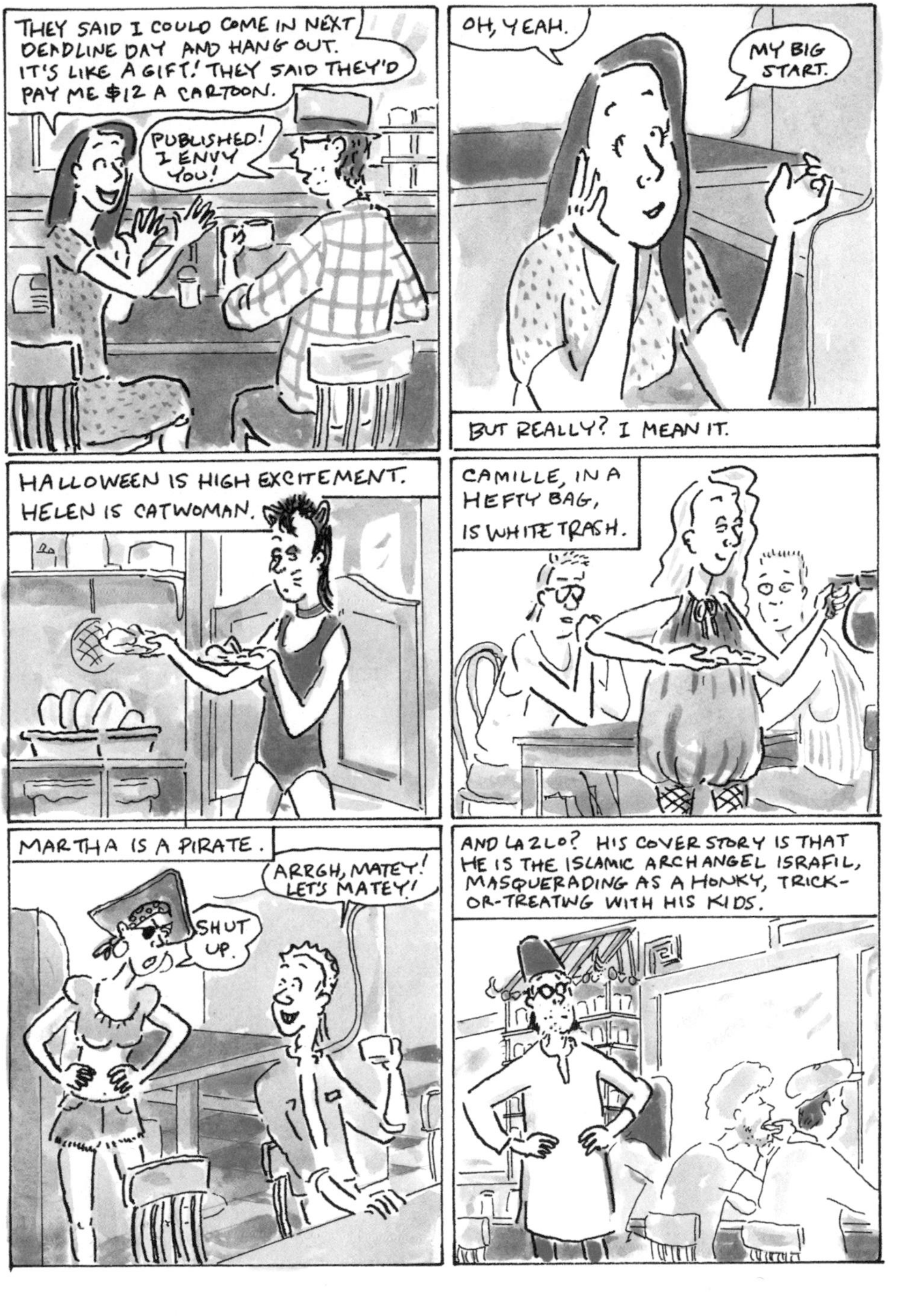
THEY SAID I COULD COME IN NEXT DEADLINE DAY AND HANG OUT. IT'S LIKE A GIFT! THEY SAID THEY'D PAY ME $12 A CARTOON.
PUBLISHED! I ENVY YOU!
OH, YEAH.
MY BIG START.
BUT REALLY? I MEAN IT.
HALLOWEEN IS HIGH EXCITEMENT. HELEN IS CATWOMAN.
CAMILLE, IN A HEFTY BAG, IS WHITE TRASH.
MARTHA IS A PIRATE.
ARRGH, MATEY! LET'S MATEY!
SHUT UP.
AND LAZLO? HIS COVER STORY IS THAT HE IS THE ISLAMIC ARCHANGEL ISRAFIL, MASQUERADING AS A HONKY, TRICK-OR-TREATING WITH HIS KIDS.

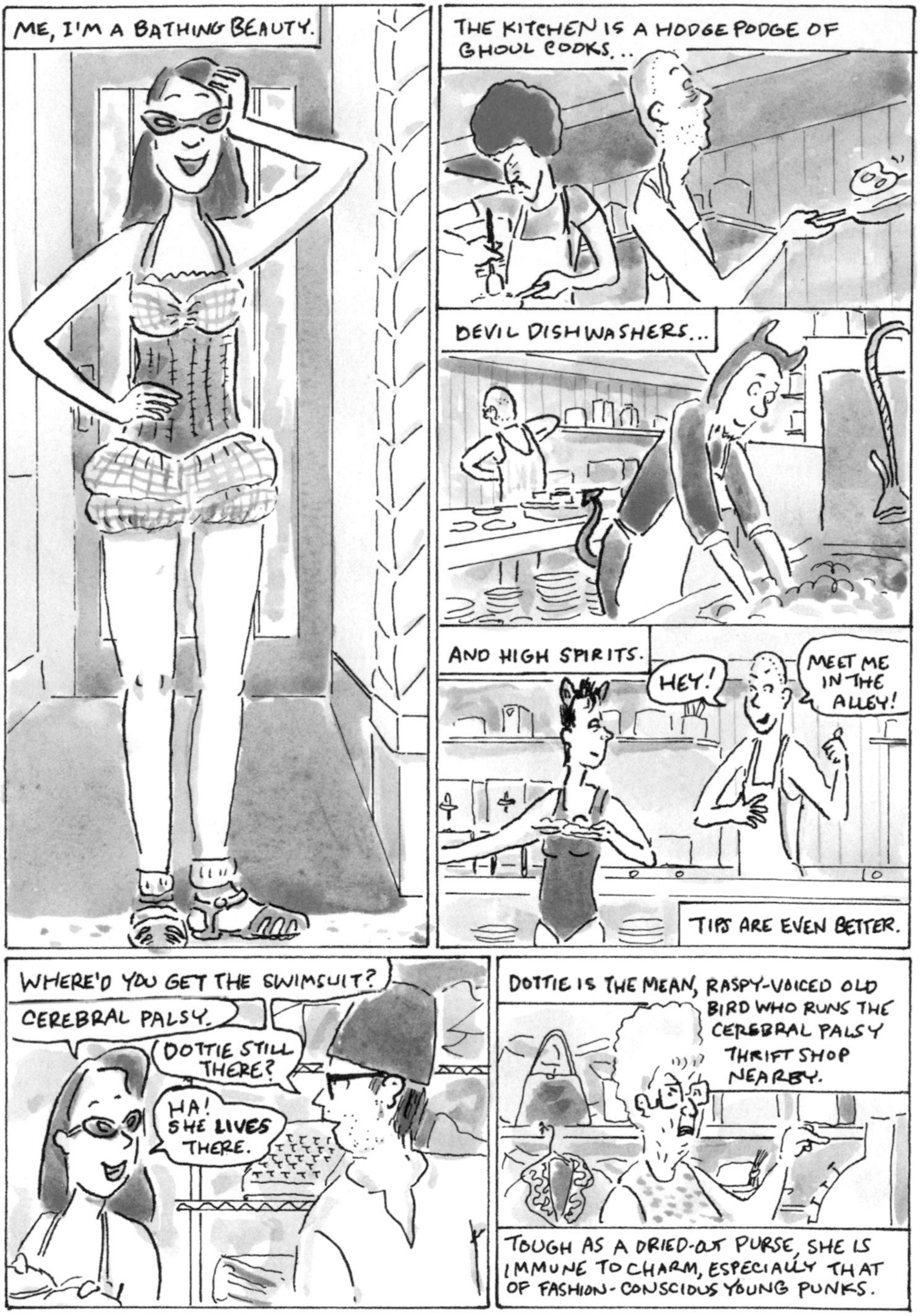
ME, I'M A BATHING BEAUTY.
THE KITCHEN IS A HODGE PODGE OF GHOUL COOKS...
DEVIL DISHWASHERS...
AND HIGH SPIRITS.
HEY!
MEET ME IN THE ALLEY!
TIPS ARE EVEN BETTER.
WHERE'D YOU GET THE SWIMSUIT?
CEREBRAL PALSY.
DOTTIE STILL THERE?
HA! SHE LIVES THERE.
DOTTIE IS THE MEAN, RASPY-VOICED OLD BIRD WHO RUNS THE CEREBRAL PALSY THRIFT SHOP NEARBY.
TOUGH AS A DRIED-OUT PURSE, SHE IS IMMUNE TO CHARM, ESPECIALLY THAT OF FASHION-CONSCIOUS YOUNG PUNKS.

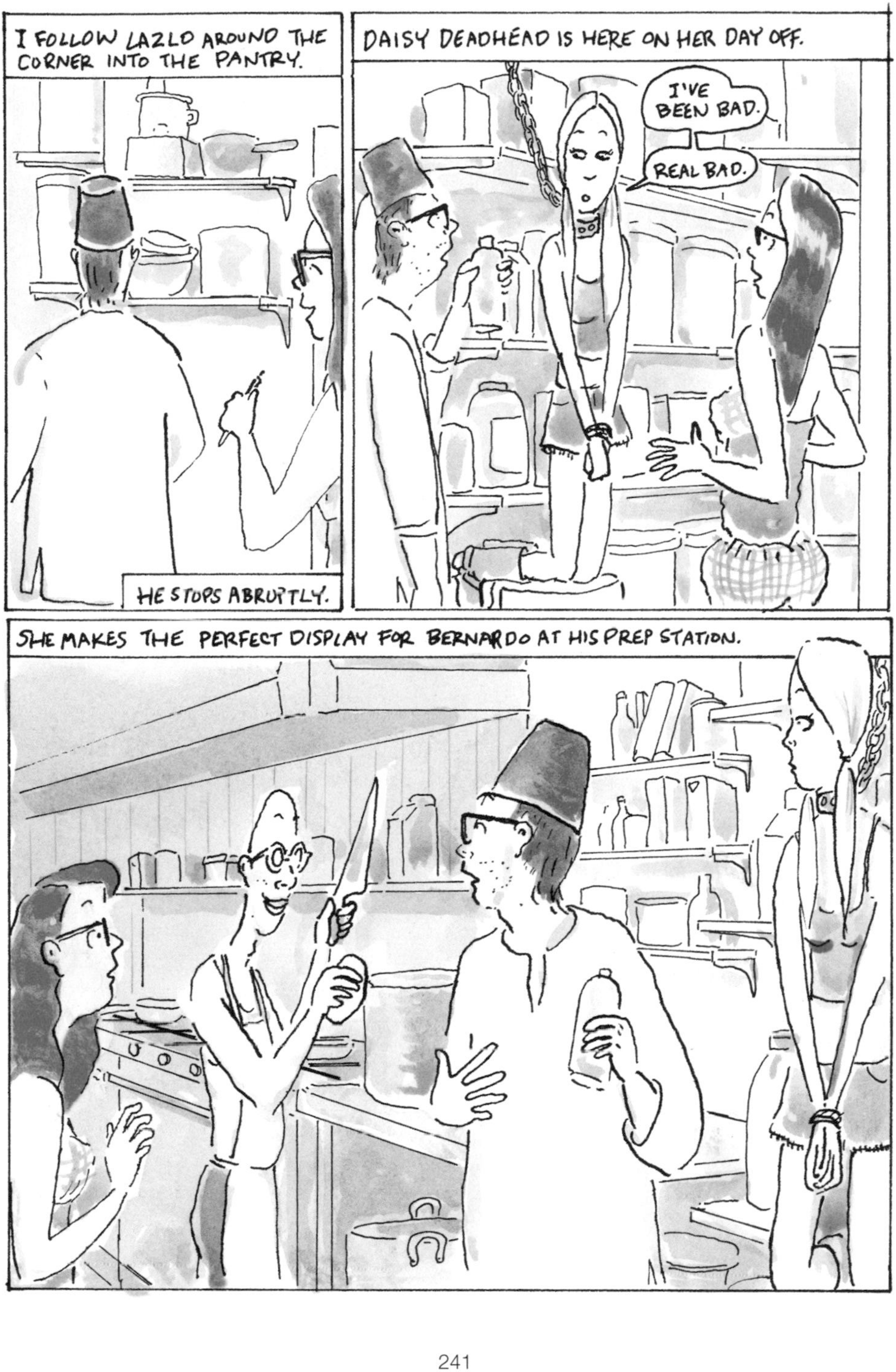
I FOLLOW LAZLO AROUND THE CORNER INTO THE PANTRY.
HE STOPS ABRUPTLY.
DAISY DEADHEAD IS HERE ON HER DAY OFF.
I'VE BEEN BAD.
REAL BAD.
SHE MAKES THE PERFECT DISPLAY FOR BERNARDO AT HIS PREP STATION.

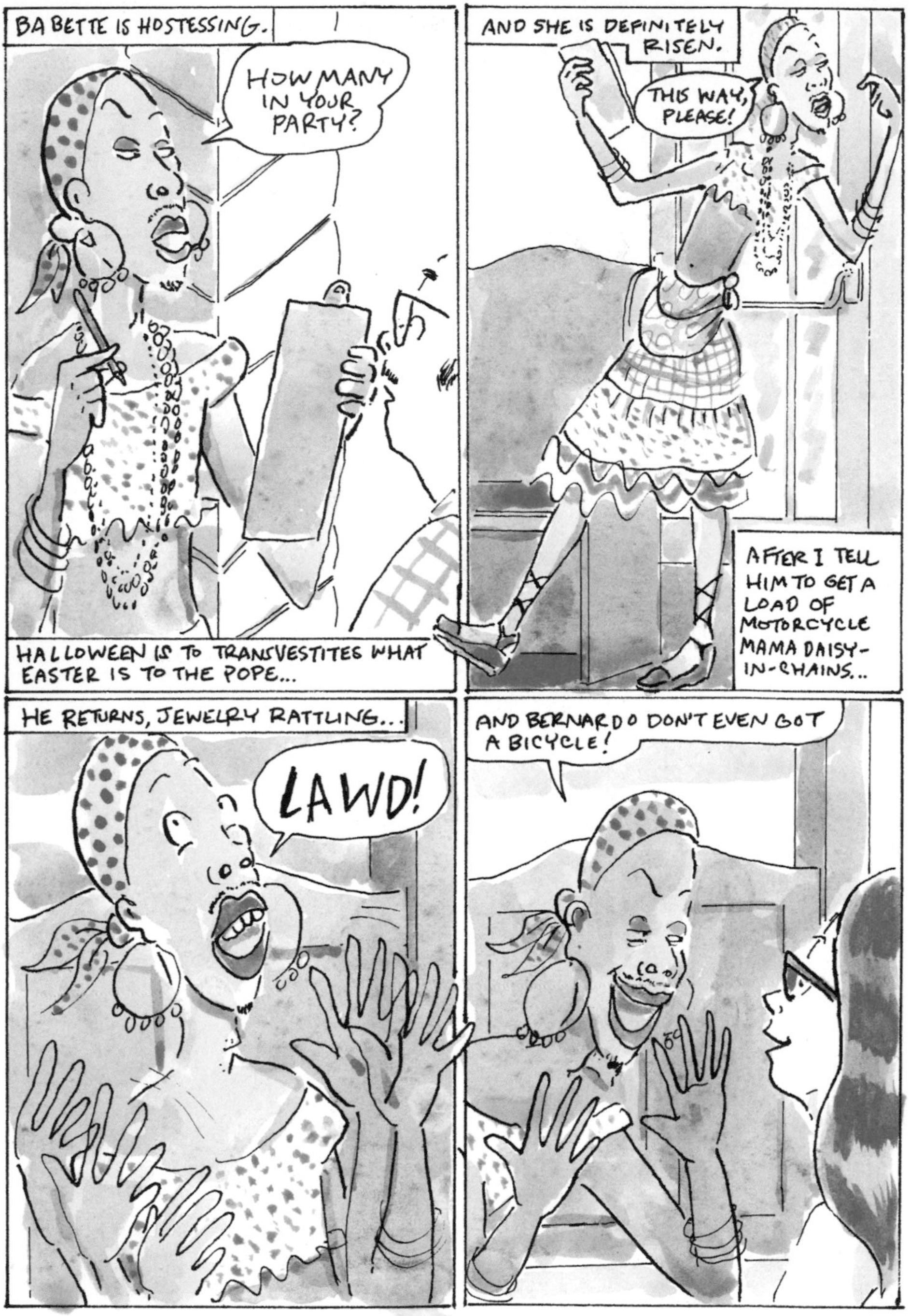
BABETTE IS HOSTESSING.
HOW MANY IN YOUR PARTY?
HALLOWEEN IS TO TRANSVESTITES WHAT EASTER IS TO THE POPE...
AND SHE IS DEFINITELY RISEN.
THIS WAY, PLEASE!
AFTER I TELL HIM TO GET A LOAD OF MOTORCYCLE MAMA DAISY-IN-CHAINS...
HE RETURNS, JEWELRY RATTLING...
LAWD!
AND BERNARDO DON'T EVEN GOT A BICYCLE!

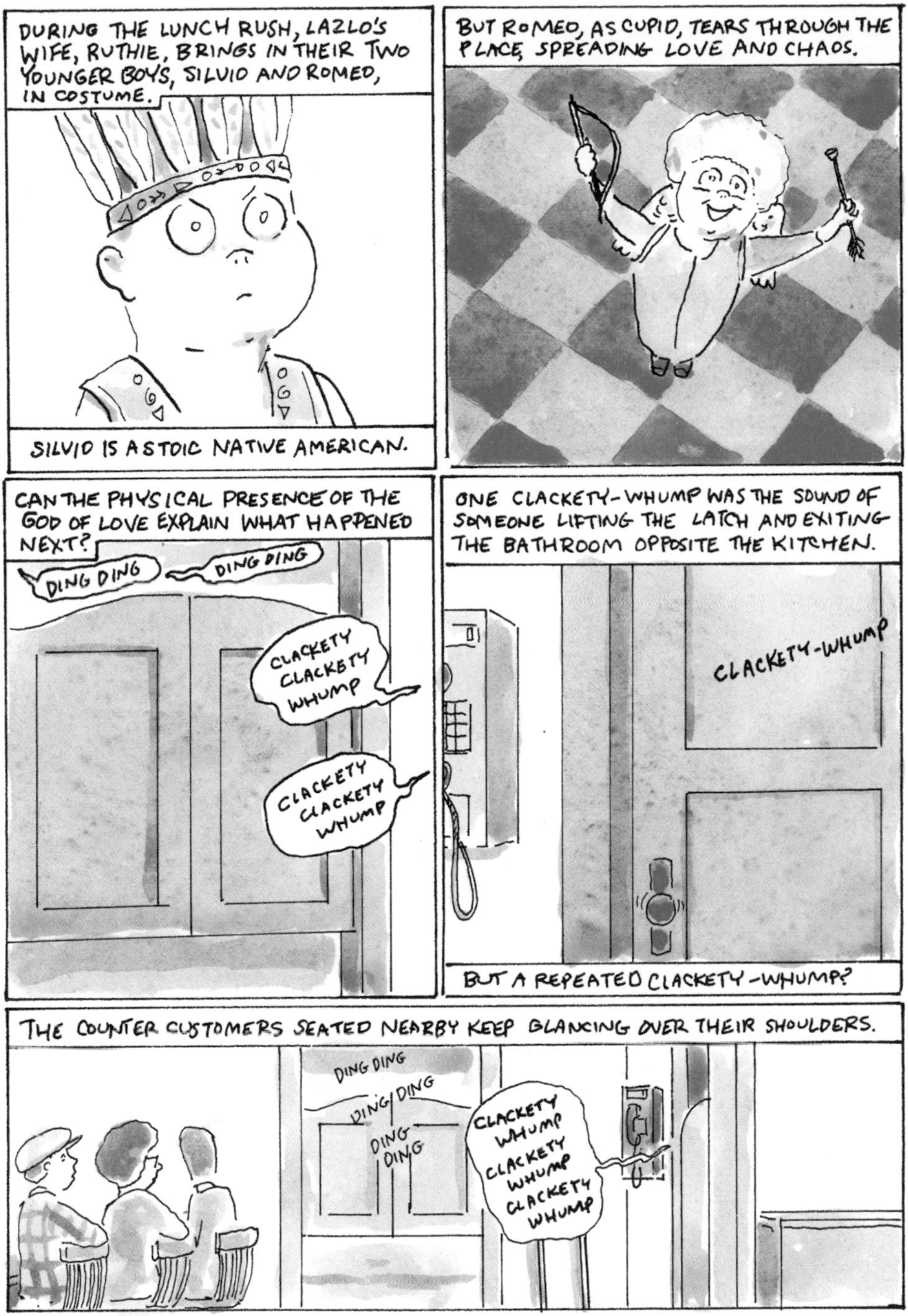

DURING THE LUNCH RUSH, LAZLO'S WIFE, RUTHIE, BRINGS IN THEIR TWO YOUNGER BOYS, SILVIO AND ROMEO, IN COSTUME.
SILVIO IS A STOIC NATIVE AMERICAN.
BUT ROMEO, AS CUPID, TEARS THROUGH THE PLACE, SPREADING LOVE AND CHAOS.
CAN THE PHYSICAL PRESENCE OF THE GOD OF LOVE EXPLAIN WHAT HAPPENED NEXT?
DING DING
DING DING
CLACKETY CLACKETY WHUMP
CLACKETY CLACKETY WHUMP
ONE CLACKETY-WHUMP WAS THE SOUND OF SOMEONE LIFTING THE LATCH AND EXITING THE BATHROOM OPPOSITE THE KITCHEN.
CLACKETY-WHUMP
BUT A REPEATED CLACKETY-WHUMP?
THE COUNTER CUSTOMERS SEATED NEARBY KEEP GLANCING OVER THEIR SHOULDERS.
DING DING
DING DING
DING DING
CLACKETY WHUMP CLACKETY WHUMP CLACKETY WHUMP

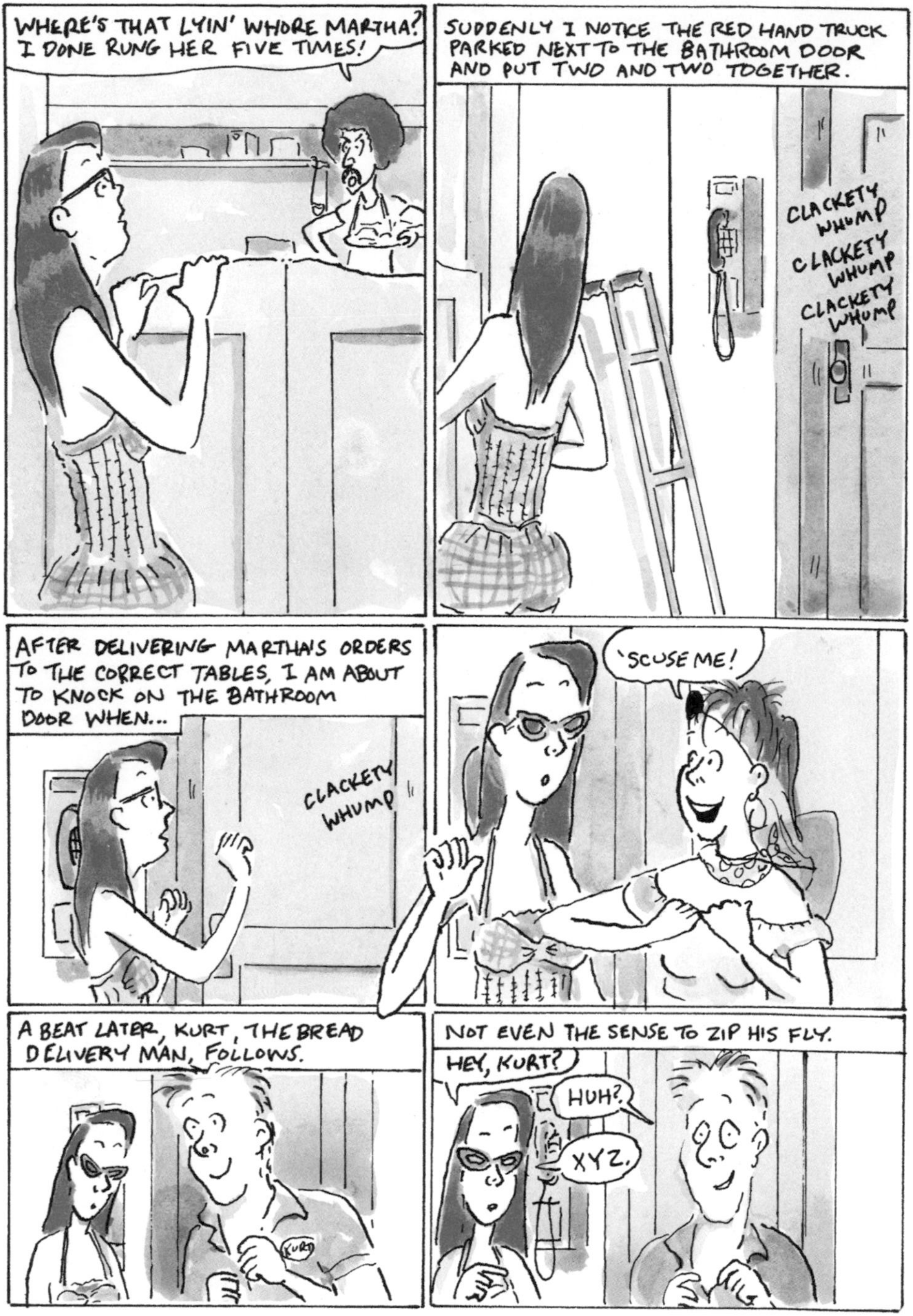
WHERE'S THAT LYIN' WHORE MARTHA? I DONE RUNG HER FIVE TIMES!
SUDDENLY I NOTICE THE RED HAND TRUCK PARKED NEXT TO THE BATHROOM DOOR AND PUT TWO AND TWO TOGETHER.
CLACKETY WHUMP
CLACKETY WHUMP
CLACKETY WHUMP
AFTER DELIVERING MARTHA'S ORDERS TO THE CORRECT TABLES, I AM ABOUT TO KNOCK ON THE BATHROOM DOOR WHEN...
CLACKETY WHUMP
'SCUSE ME!
A BEAT LATER, KURT, THE BREAD DELIVERY MAN, FOLLOWS.
KURT
NOT EVEN THE SENSE TO ZIP HIS FLY.
HEY, KURT?
HUH?
XYZ.

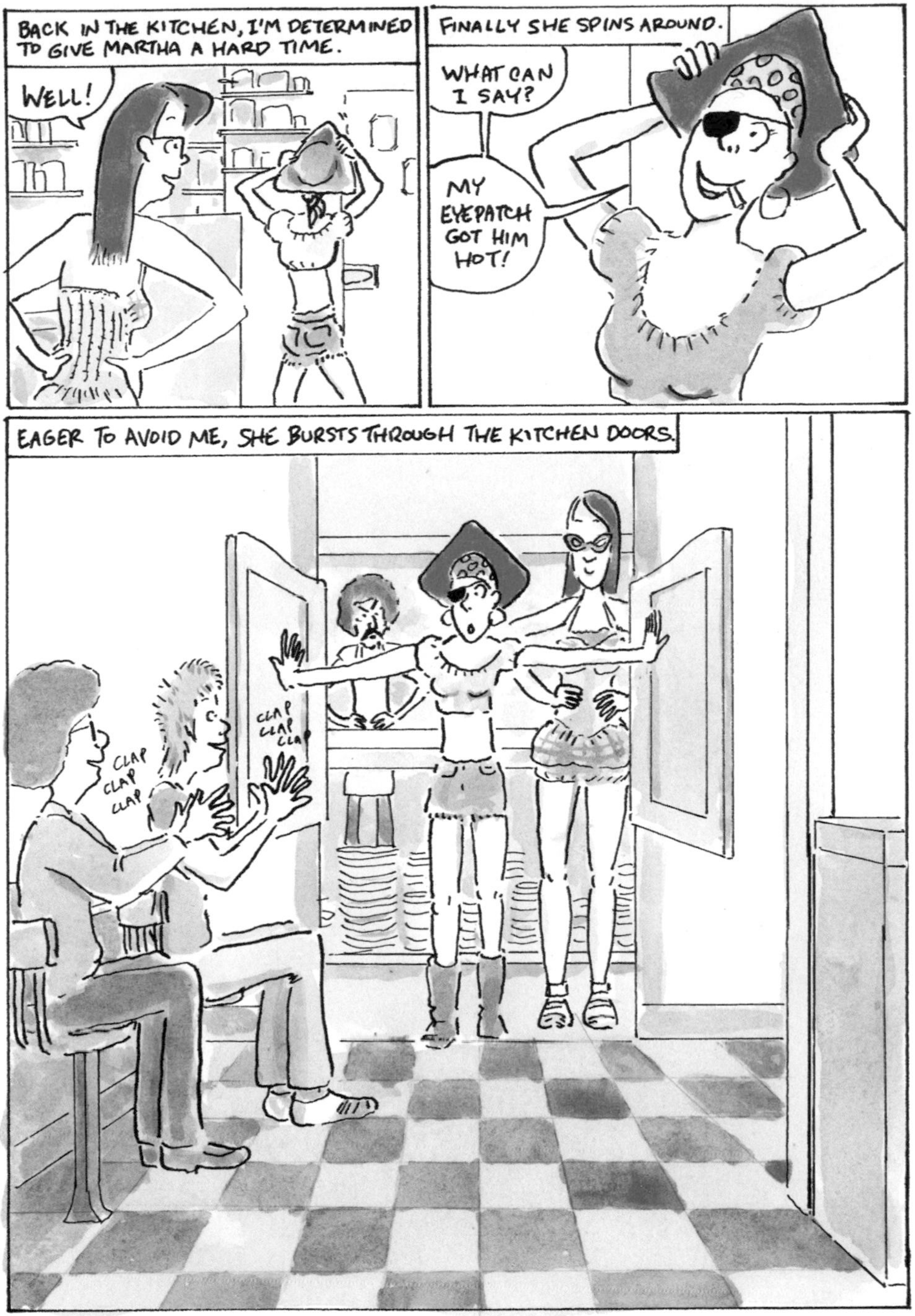
BACK IN THE KITCHEN, I'M DETERMINED TO GIVE MARTHA A HARD TIME.
WELL!
FINALLY SHE SPINS AROUND.
WHAT CAN I SAY?
MY EYEPATCH GOT HIM HOT!
EAGER TO AVOID ME, SHE BURSTS THROUGH THE KITCHEN DOORS.
CLAP CLAP CLAP
CLAP CLAP CLAP

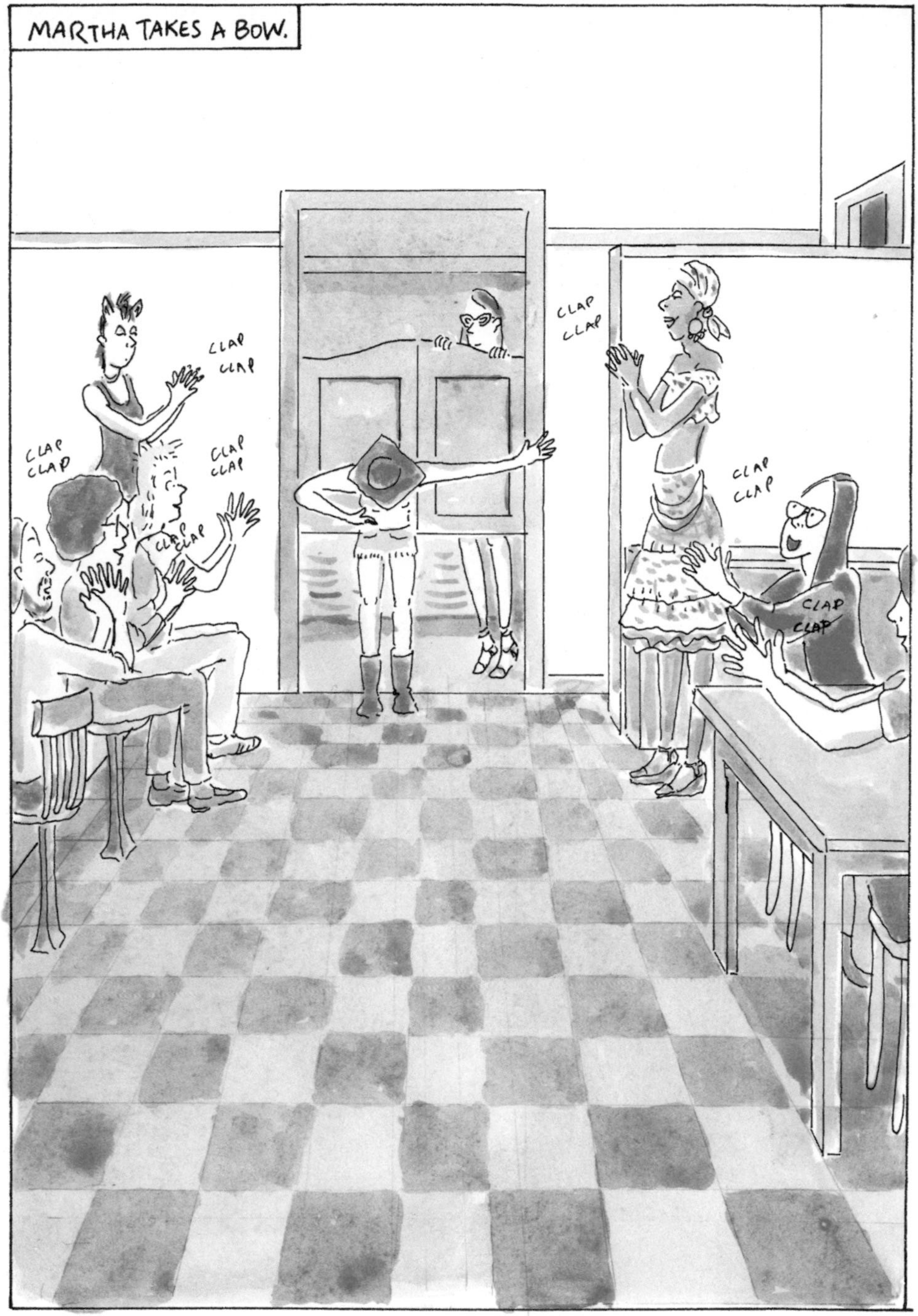
MARTHA TAKES A BOW.
CLAP CLAP
CLAP CLAP
CLAP CLAP
CLAP CLAP
CLAP CLAP
CLAP CLAP
CLAP CLAP
CLAP CLAP

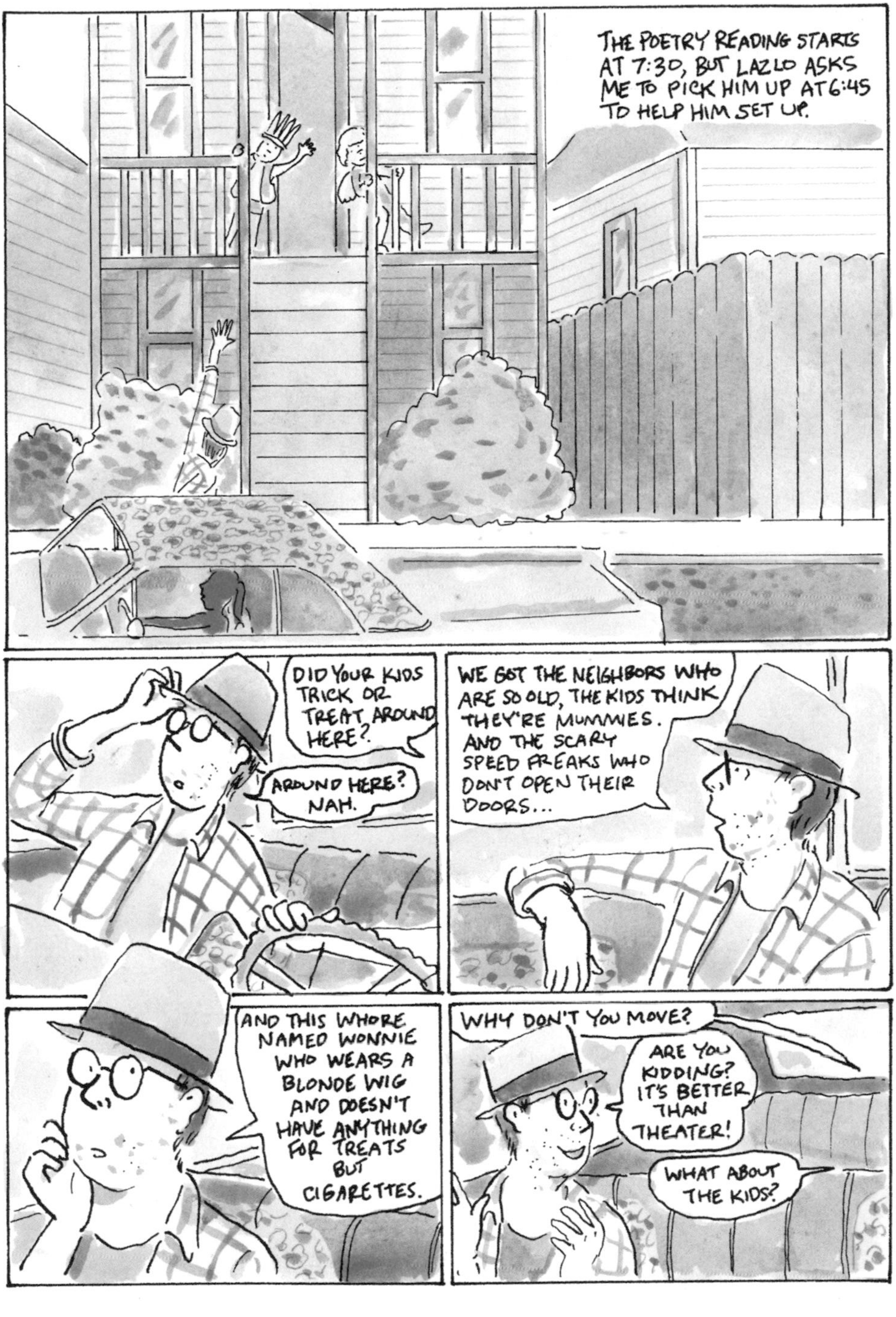
THE POETRY READING STARTS AT 7:30, BUT LAZLO ASKS ME TO PICK HIM UP AT 6:45 TO HELP HIM SET UP.
DID YOUR KIDS TRICK OR TREAT AROUND HERE?
AROUND HERE? NAH.
WE GOT THE NEIGHBORS WHO ARE SO OLD, THE KIDS THINK THEY'RE MUMMIES. AND THE SCARY SPEED FREAKS WHO DON'T OPEN THEIR DOORS...
AND THIS WHORE NAMED WONNIE WHO WEARS A BLONDE WIG AND DOESN'T HAVE ANYTHING FOR TREATS BUT CIGARETTES.
WHY DON'T YOU MOVE?
ARE YOU KIDDING? IT'S BETTER THAN THEATER!
WHAT ABOUT THE KIDS?

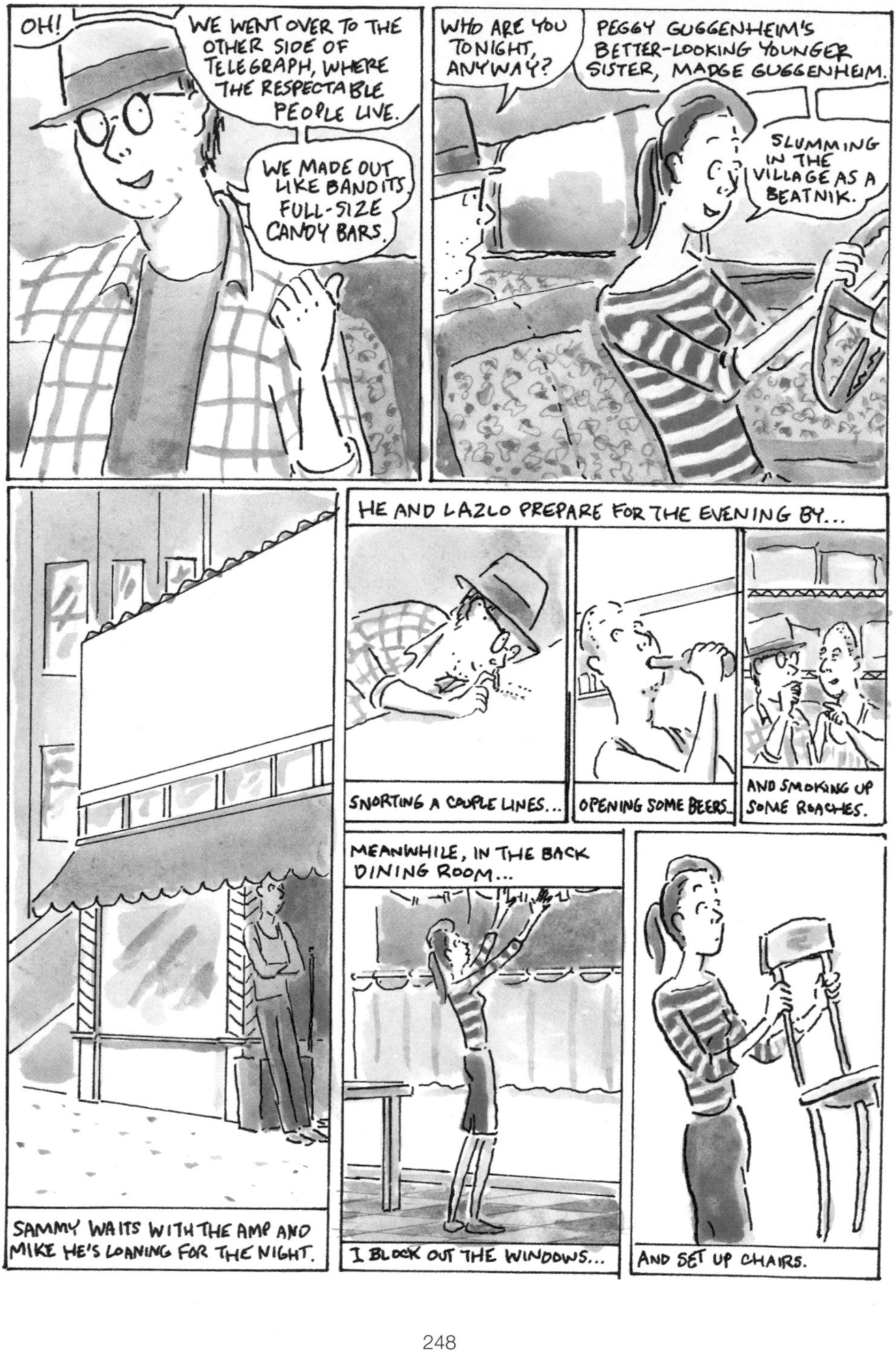

OH!
WE WENT OVER TO THE OTHER SIDE OF TELEGRAPH, WHERE THE RESPECTABLE PEOPLE LIVE.
WE MADE OUT LIKE BANDITS. FULL-SIZE CANDY BARS.
WHO ARE YOU TONIGHT, ANYWAY?
PEGGY GUGGENHEIM'S BETTER-LOOKING YOUNGER SISTER, MADGE GUGGENHEIM.
SLUMMING IN THE VILLAGE AS A BEATNIK.
SAMMY WAITS WITH THE AMP AND MIKE HE'S LOANING FOR THE NIGHT.
HE AND LAZLO PREPARE FOR THE EVENING BY...
SNORTING A COUPLE LINES...
OPENING SOME BEERS...
AND SMOKING UP SOME ROACHES.
MEANWHILE, IN THE BACK DINING ROOM...
I BLOCK OUT THE WINDOWS...
AND SET UP CHAIRS.

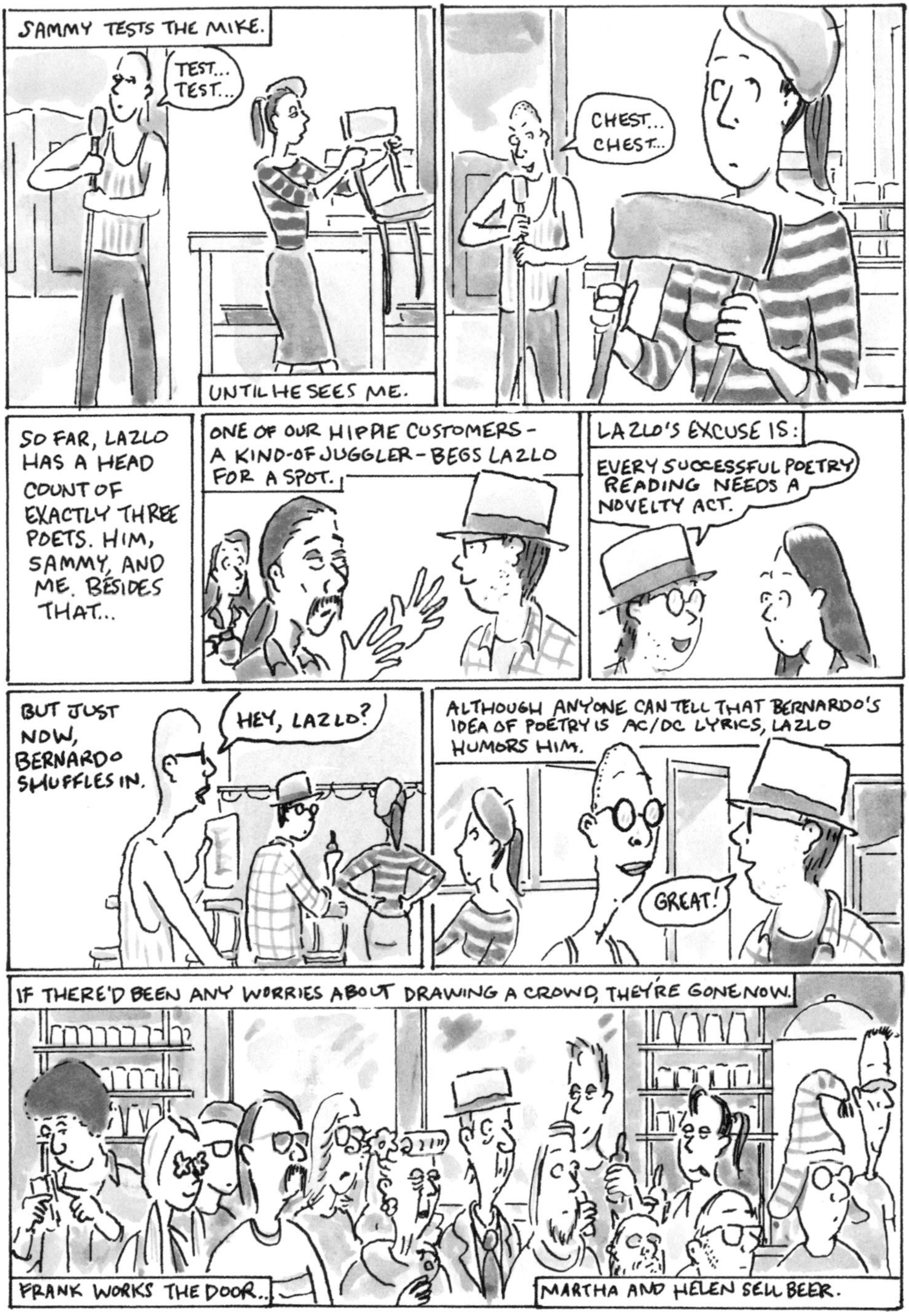
SAMMY TESTS THE MIKE.
TEST... TEST...
UNTIL HE SEES ME.
CHEST... CHEST...
SO FAR, LAZLO HAS A HEAD COUNT OF EXACTLY THREE POETS. HIM, SAMMY, AND ME. BESIDES THAT...
ONE OF OUR HIPPIE CUSTOMERS - A KIND-OF JUGGLER - BEGS LAZLO FOR A SPOT.
LAZLO'S EXCUSE IS:
EVERY SUCCESSFUL POETRY READING NEEDS A NOVELTY ACT.
BUT JUST NOW, BERNARDO SHUFFLES IN.
HEY, LAZLO?
ALTHOUGH ANYONE CAN TELL THAT BERNARDO'S IDEA OF POETRY IS AC/DC LYRICS, LAZLO HUMORS HIM.
GREAT!
IF THERE'D BEEN ANY WORRIES ABOUT DRAWING A CROWD, THEY'RE GONE NOW.
FRANK WORKS THE DOOR...
MARTHA AND HELEN SELL BEER.

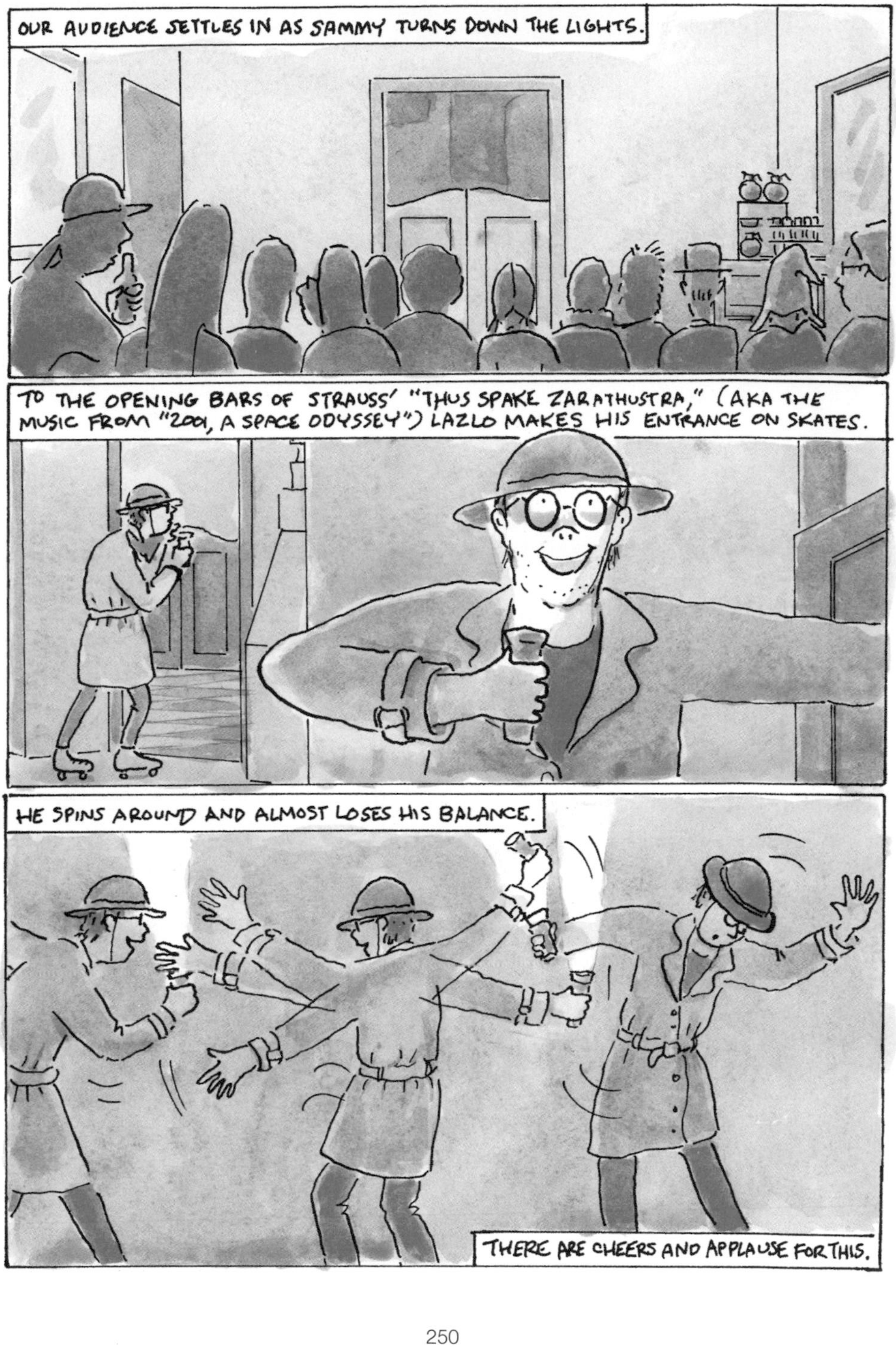
OUR AUDIENCE SETTLES IN AS SAMMY TURNS DOWN THE LIGHTS.
TO THE OPENING BARS OF STRAUSS' "THUS SPAKE ZARATHUSTRA," (AKA THE MUSIC FROM "2001, A SPACE ODYSSEY") LAZLO MAKES HIS ENTRANCE ON SKATES.
HE SPINS AROUND AND ALMOST LOSES HIS BALANCE.
THERE ARE CHEERS AND APPLAUSE FOR THIS.

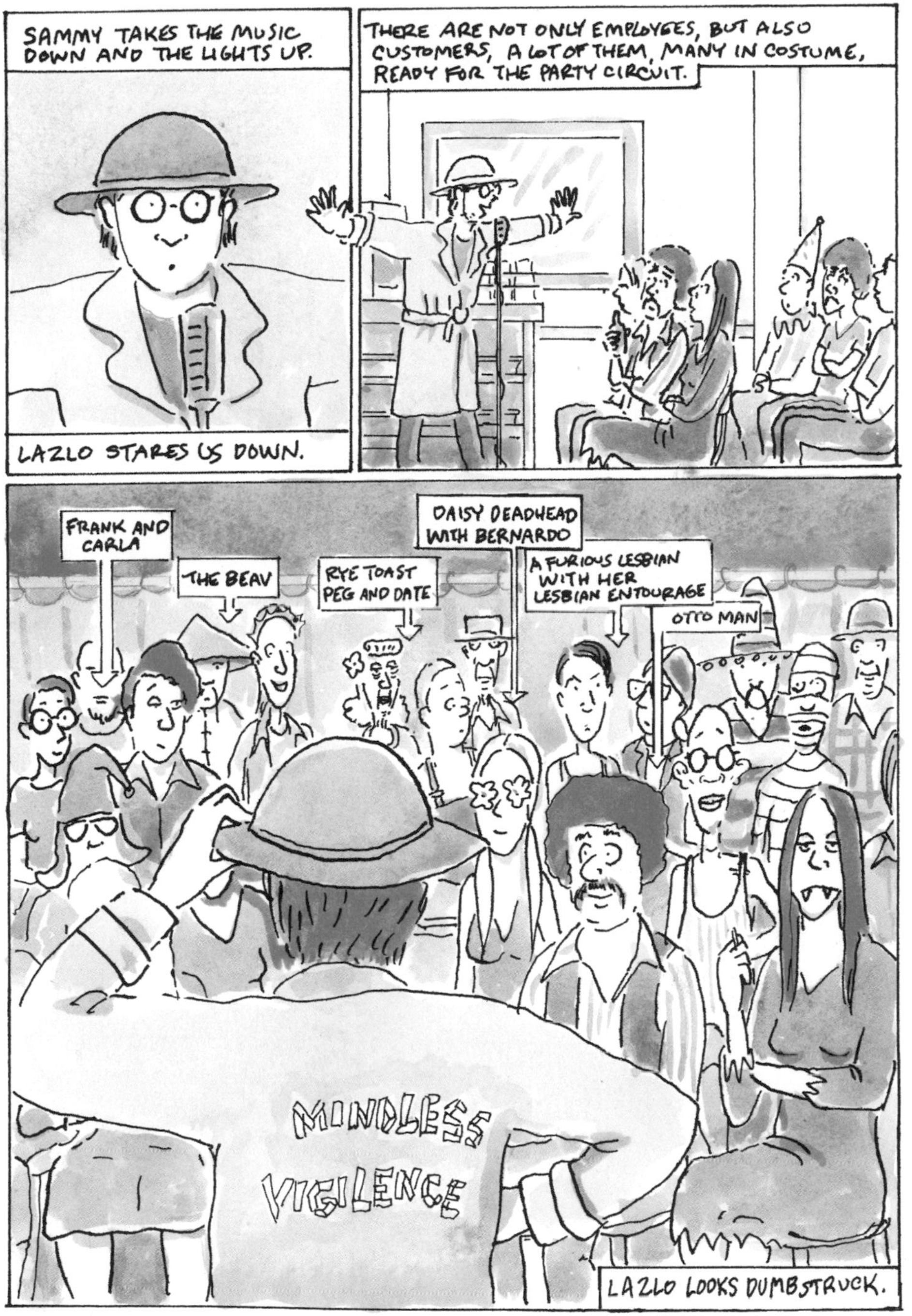
SAMMY TAKES THE MUSIC DOWN AND THE LIGHTS UP.
LAZLO STARES US DOWN.
THERE ARE NOT ONLY EMPLOYEES, BUT ALSO CUSTOMERS, A LOT OF THEM, MANY IN COSTUME, READY FOR THE PARTY CIRCUIT.
FRANK AND CARLA
THE BEAV
RYE TOAST PEG AND DATE
DAISY DEADHEAD WITH BERNARDO
A FURIOUS LESBIAN WITH HER LESBIAN ENTOURAGE
OTTO MAN
MINDLESS VIGILENCE
LAZLO LOOKS DUMBSTRUCK.

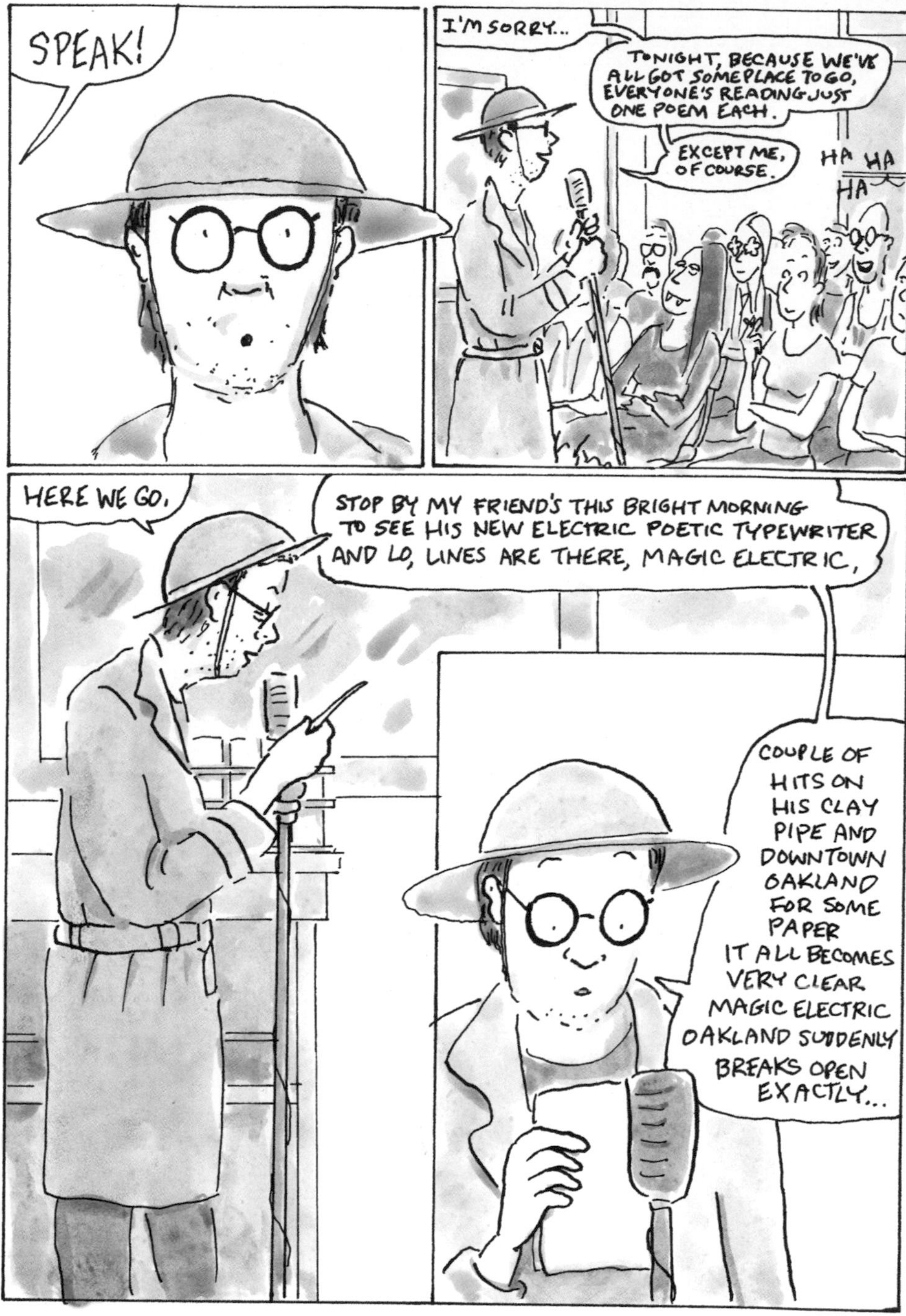
SPEAK!
I'M SORRY...
TONIGHT, BECAUSE WE'VE ALL GOT SOMEPLACE TO GO, EVERYONE'S READING JUST ONE POEM EACH.
EXCEPT ME, OF COURSE.
HA HA HA
HERE WE GO.
STOP BY MY FRIEND'S THIS BRIGHT MORNING TO SEE HIS NEW ELECTRIC POETIC TYPEWRITER AND LO, LINES ARE THERE, MAGIC ELECTRIC,
COUPLE OF HITS ON HIS CLAY PIPE AND DOWNTOWN OAKLAND FOR SOME PAPER IT ALL BECOMES VERY CLEAR MAGIC ELECTRIC OAKLAND SUDDENLY BREAKS OPEN EXACTLY...

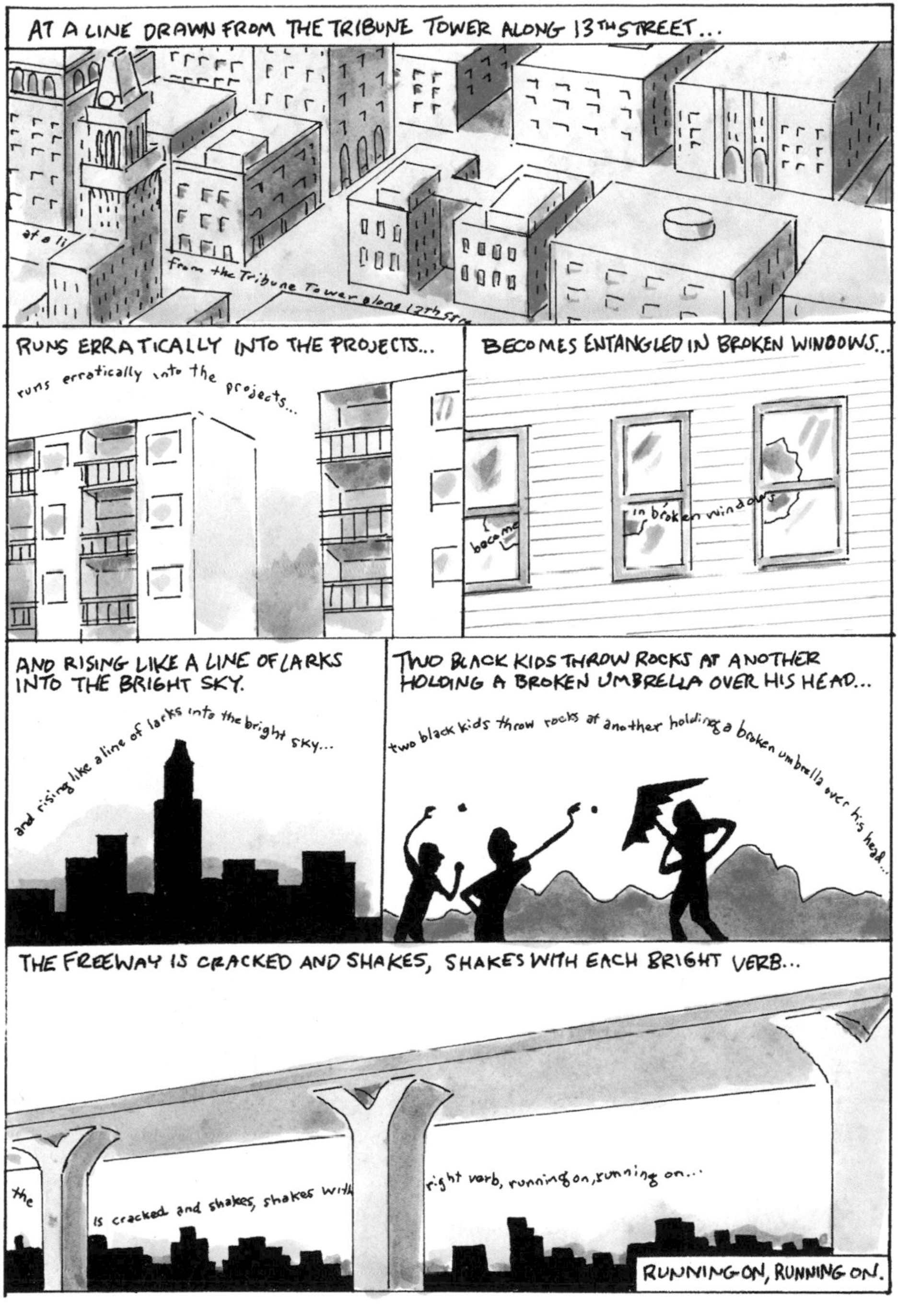
AT A LINE DRAWN FROM THE TRIBUNE TOWER ALONG 13TH STREET...
at a li
from the Tribune Tower along 13th St
RUNS ERRATICALLY INTO THE PROJECTS...
runs erratically into the projects...
BECOMES ENTANGLED IN BROKEN WINDOWS...
become
in broken windows
AND RISING LIKE A LINE OF LARKS INTO THE BRIGHT SKY.
and rising like a line of larks into the bright sky...
TWO BLACK KIDS THROW ROCKS AT ANOTHER HOLDING A BROKEN UMBRELLA OVER HIS HEAD...
two black kids throw rocks at another holding a broken umbrella over his head...
THE FREEWAY IS CRACKED AND SHAKES, SHAKES WITH EACH BRIGHT VERB...
the
is cracked and shakes, shakes with
right verb, running on, running on...
RUNNING ON, RUNNING ON.

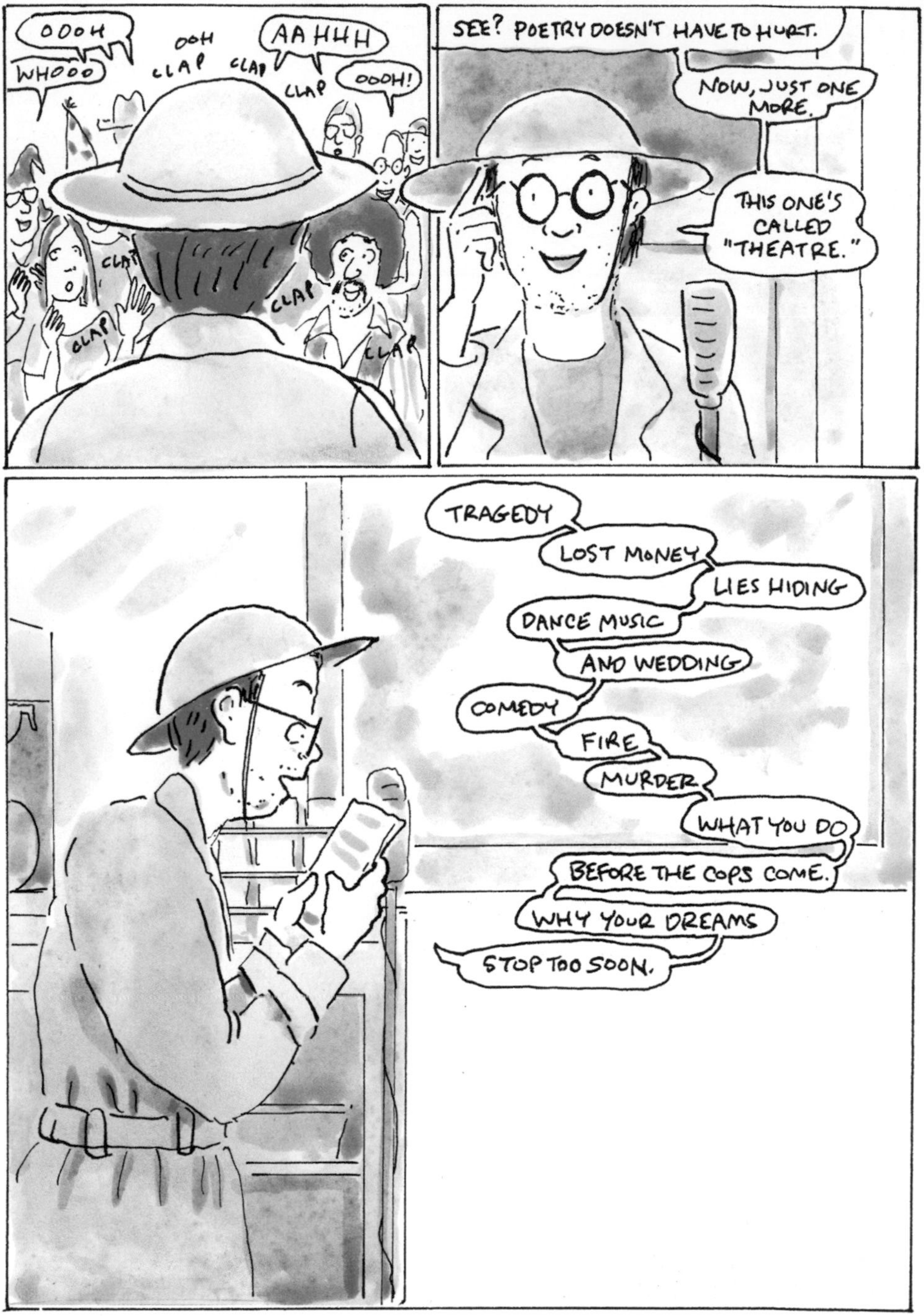
OOOH
WHOOO
OOH
CLAP CLAP
AAHHH
CLAP
OOOH!
CLAP
CLAP
CLAP
CLAP
SEE? POETRY DOESN'T HAVE TO HURT.
NOW, JUST ONE MORE.
THIS ONE'S CALLED "THEATRE."
TRAGEDY
LOST MONEY
LIES HIDING
DANCE MUSIC
AND WEDDING
COMEDY
FIRE
MURDER
WHAT YOU DO
BEFORE THE COPS COME.
WHY YOUR DREAMS
STOP TOO SOON.

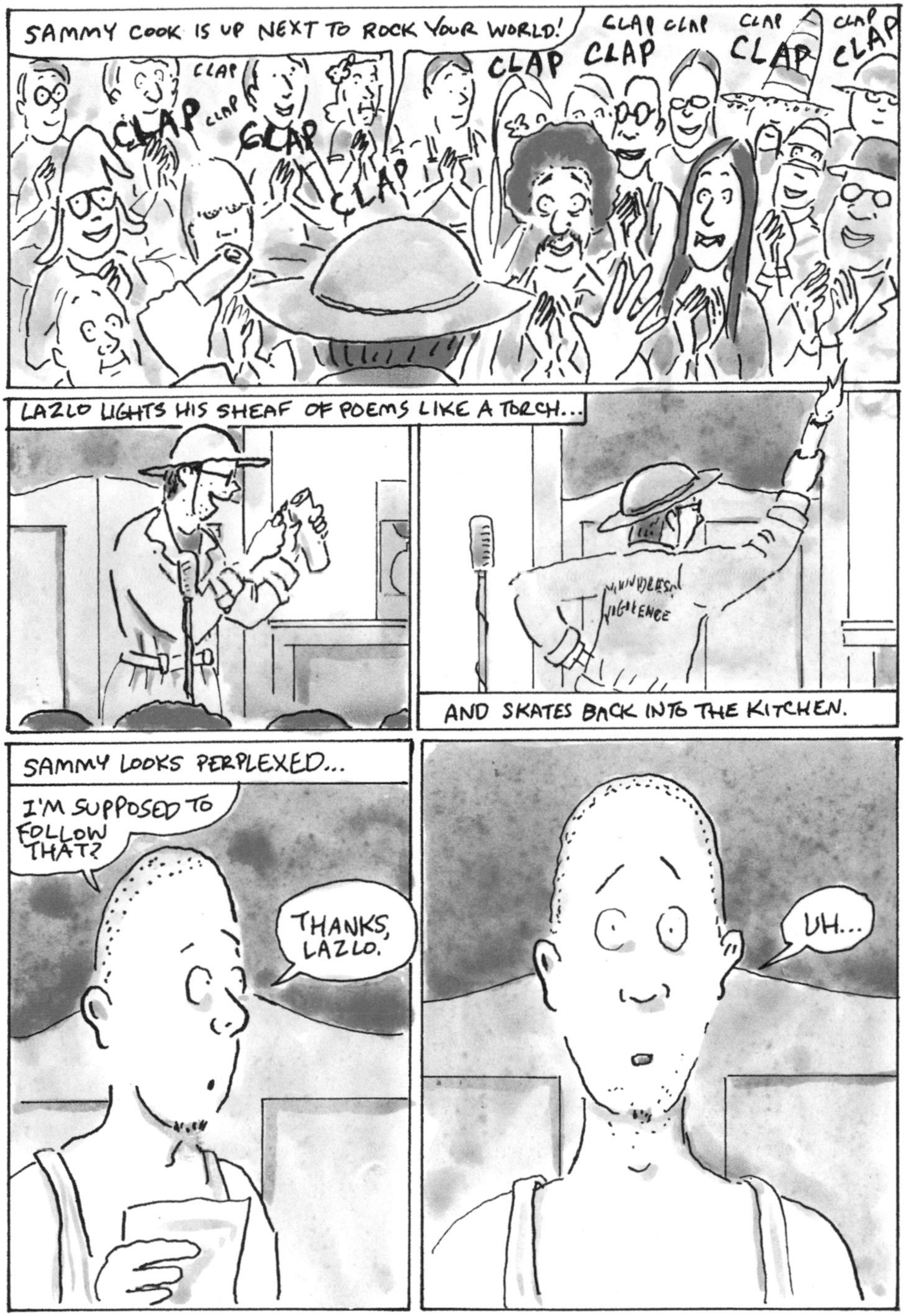

SAMMY COOK IS UP NEXT TO ROCK YOUR WORLD!
CLAP CLAP CLAP CLAP CLAP CLAP
CLAP CLAP CLAP CLAP CLAP CLAP CLAP
LAZLO LIGHTS HIS SHEAF OF POEMS LIKE A TORCH...
AND SKATES BACK INTO THE KITCHEN.
SAMMY LOOKS PERPLEXED...
I'M SUPPOSED TO FOLLOW THAT?
THANKS, LAZLO.
UH...

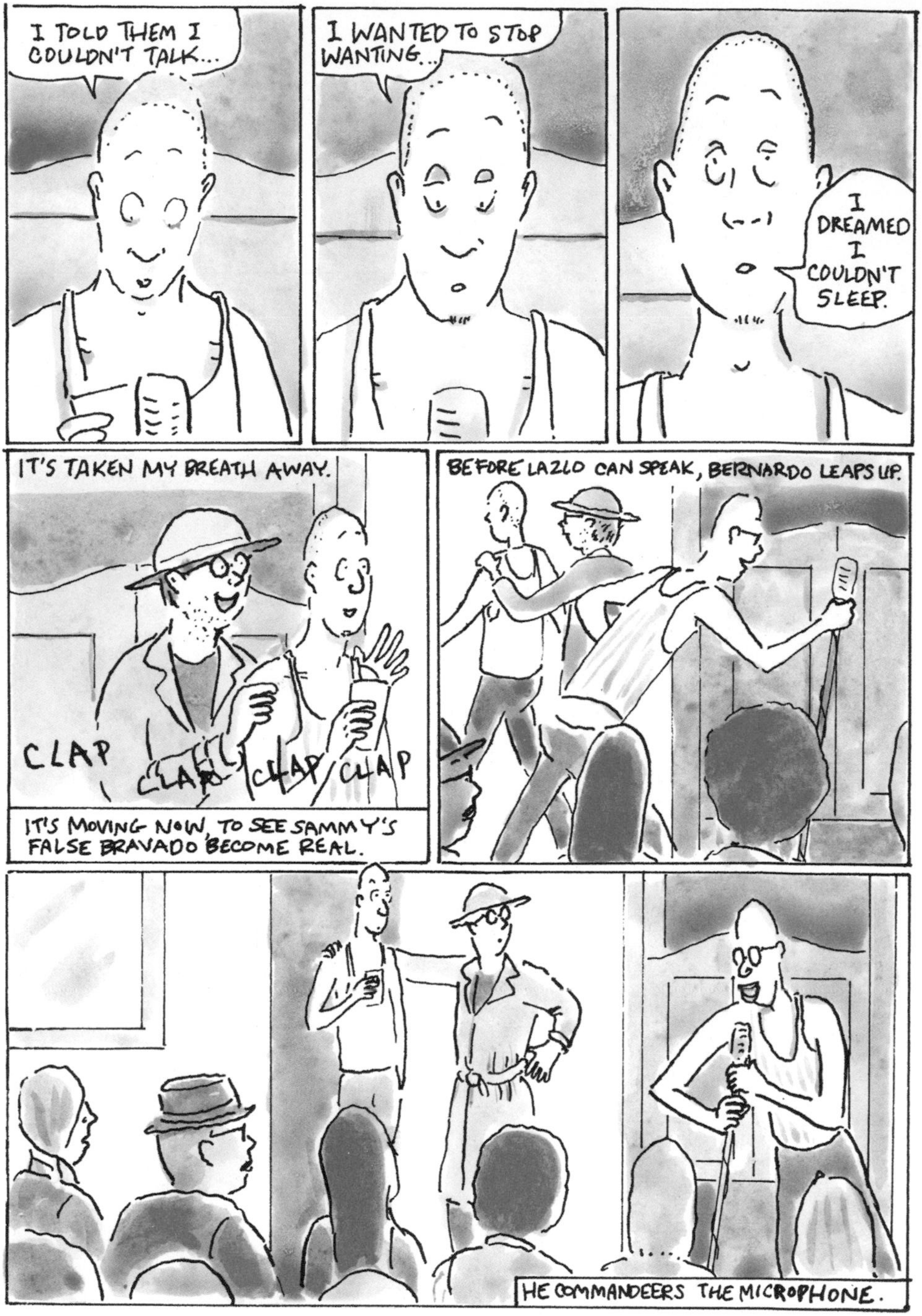
I TOLD THEM I COULDN'T TALK...
I WANTED TO STOP WANTING...
I DREAMED I COULDN'T SLEEP.
IT'S TAKEN MY BREATH AWAY.
CLAP
CLAP
CLAP
CLAP
IT'S MOVING NOW, TO SEE SAMMY'S FALSE BRAVADO BECOME REAL.
BEFORE LAZLO CAN SPEAK, BERNARDO LEAPS UP.
HE COMMANDEERS THE MICROPHONE.

ALL MY LIFE THINKING SCARED ME.
THEY TOLD ME IF YOU TALK TO YOURSELF YOU'RE CRAZY.
POETRY IS WORSE.
IT MIGHT NOT EVEN BE ME
TALKING.
HE LEAVES THE STAND ABRUPTLY.
THAT'S ALL.
CLAP CLAP CLAP CLAP CLAP CLAP
WHOO!
CLAP CLAP CLAP CLAP
AS LAZLO MAKES HIS WAY BACK TO THE MIKE, I CHECK OUT BOTH OF BERNARDO'S MAIN SQUEEZES...
LESBIAN
DAISY DEADHEAD
EACH SURE THAT SHE IS BERNARDO'S MUSE.

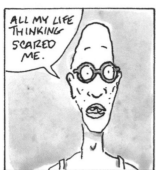

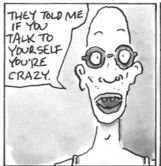

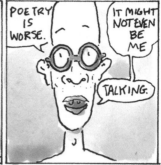

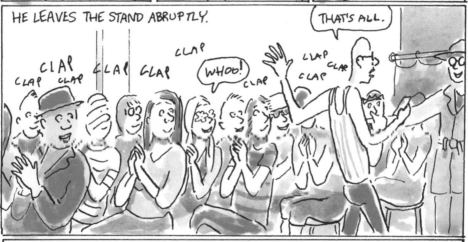

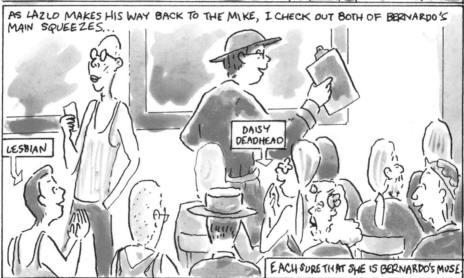

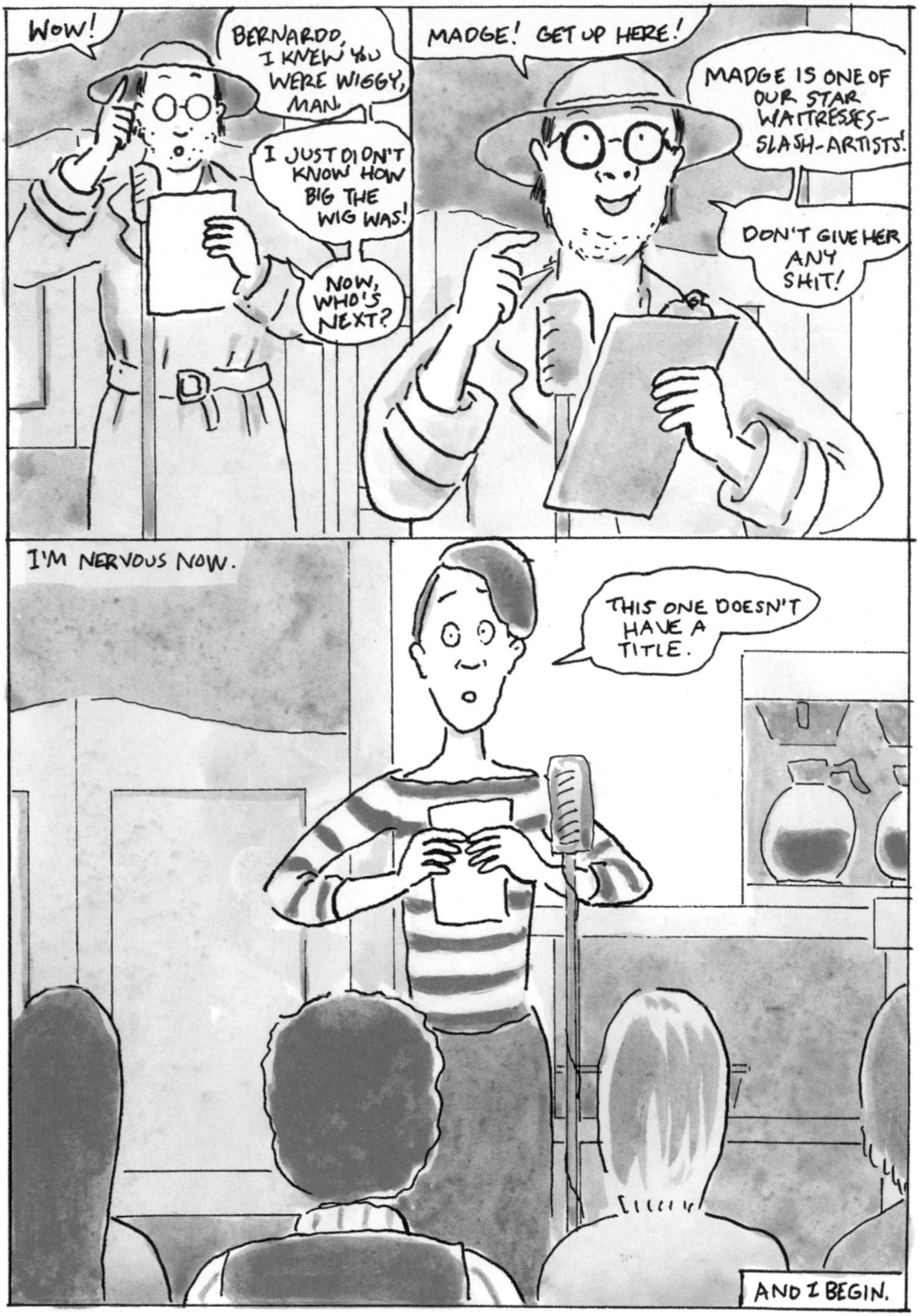
WOW!
BERNARDO, I KNEW YOU WERE WIGGY, MAN.
I JUST DIDN'T KNOW HOW BIG THE WIG WAS!
NOW, WHO'S NEXT?
MADGE! GET UP HERE!
MADGE IS ONE OF OUR STAR WAITRESSES-SLASH-ARTISTS!
DON'T GIVE HER ANY SHIT!
I'M NERVOUS NOW.
THIS ONE DOESN'T HAVE A TITLE.
AND I BEGIN.

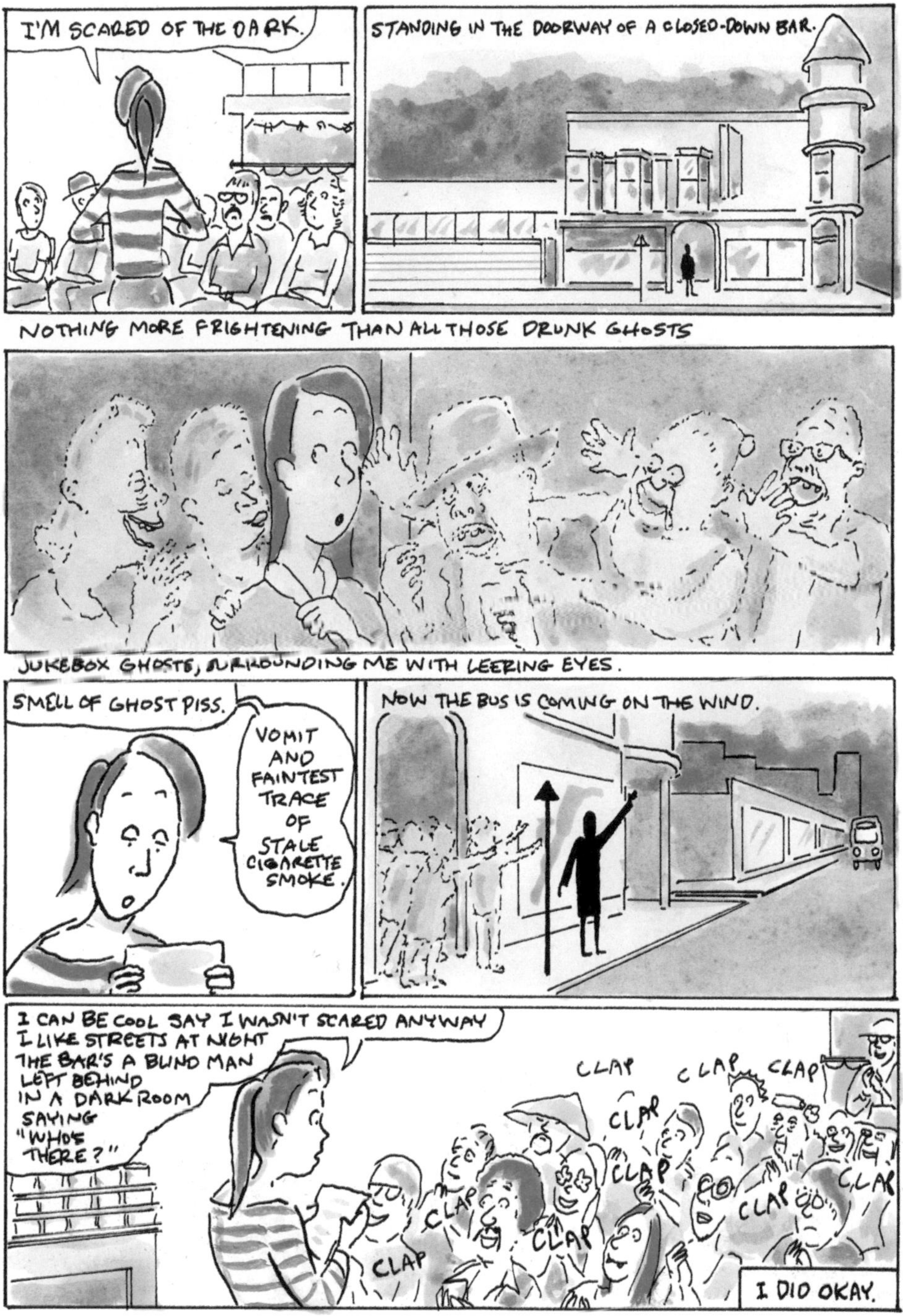
I'M SCARED OF THE DARK.
STANDING IN THE DOORWAY OF A CLOSED-DOWN BAR.
NOTHING MORE FRIGHTENING THAN ALL THOSE DRUNK GHOSTS
JUKEBOX GHOSTS, SURROUNDING ME WITH LEERING EYES.
SMELL OF GHOST PISS.
VOMIT AND FAINTEST TRACE OF STALE CIGARETTE SMOKE.
NOW THE BUS IS COMING ON THE WIND.
I CAN BE COOL SAY I WASN'T SCARED ANYWAY I LIKE STREETS AT NIGHT THE BAR'S A BLIND MAN LEFT BEHIND IN A DARK ROOM SAYING "WHO'S THERE?"
CLAP CLAP CLAP CLAP CLAP CLAP CLAP CLAP CLAP CLAP CLAP
I DID OKAY.

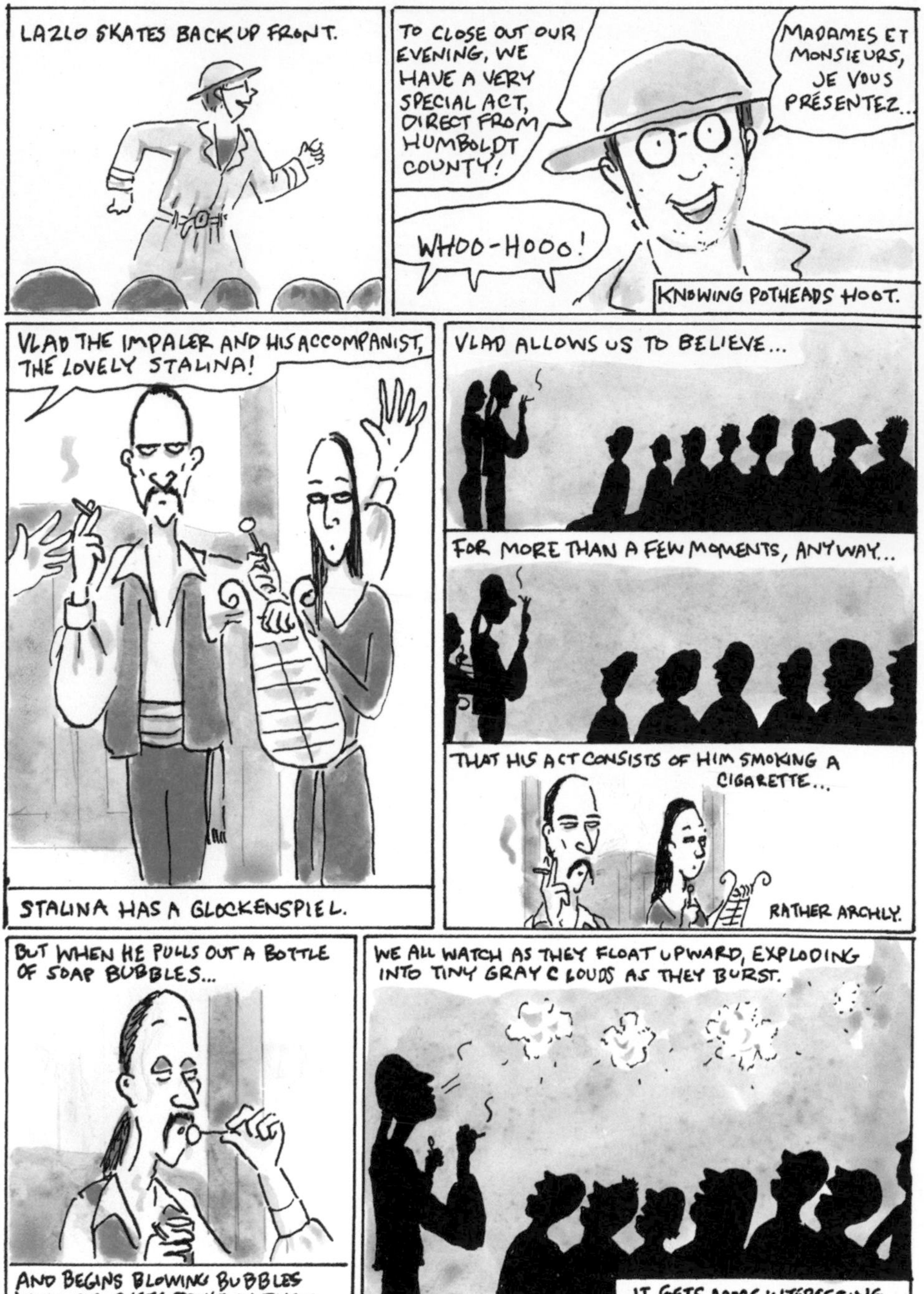

LAZLO SKATES BACK UP FRONT.
TO CLOSE OUT OUR EVENING, WE HAVE A VERY SPECIAL ACT, DIRECT FROM HUMBOLDT COUNTY!
MADAMES ET MONSIEURS, JE VOUS PRÉSENTEZ...
WHOO-HOOO!
KNOWING POTHEADS HOOT.
VLAD THE IMPALER AND HIS ACCOMPANIST, THE LOVELY STALINA!
STALINA HAS A GLOCKENSPIEL.
VLAD ALLOWS US TO BELIEVE...
FOR MORE THAN A FEW MOMENTS, ANYWAY...
THAT HIS ACT CONSISTS OF HIM SMOKING A CIGARETTE...
RATHER ARCHLY.
BUT WHEN HE PULLS OUT A BOTTLE OF SOAP BUBBLES...
AND BEGINS BLOWING BUBBLES WITH CIGARETTE SMOKE IN THEM...
WE ALL WATCH AS THEY FLOAT UPWARD, EXPLODING INTO TINY GRAY CLOUDS AS THEY BURST.
IT GETS MORE INTERESTING.

HE DEFTLY JUGGLES LARGER SMOKE-FILLED BUBBLES...

WITHOUT BREAKING ONE, AS STALINA PLAYS "DANCE OF THE SUGARPLUM FAIRIES."

HE FINALLY CREATES ONE GIANT SMOKE-FILLED POLYHEDRON...

AND AS THE MUSIC BUILDS TO A FINALE...

HE RELEASES THE MOLECULAR MODEL AND IT SPINS OVER OUR HEADS...

UNTIL IT POPS AND RAINS DOWN SMOKE, RIGHT ON MUSICAL CUE.

WHOOO!

CLAP CLAP   CLAP   CLAP CLAP CLAP CLAP CLAP

VLAD AND STALINA TAKE MANY VOWS.

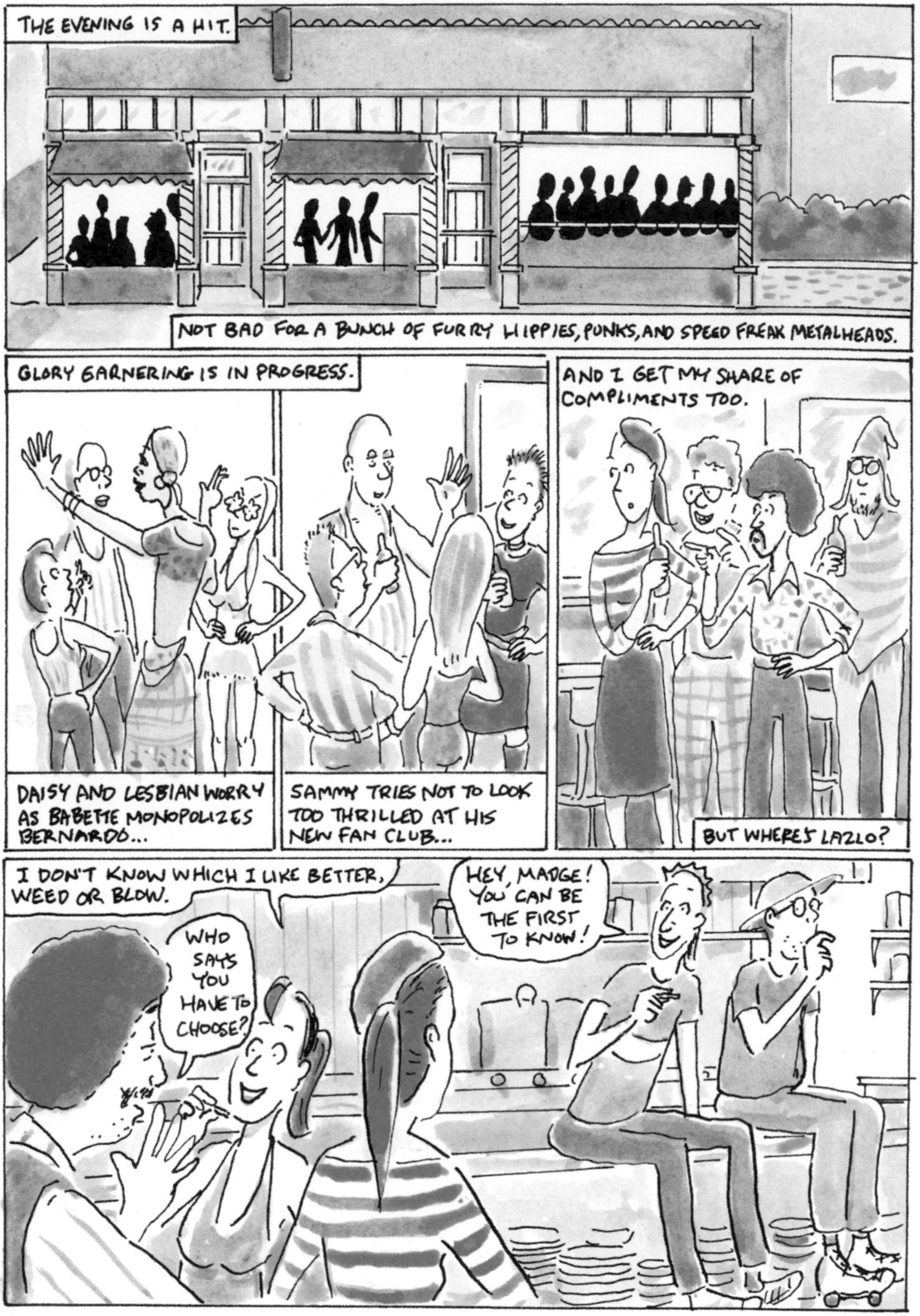
THE EVENING IS A HIT.
NOT BAD FOR A BUNCH OF FURRY HIPPIES, PUNKS, AND SPEED FREAK METALHEADS.
GLORY GARNERING IS IN PROGRESS.
DAISY AND LESBIAN WORRY AS BABETTE MONOPOLIZES BERNARDO...
SAMMY TRIES NOT TO LOOK TOO THRILLED AT HIS NEW FAN CLUB...
AND I GET MY SHARE OF COMPLIMENTS TOO.
BUT WHERE'S LAZLO?
I DON'T KNOW WHICH I LIKE BETTER, WEED OR BLOW.
WHO SAYS YOU HAVE TO CHOOSE?
HEY, MADGE! YOU CAN BE THE FIRST TO KNOW!

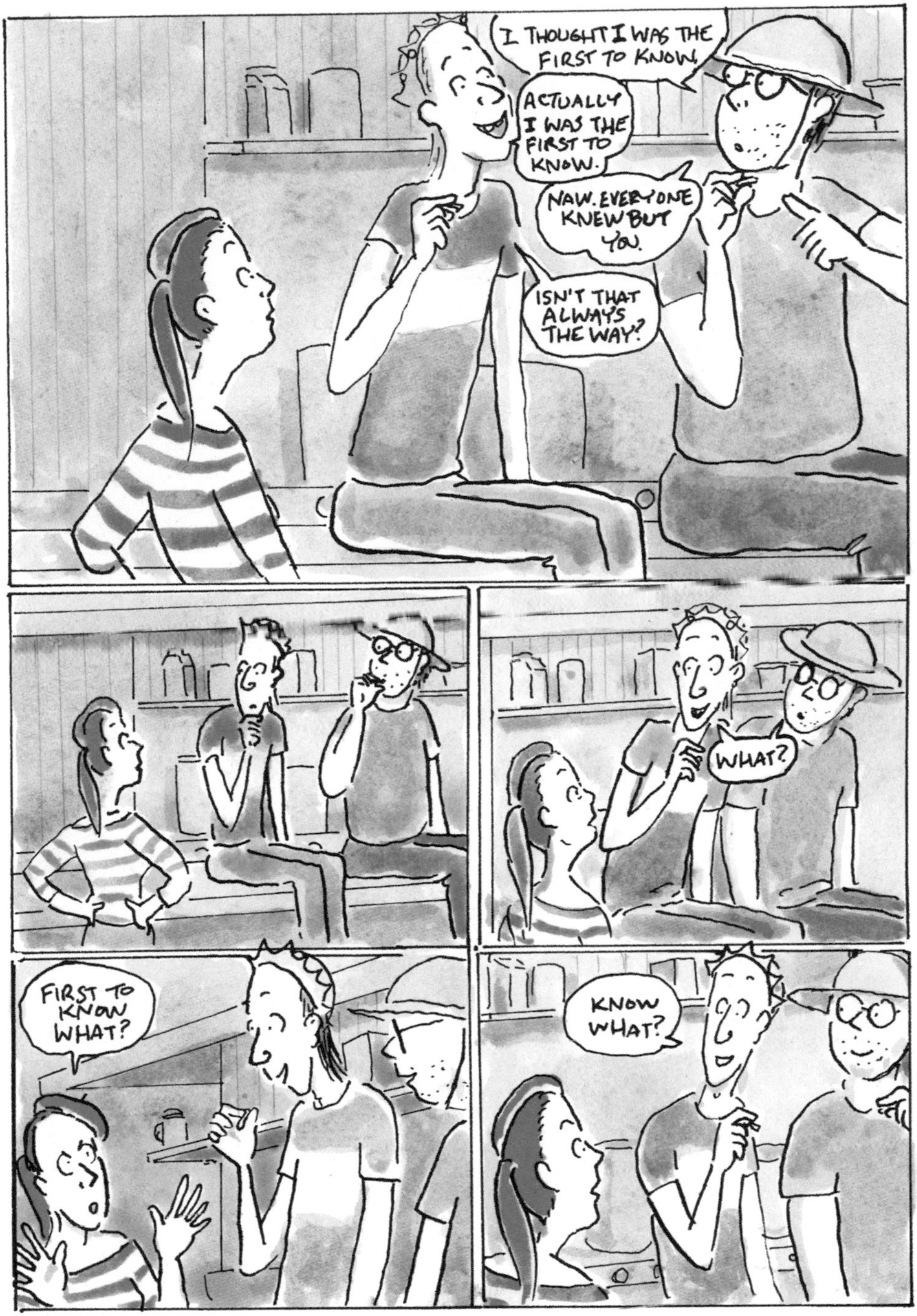
I THOUGHT I WAS THE FIRST TO KNOW.
ACTUALLY I WAS THE FIRST TO KNOW.
NAW. EVERYONE KNEW BUT YOU.
ISN'T THAT ALWAYS THE WAY?
WHAT?
FIRST TO KNOW WHAT?
KNOW WHAT?

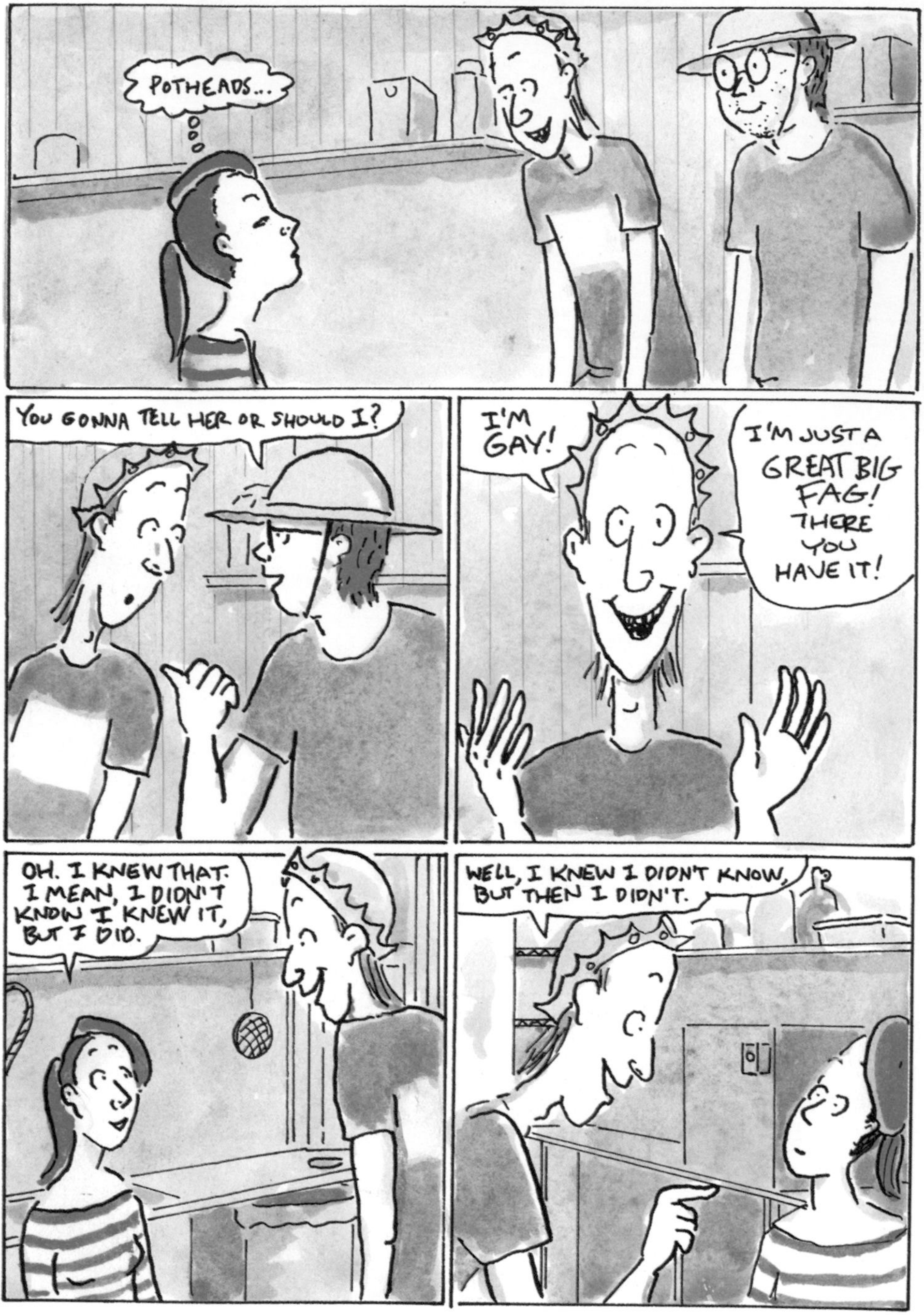
POTHEADS...
YOU GONNA TELL HER OR SHOULD I?
I'M GAY!
I'M JUST A GREAT BIG FAG! THERE YOU HAVE IT!
OH. I KNEW THAT. I MEAN, I DIDN'T KNOW I KNEW IT, BUT I DID.
WELL, I KNEW I DIDN'T KNOW, BUT THEN I DIDN'T.

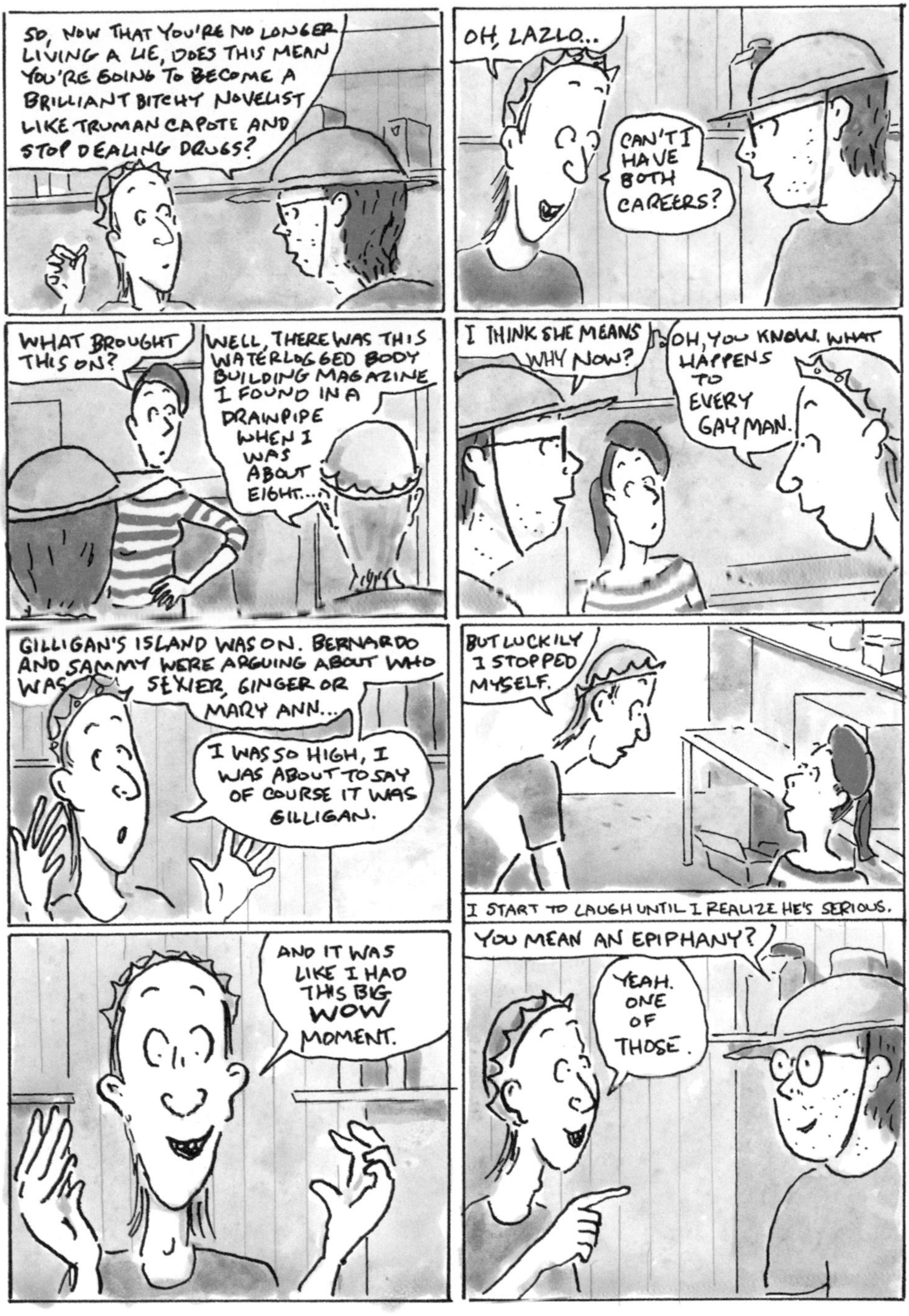
SO, NOW THAT YOU'RE NO LONGER LIVING A LIE, DOES THIS MEAN YOU'RE GOING TO BECOME A BRILLIANT BITCHY NOVELIST LIKE TRUMAN CAPOTE AND STOP DEALING DRUGS?
OH, LAZLO...
CAN'T I HAVE BOTH CAREERS?
WHAT BROUGHT THIS ON?
WELL, THERE WAS THIS WATERLOGGED BODY BUILDING MAGAZINE I FOUND IN A DRAINPIPE WHEN I WAS ABOUT EIGHT....
I THINK SHE MEANS WHY NOW?
OH, YOU KNOW. WHAT HAPPENS TO EVERY GAY MAN.
GILLIGAN'S ISLAND WAS ON. BERNARDO AND SAMMY WERE ARGUING ABOUT WHO WAS SEXIER, GINGER OR MARY ANN...
I WAS SO HIGH, I WAS ABOUT TO SAY OF COURSE IT WAS GILLIGAN.
BUT LUCKILY I STOPPED MYSELF.
I START TO LAUGH UNTIL I REALIZE HE'S SERIOUS.
AND IT WAS LIKE I HAD THIS BIG WOW MOMENT.
YOU MEAN AN EPIPHANY?
YEAH. ONE OF THOSE.

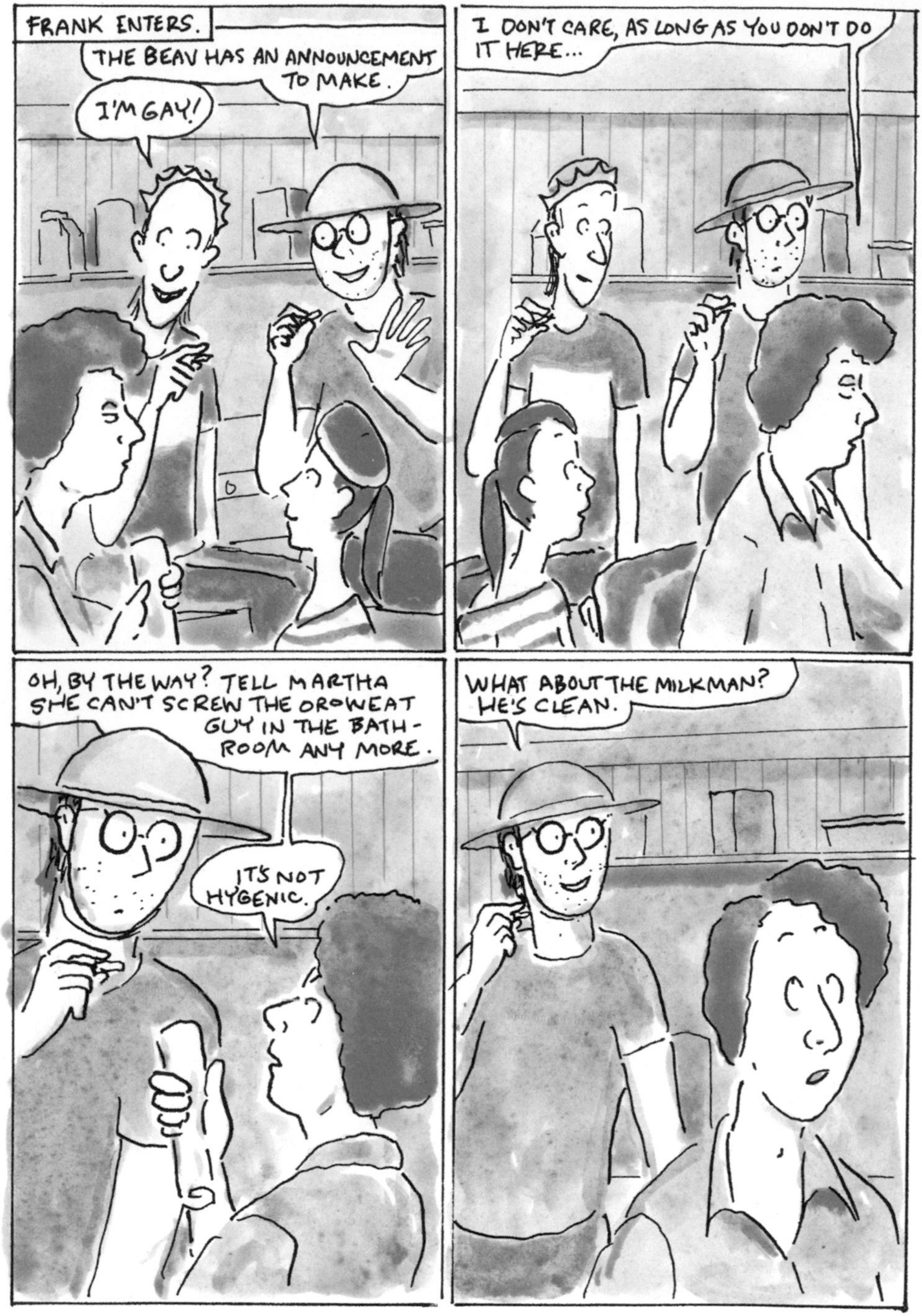
FRANK ENTERS.
THE BEAV HAS AN ANNOUNCEMENT TO MAKE.
I'M GAY!
I DON'T CARE, AS LONG AS YOU DON'T DO IT HERE...
OH, BY THE WAY? TELL MARTHA SHE CAN'T SCREW THE OROWEAT GUY IN THE BATH-ROOM ANY MORE.
IT'S NOT HYGENIC.
WHAT ABOUT THE MILKMAN? HE'S CLEAN.

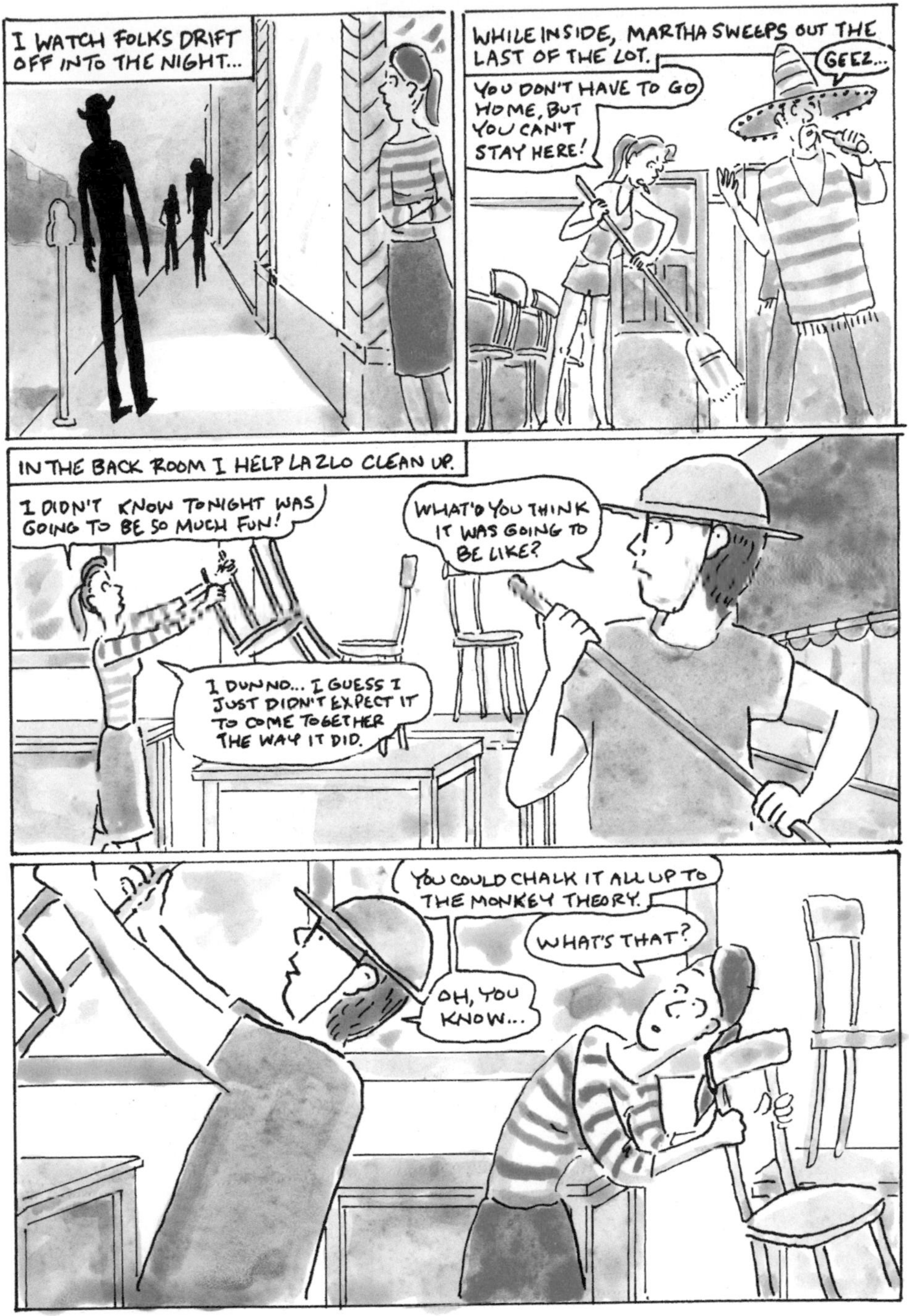
I WATCH FOLKS DRIFT OFF INTO THE NIGHT...
WHILE INSIDE, MARTHA SWEEPS OUT THE LAST OF THE LOT.
YOU DON'T HAVE TO GO HOME, BUT YOU CAN'T STAY HERE!
GEEZ...
IN THE BACK ROOM I HELP LAZLO CLEAN UP.
I DIDN'T KNOW TONIGHT WAS GOING TO BE SO MUCH FUN!
WHAT'D YOU THINK IT WAS GOING TO BE LIKE?
I DUNNO... I GUESS I JUST DIDN'T EXPECT IT TO COME TOGETHER THE WAY IT DID.
YOU COULD CHALK IT ALL UP TO THE MONKEY THEORY.
WHAT'S THAT?
OH, YOU KNOW...

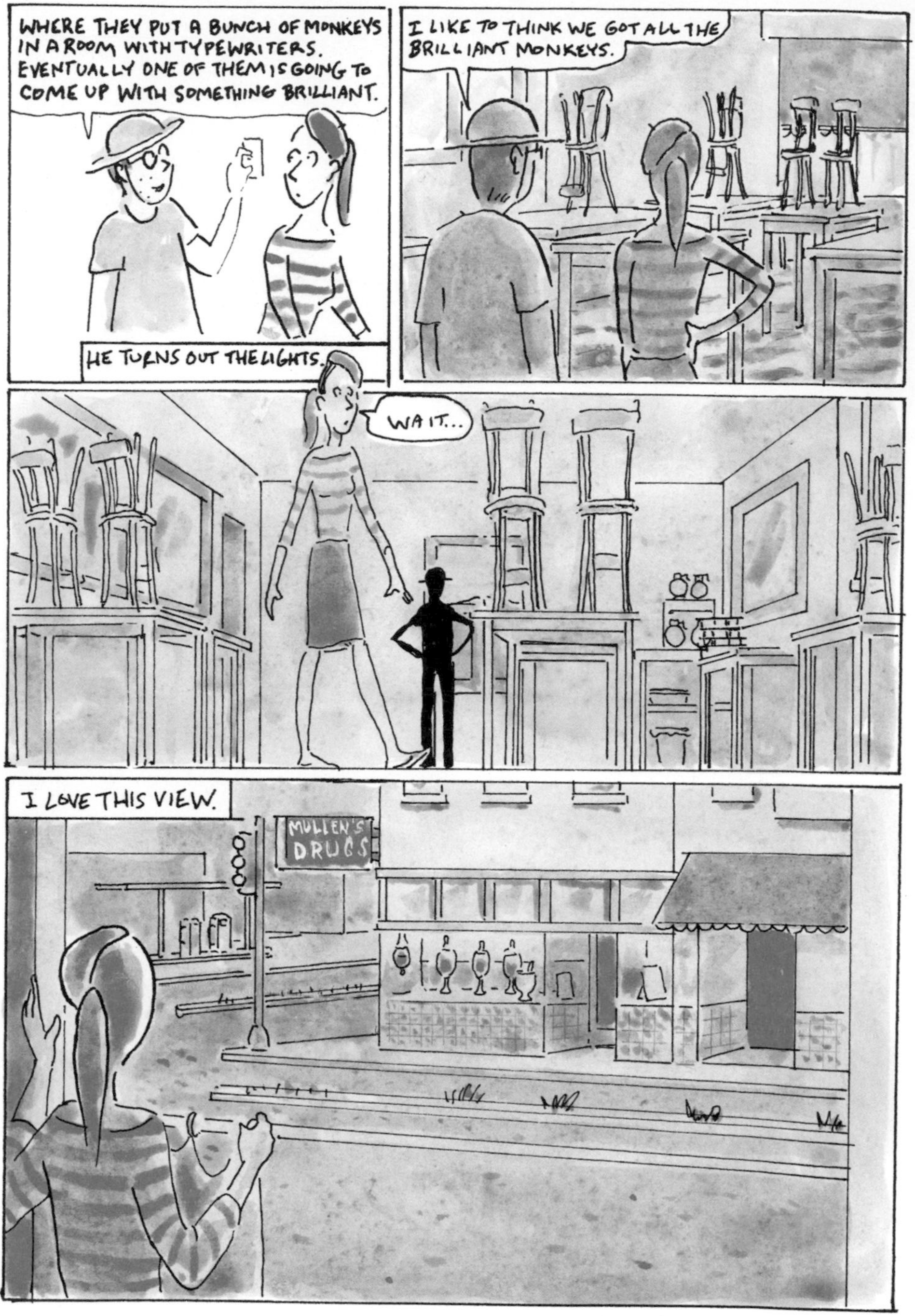
WHERE THEY PUT A BUNCH OF MONKEYS IN A ROOM WITH TYPEWRITERS. EVENTUALLY ONE OF THEM IS GOING TO COME UP WITH SOMETHING BRILLIANT.
HE TURNS OUT THE LIGHTS.
I LIKE TO THINK WE GOT ALL THE BRILLIANT MONKEYS.
WAIT...
I LOVE THIS VIEW.
MULLEN'S DRUGS

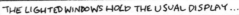

ANCHORING THE CORNER OF 40TH STREET IS THIS BEACON IN THE NIGHT:

MULLEN'S DRUGS

THE LIGHTED WINDOWS HOLD THE USUAL DISPLAY...

APOTHECARY JARS AND A MORTAR AND PESTLE BIG ENOUGH FOR A GIANT.

ABOVE THIS, IN THE APARTMENT WINDOWS, BEHIND CURTAINS, IS A SHADOW PLAY OF LIVES.

AT THE OTHER END IS ART'S COCKTAILS, PROMISING A DIFFERENT OBLIVION.

ART'S COCKTAILS

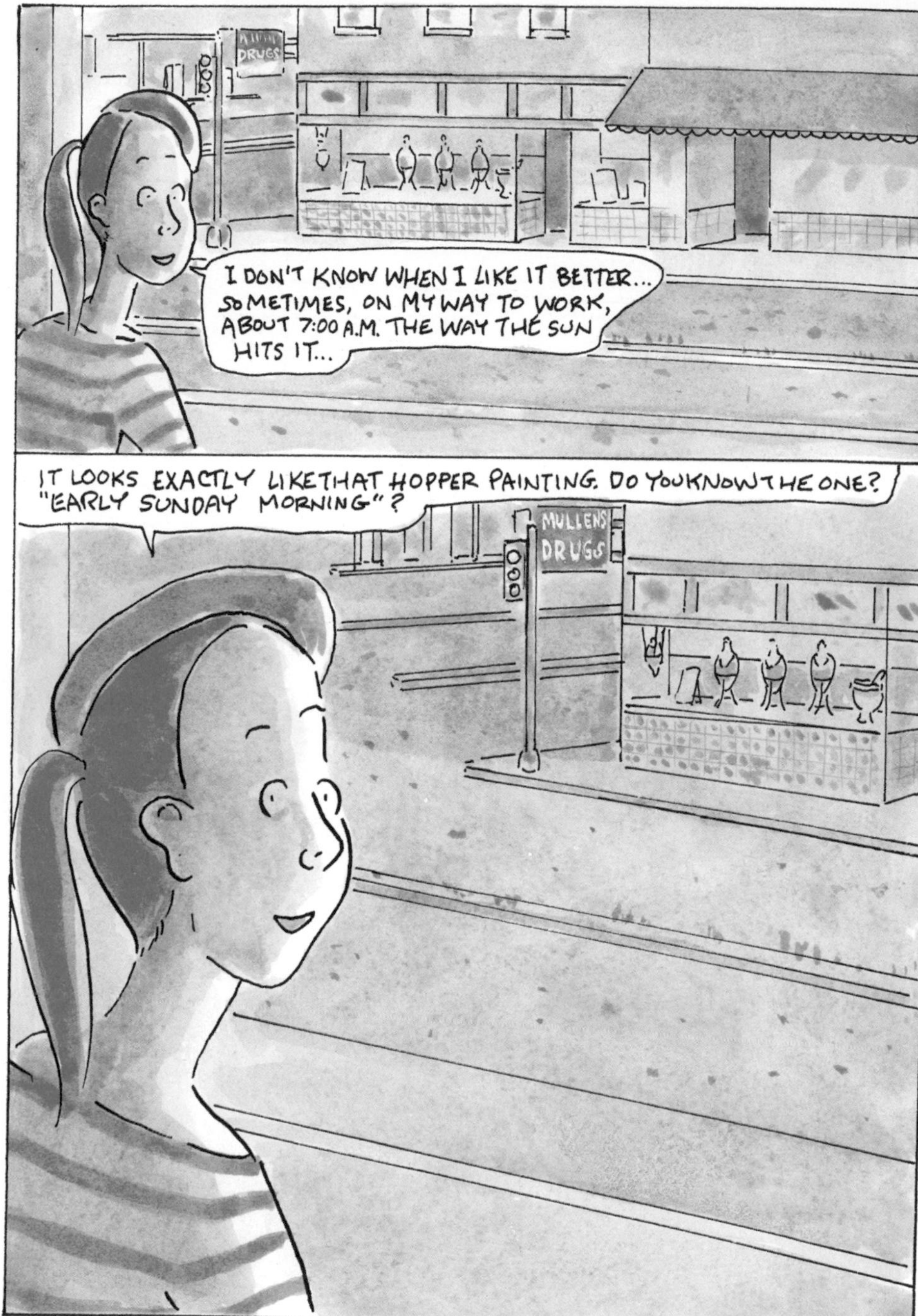
DRUGS
I DON'T KNOW WHEN I LIKE IT BETTER... SOMETIMES, ON MY WAY TO WORK, ABOUT 7:00 A.M. THE WAY THE SUN HITS IT...
IT LOOKS EXACTLY LIKE THAT HOPPER PAINTING. DO YOU KNOW THE ONE? "EARLY SUNDAY MORNING"?
MULLENS DRUGS

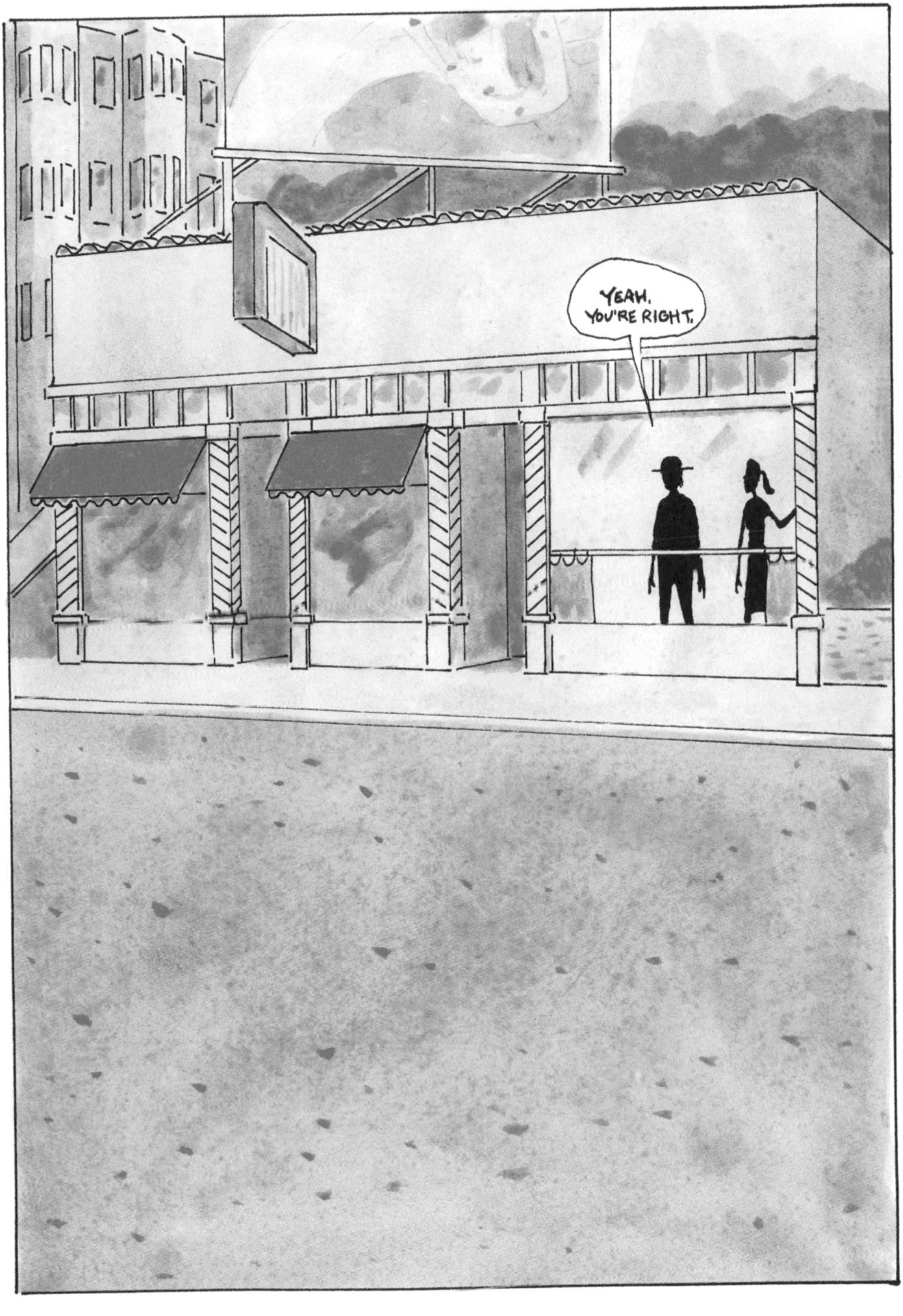
YEAH. YOU'RE RIGHT.

PHOTO BY WAYNE WHITE

MIMI POND IS A CARTOONIST, ILLUSTRATOR, AND WRITER. SHE HAS CREATED COMICS FOR THE **LOS ANGELES TIMES, SEVENTEEN MAGAZINE, NATIONAL LAMPOON,** AND MANY OTHER PUBLICATIONS. TELEVISION CREDITS INCLUDE THE FIRST FULL-LENGTH EPISODE OF **THE SIMPSONS,** "SIMPSONS ROASTING ON AN OPEN FIRE," AND EPISODES FOR THE SHOWS **DESIGNING WOMEN** AND **PEE-WEE'S PLAYHOUSE.** SHE LIVES IN LOS ANGELES WITH HER HUSBAND, THE ARTIST WAYNE WHITE.

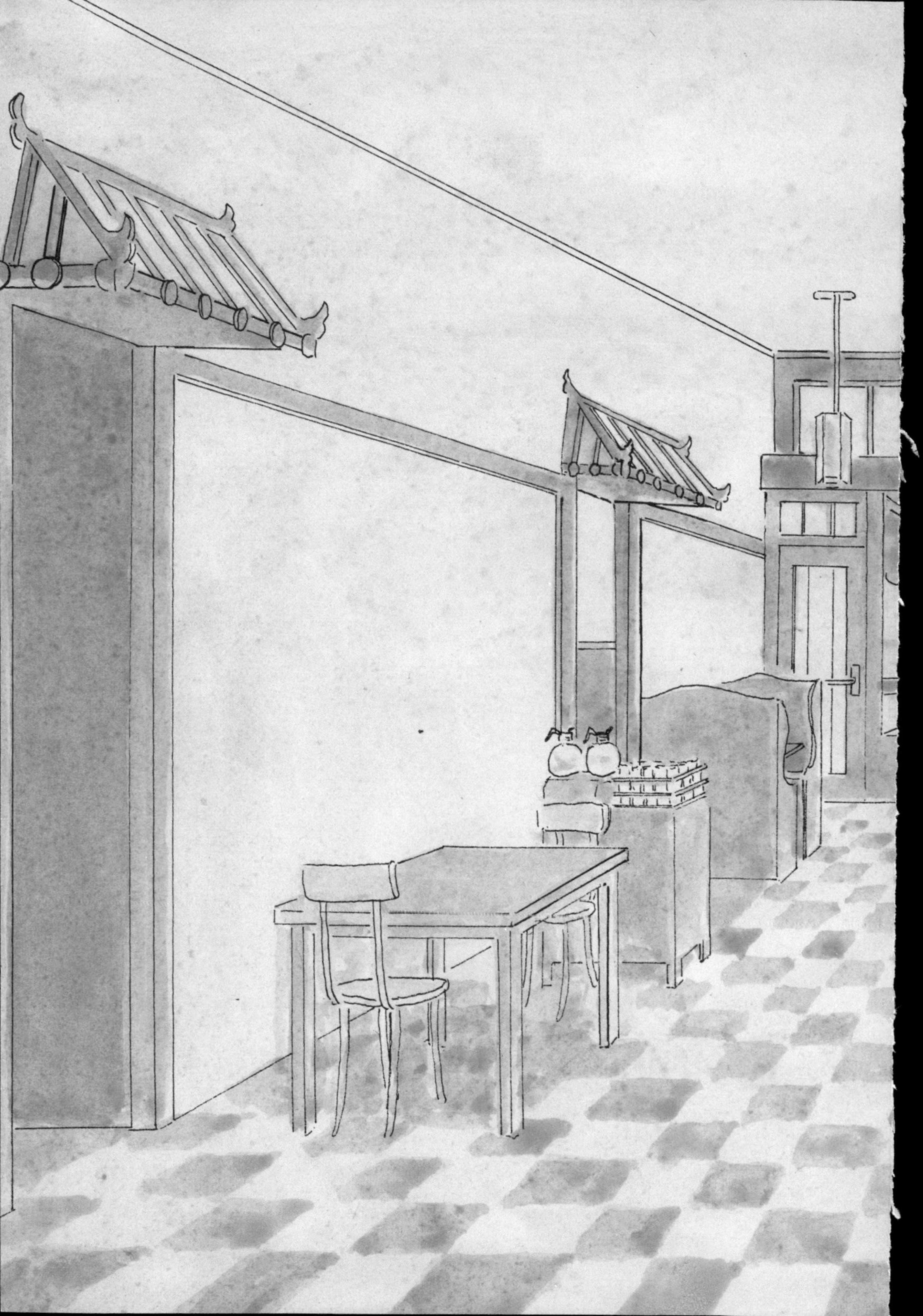